AGENTS OF REPRESSION

AGENTS OF REPRESSION

The FBI's Secret Wars Against
the Black Panther Party and
the American Indian Movement

by
Ward Churchill and
Jim Vander Wall

South End Press   Boston, MA

Editing, design, and layout by the South End Press collective
Cover photos by Kevin Barry McKiernan (top), Dick Bancroft (bottom left), and *The Guardian* (bottom right).
Cover by Todd Jailer

Library of Congress Cataloging-in-Publication Data

Churchill, Ward.
Agents of repression : the FBI's secret war against the Black Panther Party and the American Indian Movement / by Ward Churchill and Jim Vander Wall.
p. cm.
Bibliography: p.
Includes index.
ISBN 0-89608-294-6   ISBN 0-89608-293-8 (pbk.)
1. United States. Federal Bureau of Investigation. 2. Black Panther Party. 3. American Indian Movement. 4. Police power--United States. I. VanderWall, Jim. II. Title.
HV8141.C46 1988   88-16844
363.2'32--dc19   CIP

South End Press/ 116 Saint Botolph St./ Boston, MA 02115

98 97 96 95 94 93   4 5 6 7 8 9

Table of Contents

Dedication

This book is respectfully dedicated to the memory of Anna Mae Pictou Aquash, Micmac warrior woman, assassinated on Pine Ridge, February 1976 and to Naiche Wolf Soldier, strong warrior and good friend who passed into the spirit world as we were writing.

It is also offered in memory of the others, many mentioned herein, who have fallen, and with the renewed commitment to the struggles of Leonard Peltier, Geronimo Pratt and the thousands of kindred POWs/political prisoners/fugitives who mark the modern landscape of American "justice." One day justice *will* prevail.

Daughter of the Earth:
Song for Anna Mae Aquash

She came down from the North Country, from Canada
Where the northern lights shine shimmering above the fir
The strength of the continent was deep inside her heart
Strength that was needed in these times

She came to help the people as they struggled to be free
From the ones who sought to kill the land for money
They said they owned our Mother Earth and called it USA
Born of broken treaties and murder

Oh Anna Mae, oh Anna Mae
I feel your spirit and sometimes I can hear it
Saying keep on strong, keep on going on
Daughter of the Earth

The FBI had told her they would kill her if they could
Like so many others before her
But she was not afraid of them, her path was clear and true
"I am a woman working for my people"

So they shot her down and left the body lying in a field
Believing in the power of the metal gun
But the power lies within the land, it can't be owned or sold
And gives us what survives beyond our lives

Oh Anna Mae, oh Anna Mae
I feel your spirit and sometimes I can hear it
Saying keep on strong, keep on going on
Daughter of the Earth

Whenever I am frightened I just think of her
Her courage in confronting the death machine
To live for what sustains us all, to work to keep it whole
To die because some want to see it broken

Oh Anna Mae, oh Anna Mae
They stole your life away but they can't steal what you had to say
To keep on strong, keep on going on
Daughter of the Earth

Oh Anna Mae, oh Anna Mae
I feel your spirit and sometimes I can hear it
Saying keep on strong, keep on going on
Daughter of the Earth

—Ellen Klaver

About the Authors

Ward Churchill is coordinator, with Glenn Morris, of the Colorado chapter of the American Indian Movement and, with Winona LaDuke, of the Institute for Natural Progress. He has served as a delegate, in Geneva, Havana, and Benghazi, for the International Indian Treaty Council, a United Nations Class II (Human Rights Consultative) Non-Governmental Organization. Churchill has edited *Marxism and Native Americans* (South End Press, 1983) and coauthored, with Elizabeth Lloyd, *Culture versus Economism: Essays on Marxism in the Multicultural Arena* (Indigena Press, 1984), as well as authoring some 85 articles and essays. He is also director of the Educational Development Program at the University of Colorado/Boulder.

Jim Vander Wall is a member and co-founder of the Denver Leonard Peltier Support Group. He has been an active supporter of the struggles of Native Peoples for sovereignty since 1974 and has written several articles on the case of Leonard Peltier.

Acknowledgements

No two individuals ever assemble a book of this sort alone. In this case, where the "project" spans a decade and the events depicted are not only ongoing but "secret" and highly interrelated with other complex and secretive matters, the number of those making a tangible contribution undoubtedly runs into the hundreds. Among those who have proven most important and unstinting in their offerings of valuable insight and commentary concerning our manuscript, leads to additional or corroborating information, and who have typically opened both their files and their homes to us are Dennis and Kamook Banks, Faye Brown, Dino Butler, Nilak Butler, Dan Debo, Vine Deloria, Jr., Bruce Ellison, Roger Finzel, Sue Gegner, Cate Gilles, Murv Glass, Jr., Lew Gurwitz, Jeff Haas, Candy Hamilton, Stuart Hanlon, Eric Holle, Ellen Klaver, Bill Kunstler, Winona LaDuke, Larry Leaventhal, Joe and Vivian Locust, Jonathan Lubell, Peter Matthiessen, Lorelei Means, Ted Means, Russ Means, Janet McCloud, Nick Meinhart, Jim Messerschmidt, Glenn Morris, Theda Nelson, Mary O'Melveny, Kevin McKiernan, Leonard Peltier, Geronimo Pratt, Ellen Ray, Paulette D'Auteuil-Robideau and Bob Robideau, Steve Robideau, Bill Schaap, Paul Scribner, J.D. Starr, Flint Taylor, John Thorne, Madonna Thunderhawk, John Trudell, Aaron Two Elk, Rex Weyler, and Rick Williams. To scores of others who made similar contributions, we are also grateful.

Portions of the material contained herein have been published elsewhere by the authors in other forms. We would therefore like to express our gratitude to *Akwesasne Notes, CovertAction Information Bulletin, Earth First!, Environment, Insurgent Sociologist, Issues in Radical Therapy, The Journal of Ethnic Studies, The New Scholar, The Other Side, Rolling Stock, Socialist Review, Talking Leaf* and *Zeta Magazine* for their various assistance and permission to reprint. In terms of editing, technical assistance and general support, we'd like to thank the entire South End Press collective—Todd Jailer, Mike Albert and Lydia Sargeant in particular—as well as editor friends such as Bob Sipe, Tim Lange, S.K. Levin, Jennifer Dorn and Mark Olson, each of whom made a contribution along the way. Finally, we'd like to express our deepest gratitude to our partners, M.A. Jaimes and Jennie Vander Wall, for their consistent support during this effort and their many constructive criticisms of both what we were saying and how we were saying it.

The book could never have been completed without the input and guidance of all the above. Errors, factual or interpretive, however, remain solely the responsibility of the authors.

Glossary

AIM: The American Indian Movement, an indigenous liberation organization targeted for a massive COINTELPRO by the FBI.

APC: Armored Personnel Carrier, a tank-like military vehicle utilized to transport troops into battle at high speeds and in relative safety. During the late 1960s and on through the 1970s, APCs came to be used for "ground control," etc., within the U.S. They were deployed by the FBI against AIM on Pine Ridge and not withdrawn until 1976.

AR-15: Civilian variation of the U.S. military's M-16 rifle. AR-15s are usually, but not always, semi-automatic rather than fully automatic.

ASAC: Assistant Special Agent in Charge, the official title for an FBI agent in a supervisory position, often heading a resident agency or major investigation.

AUSA: Assistant U.S. Attorney, the attorney usually responsible for prosecuting federal cases.

BAYRU: Bay Area Radical Union, a "united front" of radical organizations emerging in northern California during the late 1960s; targeted by a COINTELPRO.

BIA: The Bureau of Indian Affairs, mechanism by which the U.S. administers American Indian reservations as internal colonies, and Indian people as colonial subjects.

BLA: The Black Liberation Army, originally dubbed the Afro-American Liberation Army, a clandestine armed formation which emerged from the shattering of the Black Panther Party by COINTELPRO.

"Black Nationalist Hate Groups": FBI newspeak designating black rights organizations in the U.S. including Dr. Martin Luther King's Southern Christian Leadership Conference.

Black P. Stone Nation: Formerly the Blackstone Rangers, a black street gang duped into physically attacking the Black Panther Party in Chicago by a COINTELPRO operation.

BSUs: Black Student Unions, campus-based organizations sympathetic to the Black Panther Party, targeted by COINTELPRO.

BoI: The U.S. Bureau of Intelligence, the predecessor organization to the FBI, and the entity which actually coordinated the infamous Palmer Raids against radicals during 1919-1920. The BoI is where J. Edgar Hoover got his start.

BPP: The Black Panther Party, originally the Black Panther Party for Self-Defense, a black liberation organization massively targeted by COINTELPRO.

"Catholic Left": A loose affiliation of Catholic pacifists opposed to the Vietnam war, designated by the FBI as "terrorists" and targeted by COINTELPRO.

CSS: Criminal Conspiracy Section of the Los Angeles Police Department. During the late 1960s and early 1970s, CSS was tightly interlocked with the FBI as a local appendage of COINTELPROs aimed at the Black Panther Party and other radical organizations.

CII: Criminal Intelligence and Investigation Unit of the California State Police. CII interlocked with CSS and the FBI in conducting operations against the California left from roughly 1967-1975.

CISPES: Committee in Solidarity with the People of El Salvador. An organization opposing U.S. intervention in Central America and consequently subjected to COINTELPRO-type attention by the FBI. The Bureau is presently rationalizing its conduct *vis-a-vis* CISPES on the grounds that it thought the organization might be guilty of "seditious conspiracy" (see definition below).

COINTELPROs: FBI domestic Counterintelligence Programs designed to destroy individuals and organizations the FBI considers to be politically objectionable. Tactics included all manner of official lying and media disinformation, systematically levying false charges against those targeted, manufacturing evidence to obtain their convictions, withholding evidence which might exonerate them, and occasionally assassinating "key leaders." The FBI says COINTELPRO ended in 1971; all reasonable interpretations of FBI performance indicate it continues today, albeit under other code-names.

COMINFIL: Communist Infiltration investigations. The FBI code-name for investigations undertaken against organizations suspected of being infiltrated by "communists." Exactly what a communist is is never quite spelled out. COMINFIL has thus served as an umbrella rationale for domestic intelligence and counterintelligence operations.

Control Units: Behavior modification centers within federal prisons where brainwashing is practiced, usually intended to obtain the "ideological conversion" of politically objectionable individuals. Prime examples are the Marion, Illinois facility for men and the Lexington, Kentucky facility for women (closed in 1988). Similar facilities are proliferating in West Germany and in Canada, where they are known as Special Handling Units (SHUs).

CPUSA: Communist Party, USA, an old left organization targeted by COINTELPRO.

CS: A type of "tear gas" commonly used for "crowd control" in the U.S. Under certain conditions, CS can be lethal.

ELSUR: FBI code term for Electronic Surveillance, usually related to "national security" and often illegal.

FALN: *Fuerzas Armadas de Liberación Nacional,* a Puerto Rican independence organization targeted by COINTELPRO.

FBIHQ: FBI Headquarters, in the huge J. Edgar Hoover Building in Washington, D.C., which serves as the nerve center of FBI operations.

Field Offices: FBI area command and control centers, scattered throughout the U.S. and its colony, Puerto Rico.

FOIA: The Freedom of Information Act, a statute intended to allow citizen access to FBI files (especially ones maintained on themselves), typically ignored by the Bureau other than in cases where a specific court order is obtained.

"Friends of the Bureau": An FBI euphemism referring to the many reporters and editors who will print or say whatever the Bureau wants, passing off the result as "objective journalism."

General Index: The listing of all FBI files, in which the majority of U.S. citizens appear.

GIU: Gang Intelligence Unit of the Chicago Police Department; during the late 1960s, the GIU was merely the local euphemism for "red squad."

GOONs: "Guardians of the Oglala Nation," a paramilitary force created on the Pine Ridge Sioux Reservation by then Tribal President Dick Wilson in 1972. Federal funds and arms were provided for this project. The GOONs quickly became the FBI's surrogate in carrying out the physical repression of AIM and its supporters, more than 60 of whom were murdered between 1973 and the end of 1976.

"in error...": an FBI euphemism offered whenever it is conclusively demonstrated that its representatives have deliberately lied to the press, Congress and public. This is sometimes referred to as "mis-speaking" when the false statement is made in court and under oath (see below).

internal security: The FBI euphemism covering the suppression of political diversity in the U.S.

ION: The Independent Oglala Nation, the basic grassroots organization supporting AIM on Pine Ridge, 1973-1976.

IWW: The Industrial Workers of the World ("Wobblies"), an anarcho-syndicalist labor union accused of "sedition" and destroyed by a major counterintelligence effort during World War I.

June Mail: The FBI code-name for transcripts of telephone conversations recorded by wiretap (often justified on the basis of COMINFIL or "national security" programs, or just plain illegal).

JTTF: The Joint Terrorist Task Force, created in the late 1970s as an interlock between the FBI and the New York City red squad to engage in COINTELPRO-type activities.

Key Agitator Index: The list of FBI files devoted to individuals considered so politically objectionable by the Bureau that they must be "neutralized."

Laws: A set of rules, many of which are systematically violated by the FBI and associated organizations as an expedient to enforcing others. Those caught by the FBI while breaking laws are usually heavily penalized (along with a number who are merely made to *appear* to have done something wrong); FBI agents who are caught breaking laws are, of course, also punished severely. In one case, an agent was suspended without pay for two weeks.

"mis-speak": An FBI euphemism meaning the statement of an agent caught in the act of committing perjury.

M-16: The standard U.S. military rifle. The M-16 fires a very light-weight .223 calibre slug at extremely high velocity, a characteristic which causes the projectile to be quite unstable and to tumble upon striking its target. Wounds inflicted by the M-16 are thus typically "super lethal." In sum, the M-16 is the U.S.'s way of getting around the international law prohibiting military use of comparably designated ammunition components such as hollow points, dum-dums and soft-nose bullets.

National Security: An "intelligence community" euphemism meaning that illegalities engaged in by intelligence operatives can be kept secret for purposes of "securing the nation" (from *what* is never quite made clear). The effect is simply to place intelligence operatives outside the law, free to do whatever they wish and then legally cover it up.

NoI: The Nation of Islam, a Black Muslim church in the U.S., targeted by COINTELPRO during the 1960s.

Omega 7: An anti-Castro Cuban terrorist organization formed and financed by the CIA to carry out covert opertions in this hemisphere. In the U.S., Omega 7 has been implicated in terrorist bombings, assassinations and large-scale narcotics trafficking.

OSCRO: Oglala Sioux Civil Rights Organization, a formation of traditionalist opponents of the Wilson regime on Pine Ridge, targeted by COINTELPRO during the mid-1970s.

OSS: Office of Strategic Services, predecessor organization of the CIA.

Oversight Bodies: Sometimes referred to as oversight committees. Entities which are occasionally created by Congress to give the impression that the FBI has been "brought under control," apparently so named because their function is to *overlook* FBI misconduct, while actually doing little or nothing to constrain the Bureau's latitude of operation.

O-wing: The control unit of the California State Prison at San Quentin.

prison: A place where the FBI puts those with whom it disagrees politically, but to which its agents are never sent, no matter what crimes they have committed.

Public Information Officer: The FBI classification for the agent whose specialty is providing intentionally inaccurate "facts" (disinformation) to the media; the FBI counterpart of military psychological operations (PSYOPs) specialist.

Quantico: The FBI training facility in Virginia, near the training center for Marine Corps Officers, where FBI, state and local police, and other law enforcement personnel are trained in SWAT and counterinsurgency techniques.

Racial Matters Sections: The COINTELPRO components of FBI Field Offices aimed at black political organizations.

RAM: Revolutionary Action Movement, a Philadelphia-based black liberation organization targetted by a major COINTELPRO.

Resident Agencies: Local FBI command and control centers, immediately subordinate to field offices, existing in most U.S. cities of more than 30,000 population.

RESMURS: An FBI code name, supposedly covering investigations of murders on the Pine Ridge Sioux Reservation. Although more than 60 murders occurred on Pine Ridge between 1973 and 1976, RESMURS investigated none of them. Instead, the term involved only the investigation of the deaths of two agents—Ronald Williams and Jack Coler—whom a jury in Cedar Rapids, Iowa later determined had not been murdered at all.

RNA: The Republic of New Afrika, a black liberation organization heavily targeted by COINTELPRO.

RU: The Revolutionary Union, a successor organization to BAYRU in northern California in the early 1970s; targeted by COINTELPRO.

SA: Special Agent, the official designation of an FBI agent.

SAC: Special Agent in Charge, the official designation of the FBI agent heading a field office.

Sanctuary Movement: A church-based, pacifist effort devoted to arranging refuge in North America for victims of U.S. intervention in Central America; currently designated by the FBI as "terrorist infiltrated." To the extent that the movement has been infiltrated by the FBI, this is perhaps a correct designation.

SAO: The Secret Army Organization, a right-wing organization created and controlled by the FBI during the early 1970s for purposes of carrying out the physical repression of radical organizations and individuals in the Southwest.

SCLC: The Southern Christian Leadership Conference, Dr. Martin Luther King's civil rights organization, targeted by COINTELPRO.

SDS: Students for a Democratic Society, a New Left organization targeted by COINTELPRO.

Security Index: The listing of all FBI files devoted to individuals considered politically objectionable by the Bureau.

Sedition Act: Sometimes called the "alien and sedition act." A World War I law, still in effect, making it a crime to advocate the overthrow of the federal government. This curious repeal of Thomas Jefferson's assertion that citizens are *obligated* to revolt at any time the government becomes repressive or burdensome has been consistently used by the FBI to "justify" COINTELPRO-type activities.

Seditious Conspiracy: A nebulous but sinister-sounding concept of "criminality" by which the FBI has sought to justify virtually any form of political repression in which it wishes to engage.

Serbo-Croatian Liberation Front: A mysterious right-wing terrorist organization, possibly fabricated by the FBI, used to make the formation of the JTTF appear non-political in nature.

SII: State Investigations and Intelligence unit of the California Attorney General's office. SII interlocked with CSS, CII and the FBI in the campaign to crush California radicalism during the late 1960s and early-to-mid 1970s.

Silo-Plowshares: A Chicago-based pacifist organization opposed to nuclear weapons and U.S. intervention in Central America and currently designated by the FBI as "terrorist."

Smith Act: A 1940s law, still in effect, making it illegal to say things counter to government policy in times of war or national emergency. Often used by the FBI as a COINTELPRO rationale.

SNCC: Student Non-violent Coordinating Committee, a civil rights organization targeted by COINTELPRO. In 1966, after SNCC's casualty rate had reached an absurd level, the organization was redesignated as the Student *National* Coordinating Committee.

SOG: Military Special Operations Group created to conduct unorthodox counterinsurgency in Southeast Asia during the late 1960s. Shortly thereafter, SOGs were created within Federal police forces to conduct counterinsurgency operations against the U.S. population itself.

Soledad Brothers Defense Committee: A prisoners' rights organization in northern California, targeted heavily by COINTELPRO during the early 1970s.

SPU: Special Prosecutions Unit of the Cook County, Illinois State's Attorneys Office. The SPU was devoted, during the late 1960s, to the physical repression of the Chicago Black Panther Party.

subversive: FBI newspeak for anyone with a dissident political view.

"surreptitious entry": FBI euphemism meaning burglary performed by agents.

SWAT: Special Weapons and Tactics teams, paramilitary units which have proliferated within most U.S. police organizations since 1970.

SWP: Socialist Workers Party, an old left, Trotskyite organization targeted by COINTELPRO.

terrorist: An FBI term, presently utilized by the entire government, meaning anyone engaging in resistance (armed or otherwise) to physical repression by the U.S.

"unfriendly journalists": FBI euphemism covering reporters and editors who publish facts the Bureau does not wish to have known, or who refuse to publish FBI-approved disinformation. Investigations are usually opened on such uncooperative characters, and a few have been subjected to COINTELPROs.

The United Front: A southern Illinois civil rights organization targeted by COINTELPRO during the early 1970s.

US: The United Slaves organization, a black nationalist group in southern California duped into physically attacking the Black Panther Party through an elaborate COINTELPRO.

USA: United States Attorney, chief federal prosecutor in a given area who usually works closely with the FBI in criminal prosecutions.

Venceremos: A multi-ethnic radical organization which grew out of RU in the mid-1970s; targeted by COINTELPRO.

Weatherman: An armed formation which emerged from SDS in 1969, the period in which COINTELPRO was approaching its zenith. Weatherman was later known as the Weather Underground Organization or WUO.

Young Lords: A former street gang turned Puerto Rican independence organization, targeted by COINTELPRO.

Young Patriots: A white Chicago street gang turned political, targeted by COINTELPRO.

YSA: Young Socialist Alliance, youth wing of the SWP, targeted by COINTELPRO.

Beyond the Myth

In recent years, a campaign of falsehood and vilification has been directed against the FBI by some ignorant and subversive elements. In the world-wide struggle of free peoples, the truth is still one of the most potent weapons. And the record of the FBI speaks for itself.

—J. Edgar Hoover, Introduction to *The FBI Story*

A persistent fiction remains fixed in the public mind that the Federal Bureau of Investigation (FBI) is a highly successful crime-fighting machine, composed of honest and brave individuals, utterly committed to the preservation, protection and embodiment of the lofty "American ideals" of liberty and justice for all. This myth was largely the creation of J. (John) Edgar Hoover, the Bureau's founder and director from the moment of its inception during the winter of 1918-19 until the moment of his death on the morning of May 2, 1972. More than any other individual, living or dead, it was Hoover who modeled "America's police force" after his own image, or, at any rate, after the public fantasy he elected to project for himself. And, more than any other, it is Hoover's strange legacy which continues to temper, not only the realities of the Bureau's functions, attitudes and existence, but public perceptions of these.

Much of the FBI's fabled reputation as the ultimate in crime-stopping organizations accrues from the so-called "national crime wave" of the early-to-mid 1930s. It is now known that much of the context involved in creating this impression was manufactured by Hoover. As Sanford Ungar observes in his benchmark study of the Bureau,

As early as 1932, Hoover was boasting in his congressional testimony about the value and usefulness of the [FBI's] *Uniform Crime Report*, launched in 1930 to meet the need for national crime statistics and compiled from figures submitted by local police departments. The purpose, the director said, was "to determine whether there is or is not a crime wave and whether crime is on the increase or decrease." From that time on, it was invariably on the increase, and the FBI took it upon itself to chart the nature and degree of the increase, any geographical variations in the rise, and other significant trends that seemed to emerge.[1]

Having established the "fact" of a rampant national crime wave by 1933, as well as the Bureau's preeminent role in defining its characteristics, Hoover proceeded to divert public attention *away* from the then-emergent urban syndication of racketeer-

1

ing being pioneered by such criminal visionaries as Meyer Lansky and Salvatore Lucania (aka Charlie "Lucky" Luciano).[2] This was accomplished through the development of a truly brilliant public relations gimmick designating, often on a week-by-week basis, one or another member of the nation's underworld as being "Public Enemy Number One." Virtually without fail, this dubious distinction was attached to the leaders of a gaggle of relatively small-time rural gangs busily defraying the personal costs of the Great Depression by resort to a series of sensational kidnappings and bank robberies. While the actors in this backwoods melodrama had far more in common with the Dalton, Younger, and James gangs of the 19th century Wild West than with the sleek new urban combines which represented the cutting edge of 20th century American criminality (an edge Hoover claimed to be blunting via the Bureau's "war on crime"), they were flashy, essentially easy prey for federal lawmen and thus afforded almost unlimited opportunities for the FBI to obtain "good press."

As Hoover must have seen it, no doubt accurately enough, tracking down the likes of John Dillinger, Charles "Pretty Boy" Floyd and Lester M. "Babyface Nelson" Gillis would be a "quick and dirty" affair, a matter making infinitely more media sense than breaking the Bureau's teeth—and underscoring its inadequacies as a criminal investigation agency—by engaging in frustratingly lengthy, boring and "low-yield" pursuit of the increasingly low-key and sophisticated big city mobsters. This proved all the more true when the "most wanted" desperadoes themselves began to provide unwitting and unexpected public relations boons to the Bureau. A prime example of this occurred on the morning of September 26, 1934, when, at the moment of his capture, George "Machine gun" Kelly coined the catchy term "G-men" to describe his pursuers.[3] From such stuff are legends made and, by the end of the decade, the Bureau had completed construction of a hyped-up profile of itself as a "gang-busting" entity which has survived to the present day.

In many ways, the veracity of the Bureau's account of its anti-crime performance can be accurately assessed through reflection upon Hoover's handling of his own role in this regard. As Ungar describes the matter:

> Occasionally the Director was criticized—for example, by Senator Kenneth McKeller of Tennessee in 1936—for having little, if any, experience himself in investigation and detection of crime and for never having made an arrest. As one sympathetic Hoover biographer, Ralph de Toledano, puts it, after McKeller's criticism, "Hoover was boiling mad. He felt his manhood had been impugned." In response, he staged a dramatic trip to New Orleans and supposedly led a raiding party to capture a member of the "Barker Gang," Alvin Karpis. Later, thanks to arrangements made by his friend, columnist Walter Winchell, he repeated the performance in New York for the capture of rackets boss Louis "Lepke" Buchalter. Such gestures grabbed headlines and calmed his critics. It was only years later that it became known that Hoover strolled into both situations after the danger was past and that he played a purely symbolic role.[4]

The patent success of such self-aggrandizing and deceptive promotions of the Bureau appears to have honed Hoover's already keen media instincts to the veritable razor's edge. It became a tacitly official FBI policy to "cooperate" with any group

The October 1937 cover of *G-Men*, a popular pulp magazine which, from its beginnings in 1935 until it folded in 1953, was used by FBI propagandists to pump up the Bureau's public image. Note that this issue initiates a series entitled "Famous Cases of J. Edgar Hoover," the Director's response to his critics.

or individual technically competent (and inclined) to "portray the Bureau in a favorable light." For example, the NBC radio program *Monitor* devoted a five minute weekly prime-time slot to one or another aspect of FBI operations for nearly two decades; when it was finally dropped by NBC in 1964, this segment was picked up by ABC and continued to air under the title *FBI Washington* well into the 1970s. And, as Ungar notes, "In the 1940s and early 1950s the Bureau also participated—even supplying agents as actors—in a number of commercial films glorifying its exploits, including *The House on 92nd Street*, *Walk a Crooked Mile*, and *Walk East on Beacon*."[5] There followed, during the 1960s, the ABC television series *The FBI*, ostensibly produced by Quinn/Martin (selected by the Bureau for this job because of their earlier success with *The Untouchables* feds/gangsters series) even though it "was developed with the avid participation and effective control of the Bureau...Every script was funneled through the Los Angeles Field Office and sent to Washington for suggested changes and final approval...[by] headquarters."[6]

Simultaneously, journalists and other writers deemed "friends of the Bureau" were solicited to write what—and *only* what—Hoover wished to have known about the FBI. In exchange, they were systematically provided exclusive or privileged information for reporting purposes, information which was just as regularly denied less ingratiating members of their profession:

> The Bureau's particular relationship with people it classified as "friendly media representatives" involved routine and frequent violations of the "attorney general's guidelines" that officially restricted what the FBI could release about any pending or sensitive investigation...[7]

This, in combination with other favors typically granted by the Bureau to those in its corner, led, not unnaturally, to literally miles of newsprint regurgitating verbatim, and as *fact*, the FBI's assessments, both of itself and of a wide range of other matters. Additionally, it prompted a seemingly endless stream of "nonfiction" books which appear to have been penned solely for the purpose of portraying the Bureau and its director in the most flattering possible posture. Among the very worst of these spoon-fed puff pieces have been Frederick L. Collins' *The FBI in Peace and War*, *The Story of the FBI* (compiled by the editors of *Look* magazine), Andrew Tulley's *The FBI's Most Famous Cases*, and Don Whitehead's *The FBI Story* and *Attack on Terror*.[8]

The carrots, of course, were coupled with sticks. All the while Hoover's Bureau was directly assisting its media friends in painting a false but rosy portrait of it, it was equally assiduous in suppressing the exposure of countervailing viewpoints, or even of reasonably neutral information which, for whatever reasons, the Director wished withheld from public consumption. As early as 1940, Hoover began asserting a link between criticism of the Bureau and "unAmericanism," as when he went on radio to announce that, "Your FBI is respected by the good citizens of America as much as it is feared, hated and vilified by the scum of the underworld, Communists, goose-stepping bundsmen, their fellow travelers, mouthpieces, and

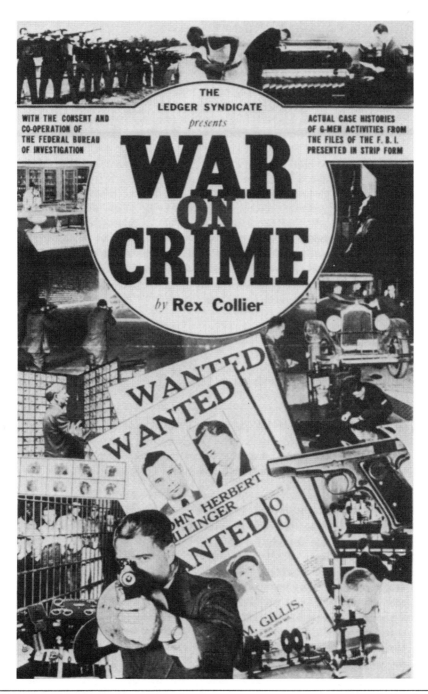

The cover of a 1935 promotional flyer for *War on Crime*, a Bureau-fostered potboiler devoted to heightening the FBI's public image as a "gang-busting" organization. Note the prominence accorded bank robber John Dillinger.

stooges," or, on another occasion, when he compared suggestions that Bureau performance might be less than perfect in some areas to "the sort of material I might
expect to see on the front page of *The Daily Worker* or *Pravda*."[9]

A close conformity to the FBI's informational "standards" was achieved within
the cost-intensive (and thus most vulnerable) movie-radio-television industry during
the so-called "McCarthy era" of the late 1940s and early 1950s, a matter facilitated
by the active connivance of the Bureau.[10] Newspaper and magazine writers buckled
under similar, if less obvious, forms of coercion, tactics which were continued long
after the McCarthy era formally ended. For instance, it is a matter of record that
Hoover personally attempted to secure the firing of reporter Jack Nelson of the *Los
Angeles Times* in 1970, when the journalist contended (accurately) that the Bureau
had provoked a Mississippi firebombing directed at civil rights activists by the Ku
Klux Klan.[11] Such methods were/are still being utilized after Hoover's death, as when
(in 1974) agents visited the editorial offices of the Anaheim, California, *Bulletin*,
to "correct" an article expressing concern over the rampant proliferation of the FBI's
computer networking capabilities; in the same fashion and the same year, there was
a heavy-handed effort to induce editorial alterations of *Chicago Tribune* stories critical of the Bureau's handling of the Patricia Hearst case.[12]

In terms of book publishing, the Bureau has also been highly active in undermining anything it does not wish to be seen by the public. As has been said elsewhere, "[The FBI] tried to discredit any 'negative' book or article that it thought
would hurt its public image."[13] For instance:

> Once the Bureau had finished its job of discrediting Max Lowenthal's *The Federal
> Bureau of Investigation*, which originally appeared in 1950, it became difficult to find
> copies of the book on bookstore shelves; articles appeared in a number of newspapers
> dealing with Lowenthal's statements in terms remarkably similar to official Bureau
> responses...Lowenthal's eventual reward, incredibly, was a subpoena from the House
> Un-American Activities Committee. Much of Lowenthal's technique, and some of his
> material, was incorporated by Fred Cook into *The FBI Nobody Knows*, published in
> 1964, and as a result he too was severely dealt with...[14]

In the end, the FBI "kept thorough files of the 'negative' articles that had appeared under anyone's by-line, sometimes supplemented with personal material
about the author. When Ovid Demaris, for example, who was writing a book about
Hoover, went to interview Attorney General William Saxbe about the FBI, the Bureau
sent in a file of 'background material' about the author in advance."[15]

Former agents who chose to publish "the inside scoop" on Bureau fallacies
have been subjected to especially venomous treatment. When William Turner attempted to promote his 1970 book, *Hoover's FBI: The Men and the Myth*, on radio
and television, the Bureau organized a special call-in campaign for live appearances devoted to discrediting not only the study, but most especially the character of its
author as well. Essentially the same methods were employed *vis a vis* Norman

Ollestad's *Inside the FBI*, as well as Bernard Connors' fictionalized *Don't Embarrass the Bureau*, to name but two others.[16] The FBI's position in such matters is clearly that those who have had the greatest opportunity to learn the difference between the truths and untruths of its domain—by virtue of having worked there—have the *least* right to talk about it. Such an interesting perspective on the public's right to know has, by now, spread to other sectors of the "intelligence/police community" as well; witness the Central Intelligence Agency's (CIA's) persistent courtroom efforts over the past fifteen years to stifle the voices of former employees attempting to share their hard-won insights with the public at large.[17]

So intensive was the Bureau's permanent public relations campaign that an entire unit—euphemistically dubbed the "Criminal Records Division," now redesignated the "External Affairs Division"—was created to handle it. By 1975, the tangible budget underwriting this effort had swollen to $2,868,000, a matter explained by FBI officials as being brought about by the need for "employing all communications media to increase public awareness of the responsibilities and services of the FBI, and to alert the public to criminal and subversive dangers threatening society, thereby encouraging citizen cooperation in combatting these elements, which constitute critical and costly problems to each member of society."[18]

The capstone to this whole, somewhat intricate, structure of Bureau propagandism was always the edifice of Hoover himself. As Ungar frames the matter,

> One crucial element in the Bureau's image-building was the material turned out in the Director's name. Apart from the endless flow of magazine and law review articles, there were the Hoover books…While epics like *Masters of Deceit* were an important part of the Bureau's long-range efforts, the FBI was always good at grabbing daily headlines, too. In 1940, Hoover himself called New York reporters to the field office there to reveal the discovery of a 'plot' in which seventeen members of a 'Christian Front' organization—including some part-time soldiers, a telephone mechanic, a baker, a chauffeur, and others—were allegedly planning to wipe out the New York police and all the nation's Jews, seize the gold stocks, take over all public utilities, and set up a dictatorship.

Hoover is quoted as saying, at this press conference *cum* public lynching, that "We have all the evidence we need to substantiate every claim we have made."[19] This turned out to be a blatant falsehood, of course; after the initial splatter of Bureau-flattering headlines, nothing much ever came of this typically absurd case.[20]

Meanwhile, as the Bureau and its Director postured and preened, the real business of organized crime in America proliferated steadily. Hoover's response to this reality, far from refocusing his agency's considerable resources toward combatting the problem, was—as was his practice with anything which interfered with the tidiness of FBI mythology—to simply insist, often loudly, that the whole issue was a hoax: "No single individual or coalition of racketeers dominates organized crime across the nation."[21] His position remained the same, regardless of the most obvious facts. As has been noted elsewhere,

Although J. Edgar Hoover never wrote a book or article, he is credited with a number of each. Here, his by-line appears on a pair of texts developed in the Bureau propaganda mills and intended to whip up anti-communist sentiment among the American public.

Neither the investigation of Murder Incorporated in Brooklyn in the early 1940s [of which, as was mentioned above, Hoover was ostensibly a direct participant], nor the work in the 1950s of New York District Attorney Frank S. Hogan and the Federal Bureau of Narcotics, nor the inquiry conducted by Senator Estes Kefauver of Tennessee could persuade the Director to say otherwise.[22]

By the early 1960s, when U.S. Attorney General Robert F. Kennedy and Arkansas Senator John McClellan teamed up for a serious probe of crime syndicate operations, the Bureau's recalcitrance in cooperating with such efforts had become so notorious among government insiders (and gangsters) that, contrary to the FBI's carefully cultivated PR profile, "the [Justice Department and Senate Committee] stereotype of the FBI agent was someone who kept looking for those stolen cars and deserters while more complex, organized violations of the law passed under his nose," and that "the Bureau's focus was…hopelessly misdirected or, at best, out of date."[23] The situation was epitomized by an exchange between Kennedy and John Francis Malone, Bureau Assistant Director in Charge of the FBI's New York office:

Kennedy: Mr. Malone, could you bring me up to date on what's been happening with organized crime [in New York]?

Malone: To tell you the truth, Mr. Attorney General, I'm sorry, but I can't because we've been having a newspaper strike here.[24]

Such comical aspects notwithstanding, the core of the Bureau's policy regarding organized crime was neither funny nor merely incompetent. To the contrary, when U.S. Attorney General William P. Rogers attempted, during the late 1950s, to field a nation-wide federal task force to crack what was then becoming known as "the Mafia," several of the interagency group's leaders ended up complaining bitterly that their effectiveness had been deliberately "stymied" by the FBI. As Richard B. Ogilvie, head of the Rogers Task Force's Midwest office, and later Cook County (Chicago) Sheriff as well as Governor of Illinois, subsequently put it:

Hoover was very cool to the whole idea [of going up against either the national crime syndicate, or even that element of it represented by the reconstituted remnants of the old Al Capone mob in Chicago]…He ordered the FBI files, containing the very information we needed on organized crime, closed to us…The FBI is still organized to fight a [rural] crime pattern of the twenties and thirties. It is not set up to do battle with the criminal syndicate—the organized conspiracy that drains $22 billion a year from the United States [this dollar amount dates from 1958-59; the cashflow of the syndicate has multiplied several-fold since then].[25]

A decade later, during the Johnson administration, when U.S. Attorney General Ramsey Clark again attempted to assemble an effective system of multi-agency regional strikeforces by which the federal government could hope to "smash the mob," the FBI's posture remained deeply subversive to the whole idea. As Ungar recounts,

> Hoover declined...to permit Bureau agents to participate in the strike forces. He did not want the [Bureau] responsible to anyone outside the Bureau's [*i.e.* his own] chain of command...[H]e feared the FBI agents might be surrendering control over the information they gathered [that is, to others who might then be in a position to challenge the public mythology of the Bureau's preeminence in crime fighting].[26]

Nor have things changed appreciably since Hoover's death, some fifteen years hence. The Bureau still appears quite content to ride upon its "gangbuster" laurels, offering guided tours of its massive facility—"The J. Edgar Hoover Building"—in Washington, D.C., featuring a brief film "history" of FBI exploits and a model firing range complete with life-size pop-up "John Dillinger" targets, as well as handouts of the latest Ten Most Wanted Fugitives list. The Hoover-engineered interlock between the Bureau and the media seems to have survived his demise, essentially intact. In fact, it has arguably evolved further and has expanded handily, which may account for the ongoing lack of critical commentary concerning the FBI's signal lack of success (or even energy) in pursuing organized crime figures/orgainzations, as well as the "short memory" accorded the Bureau's "excesses" (the conventional euphemism employed to cover its criminal acts) by the press and electronic media over the past decade.

In the end, nothing can be imagined which better serves to validate Hoover's contention, quoted at the outset, than the performance of the Director and his Bureau themselves. Theirs has truly been a record of conducting a "campaign of falsehood...by ignorant and subversive elements" with regard to the FBI. From here, we can only concur with Hoover's assessment that "the record of the FBI speaks for itself." For these reasons, we would like to close this section of our introduction by going beyond the self-congratulatory public myth of the FBI, squarely into the realm of reality expressed by a longtime local police detective who has spent the bulk of his adult life on special "mob squads" trying to jail members of New York's "Five Families" criminal combine:

> The bastards...the bastards sandbag us every time. We work for months setting something up and the feds blow it for us...They sell us out every time. I swear to Christ they tip 'em off...We ask for help, and whadda we get? We get spit, that's what we get. And then these bastards come around with their greasy smiles, and tell us what *we* should be doin' to help *them*...The "crime fighters," my ass. They couldn't fight crime if it had 'em by the throat...They're *worse* than the fuckin' hoods.[27]

To this, as concerns the FBI as an instrument preventing the organized criminal aspects of our society, we have nothing to add.

* * *

It undoubtedly seems odd that, given the thoroughly dismal record of FBI ineptitude and duplicity, willful deception of both the public and its hypothetical "supervisors" in government, manipulation and just plain arrogance, all over an extended period of time, the Bureau has managed to grow and prosper. Moreover, the question arises as to why, given all this, somewhere within the government itself, some one group did not, at some point, simply become fed up enough with the Hooverian ethos to bring about a substantial shake-up of the Bureau. Better yet, in view of the FBI's abject failure—demonstrably known to a range of insiders extending from ex-agents to local police, and onward through the Congress and assorted Attorneys General to several Presidents—in accomplishing what it perpetually touted as its "primary mission," has the Bureau not simply been dissolved altogether?

We feel that the reasons for this are several, and of varying degrees of importance. First, of course, is the sad fact that bureaucracies, once activated, evidence a life and dynamism of their own. Independent of any theoretical basis for their existence (or absence of same), they are known to be exceedingly difficult to contain, and can seldom be shown to have disappeared entirely, regardless of the effort expended in such directions. This is all the more true when they are headed over a sustained period by a bureaucrat *par excellence* such as J. Edgar Hoover, a man who—by accounts of friend and foe alike—was superbly equipped to maneuver in Washington's corridors of power in such fashion as to guarantee the survival of both himself and his organization. The matter is, to be sure, further complicated when it is noted (as it was in the preceding section) that Hoover's bureaucratic acumen was coupled with an adroit casting of his agency before the public, not as a functional element of governance per se, but as a veritable public institution, in and of itself. Once enshrined, the Bureau became—for both political and emotional reasons—a very difficult entity to dismantle, or even control.

This institutional or "surface" dynamic, important as it may be in solving the riddle of why an agency as apparently defective as the FBI has not only survived but mushroomed over the years, is nonetheless surely outweighed by a deeper and more sinister factor. As William Preston, Jr. has observed, "Hoover's first General Intelligence Division index of the 1920s had 450,000 names; there may be 20 million today."[28] Much, or most, of the information contained in personal files maintained under each of the indexed names has never pertained in any form whatsoever to criminal activities, either real or suspected by the Bureau. Rather, Hoover's agents devoted themselves (at their Director's behest) to collecting "intelligence" concerning the day-to-day private lives (*i.e.* sexual practices, credit histories, and the like) of literally millions of Americans. Among those targeted for such handling were hundreds of members of Congress, Senators, government employees, Attorneys General, and Presidents, both seated and aspirant. Under such circumstances, Hoover's vaunted bureaucratic expertise was always enhanced by what is commonly and properly referred to as blackmail; those who might seek to mount an effective challenge to the Director's wishes might well find the "seamier" side of their private existence exposed to the full glare of public scrutiny. On such details do family reputations, marriages, and political careers often rest, a matter which effectively— and not altogether unnaturally—precluded any real possibility of consolidated and concerted governmental action to bring either Hoover or his Bureau to heel over a period of several decades.[29]

Still, there was a point, after Hoover's death and in the midst of the "post-Watergate" congressional hearings of the mid-1970s, when the Bureau itself stood somewhat exposed and vulnerable, a bit of its own dirty linen hung out in public, its utilization of file information discredited before all who had cause to fear it. The possibility existed for governmental action of the sort which might have brought the FBI in line with its proclaimed role, and to have ensured the nature of its future performance. The various committees, however, each in turn abandoned their investigations of Bureau behavior well short of their logical conclusions and—in some instances—tabled or otherwise aborted them altogether. Rather than seizing the opportunity of dismantling the mythology erected by Hoover which allows the FBI to function without interference, the government hurriedly closed ranks (with very few exceptions) to leave intact the image of the Bureau—corrupt as it was known to be—without permanent or "undue" damage or disruption.[30] By the late 1970s, a spate of legislation and executive orders was enacted to insure that *none* of the FBI's functions developed under Hoover was in any real way "impaired" by even the half-hearted constraints imposed during the "Watergate era."[31]

None of this is explained by resort to the Hooverian apparatus of blackmail, by the sheer dynamics of bureaucracy, by the extent of misplaced public support for the Bureau, or even by a combination of all these factors. By 1975-76 at the latest, much of the FBI's bureaucratic impetus had been squandered along with that of the Nixon administration, and the members of government can by-and-large be viewed as having *voluntarily* returned themselves to the risk of being blackmailed by a "subordinate agency." Public support, as always in such matters, required significant engineering by "all concerned parties." There was, on the face of it, nothing at all inherent in the situation which emerged. Consequently, it is reasonable to assume that another, overarching factor must have been at work.

In this book, we will describe in some detail certain aspects of what we see as the "bottom line" to this otherwise mysterious conduct on the part of the government in not only allowing but actively assisting the Bureau in continuing to increase the level of its dirty "business as usual" since Watergate. In doing so, we seek to go as far beyond the myth of the FBI as a crime-fighting agency as is possible, given the information available to us. We posit that Hooverian propaganda was never so much an overstatement of the Bureau's gang-busting exploits, or even a pure fabrication, as much as it was a deliberate and sophisticated ruse, a calculated and intentional diversion of public attention away from the FBI's *real* purpose from the first day of its existence. Specifically, we argue that the Bureau was founded, maintained and steadily expanded as a mechanism to forestall, curtail and repress the expression of political diversity within the United States. Viewed as an essential component of enforcing the socio-political *status quo,* the Bureau's receipt of unwavering governmental support regardless of its "abuses," even at the moment when it was conclusively demonstrated to have so far exceeded its authority as to have temporarily threatened the stability of the *status quo* itself, begins to make the most fundamental kind of sense.

As our major vehicle in articulating this state of affairs, we have opted to focus our attention upon FBI operations conducted against a single, non-criminal organization (the American Indian Movement—AIM) in a given locale (the Pine Ridge Sioux Reservation, South Dakota) and during a sharply demarcated period (1972-76). We have done so for a number of reasons. Among these are the facts, as we hope to show quite plainly, that this particular exercise by the FBI seems to have been the culmination of all other Bureau experiments in political repression, many of which we take up in detail or in passing. Not coincidentally, it appears to have been among the most virulent, and certainly the most lethal on a per capita basis, of all the FBI's similar "programs" and "projects." Again, unlike many of the other examples we mention, the anti-AIM effort has received virtually no congressional attention, however limited this may have been with regard to other cases; the only formal investigation of the matter—aside from Senator James Eastland's one-member, one-witness "committee hearing" in 1975—was suspended the day before it was scheduled to begin. Finally the authors are, and have been for many years, directly involved in AIM work, one as a member, the other as a very active supporter. The particular focus of our study is therefore both natural and, perhaps, inevitable.

In discussing the details of the FBI assault upon AIM and the general population of Pine Ridge, we attempt not only to explain *what* happened there, but also *why* it happened. Although certain elements of this last are quite specific to American Indians in their peculiar relationship to the United States, we believe a great deal more may be subject to a much broader interpretation. Hence, we feel we offer an implicit explanation of how and why such a thing not only has happened before, but is entirely likely to happen again, absent a radical redefinition of the function and powers of "our" federal police. In this sense, the book is written, not only as a medium through which to understand given historical experiences, but also as a warning that these experiences are neither necessarily isolated by group nor relegated to the past. The events are recent, the wounds still fresh. Our desire is that people read what follows and become angry. Heed the dangers, grow angry and make your plans accordingly.

—Ward Churchill and Jim Vander Wall
Boulder, Colorado, 1988

Part I

The FBI as Political Police:
A Capsule History

The study of history often involves the examination and re-examination of events and processes that are reasonably well known...a function of this study is to provide a context of understanding...to apprehend and assign meaning in events or processes which have heretofore been little known, or even unknown.

—E.P. Thompson

Single acts of tyranny may be ascribed to the accidental opinion of the day; but a series of oppressions, begun at a distinguished period and pursued unalterably through every change of ministers too plainly proves a deliberate, systematical plan of reducing us to slavery.

—Thomas Jefferson

Chapter 1

Birth and Formation

During its first three and a half months in existence, the GID [General Intelligence Division of the U.S. Department of Justice, the official title under which J. Edgar Hoover's Federal Bureau of Investigation was conceived in 1919] compiled personal histories of some sixty thousand individuals thought to be radicals; before long the special indices grew to include more than two hundred thousand names. The division's translators also perused some five hundred foreign-language newspapers in order to keep up with "radical propaganda."

—Sanford J. Ungar, *FBI*

The roots from which the Federal Bureau of Investigation eventually grew seemed innocuous enough. In 1871, the United States Congress appropriated the sum of $50,000 with which the newly formed (1870) Department of Justice was authorized to engage in "the detection and prosecution of those guilty of violating Federal Law."[1] Early departmental practice was to handle investigative chores through the expedient of retaining personnel from the Pinkerton Detective Agency. However, this practice was banned by Congress in 1892 as representing a conflict of interest, a circumstance which led to the department's investigations being patched together via the borrowing of Customs Bureau, Department of Interior, and Secret Service agents over the next decade.[2] By 1903, the lack of success attendant to such procedures was so spectacular that Acting U.S. Attorney General James C. McReynolds, in a letter responding to a request from a distraught father seeking assistance in locating his kidnapped daughter, was forced to write: "You should furnish me with the names of the parties holding your daughter in bondage, the particular place, and names of witnesses by whom the facts can be proved."[3]

In 1906, Attorney General Charles S. Bonaparte (grandson of Napoleon's brother) went before Congress to complain that "a Department of Justice with no force of permanent police in any form under its control is assuredly not fully equipped for its work," and to request that Congress authorize him to create "a small, carefully selected and experienced force under [the Justice Department's] immediate orders" to accommodate investigatory functions.[4] Although Congress was less than enthusiastic in its response—several of its members having been recently indicted and convicted in a federal land fraud case—Bonaparte proceeded by a departmental order dated July 26, 1906 to establish what was called the "Bureau of Investigation" (BoI). It was then left to his successor, George W. Wickersham, to articulate with some precision the areas of responsibility assigned this new group. This he accomplished in his 1910 *Report to Congress*:

> [The BoI is intended to enforce] the national banking laws, antitrust laws, peonage laws, the bucketshop law, the laws relating to fraudulent bankruptcies, the impersonation of government officials with intent to defraud, thefts and murders committed on government reservations, offenses committed against government property, and those committed by federal court officials and employees, Chinese smuggling, customs frauds, internal revenue frauds, post office frauds, violations of the neutrality act...land frauds and immigration and naturalization cases.

To this roster of jurisdiction, Congress promptly added (the same year) responsibility for enforcement of the so-called "White Slave Traffic Act"—also known as the "Mann Act," after its author, Illinois Representative James Robert Mann—a piece of legislation aimed at breaking up a thriving interstate prostitution racket.[5] The most immediate effect of this so far as the Justice Department was concerned was the initiation of a steady increase in BoI resources and personnel. This trend escalated with the advent of the First World War in 1914, as enforcement of the then-stringent Neutrality Act and similar laws became a significant issue. On July 30, 1916, sabotage also became a major factor in BoI expansion, with the detonation of approximately two million pounds of dynamite destined for France and Great Britain by German agents on New York Harbor's Black Tom Island.[6]

In April 1917, the United States formally entered the war against Germany and the Austro-Hungarian Empire, and Woodrow Wilson—while quashing a Justice Department proposal to try civilians accused of interfering with the war effort by military court martial—signed into law the so-called "Espionage Act," including a clause making it illegal to tender "seditious utterances" during the course of the hostilities. This was quickly followed, in 1918, by the passage of the "Alien Act" (or "Alien and Sedition Act," as it is sometimes called) designed to "exclude and expel from the United States aliens who are members of the anarchist classes."[7] For the BoI, all of this meant a more-or-less instant increase in its allocated strength, from three hundred agents to approximately four hundred, and:

> To the consternation of many national leaders, the Justice Department and its growing Bureau fell into league with one of the most prominent vigilante organizations, the American Protective League. In 1917 its founder, Chicago advertising executive A.M. Briggs, persuaded...chief of the Bureau, A. Bruce Bielski, that a volunteer organization of loyal citizens should help the overloaded Bureau with its wartime work, and...Bielski in turn convinced Attorney General Thomas W. Gregory that this would be a good idea. With the prestige of official sanction, the APL grew spectacularly— until it had two hundred and fifty thousand members in chapters spread across the country. They paid a dollar to get a badge that first said Secret Service Division and later (after the Treasury Department protested about possible confusion with its real Secret Service) Auxiliary to the U.S. Department of Justice.[8]

One of the very first targets of this new quasi-official amalgam of federal agents and right-wing vigilantes was the anarcho-syndicalist Industrial Workers of the World (IWW, popularly referred to as "Wobblies"), an organization which had made substantial progress—particularly within the multi-lingual milieu of recent immigrants—in organizing the American workforce into "one big union" and which was outspokenly opposed to the war. As Howard Zinn recounts:

> In early September 1917, Department of Justice agents made simultaneous raids on forty-eight IWW meeting halls across the country, seizing correspondence and literature that would become courtroom evidence. Later that month, 165 IWW leaders were arrested for conspiracy to hinder the draft, encourage desertion, and intimidate others in connection with labor disputes. One hundred and one went on trial [en masse] in April 1918; it lasted five months, the longest criminal trial in American history up to that time...[T]he jury [several selected from the ranks of the American Protective League] found them all guilty. The judge sentenced [IWW president William "Big Bill"] Haywood and fourteen others to twenty years in prison; thirty-three were given ten years, the rest shorter sentences. They were fined a total of $2,500,000. The IWW was shattered.[9]

Nor was this repression deemed enough. The vigilante groups, operating with virtual legal impunity, set about eradicating whatever IWW organizers escaped the federal dragnet. For example, there is the case of Frank Little:

> Following a speech at the ball park in Butte [Montana] on July 31, 1917, Little went to his room at the Finn Hotel. That night, six masked and armed men broke into his room, beat him, and dragged him by a rope behind their automobile to a Milwaukee Railroad trestle on the outskirts of Butte. There he was hung. On his coat was pinned a card: "First and last warning! 3-7-77. D-D-C-S-S-W." It was said that the numbers referred to the measurements on a grave and the initials corresponded to the first letters of the names of other strike leaders in Butte, thereby warning them of similar treatment if their strike activities were not stopped. No attempt was made to find Little's assailants.[10]

In the same fashion, Wesley Everest—who, far from being subversive to the U.S. military effort, had returned from France a much-decorated hero—was captured on November 7, 1919 by a mob of self-described "patriots" in Centralia, Washington. They first "smashed his teeth with a rifle butt," then drove him to a railroad bridge, [where] he was mutilated, hanged three times and his body sprayed with bullets...The coroner's report listed his death as suicide."[11]

Numerous independent anarchists and non-IWW radicals were also subjected to the "cleansing" of BoI and vigilante operations. One of the first to go was the populist-socialist, Eugene V. Debs, who was arrested after making an anti-war speech in June of 1918; tried and convicted under the provisions of the Espionage Act, he was sentenced to ten years in Federal Prison. Emma Goldman and her lover, Alexander Berkman, both anarchists, were sentenced to ten years in prison for publicly opposing the draft (he had already been incarcerated for fourteen years in Penn-

sylvania, and she for a year on Blackwell's Island, as a result of her "labor agitation");
both were ultimately deported as "undesirable aliens" in December of 1919.[12] In
North Dakota, during July 1917, socialist Kate Richards O'Hare announced that, "the
women of the United States are nothing more or less than brood-sows, to raise
children to get into the army and be turned into fertilizer."[13] She was immediately
arrested, tried and convicted of a "seditious utterance," and sentenced to five years
in the Missouri State Penitentiary. In South Dakota, at about the same time,

> ...a farmer and socialist named Fred Fairchild, during an argument about the war, said,
> according to accusers: "If I were of conscription age and had no dependents and were
> drafted, I would refuse to serve. They could shoot me, but I would refuse to fight."
> He was tried under the Espionage Act, sentenced to a year and a day in Leavenworth
> Penitentiary. And so it went, multiplied two thousand times [the number of prosecu-
> tions under the Espionage Act].[14]

The focus of the BoI and its Protective League partners was also posed much
more broadly than merely organized or self-professed radicals. For example:

> One of the more extensive and shocking uses of the league was to help the Bureau
> of Investigation in 1918 with dragnet "slacker raids," intended to haul in young men
> who had failed to register for the draft. Thousands of people were arrested, especial-
> ly in New York and Chicago, and jailed overnight for the simple offense of not having
> a draft card in their possession at the time they were approached by the police, Bureau
> agents, APL auxiliaries, or specially deputized off-duty soldiers and sailors. Only one
> in every two hundred of them turned out to be genuine draft dodgers...[T]he abuse
> was repeated in September of the same year. It became clear that the Bureau, perhaps
> out of mere enthusiasm for its tasks, was getting out of control.[15]

Actually, the last sentence above is probably uncharitable to the BoI insofar
as there is considerable indication that Attorney General Thomas W. Gregory had
seized upon the national war fever to act in concert with major financial supporters
of the Democratic Party to "make America safe for industry," crushing the radical
opposition once and for all. Conveniently, during the war, radicals in the U.S. could
be targeted for wholesale elimination, not as threats to big business—an approach
which all but assured massive public resistance—but as a "menace to national
defense." The slacker raids and similar broadly focused gambits were designed,
more than anything, to intimidate the general public to a point where there was a
greatly diminished possibility of a popular radical resurgence after the war. In this
sense, the BoI, rather than "getting out of control," was simply accomplishing its intended goals for the Wilson administration.

The war, however, ended before the plan could be fully completed. Since a
peacetime repression of the magnitude visited upon domestic dissidents during
1917-18 was somewhat problematic, extraordinary measures were called for in continuing the BoI's political operations and Gregory turned the matter over to his successor as Attorney General, A. Mitchell Palmer. Palmer proved equal to the task, as

The front page of the *New York Times,* June 3, 1919. Although the Attorney General himself may have orchestrated the "anarchist bombing campaign" at issue, such scare tactics conditioned the public to accept the massive anti-left repression—the Palmer Raids—which shortly followed. Young J. Edgar Hoover, who served as an immediate assistant to Palmer at this time, seems to have learned much as a result of his experience.

is evidenced by BoI orchestration of an "anarchist" bombing campaign aimed at various corporate and governmental facilities around the country during the first half of 1919, and culminating in a blast at the Attorney General's own Washington, D.C. residence on June 3 of that year. Anarchist leaflets were scattered prominently about the smoking ruins of Palmer's home, as they had been at the sites of previous explosions, and the bomber himself had been blown up, disfigured beyond all possible recognition.[16] The following day, Wilson advisor Joseph Tumulty initiated the serious business of whipping up public sentiment for a new anti-radical program, stating:

> What happened in Washington last night in the attempt on the Attorney General's life is but a symptom of the terrible unrest which is stalking the country...[G]rowing steadily, from day to day, before our very eyes, [is] a movement that, if it is not checked, is bound to express itself in an attack upon everything we hold dear.[17]

For his part,

> Palmer declared war on the radicals. He named William J. Flynn, the former director of the Secret Service, to take over the Bureau and involve it [even] more actively in the fight against subversion. Francis P. Garvin became an assistant attorney general in charge of a new General Intelligence Division (GID) that would concentrate on radical and subversive activities. Garvin's direct assistant was a twenty-four-year-old up-and-coming Justice Department lawyer named John Edgar Hoover.[18]

Within six months they were ready to move:

> Palmer's men, on the night of December 21, 1919, picked up 249 aliens of Russian birth (including Emma Goldman and Alexander Berkman), put them on a transport, and deported them to what became Soviet Russia. The Constitution gave no right to Congress to deport aliens, but the Supreme Court had said, back in 1892, in affirming the right of Congress to exclude Chinese, that as a matter of self-preservation, this was a natural right of the government.[19]

This was only a minor preview of what was to follow almost immediately:

> [Palmer] used the Bureau to conduct one of the most extraordinary adventures in American legal history, the "Red Raids" which later became known as the "Palmer Raids," the attorney general's personal monument...On the night of January 2, 1920, the Bureau swept down on suspected radicals in twenty-three different cities; an estimated ten thousand people were arrested, many of them new immigrants who barely spoke English and had simply chosen an unfortunate place to gather that evening for recreation or night classes. They were confused and frightened to find themselves arrested as criminal anarchists and then held in squalid cells. Some of the "aliens" who were picked up were actually American citizens; but in the deplorable conditions in which the victims of the Palmer Raids were held, it was some time before they could make themselves known and heard.[20]

Ultimately, "the raids went on for nearly a year; from July 1919 to June 1920, warrants were issued for 6,000 alien radicals, 4,000 [of whom] were arrested but fewer than 1,000 deported."[21] And the ramifications, of course, went much further. As is noted elsewhere,

> One of those "rounded up" was an anarchist by the name of Andrea Salsedo. After his arrest he was held for eight weeks in a New York Bureau office, not allowed to have contact with his family, friends or a lawyer. Shortly thereafter his crushed body was

found on the pavement below the building. Bureau agents stated he had committed suicide by jumping from the fourteenth floor window.[22]

Two of the more vocal cynics concerning the nature of Salsedo's death were Boston-area anarchists Nicola Sacco and Bartolomeo Vanzetti, who were promptly silenced on the matter by being arrested on charges of murdering a guard during a robbery in which they, in all probability, had no part whatever. However, they:

> ...went on trial, were found guilty, and spent seven years in jail while appeals went on...The trial record and surrounding circumstances suggested that Sacco and Vanzetti were sentenced to death because they were anarchists and foreigners. In August 1927...they were electrocuted.[23]

Although he left office shortly after concluding his raids—stating that, "I apologize for nothing the Department of Justice has done in this matter. I glory in it"—what Palmer had wrought would long outlive his tenure. Ungar observes,

> In the end, the Palmer Raids had a threefold legacy: they did succeed in substantially weakening the spirit and organizational abilities of communists and other extreme left-wing groups in the United States, and they demonstrated that the use of methods that stretched and went beyond the law were a great help and an efficient tool in undermining "subversives." At the same time, the raids brought substantial additional disrespect upon the growing Bureau of Investigation and a cloud of distrust over the supposedly impartial Department of Justice. They also established the vague and dangerous precedent that the line may sometimes be blurred between straightforward law enforcement and the use of judicial processes to achieve political ends.[24]

The Bureau had come a long way since Wickersham tendered his list of jurisdictions barely a decade before.

It was into this atmosphere of blatant use of Justice Department police power to enforce the socio-economic *status quo* that J. Edgar Hoover—the man who apparently researched and articulated (via internal departmental memoranda) the "legal basis" for the Palmer Raids—thrust himself forward. He was made the permanent head of the component of the BoI most specifically preoccupied with suppressing political diversity. The General Intelligence Division was about to give way; it was time for the Federal Bureau of Investigation to be born.

The Bureau's Early Years

With the swearing in of President Warren G. Harding in 1921, Harry M. Daugherty became Attorney General. One of his first acts was to replace BoI Director Flynn with William J. Burns, another former head of the Secret Service and, after his retirement from that position in 1909, proprietor of a national detective agency bearing his name; Burns' primary claims to fame seem to have been having been convicted of surreptitious entry of a subject's office (in his mind, an avowedly proper investigative technique) and the running of a successful double-blind operation—

collecting information for England concerning Germany's North American activities and vice versa—during World War I. He, in turn, quickly gathered about himself a cabal of similar characters, notably one Gaston Bullock Means (no relation to the Means family of the Pine Ridge Reservation, covered later), "a con man who was in the midst of an extraordinary career during which he swindled people out of hundreds of thousands of dollars [and who had served as a German spy during the war]."[25] The functions of this new ensemble have been described elsewhere:

> ...Bureau men, under Burns' leadership, randomly wiretapped, broke into offices and shuffled through personal files, and kept tabs on people's private lives. The most likely targets were "enemies"—people who criticized Daugherty, the Department of Justice, and the Bureau of Investigation; senators who asked too many questions; and other competing government departments. What little standards there might have been for agents' performance were thrown out, and Bureau investigators sometimes beat prisoners to obtain confessions...To a Bureau that was already ideologically politicized Burns added a partisan twist. He kept records on the party affiliations and political connections of individual agents and added to the force on the basis of specific recommendations from friendly congressmen.[26]

J. Edgar Hoover, as head of the GID, was also designated as BoI assistant director immediately under Burns, and may thus be considered as being a party— by virtue of acquiescence, if nothing else—to such goings on. In truth, however, his major preoccupation seems to have remained very much with pursuing the GID's own special mission of "radical bashing" in the interest of government and big business. For example, during the massive railroad strike of the early 1920s,

> Attorney General Daugherty obtained a sweeping injunction from federal district court in Chicago that banned any "acts or words" that would interfere with railroad operations...[Hoover's GID] agents were sent out to enforce the injunction, and infiltrated the ranks of strikers to search for evidence of violations. Some twelve hundred unionists were arrested and many charged with contempt of court, and the Bureau was largely credited with breaking the back of the strike, an accomplishment of which Daugherty and Burns were proud.[27]

On a somewhat lesser scale, but during the same period, the GID responded to a request from the governor of Louisiana to curb the more radical activities of the Ku Klux Klan, which were seen as disrupting proper business within the state: "[T]he [GID] agents penetrated the Klan and—because there were no directly applicable federal statutes—searched out a few local officials not tied to the Klan who were willing to accept evidence gathered by federal investigators and use it to prosecute in court...[T]he organization, like the communist parties before it, was already substantially weakened."[28] Largely as a result of Hoover's success in the arena of ideological suppression, by 1923 the GID had accrued an annual budget of over $2.25 million and a staff of 697, enabling it to establish a permanent and efficient network of paid informers to infiltrate organizations considered "politically undesirable."[29]

The crunch came when Daugherty overstepped himself, employing outright "Red smear" tactics against a mainstream, rather than radical, political opponent:

> The Red smear was but one tactic...used by the Bureau against freshman Senator Burton K. Wheeler of Montana, a Democrat who had been elected in 1922 with the assistance of the left-leaning Montana "Non-Partisan League"...Shortly after his arrival in Washington, Wheeler took on the corrupt Department of Justice in speeches on the Senate floor. The Republican National Committee promptly counterattacked against the newcomer and, apparently using material provided by the Bureau, claimed that during his earlier term as United States attorney in Montana, Wheeler had permitted the state to become "a hotbed of treason and sedition." At the same time, Bureau agents hid in the bushes outside Wheeler's Washington home to spy on him, ransacked his Capitol Hill office, and tried to lure him into a compromising situation with a woman in an Ohio hotel room. Eventually, as a reprisal for the Senate investigation of the Justice Department which Wheeler was mounting, the department got a federal grand jury in Montana to bring an indictment against Wheeler for allegedly using his influence to obtain oil and gas leases for a prospector who was a friend and client.[30]

Congress, readily perceiving that application of such methods against themselves (as opposed to "the radical fringe") represented a "dangerous exercise" on the part of a government agency, promptly retaliated. In the hearings which followed, "Burns...acknowledged that the Bureau had been baldly used in an effort to bring a vendetta against Wheeler, to discredit the Senator before he could release his revelations about the Justice Department; another witness testified that Bureau agents had candidly acknowledged they were out to 'frame' Wheeler."[31] In the end, Wheeler was acquitted of the spurious charges against him, while Daugherty was dismissed from office, implicated in the Teapot Dome scandal of 1923-24; Burns and thugs like Means went with him.[32] For his part, the graceful side-stepper J. Edgar Hoover was once again able to avoid being overly tarred with the brush of his own involvements.

The new Attorney General, Harlan Fiske Stone, ushered in with the administration of Calvin Coolidge in 1924, was quick to put a new face on the Department of Justice. Disavowing the "abuses" of his predecessors, he launched a much-touted search for external personnel to fill senior departmental positions, including—unsuccessfully, as it turned out—that of BoI director. Hence, when appointing Hoover to head all Justice Department investigative and police functions on May 10, he was careful to state for publication that, "the Bureau of Investigation is not concerned with political or other opinions of individuals. It is concerned only with their conduct and then only with such conduct as is forbidden by the laws of the United States. When a police system passes beyond these limits, it is dangerous to the proper administration of justice and human liberty, which it should be our first concern to cherish," and to announce that Hoover's first condition in accepting the position was that, "the bureau must be divorced from politics."[33] The new BoI director himself went rather further in an ostensibly internal departmental memorandum, leaked to the public:

It is, of course, to be remembered that the activities of Communists and other ultra-radicals have not up to the present time constituted a violation of federal laws...and consequently, the Department of Justice, theoretically, has no right to investigate such activities as there has been no violation of federal laws. [This was an extermely interesting commentary from a man who'd "made his bones" devising an ostensibly legal basis for the Palmer Raids, union-busting and anti-Klan activities over the preceding five years.][34]

Laudable as these lofty statements may be, and accurate as they are in their expression of juridical content, all indications are that they were intended sheerly for public consumption, the reality being rather different. Hoover, apparently sensing that "American radicalism was practically destroyed by the Palmer Raids and the resulting deportations, trials and counterintelligence activities,"[35] and that his new charge truly required "a period of benign obscurity"[36] in which to rest and refit, seems merely to have launched a program of infrastructure development rather than abandonment of ideological warfare *per se.*

In this endeavor he displayed a certain genius. One of his first moves was to obtain the redesignation of the BoI as the FBI, insuring that it "would be spoken and thought of as distinct from, although always lodged within, the Justice Department."[37] Thus freed of immediate oversight within his domain, Hoover instituted a purge of employees judged incompetent, unreliable or simply as political hacks, replacing them with individuals possessing accounting, legal or other "outstanding" qualifications. Such offers were first made attractive by his rapidly assembling "a career service in which salaries and retirement benefits would be better than in any comparable agency, or elsewhere";[38] he then coupled them with a behavioral/disciplinary code which was/is unrivaled in both rigidity and severity. Finally, he created an extremely centrist organizational form by inaugurating "the tradition in which everything, large or small, was done in the Director's name."[39]

From here, Hoover began to establish the mechanisms by which the FBI could become the *de facto* regulator of the national policy in coming years. One of these, already mentioned, was the prioritization of what was to become the Files and Communications Division (FCD) which, by 1975, maintained some six and one half million "Active Investigation" files (as well as an undisclosed, but certainly much higher, number in other categories) and a "General Index" containing an estimated fifty-eight million cards. In total, the Bureau's contemporary stock of file information on American citizens—most of it pertaining to non-criminal activities—takes up literally miles of filing space in the huge J. Edgar Hoover Building,[40] despite recent intensive efforts at computerization and the fact that much file material is now retained at field offices around the country, rather than being sent to headquarters.

Another such innovation was the modernization and conversion of the old BoI Identification Division to what became known as the Division of Identification and Information (DII). Hoover dumped the archaic Bertillon system of using a complex arrangement of body measurements (length and width of head, left foot, left index finger, etc.) in favor of exclusive reliance upon the fingerprint technique. The base for this was created through the acquisition of 810,188 sets of prints maintained by the International Association of Police Chiefs and rapidly expanded after Congress, in 1930, passed a bill authorizing the Bureau to collect the prints of law-abiding citizens, as well as those of real or suspected criminals. For example, every individual who has been in the armed forces during the past fifty-seven years has his/her fingerprints submitted to the DII by the Department of Defense. By the time the DII celebrated its fiftieth anniversary in 1974, its collection contained the prints of approximately 159,000,000 Americans, and more were arriving at the rate of about 3,000 sets per day; it also employed more than 3,000 people dispensing them to some 7,300 "subscribing agencies" nationwide.[41]

The beauty of all this, from Hoover's point of view, was that it could be easily rationalized as part of the "war against crime" and "gangbuster" image (covered in our Introduction), which he was then beginning to cultivate as a cover for his Bureau's real purposes. A glimpse of this may be obtained in noting that Hoover drew upon his rapidly proliferating file information not to fight crime, but to "advise President Herbert Hoover that the 'bonus army' of desperate and destitute veterans that descended on Washington in 1932 [in the depth of the Great Depression] were made up mostly of 'criminals and communists'—advice that may have led the President to his disastrous authorization of military action to clear the demonstrators out of the capitol."[42] Another example occurred when "[t]housands of people applying for jobs with the Works Progress Administration (WPA) [a federal anti-Depression agency] in the late 1930s were matched with criminal records [courtesy of the DII] and were not hired."[43] It apparently mattered not at all to Hoover that many of these "criminal records" derived from his own program of bogus GID arrests during the 1920s; starvation was most likely seen as a fit fate for such undesirables.

Perhaps the only fullblown effort at selective political repression engaged in by the Bureau was the initiating of "a campaign against Marcus Garvey which resulted in his frameup on false charges, and ultimately [in 1927] his deportation as an 'undesirable alien,'"[44] a strategy which severely diminished the potential of his then-vibrant Universal Negro Improvement Association.[45] Meanwhile, the DII kept tabs and accumulated increasing amounts of sensitive information on all manner of socialists, communists, union organizers, black activists, anarchists and other "ultraradicals" as they painstakingly rebuilt their shattered movements. Whatever hiatus had prevailed ended formally on September 10, 1936 when Hoover dictated a "strictly confidential" memo:

> In talking with the Attorney General today concerning the radical situation, I informed him of the conference I had with the President on September 1, 1936, at which time the Secretary of State was present and...at the President's suggestion, requested of me, the representative of the Department of Justice, to have investigation made of the subversive activities in this country.[46]

The September 1937 cover of *Feds* magazine, another of the Bureau's 1930s propaganda vehicles. Note the pitch for "loyal Americans" to submit their fingerprints to the FBI.

By 1938, the FBI had launched significant and tacitly illegal (given that no federal statutory authority existed for such practices) investigations of supposed subversion in the maritime, steel, coal, textile, fur, automobile and newspaper industries, as well as various educational institutions, organized labor, assorted youth groups, black organizations, governmental affairs and the armed forces, according to another classified memorandum submitted by Hoover to Attorney General Homer Cummings and President Franklin D. Roosevelt.[47] More explicit illegality was involved in the methods of intelligence-gathering themselves; wiretapping (in direct contravention of the Federal Communications Act of 1934), bugging, mail tampering/opening and breaking-and-entering were a few of the expedients routinely applied by agents, whose investigative output was promptly summarized and transmitted "upstairs" to the White House.[48] It was also on such basis that spectacles like the "Christian Front Case," mentioned in our Introduction, were put before the public, conditioning national sentiment to accept growing national police power "for the common good."

The first device employed in returning the FBI to its status as a fullblown instrument of political repression was the Espionage Act which had proven so fruitful in this regard during the First World War:

> [W]hereas the Bureau had averaged only about thirty-five espionage cases a year between 1933 and 1937, the number increased in Fiscal Year 1938 to two hundred and fifty cases. By January 1940, appearing before the House Appropriations Committee, the Director was predicting that espionage cases might run as high as seventy thousand a year, most of which would require some degree of [FBI] investigation. Congressional appropriations for the Bureau's work increased dramatically.[49]

Shortly thereafter, Congress also passed the Smith Act—named after Representative Howard W. Smith of Virginia, its author—which was modeled on the New York Criminal Anarchy Act of 1902, and which made it a crime "to knowingly or willfully advocate, abet, advise or teach the duty, necessity, desirability or propriety of overthrowing or destroying any government in the United States by force or violence, or by assassination of any officer of such government." The new act was aimed not only at both speech and print, but "it took the Espionage Act prohibitions against talk and writing which would lead to refusal of duty in the armed forces and applied them to peacetime."[50]

Hoover thereupon informed the subcommittee overseeing the Bureau budget that "he had revived the old General Intelligence Division of the Palmer Raid days, renaming it the Security Division [later the Domestic Intelligence Division, and today known simply as the Intelligence Division]. Under its auspices, the Bureau would keep a 'general index,' alphabetical and geographical, which would permit the immediate location of anyone it wanted to investigate in the name of national security";[51] the real functions of the DII and FCI were thus finally and fully revealed. The Director also had a "warm-up case" to display before Congress:

Despite J. Edgar Hoover's puritanical posturing *vis a vis* those he perceived as political "deviants," the Director was known to steadily indulge his thirst for "the fast life." Here, he is being capped for New Year's Eve, 1937, by a starlet in one of the many expensive nightclubs he frequented. Hoover was also addicted to betting the ponies. (Photo: *Washington Post*)

For some time the FBI had investigated those who recruited Americans to go to Spain with the Abraham Lincoln Brigade to fight on the Loyalist side of the Spanish Civil War, but nothing ever came of the cases. Finally, in February 1940, a federal grand jury in Detroit indicted eleven men and one woman, all with possible communist connections, on charges of raising a foreign army in the United States...The Bureau arrested all the suspects in simultaneous raids at 5 A.M., although a federal judge would not be available for their arraignment until 3 P.M...both in the Detroit arrests and in parallel raids conducted by the FBI in Milwaukee and New York City, agents searched homes and offices without warrants. The Detroit defendants were apparently prevented from telephoning their lawyers, and when the United States marshals took custody of them, they were handcuffed to a long chain for the trip to court.[52]

Although Attorney General Robert H. Jackson—later to become Chief Justice of the international tribunal trying Nazi war criminals (including civil authorities, such as Gestapo leadership) at Nuremberg, Germany in 1946-47 and, subsequently, a Justice of the U.S. Supreme Court—shortly dropped all charges against those arrested in the FBI roundup, he simultaneously cleared the Bureau (which had been compared to the Gestapo in a *New Republic* editorial of the period) of any wrongdoing.[53] Hence, the way was clear for Hoover to move ahead: "In Minneapolis in 1943, eighteen members of the Socialist Workers Party were convicted of belonging to a party whose ideas, expressed in its Declaration of Principles, and in the *Communist Manifesto*, were said to violate the Smith Act. They were sentenced to prison terms [of ten years each], and the Supreme Court refused to review their case."[54]

All told, as Hoover reported to the House Appropriations Committee in 1946, the activities of the FBI during the Second World War had included the investigation of some 19,587 cases of alleged subversion or sabotage, 2,447 of which turned out to be *bona fide* in his view; these brought convictions in a "mere 611" cases, "with sentences aggregating 1,637 years and fines of $251,709."[55] Many of these cases were somewhat ludicrously posed as "anti-Nazi" successes (as opposed to anti-leftist actions), such as the travesties in which the Bureau claimed credit for apprehending teams of German saboteurs landed by submarine along the Eastern Seaboard (off Long Island, Florida, and Maine). In each instance, it was later revealed that the Germans had marched themselves directly to the authorities to surrender with no prompting on the part of the Bureau; in the Long Island case, "incredulous FBI men had at first refused to believe their stories."[56]

In contrast to its showy prosecution of leftists and small fry Nazi sympathizers, the Bureau was either unwilling or unable to curtail the activities of U.S.-based transnational corporations which seriously threatened national security. For example:

- Standard Oil subsidiaries supplied petroleum products and chemicals to the Axis powers throughout World War Two. This included the use of Standard Oil tankers to refuel German U-boats which were sinking Allied shipping.[57]

- International Telephone and Telegraph (ITT) produced a wide array of electronic devices for the *Wehrmacht* [Germany's armed forces] including 30,000 artillery shell fuses per month which were used to kill American G.I.s. They also built the Focke-Wulf bombers which claimed thousands of Allied lives.[58]

- General Motors, besides building trucks and cars for the *Wehrmacht*, manufactured the engines for the Junkers Ju.88 bombers, one of the deadliest weapons in the Nazi arsenal.[59]

The provision of such "aid and comfort" to the enemies of the U.S. in wartime is treason in the narrowest legal sense of the word. The Bureau, despite its responsibility to investigate such crimes, did little to impair these activities.[60] When, in 1944,

Hoover received a gift from ITT Director Sosthenes Behn, of his book *Beyond Our Shores the World Will Know Us,* Hoover responded cordially: "...the book...has arrived. I do want to express to you my heartfelt appreciation for your thoughtfulness in making this splendid volume available." Behn, besides heading a corporation which was manufacturing weapons for Hitler, had been linked by the Bureau's own files to Nazi intelligence operations.[61]

In at least one case, the Bureau's activities are known to have severely impaired the fight against corporate collaboration with the Nazis. In 1940, at the behest of ambassador-at-large William Bullitt, a Nazi sympathizer, Hoover undertook an investigation of State Department official Sumner Welles. Welles had been so effective in his opposition to the support of the Nazis by transnational corporations that Charles Higham in his book, *Trading with the Enemy,* called Welles "the single most powerful force against world fascism."[62] Hoover knew that Welles was a bisexual and over the next three years the Bureau amassed a file on his homosexual activities, including encounters set up by the Bureau to compromise Welles. Using the results of this investigation, pro-Nazi forces were able to pressure Roosevelt into demanding that Welles resign.[63]

Regardless of the realities inherent to the Bureau's posture and performance which may be retroactively discerned, the FBI had by the end of the Second World War come to be popularly perceived "as a bulwark of American democracy, the fearless protector and defender of [the nation] in troubled times, the agency that would stand behind its country, right or wrong."[64] This circumstance allowed Hoover the opportunity to consolidate what Ungar terms his "monolith," an agency expressing what are undoubtedly the most reactionary tendencies in domestic American history.

Consolidation

On March 22, 1947, President Harry S. Truman issued Executive Order (E.O.) 9835, initiating a program to seek out "infiltration of disloyal persons [*i.e.* communists]" within the United States government; the order required the Justice Department to draw up a list of organizations to be considered "totalitarian, fascist, communist or subversive...or seeking to alter the government of the United States by unconstitutional means." Not only membership in, but also "sympathetic association with" these organizations would be considered *prima facie* evidence of "disloyalty," leading to immediate dismissal from federal employment, or worse. By 1954, the FBI placed hundreds of groups—including the Chopin Cultural Center, the Cervantes Fraternal Society, the Committee for Negro Arts, the Committee for the Protection of the Bill of Rights, the League of American Writers, the Nature Friends of America, the Washington Bookshop Association, and the Yugoslav Seamen's Club—on the proscription list. Tied to the recent proclamation of the "Truman Doctrine"—the policy enunciated during the spring of 1947, to provide military and economic aid to "free peoples who are resisting attempted subjugation by armed minorities or by outside [*i.e.* Soviet] pressures"—E.O. 9835 was part of a much broader governmental effort to reinforce the American politico-economic preeminence which had emerged during Second World War:

> The United States was trying, in the postwar decade, to create a national consensus—excluding the radicals, who could not support a foreign policy aimed at suppressing revolution—of conservatives and liberals, Republicans and Democrats, around the policies of the cold war and anti-Communism. Such a coalition could best be created by a liberal Democratic President, whose aggressive policy abroad would be supported by conservatives...if the anti-Communist mood became strong enough, liberals could support repressive moves at home which in ordinary times would be seen as violating the tradition of liberal tolerance.[65]

Using the prevailing *zeitgeist*, J. Edgar Hoover was quickly able to "define [his] own parameters" in crucial areas of "internal security" and domestic counterintelligence. This included an outspoken opposition—on the grounds of "potential subversion"—to the locating of the United Nations headquarters in New York during 1947-48.[66] During the same years, he purported to have "proof positive" that Philip Jaffe, the editor of an esoteric journal titled *Amerasia,* had conspired with the U.S. Communist Party leader Earl Browder, a State Department China specialist and a Navy lieutenant to leak top secret government documents to Mao Tse Tung's soon-to-be-victorious insurgents in China, a matter which he claimed had played into the "loss of China to Communism." While a federal grand jury found these charges essentially baseless, and that both the FBI and the OSS (Office of Strategic Services, predecessor organization to the CIA) had violated the rights of the accused by conducting a series of warrantless searches of their homes and offices, the ploy was an obvious boon.[67] It also seems likely that such gestures, "playing well in Peoria" as they were, did much to establish the context within which policy-makers could confidently go beyond the "containment strategy" articulated by the Truman Doctrine to the far more militant "rollback strategy"—and attendant U.S. military buildup—posited in such planning documents as the National Security Council's NSC 68 of April 1950.[68] They must also be related directly to the passage, also in 1950, of the Republican sponsored Internal Security Act—also known as the McCarran Act after its sponsor, Senator Pat McCarran of Nevada, although it had actually been crafted by junior Congressmen Karl Mundt of South Dakota and Richard M. Nixon of California—requiring that all members of "Communist-front" or "Communist-action" organizations be registered with the federal goverment, and the corresponding proposal by Democratic Senators Hubert Humphrey and Herbert Lehman that special "detention centers" (*i.e.,* concentration camps *a la* Dachau) be established for the housing of those registered, without trial, at any time the President wished to declare an "internal security emergency."[69] All of this coupled tidily with Section 533, Title 28 of the U.S. Code which authorizes the Attorney General to order investigations of individuals and groups, even when prosecution is not contemplated.

As Howard Zinn observes:

In this atmosphere, Senator Joseph McCarthy of Wisconsin...[s]peaking to a Women's Republican Club in Wheeling, West Virginia, in early 1950...[could hold] up some papers and [shout]: "I have in my hand a list of 205—a list of names that were made known to the Secretary of State as being members of the Communist Party and who nevertheless are still working and shaping policy in the State Department." The next day, speaking in Salt Lake City, McCarthy claimed he had a list of fifty-seven (the number kept changing) such Communists in the State Department. Shortly afterward, he appeared on the floor of the Senate with photostatic copies of about a hundred dossiers from State Department loyalty files. The dossiers were three years old, and most of the people were no longer with the State Department, but McCarthy read from them anyway, inventing, adding, and changing what he read. In one case, he changed the dossier's description of "liberal" to "communistically inclined," in another from "active fellow traveller" to "active Communist," and so on...

McCarthy kept on like this for the next few years. As Chairman of the Permanent Investigations Subcommittee of a Senate Committee on Governmental Operations, "he investigated the State Department's information program, its Voice of America, and its overseas libraries, which included books by people McCarthy considered Communists. The State Department reacted in panic...forty books were removed, including *The Selected Writings of Thomas Jefferson*...Some books were burned." [70]

Although Hoover is known to have personally disliked McCarthy, considering him a "thoroughly unsavory" character,[71] he was quick to avail himself and his Bureau of the advantages afforded by the Senator's witch-hunt:

The FBI took a lot of its cues in the internal security field from the House Un-American Activities Committee [HUAC], which was still going strong in the 1950s and, in the executive branch, the Subversive Activities Control Board [SACB]. Together with those panels and, for a time, Senator Joseph McCarthy's subcommittee investigating Communist influence in government, the Bureau became part of a sort of internal security establishment within the federal government...Although the FBI was a supposedly impartial, fair-minded agency, it became firmly entrenched...on the right end of the political spectrum. They whipped the Red scare back into existence, and any person they considered too radical, or even liberal, was liable to be labeled "pink," investigated by the Bureau, and hauled before HUAC, the SACB, or a grand jury.[72]

Considerable momentum for this had been gained with the outbreak of the Korean "Conflict" in 1950 (with the communist North Koreans attempting to regain by force of arms the southern portion of their peninsula, occupied by the U.S. since 1945) and by two prominent "communist spy cases" pursued—and perhaps largely fabricated—by the Bureau. The first of these, acted out with much public fanfare during the late 1940s, involved a pair of supposedly highly placed former Communist Party members, Elizabeth Terrill Bentley and Whitaker Chambers (at the time an editor of *Time* magazine), who "recanted" by naming Alger Hiss, a State Department official, William W. Remington of the War Production Board, and Harry Dex-

ter White, an assistant secretary of the treasury and official of the International
Monetary Fund, as members of a "Russian spy ring." The charges themselves were
never proven, but "Hiss finally went to prison on a perjury conviction [for which he
served four years], as did Remington (who died after he was attacked in Lewisburg
Penitentiary), and White was substantially discredited before he died of a heart attack
a few days after testifying before HUAC."[73] As of this writing, and despite subsequent
selective release of FBI documents relating to the case, serious questions remain
concerning the Bureau's role in the matter.[74]

The second case, prosecuted during the summer of 1950, involved a man
named David Greenglass, a former machinist with the Manhattan (atomic bomb)
Project in Los Alamos, New Mexico, who was dragged into one of many loyalty investigations occurring at the time, and Harry Gold, already serving a thirty year sentence on an apparently genuine espionage conviction passed down in 1945. Possibly
in exchange for reduced time served on their sentences—Gold was released after
fifteen years, and Greenglass did only about seven and one-half years—both men
testified that Julius and Ethel Rosenberg (she being Greenglass' sister) had been the
prime movers in providing documents disclosing "the secret of the bomb" to the
USSR. Also charged was Morton Sobell, a nuclear scientist, accused by Max Elitcher,
best man at Sobell's wedding, but himself under an espionage indictment (the charges were later dropped). The case against Sobell was so weak that his defense counsel declined even to bother presenting a defense; the case against the Rosenbergs
looked little better. Nonetheless, in the heat of the times, the jury convicted them
all, and the judge sentenced Sobell to thirty years in prison; he eventually served
nineteen years in Alcatraz and other maximum security facilities before being
released. The Rosenbergs were sentenced to death and electrocuted at New York's
Ossining ("Sing Sing") prison on June 19, 1953.[75] As with the Hiss case, the Rosenberg affair is plagued with unresolved questions concerning the justice of the conviction and the FBI's true role in obtaining it, as well as issues concerning
judge-prosecutor conferences and certain "assurances" provided by Chief Justice of
the Supreme Court Fred Vinson to Attorney General Herbert Brownell.[76]

The context of repression was glamorized and rendered palatable to the public
through an intensive and sustained media campaign:

> The whole culture was permeated with anti-Communism. The large-circulation
> magazines had articles like "How Communists Get That Way" and "Communists Are
> After Your Child." *The New York Times* ran an editorial: "We would not knowingly
> employ a Communist party member in the news or editorial departments...because
> we could not trust his ability to report the news objectively or to comment on it honest-
> ly." An FBI informer's story of his exploits as a Communist who became an FBI agent—
> "I Led Three Lives"—was serialized in five hundred newspapers and put on television.
> Hollywood movies had titles like *I Married a Communist* and *I Was a Communist for
> the FBI*. Between 1948 and 1954, more than forty anti-Communist films came out of
> Hollywood...Young and old were taught that anti-Communism was heroic. Three mil-
> lion copies were sold of a book by Mickey Spillane published in 1951, *One Lonely
> Night*, in which the hero, Mike Hammer, says: "I killed more people tonight than I

have fingers on my hands. I shot them in cold blood and I enjoyed every minute of it...They were commies...red sons-of-bitches who should have died long ago..."[77]

The FBI never really broke with the McCarthyites until the spring of 1954, when "he [McCarthy] began to hold hearings to investigate supposed subversives in the military. When he began attacking generals for not being hard enough on suspected Communists, he antagonized Republicans as well as Democrats [this *was*, after all, in the midst of the Republican administration of former General Dwight D. Eisenhower], and in December 1954, the Senate voted overwhelmingly to censure him for 'conduct...unbecoming a Member of the United States Senate.'"[78] It is important to note that the censure avoided criticizing either McCarthy's rabid anti-Communist campaign of lies or abridgement of the rights of citizens, but upon his abuse of the generals and refusal to appear before a Senate Subcommittee on Privileges and Elections; at about the same time, liberal Democratic Senator Hubert Humphrey was arguing for legislation to make the Communist Party, USA flatly illegal.[79] Meanwhile, the Bureau had engaged in some 6.6 million "security investigations" of Americans between March 1947 and December 1952 (after which they supposedly tapered off dramatically).[80] In just one of its more important programs of the period, "Communist Infiltration," referred to by the acronym COMINFIL, the Bureau placed hundreds of informers within "the entire spectrum of the social and labor movements in the country,"[81] actualizing in real life Orwell's fiction that "Big Brother is watching" (and three full decades before the author's target date of 1984).

As its colleagues—and rivals—in reaction faded during the later 1950s, it was the FBI which inherited their collective mantle. It emerged from the McCarthy period unified and consolidated as a political police apparatus, its mechanisms of repression fully developed, and ideologically prepared to enforce as a permanent feature what C. Wright Mills has described as "the great stillness" of conscience which had enveloped American life over the preceding decade.[82]

Chapter 2

The COINTELPRO Era

The COINTELPRO operations of the 1960s were modeled on the successful programs of earlier years undertaken to disrupt the American Communist Party...[which] continued through the 1960s, with such interesting variations as Operation Hoodwink from 1966 through mid-1968, designed to incite organized crime against the Communist Party through documents fabricated by the FBI, evidently in the hope that criminal elements would carry on the work of repression and disruption in their own manner, by means that may be left to the imagination.

—Noam Chomsky, *COINTELPRO*

Although, by definition, the focus of the FBI's counterintelligence functions have always been administratively lodged in its Counterintelligence Division (CID) and legally restricted to "hostile foreign governments, foreign organizations and individuals connected with them,"[1] such proprieties have never been observed. To the contrary, it is clear that virtually from the day Franklin Delano Roosevelt authorized the Bureau's return to investigation of subversives, Hoover cultivated a very real confluence of such activities between the CID and that unit of the FBI established to control purely domestic political dissent, the Internal Security Division (ISD). Acronymically, these domestic counterintelligence programs were designated as COINTELPROs and, throughout the 1940s and 1950s, were directed almost exclusively at the Socialist Workers Party (SWP) and the Communist Party, USA (CPUSA).[2] According to William C. Sullivan, a former head of the CID and, along with Cartha D. "Deke" DeLoach, a major architect of COINTELPRO:

We were engaged in COINTELPRO tactics, to divide, conquer, weaken, in diverse ways, an organization. We were engaged in that when I entered the Bureau in 1941.[3]

While in strict FBI parlance a COINTELPRO refers to a specific secret and typically illegal operation (there were many thousands of individual COINTELPROs executed between 1940 and 1971), in popular usage the term came to signify the whole context of clandestine political repression activities, several of them—such as unwarranted electronic surveillance—related to but never formally part of COINTELPRO at all.[4] Regardless of its precise technical meaning in "Bureauese," COINTELPRO is now used as a descriptor covering the whole series of sustained and

37

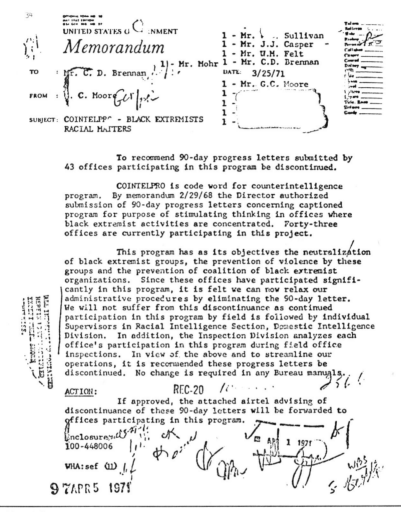

A COINTELPRO memo.

systematic campaigns directed by the Bureau against a wide array of selected domestic political organizations and individuals, especially during the 1960s.[5] According to William Kunstler, there were more than 2,370 separate "literary" COINTELPROs during the 1960s alone. An FBI memorandum from C.D. Brennan to W.C. Sullivan, dated April 27, 1971 and captioned COUNTERINTELLIGENCE PROGRAMS (COINTELPROS) INTERNAL SECURITY—RACIAL MATTERS also uses the term in a different way, listing seven sustained and overarching operations as coming under the heading prior to that date. These were: COINTELPRO—Espionage; COINTELPRO—New Left; COINTELPRO—Disruption of White Hate Groups;

William C. Sullivan, an architect of COINTELPRO, during the period when he was charged with orchestrating the FBI's campaign to destroy Dr. Martin Luther King, Jr., and the Civil Rights Movement in the South.

COINTELPRO—Communist Party, USA; Counterintelligence and Special Operations; COINTELPRO—Black Extremists; Socialist Workers Party—Disruption Program.

In collaboration with local police units (often specifically created for this purpose with the assistance of the FBI) and reactionary "private" groups (many of which were spawned or expanded with Bureau support), COINTELPRO efforts were marked—in varying degrees of intensity—by utilization of the following "methods" against the Bureau's political targets:

Eavesdropping

A massive program of surveillance was carried out against organizations and individuals via wiretaps, surreptitious entries and burglaries, electronic devices, live "tails" and mail tampering. The purpose of such activities was never intelligence gathering *per se*, but rather the inducement of "paranoia" among those targeted by making them aware they'd been selected for special treatment and that there was "an FBI agent behind every mailbox." This phrase actually originates in uncensored FBI documents obtained when a group calling itself the Citizens' Commission to Investigate the FBI finally turned the Bureau's methods around, breaking into the FBI's Media, Pennsylvania office on the night of March 8, 1971 and removing thousands of pages from classified files. The use of the word "paranoia"—which turned out to be a staple of FBI political repression vernacular—is taken from a brief entitled "New Left Notes, Philadelphia, 9/16/71, Edition No. 1," as is the verbiage concerning agents and mailboxes. It was within the Media documents, summarized during the following week in the *Washington Post*, that the public was first made aware of the existence of COINTELPRO as an official entity.[6]

Bogus Mail

Fabrication of correspondence between members of targeted groups, or between groups, was designed to foster "splits" within or between organizations; these efforts were continued—and in many cases intensified—when it became apparent that the resulting tension was sufficient to cause physical violence among group members. An example of this, covered under the heading "The Effort to Disrupt the Black Panther Party by Promoting Internal Dissention, 2) FBI Role in the Newton-Cleaver Rift," was taken up by the U.S. Senate Select Committee to Study Government Operations. The Select Committee report recounts the systematic fabrication and transmittal of letters and other documents expressly intended to push ideological disagreements between Party leaders Huey P. Newton and Eldridge Cleaver into the realm of open hostility. For instance, in a Memorandum from the Los Angeles field office to FBI headquarters on December 3, 1970 (p. 2) it is recommended that a letter be forged and sent—ostensibly by a disgruntled Party member—to Eldridge Cleaver, then in exile in Algeria; the letter should attempt to:

> ...provoke Cleaver to openly question Newton's leadership...It is felt that distance and lack of personal contact between Newton and Cleaver do offer a counterintelligence opportunity that should be probed...[Additionally] each division [of the FBI] should write numerous letters [under similar circumstances] to Cleaver criticizing Newton's leadership. It is felt that, if Cleaver received a sufficient number of complaints regarding Newton it might...create dissension that later could be more fully exploited.

Headquarters approved this COINTELPRO by a Memorandum routed to the Los Angeles, San Francisco and Washington field offices on December 5, 1970, increasing dissemination of the idea to include Atlanta, Boston, Chicago, Detroit, and New York field offices by Memorandum on December 31, 1970. This was but one of nearly a hundred similar and well-documented correspondence efforts undertaken with regard to the Newton-Cleaver factional fight alone.[7]

Indication of the nature of the "counterintelligence opportunities" which the Bureau felt "later could be more fully exploited" with regard to fostering such dissension is provided in Peter L. Zimroth's *Perversions of Justice:*

> During the next several months, the rift in the Party widened. Two Black Panther Parties emerged—one led by Newton and [Bobby] Seale, and one led by Cleaver in Algeria...On March 8, 1971, Robert Webb, a Panther loyal to Cleaver, was shot in New York. One month later, Samuel Napier, loyal to Newton, was scalded, shot to death, and then set on fire in the Party's office in Queens.

Eldridge Cleaver, Minister of Information of the Black Panther Party, editor for *Ramparts* magazine and 1968 candidate for the U.S. Presidency for the Peace and Freedom Party. This photo was taken shortly before a COINTELPRO resulted in Cleaver being driven from the country and set at odds with BPP leader Huey P. Newton. (Photo: *U.S. News and World Report*)

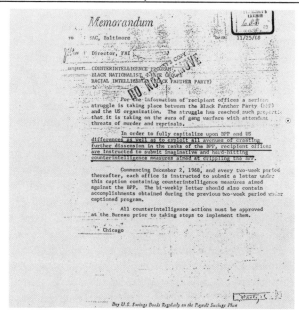

COINTELPRO memo directed against the BPP and US Organization.

The split, deliberately exacerbated by the FBI, is also directly related to several other homicides, covered elsewhere in this book.[8]

"Black Propaganda" Operations

"Black Propaganda" refers to the fabrication and distribution of publications (leaflets, broadsides, etc.) "in behalf of" targeted organizations/ individuals designed to misrepresent their positions, goals or objectives in such a way as to publicly discredit them and foster intra/inter-group tensions. A classic case of this is covered in Congress' *The FBI's Covert Action Program to Destroy the Black Panther Party*,[9] under the heading "The Effort to Promote Violence Between the Black Panther Party and Other Well-Armed, Potentially Violent Organizations." Among the methods employed was the production and distribution of a series of cartoons (see samples) attributed to the Black Panther Party (BPP) and Ron Karenga's United Slaves Organization (US), with each side supposedly caricaturing the other in extremely negative fashion. This was part of an overall Bureau effort undertaken, as explained by Hoover in a Memorandum to Baltimore and thirteen other field offices, dated November 25, 1968, "In order to fully capitalize upon BPP and US differences as well as to exploit all avenues of creating further dissension within the ranks of the BPP." Hoover also noted that "recipient offices are instructed to submit imaginative and hard-hitting counter-intelligence measures aimed at crippling the BPP" within what he described as a context of "gang warfare" and "attendant threats of murder and reprisal" associated with the BPP-US dispute.

Small wonder that, when Los Angeles Panther leaders Jon Huggins and Alprentice "Bunchy" Carter were killed by US gunmen in UCLA's Campbell Hall on January 17, 1969, the Bureau assigned itself a good measure of "credit" and recommended a new round of cartoons designed to "indicate to the BPP that the US organization feels they are ineffectual, inadequate, and riddled with graft and corruption" (Memorandum from San Diego field office to headquarters, February 20, 1969). Similarly, when US members wounded two Panthers in an ambush in San Diego on August 14, 1969, and killed another, Sylvester Bell, in a follow-up action the next day, the Bureau again congratulated itself on this "success," observing: "In view of the recent killing of BPP member Sylvester Bell, a new cartoon is being considered in hopes that it will assist in the continuance of the rift between the BPP and US," as part of "Efforts being made to determine how this situation can be capitalized upon for the benefit of the Counterintelligence Program" (Memorandum from the San Diego field office to headquarters, August 20, 1969).

It should be noted that the murderers of Huggins and Carter—the brothers George and Joseph Stiner, and a man named Claude Hubert—are believed to have been police infiltrators of US, injected as an expedient to raise the level of tension between US and the BPP. In large part, this suspicion has been raised by categorical assertions to this effect by a murky former agent provocateur placed inside the BPP during the critical period, and code-named "Othello"; Othello himself

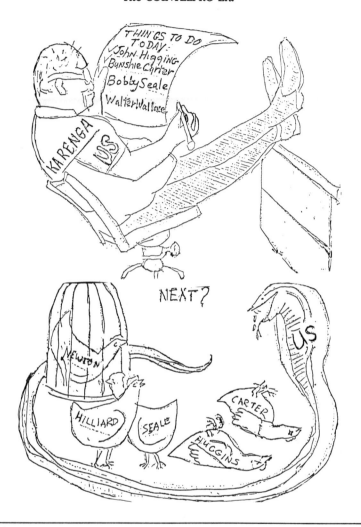

Samples of cartoons produced and distributed by the FBI as part of a COINTELPRO designed to create a "shooting war" between the BPP and the US Organization in Southern California.

is variously thought to be Louis Tackwood or Darthard Perry. Within the known context of overall COINTELPRO operations against the BPP, such a possibility would not be atypical, and should consequently not be discounted.[10]

Disinformation or "Gray Propaganda"

The FBI systematically released disinformation to the press and electronic media concerning groups and individuals, designed to discredit them and foster tensions. This was also seen as an expedient means of conditioning public sentiment to accept Bureau/police/vigilante "excesses" aimed at targeted organizations/individuals, and to facilitate the conviction of those brought to trial, even on conspicuously flimsy evidence. Such activities were so pervasive that one hardly knows where to begin in describing them. To provide a single, typically juvenile illustration, consider the text of the following Memorandum from G.C. Moore to W.C. Sullivan, routed to seven other ranking Bureau officials as well, written October 10, 1968 and proposing a media COINTELPRO against the Black Panther Party:

PURPOSE:

To recommend attached item be given news media source on a confidential basis as a counterintelligence measure to help neutralize extremist Black Panthers and foster a split between them and the Student Nonviolent Coordinating Committee (SNCC).

BACKGROUND:

There is a feud between the two most prominent black nationalist extremist groups, the Black Panthers and SNCC. Attached item notes that the feud is being continued by SNCC circulating the statement that:

"According to zoologists, the main difference between a panther and other large cats is that the panther has the smallest head."

This is biologically true. Publicity to this effect might help neutralize Black Panther recruiting efforts.

ACTION:

That attached item, captioned "Panther Pinheads," be furnished to a cooperative news media source by the Crime Records Division on a confidential basis. We will be alert for other ways to exploit this item.

The operation was approved the following day and the article appeared in newspapers nationally over the following month. While its impact on Panther recruitment efforts is difficult to quantify, it does seem to have been "helpful" in finalizing the split between the Panthers and SNCC.

Harassment Arrests

The repeated arrest of targeted individuals and organization members on spurious charges was carried out, not with any real hope of obtaining convictions (although there was always that possibility, assuming public sentiment had been sufficiently inflamed), but to simply harass, increase paranoia, tie up activists in a series of pre-arraignment incarcerations and preliminary courtroom procedures, and deplete their resources through the postings of numerous bail bonds (as well as the retention of attorneys). Again this was so pervasive a tactic that it is impossible to give

Maxwell Sanford, director of U.S. operations for RAM, was also the founder of a BPP chapter in New York City, August 1966.

a comprehensive summary of its use during the 1960s. Perhaps the best single example of its employment with precision, and with focus upon a given organization, involves the destruction of Maxwell Sanford's Revolutionary Action Movement (RAM), an incipient national-level black formation based primarily in Philadelphia, during 1967. The report on this COINTELPRO, provided by Memorandum from the Special Agent in Charge (SAC) of the Bureau's Philadelphia office to the Director on August 30, 1967 speaks for itself:

I. RAM

This division during the summer of 1967 has had the opportunity to observe an attempt by an extremist Negro group (RAM) to affect peace of the city. Some of the steps taken against RAM may be of possible use elsewhere under the current program [COIN-TELPRO]. It is pointed out that in a fast moving series of situations, the police may have to "play it by ear," which may reduce Bureau control of the action taken. Actions herein set out were carried out by either the Intelligence Unit or the Civil Disobedience Unit (CDU) of the Philadelphia PD, the largest role being played by CDU...

When activity started with the appearance of known Negro extremists native to Philadelphia at the [name deleted] residence, a full-time surveillance by police went into effect.

Cars stopping at [name deleted] residence were checked as to license numbers. When they left the residence area, they were subject to car stops by uniformed police. The occupants were identified. They then became the target of harassment. As an example, the following case is cited:

[One and one-half lines deleted.] He was located passing out RAM literature at a local school. He was interrogated. He was arrested as a narcotic user on the basis of alleged needle marks. He was subsequently released to a magistrate.

Any excuse for arrest was promptly implemented by arrest. Any possibility of neutralizing a RAM activist was exercised.

[Name deleted] was arrested for defacing private property when he painted "Black Guard" on a private building. His companion was also arrested. A charge of carrying a concealed deadly weapon, a switch-blade knife, was pushed against the companion. His probation officer was contacted, his parole revoked, and he was returned to prison for several years.

When surveillance reflected the arrival of a new group in town, they were brought in for investigation and their residence searched.

Certain addresses used by [name deleted] as mail drops in Philadelphia had been determined to be the addresses of known Negro extremists. When a young Negro was arrested for passing out RAM printed flyers and was charged with inciting to riot these addresses appeared in statements to police. Search warrants were secured. While the search of the first four only eliminated their use as main drops, the fifth contained RAM and Communist literature and a duplicating machine with a RAM leaflet on the plate. Three persons were arrested at this last address.

Legal searches of the home of [name deleted] and other RAM members produced a volume of literature of such nature that the District Attorney authorized arrest of [name deleted] and five other RAM members. They are still in prison.

Other RAM people were arrested and released on bail, but they were re-arrested several times until they could no longer make bail.

The above activities appear for the present to have curtailed the activities of this [deleted] group. It was apparently a highly frustrating experience for the person involved.

[Two lines deleted] was advised that he was again under arrest and that his wife and sister were also under arrest, he lay down on the floor of his residence, beat the floor with his fists and cried…

The above action by local police units [controlled by the FBI] is cited as an example of an effective counterintelligence technique. In other cities where close police cooperation exists, it may be possible to suggest similar operations and to police officers interested in such a violence-prone organization not only information concerning it but ideas relative to its vital or weak sections and profitable points of attack…

III. FUTURE ACTION PLANNED BY PHILADELPHIA

1. Pursuant to Bureau instructions, this office will commence interviewing RAM members. About a dozen are presently incarcerated in Philadelphia and these will be the first interviewed.

2. Philadelphia is presently reviewing and analysing a list of names and addresses compiled from three private address books taken from [name deleted] at the time of his

three arrests since returning to Philadelphia. Selective interviews will be made and analysis may lead to other counterintelligence suggestions.

3. [name deleted] and most RAM activists in Philadelphia appear to be in prison. Philadelphia will have to evaluate the situation more fully to determine the extent of vitality remaining in RAM in this area before it will be in a position to advance further suggestions under this program [COINTELPRO].

Aside from the patent and deliberate violations of such constitutionally safeguarded rights as freedom of speech, press and assembly described in the preceding, RAM's membership was never targeted because of any suspected criminality. Despite the rhetoric concerning their being "violence-prone," few arrests and no convictions were ever obtained against group members on such charges (even the so-called "switch-blade knife" at issue turned out to be a pen-knife with a blade-length of less than three inches). RAM was destroyed as an organization for no reason other than that of possessing an ideological perspective which was in opposition to the political *status quo* in the United States.

Infiltrators and Agents Provocateurs

This widely used tactic involved the infiltration of targeted organizations with informers and agents provocateurs, the latter expressly for the purpose of fomenting or engaging in illegal activities which could then be attributed to key organizational members and/or the organization as a whole. Agents provocateurs were also routinely assigned to disrupt the internal functioning of targeted groups and to assist in the spread of disinformation. Once again, examples are legion. Initially, there seemed to be an inclination on the part of the Bureau to utilize such personnel, at least in part, *a la* Herbert "I Led Three Lives" Philbrick during the early 1950s, as vehicles to promote bogus "exposés" designed to discredit radicals "from within" their own organizations. An early instance of this concerned Phillip Abbott Luce, ostensibly a member of the Progressive Labor Party, who surfaced in 1965 to offer a series of highly inaccurate "revelations" on left thinking and practice before the House Un-American Activities Committee; Luce subsequently authored a book with FBI assistance, *The New Left*,[11] containing much of the same material. Later examples of this include William Tulio Divalo with Joseph James, *I Lived Inside the Campus Revolution*,[12] and Larry Grathwohl (as told to Frank Reagan), *Bringing Down America: An FBI Informer with the Weathermen*.[13]

Literally thousands of infiltrators were used against the Left in the 1960s. According to the *New York Times*,[14] the Bureau deployed 316 informers between 1960 and 1976 within the Socialist Workers Party (SWP) and its youth wing, Young Socialist Alliance (YSA), alone. Forty-two of these FBI plants had held office within the SWP or YSA and had thus participated in shaping the very organizational policies which the Bureau claimed it was necessary to investigate; as of June 1976, more than sixty infiltrators were still active within SWP and YSA. At one point in early

1969, San Francisco attorney Charles Garry observed that between sixty and seventy infiltrators were working within the Black Panther Party, nationally.[15] When one considers the similar infiltration levels of other organizations of the period—SDS, SNCC, Student Mobilization, the Resistance, the Moratorium, Youth Against War and Fascism, La Raza, the Black Student Unions, various civil rights organizations, Yippies, and so on—the implications become clear in terms of the alarming numbers involved.

As Ungar puts it,

> Critics would later suggest that...informants...recruited during the advanced stages of New Left development, had become classic *agents provocateurs*, who entered the protest movement at the government's urging and helped stimulate violent incidents which could be used to justify severe, perhaps repressive, police response. In a film prepared for the Public Broadcasting [System] in 1971, journalist Paul Jacobs interviewed three men who insist their agent contacts encouraged them to join in bombings and burnings, or to propose that the groups they infiltrated commit criminal acts. As one of the men put it to Jacobs, "The FBI agent...told me to burn the buildings...so that the state troopers would have an excuse to come on campus and crush...the rebellion on campus."[16]

Among known provocateurs, one of the more notorious was "Tommy the Traveler" Tongyai, who roamed from campus to campus across the Northeast in the late 1960s, agitating for the bombing of military research facilities, the burning of ROTC buildings, and the like. He was paid to do so by the FBI.[17]

"Pseudo-Gangs"

There is some indication that the Bureau had begun to spawn "pseudo-gangs," phony organizations designed to "confuse, divide and undermine" as well as do outright battle with authentic dissident groups by the end of the COINTELPRO era. Researcher Ken Lawrence quotes British counterinsurgency expert Frank Kitson (who coined the term) as observing:

> There is some evidence to the effect that pseudo-gangs of ultra-militant black nationalists are operating now in the United States.[18]

Lawrence goes on to note,

> One FBI provocateur based in Tampa, Florida, named Joe Burton created organizations all over the United States and Canada between 1972 and 1975. His home base group in Tampa was called Red Star Cadre. Most of its far-flung affiliates, but not all, presented themselves as Maoist; some were ostensibly pro-Soviet or pro-Cuba. The FBI used these front groups sometimes to disrupt legitimate revolutionary movements in the U.S., other times to unify with and spy on them.[19]

Bad-jacketing

"Snitch-jacketing" or "bad-jacketing" refers to the practice of creating suspicion—through the spread of rumors, manufacture of evidence, *etc.*—that *bona fide* organizational members, usually in key positions, are FBI/police informers, guilty of such offenses as skimming organizational funds and the like. The purpose of this tactic was to "isolate and eliminate" organizational leadership; such efforts were continued—and in some instances accelerated—when it became known that the likely outcome would be exteme physical violence visited upon the "jacketed" individual(s). Bad-jacketing was a very commonly used technique. For instance, in a COINTELPRO proposal submitted on July 10, 1968 by the SAC, New York, to the Director, it was recommended that:

> ...consideration be given to convey the impression that [SNCC leader Stokely] CARMICHAEL is a CIA informer. One method of accomplishing [this] would be to have a carbon copy of informant report reportedly written by CARMICHAEL to the CIA carefully deposited in the automobile of a close Black Nationalist friend...It is hoped that when the informant report is read it will help promote distrust between CARMICHAEL and the Black Community...It is also suggested that we inform a certain percentage of reliable criminal and racial informants that "we have heard from reliable sources that CARMICHAEL is a CIA agent." It is hoped that these informants would spread the rumor in various large Negro communities across the land.

The proposal, which was approved the next day, also contained a report on another COINTELPRO directed at Carmichael:

> On 7/4/68, a pretext phone call was placed to the residence of STOKELY CARMICHAEL and in absence of CARMICHAEL his mother was told that a friend was calling who was fearful of the future safety of her son. It was explained to Mrs. CARMICHAEL the absolute necessity for CARMICHAEL to 'hide out' inasmuch as several BPP members were out to kill him, and it was probably to be done sometime this week. Mrs. CARMICHAEL appeared shocked upon hearing the news and stated she would tell STOKELY when he came home.

One result of Carmichael's bad-jacketing may be detected in the statement of Black Panther Party Minister of Defense Huey P. Newton on September 5, 1970 that, "We...charge that Stokely Carmichael is operating as an agent of the CIA."[20]

While such exercises may seem on their face to be merely slimy, the more lethal implications were brought out clearly by an FBI infiltrator named Thomas E. Mosher who had penetrated the Bay Area Radical Union in 1969 and "insinuated [himself] into a relationship with the national office of the Black Panther Party." As he later explained to the Senate Internal Security Committee during March 1971, Fred Bennett, a prominent Bay Area Panther and "general in George Jackson's People's Army," had been successfully bad-jacketed as a police informer at some point in mid-1969. Consequently, Bennett was executed by Jimmie Carr, another ranking Panther and People's Army commander, at a remote training facility in the

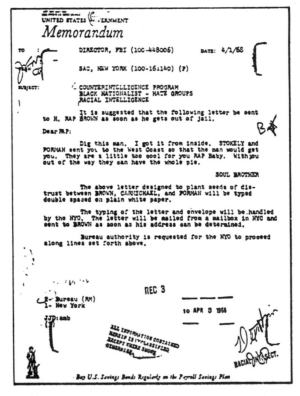

SNCC leader, and later Prime Minister of the BPP, Stokely Carmichael, during the period when a number of COINTELPROs were aimed at "neutralizing" him. The accompanying memo describes an FBI plot to create a violent dispute between Carmichael and colleague H. Rap Brown, in which the FBI hoped that one or both leaders would be physically eliminated. (Photo: *The Black Panther*)

Santa Cruz Mountains during November of that year. Carr and a subordinate Panther named Jimmie Johnson then burned the body and scattered the ashes. Mosher was apparently quite upset insofar as he had notified his FBI liaison of this, even going so far as to lead agents to the cremation site (where they verified the story), and yet no action had been taken against either Carr or Johnson. As it turns out, this seems to have been because a bad-jacket operation was also under way against Carr; by early 1972, the idea had successfully been implanted in movement circles that Carr was a police agent and was skimming funds from the People's Army. He was assassinated in his own San Francisco front yard on April 6 of that year by Richard Rodriguez (a Southern California Panther) and Lloyd Lamar Mims (an L.A. Panther), both of whom offered the explanation that "Carr was a police agent." Evidence has never been produced that either Bennett or Carr provided information to any police agency.

Both incidents are well covered in Jo Durden-Smith's *Who Killed George Jackson?* which offers the following insight on the counterintelligence method at issue here:

> This 'bad-jacketing' technique, well known in prisons where guards are adept at turning members of a group against each other, also creates a pressure point. When a man is abandoned by his comrades because of a rumor slipped into the prison grapevine, when suspicion and rancor suddenly replace old loyalties, it is easier to turn him into a stoolie, the cooperative, compliant informer...[21]

Bad-jacketing may thus be viewed as a very flexible and adaptable tool for FBI operations such as COINTELPRO, especially when coupled with incidents such as the Bennett and Carr murders.

Fabrication of Evidence

A widely used FBI tactic has been the fabrication of evidence for criminal prosecution of key individuals, and the withholding of exculpatory evidence which might serve to block conviction of these individuals. This includes the intimidation of witnesses and use of coercion to obtain false testimony.

There are numerous examples of this on record, including the so-called "Chicago Eight" (later "Chicago Seven") conspiracy trial—of David Dellinger, Tom Hayden, Rennie Davis, Abbie Hoffman, Jerry Rubin, John Froines, Lee Weiner, and originally, Bobby Seale—on charges of "interstate travel with intent to incite riot" during the 1968 Democratic Convention in Chicago. Among other things, the Bureau concocted a threatening letter to jurors, signed "The Black Panthers," and called obviously bogus witnesses Robert Pierson and William Frapolly in its efforts to obtain convictions.[22] Another example of similar—if less flamboyant—FBI evidentiary methods in federal political cases was the conspiracy trial of Benjamin Spock, *et al.*[23]

Bobby Seale (left), Chairman of the BPP, and Huey Newton, the BPP Minister of Defense, outside the Party's Oakland headquarters in 1967. Both men were the victims of sustained COINTELPRO operations. (Photo: *Ramparts*)

The Bureau also became deeply immersed in providing similar "assistance" to local prosecutors going after nationally-targeted dissidents in the courtroom, including, for instance, the 1970-71 case of New York's "Panther 21"[24] and the simultaneous murder-conspiracy trials of Panther leaders Bobby Seale and Ericka Huggins in New Haven, Connecticut.[25] That each of these legal travesties ultimately resulted in the acquittal of the defendants attests far more to the abilities of the respective juries to perceive the baldness of the government approach than to any restraint on the part of the FBI in attempting to miscarry justice.

Although such political trials were never formally a part of COINTELPRO, their relationship to it is brought out quite clearly by the Seale-Huggins case. In this matter, the murder victim was a young Panther candidate from New York named Alex Rackley who had been bad-jacketed as a police infiltrator. The perpetrator of the bad-jacketing, as well as Rackley's interrogator—the youngster had been shackled to a bed and scalded for days prior to being shot to death—and executioner was an ostensible Panther captain named George Sams. Sams, as it turned out, had been a paid FBI informer for a period of time never disclosed by the Bureau;[26] Seale and Huggins seem to have been drawn into the matter almost as a "dividend" or afterthought. It should be noted that Sams ultimately took a plea bargain which resulted in his doing light time in the Rackley murder, while New Haven Panther Captain Lonnie McLucas and others were convicted as accessories, receiving heavy sentences.

Assassinations

The Bureau has been implicated as cooperating in the outright physical elimination—assassination—of selected political leaders, either for "exemplary" reasons or after other attempts at destroying their effectiveness had failed. The Bureau almost always used surrogates to perform such functions, but can repeatedly be demonstrated as having provided the basic intelligence, logistics or other ingredients requisite to "successful" operations in this regard.

Understandably, this is the murkiest of all COINTELPRO areas, and the one from which congressional investigators have shied most consistently and sharply. However, certain COINTELPRO techniques already discussed—and acknowledged by Congress—had the effect of generating *de facto* Bureau-fostered assassinations. Others, such as the Hampton-Clark murders covered elsewhere in this book, are even clearer. While FOIA files and congressional investigations have not revealed any "smoking guns," FBI intentions in this regard are clarified in a Bureau document transmitted by the SAC, San Diego to the Director (date deleted):

> Shootings, beatings and widespread unrest continues [sic] to prevail in the ghetto area of southeast San Diego. Although no specific counterintelligence action can be *credited* with contributing to this over-all situation, it is felt that *a substantial amount of this unrest is attributable to this program* [emphasis added].

There can be little doubt that political assassination was a weapon in the COINTELPRO arsenal.

The Expansion of COINTELPRO Operations

The first solid indication that Hoover had determined to broaden the Bureau's COINTELPRO activities to cover more than the SWP and CPUSA during the post-McCarthy period came in the form of a 1960 document stating that:

> The Bureau is considering the feasibility of instituting a program of disruption to be directed against organizations which seek independence for Puerto Rico...In considering this matter, you should bear in mind that the Bureau desires to disrupt the activities of these organizations and is not interested in mere harassment.[27]

Shortly thereafter, the New York field office responded with the recommendation of a counterintelligence program to sow "disruption and discord" within the targeted groups, to bring about conditions "creating doubts as to remaining with the independence movement" and to cause "defections from the independence movement" by "exploiting factionalism within an organization."[28] This COINTELPRO was approved by Hoover for "Immediate Action" on the day of receipt. By mid-1961, the FBI was "delving deeply" into the "weaknesses, morals, criminal records, spouses, children, family life, educational qualifications and personal activities other than independence activities" of those leading the effort to achieve Puerto Rican decolonization, in order to discredit them personally.[29]

At about the same time, Hoover moved to initiate similar operations against the growing civil rights movement in the Southeast, placing Dr. Martin Luther King's name in Section A of the Reserve Index (one step below the Security Index) on May 11, 1962 and advising the Atlanta field office that he should be added to their pick-up list for handling under the provisions of the Detention Act in the event of a national emergency.[30] At the time, the Bureau attempted to rationalize this as being due to King's "association with known Communists"—namely, two friends and long-time activists named Stanley Levinson and Jack O'Dell—despite the fact that a detailed thirty-seven-page report submitted by the Atlanta office on April 25 had determined that neither King nor his Southern Christian Leadership Conference (SCLC) were under any sort of communist influence.[31] In fact, many of the Bureau's contentions concerning Levinson and O'Dell were later proven to be untrue.[32]

Nonetheless, the Bureau proceeded to implement a full-scale COMINFIL (Communist Infiltration) investigation of King and the SCLC, including round-the-clock electronic surveillance, and tied them into an ongoing COINTELPRO, originally aimed at the CPUSA. In the latter instance, the Crime Records Division disseminated a false story to the national media on October 24, 1962 stating that "a concealed member of the national committee of the Communist Party," Jack O'Dell, was serving as "acting executive director" of the SCLC. The story appeared in the *Augusta Chronicle, Birmingham News, St. Louis Globe Democrat, New Orleans Times-Picayune* and *Long Island Star Journal.*[33] O'Dell, whose role in SCLC seems to have been the development of mailing lists—from New York rather than Atlanta—was forced to resign even this position.[34]

King's response was to talk candidly with a reporter from the *New York Times* agreeing with the assessment of historian Howard Zinn that, "with all the violations by local police of their constitutional rights...the FBI has not made a single arrest in behalf of Negro citizens."[35] King then went further by observing that most agents assigned to the South, none of whom was black, were themselves southerners who shared the racial sentiments of the rednecks, klansmen, and police who confronted civil rights activists: "If an FBI man agrees with segregation, he can't honestly and objectively investigate."[36] The Bureau hierarchy exploded with fury when these words hit the papers. ISD head DeLoach announced that King "obviously uses lies, deceit, and treachery as propaganda to further his own causes...The fact that he is a vicious liar is amply demonstrated by the fact that he constantly associates with and takes instructions from Stanley Levinson who is a hidden member of the Communist Party."[37] Hoover dubbed King "the most notorious liar in the country."[38] At the same time, agents in Birmingham, Alabama actually *were* passing information to the Ku Klux Klan, via a police liaison they knew to be a klansman, facilitating physical attacks on civil rights workers, thus going far beyond what King had asserted in theory.[39]

From this point on, the Bureau began

> ...putting a "trash cover" on the SCLC office; investigating King's bank and charge accounts; instituting electronic surveillance on an Atlanta hideaway apartment often used by King; installing a bug in King's office; looking for personal weaknesses among SCLC employees that could be used to win their cooperation with the Bureau; sending a forged letter in King's name to SCLC contributors warning them that an IRS investigation was about to begin; and attempting to intensify a well-known mutual dislike of King and NAACP head Roy Wilkins.[40]

SCLC accountant James A. Harrison (code-named AT 1387-S by the FBI) was recruited to serve as a paid informant and, "[w]eekly, he would meet with Atlanta agent Alan G. Sentinella, who in May of 1965 had taken over primary responsibility for the King, SCLC, and 'Communist Influence in Racial Matters' cases from Robert R. Nichols."[41] Despite such massive and sustained coverage, the Bureau was unable to develop either incriminating evidence against King/SCLC, or to derail the civil rights agenda.

Consequently, the FBI was forced to rely upon tapes generated by a bug illegally placed in King's room at the Willard Hotel in Washington, D.C. during January of 1963, purportedly revealing him consorting with prostitutes.[42] Although the "issue" involved was moral rather than legal, Hoover was apparently convinced that the content of these tapes would "destroy the burrhead [King],"[43] and that the SCLC leader was a "tom cat" possessed by "obsessive degenerate sexual urges." The Bureau first attempted to use this material to discredit King among Washington's political circles.[44] When this failed, Hoover authorized COINTELPRO head William C. Sullivan[45] to fabricate an anonymous letter which read in part:

Dr. King, accompanied by Andrew Young, at FBI headquarters on December 1, 1964, to meet with J. Edgar Hoover, only days after Hoover described him as "the most notorious liar in the country." The Bureau's vendetta continued until his assassination. (Photo: *Washington Post*)

Cartha "Deke" DeLoach, a ranking FBI COINTELPRO specialist, during the period when he ordered the launching of a secret smear campaign accusing Dr. King of being a "sex pervert."

KING,

In view of your low grade...I will not dignify your name with either a Mr. or a Reverend or a Dr...

No person can overcome facts, not even a fraud like yourself...I repeat—no person can successfully argue against facts. You are finished...

King, there is only one thing left for you to do...You are done. There is but one way out for you. You better take it before your filthy, abnormal fraudulent self is bared to the nation.[46]

This recommendation that King commit suicide was packaged along with the highlights from the bugging tapes prepared by FBI audio technician John Matter on Sullivan's instructions and turned over to COINTELPRO operative Lish Whitsun. The latter carried it by plane to Miami, where he mailed it to King's home address.[47] It was discovered by Coretta Scott King on January 5, 1965.[48] When this failed to force King to kill himself, the Bureau escalated its efforts:

The Bureau crime records division, headed by DeLoach, initiated a major effort to let newsmen know just what [it] had on King. DeLoach personally offered a copy of the King surveillance transcript to *Newsweek* Washington bureau chief Benjamin Bradlee...Others who were offered transcripts, photos, or the recordings themselves included David Kraslow of the *Los Angeles Times*, John Herbers of the *New York Times*, Chicago columnist Mike Royko, Eugene Patterson of the *Atlanta Constitution*, and Lou Harris of the *Augusta Chronicle*.[49]

For once, however, the FBI's program of defaming opposition leaders was too raw even for the minions of American media, and the smear campaign was ultimately left to rightwing hacks such as Victor Riesel.[50]

There can be little wonder, then, why King would have come to feel that, "they are out to get me, to harass me, break my spirit,"[51] or that the Church Committee would later conclude "it is highly questionable whether the FBI's stated motivation was valid"[52] in hounding the SCLC leader to his grave. For that matter, it is hardly surprising, given the nature of the Bureau's campaign to neutralize King, that there remain serious questions—unresolved by subsequent congressional investigations—as to the FBI's role in King's assassination in Memphis on April 4, 1968.[53]

Of course, the anti-King/SCLC campaign represented only a tiny portion of the COINTELPRO iceberg. On other "fronts," the Bureau was busily undermining the electoral efforts of SWP candidates such as Fred Halstead and John Clarence Franklin,[54] and concocting incredible conspiracy charges against groups such as the Berrigan brothers' "Catholic left network," attempting to neutralize them through a welter of disinformation and lengthy criminal proceedings.[55] New Left organizations from Students for a Democratic Society (SDS) to the pacifist Clergy and Laity Concerned were also subjected to considerable destabilization efforts which reflected clearly that the preponderance of FBI resources was directed to such politically repressive ends.[56] However the real thrust of COINTELPRO was aimed at the black liberation movement. This was brought out unequivocally by Hoover in a 1967 memo establishing an intensive national counterintelligence program targeting "black nationalist—hate groups":

> The purpose of this new counterintelligence endeavor is to expose, disrupt, misdirect, discredit, or otherwise neutralize the activities of black nationalist, hate-type organizations and groupings, their leadership, spokesmen, membership, and supporters...[57]

In another Memorandum, sent out under the same caption early in 1968, the Director called upon his COINTELPRO operatives to, among other things,

> ...prevent the coalition of militant black nationalist groups...prevent militant black nationalist groups and leaders from gaining *respectability*...Prevent the *rise of a black "messiah" who would unify and electrify, the militant black nationalist movement. Malcomb X*[sic] *might have been such a "messiah;" he is the martyr of the movement today. Martin Luther King, Stokely Carmichael and Elija Muhammed* [sic] *all aspire to this position. Elija Muhammed is less of a threat because of his age. King could be a very real contender for this position should he abandon his supposed "obedience" to "white, liberal doctrines" (nonviolence) and embrace black nationalism. Carmichael has the necessary charisma to be a real threat in this way* [original emphasis].[58]

As we know, King was assassinated and Carmichael was neutralized through bad-jacketing at about the same time (see note 20). It has been convincingly argued that the Bureau was involved in the orchestration of the assassination of Malcolm X.[59] As for Elijah Muhammad, leader of the Nation of Islam (NOI), age was not the only factor in his being "less of a threat":

> The Bureau began wiretap surveillance of Elija Muhammed's [*sic*] Chicago's residence in 1957, with the authorization of Attorney General Herbert Brownell, on the grounds that members of the NOI "disavow allegiance to the United States" and "are taught they need not obey the laws of the United States."...When Elija Muhammed bought a winter home in Arizona in 1961, a wiretap and microphone were installed there. Both forms of surveillance continued for several years...Elija Muhammed was targeted for special attention when the Bureau established a "Black Nationalist Hate Group" COINTEL program in 1967 and 1968. The Bureau...played assorted COINTEL tricks on the organization as early as the late 1950s.[60]

Other black leaders, such as H. Rap Brown of the Student National Coordinating Committee (SNCC), were subject to endless legal harassment[61] or, like the Reverend Charles Koen of the Cairo (Illinois) United Front, to deliberate public and private smear campaigns.[62] In the case of black activist-comedian Dick Gregory, conscious efforts were made to render him subject to physical retribution by the mafia.[63] Organizations such as the Revolutionary Action Movement (RAM: see note 18), the

Republic of New Afrika (RNA), and even the Black Student Unions (BSUs) on various campuses came in for systematic "special handling."

Concerning the black student organization at the University of California at Santa Barbara (UCSB):

> The documents reveal that the FBI: 1) "Planted" a paid informant in the BSU, possibly with the knowledge and complicity of the UCSB administration. The informant, registered as a "student," worked undercover for at least a year. 2) Opened files on every BSU member at that time (these files were not released). 3) That the FBI had some part in the "BSU Busts" of 1969 which student activists regard as "frame-ups" (the charges were thrown out)...The FBI requested that the police inventory any radical literature found at the apartments where the BSU members were arrested...[4)] The files reveal that various UCSB administrators and staff members were sources of "intelligence" on the BSU and BSU members...5) That members of the District Attorney's Office, including the current District Attorney, Stanley Roden, reported information on the BSU to the FBI. 6) that the FBI placed one BSU member on the "Security Index," to be arrested and placed in a concentration camp in the event of a "national emergency"...The files were released to Murv Glass, 1976 BSU President, under the Freedom of Information Act.[64]

The Santa Barbara documents indicate similar activities conducted regarding the BSUs at Berkeley, San Francisco State, UCLA, and Cornell.

The actions against the RNA are illustrated in a Memorandum from SAC, Jackson (Mississippi) to Director, FBI, dated December 2, 1970 and captioned COUNTERINTELLIGENCE OPERATIONS BEING EFFECTED, TANGIBLE RESULTS (REPUBLIC OF NEW AFRICA [sic]). The document notes that, "Since March, 1968...the RNA has been trying to buy and lease land in Mississippi...(Counter-intelligence measures has [sic] been able to abort all RNA efforts to obtain land in Mississippi)." It goes on to observe that "RICHARD HENRY, aka Brother Imari, leader of the RNA, accompanied by many out-of-state supporters to hold a national RNA meeting 'on the land of the nation in Mississippi.' This conference was disruptive and ineffective due to Jackson Division, Bureau-approved counterintelligence measures." It goes on to observe that Imari had arranged the lease of a 560 acre land parcel from "a Negro male who was retiring" and that "RNA leaders, including Brother IMARI, were delighted over this land purchase or leasing prospect," but "Jackson informants were directed by contacting Agents to approach [the land owner] privately and indicate to him that his selling land to Brother IMARI would not be a wise endeavor. Additionally, on 10/9/70, [the land owner] was interviewed by Bureau Agents..." The report concludes that, "As a result of the above counterintelligence efforts, the land which the RNA had almost finalized plans regarding purchasing or leasing in rural Hinds County, Miss., has not been sold or leased to them...as a result of the above, intensive efforts of the RNA to obtain land in Mississippi over the past two and one-half years are still totally unsuccessful." A final note in this matter is that Imari spent nearly a decade in courts and prisons as a result of a shootout with police occurring in 1972, as the RNA continued—in increasingly

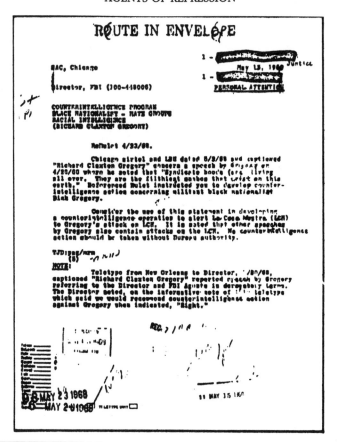

COINTELPRO memo against Dick Gregory.

Members of the RNA 11 are led through the streets of Jackson, Mississippi in chains. Arrested after a COINTELPRO-fostered shootout, they were railroaded into a variety of lengthy prison sentences. (Photo: *Guardian*)

frustrated fashion—to press its legal right to purchase property in that state. Such are the ongoing wages of COINTELPRO.

In the end, COINTELPRO was officially suspended by Hoover in 1971, in order to avoid "embarrassment to the Bureau" in the wake of the break-in at the Media, Pennsylvania resident agency. In the meantime, what former Vice President Spiro Agnew and Attorney General John Mitchell called "the chilling effect" on political dissent had been demonstrably achieved: the movement for social change loosely described as the "New Left" had been shattered, its elements fragmented and factionalized, its goals and methods hugely distorted in the public mind, scores of its leaders and members slain, hundreds more languishing in penal institutions as the result of convictions in cases which remain suspect, to say the least.

Some of the worst examples of FBI-engineered convictions are: black anarchist *Martin Sostre*, imprisoned for thirty to forty-one years for selling narcotics from his radical bookstore/meeting place in Buffalo, New York (Sostre was head of a community anti-drug campaign); *Wayland Bryand, Ronald Williams,* and *Harold Robertson,* members of the Alabama Black Liberation Front, who were sentenced to twenty years each for defending themselves against a nightriding "sheriff's posse" (this is tied to the earlier mentioned collusion of the FBI and Klan in Birmingham, Ala.); *Ahmed Evans,* sentenced to death for having returned fire against a police arms raid directed against his home in Cleveland (prior to the raid, Evans was identified as a "key black agitator" by the FBI which worked closely with the unit which conducted the raid); *Lee Otis Johnson,* a SNCC organizer in Texas, sentenced to thirty years for allegedly passing a single joint of marijuana to an undercover agent; *Connie Tucker,* leader of the Junta of Militant Organizations (JOMO), sentenced to five years for allegedly possessing enough marijuana to construct two joints (only the rolling papers were introduced into evidence at her trial); *John Sinclair,* head of the Detroit White Panther Party, sentenced to nine and one-half to ten years for possession of two joints of marijuana (this, despite a court ruling that the evidence presented amounted to entrapment by an undercover agent; notwithstanding the trivial nature of his "offense," Sinclair was incarcerated in a remote maximum security prison; the FBI attempted to build a case against him for planning to bomb the Detroit CIA office while he was imprisoned). But the most vicious and unrestrained application of COINTELPRO techniques during the late 1960s and early 1970s was clearly reserved for the Black Panther Party (BPP), the subject of our next chapter.

Before proceeding to a more detailed scrutiny of a particular COINTELPRO, we would do well not to become greatly heartened by the thought that the FBI's counterintelligence efforts along such lines were terminated at the onset of the 1970s (a theme to which we will return repeatedly throughout the course of this book). We do, after all, have numerous indicators to the contrary, not least of which is the following passage from a Bureau document:

> Over the years, our approach to investigative problems in the intelligence field has given rise to a number of new programs, some of which have been most revolution-

ary, and it can be assumed that with a continued aggressive approach to these problems, new and productive ideas will be forthcoming. These ideas will not be increased in number or improved upon from the standpoint of accomplishments merely through the institution of a program such as COINTELPRO which is given another name, and which, in fact, only encompasses everything that has been done or will be done in the future.[65]

Such a statement should be understood in light of the assertion under oath of former COINTELPRO operative Wesley Swearingen that, "The Program had been 'officially' [publicly] discontinued in April, 1971, but agents...continued to carry out the Program's objectives."[66] COINTELPRO up to the point of its official demise seems to aptly sum up the Bureau's history and represents "one of the sordid episodes in the history of American law enforcement," as Senator Frank Church once put it. The problem, however, is that there is no real indication it ever truly ended. There is not, and never has been, after all, any other substantive basis for the FBI's existence.

Chapter 3

COINTELPRO-Black Panther Party

A top secret *Special Report* for the president in June 1970 gives some insight into the motivation for the actions undertaken by the government to destroy the Black Panther Party. The report describes the party as "the most active and dangerous black extremist group in the United States." Its "hard core members" were estimated at 800, but "a recent poll indicates that approximately 25 per cent of the black population has a great respect for the BPP, including 43 per cent of blacks under 21 years of age." On the basis of such estimates of the potential of the party, the repressive apparatus of the state proceeded against it to ensure that it did not succeed in organizing as a substantial social or political force. We may add that in this case, government repression proved quite successful.

—Noam Chomsky, *COINTELPRO*

My first assignment with CCS was when I was liaison between CCS and Ron Karenga's organization, US. I contacted Ron Karenga and gave him orders to the effect that was given to me, that he was to curtail the Panther Party's growth, no matter what it cost, and that no 'rangatang'—that was what we called those people—will ever be convicted of murder.

—Louis E. Tackwood, *The Glass House Tapes*

In November of 1968, J. Edgar Hoover dispatched a Memorandum calling upon his field agents "to exploit all avenues of creating...dissension within the ranks of the BPP" and stating that "recipient offices are instructed to submit imaginative and hard-hitting counterintelligence measures aimed at crippling the BPP."[1] Some of the responses developed by the Bureau's COINTELPRO specialists in complying with this directive have been summarized in Chapter 2 and are probably still culminating as is indicated by the March 1987 sentencing of BPP founder Huey P. Newton to three years imprisonment for being a "felon in possession of a firearm."[2] The period of 1968-71, however, seems to have encompassed the great bulk of the worst of the FBI's anti-Panther activity and we will therefore offer three vignettes drawn from those years as being illustrative of the whole tenor of COINTELPRO-BPP.

Chicago BPP leader Fred Hampton addressing a "Free Bobby Seale" rally, October 1969.

The Assassinations of Fred Hampton and Mark Clark

Fred Hampton, as Noam Chomsky has observed, was "one of the most promising leaders of the Black Panther Party."[3] He'd come to the BPP's embryonic Chicago chapter—founded by SNCC organizer Bob Brown in late 1967—from suburban Maywood, where he'd been a high school leader and NAACP activist, at the beginning of 1968. When Brown left the Party with Stokely Carmichael in the FBI fostered "SNCC/Panther split" (see Chapter 2), Hampton assumed the Illinois state BPP Chairmanship, a matter which automatically rendered him a national BPP Deputy Chairman. As the Panther leadership across the country began to be decimated by the impact of COINTELPRO, Hampton's prominence in the national hierarchy increased rapidly and dramatically.[4]

Already in late 1967, the Bureau's Chicago SAC, Marlin Johnson, had instructed his Racial Matters Squad to open a file on the nineteen-year-old, a manila folder which was expanded to twelve volumes containing more than 4,000 pages over the remaining two years of Hampton's life. At the same time, an informant was planted in the Maywood NAACP office.[5] At least as early as February, 1968, Johnson also requested the installation of a wiretap on the phone of Hampton's mother, Iberia.[6] By

May, Johnson had placed the young Panther's name on the "Agitator Index" and saw to it that he was designated as a "key militant leader" for Bureau reporting purposes.[7]

In late 1968, Special Agent (SA) Roy Mitchell was assigned to augment the Chicago field office's Racial Matters Squad, headed by SA Robert Piper. One of Mitchell's first acts in his new job was to bring in an individual named William O'Neal, recently arrested twice; on one occasion for interstate car theft, and the other for impersonating a federal officer (e.g., he had manufactured and used phony FBI identification). Apparently in exchange for a monthly stipend and the dropping of these charges, O'Neal agreed to infiltrate the Chicago BPP as a counterintelligence operative.[8] To this end, he went to the Panther headquarters at 2350 Madison Street on the day it opened and joined the chapter.[9] The infiltrator was quickly accepted and placed in positions of confidence by Hampton and Chicago Minister of Defense Bobby Rush, as is evidenced by the speed with which he became Director of Chapter Security and Hampton's personal bodyguard. According to SA Mitchell, by February 1969, O'Neal was functioning as the "number three man" in the Chicago BPP and was in line for national Party office.[10]

One of the talents which seems to have bothered the Bureau most about Hampton was his undeniable effectiveness as an organizer and ghetto diplomat. By December 1968, O'Neal was reporting (accurately) that the Chairman was on the verge of negotiating a merger between the still-small BPP and a sprawling South Side street gang, several thousand members strong, known as the Blackstone Rangers (at that time in the process of changing its title to the "Black P. Stone Nation").[11] As it was obvious that Hampton's agenda was to bring about the politicization of the Rangers, their constructive engagement in community work and a corresponding sudden, massive surge in the Panthers' local political clout—indeed, the merger would have served to double the Party's *national* membership—a major COINTELPRO was quickly implemented to head things off. SAC Johnson secured approval from Hoover to prepare and mail an anonymous letter to Jeff Fort, head of the Rangers, which read:

Brother Jeff:

I've spent some time with some Panther friends on the west side lately and I know what's going on. The brothers that run the Panthers blame you for blocking their thing and there's supposed to be *a hit out on you*. I'm not a Panther, or a Ranger, just black. From what I see these Panthers are out for themselves not black people. I think you ought to know what they're up to, I know what I'd do if I was you. You might hear from me again [emphasis added].

(sgd) A black brother you don't know[12]

Predictably enough, relations between the BPP and Rangers degenerated into antagonism, with Fort offering to "blow [Hampton's] head off,"[13] and O'Neal energetically pursuing his role as "militant" in exacerbating the problem.[14] The infiltrator also used the same method, this time openly accusing the gang leader of being "an undercover cop," in destroying merger discussions with the Vice Lords[15] and providing the information by which SA Mitchell constructed another anonymous, threatening letter to the head of the Mau Maus.[16] In March, the COINTELPRO was broadened to include the sending of menacing letters to Hampton:

Brother Hampton:

Just a word of warning. A Stone friend tells me [name deleted] wants the Panthers and is looking for somebody to get you out of the way. Brother Jeff [Fort] is supposed to be interested. I'm just a black man looking for blacks working together, not more of this gang banging.[17]

On April 2, 1969, O'Neal personally instigated the first armed clash between the BPP and Rangers,[18] an action which perhaps reflected enthusiasm over a pay raise, approved by the Bureau on March 11, "for quality of services rendered".[19]

With the Panthers effectively isolated from their preferred powerbase in the ghetto,[20] the Bureau went to work undermining the BPP's ties to other radical organizations in the city. In late March 1969, Johnson, Piper and Mitchell explicitly instructed O'Neal to "create a rift" between the Party and SDS, whose national office was located at 1608 West Madison, just down the street from BPP's Chicago headquarters.[21] They followed up by releasing a batch of racist cartoons in the Panthers' name (as they had in San Diego; see Chapter 2) intended to alienate white activists[22] and, in mid-April, launched yet another disinformational COINTELPRO in an attempt to forestall the actualization of a "Rainbow Coalition" in the city composed of the BPP, SDS, the Young Lords (a Puerto Rican organization) and the Young Patriots (a white group).[23]

During this period, SA Mitchell also utilized a "special relationship" he had developed with the Chicago Police Department's (CPD's) Gang Intelligence Unit (GIU, the local "red squad") and Cook County State's Attorney Edward V. Hanrahan to direct local police toward anti-Panther activities.[24] In April 1969, Hanrahan responded by focusing the attention of his Special Prosecutions Unit (SPU) on the black community and "street gangs," notably the BPP.[25] SPU head Richard Jalovec thereupon created an elite unit within his organization to conduct what the State's Attorney had termed "a war on gangs."[26] The new unit was commanded by CPD Sergeant Daniel Groth,[27] detached from the police for this "special duty," and was initially composed of George Jones and John Ciszewski (both from GIU), Edward Carmody, Phillip Joseph "Gloves" Davis,[28] John Marusich, Fred Howard, and William Kelly.[29] Mitchell then revealed to Hanrahan, Jalovec and Groth that O'Neal was a BPP infiltrator and established the mechanism by which the SPU elite unit would be fed FBI intelligence on the BPP.[30] The unit seems to have had no other real target.

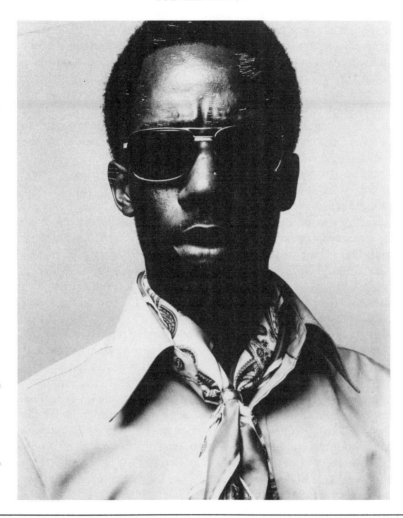

FBI infiltrator William O'Neal rose rapidly through the ranks of the Chicago BPP to become Chief of Security and Fred Hampton's personal bodyguard. O'Neal provided a detailed floorplan of Hampton's apartment used by police in the Panther leader's assassination. O'Neal is also suspected of having drugged Hampton prior to the raid, rendering him defenseless. (Photo: *Chicago Sun Times*)

Meanwhile, O'Neal stepped up his activities as an agent provocateur. He devised a "security plan," with the connivance of Mitchell, for the BPP office which involved nerve gas and the electrocution of interlopers (emphatically rejected by both Hampton and Rush),[31] and constructed an "electric chair" with which to "deal with informers" (also rejected). O'Neal later bullwhipped a Party member he branded an informer in the absence of the BPP leadership.[32] In March 1969, he proposed to acquire an aircraft or mortar with which to "bomb city hall" (rejected),[33] and began increasingly to encourage party members such as Robert Bruce and Nathaniel Junior to engage in illegal "fundraising" acts such as burglary and armed robbery, offering to train them in such "arts."[34] Once Bruce had taken him up on the proposition and had become a fugitive as a result, O'Neal transported sophisticated explosive devices and other weapons to him in Canada (at Bureau expense) and later harbored him at his father's West Side residence for several weeks.[35] In April, he was arrested for having openly threatened the life of a woman—in his capacity as a "Panther official"—but was quickly released.[36] SAC Marlin Johnson personally authorized the entire gamut of illegal and/or questionable activities.[37]

O'Neal also became increasingly preoccupied with "improving" Panther armaments. It was his habit to "set an example" by wearing a .45 automatic in a shoulder holster and he maintained a personal inventory of two 12 gauge shotguns and an M-1 carbine "for security" at BPP headquarters.[38] In June of 1969, he acquired other carbines, apparently using falsified documents, and initiated a weapons training program for Party members at a farm in Michigan.[39] He advocated that BPP cadres "always go armed."[40] The infiltrator was largely responsible for the widely publicized cache of arms "discovered" by the Bureau when SAC Johnson personally led a raid on the Monroe Street office in June, "searching for a fugitive" named George Sams, who was himself one of the FBI's BPP infiltrators.[41]

During this campaign, Johnson received repeated directives marked to his personal attention from J. Edgar Hoover, demanding that he instruct his COINTELPRO personnel to "destroy what the [BPP] stands for"[42] and "eradicate its 'serve the people' programs."[43] In May and June of 1969, the Director specifically and repeatedly instructed Johnson to destroy the Panthers' broadly acclaimed Free Breakfast for Children Program in the city, and the SAC assigned responsibility for this mission to Piper and Mitchell.[44] COINTELPRO activities were also geared up against the BPP Liberation School and community political education classes,[45] as well as against distributors of the Party newspaper, *The Black Panther*.[46] O'Neal and other infiltrators were ordered to steal BPP financial records, books, literature, tapes, films and other materials at every opportunity.[47]

Nor were the local police idle. Although no criminal charges were being pursued or criminal acts alleged prior to the event, the CPD forced an armed confrontation with Party members on July 16, 1969 which left Panther Larry Robeson mortally wounded and six others arrested on serious offenses.[48] On July 31, the police followed up by raiding and ransacking the Monroe Street office, smashing typewriters, destroying food and medical supplies for the Panther health clinic and breakfast program, setting several small fires, and beating and arresting several Panthers for "obstruction." The procedure was repeated on October 31.[49] On all three occasions, the FBI provided sensationalized accounts to the press.[50] Hampton had been successfully prosecuted in May by Hanrahan's attorneys in a dubious case involving the alleged theft of $71 worth of ice cream in Maywood during late 1967.[51] Convicted, sentenced to two to five years and shipped immediately to Illinois' Menard prison,[52] he managed, however, to obtain an appeal bond and was released in August.[53]

Throughout the fall of 1969, Hampton maintained an increasingly demanding speaking schedule,[54] organized weekly rallies at Chicago's federal building on behalf of Panther national Chairman Bobby Seale (at the time a defendant in the Chicago 8 conspiracy trial), worked with the Chicago BPP's Minister of Health Ronald "Doc" Satchel in establishing a free People's Clinic on the West Side, taught political education classes at the Liberation School and attended the Breakfast for Children Program every morning at 6 a.m.[55] He also began a community control of police project and launched an investigation into the police slayings of two black youths, the Soto brothers.[56] In early October, in order to be nearer to Party headquarters, Hampton and his fiance, Deborah Johnson, who was pregnant with their child, rented a four and one half room apartment at 2337 West Monroe Street.[57] Within a week, O'Neal was reporting that much of the Panthers' "provocative" arms stockpile had been removed from the BPP office and was being stored at the apartment, as well as the fact that the place was being used as a "crash pad" for visiting party members and those whose business kept them late at headquarters.[58]

In early November, the Chicago Chairman traveled to California on a speaking engagement for the UCLA Law Students Association,[59] meeting with the remaining BPP national hierarchy while there. He was told he was to be appointed to the Party's Central Committee, assuming David Hilliard's position as Chief of Staff and becoming the Panthers' major spokesperson in the near future.[60] O'Neal reported this development to SA Mitchell immediately upon Hampton's return[61] and the news was apparently placed in the context of FBI assessments that, despite the level of repression and destabilization already visited upon it, Hampton's release from prison had led to a resurgent Chicago BPP chapter becoming one of the strongest in the country, with one of the most successful Serve the People programs.[62] Stronger measures were clearly needed if Hampton's effectiveness and imminent ascendency to national leadership were to be thwarted.[63]

In mid-November, SA Mitchell met with O'Neal at the Golden Torch restaurant in downtown Chicago, having the infiltrator draw up a detailed floorplan of Hampton's apartment, including furniture placement and the location of the bed shared by the Chairman and his fiance, as well as the location of their bedroom windows (see illustration).[64] Back at the field office, Mitchell attached the diagram to a memo itemizing the weapons O'Neal had earlier reported as being stored in the apartment, and possibly a newspaper clipping concerning a recent South Side shootout in which Spurgeon "Jake" Winters, a former Panther, and CPD officers Rappaport and Gilhouley were killed.[65] He then appears to have gone "shopping."

Mitchell first met with Walter Bisewski and other members of the GIU who were assigned to anti-BPP work on November 19.[66] The GIU initially expressed interest in staging an "arms (shooting) raid" on the Hampton apartment largely, it seems, because it was under the impression that the Panthers were responsible in the deaths of Rappaport and Gilhouley.[67] SAC Johnson and SA Piper then approved

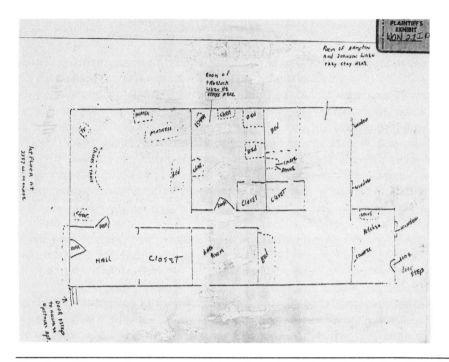

Floorplan of Hampton's apartment used by police raiders, drawn by S.A. Roy Mitchell from information obtained by O'Neal.

Mitchell's "cooperation" in the venture.[68] On November 24, however, GIU head Thomas Lyons correctly reached the conclusion that neither Hampton nor the BPP were involved in the fatal shootout and, apparently feeling used by the Bureau, cancelled the planned action at the last moment.[69] Undaunted, Mitchell then took the FBI's agenda to Jalovec at the SPU who responded favorably and, at the end of November, the two men met with Daniel Groth to go over O'Neal's floorplan and discuss details of a raid.[70] At 10:30 p.m. on December 2, Groth met with an informant—believed to have been O'Neal—who provided additional details for planning purposes.[71] Groth, Jalovec and State's Attorney Hanrahan then began a series of discussions which resulted in a scenario where Groth would lead an augmented unit of fourteen men (as opposed to his usual eight; the add-ons selected were Joseph Gorman, William Corbett, Raymond Broderick and Lynwood Harris of the SPU, plus a pair of police from other special units who were not to enter the apartment itself) equipped with a submachine gun on a predawn raid scheduled for December 4.[72] Hanrahan secured an "illegal weapons" warrant on the late afternoon of December 3 and, the same day, Johnson and Piper reported the whole affair in a joint memo to Hoover as a "positive course of action…being effected under the counterintelligence program."[73]

Meanwhile, the BPP went about its normal business. Hampton taught a political education course at the Church of Epiphany, attended by most chapter members, on the evening of December 3.[74] Afterwards, as was typical, several Panthers retired to the Monroe Street apartment to spend the night. These included Hampton and Deborah Johnson, Blair Anderson (a former Blackstone Ranger recruited to the BPP by its chairman), "Doc" Satchell, Harold Bell (Rockford Defense Captain), Verlina Brewer, Louis Truelock, Brenda Harris, and Mark Clark, a Defense Captain from the Party's downstate Peoria chapter; Deputy Defense Minister Bobby Rush was supposed to have been there, but was called away at the last moment on family business.[75] Upon arrival, they were met by O'Neal, who had earlier reported to SA Mitchell by telephone on the matter of Hampton's sleeping habits.[76] O'Neal had also prepared a late dinner, including Kool-aid, which was consumed by the group prior to their beginning to go to bed sometime around midnight.[77] O'Neal left at this point and, at about 1:30 a.m., Hampton fell asleep in mid-sentence during a telephone conversation with his mother conducted from his bedroom.[78]

Groth assembled and briefed his force at approximately 4 a.m. on the morning of December 4, using O'Neal's floorplan and other information provided by Mitchell.[79] The raiders then departed for Monroe Street with utmost secrecy and very heavily armed.[80] Once there, they divided into two "subteams" with eight of their number deployed to the front of the apartment and six to the rear.[81] At about 4:30, they launched an outright assault upon the Panthers, as Gloves Davis kicked open the front door and promptly shot Mark Clark pointblank in the chest with a .30 calibre M-1 carbine.[82] Clark, who had apparently nodded off in a front room with a shotgun across his lap, barely had time to stand up before being killed more-or-less instantly. His reflexive response to being shot discharged the shotgun. It was the only round fired by the Panthers during the raid.[83]

Davis immediately proceeded to pump a bullet into eighteen-year-old Brenda Harris, who was lying (unarmed) in a front room bed;[84] Groth hit her with a second round.[85] Gorman, joined by Davis and his carbine, then began spraying automatic fire from his .45 calibre Thompson submachinegun through a wall into the bedrooms.[86] All forty-two shots fired by the pair converged on the head of Hampton's bed, pinpointed in O'Neal's floorplan;[87] one of the slugs, fired by Davis, struck Hampton in the left shoulder, seriously wounding him as he slept.[88] While this was going on, the second subteam, firing as they came, crashed through the back door.[89] This was followed by a brief lull in the shooting, during which Carmody and another (unidentified) raider entered Hampton's bedroom. They were heard to have the following exchange:

That's Fred Hampton...
Is he dead?...Bring him out.
He's barely alive; he'll make it.[90]

Fred Hampton's body, sprawled in the doorway of his bedroom. According to survivors, Hampton had been wounded in his sleep by police gunfire, executed by two close-range bullets in the head, and dragged to the doorway by his wrist. (Photo: Chicago Police Dept.)

Chicago police, delighted with their job, remove Hampton's body during the predawn hours of December 4, 1969. (Photo: *Chicago Tribune*)

Two shots were then heard, both of which were fired pointblank into Hampton's head as he lay prone, followed by Carmody's voice stating, "He's good and dead now."[91] The chairman's body was then dragged by the wrist from the bed to the bedroom doorway, and left lying in a spreading pool of blood.[92] At that point, the raiders "mopped up," with Gorman directing fire from his submachine gun at the remaining Panthers, again, who were attempting to cover themselves in the apartment's other bedroom.[93] "Doc" Satchell was hit four times in this barrage, and Blair Anderson twice. Seventeen-year-old Verlina Brewer was also hit twice.[94] The victims were then beaten and dragged bodily to the street, where they were arrested on charges of attempting to murder the raiders and aggravated assault.[95]

At 9:26 a.m., SAC Marlin Johnson dispatched an "Urgent" teletype to FBI headquarters, informing Hoover of the deaths of Hampton and Clark, and that the surviving apartment occupants were facing serious charges.[96] He then instructed SA Piper to send Mitchell and another (unidentified) agent to meet with State's Attorney Hanrahan.[97] After a thirty minute discussion with the FBI men in his library, Hanrahan convened a press conference, with Groth and the rest of the SPU team present, at which time he announced that his raiders had been "attacked" by the "violent" and "extremely vicious" Panthers and had "defended themselves" accordingly; he called upon all "law abiding" citizens to support the actions of his office.[98] At almost the same moment, the survivors were being assigned bail of $100,000 each, a matter which was not resolved until all of the charges were dropped five months later.[99]

On December 8, Hanrahan conducted a second press conference in which he lauded the raiders for their "remarkable restraint," "bravery" and "professional discipline" in not killing all the Panthers present.[100] He then contacted *Chicago Tribune* editor Clayton Kirkpatrick, a long-time "friend of the FBI," and asked that the paper run—as an "exclusive"—unedited and prominently displayed, the SPU version of the raid.[101] Kirkpatrick complied with this request by assigning reporters Robert Wiedrich and Edward Lee to produce a verbatim interview with Daniel Groth which, along with several photos provided by the SPU purporting to show bullet holes made by shots fired at the raiders by the Panthers, was run under a banner headline on page one.[102] On December 11, the same day the *Tribune* story appeared, Hanrahan also arranged for Groth and his team to "re-enact" the raid for CBS-TV under direct supervision of SPU head Jalovec;[103] this bit of "investigative journalism" was run during prime time on Chicago's channel two that same evening, "demonstrating conclusively" how the raiders had acted admirably and only in self-defense.[104]

By the next day, however, less "cooperative" reporters had unearthed the fact that the SPU's "photographic evidence" was fabricated; the dark spots which supposedly were Panther-made bullet holes were actually old nailheads showing up starkly against the apartment's pale doors.[105] In the ensuing uproar, Hanrahan called yet another press conference, this time responding angrily and evasively, standing "100 percent behind the police" while instructing CPD Superintendent Conlisk to

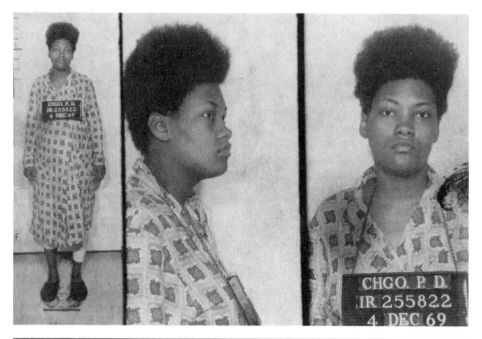

Deborah Johnson, fiance of Fred Hampton, while being booked on charges of "assaulting" the police officers who had just murdered her husband-to-be. (Photo: Chicago Police Dept.)

undertake an immediate Internal Police Investigation (IID) in order "to lay this matter to rest, once and for all."[106] This was conducted so speedily and in such a fashion by Capt. Harry Ervanian and Lt. Robert Kukowski of the CPD, in cooperation with a department ballistics expert, John Sadunas, that the investigators were later forced to admit under oath that it had been a "whitewash" and "the worst investigation" that either had ever seen.[107] Hanrahan, of course, immediately went public with the assertion that the IID finding "completely exonerated" his raiders from "any taint or implication of wrongdoing."[108]

The Chicago Bureau office, meanwhile, apparently feeling secure from the buffeting being absorbed by Hanrahan and the SPU, was busily establishing its central role in the murders for the edification of headquarters. On December 11, SA Piper sent a letter to Hoover stating that the Groth team could not have acted other than with intelligence information provided by Mitchell and himself via O'Neal, and that "this information was not available from any other source."[109] He noted that "the chairman of the Illinois BPP, Fred Hampton," was killed in the raid, and that this "success" was due, in large part, to the "tremendous value" of O'Neal's work inside the Party.[110] He thereupon requested payment of a cash "bonus" to the infiltrator for services rendered, a matter which was quickly approved in Washington.[111] For his part, in an apparent attempt to provide some *post hoc* justification for the acts of the

SPU raiders, Mitchell wrote a covering memo on December 12 (approved by Piper) claiming that he had informed the State's Attorney's Office as early as "December 1 or 2" that there were "illegal weapons" in Hampton's apartment, a "fact" he omitted from *all* related (internal) memoranda.[112]

On December 13, SAC Johnson, in a ploy remarkably similar to Hanrahan's IID investigation, recommended that a Federal Grand Jury be empaneled to consider whether Panther civil rights had been violated during the raid.[113] Attorney General John Mitchell responded by immediately assigning Jerris Leonard, chief of the Justice Department's Civil Rights Division—and a director of a secret interagency intelligence operation[114]—to head up the effort, which was initiated on December 21.[115] While the Grand Jury was gearing up, a special "Blue Ribbon" inquest was also staged by the Cook County Coroner's office.[116] During these relatively short proceedings, and apparently under the tutelage of Hanrahan and Jalovec, Groth, ballistics expert Sadunas, and Sadunas' supervisor, John Koludrovich, perjured themselves on a number of critical points (*e.g.*: Sadunas "matched" two *police* shotgun shell casings to "Brenda Harris'" weapon) while the other raiders provided corroborating testimony.[117] As a result, the assassinations of Hampton and Clark were officially labeled as "justifiable homicides" and no murder indictments were returned against the SPU.

Marlin Johnson testified before the Federal Grand Jury on February 11, 1970, contending that the Bureau's involvement in the "Hampton-Clark affair" had been, at most, extremely peripheral. He neglected to mention FBI infiltration of the Party, provision of the Monroe Street floorplan to the SPU, or any other COINTELPRO-related activity.[118] While his SAC was perjuring himself, SA Roy Mitchell was constructing another memo to headquarters requesting authorization to continue O'Neal on the payroll at $575 per month; as justification, he recited those facts his boss "failed to remember" under oath.[119] Within such a travesty, it is hardly surprising that Hanrahan was able to "cut a deal" with Leonard whereby the "whole matter could be laid to rest forever," an arrangement summarized in a memo to headquarters prepared by an FBI agent named Trevanius at Johnson's instruction on April 8, 1970:

> AAG Jerris Leonard, Civil Rights Division, Department of Justice, at Chicago, advised SAC Marlin Johnson in the strictest confidence that no indictments of police officers are planned in captioned matter. AAG Leonard has a firm commitment to meet with Edward V. Hanrahan, States Attorney, Cook County, Illinois, within one week whereupon, on the basis of Federal District Court order Hanrahan will receive testimony of State's Attorney's Police before FGJ.

> The above is based on an agreement whereby Hanrahan will dismiss the local indictments against the BPP members. Hanrahan is given thirty days to dismiss the local indictment which will be based upon [a] change of testimony of John Sidunas [sic] of the Chicago Police Crime Lab.[120]

The *quid pro quo* appears to have been that Hanrahan and his raiders would "walk" in exchange for their continued silence concerning the facts and nature of FBI involvement in the murders. Thus, upon the conclusion of three official and highly publicized investigations of the Hampton-Clark assassinations, each of which purported to extend a clean bill of health over the murderers and their superiors, it was left to the dead men's families and surviving Panthers to bring out the real facts, in civil rather than the far more appropriate criminal court framework. Proceeding on the basis of the most obvious problems with the state-federal position,[121] Iberia Hampton *et al.* secured the services of attorneys Flint Taylor, Dennis Cunningham and Jeff Haas of the People's Law Office in Chicago and entered a $47.7 million damage suit against Edward V. Hanrahan *et al.*[122]

Utilizing the context of at least limited public revelation of COINTELPRO fostered by the Media, Pennsylvania break-in, an FOIA suit brought by newsman Daniel Shorr, the Church Committee's investigations of domestic intelligence operations and the newly functional Freedom of Information Act as a basis by which to secure a portion of the relevant but hitherto withheld FBI documents, Taylor and Haas were able to move things along in the civil arena. For example, disclosure of O'Neal's identity was finally forced in 1973 (in an unrelated case, involving the murder of a drug dealer), and details of his role as an infiltrator emerged more or less steadily thereafter.[123] Still, the whole affair proceeded with excruciating slowness:

> During the trial, the Defendants and their lawyers participated in massive obstruction and coverup. The Defendants stonewalled and were repeatedly evasive, recalling almost nothing. They were aided and abetted by repeated objections by their lawyers and the "rulings" of the Trial Court. Defendant MITCHELL "forgot" a recent three-day meeting with [defense lawyer] Kanter and O'NEAL, and only avoided perjury by "correcting" his testimony at the next session. Defendants PIPER and MITCHELL combined with their attorneys to suppress at trial over 90% of the documentary evidence that the Court had ordered produced—evidence which held the key to their culpability.[124]

A classic case of FBI obstructionism occurred when Richard G. Held, who had replaced Marlin Johnson as SAC, Chicago, upon the latter's retirement in 1970, contended under oath that his office had already delivered all pertinent documents concerning Bureau involvement with Hampton. When Taylor and Haas promptly produced copies of documents other than those Held was claiming represented an essentially complete disclosure, the new SAC was ordered by the court to reconsider his position and quickly came up with several handcarts loaded with boxes of heavily deleted material, numbering some 100,000 pages in all.[125] Despite such blatant examples of government misconduct, Federal Judge J. Sam Perry opted (after an 18-month civil rights trial) to enter *directed* verdicts of acquittal on all counts in 1977.[126]

Tenacious, Taylor and Haas appealed this decision to the U.S. Seventh Circuit Court and, in 1979, were able to sufficiently demonstrate judicial impropriety and the appearance of an FBI conspiracy to murder Hampton and obstruct justice that a retrial was ordered.[127] The defendants (Hanrahan, *et al.*) then appealed this outcome to the U.S. Supreme Court, contending that any further probing of the case "would endanger the lives of informants who had participated"; the high court denied *certiorari* in 1981, refusing to hear the appeal. With both sides becoming rather battle-weary, the case was finally arbitrated in 1983, absent a jury, with presiding judge John F. Grady ruling that there *had* in fact been an active governmental conspiracy to deny Hampton, Clark and the BPP plaintiffs their civil rights. The defendants as a group were found to have been culpable, sanctions were imposed upon the FBI for its coverup activities, and an award of $1.85 million went to the survivors and families of the deceased.[128]

Needless to say, the victory was somewhat pyrrhic. None of the perpetrators of the crime at issue ever served so much as a day in jail for *any* of their offenses, and the political purposes of the COINTELPRO which entailed the assassinations had long since been achieved. The December 4, 1969 raid had broken the back of the Illinois BPP, and the Party in Chicago passed into oblivion.

The Case of Geronimo Pratt

Louisana born and raised, Elmer Gerard ("Geronimo" or "G") Pratt enlisted in the U.S. Army in 1965 at the age of seventeen. He became a paratrooper and underwent considerable training in light weapons and irregular warfare before being assigned to the 82nd Airborne Division's Long Range Reconnaissance Patrol (LRRP) unit in late 1966, operating in Vietnam's Central Highlands region and "cross border" in Cambodia and Laos. Over the following eighteen months (the duration of his enlistment), Pratt participated in a series of highly classified missions, garnering some eighteen combat decorations—including the Silver Star, Bronze Star (for valor), Vietnamese Cross of Gallantry and the Purple Heart—while becoming increasingly disenchanted with the nature of the war, the military system and the social order which spawned them.[129]

Availing himself of an "early out" discharge from the Army in exchange for his double tour in Southeast Asia, he relocated from Louisiana to Los Angeles in August of 1968. Using his benefits under the G.I. Bill, he enrolled at UCLA through the High Potential Equal Opportunity Program (EOP), taking an active role in the campus Black Student Union (BSU) and becoming acquainted with local BPP leaders Jon Huggins and Bunchy Carter. The latter in particular nurtured a close personal friendship, and recruited Pratt into the Party during the fall.[130] At about the same time, J. Edgar Hoover went on record describing the BPP as "the greatest threat to the internal security of the country,"[131] and began issuing secret directives to destroy the Party via various COINTELPRO expedients.

Pratt was an active member of the Los Angeles BPP (LA-BPP) Chapter during the period of the Bureau disinformation campaign which resulted in a "shooting war" between the US organization and the Panthers (see Chapter 2). His primary

The Oakland BPP office after it was riddled with gunfire by a group of "off-duty" police. (Photo: *The Berkeley Barb*)

Los Angeles BPP leaders Alprentice "Bunchy" Carter (left) and Jon Huggins (right) were gunned down January 17, 1969 in Campbell Hall, UCLA, by members of Ron Karenga's US Organization, provoked by a carefully orchestrated COINTELPRO. (Photo: *The Black Panther*)

function at the outset seems to have been to handle the southern California end of BPP Minister of Information Eldridge Cleaver's presidential campaign on the Peace and Freedom Party ticket, a process which resulted in his becoming close to Cleaver and his wife, Kathleen, prior to the BPP leader's going into exile over an alleged parole violation during November 1968.[132] It was undoubtedly through this association that Pratt also rapidly became personally familiar with others in the Panther national hierarchy, including both Bobby and John Seale, David and June Hilliard, and George Murphy.

By the end of the year, Pratt seems to have proven himself so effective at his political work that, when Carter and Huggins were assassinated by US gunmen on January 17, 1969, it was discovered that Carter had left an audio tape (prepared for such an eventuality) designating the ex-GI his successor as head of the LA-BPP. Pratt was also named by Carter to succeed himself and Huggins as chapter representative on the national Panther Central Committee.[133] It was at precisely this point that he appears to have been personally targeted for "neutralization" through the application of COINTELPRO techniques; the medium through which this was accomplished seems to have been through the same FBI/CCI/CCS/SSI federal/state/local police combination deployed against George Jackson, the Soledad Brothers Defense Committee and other radical California groups (see next section).[134]

Pratt was almost immediately designated a "Key Black Extremist" by the L.A. Bureau office and placed in the National Security Index.[135] As a consequence, he was targeted not only for neutralization by the FBI, but, as former Panther infiltrator Louis Tackwood had pointed out, this automatically placed him "on the wall" of the Los Angeles Police Department's (LAPD) Criminal Conspiracy Section (CCS) "glasshouse" (headquarters) as an individual to be eliminated by local police action.[136] As Tackwood explained the CCS operation:

> The room is broken up into divisions, see my point? Black, white, chicano and subversives. Everybody's there. And every last one of the walls has pictures of them. This one black, the middle all white, and the chicanos all on this side. Most of the files are on the walls, you see?...They got everybody. Panthers, SDS, Weathermen. Let me explain to you. They got a national hookup. You see my point? And because of this national power, they are the only organization in the police department that has a liaison man, that works for the FBI, and the FBI has a liaison man who works with the CCS.[137]

The inevitable consequence of this was that the new LA-BPP was placed under intensely close surveillance by the FBI[138] and subjected to a series of unfounded but serious arrests by the Bureau's local police affiliates at CCS:

- On April 4, 1969, Pratt and his second in command, Roger "Blue" Lewis, were arrested "on a tip" by the LAPD, for "possession of an explosive device" (a pipebomb) while driving in a car; the matter did not go to trial until 1972, under circumstances which will be described below.[139]

Louis Tackwood, an infiltrator/provocateur within the BPP who subsequently went public with the story of how the FBI and local police agencies were conspiring to destroy the Panthers, shed much light on the nature of the COINTELPRO used against Geronimo Pratt. Tackwood was also involved in the assassination of George Jackson inside San Quentin prison. (Photo: *The Black Panther*)

NOW, GERONIMO ... WHO WERE YOU CALLIN' A PORK CHOP NIGGER ?

Two of the cartoons produced and distributed by the Los Angeles office of the FBI during the COINTELPRO against Geronimo Pratt, designed to continue to provoke the lethal tension between the Panthers and the US Organization which had already claimed the lives of Bunchy Carter, Jon Huggins, Sylvester Bell and others.

- On April 23, 1969, he was arrested along with FBI Panther infiltrator Julio C. Butler and three *bona fide* Party members on charges of having kidnapped another BPP member, Ollie Taylor; acquittal in this matter occurred in April of 1971.[140]

- On June 15, 1969, Pratt and several other Party members were questioned on suspicion of murdering Frank "Captain Franco" Diggs, a Party member whose bullet-riddled body was discovered in a vacant lot in the San Pedro area south of Watts on December 19, 1968; this seems to have been a pure harassment bust (as well as another tactic of projecting the image of "Panther violence" into the media), and charges were quickly dropped. Under the conditions of FBI-fostered US assaults upon LA-BPP members prevailing at the time—this was less than a month before the Carter/Huggins murders, as well as the murder of Sylvester Bell in San Diego—it would have been much more likely to suspect Karenga's US organization than Pratt. No one has ever been prosecuted in the death of Captain Franco.[141]

Pratt was also made the subject of a personalized series of COINTELPRO cartoons (see illustration) designed to make him a target for the attentions of US. Nonetheless, there is considerable evidence that he initially attempted to steer the LA-BPP away from any overemphasis on armed struggle; during his early tenure, he is known to have worked very hard to maintain the Chapter's Free Breakfast for Children Program, community education and health care efforts. At the same time Elaine Brown undertook the extraordinary (for a Panther leader) step of instructing BPP cadres to cooperate in the police investigation of the Carter/Huggins assassination, testifying against other black people (from US) in open court.[142] The FBI's response to such efforts was to open a conspiracy investigation of Pratt with regard to the robbery of a Bank of America facility already known by the Bureau to have been carried out by US members.[143]

This was followed very closely by a Bureau effort to ensnarl both Pratt and Roger Lewis in a violation of the 1940 Smith Act and plotting of "insurrection."[144] The LA-FBI office, apparently on the basis of its own contrived image of the Panther leader's "violence" and "criminality," then prepared a "biography" of Pratt to accompany its recommendation that he be elevated to "Priority I" status in the National Security Index and an announcement that he was forthwith being included in the FBI's "Black Nationalist Photo Album" across the country; although much is made of his military record in this document, virtually no evidence is offered to validate the notion that he represented the sort of acute threat to national security associated with a top SI rating.[145] Nevertheless, the recommendation was approved within forty-eight hours.[146] As he entered his sixth month as leader of the LA-BPP, Pratt was thus explicitly singled out for neutralization by the head of the Bureau's LA-COINTELPRO section, Richard Wallace Held (son of Richard G. Held who orchestrated the coverup of FBI involvement in the Hampton-Clark assassinations; see above).[147]

Largely because of this blatant pattern of Bureau and cooperating police attempts to eliminate him, Pratt came to recognize the absolute impossibility of securing social change (or even elementary justice) "through the system" (see note 132, this

FBI agent Richard W. Held (son of Richard G. Held), a COINTELPRO specialist who worked in Los Angeles against Pratt and the BPP; as SAC in San Juan, Puerto Rico; and most recently as SAC in San Francisco.

chapter). By July of 1969, he increasingly acknowledged the necessity of "meeting fire with fire" and became associated with the "Afro-American Liberation Army," an entity which later became better known as the Black Liberation Army (BLA).[148] The final catalyst in this transformation undoubtedly occurred on December 8, 1969, when, as has been described elsewhere:

> Four days after a similar raid on a Panther apartment in Chicago (a raid which left Mark Clark and Fred Hampton dead), forty men of the Special Weapons and Tactics (SWAT) squad, with more than a hundred regular police as backup, raided the Los Angeles Panther headquarters at 5:30 in the morning...(No suggestion has been made that the two raids were linked. But it's interesting to note that Fred Hampton had been in Los Angeles one or two days before his death, meeting with Geronimo Pratt, whom Tackwood says was the main target of the second raid.) The Panthers chose to defend themselves, and for four hours they fought off police, refusing to surrender until press and public were on the scene. Six of them were wounded. Thirteen were arrested. Miraculously, none of them were killed.

Interior and exterior views of the Los Angeles BPP office shortly after the December 8, 1969 police assault. A jury subsequently found all Panthers who had participated in the shoot-out innocent of any major crimes. (Photos: *The Black Panther*)

The pretext of the raid was twofold. The police, first of all, claimed that on November 28, 1969, George Young and Paul Redd had thrown a police sergeant out of Panther headquarters at gunpoint, and that, later in the day, Geronimo Pratt had taken a bead on a passing police car with a machinegun. Arrest warrants for all three had been sworn out a week before the raid. Second, the SWAT assault group was armed with a search warrant (as well as an armored personnel carrier, AR-15 automatic rifles, helicopters, tear gas and dynamite). They were to search for stolen weapons...[I]n getting the search warrant, police deliberately misled Municipal Court Judge Antonio Chavez. The reason CCS Sergeant Raymond Callahan gave for the prospective search was that he wanted to look for six machineguns and thirty M-14s stolen from Camp Pendleton marine base, as well as the weapons used in what he called "the assault on officers." In an affidavit under oath, Callahan told Judge Chavez that George Young had been at Camp Pendleton when the machineguns and M-14s were stolen and that he later went AWOL. What he didn't tell him was that Young was in the stockade at the time of the theft and he knew it. "I didn't think it was important," he later said.[149]

The similarities between the Chicago and Los Angeles raids are undeniable, with a special local police unit closely linked to the FBI involved in both assaults (SPU in Chicago, CCS in Los Angeles; Ray Callahan would thus serve as Daniel Groth in this matter), spurious warrants seeking "illegal weapons" utilized on both occasions (and based on Bureau "tips," as we shall see), predawn timing of both raids to catch the Panthers asleep and a reliance upon overwhelming police firepower to the exclusion of all other methods. Both raids occurred in the context of an ongoing and highly energetic anti-BPP COINTELPRO, and—as in the Hampton assassination—bullets were fired directly into Pratt's bed. (Unlike the Chicago leader, however, Pratt was sleeping on the floor, the result of spinal injuries sustained in Vietnam.)[150] In both instances, the FBI had managed to place an infiltrator/provocateur very high within the local BPP chapter—O'Neal in Chicago, in Los Angeles it was Melvin "Cotton" Smith, number three man in the LA-BPP—who provided detailed floorplans, including sleeping arrangements of the Panther facility, prior to the raid.[151] And, in both cases, surviving Panthers were immediately arrested for their "assault upon the police."[152]

When the resultant "case" against the L.A. Panthers was finally prosecuted in July, 1971:

...there was a "surprise" development. Melvin "Cotton" Smith turned up as a star witness for the prosecution. According to Deputy District Attorney Ronald H. Carroll, Smith had turned State's evidence to escape prosecution...[However] on November 22, 1971, Tackwood testified...he had started working for [CCS Sergeant R.G.] Farwell in the fall of 1969, before the December 8 raid, and had been told by Farwell that [FBI infiltrator] Cotton Smith was to be Tackwood's contact. Since Smith's testimony was crucial to the State's case, Tackwood's exposure of Smith's real role was a devastating blow to the prosecution.[153]

One consequence of this revelation was that, after eleven days of deliberation, the jury returned acquittals (or failed to reach any verdict whatsoever) relative to charges of conspiring to assault and murder police officers brought against all thirteen Panther defendants. Oddly, nine of the defendants, including Pratt, were convicted of the relatively minor and technical charge of conspiring to possess illegal weapons.[154] In addition, as has been noted elsewhere:

> In order for the armed police assault on the Panther headquarters to have been justified, the police contention that the Panthers had fired on them first would have had to have been true, in which case at least some of the Panthers would have been guilty of conspiracy to commit murder and assault charges...The failure of the jury to return guilty verdicts on these charges represented a total repudiation of the CCS [and FBI] "conspiracy" theory that led to the raids on December 8.[155]

Pratt spent more than two months in jail following the shootout, until some $125,000 in bail could be raised to secure his release.[156] It was apparently during this incarceration that he began the series of personal notes which were later edited and released as an underground book, *The New Urban Guerrilla*, and a contribution to the "BLA Manual" entitled *Humanity, Freedom, Peace.*[157] Upon his release, he made a whirlwind national speaking tour and then dropped out of sight (while remaining mostly in Los Angeles).[158] During this period he reputedly began to associate with George Jackson's emergent People's Army in northern California.[159] The Bureau, which attempted to "turn" the Panther leader into an informer while he was in lockup, now opted to launch a COINTELPRO to bad-jacket him:

> For the information of the Bureau, in view of PRATT's adamant expression of hatred toward law enforcement personnel in general, no consideration is being given to reinterview PRATT for the purpose of development as a PRI [informer]. It is noted, however, that constant consideration is given to the possibility of utilization of counterintelligence measures with efforts being directed toward neutralizing PRATT as an effective BPP functionary.[160]

That this attempt was undertaken (through the efforts of FBI infiltrator Cotton Smith) is borne out by the sudden subjecting of Pratt to a battery of "loyalty tests" (which he passed), administered by representatives of the BPP national hierarchy in June of 1970.[161] His outspoken alignment with Eldridge Cleaver, in combination with the lingering suspicions created by the bad-jacketing, served to bring about his formal expulsion from the BPP when, "on August 5, Huey Newton came out of jail, and [soon] issued orders 'to wash everybody who's a [Cleaver] man...right out of the Party.'"[162] This, of course, was a situation directly connected to the earlier mentioned COINTELPRO exacerbating the so-called "Newton-Cleaver split" within the BPP (see Chapter 2), a process which had not yet culminated and which temporarily resulted in Cleaver also distancing himself from Pratt and others.[163] It was at this juncture that the abortive Marin County Civic Center action involving Jonathan Jackson and the People's Army occurred (see next section), and Pratt left California to "cool out" and reconsider matters from the vantage point of Texas, a move which

Melvin "Cotton" Smith, an infiltrator/provocateur who became Security Chief of the Los Angeles BPP, had much to do with putting Geronimo Pratt into position for COINTELPRO neutralization. Smith is currently serving a life sentence for murder. (Photo: *The Black Panther*)

Geronimo Pratt (in hat) and Huey Newton on August 5, 1970, the day Newton was released from prison pending retrial on his conviction for the murder of Oakland policeman John Frey. This was shortly.before the FBI's COINTELPRO set the two against each other, leaving Pratt isolated from the BPP. (Photo: *The Black Panther*)

caused him to miss a court appearance concerning the "pipe bomb case." (Codefendant Roger Lewis went to trial, was convicted and sentenced to three years.)[164]

With Pratt isolated from the BPP, and correspondingly vulnerable, the FBI moved quickly to finish him off. On September 14, Assistant U.S. Attorney Michael A. Heuer obtained a federal warrant on the charge of interstate flight to avoid prosecution,[165] and a nation-wide manhunt was begun. Meanwhile, a grand jury was convened in Los Angeles to hear evidence prepared by CCS detective Callahan intended to result in his indictment on murder charges (according to both Tackwood and Cotton Smith, there had been a considerable controversy in CCS and the FBI over exactly *what* murder to use in preparing a case against Pratt), a result which was obtained on December 4, 1970.[166] "Coincidental" to the secret grand jury finding, his whereabouts were pinpointed in Dallas by the FBI on December 8, and:

> ...when the FBI found out...where G was hiding, they didn't bust him, they called here [to Los Angeles]. And you know who busted him?...Not the FBI, but the CCS, and in Texas! And brought him back. No extradition whatsoever...With all those charges, he could have fought extradition for years. They kidnapped him. Arrested down there, and they kidnapped him...CCS, they're like federally sponsored. Like J. Edgar Hoover says, "They're my boys, they're my boys."[167]

The problematic manner of Pratt's removal from Texas to California was compounded by the fact that CCS detectives Callahan and Mahoney, who handled the procedure, "neglected" to mention his murder indictment; he did not learn that he was charged until he was arraigned in the matter (in Los Angeles) on December 16.[168] He was incarcerated without bond, a situation dramatically worsened when, on January 23, 1971, Huey P. Newton, reacting to escalating COINTELPRO efforts to consummate the split between his adherents and those of Cleaver, used *The Black Panther* as a medium through which to publish a full page story announcing the expulsion of Pratt, his wife Sandra, and LA-BPP members Will Stafford, Wilfred Holiday and George Lloyd from the Party.[169] Pratt was personally denounced (for public consumption) as being extremely violent and all BPP members were forbidden to endeavor to "aid or communicate with those expelled."[170] Geronimo Pratt was thus effectively cut off altogether from the outside world and denied any possibility of substantial assistance as the noose tightened about his neck.

Over the next few weeks, the Cleaver-Newton COINTELPRO reached its fruition as Newton appeared live on San Francisco television station KGO's "Jim Dunbar Show," with Eldridge Cleaver connected from Algiers by long-distance telephone; the two faction leaders then publicly "had it out" over the airways concerning—among other things—the purging of Pratt and other "Cleaverite" members from the BPP. The "split" was official.[171] Throughout the spring, the Bureau also persistently but unsuccessfully attempted to tie Pratt to the 1969 Camp Pendleton armory robbery, a failure which left the prosecution unable to obtain serious convictions when the December 8 shootout case finally went to trial in May of 1971.[172] Rough stasis was maintained until November 11, when Pratt was informed that his wife, Sandra (known as "Red"), eight months pregnant, had been murdered, her bullet-riddled body stuffed in a sleeping bag and dumped alongside an L.A. freeway; he was allowed neither to view the body nor attend the funeral, and no serious police investigation of her homicide seems to have occurred.[173]

A lull again prevailed through the spring of 1972, with Pratt's acquittal on all major charges against him except for the murder indictment. In June, however, this matter came to trial with the former BPP leader represented by a relatively inexperienced court-appointed attorney, Johnnie Cochran (assisted by attorney Charles Hollopeter), in whom he professed little confidence. Virtually no defense funds or external support were raised.[174] His misgivings over the situation were well founded, given the welter of COINTELPRO complexity which attended the prosecution from start to finish.

On its face, the case was forthright enough. At a little after 8 p.m. on December 18, 1968, two black men robbed and shot a white couple, Caroline and Kenneth Olsen, on a Santa Monica, California tennis court. Caroline Olsen died one week later. Pratt was accused of "the tennis court murder" in a letter dated August 10, 1969, addressed to LAPD Sergeant Duwayne Rice by an "underworld informant" and marked "Do Not Open Except In Case of My Death" (a common enough street-snitch ploy to protect longevity). Unaccountably—given that the informant had not died—Rice opened and read the accusation on October 20, 1970, and turned the letter over to CCS detective Ray Callahan for presentation to the grand jury which secretly indicted Pratt on December 4 (a standard practice in the indictment of a fugitive). The informant then testified at the trial that Pratt, in direct personal conversation with him, had "bragged" of the crime. He further testified that a .45 calibre Colt automatic seized by the LAPD in the January 17, 1970 raid upon the Ericka Huggins residence, belonging to Pratt but not ballistically matching the tennis court murder weapon, was actually the gun in question, Pratt having "changed the barrel" in order to alter its ballistic pattern.[175] A second informant, who did not testify, corroborated this testimony.

Kenneth Olsen, the surviving victim, then identified Pratt as the murderer in open court, as did Barbara Reed, a shopkeeper who had seen the gunmen prior to the shooting. Mitchell Lachman, who had been near the tennis court on the evening of the murder, testified the gunmen fled in a vehicle matching the description of Pratt's white over red GTO convertible. Pratt's main line of defense was (and is) that he was in Oakland, some 400 miles north of Santa Monica, attending a BPP national leadership meeting on the evening in question. Presentation of this alibi was, however, severely hampered by the COINTELPRO-induced refusal of many of those also in attendance—such as David, June, and Pat Hilliard, Bobby and John Seale, Nathan Hare, Rosemary Gross and Brenda Presley (all of the Newton faction)—to testify on his behalf.[176] Kathleen Cleaver, also in attendance at the meeting, did testify that Pratt was in Oakland from December 13-25, 1968, but even her efforts to do so had been hampered by COINTELPRO letters to her husband "explaining" that it was "too dangerous" for her to return to the United States during the trial.[177] With

Kathleen Cleaver, wife of BPP Minister of Information Eldridge Cleaver, was prevented from offering full assistance to Pratt during his murder trial by a COINTELPRO aimed at splintering the Panthers as a united organization. (Photo: *Ramparts*)

the weight of testimony heavily on the side of the prosecution, Pratt was convicted of first degree murder on July 28, 1972;[178] the sentence imposed was seven years to life (standard under California's indeterminate sentencing guidelines).

Of course, there were certain problems with the case which went beyond the Bureau-imposed constraints attending Pratt's attempts to assemble defense witnesses. For instance, it did occur to the defense that if the FBI were tapping the phones of, or otherwise electronically surveilling, the BPP national offices in Oakland during December of 1968—as seems likely—the Bureau itself might well be able to substantiate Pratt's whereabouts on the crucial night. The FBI, however, submitted at trial that no such taps or bugs existed, an assertion which was later shown to be untrue.[179] The Bureau then refused to release its JUNE logs from the taps, on "national security" grounds, until forced to do so by an FOIA suit brought by attorneys Jonathan Lubell, Mary O'Melveny and William H. O'Brien.[180] At that point (1981), the transcripts were delivered, minus *precisely* the records covering the period of time which might serve to establish Pratt's innocence; "The FBI has indicated (not by affidavit) that the transcripts of the conversations recorded by these telephone taps have been lost or destroyed," according to the frustrated judge.[181]

Then there was the matter of the identity of the State's star witness, who first accused Pratt of the tennis court murder in his letter to Rice, testified to Pratt's "confession" of the crime (*i.e.*, "bragging") and finally reconciled the prosecution's ballistics difficulties. He was none other than the infiltrator/provocateur, expelled from the BPP by Pratt, Julius C. (aka Julio) Butler. At the trial, the prosecution went considerably out of its way to bolster Butler's credibility before the jury by "establishing" that the witness was *not* a paid FBI informant (although they were willing to allow that he'd been a deputy sheriff prior to joining the BPP):

> *Q:* And when you were working for the Black Panther Party, were you also working for law enforcement at the same time?
> *A:* No.
> *Q:* You had severed any ties you had with law enforcement?
> *A:* That's correct.
> *Q:* Have you at any time since leaving the Sheriff's Department worked for the FBI or the CIA?
> *A:* No.
> *Q:* Are you now working for the FBI or CIA?
> *A:* No.[182]

This testimony was entered despite the fact that Los Angeles FBI Field Office informant reports concerning one Julius Carl Butler show he performed exactly this function, at least during the period beginning in August of 1969 (the time when he ostensibly made his initial accusation against Pratt) until January 20, 1970 (after Pratt was jailed without bond on the Olsen murder charge). During the whole of 1970, he filed monthly reports with the Bureau, he was "evaluated" by the FBI as an informant during that year, and his PRI file was not closed until May of 1972 (immediately prior to his going on the stand).[183] Louis Tackwood has consistently contended that Butler was an FBI infiltrator of the BPP from the day he joined the Party in early 1968 and that he actively worked with CCS detectives Ray Callahan and Daniel P. Mahoney to eliminate Pratt.[184] It should be noted that, since the trial, Butler has been able to complete law school and enter the California bar, despite guilty pleas to four felony charges.[185]

The supposed informant corroboration of Butler's testimony, it was later revealed, was obtained from Cotton Smith, already unmasked as an infiltrator/provocateur during the 1971 shootout trial and thus unable to credibly take the stand in the Olsen murder case. In 1985, Smith totally recanted his allegations against Pratt, stating unequivocally that the former Panther leader had been "framed," but by "the FBI rather than local police"; he specifically named LA-FBI COINTELPRO operative George Aiken as having been instrumental in the affair.[186] At the trial, the Bureau also submitted that Pratt was *not* the target of COINTELPRO activity; several hundred documents subsequently released under the FOIA demonstrate this to have been categorically untrue. Further:

> On 18 December 1979, eight years after Pratt's trial, the California Attorney-General's office filed a declaration in court that his defense camp had been infiltrated by *one* FBI informant. The Deputy Attorney-General wrote to the court and defense counsel on 28 July 1980, enclosing a copy of a letter of the same date from the Executive Assistant Director of the FBI. This letter revealed that two had been in a position to obtain information about Elmer Pratt's defense strategy.[187]

As to Kenneth Olsen's positive identification in court of Pratt as his assailant and his wife's murderer, both he and the District Attorney omitted mention of the fact that he had positively identified another man—Ronald Perkins—in a police lineup very shortly after the fact, on December 24, 1968; they had similarly neglected to mention that LAPD personnel had "worked with" Olsen from photo spreads for some months prior to the trial, with an eye toward obtaining the necessary ID of Pratt.[188] Again, both the prosecutors and Mrs. Reed, the other witness who offered a positive ID on Pratt, "forgot" comparable police coaching, and all parties to the State's case somehow managed to overlook the fact that both Olsen and Redd had initially (and repeatedly) described both gunmen as "clean shaven," while Pratt was known to have worn a mustache and goatee for the entirety of his adult life.[189] This leaves Lachman's testimony that the assailants fled the scene in a white-over-red convertible "like" (but not necessarily) Pratt's; even if it *were* the same car, it was well established—and never contested by the State—that virtually the whole LA-BPP had use of the vehicle during the period in question.[190]

Despite the obvious and extreme problems with this case, Pratt's first appeal was denied by the California Court of Appeals on February 1, 1974, with the exception that sentence was set for rehearing before trial judge Kathleen Parker due to the fact that he had been under 21 years of age at the time of the alleged crime; sentence was sustained on January 10, 1975. Meanwhile, the California Supreme Court denied a petition for hearing on April 17, 1974, and the U.S. Supreme Court denied a petition for *certiorari* in the same year.[191] On November 20, 1979, Pratt filed a writ of *habeas corpus* through the office of San Francisco attorney Stuart Hanlon, in Los Angeles Superior Court; the argument, based on FOIA disclosure of COINTELPRO documents and governmental misrepresentation at trial, was heard once again by Judge Parker, and denied on January 18, 1980 (along with a request for an evidentiary hearing in the matter).[192] Consequently, an identical writ was filed with the California Court of Appeals on April 10, and denied on December 3, 1980.[193] On April 1, 1981, the California Supreme Court joined in denying the writ and evidentiary hearing.[194]

Perhaps a portion of the various courts' inability to see the obvious in the Pratt case has to do with the FBI's (and its associates') continued desire to obfuscate it. For instance, in a continuation of *habeas corpus* proceedings in 1985, Stuart Hanlon was (finally) allowed to depose certain COINTELPRO principals such as the LA-FBI's Richard W. Held, Brendan O. Cleary and Richard H. Bloesner, as well as Ray Callahan and Daniel P. Mahoney of CCS. Each displayed a truly remarkable inability, for all their professional training in "recall," to remember much of anything they ever did with regards to their jobs. The following excerpt from the testimony of Held is indicative of the whole:

Hanlon: Mr. Held, you were—without going into what it was—you were the COINTELPRO agent in Los Angeles for a period of time; is that correct?

Held: That was, I was responsible for coordinating that amongst other things that I did, that is correct.

Hanlon: In that role, you were aware, were you not, of a list known as "Key Black Extremists?"

Held: I don't recall that list, Mr. Hanlon.

Hanlon: Let me ask it again. Were you aware that there was a list out of Washington designating certain persons as "Key Black Extremists?"

Held: I vaguely recall that. Now, of what significance that was in terms of what kind of investigative attention that would have called for, I don't recall if any.[195]

Or at another point:

Held: No. I don't recall. I remember my contacts with Mr. [Julius C.] Butler in a general fashion, but I don't recall any—I recall that regardless of any documents they showed me, but I don't recall—I don't recall the document.[196]

Nor has justice been better regarding parole. Pratt's first hearing on the matter occurred in February 1978. Chairperson of this three-person panel was Ray Brown, former head of the Oakland Police Department's anti-BPP Squad (that smaller city's approximation of L.A.'s CCS) from 1967-72. Although petitioned to do so, Brown refused to disqualify himself, and the panel unanimously decided to deny Pratt a release date.[197] The performance has been repeated on each occasion since, including the former Panther leader's last hearing, in April 1987.[198]

One reason for the seemingly blanket recalcitrance of the authorities—federal, state and local—in extending even the most elementary pretense of justice in the Pratt case may revolve around his quiet refusal to abandon the political principles which caused him to become a COINTELPRO target in the first place. In 1973, he refused the honor of his participation in his trial on the 1969 "pipe bomb" charges, was convicted (essentially *in absentia*) and, like Roger Lewis, was sentenced to three years. Shortly after he was transferred from Folsom Prison to San Quentin, in March of 1974, the FBI began a new investigation of him, "based upon information which indicates that the captioned individual [Pratt] is engaged in activities which could involve a violation of Title 18, United States Code, Section 2383 (Rebellion and Insurrection), 2384 (Seditious Conspiracy), or 2385 (Advocating Overthrow of the U.S. Government)"; specifically at issue were his continuing linkages to the BPP Cleaver faction, as well as his alleged leadership position within the Black Guerrilla Family, a group evolved from George Jackson's "inside" organization (Jackson adherents James Holiday, Hugo Pinnell, Johnny Spain and David Johnson were also mentioned by name in this regard).[199]

Whatever the particulars of official motivation in the handling of the Pratt case, it must be assessed within the overall COINTELPRO-BPP context, especially a counterintelligence-related instructional memo, dated October 24, 1968, and sent by Bureau headquarters to all field offices. It reads in part:

Geronimo Pratt in 1987, in the San Quentin prison where he has spent the past eighteen years of his life, five years in solitary confinement, for a crime he did not commit. (Photo: *Los Angeles Times*)

Successful prosecution is the best deterrent to such unlawful activities [as dissident political organizing]. Intensive investigations of key activists...are logically expected to result in prosecutions under substantive violation within the Bureau's jurisdiction.[200]

To this, the Church Committee's rejoinder in its investigation of the Bureau's COINTELPRO illegalities still seems quite appropriate: "While the FBI considered Federal prosecution a 'logical' result, it should be noted that key activists were chosen not because they were suspected of having committed or planning [sic] to commit any specific Federal crime."[201]

The George Jackson Case

Although its details are hardly as clear as those of the Hampton-Clark and Pratt cases, nothing defines the scope and intentions of the FBI's campaign to repress the Black Panther Party as well as the contours of the grand plot which have emerged since the assassination of BPP Field Marshal George L. Jackson in California's San Quentin prison on August 21, 1971.[202] As has been noted elsewhere, Jackson—who had served some ten years of an indeterminate sentence (one year to life) accruing from a $70 gas station robbery committed when he was eighteen years of age and who had been named as a defendant in the Soledad Brothers case[203]—had become an international *cause celebre* and a focal point of the movement against black oppression, largely as a result of the eloquence of his book, *Soledad Brother.*[204] Insofar

George Jackson, author of *Soledad Brother* and *Blood in My Eye*, BPP Field Marshal and founder of the People's Army, prior to his assassination in San Quentin on August 21, 1971. (Photo: Random House)

as he was both a major movement symbol and, by virtue of being entombed in a maximum security prison, a stationary target who would necessarily limit the mobility of his supporters, Jackson was a made-to-order victim of some of COINTELPRO's most wicked blows.

According to Louis Tackwood and other police infiltrators of the BPP, the FBI, in conjunction with collaborating California law enforcement agencies such as the LAPD's CCS, as well as the State of California's Sacramento-based Criminal Identification and Investigation (CII) section, and Special Investigations and Identifications (SII) unit—the same combination brought to bear against Geronimo Pratt—hatched a plan to utilize the support apparatus attending Jackson as the means to destroy not only the "guts" of the Panthers, but affiliated entities as well. As reconstructed by Jo Durden-Smith from Tackwood's interviews,[205] this police consortium planned to utilize the highly placed infiltrator Cotton Smith to initiate a gambit wherein teams of Panthers belonging to what George Jackson had taken to calling the "People's Army" would enter a courtroom and take hostages who could be exchanged for the Soledad Brothers and transportation to a "non-imperialist country," probably Algeria.[206] On the day of this grand event, the police would be ready and, "The Panthers would be destroyed, their soldiers killed, their organization discredited, their supporters embroiled in a massive conspiracy prosecution."[207]

This plan, however, went somewhat awry. The courtroom nearest San Quentin, contained in the Marin County Civic Center at San Rafael, California, was selected, logically enough, and Cotton Smith duly transported appropriate weaponry into the area. A date was chosen in which three black prisoners from San Quentin would actually be in court, and things were set to go. Durden-Smith erroneously contends Geronimo Pratt canceled the operation at the last moment; the LA-BPP leader was not involved, however, in any capacity at all. In any event, the cancellation occurred with such haste that Smith was unable to notify his contact agents in either the FBI or CCS. Worse, no one thought to inform Jackson's seventeen-year-old brother Jonathan, who was scheduled to participate in the action to free George. As Tackwood put it, "He goes in, looking for the fellers. See my point? And there ain't no motherfucking body there. So, 'stick 'em up.' He goes into his little act. Poor dum-dum."[208]

Trying to put the best face on what must have been a bewildering situation, Jonathan Jackson armed the three prisoners—William Christmas, Ruchell Magee and James McClain—taking Judge Harold J. Haley, Assistant District Attorney Gary Thomas and three jurors hostage. The group then prepared to leave, demanding and receiving assurance from the local sheriff that they would not be fired upon. In the meantime, however, CCS representatives and, apparently by prearrangement, a whole contingent of San Quentin's sharpshooters arrived on the scene.[209] As Durden-Smith describes it:

> Outside the civic center…were sergeants Mahoney and Callahan of Los Angeles CCS. They knew nothing of the last minute change in the plan. As far as they were concerned, "the shit was going to hit the fan." They were to force a confrontation between the police and the [Panthers] any way they could…So, when the small group of kid-

nappers walked out into the Marin Civic Center car park around eleven o'clock on the morning of August 7, 1970, with Jonathan Jackson bringing up the rear, the sergeants reacted first with surprise: the group was smaller than it should have been. Soon they fired the disputed first shot, the shot that led to four deaths in nineteen seconds.[210]

Killed in the fusillade of bullets were Jonathan Jackson, inmates William Christmas and James McClain, and Judge Haley. Assistant District Attorney Thomas was paralyzed for life, while Ruchell Magee and a juror were also badly wounded. Although the COINTELPRO had fallen short of its original objectives, it still represented a not inconsiderable propaganda coup and opened the door for followup actions against Panther supporters. One of those in line for elimination in this regard was Stanford University professor Bruce Franklin, head of the Revolutionary Union (RU; formerly Bay Area Radical Union or BAYRU), and later founder of the Venceremos organization; Franklin was first dismissed from his teaching position on January 22, 1972 and then indicted in early 1973 along with several other Venceremos leaders of having abetted the escape of a California prisoner. It was more than a year before they were acquitted, by which time the organization had for all practical purposes dissolved.[211]

A more immediate target in the aftermath of the "Marin County Shootout" was Angela Davis. A former UCLA professor who had been dismissed for her affiliations with the Communist Party and BPP in Los Angeles, Davis was head of the Soledad Brothers Defense Committee and an increasingly effective spokesperson for the movement as a whole. She was charged with murder on the day following the shootout, although FBI and CCS surveillance located her in San Jose rather than San Rafael on the morning of August 7. The only "evidence" ever posited to link her to the event was that Jonathan Jackson, who served as her bodyguard from time to time, entered the courtroom in possession of a shotgun and two handguns which she had earlier purchased (legally). Nonetheless, a warrant was issued for her arrest in California and, as she declined to surrender under the circumstances then prevailing, she was designated as the FBI's "most wanted fugitive."[212]

Davis was captured in a New York hotel room by FBI agents on the night of October 13, 1970 and held (for a time in an isolation cell) in the city's Women's House of Corrections without bond. As her attorneys argued to block extradition and to serve a writ of *habeas corpus* due to lack of evidence against her, California altered the charges against her to reflect participation in a conspiracy to commit murder (rather than murder, *per se*) and President Richard M. Nixon went on nation-wide television to congratulate J. Edgar Hoover for the Bureau's apprehension of this "terrorist." Her various appeals having been hustled all the way through the U.S. Supreme Court in record time and denied at each step along the way, she was transported in the dead of night back to California in mid-December. She was held in the Marin Civic Center's jail without bond before and during her trial as a co-conspirator with Ruchell Magee.[213] At the time the jury reached the obvious conclusion, acquitting her of all charges, she had been incarcerated for more than a year, and Soledad Brothers funding had been severely strained in her defense.

Angela Davis and Jonathan Jackson at a Soledad Brothers rally, spring 1970. Davis was proclaimed by the FBI and Richard Nixon to be one of the nation's "most wanted terrorists." She was ultimately acquitted of all charges. (Photo: Wide World)

Meanwhile, as he has flatly put it, Tackwood was proceeding with his "mission to kill George Jackson."[214] This seems to have taken the form of orchestrating an escape attempt by Jackson who, quite naturally, had become increasingly convinced he was to be assassinated inside San Quentin. A portion of this activity appears to have been the "smuggling" of fake explosives and possibly a faulty .38 calibre revolver to the desperate inmate.[215] Prison authorities appear to have allowed this to happen. In Tackwood's version,

> It was a plot, see, between the CII and the guards. The guards hate him, they hate his guts. He's accused of killing a guard, remember that. And they hate him, at least some of them do. They harass him at all times, give him all the hell they can, illegally. Then they kill him. Poor old George.[216]

Again, the plan went awry as Jackson, who was a karate expert, overpowered his executioners at the moment it became obvious that the "hit was on." Consequently, three guards were killed and three others barely survived the altercation before Jackson was gunned down while running across the prison's O-wing courtyard.[217] In the aftermath, the police again misstepped, this time in attempting to spread the impact of the event more broadly across the movement. Although several inmates testified to Jackson's wielding a small .38 revolver—which several guards also initially reported—the state's utterly implausible official claim was that Jackson had utilized a huge 9 mm. Spanish Astra automatic, traced to BPP Field Marshal Landon Williams, in undertaking his escape attempt.[218] Further, it was contended that the weapon had been carried into the prison on the crucial morning by attorney Stephen Bingham, past San Quentin's array of metal detectors and other security measures, and delivered to Jackson in a visiting room; the prisoner then supposedly placed the pistol atop his head, under an Afro wig, and carried it through additional metal detectors and a physical search before pulling it out and commencing to commit mayhem.[219] Still, Jackson was dead, Bingham forced underground and Williams arrested as a result.[220]

By all accounts, the "California left" was largely broken as a result of this progression of contrived, but apparently gratuitous violence. The Black Panther Party, Revolutionary Union, Venceremos, California Prison Rights Movement and a host of other West Coast radical organizations, all of which were vibrant at the point the FBI/CCS/SII/CII combine went to work, have each either ceased to exist or have been reduced to tiny sectarian cults. This active destruction of the U.S. left correlates well with Louis Tackwood's warning that,

> They [the police intelligence agencies] have an overall plan...their major plan is they want a full Police State. I don't just mean California, I mean all over. They talk about it all the time. Total Police State, you see my point...I'm saying the people who are involved right now are looking to the future. Wow, when we do get this police thing, whew, look out. They got a plan working right now...It's in the planning stage right now...Even if tomorrow morning you say martial law wasn't in effect, they'd still have

been out there and they got control right now. In other words, like I mean, this would be a Police State for ever afterwards.[221]

Arguably, COINTELPRO-BPP was J. Edgar Hoover's personal monument, the ...ne of ugliness to a career characterized by the craft and construction of an ...devoted to violent repression in the name of all that is good and sacred. ...his passing, and the spate of Watergate era investigations of Bureau ac-...ll the supposed "reforms" these entailed, did little or nothing to alter ...il nature of what Hoover had wrought. Lead cannot, after all, be ...gold by the waving of the alchemist's wand. The full horror and ...OINTELPRO-BPP were discretely and, all too often, conveniently ...er's "outfit" was left intact, ritually chastised perhaps, but un-...esses," its priorities and ideology unscathed. The fields so ten-...ies such as the Church Committee were allowed (or forced) ...planting had barely begun.

...inions had learned their lessons well. With generations of ...; the public sensibility, of casting lies as truth and truth as ...at beyond the most cursory genuflections to power neces-si...   ...here would be little but business as usual for the Bureau. Mo..   ...their repressive skills in COINTELPRO-BPP, they were eagei...   ...of this most lethal and effective exercise in gutting politi-cal div...   ...t settings and before a broader cross-section of agents. Hence, i.   ..., even as its leaders proclaimed that the "excesses" of COINTELPRO would "never happen again," the FBI shifted its focus from the urban ghettos to the remote expanse of the northern plains. The Bureau was setting out on its next and "greatest" COINTELPRO ever: the quelling of an "Indian uprising" on the Pine Ridge Sioux Reservation in South Dakota.

Part II

A Context of Struggle

When the prairie is on fire you see animals surrounded by the fire; you see them run and hide themselves so they will not burn. That is the way we are.
—Najinyanupi (Surrounded), Oglala Lakota, 1876

Even the most sympathetic non-Indians [have] been schooled to deny this claim to international status made by the Indian tribes. Most of the literature on Indians has concentrated on the fierce and gallant fight of the Plains tribes against General Custer and the United States cavalry; the early part of American history, when Indians were the equals or superiors of the colonists, has rarely been written. Rather than a claim to international status, most non-Indian readers [have] been led to believe that, following the Indian Wars, the Indians meekly marched off to reservations and lived in peace. The whole implication of the traditional Indian stereotype [is] that the Indians had become the best of American citizens within a decade of Wounded Knee [1890].
—Vine Deloria, Jr., Hunkpapa Lakota, 1972

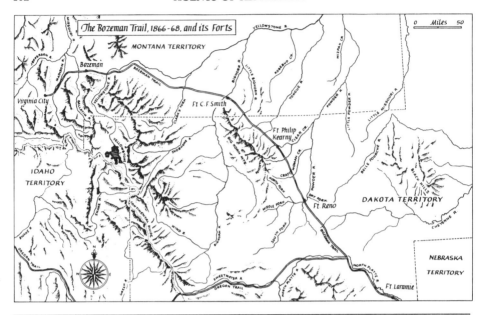

Map 1: The Bozeman Trail, 1866-1868.

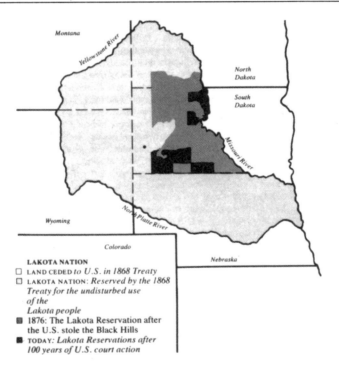

Map 2: The Great Sioux Nation as defined by the 1868 Fort Laramie Treaty.

Chapter 4

Why Pine Ridge?

> The white man made us many promises, but he only kept one. He promised to
> take our land, and he took it.
> —Mahpiya Luta (Red Cloud), Oglala Lakota Leader, 1882

After half a century shaping its repressive techniques amidst the urban clamor of mass society, it undoubtedly seems incongruous, even inexplicable, that the FBI should have suddenly refocused its energies to attack a small and impoverished people residing on a parcel of barren real estate far out in the American hinterland. Upon closer examination, however, explanations—historical, topical and speculative—can be found for the Bureau's actions.

Historical Background

Today, it has become almost a matter of conventional wisdom that "Vietnam was the first war the U.S. ever lost." Actually, a far better case could be made that this crucial (and humiliating) event occurred a century earlier, in 1868, following the so-called "Red Cloud War" in what are now the states of Wyoming and Montana. The United States, in patent violation of the territorial guarantees extended to the Lakota (western Sioux) under the Fort Laramie Treaty of 1851,[1] had moved to open up a "direct route" northward from the fort, across the prime buffalo graze lying between the Black Hills and the Big Horn Mountains, to the newly discovered gold fields near Virginia City (see Map 1). Beginning in 1865, the U.S. Army was instructed to establish a string of posts along this route—known as the "Bozeman Trail"—to protect it from the "depredations" (*i.e.*, defensive responses) of the Indians whose legally recognized homeland had thus been invaded.[2]

Under the political leadership of Red Cloud, the Oglalas, the largest of the seven groups of Lakota,[3] forged a unified military response to this invasion and threat to their traditional buffalo economy. In short order, the Lakota had also consolidated a defensive alliance with the Arapaho and Northern Cheyenne, two other Indian nations whose 1851 treaty areas were violated by the U.S. offensive actions.[4] During 1866, the warriors of this powerful confederation halted all traffic along the Bozeman Trail, isolating and laying siege to the military posts along it, and annihilating the troops of Captain William C. Fetterman outside Fort Phil Kearny on December 21.[5]

By mid-1867, after two major engagements known as "The Hay Field Fight" (near Fort C.F. Smith) and "The Wagon Box Fight" (near Fort Phil Kearney) and with the realization that it had seriously underestimated the Indians' ability to work in concert and mount a sustained campaign, the U.S. began a series of overtures for peace negotiations intended to avert a full-scale military disaster. Red Cloud refused to so much as discuss negotiations until all troops were withdrawn from the con- tested areas.[6] The Oglalas then burned the abandoned army posts to the ground before going to Fort Laramie to sign a new treaty on April 29, 1868. As Dee Brown has observed: "For the first time in its history the United States Government had negotiated a peace which conceded everything demanded by the enemy and which extracted nothing in return."[7]

By provision of the new treaty,[8] ratified by Congress on February 16, 1869, the Lakota homeland—centering on the sacred Black Hills (*Paha Sapa*, in Lakota)—was reserved for their exclusive use and occupancy in perpetuity. This was accomplished under two separate articles:

Article 2: The United States agrees that the following district of country to wit, *viz:* commencing on the east bank of the Missouri River where the forty-sixth parallel of north latitude crosses the same, thence along low water mark down said river, and along the northern line of Nebraska to the one hundred and fourth degree of longitude west from Greenwich, thence north on said meridian to a point where the forty-sixth parallel of north latitude intercepts same, thence east along said parallel to the place of the beginning; and in addition thereto, all existing reservations on the east bank of said river shall be, and the same is, set apart for the absolute and undisturbed use and occupation of the Indians herein named, and for such other friendly tribes or individual Indians as they may be willing, with the consent of the United States, to admit amongst them; and the United States now solemnly agrees that no persons except those herein designated and authorized so to do, and except officers, agents and employees of the government as may be authorized to enter upon Indian reservations in discharge of duties enjoined by law, shall ever be permitted to pass over, settle upon, or reside in the territory described in this article.

Article 16: The United States hereby agrees and stipulates that the country north of the North Platte River and east of the Big Horn Mountains shall be held and considered to be unceded Indian territory, and also stipulates and agrees that no white person or persons shall be permitted to settle upon or occupy any portion of same; or without consent of the Indians first had and obtained, to pass through same.

Under Article 17, it was expressly articulated that the 1868 treaty in no way negated Lakota title to lands secured under the 1851 treaty, or those entered into even earlier.[9] Also, under Article 12, it was provided that:

No [subsequent] treaty for the cession of any portion of the reservation herein described which may be held in common shall be of any validity or force as against said Indians,

Red Cloud, chief of the Oglala Lakota, "the first and only Indian leader in the West to win a war with the United States." (Museum of the American Indian, Heye Foundation)

unless executed and signed by at least three-fourths of all the adult male Indians [the gender provision was a U.S., rather than Lakota, stipulation], occupying or interested in the same; and no cession by the tribe shall be understood or construed in such manner as to deprive, without his consent, any individual member of the tribe of his rights to any tract of land selected by him.

Hence, Red Cloud had led his people into a situation in which they were assured of a substantial land base comprising at least 3% of what is now the continental United States (see Map 2), which could not be alienated other than through the democratic consent of the Lakota, and the borders of which were guaranteed by the U.S. Perhaps of equal importance, the Red Cloud War had caused the U.S. to strongly reaffirm its recognition—by virtue of its executing and ratifying the 1868 treaty at all—of the Lakota as a fully sovereign national entity in their own right.[10] By all accepted standards of international custom and convention, this should have been the end of the matter.

Contrary to myth, "General" George Custer never rose higher in rank than Lt. Colonel. On June 25, 1876, Custer attempted to secure glory by slaughtering what he thought was a fleeing group of Lakota and Cheyenne women and children, a miscalculation that resulted in the death of his entire command. (Photo: U.S. Army)

The first real sign of trouble with regard to the 1868 Fort Laramie Treaty came in 1872, when a Jesuit missionary Jean De Smet, who had been trespassing on Lakota land, confided to *Sioux Falls* (S.D.) *Times* editor Charles Collins that he believed there to be considerable mineral deposits in the Black Hills.[11] By 1874, area newspapers were clamoring for "improvement and development of one of the richest and most fertile sections of America," and demanding to know "what is to be done with these Indian dogs in our manger?"[12] In Washington, D.C., Congressman Moses K. Armstrong introduced a bill providing for the purchase of the Black Hills[13] and, should the Lakota prove reluctant in agreeing to the proposition, General Alfred M. Terry issued Special Order 117, sending Lt. Colonel George Armstrong Custer and his entire 7th Cavalry regiment from Fort Abraham Lincoln (on the Missouri River in what is now North Dakota) directly into the Lakota holy land.[14]

Custer showed a certain trepidation in undertaking this adventure, asking for and receiving two companies of infantry to reinforce his approximately 700 mounted troops and delaying his departure for more than a month in order to train his command and await the arrival of improved weaponry.[15] Despite his worries, however, his only interaction with the Indians came in the form of a 200 person protest delegation led by Tatokala Inyanka (Running Antelope) before the outset; the Lakotas merely monitored his column's progress thereafter.[16] When he did move, he took along a contingent of civilian geologists and other scientific experts whose presence gave clear indication of the expedition's ulterior motive: an assessment of whether mineral wealth might lie within the Black Hills.[17]

Although there are serious questions as to whether gold was actually discovered by anyone in Custer's party, on August 2 the Colonel dispatched "Lonesome Charlie" Reynolds (one of his scouts) to carry out word that the precious metal had been found near present-day Rapid City, S.D.[18] This led immediately to banner headlines such as that of the *Yankton Press and South Dakotan* on August 13, 1874:

STRUCK IT AT LAST!

Rich Mines of Gold and Silver Reported Found by Custer

PREPARE FOR LIVELY TIMES!

Gold Expected to Fall 10 per Cent - Spades and Picks Rising - The National Debt to be Paid When Custer Returns

Such sensationalism set a swarm of miners scurrying for the Black Hills,[19] and brought about a second government foray, "The Jenny Expedition," during the spring and summer of 1875.[20] Custer continued to fuel the fires of greed via his contributions to the Eastern press.[21] Sensing that war was imminent after another federal treaty commission failed to secure Lakota agreement to sale of the Hills on September 29,[22] most of the Lakota fighters began moving into the Powder River country of Montana (in Unceded Indian Territory) where they were joined by the bulk of the Arapaho and Northern Cheyenne. The Indians gathered to consolidate their strength and consider their options in the face of what had become another outright invasion of their national territory.[23]

On November 22, 1875, Secretary of War W.W. Belknap announced that there would be war with the Lakota "unless something is done to obtain possession of [the Black Hills] for the white miners who have been strongly attracted by reports of rich deposits of [gold]."[24] This was followed by a December 3 warning, issued by Commissioner of Indian Affairs Edward P. Smith, that all Indians in the Powder River Country were to return to the agencies by January 31, 1876, or "military force would be sent to compel them."[25] On February 7 of the next year, the U.S. War Department authorized General Philip ("the only good Indian is a dead one") Sheridan, commander of the Military District of Missouri, to begin operations against "the hostile Sioux," particularly those led by Tatanka Yotanka (Sitting Bull), the Hunkpapa spiritual leader, and Tesunke Witko (Crazy Horse) of the Oglalas.[26] The following day, Sheridan issued orders for Generals Crook and Terry to start preparing a campaign—to "commence with the spring thaws"—aimed in the direction of the headwaters of the Powder, Tongue, Rosebud, and Bighorn Rivers, "where Crazy Horse and his allies frequent."[27]

The plan was that Crook would march northward with about 1,000 men along the old Bozeman Trail while Colonel John Gibbon would move in from the west with another 1,200. Custer, proceeding from his base at Fort Abraham Lincoln with the 750 men of his 7th Cavalry, would converge with the other two columns from the east. The Lakotas, Cheyennes and Arapahos would thereby be caught and crushed in a massive vise (see Map 3).[28] The only problem for the army's strategists was that they had not reckoned with the depth of experience attained by Indian

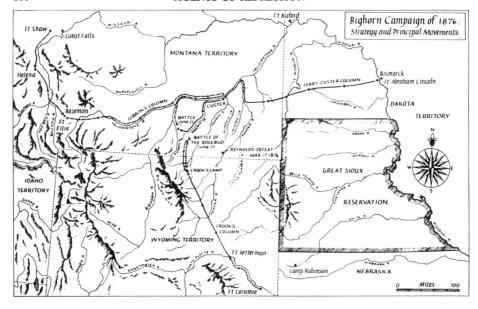

Map 3: The Bighorn Campaign of 1876.

leaders such as Crazy Horse and the Hunkpapa, Pizi (Gall), during and since the Red Cloud War.[29]

Crazy Horse elected to confront the soldiers piecemeal. As it is put elsewhere:

> On the morning of June 17, [Crook's] troops broke camp in Dead Canyon Valley, on the Rosebud. Waiting on the bluffs were 1,500 fighting men of the Sioux and Cheyenne tribes, under Crazy Horse. Shortly after eight o'clock the battle was joined...Crazy Horse threw in wave after wave of his warriors. The floor of the valley was a maelstrom of smoke, dust and furiously moving masses of men and horses...The armies broke apart after the long day's fighting...[and] it was Crook who had to retreat the next day, with heavy losses...[30]

On June 25, it was Custer's turn as he divided his men into three parts in order to launch what he believed would be a surprise attack on a very large village, mostly obscured by trees, along the valley of the Little Bighorn River.[31] Mistaking the flight of women and children before his advancing troops as a general Indian retreat, and apparently with no real sense of the size of the community he was attacking, he ordered the 215 men of his personal group into a charge.[32] Crazy Horse, Gall, and Ese Heoohnesee (Two Moon) of the Cheyenne quickly annihilated this unit, ridding themselves of the hated "Yellow Hair" once and for all.[33] The second component of troops, commanded by Major Marcus Reno, had also charged (at Custer's orders) and narrowly averted a similar fate, surviving with heavy losses only through the luck of reaching a rocky bluff where they were able to hold out until reinforced by the remaining 7th Cavalry troopers under Captain Frederick Benteen.[34] Even then, they might well all have perished had the Indians not withdrawn at the approach of Crook's column two days later.[35]

For the second time in a decade, the U.S. Army had been soundly defeated in the field while waging war to expropriate the landholdings of a "squalid bunch of savages."[36] It was a blow from which the martial pride of the nation seems never to have recovered. At the time, as Dee Brown notes:

> When the white men in the East heard of Long Hair's defeat, they called it a massacre and went crazy with anger. They wanted to punish all the Indians of the West. Because they could not punish Sitting Bull and the war chiefs, the Great Council in Washington decided to punish the Indians they could find—those who remained on the reservations and had taken no part in the fighting...On July 22 the Great Warrior Sherman received authority to assume military control of all reservations in Sioux country and to treat the Indians as prisoners of war.[37]

On August 15, 1876, Congress also dispatched another commission to secure the "agreement" of these Lakota POWs to the cession of the Black Hills to the United States. This time, they utilized a rather interesting negotiating concept: rations to the captives were cut off, pending their signing of a document "legally" relinquishing title to their land.[38] Under such duress, Red Cloud, Spotted Tail and perhaps 10% of the other adult Lakota males alive at the time signed in exchange for subsistence rations and, in 1877, Congress used this as the basis for legislation (19 *Stat.* 254) formally incorporating the Black Hills portion of South Dakota and the Unceded Indian Territory of Nebraska, Wyoming and Montana as U.S. property (see Map 2 for what remained of Lakota Territories after this act).

The warring Indians to the north, meanwhile, had broken up into small groups, mostly to secure forage for their horses and to hunt for winter provisions. This prompted Sheridan to order a winter campaign—such as he'd earlier prosecuted with great success against the Southern Cheyenne, Comanches and Kiowas on the southern plains—in which the Indians, immobilized by the cold and snow, might be slaughtered on a village-by-village basis.[39] Actually, the first such incident occurred on September 9, 1876, when more than 100 of Crook's 3rd Cavalry, under Captain Anson Mills, surprised and destroyed a small Oglala village headed by Tesunke Milahanska (American Horse) at Slim Buttes, S.D.[40] On November 25, Colonel Ranald McKenzie, imported especially for the task, fell upon Tahmela Pashme's (Dull Knife) Cheyenne village in precisely the same fashion.[41] And so it went throughout the long winter.

Facing a form of warfare waged during their most vulnerable season and directed essentially at their noncombatant elders, children and women, Sitting Bull and Gall led their followers across the border into Canada during February 1877 (a sanctuary from which they drifted back over the next several years, with Sitting Bull himself not returning until 1881).[42] Crazy Horse and his group flatly refused to abandon the Powder River Country and the army showed itself to be singularly unable

Tesunke Witko (Crazy Horse), the Oglala leader who destroyed Custer, shortly after he brought his followers into Fort Robinson, Nebraska in May of 1877. Duped into "surrendering," Crazy Horse was assassinated by BIA police. (Photo: S.J. Morrow, collection of the University of South Dakota)

to defeat them. Hence, Crook—with Sheridan's endorsement—resorted to a political cal ruse, sending word to the Oglala holdouts that, in exchange for the cessation of hostilities, the government would guarantee them a permanent reservation comprised of the Powder River area and renegotiate the 1868 treaty territory.[43]

As this was the crux of their dispute with the U.S., Crazy Horse's people came in to the Red Cloud Agency (located near Camp Robinson, Neb.) on May 6, 1877. Given their understanding of the conditions underlying their action, they conducted themselves as warriors who had carried their fight to successful conclusion rather than a defeated rabble; Mari Sandoz quotes one army officer who was present as exclaiming, "My God! This is a triumphal march, not a surrender!"[44] In accordance with their agreement, the Indians turned in their weapons and horses, pledging that they had no wish to engage in further warfare. The duplicity of the Crook-Sheridan overture then became grossly apparent as Crazy Horse was assassinated (by a special force of Oglalas, employed by the U.S. Department of Interior) on September 5;[45] there is no evidence that the government ever seriously considered allowing the Indians to return to the Powder River.

With the Lakotas safely disarmed and immobilized, their leadership coopted, killed in battle, assassinated or driven into exile, and the bulk of their land expropriated, the government launched an offensive intended to undercut their cultural integrity and free even more territory for "settlement." Commissioner of Indian Affairs Hiram Price enunciated the basis for their racist policies in 1882: "To domesticate and civilize wild Indians is a noble work. But to allow them to drag along, year after year, in their old superstition, laziness and filth instead of elevating them in the scale of humanity would be a lasting disgrace."[46] Congress followed the impoundment of the Lakota sacred sites in the Black Hills by passing legislation in 1883 which outlawed virtually the entire range of their major spiritual ceremonies. The Sun Dance, give-away feasts, the Lakota manner of burying the dead, and the building/use of sweatlodges all became criminal matters, punishable by jail sentences.[47] At the same time, it became standard practice to abduct Indian children from their families and communities at an early age, forcibly shipping them to remote boarding schools where they were indoctrinated in non-Indian values and worldview, and where even the speaking of their own language was prohibited.[48]

In 1885, the so-called Major Crimes Act (18 U.S.C.A. § 1153) was passed, completely usurping the already subordinated principle of Lakota sovereignty by unilaterally extending federal jurisdiction over seven felonies (murder, rape, assault, larceny, burglary, fraud, and embezzlement) when these were committed in reserved Indian areas.[49] This was followed, in 1887, by the General Allotment Act (25 U.S.C.A. § 331), more popularly known as the "Dawes Act" (after its sponsor, Massachusetts Senator Henry M. Dawes), which largely dissolved the traditional Indian custom of using and occupying (*i.e.,* holding) land in common; instead, each federally recognized tribal member was alloted an individual real estate parcel—usually 160 acres—and reservation land not thus divvied up was declared to be "surplus" and "legally" open to non-Indian corporate acquistions and/or homesteading.[50] Under the "civilizing" provisions of the Dawes Act, about half the remaining Great Sioux Reservation was lost (see Map 4) and, as Vine Deloria, Jr. and Clifford M. Lytle point out:

> As a consequence of the allotment policy, Indian landholdings were reduced from 138 million acres in 1887 to 48 million in 1934. Of this 48 million acres, nearly 20 million were desert or semiarid and virtually useless for any kind of annual farming ventures...[Further, the Act] gave the secretary of the interior almost dictatorial powers over the use of allotments since, if the local [federal Indian] agent disagreed with the use to which lands were being put, he could intervene and lease the land to whomsoever he pleased.[51]

Under the heel of such a conqueror, the forms of Lakota resistance shifted to desperation. In October 1890, two Minneconjous, Mato Siglapsanpsan (Kicking Bear) and Tatanka Hu Iyucan (Short Bull), visited Sitting Bull at his home on the Standing Rock Reservation. They had recently traveled to Utah in order to learn the powerful spiritual vision called the "Ghost Dance" espoused by a Paiute messiah known as Wovoka (the Cutter), and passed their information along to the great Hunkpapa leader.[52] Sitting Bull, who had been searching for a way of galvanizing his people's flagging morale, seized upon Wovoka's theme:

> The Great Spirit had sent the white man to punish the Indians for their sins. The Indians now had been punished enough and deliverance was at hand, but the whites had been bad ever since they killed Jesus. Dancing could preserve the Indians from sickness, and the white man's bullets could no longer penetrate Indian skins. Red paint

Tatanka Yotanka (Sitting Bull), the Hunkpapa Lakota spiritual leader, led his people into Canada in 1877 rather than surrender to the U.S. The last of the original Lakota "recalcitrant" figures, Sitting Bull was assassinated on the Standing Rock Reservation by BIA police on December 15, 1890. (Photo: D.F. Berry, collection of the University of South Dakota)

from the Paiute messiah was also widely used for protection. A deep landslide would hold the whites down with sod and broken timber, and any who escaped would become fish in the rivers. The earth would tremble with the avalanche or flood. They must wear "ghost shirts" painted with the sun and moon and stars.[53]

Dee Brown adds that the dancers believed if they pursued this vision with appropriate fervor and danced with sufficient zeal:

In the next springtime, when the grass was knee high, the earth would be covered with new soil which would bury all white men, and the land would be covered with sweet grass and running water and trees. Great herds of buffalo and wild horses would come back. The Indians who danced the Ghost Dance would be taken up in the air and suspended there while a wave of new earth was passing, and then they would be set down among the ghosts of their ancestors on the new earth, where only Indians would live.[54]

Needless to say, under the circumstances, Sitting Bull had no great difficulty in attracting a mass of adherents to such sentiments, and the ceremonies were shortly spreading throughout the Lakota reservations. Although the Ghost Dance plainly lacked a military dimension,[55] the government—more concerned with the revitalization of Lakota socio-cultural cohesion it represented than with any con-

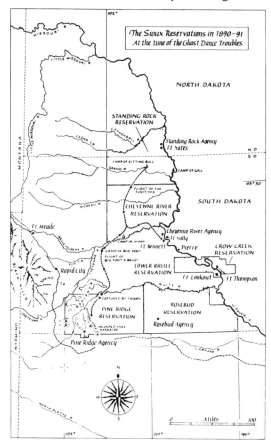

Map 4: The Sioux Reservations during 1890-1891.

ceivable physical threat—chose to view the phenomenon as an "incipient uprising." On October 30, Indian agent D.F. Royer telegraphed his superiors in Washington that "the situation [could] be saved only by the arrival of six to seven hundred troops"; by November 15, the number had risen to "one thousand," and the "Army at once began moving units into the region, most of them around the Pine Ridge agency [the replacement for the Red Cloud agency at Camp Robinson], until in a matter of days it had almost three thousand men in the field."[56]

On December 12, 1890, Lt. Colonel William F. Drum, commanding Fort Yates (N.D.) on the Standing Rock Reservation, received orders from General Nelson A. Miles "to secure the person of Sitting Bull. Call upon the Indian agent [James McLaughlin] to cooperate and render such assistance as will be best to promote the purpose in view."[57] McLaughlin complied by mobilizing the special Indian police who had participated in the assassination of Crazy Horse. Led by a Hunkpapa named Natableca Tatanka (Bull Head), on December 15 the unit traveled to Sitting Bull's residence and killed him. A troop of cavalry intervened to prevent Sitting Bull's enraged followers from slaughtering the Bull Head party on the spot.[58]

With the assassination of Sitting Bull, the Ghost Dancers scattered in panic, the troops fanning out in pursuit. On December 17, a group of about 100 fleeing Hunkpapas arrived at the camp of the Minneconjou leader Si Inskokeca (Big Foot), whose arrest—as a "fomenter of disturbances"—had been ordered the same day by the War Department.[59] The combined group, numbering perhaps 350, then began to move in a southwesterly direction (see Map 4), attempting to reach the Pine Ridge agency. On December 28, they were intercepted on Porcupine Creek, near Pine Ridge, by four companies of the 7th Cavalry under Major Samuel Whitside. Big Foot, ill with pneumonia, instructed his followers to offer no resistance, surrender their weapons, and follow the soldiers into camp a few miles to the south on Wounded Knee Creek.[60] They were met there by four more companies of the 7th under Colonel George Forsyth, as well as a company of scouts and a battery of four Hotchkiss guns.[61] The following morning, the soldiers again demanded that the Indians give up their weapons, this time impounding axes, knives and even tent pegs.[62] The soldiers then opened fire on their defenseless captives.

> No one knows how may Indians were killed on this miserable field, because by the time anyone could count the bodies, some had already been removed. But the number was very close to three hundred, about two thirds of them women and children...Women and children attempted to escape by running up a dry ravine, but were pursued and slaughtered—there is no other word—by hundreds of maddened soldiers, while shells from the Hotchkiss guns, which had been moved to permit them to sweep the ravine, continued to burst among them. The line of bodies was afterward found to extend for more than two miles from the camp—and they were all women and children. A few survivors eventually found shelter in brushy gullies here and there, and their pursuers had scouts call out that women and children could come out of their hiding places because they had nothing to fear...some small boys crept out and were surrounded by soldiers who butchered them.[63]

In the aftermath of Wounded Knee, all forms of Lakota resistance became highly covert for nearly twenty years. Even then, its public articulation came through the rather innocuous medium of a series of books authored by Charles Eastman (Ohiyesa), a Santee Dakota who had helped bury the bodies of the Big Foot group in 1890.[64] By the early 1920s, American Indians throughout the United States appeared so subdued that Congress felt it possible to undertake their formal and unilateral absorption into the U.S. polity itself, via the so-called Indian Citizenship Act of 1924 (8 U.S.C.A § 1401 [a] [2]).[65] This was followed by passage of the Indian Reorganization Act (25 U.S.C.A. § 461, also known as the Wheeler-Howard Act), through which Congress presumed to dispense with traditional Indian forms of governance altogether; these were "legally" supplanted by "tribal councils"—consciously patterned after corporate boards—which Congress felt to be superior for its own agenda of utilizing reserved Indian land and resources "for the common good."[66]

The Big Foot band, before and after. Above, assembled on the Cheyenne River Sioux Reservation in August 1890; below, after being massacred by the 7th Cavalry at Wounded Knee on December 29, 1890. (Photos: U.S. Army)

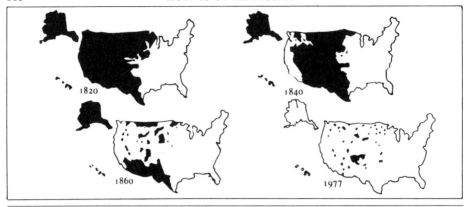

The diminution of Indian lands since the European invasion of 1492, when all of what is now the United States was inhabited by Indian peoples. The federal government is manifestly unwilling to live up to its treaty obligations regarding even the tiny residue presently remaining in Indian hands. These maps are largely derived from Royce, Charles C., *Indian Land Cessions in the United States,* 1890.

In 1942, the Oglala Lakotas on Pine Ridge, were treated to an example of the sort of obligation such status entailed. The northwestern one-eighth of the reservation was impounded by the War Department, to be used as an aerial gunnery range for the duration of World War II. As of this writing (some forty-three years after the end of the war), the land has not been returned, a situation which may well have received major impetus on August 2, 1946, when Congress passed the Indian Claims Commission Act (60 *Stat.* 1049). The expressed purpose of this legislation was to establish a mechanism by which to apply a veneer of legality and respectability to all historical U.S. seizures of Indian land, *regardless* of the conditions or legality attending these expropriations at the time they took place. The method employed by the commission was to provide monetary compensation to Indian victims of government land thefts (or their descendants) at prices deemed "fair" by the government; such dollar compensation was formally construed as ending Indian land claims/land rights, "quieting title" for the non-Indian holders of Indian land. Recovery of illegally taken lands by Indians was specifically prohibited within the practice of the commission.[67]

As Shoshone activist Josephine C. Mills stated in 1964, "There is no longer any need to shoot down Indians in order to take away their rights and land...legislation [in combination with] the Indian Claims Commission [is sufficient to do] the trick legally."[68] This procedure required Indians to be, if not exactly cooperative, then at least quiescent in the finalization of their disenfranchisement. A Damoclean sword was required to keep them properly subdued. Hence, in June of 1953, Representative William Henry Harrison of Wyoming introduced the "Termination Act" (67 *Stat.* B132) which stipulated:

> [It is] the sense of Congress that, at the earliest possible time, all of the Indian tribes and the individual members thereof located within the States of California, Florida,

New York, and Texas, should be freed from Federal supervision and control and all disabilities and limitations specifically applicable to Indians.

Decoded, this language simply meant that Congress had empowered itself to dissolve ("terminate") at its discretion Indian nations within the four designated states. At the second session of Congress, during January 1954, the act was amended to extend this power over the remaining states and Republican Senator Arthur V. Watkins of Utah then spearheaded a drive to apply it. In short order, several Indian nations—including the Menominee, Klamath, Siletz, Grande Ronde, several small Paiute bands, and a number of the Rancherias in California—were declared no longer to exist.[69] In such a context of raw coercion, Congress availed itself of the opportunity to trample the remaining residue of Indian sovereignty, passing, in August 1953, Public Law 280 (67 *Stat.* 588), a bill which subordinated Indians not only to the federal government, but often to states as well.[70]

As all this was going on, Colonel Lewis A. Pick of the Army Corps of Engineers and William Glenn Sloan, assistant director of the Bureau of Reclamation regional office in Billings, Montana, were putting into effect a proposal to harness the Missouri River—wholly owned by the Lakotas in the high plains area—via a series of dams and reservoirs. The "Pick-Sloan Plan" approved by Congress in 1944 not only preempted Lakota water rights, but would have flooded substantial portions of the best land in the Standing Rock, Cheyenne River, Crow Creek, Yankton and Rosebud Reservations as well. Although undoubtedly somewhat "chilled" by the legislative intimidation emanating from Washington, D.C., the Lakotas proved to be less than resigned to such a fate.[71]

Proceeding on the basis of a Court of Claims suit filed in 1921 regarding the Black Hill regional expropriation,[72] they brought their case before the Claims Commission in 1947. Counter to the working assumptions of the commission, they argued that *only* the Lakota could provide a legal foundation from which the Pick-Sloan plan might be carried through, that the commission held no such legal prerogative and that the federal government held no inherent legal right to do anything at all in western South Dakota on its own initiative. Further, they adopted the position that monetary compensation for their treaty lands was unacceptable, that they required the return of all land guaranteed by treaty, and suggested that they would decline any compensatory payment. They have never abandoned this position.[73]

This nationalist vigor on the part of the Lakotas belied the myth of "the vanishing Red Man" promoted within the U.S. throughout the 20th century,[74] and confronted federal policymakers with a thorny problem: either they would have to pull back somewhat from their drive to accomplish the final usurpation of Native America, or follow through on their threat of termination by dissolving one of the best known of all Indian nations. This would have to be undertaken in the full glare of world opinion, with all the embarrassment this might entail, a circumstance guaranteed to be used to maximum propaganda advantage by cold war adversaries.[75]

The first federal response was a period of relative inaction, perhaps in the hope that the difficulty would simply disappear.

But, by the 1970s, the incipient conflict was coming to a head. Not unnaturally, in an era marked by irregular warfare and covert operations both at home and abroad, the government began to weigh its options in terms of possible clandestine alternatives to the policy poles remarked above. Regardless of other factors, it was perceived in some sectors of the federal bureaucracy that the time had come to resolve once and for all the issue of the recalcitrant Lakota, a people which had, after all, administered deep and lasting wounds to U.S. martial pride. Here, the logical target would be the Oglalas of Pine Ridge, the segment of the Great Sioux Nation which had all along been viewed—perhaps correctly—as the keystone of Lakota nationalism and resistance.

Topical Factors

By 1970, the dynamic of historical antagonism shaping U.S.-Lakota relations was being exacerbated by the rise of an overt activism and militancy among younger Indians across the country. Beginning in the mid-1960s, a Cherokee college student named Clyde Warrior, who described himself as "an academic Aborigine," became increasingly effective in asserting a vision of pan-Indian nationalism; paralleling the SNCC demands for Black Power articulated by Stokely Carmichael and H. Rap Brown, Warrior's National Indian Youth Council (NIYC) pushed "Red Power" through its newspaper, *ABC: Americans Before Columbus.*[76] A new generation of Indians began to consider direct confrontation with the federal government, using a synthesis of their own traditions and the tactics deployed by the civil rights, antiwar and new left movements. They were inspired by Warrior's writing:

What can you do when a society tells you that you should be nonexistent? As I look at it, the situation will not change unless really violent action comes about. If this country understands violence then that is the way to do it. Some of the young Indians are already talking revolution. "We have tried everything else," they say. "The only thing left is our guns. Let's use them."[77]

Although such posturing was obviously rhetorical, it was effective. Even such essentially conservative organizations as the National Congress of American Indians (NCAI) became energized during the period as, under the leadership of Lakota law student Vine Deloria, Jr., it began to issue increasingly sharp criticisms of federal Indian policy.[78] In Oregon and Washington, younger Indian activists such as Janet McCloud (Suquamish) and Hank Adams (Assiniboin/Lakota) added their weight to the ongoing fishing rights struggles in the Northwest.[79] Further expressions of American Indian rights to sovereignty and self-determination forcefully emerged during these years in locations as diverse as Florida (where the Seminoles had refused to even enter into a peace accord with the U.S. until 1964), the St. Regis Mohawk Reservation in upstate New York (Mohawk treaty relations extend not only to the U.S., but to Great Britain and Canada as well), and even among such "federally unrecognized" people as the Passamaquoddys of Maine and the Yaquis in Arizona.[80]

In this atmosphere of political ferment, two Anishinabes (Chippewas) in Minneapolis, Dennis Banks and George Mitchell, founded the American Indian Movement (AIM) in 1968. The organization was self-consciously patterned after the Black Panther Party's community self-defense model pioneered by Huey P. Newton and Bobby Seale two years previously in Oakland.[81] AIM chapters quickly sprang up around the country and began to attract those who would comprise the organization's future leadership. The latter initially consisted mainly of tough young urban fighters such as Clyde Bellecourt, an Anishinabe who put together the Minneapolis organization; Joe Locust, a Cherokee who, assisted by Clyde Bellecourt's older brother, Vernon, set things rolling in Denver; and Russell Means, an Oglala who organized Cleveland AIM and enlisted virtually his entire family: brothers Ted, Dale ("Dace") and Bill, as well as cousin Madonna Gilbert (Thunderhawk).[82] Within two years, as with the BPP, the AIM agenda had shifted from the local to national arena; however, it had deliberately refocused its attentions from the locus of its city origins to the rural reservations, thus linking itself directly to the issue of treaty rights and the more traditional segments of Indian society.[83]

The AIM impetus received a decided boost in November 1969, when an *ad hoc* group calling itself Indians of All Tribes (IAT) occupied Alcatraz Island in San Francisco Bay. Headed by Richard Oaks, a Mohawk, and a young Santee Dakota AIM member named John Trudell, IAT demanded title to Alcatraz under provision of an act passed on July 31, 1882 (22 *Stat.* 181) which indicated that abandoned federal facilities—such as the empty prison situated on the island—should be utilized for Indian schools. They also relied upon Title 25, U.S. Code 194: "In all trials about the right of property in which an Indian may be party on one side, and a white person on the other, the burden of proof shall rest upon the white person, whenever the Indian shall make out a presumption of title in himself from the fact of previous possession or ownership." IAT released a statement that its agenda consisted of utilizing Alcatraz to establish a Center for Native American studies, an American Indian Spiritual Center, an Indian Center of Ecology, a Great Indian Training School and an American Indian Museum; it also offered to buy the island from the federal government, following the standards of equity set by the U.S. in its land acquisitions from Indians:

> We, the native Americans, re-claim the land known as Alcatraz Island in the name of all American Indians by right of discovery...We wish to be fair and honorable in our dealings with the Caucasian inhabitants of this land, and hereby offer the following treaty...We will purchase said Alcatraz for twenty-four (24) dollars in glass beads and red cloth, a precedent set by the white man's purchase of a similar island about 300 years ago. We know that $24 in trade goods for these 16 acres is more than was paid when Manhattan Island was sold, but we know that land values have risen over the years. Our offer of $1.24 per acre is greater than the 47 cents per acre the white men are now paying the California Indians for their land [through the Indian Claims Commission].[84]

Richard Oaks, a Mohawk leader of the Alcatraz occupation, on the island in 1969. After the end of the action, Oaks was murdered by Michael Morgan, a non-Indian, on September 20, 1972. (Photo: *Akwesasne Notes*)

The massive publicity which attended the Alcatraz takeover, and the consequent rapid building of public consciousness and support concerning Indian issues[85] caused Congress to react in something of a panic. On December 23, 1969, House Joint Resolution 1042 (115 C.R. 215, H 12975) was passed, stipulating that "the President of the United States is directed to initiate immediate negotiations with delegated representatives of [IAT] and any other appropriate representatives of the Indian community with the objective of transferring unencumbered title in fee of Alcatraz Island to [IAT] or any other designated organization of the American Indian Community." A bit cooler, the Nixon administration "complied" with this instruction by dispatching Robert Robertson, executive director of the National Council of Indian Opportunity, to Alcatraz; in meetings on January 4 and 5, 1970, Robertson insisted that women and children be "immediately removed" from the island and that the overall IAT contingent of several hundred be reduced to a "symbolic force of 5-10 men [to be placed on the federal payroll]," as a prerequisite to further discussions.[86] The Indians refused on both counts.

On March 8, IAT upped the ante by occupying a second site, an unused section of the Fort Lawton military reservation, near Seattle. In the army's immediate eviction of the group, seventy-seven persons were arrested for trespass and other offenses; IAT, however, reoccupied the site on March 15, with twelve "ringleaders" arrested in the ensuing military response; the site was reoccupied yet again on April 2.[87] In light of the escalating situation, the Department of Interior offered what it termed as its "maximal counter-proposal" to the IAT demands—and a clear Congressional directive—on March 31: Alcatraz was to be made into a national park featuring a theme of "Indian quality," while Indians would be hired as park rangers and allowed to serve on the facility's planning board, under supervision of the Interior Secretary.[88] IAT, of course, categorically rejected this scenario:

> Our answer to the U.S. government that this island be turned into a park and that the Indian people be appointed by Walter J. Hickle to run this park...our answer is at this time, and at any other time, an emphatic NO.[89]

Despite the IAT response, Thomas E. Hannon, regional administrator of the General Services Administration (GSA) announced on May 28, 1970, that title to Alcatraz was being transferred to the Department of Interior "for purposes of establishing a park."[90]

This was followed, on May 12, by a White House order to the Coast Guard to "deny electricity to the Indians"; the water barge by which supplies reached the island was taken out of service at the same time.[91] IAT then trimmed its ranks, and both sides hunkered down for a serious siege. Ultimately, on June 14, 1971—after the long stalemate had diffused public attention—a taskforce of U.S. marshals landed on Alcatraz, arresting and removing all remaining IAT members on the island.[92] Needless to say, no national park has been actualized on the barren and deserted "rock."

Although the 19-month occupation had failed to accomplish its stated objectives, it had demonstrated beyond all doubt that strong actions by Indians could result not only in broad public exposure of the issues and substantial national/international support for Indian rights, but could potentially force significant concessions from the federal government as well. One direct result of this realization was a spate of similar seizures of unused federal and corporate properties; among these were the Pomo tribal takeover of an abandoned army radio-transmitter base near Middletown, Ca., on May 1, 1971; the whole series of occupations of Pacific Gas and Electric real estate undertaken by the Pit River Nation during 1970-73; and even the seizure of a former Nike missile base on the Chicago lakefront in 1972.[93] The surge of American Indian militancy was fueled even further by events such as the near-fatal shooting of Washington fishing rights activist Hank Adams on January 21, 1971.[94]

The lessons of this were not lost on the AIM leadership, especially not on Russell Means. As Robert Burnette, a former chairman of the Rosebud Reservation (and an activist during the period), recounts:

> [Means] revealed his bizarre knack for staging demonstrations that attracted the sort of press coverage Indians had been looking for: the capture of the *Mayflower II* on

Thanksgiving of 1970, a brief occupation of Mount Rushmore in June 1971, and an abortive attempt to seize the BIA central office on 22 September of the same year. His genius for public relations [made him increasingly] the group's spokesperson.[95]

It was perhaps initially for this reason that AIM began to gravitate towards the Means brothers' home base on Pine Ridge during the fall of 1971. An immediate outcome of this trend was that the organizational leadership was present in force when a 51-year-old Oglala named Raymond Yellow Thunder was murdered in the town of Gordon, Nebraska, in January 1972. As the matter is described elsewhere, "Yellow Thunder, drunk from a session in a Gordon bar, had been picked up by two white brothers, Melvin Hare, twenty-six, and Leslie Hare, twenty-eight. The white men drove the...Indian around in their car, beat him, abused him, tortured him, and threw him naked into an American Legion dance hall where he was further taunted. He was found dead a week later in the trunk of a car."[96] As Bill Means explains:

> When Raymond Yellow Thunder was killed, his relatives first went to the BIA, then to the FBI, and to the local police, but they got no response. Severt Young Bear [an Oglala from Pine Ridge] then...asked AIM to come...help clear up the case. We realized this was a new level. We realized we could not allow Indian people to be murdered, that we would have to change tactics. It was a turning point. We could not just carry signs and protest, but we would have to be willing to die to protect our people.[97]

Historian Alvin Josephy, Jr., capsulizes what happened next:

> In February 1972, when nothing was done to punish the tormentors and murderers of Raymond Yellow Thunder, [Russell] Means and [Dennis] Banks led some 1,300 angry Indians, mostly Sioux from Pine Ridge and Rosebud, into the town of Gordon, occupying it for three days and threatening town and state officials if they failed to carry out justice. To the relief of the frightened townspeople, two Whites [the Hares] were finally jailed in connection with the crime, a policeman was suspended, and the local authorities were persuaded to end discrimination against Indians. Although discrimination continued, AIM's reputation soared among reservation Indians. What tribal leaders had dared not do to protect their people, AIM had done.[98]

Russell Means' statement during the Yellow Thunder action that, "We've come here to Gordon today to secure justice for American Indians and to put Gordon on the map...and if justice is not immediately forthcoming, we'll be back to take Gordon *off* the map," quickly became a veritable slogan of Indian pride on Pine Ridge. It was also Means' failed 1971 BIA takeover attempt from which the concept for the next national action—"The Trail of Broken Treaties"—was born the following July, in a meeting held in conjunction with the annual Sun Dance conducted at the home of Brulé spiritual leaders Henry and Leonard Crow Dog (called "Crow Dog's Paradise") on the Rosebud Reservation. The idea was to bring together several large caravans composed of hundreds of Indians from across the country at the BIA building in Washington, D.C., immediately prior to the presidential election in November 1972. Such a convergence was virtually guaranteed to attain prime television news coverage, providing a tremendous forum for the airing of Indian grievances. Given the politically delicate timing of the event, it seemed likely that the Nixon administration might be willing to enter into serious negotiations on the subject of Indian rights.[99]

At a meeting attended by representatives of a number of Indian organizations and hosted by Joe Locust's Colorado AIM chapter in Denver from September 30 to October 2, two non-AIM members—Robert Burnette and Rubin Snake, a Winnebago from Nebraska—were chosen to codirect the Trail's executive council (AIM representation to the executive staff was provided by Ralph Ware, a Kiowa). Russell Means was selected to assemble the first caravan, originating in Seattle, and Dennis Banks was sent to San Francisco to begin working on a second.[100] They were undoubtedly assisted in their organizing tasks by sentiment aroused by the murder on September 20 of Richard Oaks, leader of IAT at Alcatraz, at the hands of a non-Indian named Michael Morgan.[101] This was fused, at least to some extent, to other recent murders which had already become hot issues in Indian Country: the Yellow Thunder case; the execution-style slaying of a 19-year-old Papago youth named Phillip Celay by Sheriff's Deputy David Bosman near Ajo, Arizona, on July 1; and the similar police-caused death in Philadelphia of a young Onondaga named Leroy Shenandoah, a U.S. Army Special Forces veteran who had served as a member of the honor guard attending the casket of John F. Kennedy.[102] Recruits, endorsements and financial support for the Trail of Broken Treaties came pouring in. As Vine Deloria, Jr., recounts:

> The caravan began [from San Francisco, Means' and Banks' efforts having been consolidated] in October and wound its way eastward, stopping at every reservation within easy driving distance of the main route. For the first time, people began to realize the extent of discontent existing on the reservations. The Bureau of Indian Affairs had been instructed to refuse to assist any of the different groups that were proceeding east. The BIA did its best to hamper the caravan. Nevertheless, as the caravan arrived at the reservations, it was generally greeted by large crowds and joined by many participants who wished to present their grievances to the government...
>
> The caravan stopped in St. Paul, Minnesota, to plan the list of grievances and hold workshops on the various phases of the march. In several days of workshops the caravan members hammered out a list of twenty points which they felt fairly and adequately summarized a reform program for the government which would receive strong support from Indians...The Twenty Points presented a framework for considering the status of Indian tribes and the nature of their federal relationship. It harkened back to the days of freedom, when the United States courted the friendship of the tribes in its desperate battle to maintain its independence from Great Britain.[103]

Armed with this document, the Trail of Broken Treaties moved on to Washington, arriving on November 3. As *Akwesasne Notes* wrote:

AIM leader Russell Means, carrying a portrait of Richard Nixon as a "shield," confronts police in front of the BIA Building in Washington, D.C. in November 1972. Such gestures were part of what was termed as Means' "bizarre knack" for attracting media attention to AIM. (Photo: *Akwesasne Notes*)

One of the first things the Trail of Broken Treaties organizers found out was that their request to hold religious services at three Arlington Cemetery sites [where distinguished Indian soldiers were buried] was rejected because it conflicted with regulations prohibiting any services "closely related" to "partisan activities"...Several thousand Indians were already in Washington—and about 2,000 more were expected to arrive in two separate caravans from North Carolina and St. Paul...[Meanwhile], the People's Involvement Corporation, a Black community organization, had loaned its large building, a former bakery, to the Caravan, and supplied the bulk of the food for the first arrivals...The sleepy group headed to the basement [of this building] to sleep, but they were confronted with another problem they hadn't anticipated: rats. Their welcoming group had been cooking for a day before the caravan arrived, all kinds of food. And the smell must have wafted throughout the city, attracting every rat in Washington to the basement...[104]

Relying on an earlier agreement reached between Assistant Secretary of Interior for the Bureau of Land Management Harrison Loesch and Robert Burnette, that "more than vocal support" would be provided by the federal government to the Trail, once it arrived in the capital, "hundreds of Caravan people went over to the BIA to see what could be arranged."[105] A Trail of Broken Treaties Steering Committee composed of Russell Means, Sid Mills (a Yakima AIM leader from Washington),

Hank Adams and others talked with Loesch and BIA officials about what might be done to accommodate the large and peaceful demonstration. Around 4 p.m., however, a contingent of BIA security guards began to attempt to clear the building of caravan members lounging around the building's ground floor awaiting word on the negotiations continuing upstairs. When the Indians refused to leave without their steering committee, the police resorted to clubs and—undoubtedly to their great surprise—were quickly overpowered and thrown out themselves. Caravan members barricaded the building against police counterattack while BIA employees scrambled out windows to escape. The police cordoned off the building in a vain attempt to prevent Indian reinforcements from getting in (ultimately the Indian occupation group "stabilized" at about 400).[106] As an infuriated Robert Burnette put it:

> Loesch was lying through his teeth [about providing federal assistance]. His intention was to put us in our place. This is the first [sic] national Indian effort we have ever made, and they don't like it. I've supported the occupation of the BIA because we have no alternative. We came here peacefully, but are being forced to do something we hadn't planned.[107]

Initially, the steering committee attempted to negotiate for alternative housing. This seemed fruitful when, on the first day of the occupation, the government offered a nearby auditorium. A Trail delegation sent to investigate the site, however, found the building locked and guarded by U.S. marshals. A GSA spokesperson explained that the auditorium's use was contingent upon the "peaceful and complete" evacuation of the BIA building. Russell Means responded that the Indians weren't going anywhere until the government allowed AIM security to occupy the auditorium.[108] By this time, the BIA occupiers had thoroughly armed themselves with clubs and makeshift spears, painted themselves for battle, and turned away Chief U.S. Marshal Wayne Colburn when he attempted to serve eviction papers during the afternoon of November 3.[109]

In ways never intended by its organizers and sponsors, the Trail of Broken Treaties had riveted the nation's attention. As had been the case at Alcatraz, public support was immediate and widespread, with even Commissioner of Indian Affairs Louis R. Bruce temporarily joining the occupation (in "an act of solidarity," as he called it; the gesture cost him his job at the hands of Interior Secretary Rogers B. Morton shortly thereafter). Under these circumstances, the steering committee dropped the question of alternative housing as an agenda item, and announced on the evening of the 3rd that, henceforth, they would negotiate *only* on the Twenty Points, retaining control of the BIA building until they had received satisfaction.[110] Deloria describes what followed:

> The next several days were critical. The caravan leaders could barely keep their followers under control. Sporadic efforts by police to harass the occupants of the building created a constant state of fear, and with each wave of harassment the building suffered additional damage as the Indians tried to plug the obvious weak points in their defenses.[111]

"John G. Arellano," posing as a hyper-militant "AIM warrior" at the BIA Building during November 1972. Arellano, a police infiltrator utilized by the FBI as a provocateur, subsequently fingered Indian leader Hank Adams on false charges. (Photo: *Akwesasne Notes*)

On November 5, White House representatives Leonard Garment and Frank Carlucci (recently appointed Reagan's Secretary of Defense after heading the National Security Council) signed an agreement to review and respond to the substance of the Twenty Points,[112] and:

> A team of negotiators led by Hank Adams...worked out a partial solution to the occupation...Finally, on November 9th, the Indians left the building under a promise by the administration that no criminal charges would be filed for events which happened during the occupation. In addition, the caravan participants received some $66,000 in travel money...[113]

"As the various groups of Indians left the building and started the trek home," Deloria continues, "government agents discovered that a substantial number of federal records were missing. During the weekend the AIM leaders had loaded a number of boxes of files into trucks and cars and had taken them out of the city."[114] He goes on to note that Hank Adams felt a deep sense of responsibility to see these records returned and "sent out word through Indian country that he would remain in Washington, D.C., and see that any papers shipped to him were returned to the proper authority."[115] He had accomplished this on two occasions (with batches of papers turned over to him after AIM had photocopied them) when he was suddenly arrested by the FBI while being assisted in returning a third batch by Les Whitten, an associate of the nationally syndicated columnist, Jack Anderson. As it turned out, Adams had been set up in an obvious case of entrapment (charges were thrown out on this basis) by an FBI infiltrator named Johnny Arellano, who had been posing as an AIM member.[116] It was at this juncture that the government began to become increasingly vocal about the damages inflicted by the occupiers upon the BIA building—the House Subcommittee on Indian Affairs contended that this was "the most severe damage inflicted upon Washington, D.C., since the British burned the city in the War of 1812"[117]—but:

> Later events would indicate that the federal government had a substantial number of agents among the protesters, and some were so militant and destructive that they were awarded special Indian names for their involvement in the protest. It became apparent why the government had been so willing to agree not to prosecute the Indians: The presence of agent-provocateurs and the intensity of their work would have made it extremely difficult for the government to have proven an intent by the real Indian activists to destroy the building.[118]

This precursor of things to come was coupled to what appears to be the launching of a much broader federal campaign to destroy the leadership of the emergent Indian movement. For example, at least as early as November 17, 1972, the White House reneged on its non-prosecution agreement. On that date, Harrison Loesch held a press conference at which he stated that he and Secretary of Interior Morton had "agreed to a full-scale prosecution" of those involved in the BIA takeover; when shown a copy of the agreement signed by White House representatives, he responded "the Secretary has indicated that he trusted that any such *recommendation* entered into by Carlucci and Garment will not be followed [emphasis added];" Morton and Loesch were publicly seconded by Attorney General Richard Kleindienst.[119] As Robert Burnette recalls, the government also used the occasion to undertake its first serious propaganda effort against AIM:

> The same day, the NTCA [National Tribal Chairman's Association, an arch-conservative, government-sponsored "Indian organization"], led by Rev. Webster Two Hawk, held its own press conference [at federal expense]. Two Hawk urged the federal government not to speak to any Indian group except his own, to prosecute those who had occupied the BIA building, to prosecute those who stole the BIA files, and to continue business as usual. Two Hawk then moderated this statement by blaming the damage on "irresponsible self-styled revolutionaries" who led the take-over. A great many right-wing groups seized upon Two Hawks' statements and presented him to an unknowing public as a responsible Indian leader.[120]

Meanwhile, realizing earlier in 1972 that Pine Ridge was becoming a focal point of AIM activity and grassroots reservation support, the BIA had thrown its weight behind the campaign for the tribal presidency undertaken by Richard "Dickie" Wilson, an Oglala stamped in the Webster Two Hawk mold. When Wilson won handily, the government was positioned to mount a strong "Indian" retaliation against AIM members returning triumphantly from the BIA confrontation in Washington:

> As Russell Means led the Oglala Sioux remnants of the Trail of Broken Treaties through the town of Pine Ridge, the seat of government of the Oglala reservation, he may have noticed a stir of activity around police headquarters. Unknown to Means, tribal presi-

dent Richard Wilson had secured a court order from the Oglala Sioux tribal court prohibiting Means or any other AIM member from speaking at or attending any public meeting...Since the Oglala Sioux Landowners Association was meeting in Pine Ridge, Means, a member of this group, decided to attend and to report what had actually happened in Washington. Before he had a chance to speak his mind, he was arrested by BIA special officer Delmar Eastman for violating this court order...This arrest was a blatant violation of the First Amendment, for it denied Means freedom of speech on the reservation where he was born and was an enrolled member.[121]

Upon his release from the tribal jail the next day, Means drove southwest to Scottsbluff, Nebraska, where he was arrested by local police who claimed to wish to hold him on a "routine" check for outstanding warrants; during the night, an empty gun was slid into his holding cell, the door was unlocked, and he was told to "make a break for it" by police. "They wanted to off me during an escape attempt," he later stated.[122] A rash of similar incidents were directed at AIM members on and around Pine Ridge Reservation during this period.

A confrontation was brewing which would pit Indian against Indian on the Pine Ridge Reservation. Clearly one side was being backed—used as surrogates—by the federal government, regardless of the legality of its tactics. By the same token, the racist local law enforcement agencies—virulent enough for some observers to describe the area as being "the Mississippi of the north"—were attacking Indians associated with AIM in more concerted fashion.[123] Federal interest in fostering such a situation lay in the probability that it would suppress and isolate—if not destroy outright—AIM, the vehicle of rising Indian militancy which threatened to derail the quiet process by which the government was extinguishing Indian land title, and raise a whole range of related issues long thought dead and buried. All the better that the location of the conflict would be Pine Ridge, allowing the dispensation of a lesson to the unruly Lakotas—especially the "haughty" Oglala traditionals—which would place them in a posture of humility forever after.

It seems likely that the federal sector was unprepared for the dogged stamina AIM would exhibit, the amount of punishment it absorbed without yielding, or the depth of its support at reservation grassroots. The official government assessment of the organization in 1972 was that:

> Some of their leaders are star-struck with self-righteousness, some are renegades, some are youthful adventurers, some have criminal records. They come forward with great gusto when there is hell to raise; otherwise, they are loosely organized, slipping from one expensive-to-the-taxpayers event to the next under the cloak of false idealism.[124]

But if government policymakers miscalculated, so did AIM. As Dennis Banks reflected later,

> It strikes me that we were incredibly naive in those days, for all our militance and radical rhetoric. We actually believed that if we raised the issues, made people aware of the truth, and stuck to our guns in a strong way, that things would change, that that's all it would take. Oh, we expected to pay dues—don't get me wrong—we were

prepared for beatings and arrests, time spent in jails and prisons to some degree or another. I guess, after Richard Oaks, you'd have to say we expected death. But somehow, we still didn't really understand the rules of the game, we weren't prepared for the *magnitude* of what happened. Part of that was maybe because we still didn't really comprehend what the stakes were.[125]

Speculative Motivations

In addition to the political agenda underscored by the federal posture on Pine Ridge by 1972, another crucial locus of consideration hinges upon more narrowly posed economic speculations. Most obviously, such concerns center upon the possible loss of projected revenues from the Black Hills region's extant enterprises. Here, the "Custer's Gold" syndrome of the 1870s—which had materialized into real wealth despite the colonel's fabrications at the time—continued to weigh in heavily. Among the hundreds of "paying" mines which had spread across the mineral-rich Hills during the succeeding century, just one (the Homestake Mine, a Hearst Corporation subsidiary in Lead, S.D.) extracted over $14 billion in ore by 1970.[126]

The massive investment made in actualizing the Pick-Sloan Plan had begun to pay off with the successful incorporation of substantial (non-Indian controlled) sections of western South Dakota into the wheat-growing "bread-basket" of the national economy by the mid-1960s.[127] Additionally, much of the 150 million-odd acres of the 1868 treaty territory supported a thriving cattle industry. The Black Hills themselves yield significant profits from logging and generate as much as a billion dollars per year from tourism.[128]

Probably far more important to federal calculations during the "energy crisis" period of the early 1970s was a process which had begun with the discovery of high-grade uranium veins near the southern Hills town of Edgemont in 1952. The quality of this find immediately prompted the Atomic Energy Commission (AEC) to initiate a mining and milling operation based at Igloo, an abandoned army ordnance depot about eight miles southwest of town and thirty miles west of Pine Ridge.[129] Local inhabitants were assured by appropriate officials that the operation represented "no public health hazard" and the AEC proceeded to feed its ore buying program (largely for weapons procurement purposes) from the Edgemont facility until it was closed due to diminishing productivity during the late-1960s. In the meantime, the AEC exhibited a cavalier attitude regarding the disposal of some 3.5 million tons of mill tailings, a sandy waste by-product which retains about 75% of the radioactivity found in the original ore, simply dumping it in piles along Cottonwood Creek, a local tributary of the Cheyenne River. On June 11, 1962, more than 200 tons of this radioactive waste were washed into the creek, on into the Cheyenne River and eastward into the Pine Ridge water table. The government remained very quiet about the potential effects of this massive contamination.[130]

By the mid-1970s, more than 5,000 speculative uranium mining leases had been let by the Interior Department in the Black Hills National Forest alone, while an additional 218,747 acres of privately held land in the area were under similar

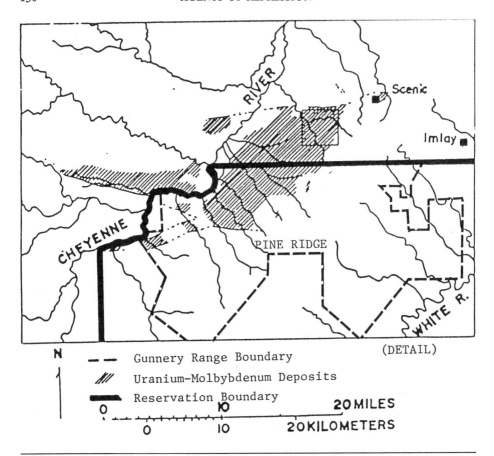

N

- - - Gunnery Range Boundary

//// Uranium-Molybdenum Deposits

━━━ Reservation Boundary

(DETAIL)

0 ————————— 10 ————————— 20 MILES

0 ————————— 10 ————————— 20 KILOMETERS

Map 5: Uranium-Molybdenum Deposits on the Pine Ridge Reservation. These deposits were identified by satellite surveys undertaken by NASA and the National Uranium Resource Evaluation (NURE) program during the early 1970s. (Derived from Gries, J.P., *Status of Mineral Resource Information on the Pine Ridge Indian Reservation, S.D.*, 1976)

contract.[131] Among the primary leaseholders were such transnational corporate giants as Union Carbide, Chevron, Anaconda/ARCO, British-Canadian Rio Algom, Wyoming Mineral/Westinghouse, Kerr-McGee and the Tennessee Valley Authority. Union Carbide, to choose but one example, was receiving $2.3 billion per year in federal subsidies to underwrite its uranium exploration efforts.[132]

The great bulk of this activity was unknown to area residents, Indian and non-Indian alike, as was the fact that, in 1971, a National Uranium Resource Evaluations (NURE, a component of the U.S. Geological Survey [USGS]) satellite orbited by NASA and using special remote sensing equipment had located an especially rich and promising deposit within the northwestern one-eighth of Pine Ridge; this was the unreturned Gunnery Range area "borrowed" by the War Department in 1942 (see

Map 5).[133] Pursuant to this discovery, a joint report quietly prepared by the USGS, Bureau of Mines and the BIA concluded that "numerous potential pay zones" and "relatively shallow drilling depths...combine to make the Pine Ridge Reservation an attractive prospecting area" for uranium, oil, natural gas, and gravel.[134] Although a spokesman for Union Carbide, which had been selected by the government to develop "the Pine Ridge prospectus" claimed that "we don't think there's much uranium there,"[135] the South Dakota State Surface Mining Licensing Office countered:

> Of course they won't tell us exactly what they have learned, but the first thing they do is take a water sample; if the water shows a relatively high level of radioactivity, then they know that the uranium is there somewhere, and they explore to find it. I know that the water samples from Pine Ridge showed a considerable amount of uranium, one of the highest. They know it's there. It's one of their prime spots.[136]

By 1975, the federal interest in Pine Ridge uranium (real or suspected) was rendered rather explicit by the illegal cession on June 24 (agreed to with neither the consent of the tribal council required by BIA regulations nor the expressed consent of three-fourths of all adult Lakotas stipulated by the 1868 treaty) by Dick Wilson of 76,200 acres of the crucial Sheep Mountain portion of the Gunnery Range. This patently unconstitutional transfer of Lakota land to the U.S. Park Service—specifically, to the Badlands National Monument—was quickly certified as legitimate by both the House and Senate: "Congress has by Public Law 90-468 authorized the additions to Badlands National Monument...consisting of lands within the exterior boundaries of the Pine Ridge Indian Reservation...which will be held by the United States in trust for the Tribe;" however, "the Tribe does *not* have the right to develop minerals on land *re*acquired under Public Law 90-468 [emphasis added]."[137]

Aside from uranium, there was also a question of coal. At about the same time prospectors were turning up uranium around Edgemont, USGS geologists were beginning to realize the extent of the huge Fort Union coal deposit, probably North America's single largest reserve of bituminous and almost entirely located beneath the surface of the 1868 treaty area (see Map 6 on following page). At the outset, coal did not figure as a particularly important strategic asset, and the Department of Interior largely contented itself with assisting corporations such as Peabody Coal in obtaining super-profits by providing them BIA-sanctioned access to Indian lands at absurdly low rates; a classic case of this was the leasing of approximately 220,000 acres of the Northern Cheyenne Reservation at $3 per acre during the 1950s.[138]

By 1970, however, with U.S. energy consumption increasing in geometric proportions, "the peaceful atom" having failed to measure up to its advance billing, OPEC consolidating its threat of curtailing the volume of high-profit oil imports and Richard Nixon beginning to promise a policy of "national energy independence" by the end of the decade, things had started to look a bit different to federal policymakers. Coal had re-emerged as a priority energy resource in the U.S. During 1971, the government sponsored Study Committee for Rehabilitating Lands Surface Mined for Coal in the Western United States returned a finding that there was little

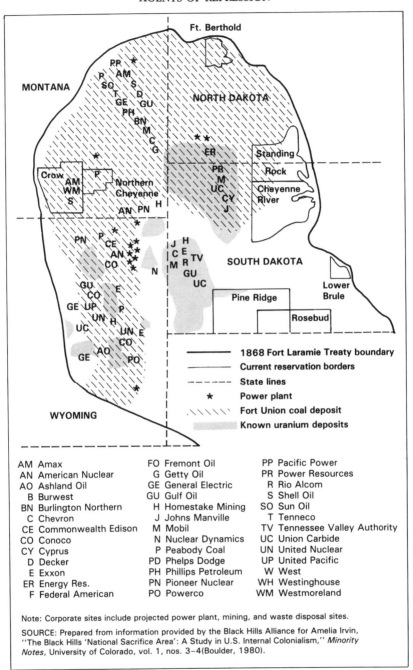

Ft. Berthold

MONTANA

NORTH DAKOTA

Standing
Rock

Cheyenne
River

SOUTH DAKOTA

Crow

Northern
Cheyenne

Lower
Brule

Pine Ridge

Rosebud

WYOMING

━━━━━	**1868 Fort Laramie Treaty boundary**	
─────	**Current reservation borders**	
─────	**State lines**	
＊	**Power plant**	
\\\\\	**Fort Union coal deposit**	
▨	**Known uranium deposits**	

AM	Amax	FO	Fremont Oil	PP	Pacific Power
AN	American Nuclear	G	Getty Oil	PR	Power Resources
AO	Ashland Oil	GE	General Electric	R	Rio Alcom
B	Burwest	GU	Gulf Oil	S	Shell Oil
BN	Burlington Northern	H	Homestake Mining	SO	Sun Oil
C	Chevron	J	Johns Manville	T	Tenneco
CE	Commonwealth Edison	M	Mobil	TV	Tennessee Valley Authority
CO	Conoco	N	Nuclear Dynamics	UC	Union Carbide
CY	Cyprus	P	Peabody Coal	UN	United Nuclear
D	Decker	PD	Phelps Dodge	UP	United Pacific
E	Exxon	PH	Phillips Petroleum	W	West
ER	Energy Res.	PN	Pioneer Nuclear	WH	Westinghouse
F	Federal American	PO	Powerco	WM	Westmoreland

Note: Corporate sites include projected power plant, mining, and waste disposal sites.

SOURCE: Prepared from information provided by the Black Hills Alliance for Amelia Irvin, "The Black Hills 'National Sacrifice Area': A Study in U.S. Internal Colonialism," *Minority Notes*, University of Colorado, vol. 1, nos. 3–4(Boulder, 1980).

Map 6: U.S. corporate interests in the greater Sioux Nation.

or no possibility of rejuvenating ("reclaiming") arid or semi-arid terrain once it had been stripmined. The Committee then stated that, in view of the goal of national energy self-sufficiency, coal-rich (but dry) western areas such as the Black Hills and "Four Corners" (of the states of Arizona, New Mexico, Colorado and Utah) regions should be considered "national sacrifice areas" for purposes of pursuing unrestricted energy resource development; the thesis was formally accepted—in a less secretive fashion—by both the National Academy of Sciences and the National Academy of Engineering in 1974.[139] With this conceptual hurdle cleared:

> In 1971, the multicorporate North Central Power Study (dutifully endorsed by the Department of the Interior) decreed that Black Hills aquifers—the only real source of water in this dry country—could sustain massive exploitation of the coal, oil and uranium resources of the region and that the Black Hills should become the nucleus of a vast multinational energy domain, producing power right in the mine fields, in forty-two huge thermal-generation plants, and exporting it eastward in a grid of power lines, all the way to Minneapolis and St. Louis.[140]

As is noted elsewhere:

> Overall, the plans for industrializing the Black Hills are staggering. They include a gigantic park featuring more than a score of 10,000 megawatt coal-fired plants, a dozen nuclear reactors, huge coal-slurry pipelines designed to use millions of gallons of water, and at least 14 major uranium mines.[141]

The slurry lines were dreamed up by a corporation called Energy Transport Systems, Inc. (ETSI) and would extend all the way from the Wyo-Dak mine near Gillette, Wyoming, to Arkansas, an operation estimated to require some 20,000 acre feet of groundwater annually and which might be expected to totally deplete regional aquifers by some point early in the next century.[142] The federal government also approved this prospect—which would serve to render the entire Black Hills region uninhabitable for the next several thousand years—as being an "acceptable price" to pay for energy development.[143]

Perhaps the federal and corporate propensity to simply write off huge portions of North America as national sacrifice areas—and indigenous inhabitants as what Russell Means later called "national sacrifice peoples"[144]—was motivated by more than sheer avarice. It is possible that, by the early 1970s, they were already aware of the extent of the nuclear contamination which their earlier uranium mining and milling operations had engendered in the immediate vicinity of the Hills (as similar activities had throughout the Four Corners region[145]). They might have viewed both the land and its people as having *already* been unwittingly expended and opted to put "the best face" on the matter. Such a federal/corporate outlook would tend to dovetail neatly with a finding of the Los Alamos National Laboratory, published toward the end of the decade:

Perhaps the solution to the radon emission problem [as well as other contamination factors related to uranium production] is to zone the land into uranium mining and milling districts *so as to forbid human habitation* [emphasis added].[146]

Certainly, the government has pursued its policies in the Black Hills as if it had accepted this conclusion, albeit too late to salvage the human inhabitants involved. For example, it has sought during the 1980s to locate nuclear waste facilities in the areas of worst radioactive contamination: a low-level dump site has been advocated at Edgemont (again, with the assurance extended to the highly irradiated local populace that such a siting represents no public health hazard), and Pine Ridge residents have long suspected that a high level (military) waste dump had been secretly positioned within a "secure" section of the Gunnery Range.[147]

Virtually all of this was intangible at the onset of the 1970s, bound up as it was in the speculations and boardroom projections of governmental and corporate planners. None of it was known to movement people and their supporters during the fall of 1972 and it would be more than five years before AIM leader Ted Means would contend that:

...at this time, we see a move by the United States to develop energy resources within what is called the Ft. Laramie Treaty Area, being the treaty of 1868 which was proclaimed by the President and ratified by Congress...The energy development is in direct violation of this treaty. And it has some very serious environmental effects on people in our area...What we see the government doing, along with these energy developments...[is to] represent the American Indian Movement as a direct threat to its corporate and illegal goals of exploitation. For this reason, we have suffered from the direct attack of the government, especially through the FBI and the court systems of the Federal Government in the state of South Dakota.[148]

The FBI seems to have understood from the beginning why AIM was to be combatted. For instance, a 1974 memorandum sent from Bureau headquarters to fifteen field offices, and devoted to describing the dangers inherent in AIM's organizational objectives, spotlights a statement by Dennis Banks on April 16 of that year, indicating that AIM would place increasing emphasis on resisting "corporate rip-offs" of Indian land and resources.[149]

In any event, all three major federal preoccupations—an historical animus directed at the Lakotas, the need to quell an incipient Oglala-focused "insurgency" which threatened to unsettle customary methods of expropriating Indian land, and a tremendous speculative economic interest in the control of the resources within the 1868 Fort Laramie Treaty area—had coalesced by late 1972 to form a firm foundation for what was to follow. The FBI was on its way to Pine Ridge in strength.[150]

Chapter 5

The Pine Ridge Battleground

There is a prophecy in our Ojibway religion that one day we would all stand together. I am elated because I lived to see it happen.
—Eddie Benton-Benai, Anishinabe, AIM Spiritual Leader, 1973

We're trying to regain what we had in the past, being human beings and being involved in human society.
—Stan Holder, Wichita, AIM Leader, 1973

The most immediate cause for the extent of government backing of Dick Wilson's 1972 election campaign was probably a series of statements by Russell Means, upon his resumption of residency on Pine Ridge that year, that he would seek the tribal presidency in 1974.[1] The Means platform focused upon Oglala sovereignty, specifically: a return of tribal decision-making to the traditional councils of elders (preempted by the Indian Reorganization Act [IRA] in 1936), a resumption of Lakota treaty-making with the U.S. and/or other nations and corresponding elimination of the BIA as Oglala liaison with the federal government (part of the Trail of Broken Treaties' 20 points); a program to recover Lakota jurisdiction and subordinate the BIA police to community control, and a program to recover Lakota treaty territory, including control of the many portions of Pine Ridge leased to non-Indians by the BIA as part of its exercise of "trust" responsibility over Indian lands.[2] Means no doubt felt a personal interest in the latter element of his agenda:

The Means brothers, for example, had inherited 190 acres of land [on Pine Ridge], but the land, like all allotments, was held in trust by the federal government, and it was leased by the BIA to a white rancher. According to Russell Means, they no longer received lease payments after 1969 when they joined AIM.[3]

From the federal governmant's perspective, support for Means personally and for his program was anathema. Consequently, the penalties summarily visited upon the Means family were broadened to include others: "On Pine Ridge...traditional supporters [across the reservation] were not receiving their lease money, and the suspected culprit was Dickie Wilson."[4] In addition, Wilson began to assemble a "flying squad" calling themselves GOONs (Guardians Of the Oglala Nation) with which to dispense physical punishment to his opponents:

> Wilson, with special powers usurped from the tribal council, began to harass AIM members and friends. One Sioux girl [sic] who supported AIM's activities had to leave her car, which bore an AIM bumper sticker, and walk for help when the car ran into a ditch. When she came back, the car was riddled with bullet holes and inoperable.[5]

The GOON squad was consolidated in November 1972 when the BIA provided Wilson with $62,000 for the expressed purpose of hiring, as he later explained to South Dakota Senator James Abourezk,

> ...an auxiliary police force...We organized this force to handle people like Russell Means and other radicals who were going to have what they called a victory dance at Billy Mills Hall [in the village of Pine Ridge] after the destruction of the BIA office in Washington, D.C...[The BIA provided these funds] to hire a small group of people to protect our buildings, bureau office, tribal offices...[6]

The need for augmented "security" corresponds with AIM supporter—and, at that time, tribal council member—Severt Young Bear's analysis:

> Right from the day [Wilson] took office, the 10th of April, 1972, people been constantly fighting him...Because of some of the under-the-table dealings...when he was a tribal council member before, and when he was in the [Oglala Sioux Tribal] Housing Authority. He was one of those guys setting up liquor on the reservation a couple of years ago...During the campaign he told these two guys from Rapid City that if he gets to be tribal [president], he promised them a housing contract of $13 million, and a liquor contract...These two white men put a little over $10,000 into his campaign. So he was throwing money around, used wine to buy votes, and that was the kind of dealing that he done.[7]

Or, to quote Rosebud Tribal President Robert Burnette:

> In the early 1960s [Wilson] and his wife fled the reservation and spent several years in the Southwest after a conflict-of-interest case in which she was the director and he was a contract plumber for the Oglala Sioux Housing Authority. He came back and was forgiven. A few years later Wilson and Robert Mousseaux, the tribal secretary, were brought up on charges of unlawfully converting tribal funds to the use of another individual. Charges against Wilson were later dismissed, but Mousseaux was convicted. [By 1973] the traditional chiefs and tribal elders had reached the end of their rope with Wilson. His misuse of tribal funds, his management of the tribe without a budget, his violation of the tribal constitution by refusing to call meetings in accordance with tribal law, and the goon squad he maintained to intimidate his opponents had antagonized even the most patient of the old Indian leaders.[8]

By January 1973, "Wilson was so busy with his war on AIM"[9] that he missed an opportunity to offset the organization's spiraling popularity on Pine Ridge and neutralize some of the traditionals' opposition to his presidency. At about 1 a.m. on

January 23, a 20-year-old Oglala named Wesley Bad Heart Bull was stabbed to death by Darld Schmitz, a non-Indian, in a gas station lot in the town of Buffalo Gap, S.D. Schmitz was arrested, but released the same day on $5,000 bond; a week later he was charged with second degree manslaughter in the slaying of the unarmed Indian youth. Bad Heart Bull's mother, Sarah, understandably upset by what she saw as the impending slap-on-the-wrist to be administered to her son's executioner, sent a request to the AIM leadership—assembled in Scottsbluff, Nebraska, at a Chicano-Indio Unity Conference sponsored by the Denver-based Crusade for Justice—that they intervene as they had in the Yellow Thunder case (see Chapter 4).[10]

AIM field coordinator Banks responded by arranging a February 6 meeting for himself, Russell Means, and Utah AIM leader David Hill (a Choctaw from Salt Lake City) with Fall River County (S.D.) state's attorney Hobart Gates. He stipulated AIM wished to discuss the upgrading of charges against Schmitz to include murder, and put out a call for Indians to demonstrate their support for such a legal move by assembling peacefully at the county courthouse in Custer (S.D.).[11] Unaccountably (at the time; less so in light of future events), an unidentified "government spokesman" caused *Rapid City Journal* reporter Lyn Gladstone to falsely state, in a story dated February 5, that the AIM action had been "called off."

Only about 200 AIM supporters materialized in the midst of a blizzard on February 6. Banks, Means and Hill proceeded with their meeting with Gates who stone-walled. Insisting justice was "already being done," he ignored eyewitness testimony that Bad Heart Bull had been killed "intentionally and in cold blood," pronounced the *pro forma* session to be at an end, and asked the three to leave his office. Means replied, "I want to know why this white man who killed an Indian is charged with second-degree manslaughter instead of first-degree murder, and the only way you're going to get me out of here is to kill me too!"[12] With that:

> All hell broke loose…A fight broke out with fists and clubs, and the Indians inside the courthouse tore nightsticks away from the police and started swinging. Banks leaped out a window and escaped in the snow. Means and Dave Hill took on the police in the courthouse and knocked eleven of them down before being beaten themselves…Outside, their followers tried to swarm up the courthouse steps and were repulsed by police, who fired teargas and used riotsticks on women as well as men…When the unequal fight had ended, twenty-seven Indians were arrested and marched away through the snowy street as smoke rolled up from burning buildings. Eleven police had been injured badly enough to see a doctor, and Means and Hill were hospitalized briefly and jailed…The whites in Custer were terrified. Would-be vigilantes vowed to shoot any AIM member on sight, and the National Guard was mobilized and three blocking positions were set up around Custer in case [AIM] returned.[13]

It was later revealed that the altercation was prearranged by the state: Fall River County Sheriff Earnest Peppin had been requested to muster an unorthodox compliment of riot-equipped deputies to deny access to the courthouse (a public building) to the Indians assembled in a heavy snowstorm. The deputies were reinforced by a hefty contingent of state police (also called for riot duty), South Dakota

Sheriff's Deputy Bill Rice and an accomplice assault Sarah Bad Heart Bull on February 6, 1973, setting off the Custer Courthouse "Riot" in which part of the town burned. AIM had come to Custer to demand that charges against Darld Schmitz, murderer of Bad Heart Bull's son, be upgraded from manslaughter. Schmitz ultimately went free while a number of AIM protesters, including Sarah, were imprisoned. (Photo: *Akwesasne Notes*)

Division of Criminal Investigation (DCI) agent Bernard Christianson was assigned to oversee the whole operation and the FBI had "observers" on hand. The hostilities outside the courthouse, timed to coincide with the attack on the AIM delegation inside, had been precipitated by a deputy shoving Sarah Bad Heart Bull down the courthouse steps. Two fires—in a courthouse annex and Chamber of Commerce building—were ignited by police teargas canisters. Among those arrested on charges such as "incitement to riot" was Sarah Bad Heart Bull; she would ultimately serve five months of a one-to-five year sentence, while her son's killer never served a day.[14]

Wilson might easily have upstaged AIM in this matter *and* registered a solid statement of his concern with the wellbeing of Oglalas simply by asserting that he too felt Schmitz should be charged with murder. Instead, he remained silent until the day of the police assault on the Indian demonstrators in Custer. At that point he chose to further align himself against his ostensible constituents "when [he] offered to send BIA police to help white law officers put down the AIM protest."[15] At the same time, he escalated GOON squad operations, making it clear that his priority continued to be a "total ban" on "AIM-related" activities on the reservation itself.[16] It was also known that he'd opened negotiations with the U.S. Park Service to transfer title to the Sheep Mountain area of the Gunnery Range (see Chapter 4) during early February and he'd come out in favor of accepting the Claims Commission settlement offer concerning the 1868 treaty territory at about the same time.[17]

In desperation, the traditionals initiated impeachment proceedings—supposedly their "fundamental right" under the tribe's BIA-drafted IRA constitution—against Wilson:

> The impeachment hearings were scheduled for February 14, 1973 before the tribal council. Although over three hundred people showed up, Wilson [who was being allowed by the BIA to preside over the process of his own possible removal] postponed the impeachment due to "road and weather conditions," and on the same day the U.S. Marshals Service, under the direction of ex-marine Wayne Colburn, moved approximately seventy highly-trained counter-insurgency Special Operations Group (SOG) troops onto Pine Ridge Reservation. The well-armed paramilitary SOG forces, described by Colburn as "a strike force deployed only at the request of the President or the U.S. Attorney General," set up a command post at the BIA building in the town of Pine Ridge, installing machine guns on the roof, and began training the BIA police in riot formation and in various weapon and tear-gas techniques...The FBI office in the South Dakota capital of Pierre sent agents Jim Dix and Bruce Erikson to Pine Ridge to work with Colburn's SOG unit. The town of Pine Ridge, Wilson's stronghold on the southern border of the reservation, became an armed camp; Wilson a besieged despot.[18]

Thus federally reinforced, Wilson rescheduled the hearing for February 22, and during the intervening week:

> [T]he U.S. Marshals, FBI, state police, BIA police, and Wilson's goon squad consolidated their grip on Pine Ridge and patrolled the area between Rapid City and the reservation. Radio communications equipment was installed between Pine Ridge and the Hacienda Motel in Gordon, Nebraska where, according to the U.S. Marshal's Log, later released in court, a SOG standby unit was stationed. On February 20 the U.S. Marshals Service Director's Office in Washington, D.C. advised the Command Post that "50 additional [SOG] men will be departing for Rapid City as soon as possible." FBI Special Agent in Charge [Minneapolis], Joseph Trimbach, arrived that day to take charge of the FBI operations.[19]

Despite this display of federal force and support for Wilson's manifest illegalities, the traditionals, headed by Oglala elders Gladys Bissonette and Ellen Moves Camp, began streaming into Billy Mills Hall, site of the impeachment hearing. They were joined by members of the reservation-based Oglala Sioux Civil Rights Organization (OSCRO), led by Gladys Bissonette's son Pedro (actually her nephew; after being orphaned, Pedro referred to Gladys as his mother), and by 10 a.m.—the appointed time for the hearing to begin—hundreds of Wilson opponents had as-

ION leaders Gladys Bissonette and Ellen Moves Camp (left) during negotiations at Wounded Knee, 1973. Although neither was identified as "leadership" by the FBI, a distinction reserved for males by the Bureau, both were subjected to extensive harrassment over the subsequent three years. (Photo: *Akwesasne Notes*)

sembled. Still in control of his own impeachment process, Wilson blithely postponed matters until 2 p.m. The U.S. Marshal's Log reveals that at this time, "All SOG units [were] on station…[U.S. Deputy Marshal Reese] Kash advises [from inside Billy Mills Hall] approximately 300 spectators there now and that a quorum of the Council has arrived…Mr. Wilson is beginning to show the film Anarchy, U.S.A.," produced and directed by the John Birch Society.[20]

By 2 p.m., more than 600 anti-Wilsonites (from an "eligible voter pool" on Pine Ridge barely exceeding 3,000) were on the scene and, in quorum, the tribal council voted to proceed with impeachment. Hobart Keith, president of OSCRO, then moved from the floor that Wilson be "suspended for ten to twenty days" while a proper trial was organized. Citing an interest in "the smooth and uninterrupted functioning of tribal government," Wilson rejected this, scheduled his impeachment trial for the following day, and proceeded to select a tribal judge to hear his own case. On February 23, in a brief session boycotted by Severt Young Bear and fifteen other council members, Wilson was "exonerated" without council quorum. The U.S. Marshal's Log laconically reports that during the afternoon of this date the command post "[r]eceived information from BIA police source that Dick Wilson was voted back into office, 4-0 vote." The same evening, Wilson extended his ban on AIM activities to include "all public meetings and demonstrations" on the reservation.[21]

On the morning of the 24th, the traditionals and OSCRO openly defied Wilson's proscription on meetings. More than 200 people—including several tribal council members—assembled in Calico Hall, near the reservation village of Oglala, and announced they would continue meeting until "something [was] done" about Dickie Wilson.[22] The gathering was put under round-the-clock surveillance by the BIA police, marshals and FBI. The U.S. Marshal's Log for that date records: "Col. Simmons, Pentagon, called [in reference to Chief U.S. Marshal Wayne Colburn]…Mr. Colburn will arrive at Rapid City Regional Airport…on military U.S. twin engine propeller aircraft. Have Mr. Colburn confirm his arrival with Col. Simmons." A 7:45

a.m. entry in the Log, dated February 26, notes: "Col. Dunn would like [Colburn] to call him at the Pentagon, 202-695-0441, Ext. 215." Not only had the head U.S. marshal injected himself directly into the Pine Ridge scenario, but this was the first concrete evidence of direct (and constitutionally illegal) involvement of the U.S. Army and Air Force in what was officially considered to be the "domestic civil disturbance" unfolding there.

AIM had withdrawn to Rapid City after the Custer incident, announcing that it was launching a campaign to "straighten out" the pattern of civil and human rights abuses against Indians throughout the region. On February 26, the traditionals requested that Russell Means return to the reservation.[23] After conferring with the Calico Hall group, Means went on to Pine Ridge, where he attempted to meet directly with Wilson. The "meeting...ended when five of Wilson's supporters [GOONs] cornered the AIM leader in a parking lot and tried to beat him up. Means broke through the cordon and escaped."[24] On the same day, Justice Department Community Relations Service official John Terronez attempted to intervene by arranging a meeting between the traditionals and Marshal Kash. According to the U.S. Marshal's Log for the February 26, Kash instructed a subordinate, Bart Schmidt, to "inform Mr. Terronez that CP [Command Post] was unable to contact me." Kash also concealed the extent of the police/military buildup: "[S]hould Mr. Terronez of the Community Relations Service request to see any of our personnel he is to be escorted to the office adjacent to Mr. Lyman's office. He is not to be admitted to the command post."

The Siege of Wounded Knee

With these overtures to peaceful dialog rebuffed by federal representatives and with Wilson publicly declaring that he would "cut off Russell Means' braids if I catch him on this reservation again,"[25] the traditionals called for AIM to return in force. Ellen Moves Camp, a Calico Hall leader, recalls:

> We decided we needed the American Indian Movement in here because our men were scared, they hung back. It was mostly the women that went forward and spoke out...All of our older people from the reservation helped us make that decision...This is what we needed, a little more push. Most of the reservation believes in AIM, and we're proud to have them with us.[26]

In a meeting attended by both Means and Dennis Banks on February 27, Pedro Bissonette of OSCRO suggested a "symbolic confrontation" by going *en masse* to the 1890 massacre site at Wounded Knee, where they would conduct a press conference and release a prepared statement demanding Congressional hearings on the 1868 Fort Laramie Treaty and BIA abuses of its provisions (with special emphasis on the conduct of Wilson's regime). With the Nixon administration's recent responses to both the Congressional directive concerning transfer of title to Alcatraz and to the Twenty Points of The Trail of Broken Treaties in mind, Banks and Means recommended the statement include language making it absolutely clear that a

GOON roadblock established near Wounded Knee, March 1973. Chuck Richards, above with binoculars, was a member of Pine Ridge's "Manson Family," known for extreme brutality, and later part of an assassination plot against AIM leader Leonard Peltier, imprisoned in Lompoc (CA) Federal Penitentiary. (Photo: Kevin Barry McKiernan)

similar stonewall would not be acceptable again. Consequently, the text was revised to state: "The only two options open to the United States of America are: 1) They wipe out the old people, women, children, and men, by shooting and attacking us. 2) They negotiate our demands."[27] With that:

One by one, the Oglala Sioux Chiefs stood up, and their names will come before you...Names like Fools Crow and Crow Dog, names like Catches...Names like Kills Enemy, Iron Cloud...We'd reached a point in history where we could not tolerate that kind of abuse any longer, where these women, these parents, these mothers couldn't tolerate the mistreatment that goes on on the reservations any longer, they could not see another Indian youngster die. They could not see another Indian man meet his death, whether he was in Chicago or Nebraska, or Buffalo Gap.[28]

A fifty-four car caravan transported perhaps 200 people directly from the meeting to the tiny hamlet of Wounded Knee, arriving at approximately 7:30 p.m. They settled in for the night in a local church and the trading post of Clive and Agnes Gildersleeve (government chartered white traders who had long been accused of "ripping off" reservation Oglalas). Others went to work notifying press and television representatives of the press conference set for the next morning. By dawn, however, those inside Wounded Knee began to notice roadblocks being thrown by GOONs across all the access routes to the hamlet. These were rapidly reinforced by BIA police contingents and, later in the morning, by additional roadblocks manned by U.S. Marshal SOG personnel and FBI observers. Sealed in, the "occupiers" removed what guns and ammunition were in the trading post and set up defensive positions of their own.[29] As Ellen Moves Camp later put it:

We didn't know we were going to be crowded in there by a bunch of guns and stuff, military and FBIs and marshals and goons. We didn't talk about going in there and taking over Wounded Knee. That was the furthest thing from our minds. But what choice did the government give us?[30]

Agnes Lamont, an Oglala elder working at a school dormitory in Pine Ridge village, later testified that the SOG unit posted to Gordon was immediately moved up and billeted in her building, displacing students. "They had blue jump-suits on," she recalled, "and they had guns."[31] By 10 p.m., SAC Minneapolis Trimbach had assumed personal command of the FBI roadblock straddling the blacktop road running between Wounded Knee and Pine Ridge. When Community Relations specialist Terronez—who had gone into the hamlet in an attempt to mediate things with AIM—returned with the statement of demands intended for press conference distribution earlier in the day, Trimbach threatened to arrest him.[32] On the same date, the U.S. Marshal's log chronicles that Colburn had secured two armored personnel carriers (APC's, military assault vehicles) from the South Dakota National Guard, and instructions from Washington "not [to] let newspaper personnel in the Wounded Knee area...no TV coverage of the Wounded Knee area, authority Attorney General [Kleindienst]...No photos of [military] personnel." Finally:

On February 28, General Alexander Haig, then Vice-Chief of Staff at the Pentagon, dispatched Colonel Volney Warner of the 82nd Airborne and Colonel Jack Potter of the Sixth Army to Wounded Knee. For the first time in their careers they were ordered to wear civilian clothes while on duty. At 3:00 a.m. the following morning, they met with Colonel Vic Jackson from the California Civil Disorder Management School, FBI agent

In the first instance since the Civil War that the U.S. Army had been dispatched in a domestic operation, the Pentagon invaded Wounded Knee with 17 armored personnel carriers, 130,000 rounds of M-16 ammunition, 41,000 rounds of M-1 ammunition, 24,000 flares, 12 M-79 grenade launchers, 600 cases of C-S gas, 100 rounds of M-40 explosives, helicopters, Phantom jets, and personnel, all under the direction of General Alexander Haig. (Photo: *Akwesasne Notes*)

Joseph Trimbach, and Wayne Colburn of the Marshals Service at Ellsworth Air Force Base outside Rapid City. Following their meeting, they flew over Wounded Knee by helicopter; by March 3, Air Force F-4 Phantom jets were making daily passes over the besieged hamlet. Colonel Warner's daily reports to the Pentagon were passed along to Fred Buzhardt, counsel for the Secretary of Defense, to General Haig, and then to the White House. Attorney General Kleindienst issued a statement through the FBI that he wanted "all individuals prosecuted. There will be no amnesty or bonds set...Prosecute everyone for any crimes possible."[33]

As Rex Weyler notes, "Documents later subpoenaed from the Pentagon revealed that Colonel Potter directed the employment of 17 APCs [in addition to those provided by the South Dakota National Guard], 130,000 rounds of M-16 ammunition, 41,000 rounds of M-40 high explosive [for M-79 grenade launchers], as well as helicopters, Phantom jets, and personnel. Military officers, supply sergeants, maintenance technicians, chemical officers, and medical teams remained on duty throughout the seventy-one day siege, all working in civilian clothes. Three hundred miles to the south, at Fort Carson, Colorado the Army had billeted a fully uniformed and armed assault unit on twenty-four hour alert."[34] Thus, from the very onset, the government posture attending "the siege of Wounded Knee" was quite sufficient to render accurate the comment of a later observer that he was witnessing "the continuing Indian wars."[35]

Although the government did its best to conceal the unconstitutional involvement of the military in the siege, it still had to rationalize the massive federal police buildup for public consumption. Initially, this was accomplished through the proclamation that AIM was holding eleven hostages in the hamlet.[36] However, when South Dakota Senators James Abourezk and George McGovern arrived on March 2, to "negotiate the safe release of these people," they were informed by one of them—Father Paul Manhart of the local church—that they were *not* hostages, and preferred to remain with the AIM people inside Wounded Knee.[37] After an all-night meeting, three people—Clive and Agnes Gildersleeve among them—came out, while McGovern was forced to conclude at a press conference on March 3 that, "They [the 'hostages'] don't want to leave because they consider that to be their home."[38] Wilber A. Riegert, eighty-six years old and supposedly another of the hostages, put it even more explicitly:

> The fact is, we as a group of hostages decided to stay and save AIM and our own property. Had we not, those troops would have come down here and killed all of those people. The real hostages are the AIM people.[39]

In response to a Pentagon query as to whether FBI-requested weapons would be used to "shoot to kill," the Bureau responded, "Rifles are for that purpose."[40] AIM sent out a communique proposing disengagement and a "mutual withdrawal of forces" from the Wounded Knee area,[41] but Justice Department spokesman Ralph Erickson "declined to reply" to the AIM offer, despite the fact that exchanges of gunfire between opposing sides had become commonplace. At the same time, Erickson incongruously expressed great concern with the safety of the U.S. marshals and FBI personnel surrounding the hamlet.[42]

As it became clear that the government did not desire a peaceful resolution to the situation, supporters initiated the laborious process of supplying the besieged with food, medicines, weapons and ammunition. This was accomplished by automobile during intermittent periods when traffic was allowed in and out of the hamlet (*e.g.*, when federal "negotiators" were present), and by the much more dangerous expedient of backpacking the materiel cross-country, through federal lines and roving GOON squads at night when car traffic was prohibited. To curtail this latter method, the GOONs (and possibly federal personnel as well) resorted to setting grass fires around Wounded Knee, in an attempt to deprive the infiltrators of natural cover and exposing them to the glare of the hundreds of flares which illuminated the area from dusk to dawn. The entire spectacle began to resemble the bridge scene in *Apocalypse Now.*

AIM leaders Dennis Banks (left) and Russell Means burn a government offer during a Wounded Knee community meeting. The Federal suggestion that the group under siege within the hamlet surrender had just been unanimously rejected. (Photo: *Akwesasne Notes*)

Nonetheless, scores of people penetrated the blockade to reinforce the thin line of warriors serving in the AIM positions, or to act as cooks, medics, *etc.* AIM's hastily constructed bunkers were strengthened steadily with the addition of layers of earth, concrete blocks and timber.[43] On March 5, at a press conference convened in the Pine Ridge tribal offices, Dick Wilson announced that "the restraints are off [on the GOON squad] from this moment," that henceforth AIM members and supporters on the reservation would be considered "free game," and that "AIM will die at Wounded Knee."[44] From inside the hamlet, Russell Means responded sardonically (to a UPI reporter) that he could not "comment on the ravings of a drunken paranoid,"[45] but it was clear matters were approaching the point of explosion.

On March 6, the Justice Department's Ralph Erickson called upon AIM "to send the women and children out of Wounded Knee before darkness falls on March 8."[46] Only two people decided to avail themselves of this "opportunity to leave" and, on March 7, Reverend Ralph Abernathy, Martin Luther King's replacement as head of the Southern Christian Leadership Conference, ventured through the federal lines to express his organization's "solidarity with AIM's objectives" and to call upon the government to allow a "peaceful resolution to the crisis."[47] Abernathy was joined in his efforts by the Reverend John Adams of the United Methodist Church, a National Council of Churches on-site representative, who spent the day desperately and unsuccessfully attempting to arrange a cease-fire with Washington.[48] Meanwhile:

It was tense in Wounded Knee on March 8, as people awaited the nightfall deadline. Two Air Force Phantom jets flew low over the village. Inside Wounded Knee, a religious ceremony was held and warriors came forward to have their faces painted by medicine men, signifying their acceptance of the possibility of death. The marshal's logs note that, "a newsman leaving Wounded Knee advises that they [sic] observe a lot more weapons than before..." Carter Camp [a Ponca from Oklahoma who served as an AIM spokesperson at Wounded Knee] said, "We in no way think we can whip the United States government, but we have every intention of selling our lives as dearly as we can." Many of the Oglala residents of the village had taken up a petition accusing the U.S. forces of holding them prisoners in the village. Now they announced they were joining with the activists. Pedro Bissonette, speaking for the Oglalas announced, "One hundred and sixty-seven have volunteered to remain and fight with us..."[49]

During the evening, an AIM perimeter patrol headed by organizational security director Stan Holder was fired upon by a federal APC; two Oglalas were wounded, becoming the first AIM casualties of the siege.[50] Despite this flare-up, however, the night passed in relative tranquility. The first intense firefight occurred on March 9, as cease-fire negotiations were once again in process, when Federal personnel and GOONs poured thousands of rounds from automatic weapons and .30-06 sniper rifles into Wounded Knee. The AIM security groups responded with hunting rifles and their sole automatic weapon, a Chinese AK-47 assault rifle brought home by a returning Vietnam veteran (the FBI contended that the firefight was precipitated by AIM firing "an M-60 machinegun," a weapon later proven never to have existed in the "AIM arsenal").[51] Although this massive exchange resulted in no further casualties, a federal marshal threatened to kill Reverend Adams who was still attempting to mediate.[52]

On March 10, conscious that "the resistance of Wounded Knee had been front-page news for two weeks" and that the previous day's show of force had done nothing to dislodge AIM from its positions, the government tried a different tack.[53] Professing confidence that "the militants," who only "sought publicity"—and who were in any event "outside agitators"—would quickly leave if provided an opportunity to exit without immediate arrest, the Justice Department announced it was lifting its roadblocks and allowing free access in and out of the hamlet.[54] However:

The ploy backfired. When the siege was relaxed [on the morning of March 11], a few people left, but over a hundred poured into the village, with them Frank Fools Crow and other Oglala chiefs and headmen...in a ceremony led by Chief Fools Crow, the community declared itself sovereign, proclaiming an Independent Oglala Nation [ION], and assigning a delegation to the United Nations. One hundred and eighty-two Oglala-Lakota people became citizens of the Independent Oglala Nation; in addition, 160 Indians of other tribes in the United States and Canada became dual citizens of both their home nation and the Oglala Nation. Seven white supporters, members of Vietnam Veterans Against the War, were given naturalized citizenship status. The Independent Oglala Nation requested other Indian nations to send delegations to Wounded Knee, and they established working committees on housing, medical care, food supply, customs and immigration, internal security, information, and defense; daily spiritual ceremonies were [scheduled], as well as council meetings.[55]

Wilson's GOONs, breaking the conditions of the March ceasefire, impound food destined for Wounded Knee. (Photo: *Kevin Barry McKiernan*)

The federal presence on Pine Ridge from 1973-1976 was consistently marked by equipment and symbolism reminiscent of Vietnam, like this Armored Personnel Carrier (APC), camouflage uniforms and macabre cow's skull. (Photo: *Akwesasne Notes*)

Several times during the day, "according to his official reports, [SAC Joseph] Trimbach tried to drive into [Wounded Knee]. On his last attempt, he was told at the [AIM] checkpoint to '...immediately leave the area and that when any law enforcement officers were found at Wounded Knee they were to be arrested.'"[56] As it turned out, four U.S. Postal Inspectors recruited by Trimbach also attempted to enter Wounded Knee that day, but were detained by AIM security and then expelled (this was to have dire consequences for AIM spiritual leader Leonard Crow Dog; see Chapter 12).[57] Infuriated at being treated in a manner he was used to imposing on others, Trimbach reacted viciously. After consulting with Bureau COINTELPRO specialist Richard G. Held (soon to coordinate the Hampton-Clark murder coverup in Chicago; see Chapter 3), imported to tender just such advice, Trimbach violated the cease-fire by redeploying his agents along the federal siege line.[58] This gambit to reignite hostilities quickly bore fruit as agent Curtis Fitzpatrick—having spotted an AIM vehicle he believed to be "either overdue at a rental agency or stolen" (it was, in fact, neither)—opened fire. Fitzpatrick was rewarded for his rashness by becoming the first federal casualty at Wounded Knee.[59] As is noted elsewhere,

> The feds made what Ed Sullivan would call "a really big show" out of Fitzpatrick's misfortune. He was flown by helicopter to Ellsworth Air Force Base at Rapid City with an enormous bandage swathed around his head and face. Oddly enough, he had been shot in the wrist.[60]

This tidy bit of widely-publicized distortion was quite sufficient to establish "a pretext for renewing hostilities and punishing AIM and the Oglala militants."[61] Held seems to have been particularly pleased with FBI performance in the destruction of the truce, given his authorship of a six-page document upon completion of a ninety-day stint as an "observer-consultant" at Wounded Knee. Circulated by Bureau headquarters on April 24, 1974, Held's "The Use of Special Agents in a Paramilitary Law Enforcement Operation in Indian Country" protested the Attorney General's "restraint" in not issuing blanket shoot-to-kill orders, criticized other federal law enforcement agencies for not being "tough enough" in the beginning as well as failing "to submit to FBI authority" during the early part of the siege (a matter "partially corrected" by the events of March 11) and positing that "the FBI will insist on taking charge at the outset" for all future "Indian uprisings."[62] Given that the BIA police and, by implication, the GOONs (see next chapter) had been under FBI control all along, Held's thesis can only be construed as suggesting that both U.S. Marshal's Service and military personnel came under increasingly direct FBI control after March 11.[63]

Beginning on March 12, the intensity of federal fire poured into Wounded Knee increased substantially, including considerable quantities of .50 calibre armor-piercing heavy machinegun ammunition capable of penetrating all but the strongest AIM defenses. On March 13, Chief U.S. Marshal Wayne Colburn, not to be outdone

Chief U.S. Marshal Wayne Colburn (left) with head federal negotiator Harlington Wood inside Wounded Knee, March 1973.
(Photo: *Akwesasne Notes*)

Oglala Sioux Tribal Council member Severt Young Bear (center) with Verona (left) and Leonard Crow Dog at Wounded Knee in April 1973. (Photo: *Akwesasne Notes*)

by his FBI counterparts, went on record that his force of some 300 men had "lost patience" with AIM and that he was "having difficulty holding them back." He went on to state, "I'm certainly going to change [AIM's] lifestyle. If this means starving, if it means being cold…that's what's going to be done."[64] A few days later, AIM security director Stan Holder observed,

> We've been receiving automatic weapons fire—M-60, its a 7.62 NATO round; M-16, the weapon used in Vietnam by the United States Armed Forces; .30 calibres, which are either mounted or built into armored personnel carriers. Then the .30-06, a normal hunting [and sniping] rifle that the white ranchers and vigilantes use—who the government says aren't there. Also shotguns used by the BIA police, and .38s, .44 magnums, things of this nature—weapons you'd find in any sporting goods store, and your military weapons used by the Federal Marshals [and FBI]. They've also been using gas, which they say they haven't been using.[65]

Later, Roger Iron Cloud, an Oglala Vietnam combat veteran, commented: "We took more bullets in seventy-one days than I took in two years in Vietnam."[66]

On March 13, Assistant Attorney General Harlington Wood arrived on the scene due to the mediation efforts of Reverend John Adams. Accompanied by Wayne Colburn, Wood entered Wounded Knee under escort and, for the next two days, met with Russell Means, Dennis Banks, and an Oglala attorney based in Rapid City, Ramon Roubideaux, among others:

> Independent Oglala Nation spokespeople demanded that Washington suspend the tribal government and hold a referendum for a new form of government. Wounded Knee supporters had collected 1400 signatures in favor of such a referendum since the siege began, almost as many as voted for Wilson in the previous election. However, the federal officials wanted only to discuss law enforcement and disarmament [of AIM].[67]

The talks stalemated. Wood declared, "There will be no movement on the part of U.S. forces to take control of Wounded Knee while negotiations are in process."[68] He then departed for Washington to confer with his superiors, promising to return "in a few days." The same evening, March 14, Senator George McGovern said, "Every reasonable effort at negotiation failed—every concession made by the government has been met by yet another AIM demand. They are seeking violence. The law must be enforced. There is no other way in a society such as ours."[69] This must have been music to Dick Wilson's ears, as he had been beside himself throughout the negotiations, observing [accurately enough] that for the federal government to deal seriously with AIM or the ION meant the undermining of his own position. During negotiations and in apparently direct collusion with the FBI, Wilson ordered the arrest and jailing of several opposition tribal council members, including Severt Young Bear.[70] With these men safely behind bars,

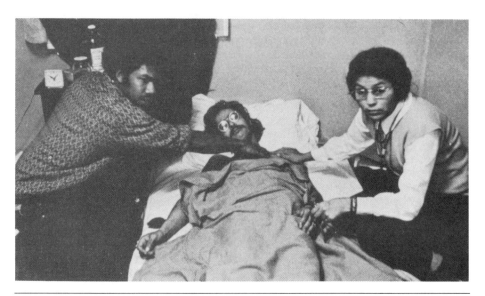

AIM medic Rocky Madrid, wounded by a federal sniper inside Wounded Knee, 1973. (Photo: *Akwesasne Notes*)

An FBI sniper engaged in the activity which resulted in the gunshot deaths of AIM members Buddy Lamont and Frank Clearwater at Wounded Knee, 1973. (Photo: *Akwesasne Notes*)

Wilson's rump council, shorn of six of its eight district chairmen, enacted several resolutions. The first asked the BIA police to remove all nontribesmen from the reservation. This meant that [not only would non-Oglala AIM members have to go, but] the churchmen trying to resolve the situation peacefully...Wilson characterized the National Council of Churches as "dope pushers"...The second resolution held AIM responsible for all acts of violence.[71]

It was clear that Wilson wanted no repeat of Wood's visit to Wounded Knee, and that the FBI concurred.

On March 17, Wood returned with what he termed "the government's best offer," an insulting proposal that:

Russell Means, Dennis Banks, Pedro Bissonette, Clyde Bellecourt, and Carter Camp [would] meet with Marvin Franklin and William Rogers of the Interior Department [to discuss "Indian issues"] in Sioux Falls [S.D.], for three to five hours. Before and after the session, a one-hour press conference would be held at the end of which the [AIM and] ION negotiators would be arrested. Simultaneous with the beginning of the talks, the occupants of Wounded Knee were to stack arms, walk out, and submit to arrest.[72]

With a smile, Wood requested that the group "think about it" overnight and then left. At about 9 p.m., perhaps to provide "incentive" to their deliberations, about 300 rounds of mixed tracer ammunition were fired at an AIM bunker. *Los Angeles Free Press* reporter Ron Ridenour, who was inside Wounded Knee at the time, recounted what happened next:

I stayed in the street and watched the battle. A Chicano medic, Rocky Madrid, was escorted to the front lines by a platoon [sic] of four men to see if anyone was wounded. Minutes later, he was returned on a stretcher with a bullet wound in his abdomen, the only casualty of that battle...Harlington Wood's broad smile of six hours ago lingered in my mind. I could see it growing broader as he probably watched it from afar.[73]

Despite such federal "coaxing," Wood's proposal was categorically rejected on March 15, with Carter Camp tabling an ION counter-proposal that a special Presidential emissary be sent to "deal with our sovereignty and our separate governments' relationship under our treaty."[74] On March 17, AIM medic Lorelei DeCora (a Minneconjou known as Lorelei Means after her marriage to Ted Means in 1973), in charge of the ION clinic at Wounded Knee, told a reporter:

We've had three guys shot; two were Oglala Sioux. One was shot in the leg with an M-16. The other was shot in the hand, but the bullet passed right through. And just a couple of nights ago, a Chicano medic who was here to support us, when they started to fire, he ran out with his medic's band, and he got hit in the stomach with an M-16 too. They're all okay. The medicine men took the bullets out.[75]

AIM's belief in and willingness to sacrifice for traditional Indian ways was now measuring up to the test of reality.

During the week following rejection of the Wood proposal, the federal perimeter was tightened, in some cases virtually to the edge of AIM's defenses. The nightly firefights were extended from their earlier duration of a few minutes to the point where they often lasted for hours. Use of Pentagon-provided "starlight" scopes for night-time sniping—used to wound medic Rocky Madrid—became prevalent, as did utilization of heavy calibre tracer ammunition which started fires in several buildings. On March 21, in an effort to curtail the media attention being paid to Wounded Knee, the Justice Department ordered the press out of the area by 4:30 p.m. daily, and initiated severe restrictions on the granting of daily press passes; on March 23, it was announced that alternative press personnel—such as Tom Cook of *Akwesasne Notes*, Mike Falk of *Liberation* magazine, Mike Schuster of Liberation News Service, and freelancer Betsy Dudley—who had chosen to report from inside Wounded Knee, faced arrest by the FBI whenever the siege ended.[76]

On another front, a nationwide effort was undertaken to cut off tangible outside support for AIM/ION, beginning on about March 20. Individuals and organizations thought to be sympathetic to the occupants of Wounded Knee were monitored around the country and, when they showed signs of mustering concrete support, they were intercepted and arrested on "routine warrant checks" and other specious charges. As Scott Burgwin, an AIM supporter arrested with four colleagues in Oregon recounts:

> We picked up food and clothing in Eugene at about 10 p.m. [and] continued that night toward Bend, Oregon. The truck broke down. We started out again at about 1:30 p.m. on Saturday, March 24. As we were leaving Bend, at about 4 p.m., about 10 or 15 FBI Agents, state troopers, and local police officers, including a matron, caused us to stop. We were ordered out of the truck by the FBI Agents who proceeded to have all five of us searched and handcuffed. The two women were together and the women were taken in separate police vehicles. Two agents questioned me in the police car...They told me it was against the law to do what I was doing. I was booked and fingerprinted. Bail was set at $16,000 for each of us...[We were told] we were charged with intent to aid and abet a riot by using interstate commerce (highways)...[77]

By March 26, there were virtually no mainstream media representatives present at Wounded Knee and all traffic to and from the hamlet had been suspended. Consequently,

> ...news coverage of the occupation [sic] came mainly from the government press conferences outside Wounded Knee, insuring officials a measure of press control. Thus when food and medicine were airlifted to Wounded Knee, the Justice Department announced that "guns and ammunition have been dropped to the militants." When police arrested "19 college-age males" for possession of "contraband" destined for Wounded Knee they did not mention that the contraband was food...This management of the news [also] meant the government no longer had to submit to open scrutiny of its actions. No reporters were on hand to record the heavy firefights or the fact that unarmed stretcher-bearers were fired upon as they carried injured Indians from the earthen bunkers to the village field hospital.[78]

On March 23, the last external delegations—those of black activist Angela Davis and a fourteen-person group from the Iroquois Six-Nations Confederacy headed by Onondaga Chief Oren Lyons—departed Wounded Knee.[79] As the last television crew (NBC) pulled out on the morning of March 26, the GOONs began setting up a "tribal road block"—actually a firing position—very close to AIM lines. Within two hours, the GOONs joined their federal cohorts in directing what was, to date, the most concentrated barrage of small-arms fire at the AIM defenses. Ken Tilsen, a Minneapolis attorney inside Wounded Knee, later observed, "We estimated we took 20,000 [rounds]" in about twenty-four hours.[80] Although AIM's return fire was sparse—"maybe 250 shots, we were really low on ammo at that point," Dennis Banks recalls[81]—it may have caused the first (and only) serious federal casualty of the siege: U.S. marshal Lloyd Grimm was struck in the torso by a .30 calibre slug from a deer rifle as he stood to fire his M-16 at an AIM bunker. More likely, Grimm was struck by a stray bullet from the rifle of a GOON positioned behind him.[82]

Tilsen, expressing concern that there was to be "a second massacre at Wounded Knee,"[83] slipped through federal lines, returned home, and began organizing the Wounded Knee Legal Defense/Offense Committee (WKLDOC, pronounced "wickle-doc"). WKLDOC was initially composed of attorneys Tilsen, Ramon Roubideaux, Beverly Axelrod (previously lawyer for Eldridge Cleaver), Mark Lane and Fran Olsen; it was to grow rapidly into a legal and investigative combine involving scores of people and provided the basis for AIM's judicial campaign over the next several years.[84] In any event, Tilsen's voice was added to others, such as those of Rosebud Tribal President Robert Burnette and the Reverend John Adams, who were desperately trying to secure a mediated settlement to the fighting at Wounded Knee, a matter which would have to occur on terms other than what Russell Means described as an offer "to fly us to jail."[85]

As federal/GOON pressure continued, Means and Banks decided to hike through the siege-line on the night of Sunday, April 1. They went directly to Crow Dog's Paradise, some eighty miles due east of Wounded Knee, which was being used as a basing area for the foot transportation of supplies to the ION (and from which a "security force" planned to depart for the battle zone in the event that an all-out federal assault should occur there).[86] Supplies of all sorts had become a serious concern for everyone inside Wounded Knee and the two AIM leaders wished to confer directly with logistics coordinators in an effort to increase the inflow of food.[87] The FBI, having managed to successfully insinuate informants into the besieged hamlet,[88] became aware of the Banks/Means trip almost immediately and just as quickly attempted to use it in a propaganda effort designed to undermine AIM's support nationally:

Talking to the press which had been denied access to the village, Solicitor General of the Department of the Interior Kent Frizzell told them that a faction of Oglalas inside the village wanted to surrender, and had used the absence of Banks and Means to "get the drop on" the more militant ones, but that following their return, Banks and Means reasserted "complete control."[89]

Angela Davis confers with Iroquois delegation headed by Onondaga chief Oren Lyons (center) while visiting Wounded Knee. (Photo: *Akwesasne Notes*)

WKLDOC lawyers (from left to right) Fran Olsen, Ramon Robideau, Mark Lane, Ken Tilsen and Beverly Axelrod. (Photo: *Akwesasne Notes*)

As a result of this false statement, the Associated Press released the following story on its national wire service on April 2:

> Pine Ridge, South Dakota—Now there's talk of mutiny among the militant Indians holding Wounded Knee in South Dakota. A government spokesman says an inform- ant inside the besieged hamlet reports there was a falling out between leaders of the American Indian Movement and leaders of the Oglala Sioux...A conflict that reached the point of armed confrontation. The spokesman says the militant group headed by Russell Means and Dennis Banks is still in control, but that about 100 Indians may decide to leave Wounded Knee.

The same evening, Means and Banks walked back into Wounded Knee, con- vened a general meeting, and videotaped a "solidarity conference" between them- selves and Pedro Bissonette (elected by the Oglala traditionals to represent the ION for this purpose). The tape made absolutely clear—as had the ceremony convened by Chief Fools Crow on March 11—that there was no split; to the contrary, all par- ties attributed the media story to "government fabrication." The following day, April 3, Ted Means played the tape in Rapid City at a press assembly covering the negotia- tions which Frizzell had been flown in from Washington to conduct, thus partially neutralizing the government media hoax. The "correction," however, failed to gain anything approaching the exposure enjoyed by the federal distortion, a matter which left a completely inaccurate perception of the situation at Wounded Knee among a broad segment of the public.[90]

With it finally clear that divide and conquer tactics were not going to work, Frizzell agreed to go to Wounded Knee to attempt serious negotiations toward resolution. The opening exchange on April 3 exposed the Solicitor General to the frustration felt by traditional Oglalas as a result of federal policies, both past and— more particularly—present:

Gladys Bissonette: [If there is to be a settlement here,] I would suggest that they remove Wilson at the same time, because we're not safe with him around.

Kent Frizzell: What I assume and consent to is a sufficient number of marshals and FBI people would remain on the Pine Ridge Reservation, and there will be no Wilson men, as such, with any authority, other than the BIA police.

Ellen Moves Camp: The BIA police is with him.

Frizzell: Well, of course, if the FBI and the marshals are here, the BIA police would be very reluctant to take any advantage because they are subjecting themselves to a civil rights complaint.

Moves Camp: They didn't do it before we came in here.

Frizzell: Well, we didn't have any FBI and marshals on board.

Federal negotiators Kent Frizzell (left) and Richard Hellstern smoking the Lakota Sacred Pipe to consummate the April agreement for a ceasefire at Wounded Knee. The pact was immediately violated by both federal forces and GOONs. (Photo: Kevin Barry McKiernan)

Wounded Knee negotiating team composed of (from left) AIM leader Russell Means, spiritual leader Wallace Black Elk, and ION leader Pedro Bissonette in early April 1973. (Photo: Kevin Barry McKiernan)

Moves Camp: There were U.S. Marshals in here since February 14, two weeks before we came in [to Wounded Knee].

Carter Camp: They put sandbags on top of the BIA office in Pine Ridge.

Bissonette: And that tribal office, upstairs—and I know you know as well as I do—is loaded with ammunition. I seen 'em loading it in. There's ammunition, boxes and boxes.

Frizzell: Well, of course the BIA is going to be under the close eye of the Department of Interior if an agreement is reached—and the Department of Justice and the marshals and the FBI.

Moves Camp: They've been there all this time—since two weeks before we came here, and the Justice Department was there!

Frizzell: Well then, what would you suggest as an alternative?

Bissonette: Throw them all in jail.

Moves Camp: Throw them all out.

Frizzell: We have no authority to do that.

Bissonette: You can take your guns back that you gave to the BIA and the goons.[91]

During that evening—in an apparent attempt to recreate the collapse of the earlier Harlington Wood ceasefire and discussions—the federal police began moving their armored personnel carriers (APCs) toward AIM bunkers, provoking a major firefight. The following day Frizzell, confronted by an enraged Carter Camp, agreed that the movement of the APCs had been "inexcusable," given that negotiations were in process. He then had to respond to the full range of FBI and marshal abuses from the AIM perspective:

Carter Camp: Yesterday you asked us if there was going to be any problem with us when it comes to this agreement. There will—if this type of thing keeps coming up. They're now using their flares as an offensive weapon to burn our houses and our fields. I have seen them shoot ten or fifteen times at the same target. We know you guys are committing offensive actions. It's only by great restraint that our warriors haven't gone out—cause you know we have the military capability of taking out these roadblocks. But we haven't made the aggressive actions that you have…You guys ask us to believe that the North Vietnamese are violating their treaty agreements over there, and they're violating the cease-fire. Right now we can see that's a bullshit lie because you guys can't even keep your treaty agreements or your cease-fire here…You shoot each other and blame the Indians. You report incoming tracers on the radio—our people don't *have* tracer bullets. You say we fire out of a church where we *know* we don't have any weapons. And that's the kind of excuse you're using for returning fire and putting "suppressing fire" on our bunkers and streets. This is a constant and everyday thing.[92]

In spite of the strength of this verbal battering (or perhaps because of it), an agreement was finally reached on April 6 which was acceptable to both AIM and ION (with the exception of Dennis Banks, who abstained from signing), as well as the U.S. government. In substance, the document provided that:

• Russell Means would submit to arrest and go to Washington, D.C., for meetings with White House representatives. A disarmament program would start as soon as Means called to report that talks were going on. There would be a thirty-to-sixty day delay in the arrests of those who would be indicted by a federal grand jury.

• A federal investigation of Indian affairs on Pine Ridge and an audit of tribal books would take place.

• The Justice Department would consider and, where appropriate, protect the legal rights of individual Oglala Sioux Indians by bringing civil suits against unlawful acts by the tribal council and the federal government.

• A presidential treaty commission would re-examine the Treaty of 1868.

• A meeting would be held in Washington in May between Indian leaders and White House representatives to discuss Indian affairs.[93]

"I pray to my Father in Heaven, as you do to your Great Spirit, that the agreement we are about to sign is not full of empty words, and the promises will be fulfilled," said Solicitor General of the Department of Interior Kent Frizzell as he smoked the Sacred Pipe of the Lakotas with AIM and ION leaders to consecrate the event.[94] Then, with a smile, he was off.

Shortly thereafter, Chief U.S. Marshal Wayne Colburn radioed that he planned to "move into Wounded Knee at 7 o'clock the next morning with a force of 180 marshals for a sweep of the village" intended to disarm the defenders, "in line with the agreement."[95] Angered, but not panicked by this proposition—which they had *not* agreed to—those inside replied that they'd understood disarmament to be a mutual provision, by which federal forces would withdraw beyond rifle shot as AIM gave up its arms, and informed Colburn that "under no circumstances" was he to attempt to enter Wounded Knee; they also demanded Frizzell's return to explain this latest "problem."[96] With that, Russell Means—duly arrested—sallied forth to Washington, as agreed; he traveled in the company of AIM spiritual leader, Leonard Crow Dog. Once there, they discovered that "the White House claimed that the surrender of weapons was a *preliminary* necessity before the talks began. Means refused to ask the defenders to give up, and the White House refused to talk until they did."[97] As he left the White House grounds, Means informed press people waiting for word of his discussions with presidential advisors that they could: "Tell them [the public] that the Indians' last treaty with the government lasted all of 72 hours. The government broke it before the ink was dry."[98]

For the next week, an uneasy stalemate existed at Wounded Knee, with the "cease-fire...broken only by occasional fire into the village by over-eager FBI agents and angry Wilson supporters."[99] By April 16, however, the government's absolute quarantine of the area was beginning to have the desired effect: most people inside the beleaguered hamlet were reduced to one meal per day, and the nightly back-packing forays were proving insufficient to reverse the dwindling of supplies. The situation had become critical.

Then, on April 17, the government attacked again in full force. At dawn Wounded Knee's night shift roving-patrol spotted three small planes coming in low over the hills, and woke up friends to greet a long awaited airdrop. The planes dropped ten parachutes and flew off. The FBI helicopter "Snoopy" opened fire on some of the families from the housing project [inside the AIM/ION perimeter] who began to gather up the bundles which had dropped near their homes. Wounded Knee warriors fired back to drive the helicopter out of range, and the firefight raged until four in the afternoon. The press at this point had access only to the government press conferences in Pine Ridge and reported the government's story that their helicopter had been fired upon without provocation and that they had refrained from firing for two hours after that.[100]

Dennis Banks recalls,

[T]he marshals ran down the hills from their bunkers. They were running toward the food drop, too. You could see them running down the hill with their guns aimed up toward them planes. But those little planes just pulled out and went away...Then one of them come back and dropped more food. The federal marshals kept running down that hill aiming their guns at that one plane. Why some of those marshals were almost down to our bunkers and some of our boys shot warning shots over them 'cause they were trying to get that food away from us. That made 'em go back, but then them crazy marshals started firing machine guns at some of the bags of food, trying to destroy them before we could bring 'em in."[101]

In the firefight which followed, a "federal spokesman quietly admitted...U.S. forces...fired at least 4,000 rounds," much of it .50 calibre armor-piercing directed at the church.[102]

Inside were:

Frank Clearwater [47] and his wife Morning Star, 37...three-months pregnant, [who] had hiked into Wounded Knee only the night before. Frank was part Apache. Morning Star was Cherokee. They were not members of the American Indian Movement, but had driven to Wounded Knee from their home in North Carolina wanting to help in whatever way they could. Some time after the airdrop, Frank went to sleep in the Catholic Church up on the hill. When the fire started up [again], he bolted up just as a federal bullet came through the wall and tore off the back of his head.[103]

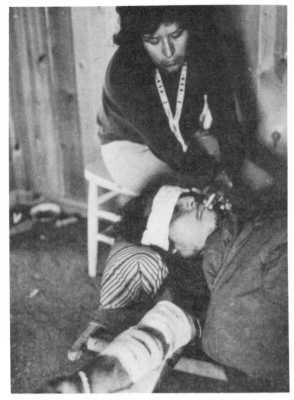

Frank Clearwater, struck in the head by a federal bullet on April 16, 1973, lies dying in the Wounded Knee Clinic. Joseph Trimbach, FBI SAC, Minneapolis, deliberately delayed Clearwater's receipt of medical aid. After the victim's death, the Bureau launched a campaign to defame his character. (Photo: Kevin Barry McKiernan)

Five other AIM members were wounded in the firefight, but the bullets "were removed by medicine men or physicians working in the Wounded Knee clinic. Although some of the injuries were serious, none of the five persons suffered permanent damage. But there was nothing that could be done for Frank Clearwater."[104] With this realization, Stan Holder radioed the federal command post that an urgent "med-evac" was needed to save Clearwater's life; "at 9:26 a.m., 'hdqts 2,' the FBI commander [Joseph Trimbach] ordered that 'no copter is to go to WK; if they have wounded, bring them out under white flag to RB-1, and they will fly them from there.' For some reason, it was not until 9:45 a.m. that this order was relayed to the Indians at Wounded Knee…Before Frank Clearwater was driven to Roadblock #1, Morning Star requested government permission to accompany her husband to the hospital. A safe conduct pass was granted. Once outside Wounded Knee, she was arrested by the FBI. They dragged her away from Frank and threw her in the overcrowded Bureau of Indian Affairs jail in Pine Ridge."[105]

Clearwater died on April 25, without ever regaining consciousness. A medic who had helped carry him from the church where he was shot to the clinic recalled how, "We were shot at all the way up the hill and all the way into the [clinic]. He had a bad injury in the back of his head, and he was taken out under two white flags, held very high, and we were shot at all the way into the clinic area."[106] Wallace Black Elk, an Oglala who, along with Leonard Crow Dog, served a medicine man in the clinic, recounted: "Part of Clearwater's neck was torn, but I didn't know if it went in his skull. I see the flesh is torn off, and he was bleeding profusely, and going into convulsions. Three other people were brought in. The second man brought in, he was shot four times...This other man, in the right arm, there were three wounds...This is the worst I've ever seen people get shot."[107] There can be little doubt that the federal use of super-lethal ammunition and the FBI's delay of medical evacuation caused Frank Clearwater's death.

Meanwhile, after a frenzy of investigation, the FBI had tracked the airlift pilots to their homes in the northeast. They were charged with interfering with federal officers in the lawful performance of their duties, conspiracy to commit offenses against the United States, and interstate travel with the intent to aid, abet, promote, encourage and participate in a riot (each count carried a possible five-year prison term and $10,000 fine; charges were later dropped).[108] Elsewhere, Russell Means—whose $25,000 bond had prevented return to Wounded Knee after collapse of the White House talks—had next sought a hearing with the House Indian Affairs Subcommittee on Wounded Knee and the Trail of Broken Treaties. About all he obtained for this effort was the abuse of the Subcommittee chair, Representative James Haley of Florida, who informed him that "you and your bunch of hoodlums belong in a federal penitentiary."[109] Means embarked on a fundraising tour which ended in Los Angeles on the day of Clearwater's death; obviously livid, he announced at a rally that he was returning to Pine Ridge to "bury Frank Clearwater's body" and, if the government tried to stop him, "they can expect a fight." With that, the FBI moved in and, after a rather wild chase amid the tangle of LA's freeways, captured him.[110] The same evening, the Bureau's Rapid City office released a false report to the press concerning Clearwater's identity; it "said he was white, not Indian, thus making him an 'outside agitator' and his death somehow not as blameworthy."[111] For his part, Dick Wilson blocked burial of Clearwater anywhere on Pine Ridge on the basis that he was "not Oglala." (Many whites and non-Oglala Indians such as Clearwater are buried on Pine Ridge; the corpse was ultimately interred in traditional style at Crow Dog's Paradise on Rosebud.)[112]

A nervous truce once again settled over the combatants as the government engaged in "damage control" public relations. Consequently, on April 20, two of Wilson's GOONs—John Hussman and Emile "Woody" Richards—stated to the press that they were "fed up," and "if the government does not move the 'militants' out of Wounded Knee by May 4, we will begin to lead commando-type raids"; Wilson affirmed that he would back them up "100%—with whatever is necessary."[113] The GOONs then set up another firing position, which they dubbed the "residents' roadblock." U.S. Chief Marshal Wayne Colburn, finally realizing that the GOONs were beyond his control, belatedly began attempting to constrain them. On April 23, GOONs at the "residents' roadblock" detained a Justice Department Community Relations Service representative. When marshals attempted to interfere, "the [GOONs] pointed their weapons at Wayne Colburn...and a shoot-out appeared im-

Dick Wilson (center) at the "Residents' Roadblock" on April 24, 1973. Chief U.S. Marshal Wayne Colburn Ordered his men to disperse the GOONs, but FBI COINTELPRO specialist Richard G. Held arrived with countermanding orders. (Photo: Kevin Barry McKiernan)

minent." Deputy Assistant Attorney General Hellstern later noted, "The discussion became so belligerent that we decided that this problem could no longer be allowed." The FBI logs for that date indicate: "[At] 6:21 p.m., USM Colburn...arrested 11 Indians on the Indian Roadblock for obstructing a Federal officer."[114]

"I'm fed up with the Department of Injustice..." Dick Wilson responded. Later "that same night, after Colburn had taken the roadblock down, more of Wilson's people put it up again. The FBI, still supporting the vigilantes, had supplied them with automatic weapons..."[115]

This event seems to have brought to a head the growing discord between the FBI and the Marshals Service concerning whose "policy" was to be followed and which agency was ultimately subordinate to the other's "command and control" at Wounded Knee. Recognizing the fact that the GOONs had become a menace to all concerned and that Pine Ridge BIA police chief Delmar Eastman was simultaneously serving as a GOON leader (as was his second in command, Duane Brewer),[116] Colburn attempted to get around the problem by "working closely with BIA units from other reservations assigned to Pine Ridge."[117] The FBI seems to have thrown its full support behind Wilson's GOONs. The GOONs' improvised weaponry was replaced by fully-automatic assault rifles and ammunition; they also began sporting government communications gear and seemed to be in possession of federal intelligence information. For example, on the night of April 23, the communications center in Wounded Knee monitored the following radio exchange between two GOON units:

Tribal Government Roadblock to Tribal Roving Patrol: How many M-16s you guys got? Where are the other guys?

Tribal Patrol to Tribal Roadblock: We got eight M-16s and some men coming up on horseback. Got a van too.[118]

Immediately thereafter, the roving patrol captured a group of "hippies" who were apparently attempting to backpack supplies in "from Crow Dog's camp," and then fought off a BIA police patrol (from another reservation) which tried to come and take custody of the prisoners. The tribal roadblock insisted that there was no GOON patrol in the area. None of those captured was ever seen again, a matter which gave rise to the suspicion on the part of many AIM people and others that they'd been summarily executed and buried in unmarked graves somewhere on the lonely reservation prairie.[119] Additionally:

Once again during the night the marshals removed the Tribal Roadblock...But the next day Richard Wilson led a group of supporters back to the site where they encountered the marshals again. The Marshal's logs report, "10:15...instructions from [Assistant Attorney General] Hellstern is that gas may be used to prevent the establishment of any new non-Federal positions." As Wilson and Colburn confronted each other, FBI [operations consultant] Richard [G.] Held arrived by helicopter to inform the marshals that word had come from a high Washington source to let the roadblock stand...As a result, the marshals were forced to allow several of Wilson's people to be stationed at the roadblock, and to participate in...patrols around the village.[120]

Obviously, the FBI was ascendant in its contest with the Marshals Service. In retrospect, it seems probable that the Bureau engaged in the peculiar behavior of supporting the GOONs against other federal law enforcement officers, not because it had any more desire than the marshals to launch a frontal assault on the AIM perimeter as demanded by the Wilsonites, but because it wished to create another situation. The large force of marshals (and their "imported" BIA police allies) were to be placed in the position of requesting to leave Pine Ridge—to get out of the crossfire, if nothing else—at about the same time that a negotiated settlement brought AIM and the ION out of their entrenchment in Wounded Knee. In this sense, *any* settlement would do from the Bureau's perspective, because it would never have to be honored; the objective was to establish a situation where the FBI and its Pine Ridge BIA police/GOON surrogate could deal with the dissidents piecemeal, at their leisure, in a virtual vacuum of scrutiny by other law enforcement agencies, and ac-

AIM medic, shot by a federal sniper while attempting to reach Buddy Lamont, is evacuated from Wounded Knee late in the afternoon of April 27, 1973. (Photo: Kevin Barry McKiernan)

AIM member Buddy Lamont (center) at Wounded Knee. On April 27, 1973, Lamont was driven from a bunker by tear gas and then severely wounded by a federal sniper. For the next several hours, snipers prevented medics from reaching him, resulting in his bleeding to death. Lamont is buried next to the mass grave of Big Foot's band, slaughtered in 1890. (Photo: *Akwesasne Notes*)

cording to the Bureau's own special rules for "counterintelligence operations" (in this case, a form of outright counterinsurgency warfare).

As a result, by late March AIM and the marshals had at times become perverse colleagues, occasionally cooperating in attempts to come to grips with the GOONs, who were by then firing regularly at both groups. For instance, on the evening of April 26, Red Arrow (the code name of the marshals' main communications bunker) was frantically collaborating with AIM security in an effort to locate the source of automatic weapons fire raking the positions of both sides:

...the rifle fire increased and confusion arose as to who was firing at whom. The marshals reported unexplained fire coming from the DMZ [the buffer zone between federal and AIM lines] which was hitting both the Wounded Knee bunkers and the government APCs. The government Red Arrow command post reached Wounded Knee security by radio saying that they had honored an agreed upon cease-fire, but that their Roadblock-6 was "still receiving fire." Wounded Knee security answered that they were "taking almost continuous automatic weapon fire" from a hill near Roadblock-6. Red Arrow answered, "Ten-four. A couple of our RBs [roadblocks] have reported firing and they don't know who is over in those positions. They report that it is being fired *into* Wounded Knee."

WOUNDED KNEE: "Roger. You think you're pretty sure we got a third party out there firing on us with automatic weapons?"

RED ARROW: "That's what it sounds like."

The [GOONs] were in the hills with government-issue automatic weapons, M-16s, firing on both government and Indian positions. The government troops poured fire into Wounded Knee that night. Wounded Knee security estimated that they took 20,000 rounds from vigilantes and marshals in twelve hours.[121]

At dawn, the marshals, unnerved and frustrated by the experience of taking fire from two sides, began pumping tear gas rounds from M-79 grenade launchers into the AIM bunkers. At about 8:30 a.m. a pair of security people were forced out of the Last Stand bunker by the gas, and one of them, Buddy Lamont, was hit by a burst of fire from an M-16. As Lamont lay bleeding, the marshals laid down a heavy suppressing fire, preventing AIM medics from reaching him for nearly three hours. By this time Lamont had bled to death.[122] As he was an enrolled Oglala, well known on Pine Ridge, the FBI was unable to mount a campaign to "discredit" his ethnicity, and Dickie Wilson was unable to block his being buried next to the mass grave of the 1890 Lakota victims of another federal assault at Wounded Knee.[123]

As the smoke cleared, another horror story emerged. At about the same time that Buddy Lamont was fatally wounded, another warrior—driven from the Little Big Horn bunker by tear gas—had been shot through both legs by a sniper's .30-06 bullet. A SOG team positioned in the DMZ to coordinate the marshals' barrage then "continued to direct fire on Little Big Horn"[124] and when a female AIM medic clearly marked with a red-cross armband tried to reach the wounded man, "the marshals at RB-4 opened up on her so that she had to take cover in a ditch...[t]he man injured at Little Big Horn did not get medical aid, as the marshals were now insisting [by radio] that the medic return directly to the clinic."[125] It wasn't till Holder managed to arrange the ceasefire allowing recovery of Lamont's body "that the man injured so many hours before could be brought in by medics."[126] By then, he'd suffered considerable blood loss and was in severe shock.

Perhaps sickened by the turn events were taking, and mindful of the GOON ultimatum that even more serious bloodletting (of which his men were to be a target) would begin on May 4, Wayne Colburn apparently used his waning influence to make a plea for a last, all-out effort for a settlement. Kent Frizzell returned and:

> Negotiations finally got underway in Wounded Knee on May 1...There were separate "military" and "political" talks...In the military talks, Dennis Banks and four members of Wounded Knee security met with the Director of the U.S. Marshals, Wayne Colburn, Assistant Attorney General Richard Hellstern, and Marshal Hall...the AIM security representatives repeatedly reiterated that disarmament was a purely tactical matter and could be handled easily, if and when a political settlement satisfactory to the Oglalas was reached...In the political talks, Leonard Crow Dog, Gladys Bissonette, Verona Crow Dog, and five other Oglalas met with Assistant Attorney General [sic., Solicitor General] Kent Frizzell, FBI agent Noel Castleman, and an attorney from the Justice Department's Civil Rights Division, Dennis Ickes. The Oglalas asked that the traditional chiefs and their lawyers be allowed into Wounded Knee for the negotiations. They proposed a meeting take place within a few days between the Independent Oglala Nation and the chiefs on one side, and White House officials on the other, at which the May treaty meetings would be arranged and an agenda for them set. The Oglalas stated that they were willing to let this proposed planning session stand as the sole guarantee of Federal good faith when [Crow Dog and Means] had traveled to Washington, following the signing of the April 5th agreement.[127]

As in April, Frizzell attempted to stonewall until AIM and ION disarmed. The Oglalas again rejected this, countering with a query concerning the disposition of the more than 150 formal civil rights complaints they'd registered against the Wilson administration prior to going to Wounded Knee.[128] Frizzell and SA Castleman resorted to visiting Buddy Lamont's aging mother Agnes and his sister, Darlene, enlisting them to ask AIM to lay down its arms. They were threatened with the alternative that more Indian people would "be killed, like Buddy." These women, along with the traditional chiefs, were admitted to Wounded Knee for further negotiations on May 2.[129] Finally, on the night of May 3:

> ...in the last few minutes of [a] four-hour session, a tentative scheme for settlement was outlined. It sketched a progression of events as follows: 1. A letter would be delivered to the chiefs from the White House promising later meetings on the treaty commission. 2. Then there would be a laying down of arms. 3. The roadblocks would be lifted to permit Buddy LaMonte's [sic] wake and funeral to take place in Wounded Knee. 4. Seventy-two hours after the funeral, those with outstanding warrants would

be arrested. 5. The treaty commission meetings would be held at Chief Fools Crow's land in the third week of May.[130]

On May 4, WKLDOC attorney Ramon Roubideaux was allowed into Wounded Knee to assist AIM and the ION in finalizing the agreement; he was the first legal counsel to be granted access since April 17.[131] Wilson's GOONs, however, gave it one last go in attempting to block any sort of peaceful resolution:

> On May 5, Hank Adams, the...treaty expert who had participated in the April negotiations, and had been working since then on the outside to help arrange a settlement, delivered a letter from Leonard Garment, Special Counsel to the President of the United States, guaranteeing the meeting with the chiefs later in May. Adams was one of those who had been ordered off the reservation by Richard Wilson, so [under threat of GOON attention] he had to hand the letter over a fence at the reservation line. Fools Crow brought the letter to Wounded Knee, and along with other leaders of the Independent Oglala Nation, signed the document they'd agreed to the night before.[132]

With the agreement signed, events moved quickly. Buddy Lamont's funeral was held on May 6 and AIM's formal "stand down" occurred the next day. Although everyone still had more than two days' grace period by provision of the May 5 agreement, the FBI began arresting people immediately. Worse, the agents attempted to prevent WKLDOC attorneys from witnessing the proceedings.[133]

About 150 people were still in the village on the last day, approximately one-third of them local residents, one-third of the Oglalas from other towns on the reservation, and one-third supporters from around the country...One by one, people were taken out of the group to be searched, questioned, fingerprinted, and photographed. No one knew until they were questioned whether they would be arrested or not.[134]

Meanwhile, a task force of marshals accompanied BIA police in a sweep of the hamlet itself. Arvin Wells, a Comanche from Oklahoma, who was one of the AIM observers of this action, recalled how "[t]hey proceeded to break into the cars people had left there, and into the homes of the original residents...Later, the government [finally] allowed the press to enter the village, and told them AIM was responsible for the destruction."[135] Eddie White Dress, an elderly Oglala resident of Wounded Knee, described how he had seen BIA police destroying their homes and cars from the window of a government bus which was taking people to jail in Rapid City, and Grace Spotted Eagle (Black Elk), an Oglala, recounted how, "We were all held up on the hill while they let the police and Dick Wilson's goons down there. So they went in and wrecked the place and blamed the American Indian Movement...they let the goon squads in so they wrecked the place, shot up our cars, and wrecked most of the local people's cars too."[136]

Among the casualties of this sort of activism was Father Manhart's Catholic church, later burned to the ground by a fire "of unknown origin."[137] The fury of the BIA police and their GOON colleagues was probably exacerbated by the fact that:

[Dennis] Banks and sixty other militants had escaped during the night, trying to slip through the heavy ring of federal and vigilante forces. Fourteen of the activists were captured with a variety of weapons. The rest disappeared without a trace...The federal officers were [also] faked out when they went to collect the weapons neatly stacked inside the village. They found a toy bow-and-arrow set, several Mattel plastic M-16s, carved wooden replicas of rifles, and eight decrepit .22s.[138]

As he had in April, Banks had once again refused to sign the May 5 agreement, taking his group out rather than interfere with the consensus of the ION. Events would shortly lend substance to his "paranoid" wariness, but in the interim the siege was over. Government promises had once again been made and, as Gladys Bissonette put it at the time:

[During the siege, there] was unity and friendship among 64 different tribes and that's more than I can say that the Pine Ridge Reservation has ever had in my lifetime. I have never seen anything like this and although we were half-starved here, we didn't mind it. We were all happy together and it is kind of sad to see everyone leave...but we know we'll be together again soon.[139]

The hated marshals were leaving Pine Ridge as fast as they could pack their gear and the traditionals were experiencing a sense of strength and possibilities which had been largely absent from the lives of even the oldest. On the other hand, Stan Holder was languishing in a cell in Rapid City under a $32,000 bond; $152,000 was assigned as the price of freedom for Pedro Bissonette, while Russell Means went for $150,000, Leonard Crow Dog for $35,000 and scores of others were being held in lieu of lesser sums.[140] According to WKLDOC attorney Karen Northcott, the nationwide tally on Wounded Knee-related arrests had, by that point, reached more than 1,200.[141] A tremendous stockpile of military and paramilitary materiel had been built up on the reservation during the siege, now available for use by the FBI, BIA police and the GOONs. And, already, resistance to this deadly combination had cost AIM and the ION fifteen seriously wounded and anywhere from two to fourteen dead at Wounded Knee. Unknown to most participants at the time, the battle had barely begun.

The Wounded Knee Aftermath

On May 17, 1973, the White House delegation arrived in the reservation community of Kyle to participate in the scheduled meeting on Chief Fools Crow's property. Although the ION/AIM intent in signing the May 5 agreement had clearly been to convene discussions with high-level government officials, "[m]ost of those in the federal team were middle-level functionaries from the Justice and Interior Departments, including Charles Soller, acting Associate Solicitor of Interior's Division of Indian Affairs; Craig Decker, trial attorney with the Land and Natural Resources Division of the Justice Department; Leslie Gay, chief of the Tribal Government section of the BIA; and Bobby Greene Kilberg, attorney and former White House con-

Oglala Lakota chief Frank Fools Crow convened a meeting with federal representatives to discuss the 1868 Fort Laramie Treaty on May 17, 1973. Although the U.S. had agreed to seriously examine treaty violations as a precondition to AIM and ION laying down their arms at Wounded Knee, this was just one more broken promise. (Photo: *Akwesasne Notes*)

sultant. They were led by Bradley Patterson, an assistant to White House counsel Leonard Garment,"[142] and had "stopped first in Pine Ridge to meet with Dick Wilson, apparently to reaffirm Washington's support for the 'duly elected government of this reservation.'"[143]

> [S]everal hundred people gathered at Fools Crow's camp...for the long awaited meetings with White House representatives. Present were many Oglalas, as well as traditional spokespeople for the seven other Teton Sioux reservations, and the other Indian nations that signed the treaty—the Cheyenne and Arapaho—and other guests, including a delegation from the Iroquois Six Nations Confederacy. In an attempt to intimidate local supporters, Dick Wilson's "goon squad" and BIA police established a roadblock on the road to Fools Crow's and required people to identify themselves as they were allowed through. Despite this, a crowd had gathered by early on the morning of the 17th. Also present were several dozen U.S. Marshals, there presumably to protect the Federal visitors.[144]

Chief Fools Crow, speaking in Lakota and translated by his assistant, Matthew King, opened by aptly framing the discussion from the Oglala point of view: "Today I met one of the good representatives of the Government. I want him to take a good look at me and my mother earth. This is my country. I want to ask him a simple question: Can we be reinstated back to the 1868 Treaty?"[145] There followed an interchange between King and Patterson, as the latter pretended not to understand the question:

Patterson: Now, what is your specific question? Is your question, "Can we, the five of us, rewrite the treaty?"

Matthew King: No. We want it reinstated. The treaty-making period was cut off by introducing the Indian Bureau in its place. We want to be reinstated back to [our] 1868 government.

Patterson: When you say the Indian Bureau, what you mean is that in 1934 you had the Indian Reorg...

King: No. 1871. 1871 [the year Congress officially ended U.S. treaty-making with Indian nations—through a rider to the Indian Appropriation Act for that year—while expressly *not* abrogating any treaty with any tribe which had *already* been ratified by the Senate].

Patterson: Well, in 1871—which are you talking about, the...

King: Before that we [were] a nation.

Patterson: Yes...

King: Making treaties with the United States.

Patterson: Act of Congress...

King: And we were a self-sustaining people.

Patterson: Right.

King: And we got along with that period of time. And after 1871 the Bureau was introduced and the Government says, "Well, you're not supposed to make any more treaties with the Government," and they...forced in the Bureau. Now, we want to be reinstated back to that period of time, and be a self-governing nation.[146]

Patterson, realizing the legal basis of the traditionals' agenda, attempted to evade, and was solidly countered by King.

Patterson: I understand. Well I'll give you an answer. In 1871, the Congress passed this law [Title 25, Section 71, U.S.C., March 3, 1871] which said as you described. No one in the Executive Branch, even the President if he were standing here personally, can change that law. The only way that law can be changed is if the Congress changes it itself.

King: If the Government could change the law in '71, when our treaties were the supreme law of the land, he could change it again.[147]

King might have added that there was really no need to change the law in this instance, or to negotiate another treaty, but only for the U.S. to belatedly begin meeting its obligations (also a matter of law) under the existing Fort Laramie Treaty.

However, the polarity of the Oglala and government positions was already locked in.

> Although the Oglalas were angry at what appeared to be a deliberate snub of their claims to sovereign status...the chiefs finally decided to [hear what the government representatives] had to say. Throughout the afternoon, the U.S. delegation gave speeches on their fields of expertise, ignoring the fact that the Sioux were challenging the entire framework of U.S.-Indian relations...Using a brightly colored map, Carl Decker [sic] lectured about the loss of Indian lands since 1868; Leslie Gay explained the Wheeler-Howard Indian Reorganization Act and reminded the people that, "in the eyes of the Government, the Oglalas are under this law." He also said that the petition to call a referendum on a new form of government for the Oglalas, on which the supporters of the Wounded Knee occupation had gathered 1,400 signatures, had been rejected by...Kent Frizzell, despite the fact that that figure was more than the required one-third of the voters in the Oglala Sioux Tribe. Frizzell's office ruled that for such a referendum the people would have to have acquired the signatures of eligible voters, rather than those registered to vote, and also questioned the submitting of the signatures of those between the ages of 18 and 21, even though they [were] to vote...in Federal elections. [In 1968, a referendum had been approved by the Secretary of Interior after being called for by a petition with only 800 signatures.][148]

The meeting continued all the next day:

> Throughout the day, Indian people spoke to the government representatives about their many concerns relating to the 1868 treaty...[and] demanded protection of Indian water and mineral rights guaranteed by the treaty; for a referendum vote by which the Sioux could choose whether they wished to remain under the BIA form of Tribal Governments or return to the independent, traditional forms; and for the Government to live up to its responsibility under the treaty to prosecute whites who harmed Indian people on treaty lands—such as the murders of Wesley Bad Heart Bull and Raymond Yellow Thunder. They also made it clear that Wilson's administration was continuing its reign of terror.[149]

In response, Bradley Patterson delivered a patronizing lecture in which he explained that Wounded Knee was "not the way the Indian people or any other people in society are really in the long run going to get any real progress,"[150] a statement which provoked WKLDOC attorney Ramon Roubideaux to offer a heated rejoinder:

> I think I should rise to point out an instance or two where I don't think you've been listening. In the first place, I don't see how you could keep from arriving at the conclusion that we have a dangerous, explosive situation here on the Pine Ridge Reservation, a situation that demands *immediate* action. Between now and November when the primary election [for Tribal offices] is held, I guarantee you that if nothing is done, you're going to have on your hands the deaths of several people on this reservation. I don't think there should be any doubt in your mind that there's been a total breakdown of Tribal Government on this reservation. The abuse of Indian people is con-

tinuing. It's an *emergency* situation, and if you don't get that out of this meeting, I don't think you've been listening.[151]

With a dismissive shrug to Roubideaux's prophetic words, Patterson gathered his entourage and left, promising to return on May 30. On that date, a single U.S. marshal drove up to Fools Crow's, delivering a letter, rather than a delegation, to the people assembled for the meeting. Signed by Nixon counsel Leonard Garment, the missive read in part:

The days of treaty-making with the American Indians ended in 1871, 102 years ago...Only Congress can rescind or change in any way statutes enacted since 1871, such as the Indian Reorganization Act...Insofar as you wish to propose any specific changes in existing treaties or statutes, the Congress is, in effect, a Treaty Commission.[152]

As with Alcatraz, The Trail of Broken Treaties, *etc.*, the substance of the issues raised at Wounded Knee had been deliberately avoided; the Indian attempt to use discussion and law as tools of social justice was sandbagged at every step. Worse, implicit in the federal position was the statement that force would be used to continue an illegitimate *status quo* for the Oglalas of Pine Ridge. The situation officially became nothing more than "a police matter" once the Oglalas and their allies emerged from their bunkers at Wounded Knee.

The provision of security for visiting federal dignitaries at Kyle was the swan song for Wayne Colburn's dwindling force of marshals on the reservation. Already, the FBI had demonstrated its primacy by causing the dropping of charges against the eleven GOONs arrested at their "residents' roadblock" by marshals on April 23. Ninety-year-old Wounded Knee resident Stella Bear Shield explained certain of the implications of this by recounting how her grandson, who had joined ION during the siege, had been subsequently arrested, made bail, and "now that [the] boy's out and he's at home, the goons have been after him. They been hitting him, beating him up and they even took shots at [the] house."[153] Ethel Merrival, a middle-aged Oglala who at the time served as a tribal attorney, amplified this:

Now we've got Dickie Wilson's goon squad running up and down the street—they [the FBI] don't do anything to them because they're Dickie's goons. That includes my nephews and two of my sons [who were GOONs]. And all these things, where can we go? I go to the FBI and [BIA] Superintendent. They say, "Those are internal affairs [of the tribe]." So does [Senator James] Abourezk. "Those are things you've got to straighten out for yourself"...Two of my granddaughters were abducted night before last by two of these goon squad—and they're so scared, they're afraid to tell. But you've got to know these things from the grassroots, from the people it happened to.[154]

Concerning the civil rights complaints which were filed with the Justice Department on these and other GOON actions during the period (including the 150 raised during the April negotiations at Wounded Knee), *not one* was ever prosecuted: "[Of the total], Dennis Ickes of the Justice Department investigated [only] 42. From these 42 complaints Ickes reported that he had 'two cases that look very good against members of the goon squad,' but no indictments were ever issued, no arrests made. Wilson was turned loose upon the traditional people—those who were not dead or in jail—once again."[155] The pattern has continued through the present day, unbroken by a single FBI-generated GOON prosecution.

The GOONs' anti-AIM activities on Pine Ridge underwent a continuous escalation in scope and virulence through the period of greatest FBI activity on Pine Ridge, roughly mid-1973 to late-1976. During this approximate three-year span, at least sixty-nine AIM members and supporters were to die violently on and around Pine Ridge, while more than 300 were physically assaulted and, in many cases, shot. Virtually all of these murders and assaults are attributed to the GOONs and their counterparts in the BIA police.[156] As has been noted elsewhere:

> Using only documented political deaths, the yearly murder rate on the Pine Ridge Reservation between March 1, 1973, and March 1, 1976, was 170 per 100,000. By comparison, Detroit, the reputed "murder capital of the United States," had a rate of 20.2 per 100,000 in 1974. The U.S. average was 9.7 per 100,000...In a nation of 200 million persons, a murder rate comparable with that on Pine Ridge between 1973 and 1976 would have left 340,000 persons dead for political reasons alone in one year; 1.32 million in three...The political murder rate at Pine Ridge [during this period] was almost equivalent to that in Chile during the three years after a military coup supported by the United States deposed and killed President Salvador Allende.[157]

Similarly, when Russell Means ran (as promised) against Dick Wilson in the 1974 election—an effort to legally depose Wilson and end GOON violence—the incumbent rigged the results. Although Means defeated Wilson decisively in the primary, 677 votes to 511, Wilson came out of the general balloting having "won" by less than 200 votes.[158] AIM asked for an investigation by the U.S. Commission on Civil Rights, which described the whole affair as "permeated with fraud" by Wilsonites.[159] The Bureau, however, did nothing to intervene, Wilson was reseated for a second two-year term and GOON atrocities continued with increasing frequency.

Throughout the entire period, 1972-76, the Bureau pleaded "lack of manpower" as the basis for its failure to come to grips with either the GOONs or Wilson's violations of his constituents' rights.[160] Yet, beginning from a standard (given the population density of its investigative area) resident office cadre of three agents in mid-1972, the Rapid City office of the FBI—under jurisdiction of which the Pine Ridge Reservation falls—nearly quadrupled (to eleven agents) in one year.[161] This beefed up force was augmented in March 1973 by a ten-man Special Weapons and Tactics (SWAT) team, assigned to the tiny village of Pine Ridge.[162] This concentration of agents, maintained for more than two years and again tripled during the first half of 1975, afforded the FBI in western South Dakota the highest ratio of agents to citizens anywhere in the United States.[163]

At the same time that the Bureau was professedly too short-handed to confront—or in most instances even investigate—the spiraling physical repression of AIM members and supporters on Pine Ridge, it evidenced no such deficiency when it came to building cases against dissidents, even on minor offenses. To the contrary, agents amassed some 316,000 investigative file classifications on those inside Wounded Knee during 1973 alone.[164] As stated in a government report:

> The events gave [immediate] rise to approximately 562 arrests, Federal grand juries indicted 185 persons and there was a total of 15 convictions, a very low rate considering the usual rate of conviction in Federal Courts and a great input of resources in these cases...While the cases were being prosecuted, an antagonism intensified between FBI Agents assigned to the cases and supporters and legal counsel for the defendants [*i.e.*, AIM].[165]

This grotesque bias in the FBI's assignment of resources on Pine Ridge reveals that constitutional guarantees of "equal protection before the law" for persons associated with AIM were simply suspended by the Bureau. Even more serious, the paucity of convictions ultimately obtained against AIM people as a result of the FBI's efforts shows quite clearly that the Bureau was engaged in its foresworn but time-honored COINTELPRO tactic of pursuing arrests and indictments against AIM, "not to obtain convictions, or to punish people the Bureau believes to be guilty of criminal acts in the strict sense. Rather, it is [done] to neutralize an organization whose politics the FBI objects to by tying the organization up in an unending series of trials and pretrial incarcerations, and in bankrupting the organization by forcing it to meet massive amounts of bail."[166]

To take a classic example of the "method" being used against AIM, Russell Means was charged with a total of thirty-seven felonies and three misdemeanors between 1973 and 1976. Of these, he was exonerated thirty-nine times. The fortieth charge, which resulted in a conviction costing him a year in the South Dakota State Penitentiary, was not filed as a result of *any* of the "criminal activities" the Bureau attributed to him. Rather, it was levied as a result of his frustrated and allegedly illegal behavior in court, near the end of the seemingly interminable Bureau-fostered trials which had drained his time, energy and other resources for more than two years.[167]

Throughout the three years of its peak activity on Pine Ridge, the Bureau justified its tactics on the basis that AIM was (and is) a public menace, a "violence prone" or even "violent" entity. In hindsight, we can readily discern that this portrait was largely the result of FBI fabrication and media manipulation, the COINTELPRO expedient of "disinformation," otherwise known as "gray propaganda." Even at the time, it should have been clear that the relative body counts involved pointed to exactly the opposite conclusion (*i.e.*: hundreds of AIM casualties, and virtually none among the GOONs, BIA police and FBI prior to mid-1975).

Nor were other COINTELPRO techniques absent from the Bureau's anti-AIM arsenal. The history of the Bureau's operations on Pine Ridge during the mid-1970s is replete with informers, infiltrators and provocateurs, the subornation of testimony and fabrication of evidence introduced in criminal proceedings, the withholding of exculpatory evidence which might have cleared (and could still prove the innocence of) targeted defendants, and bad-jacketing. In several instances, there is the strong appearance of "key individuals" associated with AIM having been assassinated, a matter distinct from the more random and generalized GOON violence allowed and/or motivated by the Bureau. Further, certain FBI personnel assigned to Pine Ridge from 1972-76—men such as Richard G. Held and his son, Richard W.—had long specialized in the design, implementation and covering-up of COINTELPROs.

The 1973 events at Wounded Knee were merely the warm-up. The clandestine war waged against AIM by the FBI in the wake of that spectacular occurrence represented the ugly culmination of two related federal processes: 1) the pattern of duplicity intermingled with raw force through which the U.S. has, by its own definition, colonized American Indian nations,[168] and 2) the ever-increasing reliance upon duplicity mixed with raw force by which the U.S. represses *all* serious opposition to its imperial *status quo*.[169] In the latter sense, AIM stands as an example for all whose politics devolve from dissent.

In 1889, the Commissioner of Indian Affairs summed up U.S. imperial intentions toward American Indians by stating, "The Indian must conform to the white man's ways, peaceably if they will, forcibly if they must. This civilization may not be the best possible, but it is the best the Indians can get. They cannot escape and must either conform or be crushed by it."[170] In 1976, Norman Zigrossi, ASAC of the Bureau's Rapid City office, expressed these sentiments in equally crystalline fashion:

> They [the Indians] are a conquered nation, and when you are conquered, the people you are conquered by dictate your future. This is a basic philosophy of mine. If I'm part of a conquered nation, I've got to yield to authority...[The FBI must function as] a colonial police force.[171]

The next section of this book will examine in some detail the functioning of Zigrossi's "colonial police force" as it endeavored to force AIM and the traditional Oglalas to "yield to authority." In so doing, the authors believe they will demonstrate beyond all reasonable doubt that, far from being terminated in 1971 (as the FBI claims), or in 1973 (as Congress ordered), COINTELPRO was both continued and intensified on Pine Ridge during the mid-1970s.

PART III

The FBI on Pine Ridge, 1972-76

It has always been the same. They always have two plans, a peace plan and a war plan. Our grandfathers told us this. If they don't get their way with the peace plan, then they bring the soldiers. It's no different today.
—Noble Red Man (Matthew King), Oglala Lakota Elder, 1980

I have become increasingly aware of the fact that Native Americans who hold traditional views and are political activists are singled out for special attention by the criminal justice system in South Dakota. Members of the American Indian Movement, in particular, are singled out for harassment. Every law enforcement agency in the state, including the highway patrol, BIA police, FBI, DCI [Division of Criminal Investigation], and seemingly all local authorities apparently agree on one thing, that the American Indian Movement is innately evil, and that they should do everything in their power to suppress the Native peoples who adhere to the goals of that organization.
—David Holman, Commissioner,
South Dakota State Criminal Justice Commission, Resignation Letter, 1977

Chapter 6

The GOONs, Cable Splicer
and Garden Plot

Police participation in clandestine right-wing terrorist organizations is quite prevalent in Latin America. These groups, such as "La Mano Blanca" (the White Hand) in Guatemala, "La Banda" in the Dominican Republic, "The Death Squad" in Uruguay and Brazil...operate, in practice, with unofficial government approval. US involvement in the organization, training, and equipping of [those] Death Squads is...quite clear.

—Center for Research on Criminal Justice,
The Iron Fist and the Velvet Glove, 1975

The idea that the FBI would support and coordinate a "private army" might, at first glance, seem far-fetched. It is, however, not without precedent. As was pointed out in Chapter 1, the Bureau made considerable use of the Pinkertons and *ad hoc* vigilante groups in breaking the backs of the various labor and radical organizations during the Red Scare period of 1918-22 and throughout the 1920s and 1930s. Again, as is noted in Chapter 2, the FBI's relation with the Ku Klux Klan in Alabama during the early- to mid-1960s—the period of greatest racist violence against civil rights workers in that state—certainly points in the same direction.

A more recent example occurred on November 3, 1979, when a mob of Klansmen and Nazis murdered five members of the Communist Workers Party (CWP) at an anti-Klan rally in Greensboro, North Carolina.[1] The names of those to be shot had been provided to the Klan by U.S. Alcohol, Tobacco, and Firearms (BATF) agent Bernard Butkovich, who subsequently assisted the killers in making their escape.[2] The hit squad itself seems to have been recruited, organized and led on its lethal mission by an FBI infiltrator, Edward Dawson.[3] The Bureau contended that the CWP assertions of federal complicity in the massacre were "utterly absurd" and concluded that there had been no conspiracy to violate the civil rights of CWP members.[4] Further, despite the fact that "Director [of the FBI William] Webster has taken a very personal interest in this case," and that the assassinations occurred in broad daylight at a heavily surveilled public event, there has been no resolution of the matter after more than eight years.[5]

The Secret Army Organization (SAO) was another paramilitary surrogate for the FBI. An ex-FBI informer, Nanda Zocchino, recounted in the January 26, 1976 editorial of the *Los Angeles Times* how the Bureau had created and financed this "crypto-fascist" group in San Diego during 1969-70. During the early-1970s the SAO engaged in a range of activities including burglary, mail thefts, bombings, kidnappings, assassination plots and attempted murder. All of this, according to Zocchino, was supervised directly by the FBI. A second informant to the San Diego FBI office, Howard Berry Godfrey, has substantially corroborated Zocchino's story, while the Bureau itself has done little to deny it.[6]

According to the Citizens Research and Investigation Committee (CRIC), the SAO was established specifically to "use violence against radicals" and, at its peak, had cadres in eleven western states.[7] One of the primary early targets of the SAO was San Diego State University economics professor Peter G. Bohmer, who received more than forty death threats before SAO member George M. Hoover fired a 9 mm. pistol into his home on the night of January 9, 1972.[8] Bohmer was out for the evening, but Hoover managed to hit a house-guest, Paula Tharp, in the right elbow, permanently disabling her.[9] Despite the facts that the SAO gunman was in the company of FBI infiltrator Godfrey at the time of the shooting and that Godfrey duly informed his Bureau handler, SA Steve Christianson, no arrest was made for more than six months.[10] Even then, the FBI seems to have been motivated not so much by the injury sustained by Ms. Tharp as by its sense that it might be losing control of the SAO, a matter evidenced by the bombing (carried out by Hoover and eight other SAO members) of San Diego's Guild Theater on June 19, 1972.[11]

In the wake of these arrests, San Diego police raids of SAO members' residences netted "large quantities of illegal explosives, handguns and rifles, including an unpacked case of M-16 rifles. The market value of these weapons was estimated at more than $60,000."[12] American Civil Liberties Union (ACLU) attorney Frederick Hetter pointed out that "Godfrey [the FBI infiltrator] supplied 75% of the money for the SAO" to acquire these weapons and munitions.[13] *San Diego Door* reporters Doug Porter and Ric Reynolds later discovered that Godfrey had also infiltrated the radical Message Information Center (under the assumed name of "Larry") as well as the Movement for a Democratic Military and that he had been assembling a list of "priority people" in the Peace and Freedom Party. He had thus placed himself in an ideal position to assign choice targets to the SAO hitmen.[14]

The GOONs

The scale and duration of GOON activities on Pine Ridge from 1972 onward, and the FBI's patent lack of response to them, suggests a similar situation. Although there is no conclusive evidence that FBI personnel participated in the initial organization of Dick Wilson's GOON squads in 1972, it is clear that the Bureau—which held preeminent jurisdiction over the reservation—made no effort at all to arrest or otherwise curtail GOONs engaged in blatantly criminal behavior (*e.g.*: sys-

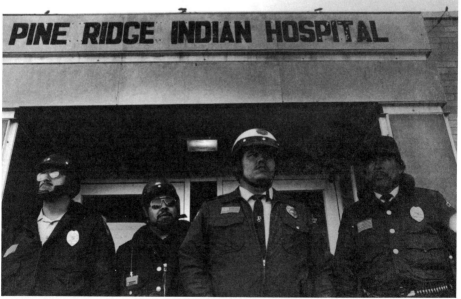

The BIA Police (above) during the period of its formation on the Sioux Reservations, when it was used to assassinate Crazy Horse and Sitting Bull (Photo: John Anderson) and (below) during the period of the "new look" when it was used by the FBI to "neutralize" scores of AIM members and supporters. (Photo: Kevin Barry McKiernan)

tematically beating up Wilson opponents, running their cars off the road, shooting up their houses and other acts of vandalism). Similarly, the Bureau obviously defaulted on a fundamental responsibility when it failed to investigate *any* of the scores of formal civil rights complaints generated by GOON activities on Pine Ridge during 1972 (see preceding chapter).

Compounding this situation was the fact that the FBI made no attempt to intervene in reservation law enforcement when it became apparent that ranking BIA police officials such as Delmar Eastman and Duane Brewer were doubling as GOON squad leaders in 1972. While the nature of GOON assaults had not yet become lethal, the structure of the politically repressive apparatus emerging on Pine Ridge bears striking resemblance in both configuration and ideological orientation to Latin American death squads.[15] The Bureau's marked inaction in the face of the growing GOON phenomenon can only be construed as a *de facto* endorsement.

By early 1973, it is evident that both the FBI and the U.S. Marshals Service had begun to offer more concrete support to the GOONs. This included acknowledgement of the "right" of the vigilante organization to establish its own roadblocks in conjunction with those of the federal government, the provision of restricted intelligence information, and agreement to the mounting of both foot and mobile GOON patrols in collaboration with those of official police units. Materially, this support appears to have included provision, either directly or through the Pine Ridge BIA police force, of relatively sophisticated military communications gear, ammunition and the GOONs' first automatic weapons (military M-16 assault rifles). Although the physical intensity of GOON assaults was increasing from January through March, 1973, the massive federal police presence on the reservation resulted in total non-enforcement of the law *vis a vis* GOON squad members.

As noted in the preceding chapter, a policy dispute between the FBI and the U.S. Marshals Service concerning control of the siege of Wounded Knee came to a head in April 1973. The marshals, sensing that they were losing control of the GOONs (as had the FBI with the SAO), began finally trying to curtail vigilante activities. This led to the first arrests of GOON squad members at the "residents' roadblock" on the evening of April 23, a matter immediately "fixed" by FBI COINTELPRO expert Richard G. Held. All indications are that, by then, the Bureau had greatly stepped up its effort to arm the GOONs with M-16s—more than compensating for the withdrawal of support by the Marshals Service—and that the GOONs turned this upgraded firepower on both AIM/ION *and* the marshals. This rendered the marshals' position on Pine Ridge untenable, led to their rapid withdrawal in early May and left the FBI in undisputed control of anti-AIM operations on the reservation. It was also on April 23 that the GOONs may have committed their first murders, summarily executing as many as a dozen AIM supporters attempting to backpack supplies into Wounded Knee; the matter remains one of the many grim mysteries attending events of Pine Ridge during the mid-1970s.

With the FBI in complete charge, the GOONs ran wild for the next two and one-half years. While the Bureau continued to arm, equip and supply the vigilan-

GOONs Salty Twiss (left) and Bennett "Tuffy" Sierra (center) in a firing position outside Wounded Knee, 1973. Both men were notorious for brutality on Pine Ridge and were involved with others, such as Emile "Woody" Richards, Francis Randall and Robert Beck in violence against AIM, OSCRO and ION members between 1972 and 1976.
(Photo: *Akwesasne Notes*)

tes, the tally of their victims reached unheard of proportions (see preceding chapter). Illustrative examples drawn from the lengthy list of GOON crimes committed, 1973-76, include the following:

- On the night of March 1, 1973, the home of Aaron and Betty DeSersa, near the reservation village of Manderson, was firebombed. Betty was severely burned in the blaze, which destroyed the DeSersa house. Aaron DeSersa was an OSCRO member and, as editor of the *Shannon County News*, had vigorously condemned Wilson and the GOONs while strongly endorsing AIM and its actions at Gordon, the BIA Building, Custer and Wounded Knee.[16]

- During the period from April to June 1973, the home of anti-Wilson tribal council member Severt Young Bear was shot up so frequently that Young Bear requested an AIM security detail be posted on his property each night. The shootings abated thereafter.[17]

- On June 19, 1973, brothers (and AIM supporters) Clarence and Vernal Cross were sitting in their car by the side of a road near Pine Ridge when they began receiving rifle fire. Clarence died of gunshot wounds. Vernal, injured but alive, was charged by Delmar Eastman with the murder of his brother (charges were later dropped). Nine-year-old Mary Ann Little Bear, who was riding past the Cross car at the time of the shooting in a vehicle driven by her father, was struck in the face by a stray round, suffering a wound which cost her an eye. Witnesses named three GOONs—Francis Randall, John Hussman and Woody Richards—as the gunmen involved.[18]

- On October 21, 1973, Agnes Lamont (whose son Buddy had been killed at Wounded Knee) and her sister, Jenny Leading Fighter, were rammed broadside while stopped at a stop sign in Pine Ridge village. Three GOON squad members were in the other car, all drunk and in possession of loaded, high-power rifles fitted with scopes. Mrs.

Leading Fighter's head and neck were injured badly enough to require several days hospitalization.[19]

- On November 10, 1973, AIM supporter Phillip Little Crow was beaten to death; a GOON was detained, charged with "voluntary manslaughter," then released.[20]

- On November 15, 1973, OSCRO member Pat Hart was shot in the stomach by a sniper; surgery lasted ten hours.[21]

- On November 20, 1973, AIM member Allison Little Fast Horse was found dead in a ditch near Pine Ridge, a .38 calibre bullet through his heart.[22]

- On February 7, 1974, a bullet fired at AIM member Milo Goings in the hamlet of White Clay, Nebraska, struck nine-year-old Harold Weasel Bear in the face.[23]

- On February 27, 1975, three WKLDOC attorneys—Roger Finzel of South Dakota (more recently of Albuquerque), William Rossmore of Connecticut, and Marsha Copleman of New Jersey—accompanied by WKLDOC researchers Kathi James and Eva Gordon, flew into the tiny Pine Ridge Airport. They were met by a client, AIM member Bernard Escamilla (then facing prosecution as a result of Wounded Knee charges), and spent the next several hours interviewing potential witnesses for his defense around the reservation. When they returned to the airport, they found their plane riddled with bullet holes. At that time, some fifteen car loads of GOONs arrived; the WKLDOC people and Escamilla attempted to take refuge in their car, but the GOONs smashed the windows and sliced open the vehicle's convertible top. The captives were then held at shotgun point until the arrival of Dick Wilson, who ordered his men to "stomp 'em." According to the attorneys' subsequent joint statement, published in the *Rapid City Journal* on February 28, they were then "stomped, kicked and pummeled to the ground. [GOONs] took turns kicking and stomping, while one slashed Finzel's face with a knife, [also] cutting...Eva Gordon's hand as she attempted to shield him." Escamilla was the most severely injured of the group, requiring two days hospitalization in Rapid City, while the rest were treated for multiple contusions and lacerations, and released. The victims identified Dick and "Manny" (Richard Jr.) Wilson, Duane and Vincent Brewer and several other GOONs as being among their assailants. The Bureau administered polygraph examinations to the *victims* (which they passed), rather than to the GOONs.[24]

- Although GOONs Fred Two Bulls and Vincent Brewer had earlier delivered a message from Dick Wilson to Chief Fools Crow to the effect that the traditional chiefs "needn't fear" personal violence from vigilantes, on the night of March 3, 1975, an unknown number of GOONs shot up the house of Fools Crow's elderly assistant, Matthew King. Two nights later, Fools Crow's own residence was burned to the ground. On March 6, the *Rapid City Journal* reported that Delmar Eastman and Duane Brewer—ostensibly responsible BIA police officials on Pine Ridge—were "unavailable for comment" on the incidents.[25]

- On the afternoon of March 21, 1975, Edith Eagle Hawk, her four-month-old daughter and three-year-old grandson were killed when their car was forced into a deep ditch alongside Highway 44, between Scenic, S.D. and Rapid City. Edith Eagle Hawk was a defense (alibi) witness for AIM member Jerry Bear Shield, who was at the time accused of killing a GOON, William Jack Steele, on March 9 (charges against Bear Shield were later dropped when it was revealed Steele had probably died at the hands of GOON associates). The driver of the car which struck the Eagle Hawk vehicle—Albert Coomes, a white on-reservation rancher who was allowed by Wilsonites to serve as an active GOON—also lost control of his car, went into the ditch and was killed. Eugene Eagle Hawk, who survived the crash, identified a second occupant of the Coomes car as being Mark Clifford, a prominent GOON. BIA and FBI reports on the matter fail to make mention of Clifford.[26]

- At about 1 a.m. March 27, 1975, Jeanette Bissonette, sister-in-law of OSCRO leader Pedro Bissonette and mother of six children, was shot and killed by sniper fire as she made her way home from the funeral wake of her friend, AIM supporter Stacy Cottier, who had been killed by random GOON gunfire a week previously. AIM members postulated that the shot was probably intended for ION leader Ellen Moves Camp, who at the time owned a dark blue automobile very similar to the one driven by Jeanette Bissonette. This killing prompted South Dakota Senator James Abourezk, who two years previously had expressed considerable opposition to AIM, to remark that, under the Wilson/FBI regime, "Pine Ridge Reservation is being run like Hitler's Germany."[27]

- On June 8, 1975, Russell Means was shot in the back by a BIA police officer who was arresting the AIM leader for "rowdy behavior." The shooting, which was termed "an accident," put a bullet through Means' kidney.[28]

- On September 10, 1975, Jim Little, an AIM supporter and former Tribal Council member (aligned with Severt Young Bear), was stomped to death by four GOONs; although the incident occurred less than two miles from the Pine Ridge hospital, it took nearly an hour for an ambulance (driven by more known GOONs) to arrive.[29]

- On November 17, 1975, BIA police officer Jesse Trueblood (a known GOON and probable psychotic) opened fire with an M-16 on the home of the Chester Stone family in Oglala. He was probably attempting to hit AIM supporter Louis Tyon, who was visiting the Stones, and with whom Trueblood had had an altercation earlier in the day. His bullets struck Chester Stone in the right arm and his wife, Bernice, in the buttocks. Tyon received a crippling wound to the left knee, while Stone's granddaughter, Deborah Mousseau, was wounded in the left arm. The Stones' 3-year-old grandson, Johnny Mousseau, was hit in the right arm which permanently maimed and disabled him. Trueblood then drove away and was found a short time later, slumped in the front seat of his car, a bullet from his own service revolver fired pointblank into his brain.[30]

- On March 1, 1976, Hobart Horse, an AIM member thought by both the FBI and GOONs to have been involved in the emergence of serious armed self-defense among Pine Ridge dissidents, was shot to death in the tiny reservation hamlet of Sharps Corners.[31]

- At about 4 a.m. on May 6, 1976, Russell Means and AIM member John Thomas were ambushed in a housing project in the town of Wagner, on the Yankton Sioux Reservation, across the Missouri River from Rosebud. According to a *Rocky Mountain News* story of the same date, a GOON hit squad composed of James Wedell, Michael Weston, Jerald Black Elk and Terry Provost (as well as an unidentified juvenile), all armed, had jumped the pair and "told the two AIM members to drop any weapons they were carrying and get down on all fours." The GOONs then fired pointblank into the bodies of their victims and "Means suffered a small calibre bullet wound in the abdomen and Thomas was hit in the neck and jaw." Both men lived through the attempted execution.[32]

In each of these cases, and literally hundreds of others (some of which will be covered under the heading of "Assassinations" in the next chapter), the FBI produced no results at all despite its vaunted "crime solving" capabilities. The result was an atmosphere on Pine Ridge which has been eloquently described by Al Trimble, an Oglala whose sharp criticism of BIA leasing practices and of the GOON squads led Dick Wilson to demand his removal as reservation BIA Superintendent (Trimble was duly fired on March 20, 1975), and who subsequently unseated Wilson in the 1976 election of the Oglala Tribal President:

Things started to [really] come apart in the fall of 1974, when Wilson tried to get around the law by trying to sell beer and liquor at a rodeo on the reservation. We confiscated three hundred cases of beer, but the feds refused to prosecute anybody, and we think they gave him back the beer, as well. Then there was the murder of Jesse Trueblood, when Manny Wilson and Duane Brewer concealed the evidence and the FBI cooperated, even though Brewer later hinted that Manny was involved in the killing. Hell, those goons were in complete charge, with their car caravans, squealing tires around, intimidating people. Dick Wilson is not the most courageous person in the world; despite all the smoke he was blowing, he never moved without a big gang of goons. And half our BIA cops were Wilson people, and they had our tribal judge in their pocket too, and those white cowboys in the area were boasting about all their guns and boasting how they were going to shoot those "longhairs" first and let the court ask any questions later...It was a totally lawless situation, the traditional Indians couldn't count on any law enforcement.[33]

Under such circumstances, it is hardly surprising that, "[b]y 1975, almost everyone on the reservation went armed, and few dared to walk around openly, even in daylight."[34] Even the Bureau was prepared to admit (secretly) that AIM and the ION traditionals had been forced to clump together in enclaves or "AIM centers" (as the FBI called them) for the purpose of the somewhat limited safety numbers and proximity might provide.[35] In this Bureau-fostered "feudal nightmare," which Senator Abourezk was to describe as constituting a state of "total anarchy," the principle of armed self-defense had, for the dissidents, become a necessity for survival.[36] This grim fact, in turn, was to play the most crucial role in the final, massive phase of escalation involved in the FBI's Pine Ridge operations (from mid-1975 through the end of 1976; see Chapter 9).

Robert Burnette, who deposed Webster Two Hawk as Rosebud Tribal President in the 1974 elections, was an insightful and highly vocal critic of the Wilson regime and FBI/GOON conduct on the adjoining Pine Ridge Reservation. (Photo: Wilfred Bailey/IFCO News)

The 1974 Tribal Elections

Another dimension of GOON activities involved the 1974 tribal election on Pine Ridge. As was noted in Chapter 5, Russell Means successfully challenged Dick Wilson in the 1973 tribal primaries, winning the opposition slot in the 1974 general election run-off for president. In the latter balloting, Wilson emerged "victorious" by a 200-vote margin. As Burnette recounts, "Drunks showed their friends crisp twenty-dollar bills they had been given to vote for Wilson. BIA policemen arrived from outlying districts and stuffed wads of paper ballots into the wooden boxes without signing the register books. One District, Potato Creek, showed forty registered voters but 83 cast votes."[37]

Although Commissioner of Indian Affairs Morris Thompson quickly validated this outcome—stating to the Associated Press that, "Based on our present information [provided by the FBI] there does not appear to be sufficient evidence of voting fraud or irregularities to warrant federal intervention."[38] The U.S. Commission on Civil Rights reached rather different conclusions as a result of its own intensive investigation of the matter. According to the Commission report:

- Many people who voted were not eligible because they were not enrolled Oglalas, a matter tied to Wilson's propensity to enlist the support of non-Indians on the reservation. An examination of 793 questionable names on the official voting records identified 154 such cases of voter fraud.

- An "undetermined number" of individuals voting in the elections, while their names did appear on the tribal roll, were either not residents of the reservation or failed to meet the one-year residency requirement of the tribal constitution.

Incumbent Tribal President Dick Wilson (center) with a pair of "campaign organizers"/GOONs during the 1974 Pine Ridge election. (Photo: Kevin Barry McKiernan)

- No method was used by poll watchers—retained by Wilson's tribal administration—to verify the identity, at the time ballots were cast, of those whose names later appeared on the official voting records.

- Wilson's administration made no attempt at all to maintain the accuracy of the tribal eligible voter list; an investigation by Senator Abourezk determined that, in 1969, the eligible voter list for Pine Ridge included 3,104 names, but that, by 1973, there were 9,518. Given that there were barely 11,000 total Oglala residents on Pine Ridge at the time, the Senator remarked that the situation was "most peculiar."

- Poll watchers were not used in certain locations during the balloting.

- No count or record was made of official ballots distributed during the election; election officials could not even tell investigators how many ballots had been printed by the Wilson administration.

- Of the three election board members, two had been "elected" by the tribal council, over which Wilson held absolute sway, after being nominated by Wilson himself. The third was simply appointed by Wilson, in a memorandum to the council signed by him, as well as two executive council cronies, Emma Nelson and Lloyd Eaglebull.

- When Means attempted to follow due process in contesting the election, Wilson—the only individual empowered to convene the tribal council to hear the complaint(s)—refused to do so.

1974 Pine Ridge campaign literature: (left) from the grassroots organization supporting AIM leader Russell Means; (right) from the Wilson faction, paid for with federal funds.

- The BIA, which had legal responsibility to do so, failed to oversee the election, and then refused to convene an investigation into irregularities in election procedures

- The election was held in a climate of fear engendered by the GOON squads. The Commission noted that harassment of suspected opponents of Wilson was endemic prior to the general election and that coercive and intimidating tactics had been applied by the GOONs in wholesale fashion on election day itself. It was noted that Wilson had stated publicly, prior to the election, that all those found to have voted for Means would be "run off the reservation" by his GOONs, and that two individuals connected with the Means campaign had been inexplicably fired from their jobs immediately after the poll results were in.

The Commission on Civil Rights recommended that the election be nullified and restaged under close supervision, and the report was routed directly to Indian Commissioner Thompson and Attorney General William Saxbe.[39] No federal action was taken either to conduct a new election on Pine Ridge or to bring charges against those implicated, a posture which undoubtedly contributed to the mayhem that erupted in the reservation town of Wanblee following the next election (see next chapter). Perhaps the closest parallel in American history to the circumstances which were allowed to prevail during the 1974 Pine Ridge election is the so-called "Pineapple Primary" of April 1928 in Chicago, fraught with comparable fraud and irregularities, and during which Al Capone's roving bands of thugs provided GOON-like services to the corrupt mayor, William Hale "Big Bill" Thompson:

Party hacks...who had managed to get themselves appointed election officials padded the voter registration lists with fictitious names under which fraudulent voters could vote. They inserted the names of unregistered voters friendly to their slate, permitted by the ward bosses, who had verified them from preelection pledge cards. They registered vagrants whose votes the bosses bought for a few dollars, assigning them false names and addresses. Before the polling booths opened, they stuffed the ballot boxes with bundles of ballots premarked in favor of their faction. They let the bosses' hirelings remove additional bundles for marking and mixing with legitimate ballots during the final tally...As the voting got underway, Capone's henchmen...cruised the polling areas in cars bearing America First stickers...With threats of mayhem they drove off voters thought favorable to the opposition.[40]

A major difference between the process in Chicago in 1928 and that evident on Pine Ridge in 1974 is that in the former example the federal government opposed the corruption, eventually deposing, and in some cases imprisoning the perpetrators. At Pine Ridge, the same government appears to have supported, covered up for and rewarded the individuals who stand analogous to "Big Bill" Thompson and Al Capone.[41]

GOON Financing

Upon his election as tribal president in 1972, Dick Wilson moved very quickly to convert Pine Ridge into a personal fiefdom. In short order, he had padded the tribal payroll with friends and relatives. His brother Jim, for example, was given a $25,000 per year job heading the tribal planning office on a reservation where the average per capita annual income was less than $1,000 and where more than half the homes had neither indoor toilets nor running water.[42] Contending that "there's nothing in tribal law against nepotism,"[43] Wilson hired his wife as director of the Pine Ridge Head Start Program,[44] and filled other well-paying positions with his other brother George, "cousin, sons, and nephew, as well as...as many of his supporters as he could pile on the payroll,"[45] while raising his own salary from $5,500 (when he took office) to $15,500 (six months later).[46] There is evidence that he was already coercing beneficiaries of his patronage to double as GOONs, a matter recorded in affidavits:

> I am employed by the Tribe in water works and well repair. George Wilson, Richard Wilson's brother, is my boss. Richard Wilson asked me and my co-workers to stand guard at the BIA building and the Tribal office. There were training sessions for this riot squad...for defending the building, using riot sticks and so on...I found out Indian people were being trained against Indian people so I didn't want to do it...The reason I and my co-workers first went to the training sessions was because we were afraid of losing our jobs...A lot of people acting as goons now are unemployed and are doing it because they need the money. [A] commander, Glen Three Stars, has never held a permanent job. As long as this keeps up, he'll have one.[47]

In October 1972, through his cohorts, Tribal Secretary Toby Eaglebull and council member Johnson Holy Rock (who drafted it), Wilson was able to get Tribal

Resolution 72-55 passed. This bit of "legislation," approved by the BIA, gave Wilson "almost dictatorial powers" and allowed him to upgrade the skills and temper of his embryonic GOON squad by enabling him to use the "Tribal Executive Committee, which he easily controlled, to transact all Tribal business, even though under the Tribal Constitution the Executive Committee could act only on 'routine matters' when the Council was not in session."[48] This amounted, in effect, to "authorization" of Wilson to make any expenditures of tribal funds he desired—regardless of the purpose and cost involved—at his own discretion.

Hence, in addition to the $62,000 BIA "seed grant" mentioned in Chapter 5, allocated to the establishment of Wilson's "Tribal Rangers" (the BIA euphemism for the GOON squads) on November 15, 1972, he was apparently able to misappropriate an undetermined amount in federal highway funds to underwrite the payroll of his private army,[49] as well as put through the purchase of some $200,000 worth of house trailers used as their accommodations.[50] Another $330,000 was spent on construction of a building intended as Wilson's personal headquarters, with office space available for GOON leaders and BIA police (the building is now used as the tribal courthouse).[51] It is exceedingly difficult to nail down exactly what was spent for what during the Wilson years, as a GAO audit later revealed that his administration kept virtually no books on its transactions.[52] Still, the federal government had every reason to be aware of at least the generalities of what was going on, almost from the outset, as is demonstrated by a letter sent by Hank Adams (then acting officially as a White House consultant) to Richard M. Nixon—with a copy circulated to the Attorney General—in November of 1972:

> [I must report] the use of federal and tribal funds to form a personal and private militia for the service of Mr. Dick Wilson on the Pine Ridge, South Dakota, Indian Reservation…It is my understanding federally-commissioned BIA [personnel] from a number of reservations are being used…Additionally, tribal funds are being used…to hire and arm a band of "special citizen deputies" [*i.e.*, GOONs]. The focus of these forces appears to be the tribal members who were part of the Trail of Broken Treaties Caravan [*i.e.*, AIM and supporters] who are now attempting to return and remain in their home communities, but who are now being threatened.

Even though preliminary audit information on Pine Ridge was available by late 1973, indicating—at best—gross financial mismanagement on the part of the Wilsonites, neither the FBI nor any other federal agency made an effort to intervene. To the contrary, the federal government continued to pump an estimated $24 million annually into Wilson's coffers over the next two years and, in 1974, to guarantee a $400,000 "tribal" loan through the Indian Bank in Washington, D.C., with which Wilson almost certainly underwrote his GOON payrolls.[53] Far from holding the Wilsonites accountable for their fiscal manipulations, the government later attempted to recover the loan monies which, predictably enough, had been defaulted upon, by levying the sum as an offset against its proposed monetary settlement of the

Black Hills Land Claim (*i.e.*, the government sought to charge the *victims* for the payroll costs of the GOON squad).

Garden Plot and Cable Splicer

The issue of the FBI relationship to the GOONs becomes all the more acute when viewed in the context of being part of a COINTELPRO-era scenario calling for the active domestic collaboration of the Bureau, the CIA, the military and other federal/local "assets" of repression in a combination the Church Committee had condemned as being inappropriate and illegal.[54] This is directly contrary to the termination of such activities recommended by the Committee (which received solemn assurance from the respective agencies that it had been long ended). A review of government documents declassified by court order reveals that the overall script guiding federal performance on Pine Ridge during the critical period may be found in a Top Secret Pentagon plan for domestic counterinsurgency operation code-named "Garden Plot." This was produced during the late 1960s, a subsection of the broader "Cable Splicer" study commissioned by the Pentagon's Directorate of Military Support (DOMS).[55]

In essence, the Garden Plot scenario called for the training of civilian police (at the Army's Senior Officers Civil Disturbance Orientation Course [SEADOC] at Fort Gordon) and the establishment of "Special Operations Groups" (SOGs) from among key non-military personnel nationally. These would be deployed as centerpieces to "law enforcement endeavors" focusing upon the suppression of dissidents whenever and wherever dissent in the United States was deemed to have "gotten out of hand." Advice and tactical consultation to these non-military formations would accrue directly from the military's irregular warfare specialists; specialized counterinsurgency equipment would be provided directly by the military, and—in the event that a given situation ultimately overshot the repressive capacities of the non-military collaborators—special counterinsurgency-trained military units would be deployed to finish the job. Tellingly, the term "SOG" is synonymous with the identification of a secret unit comprised of U.S. Army Special Forces and other elite personnel, CIA operatives and elite elements of the South Vietnamese police/military then functioning in Southeast Asia and eventually tied to the infamous "Operation Phoenix" assassination program undertaken there.[56] Another hallmark of this classified special warfare consortium was its use of mercenary and other unorthodox troop formations (*e.g.*, Montagnards, Khmer mercenaries and Nungs), to which "pseudo-gangs" such as the Klan, SAO and GOONs would be the domestic equivalent.[57]

At the same time that the SOGs were being formed, "[t]he BIA…created a Special Operations Service (SOS)…of fifty or so Indian police troops trained at the FBI national academy at Quantico, Virginia, at the CIA training facility in Los Fresnos, Texas, and at the BIA Indian Police Training and Research Center in Brigham City, Utah." According to researcher Rick LaCourse, FBI reports on Wounded Knee were routed to Leonard Garment at the White House, where they were sifted by the Office of Indian Services and forwarded to SOS Coordinator James Cooper; "[Cooper's] information [went] to eleven BIA Area Offices, each having a Chief Law Enforcement Officer [Delmar Eastman at Pine Ridge] who maintains intelligence relations with local BIA agency and reservation officials [such as Dick Wilson]."[58] Tellingly, SOS personnel from all eleven BIA area offices converged on Pine Ridge to work with FBI and SOG team members (as well as the GOON squads) shortly after the beginning of the siege of Wounded Knee.

The Garden Plot/Cable Splicer prospectus accords well with Attorney General Richard Kleindienst's dispatch of SWAT-trained FBI personnel and a sixty-five-man SOG from the U.S. Marshals Service to Pine Ridge on February 12, 1973, as well as the involvement of the Pentagon in the persons of Colonel Volney Warner and Jack Potter, sent by Alexander Haig (see Chapter 5). Warner's credentials for the job included formal counterinsurgency training at the U.S. Army Special Warfare School (Ft. Bragg, N.C.) and two tours in Vietnam specializing in application of counterinsurgency doctrine (his second tour was with civil affairs and pacification programs associated with Operation Phoenix). Warner countered a proposal advanced by (SAC, Minneapolis) Joseph Trimbach and U.S. Marshal Director Wayne Colburn— made during a secret meeting between the three at Ellsworth Air Force Base near Rapid City, S.D., during the early morning hours of March 3—that 2,000 troops be immediately introduced to the reservation. The Colonel suggested that they continue to "increase the size of FBI and Marshal forces, and [he would] give them the military supplies necessary to do the job. [If it failed], the 82nd Airborne Division would come to their rescue."[59] He would later compare the military's role at Wounded Knee to that of the Military Assistance and Advisory Command (MAAG) in Vietnam.[60]

Even before the meeting was conducted, the Air Force, acting on a request by Colburn, had initiated sophisticated aerial reconnaissance flights over the Wounded Knee area, turning the resulting photographs over to federal police. By noon of March 3, Colonel Jack Potter, Deputy Chief of Staff of the U.S. Sixth Army, arrived on the scene to facilitate the transfer of equipment from military to FBI and U.S. Marshal usage. Five hours later, Haig approved the "loan" of fifteen armored personnel carriers (APCs), the first step of an infusion of lethal paraphernalia which continued despite a DOMS staff intelligence report made the very next day (March 4) stating that:

> The [AIM] Indians do not appear intent upon inflicting bodily harm upon the legitimate residents of Wounded Knee, nor upon the Federal law enforcement agents operating in this area...[and] because of its isolated geographical location, the seizure and holding of Wounded Knee [by AIM] poses no threat to the nation, to the State of South Dakota, or the Pine Ridge Reservation itself.

The seeming paradox of devoting a massive buildup of lethal force to the suppression of a political organization under such circumstances is perhaps explained in part as the intelligence report continues, "However, it is conceded that this act [the occupation of Wounded Knee] is a source of irritation, if not embarrassment, to the Administration in general, *and the Department of Justice* [under which the FBI is lodged] *in particular* [emphasis added]."[61] All of this was, as is noted in Chapter 5, carried out with an attempt at great secrecy, in accordance with standard counterinsurgency doctrine.[62]

By March 5, there were 243 federal officers surrounding Wounded Knee, a figure that grew to over 300 by March 12. Corresponding provisions of military material included "over 130 M-16 rifles with 100,000 rounds of ammunition, 75 high-powered sniper rifles (M-14s, M-1s and Springfields, all with scopes and ammunition [these were the weapons with which AIM members Buddy Lamont and Frank Clearwater were killed and several other AIM members wounded]), helmets, flak vests, signal flares, mine detectors, C-rations, jeeps, trucks, and maintenance technicians for the APCs..."[63] On April 12, the FBI (via the Justice Department), followed up by requesting a "prepositioned package" of military equipment, including: "...200 baseball-type CS gas grenades, M-79 grenade launchers with 100 rounds of high explosives, 600 rounds of CS gas and 600 rounds of red smoke (usually used as markers in targeting air strikes), 750 pounds of dry CS and air delivery cannisters, helicopters and [additional] military advisors." The request was approved by the Defense Department on April 17, 1973 and prepositioned at Ft. Carson, Colorado rather than at Ellsworth Air Force Base as the Bureau had requested. It was this military logistics support which allowed federal forces to pour more than 500,000 bullets into Wounded Knee in seventy-one days. Simultaneously, Fred Buzhardt, General Counsel for the Defense Department, had prepared—according to a 1975 letter from former presidential advisor John Ehrlichman to actor Marlon Brando—a memo to Nixon recommending the "full scale" invasion of Pine Ridge, utilizing "tanks" and "a minimum of a division of troops [15,000-17,000 men]."[64]

It must be remembered that all this military might was focused upon less than 300 AIM members and supporters inside Wounded Knee.[65] It must also be recalled that all this accumulated military hardware, once in the hands of the FBI, remained there for the duration of its exercise on Pine Ridge, a matter readily evinced by the APCs and the Bell UH-1B "Huey" helicopters consistently utilized by the Bureau on the reservation during the summer and fall of 1975. Given this profligate mass of largely unaccounted for military weaponry, the question of how the GOONs came to be so well armed can be readily answered.

The situation on Pine Ridge closely resembled the conditions of death-squad repression prevailing in Latin America. The FBI's fostering and use of pseudo-gangs or private armies, *especially* in the context of its secret cooperation with the military, in pursuit of its covert political agenda(s), truly seems to approximate the situation in such countries as Uruguay or Guatemala.[66] In a domestic sense, the role of the FBI on Pine Ridge corresponds precisely with that of the Special Forces in Southeast Asia and that of the GOONs to the Montagnard and other "indigs" the Green Berets equipped and led there.

It was perhaps for this reason that President Richard Nixon refused, when ordered by federal Judge Fred Nichol during the 1974 "Wounded Knee Leadership

Trial" of Russell Means and Dennis Banks, to deliver tapes of Oval Office discussions of Wounded Knee. Both former FBI director L. Patrick Gray and former White House Counsel John Dean had already testified that the siege was a common conversational topic with Nixon in 1973 and that the military figured prominently in such talk. Nixon, however, sent a letter stating that "it would not be in the national interest" to make public the content of these candid, if informal, policy considerations.[67]

In sum, the actual circumstances of federal police behavior on Pine Ridge during the crucial period lends considerable support to Tim Butz's observation that, "The experiment with militarizing the police did not begin with Wounded Knee—Wounded Knee was simply a field test where the military was allowed to clandestinely control a rather large army composed of specially-trained U.S. Marshals and FBI agents."[68] This, coupled with Senator Sam Ervin's pointed warning during his Committee Hearings on Military Intelligence Domestic Operations (1975)—that the military cannot be relied on to check its own growing power—and the rather self-evident fact that the practices of the COINTELPRO era did *not* end when the FBI said they did, should be cause for a considerable sense of alarm to thinking people everywhere.

Chapter 7

Assassinations and Bad-jacketing

The only way to deal with the Indian problem in South Dakota is to put a gun to AIM leaders' heads and pull the trigger.
—William "Wild Bill" Janklow, South Dakota Attorney General (1975)

As the Hampton-Clark assassinations proved in Chicago, the FBI is not above using surrogate police agencies to bring about the physical elimination of political leaders. In other instances, such as with the SAO (see Chapter 6) in southern California, the Bureau has been known to use (or attempt to use) paramilitary civilian organizations under its control and sponsorship for such purposes. In still other situations, including the deliberate fostering of violent strife between the US organization and the BPP during the late 1960s, it has orchestrated the murder of targeted dissident leaders by rival factions within their own ethnic or political communities (*e.g.*: Jon Huggins and Bunchy Carter). Finally, as with the case of Fred Bennett, the Bureau has employed the technique of "bad-jacketing" to facilitate the execution of key individuals by members of their *own* political groupings. In some instances, all of these COINTELPRO approaches may be seen to coexist. Such was certainly the case with regard to the BPP by the early 1970s, and such was the case on Pine Ridge from late 1972 through early 1976.

As was noted in Chapter 5, a vastly disproportionate number of AIM members and supporters died violently during the period of heaviest FBI operational involvement on Pine Ridge. In Chapter 6, a number of examples illustrate the violence perpetrated by one of the Bureau's surrogate entities, the GOON squad. While much of this appears to be more or less randomly directed against the entire "dissident" socio-political constituency, and thus cannot be accurately cast within assassination activities *per se,* other examples—notably the two attempts to kill AIM leader Russell Means and the murder of Jeanette Bissonette (apparently mistaken for ION leader Ellen Moves Camp)—must be understood as attempted assassinations.

For purposes of this study, the term "assassination" will be used to connote the individually targeted political murders undertaken by individuals outside the victim's own group. "Bad-jacketing," which often results in assassinations carried out from *within* the victim's circle, is not always lethal, or lethally intended. These two distinct but related categories of COINTELPRO-type activity will therefore be handled separately in this chapter. The following examples, however, should serve to demonstrate clearly that both techniques were integral to the campaign of repression visited by the FBI upon the American Indian opposition on Pine Ridge.

Assassinations

The Case of Pedro Bissonette

On October 17, 1973, Pedro Bissonette, head of OSCRO and a leader of the ION which had emerged during the siege of Wounded Knee earlier that year (see Chapter 5), was hunted down and shot to death by BIA police. Bissonette had been arrested on April 27, 1973, near the end of the events at Wounded Knee, and charged with "interfering with a Federal Officer in performance of his duties"; the FBI had then come forth with an offer of probation in lieu of the possible ninety-year sentence the OSCRO/ION leader was facing in exchange for his "cooperative" testimony against AIM leaders to be tried for Wounded Knee-related "offenses."[1] His response was offered publicly:

> I will stand with my brothers and sisters. I will tell the truth about them and about why we went to Wounded Knee. I will fight for my people. I will live for them, and if it is necessary to stop the terrible things that happen to Indians on the Pine Ridge Reservation, I am ready to die for them...I will never lie against my people, crawl for a better deal for myself. I stand with Russell Means, Gladys Bissonette, Ellen Moves Camp, Clyde Bellecourt.[2]

Bissonette's posture and utterances were an unmitigated disaster for the Bureau's campaign to divide the AIM "outsiders" from their traditionalist ION supporters on the reservation. Worse, WKLDOC attorney Ramon Roubideaux was able to demonstrate sufficient governmental misconduct in his case that Bissonette was able to obtain a low bail release from jail.[3] As the prosecution's position began to erode, he announced that he intended not only to serve as a defense witness in the forthcoming Wounded Knee trials, but to base his testimony upon *documented* evidence proving the criminal culpability of Dick Wilson, the GOONs and the FBI in the events which had transpired on Pine Ridge up to that point.[4] Insofar as neither Wilson nor his federal colleagues was sure that Bissonette *didn't* have such evidence, this was taken as a very serious threat.

On the morning of October 17, a man (believed to be a GOON named Cliff Richards) confronted Pedro Bissonette on a sidewalk in the tiny unincorporated hamlet of White Clay, Nebraska. In the ensuing scuffle, Richards was knocked to the ground and Bissonette walked away.[5] Although White Clay is across the reservation boundary, beyond the jurisdiction of the BIA police, police chief/GOON

OSCRO/ION leader Pedro Bissonette at a press conference shortly before his death. On the night of October 17, 1973, Bissonette was shot at a BIA roadblock on Pine Ridge by GOON Joe Clifford and allowed to bleed to death before being taken to a nearby hospital. (Photo: *Akwesasne Notes*)

leader Delmar Eastman immediately ordered an intensive effort to track down the OSCRO/ION leader:

All day...there was an extensive manhunt for Pedro. The search involved about 20 police cars and several airplanes. They hunted Pedro down like an animal and murdered him in cold blood. We have not yet determined who did the actual shooting but are quite certain that the murder was engineered by BIA Special Officer Del Eastman.[6]

According to Pine Ridge BIA Superintendent Kendall Cummings, in a statement to an AP reporter made the following morning,

Pine Ridge police began looking for Bissonette on [a] warrant Wednesday afternoon [October 17]. Two officers spotted him and tried to stop him, but Bissonette fired a shot at them and they gave pursuit. Later in the evening, two officers were making a routine check of a car, and found Bissonette inside. Pedro attempted to shoot one of the officers and was shot at fairly close range.[7]

The official report of BIA police officer Joe Clifford (a known GOON) is somewhat at odds with Cummings' version, contending that Bissonette's car was stopped at a roadblock erected specifically for the purpose of "apprehending" the "fugitive." In Clifford's account, Bissonette "resisted arrest" and it became necessary to subdue him with a 12 gauge shotgun blast at pointblank range; the time of this shooting is listed as being 9:48 P.M. Clifford does not mention that Bissonette attempted to shoot anyone, although the notion of resisting arrest might conceivably be stretched to cover such an act.[8] In any event, no weapon was ever produced by the police.

WKLDOC attorney Mark Lane viewed Bissonette's body in the Pine Ridge morgue shortly before it was whisked away to Nebraska, and asserted the wounds were quite different from those reported by BIA police. (Photo: *Rapid City Journal*)

Pedro Bissonette was pronounced dead on arrival at Pine Ridge hospital at 10:10 p.m., a time which, when taken together with Clifford's report, suggests everything possible was done to rush the wounded man to medical attention to save his life.[9] Several witnesses who happened upon the scene reported, however, that Bissonette's car was already stopped at the roadblock as early as 9 p.m., and that a pool of blood was observable at that time, approximately forty-five feet from the automobile.[10] If the time of the shooting was 9 p.m., this means it took over an hour to get to the hospital—a few minutes away—an interval which allowed ample time for Bissonette to die of shock and loss of blood.

WKLDOC attorney Mark Lane rushed from Rapid City to the hospital (over an hour's drive) in order to view the remains. He was admitted to the morgue "at some point just before midnight," and discovered a pattern of seven bullet holes, "apparently from a .38 calibre pistol in a remarkably small pattern—three by five inches—any shot of which would have killed him" in Bissonette's chest.[11] Lane also reported a grazing wound to the neck of the body, three bullet holes in the hand, various body bruises indicating that a beating had been administered at some point prior to death, and what he took to be tear gas burns.[12] He immediately called Pedro's mother (and ION leader) Gladys Bissonette to initiate a family demand for an independent autopsy.[13]

However, at 3 a.m. on October 18—that is, before anyone else could view the corpse and before any sort of legal action could be taken on the matter of the independent autopsy—Bissonette's body was removed from the morgue in Pine Ridge hospital and shipped to Scottsbluff, Nebraska, on orders from Delmar Eastman.[14] When queried two days later by a reporter, Eastman responded that he'd ordered the hasty removal "under direct orders from [U.S. Attorney] Bill Clayton."[15]

Clayton, who was to play a very prominent and cooperative role in the FBI's handling of the Angie Long Visitor case (see Chapter 9) had, as it turned out, offered assurances by phone to Washington, D.C. attorney Leonard Cavise (an associate of Mark Lane) that the body would *not* be moved; this promise was made immediately prior to his issuance of instructions to Eastman to whisk the remains across the state line.[16] As a consequence, the independent autopsy sought by the Bissonette family and WKLDOC was never performed; the body was examined by BIA-retained pathologist W.O. Brown on October 20 (with a finding of a cause of death conforming precisely with that posited in Clifford's police report) and then placed in a sealed coffin.[17] The burial occurred on October 23, 1973. When Delmar Eastman's BIA police arrived they were turned away by AIM security. They eventually set up a command post across the road from which they attempted to keep the ceremony under surveillance.[18]

The FBI, considered this "an open and shut case" of justifiable homicide on the part of Joe Clifford. No investigation of Bissonette's death was ever undertaken by the Bureau, perhaps because as Dennis Banks later put it: "We lost a great man there. The federal police killed Pedro in an assassination conspiracy, and the reason was obvious: he knew too much about Wilson and the BIA and about what the police were up to, and he intended to expose them. Also, I think they decided that if Pedro was dead, AIM could no longer function on the reservation."[19]

The Murder of Byron DeSersa

On January 30, 1976, Oglala Sioux tribal attorney Byron DeSersa was killed by GOONs during a chase on the reservation. As the situation has been described elsewhere:

> In the dark winter of 1975-76, the lawlessness on Pine Ridge intensified, despite the replacement of Dick Wilson as Tribal Council president by Al Trimble, [a] former BIA Superintendent. Trimble soon found that at least 25 percent of the federal monies allocated to small businesses and job development [on the reservation] had found its way into the pockets of "two brothers," whom he did not have to name...Wilson was outraged by the three to one vote against him, and since he did not actually relinquish office until April, 1976, he made the most of the time left. After the election on January 17, the chairman of the Pine Ridge District—Wilson's stronghold—let it be known that Trimble's home town of Wanblee [in the far northeast corner of the reservation], which had worked hard against Wilson, needed "straightening out."[20]

In the early evening of January 30, three cars containing fifteen GOONs appeared on the streets of Wanblee. Each of Wilson's minions was attired in a government-issue flak vest and carried an M-16 rifle. After driving around the tiny village, making sure local residents were aware of their presence, the GOONs stopped to shoot up the house of Guy Dull Knife, an elderly but vehement Cheyenne opponent of the Wilson regime.[21] They then spotted a car driven by DeSersa and three companions and gave chase.

Byron DeSersa was a visible and vocal anti-Wilson activist, a contributor to the outspoken newspaper edited by his uncle (whose home was fire-bombed by GOONs in 1973; see Chapter 6), a known OSCRO member and AIM supporter, and a major organizer in Al Trimble's 1975 election campaign. He had also recently announced that he intended to use his legal expertise to bring the Wilsonites to justice once the new tribal government was consolidated. It was probably for all of these reasons that the DeSersa car became the focal point of GOON attention:

> Although the culprits [had already been identified] by witnesses, the BIA police made no arrests and, later...in a high-speed four mile chase, these same goons overtook a car driven by tribal attorney Byron DeSersa (a grandson of Black Elk) and shot it full of holes. "Oh Christ, I'm hit, I'm hit bad!" DeSersa cried; he could not control the car, which rolled into a ditch. His passengers fled across a field, all but George Bettelyoun, who tried to help him, crying, "They're gonna kill you!" DeSersa crawled across the seat and dragged himself out of the car, but was unable to climb the road bank. He told his passenger to save himself, which he did. DeSersa, leg nearly severed by three bullets which had splayed when they came through the car door, would have survived if he had received help; instead, he bled to death while the goons pursued his passengers through the woods.[22]

The next afternoon, two FBI agents arrived in Wanblee to "investigate the disturbance." Although George Bettelyoun identified DeSersa's killers to the agents, they did nothing to apprehend—or even interfere with—the GOONs, who were still present and had meanwhile engaged in several fire-bombings. To the contrary, the agents busied themselves questioning everyone "except those involved...and arrested Guy Dull Knife (victim of the first shooting attack) for disorderly conduct."[23]

The FBI agents told those who protested that they lacked "probable cause" to make arrests [of the GOONs], and anyway, they were only in Wanblee in an "investigative capacity." The outraged Wanblee residents finally organized their own law and gave the GOONs until sunset to get out of town; the GOONs received a BIA police escort back to Pine Ridge village.[24]

Called in to investigate the situation by Trimble, Shirley Hill Witt (Director of the Rocky Mountain Regional Office of the U.S. Commission on Civil Rights) and William Muldrow (an Equal Opportunity Specialist with that office) officially reported that:

> On Friday evening and Saturday morning, January 30 and 31...several carloads of heavily armed persons reported by eyewitnesses to be Wilson supporters arrived in [Wanblee]...Byron DeSersa, a resident of Wanblee, was shot and killed during a high-speed automobile chase, reportedly by persons recognized by passengers in DeSersa's car as being the same individuals...Attackers jumped out of their cars to chase those who were with DeSersa, and he bled to death for lack of medical attention.[25]

A later Civil Rights Commission inquiry into the circumstances of DeSersa's death concluded:

GOON leader Dale Janis at a roadblock outside Wounded Knee, 1973. Involved in a number of brutal actions against AIM and its supporters, Janis was finally convicted of manslaughter and sentenced to two years in the Byron DeSersa murder. The FBI played no role in his prosecution or conviction. (Photo: Kevin Barry McKiernan)

The BIA police simply ordered Winters [the GOON most personally responsible] out of town. The FBI was notified, but the Bureau...did nothing but drive around the area. Winters was later picked up by the Martin [South Dakota] police department.[26]

Hill Witt and Muldrow concur on this last point:

Saturday evening [January 31] one person, Charles David Winters, was arrested for the murder of DeSersa. No attempt was made [by the FBI or BIA police] to apprehend or arrest the other passengers in Winters' car, even though persons who were with DeSersa when he was shot claimed they were chased by Winters' companions after the shooting and could readily identify their attackers. Nor have further arrests been made in connection with the terrorization of the town over two days.[27]

The Winters arrest is an anomaly in the odyssey of anti-AIM GOON violence insofar as it was effected by off-reservation local police and pushed beyond federal control by Winters' near-immediate confession that he had fired the fatal shots at DeSersa.[28] More, he also implicated several of his colleagues as being directly involved in the murder before being released on $5,000 bond (compared to $125,000 bail required for release of Russell Means on non-capital, Wounded Knee-related charges in 1973; see Chapter 5). In the end, four GOONs were taken to trial: Billy Wilson (Dick Wilson's son) and Chuck Richards (his son-in-law) were both acquitted on the basis of "self-defense," although neither Byron DeSersa nor his passengers had been armed at the time of the murder; Winters and GOON leader Dale Janis were allowed to plea bargain to second degree manslaughter and ultimately served two years each for what had clearly been cold-blooded murder.[29]

Anna Mae Pictou and Nogeesik Aquash during their marriage ceremony, conducted by AIM spiritual leader Wallace Black Elk, inside Wounded Knee, 1973. (Photo: Kevin Barry McKiernan)

The Execution of Anna Mae Aquash

On February 24, 1976, the body of AIM member Anna Mae Pictou Aquash (a Micmac from Nova Scotia) was discovered near Highway 73, close to the village of Wanblee, in a deserted area of Pine Ridge. Her body was found by a Lakota rancher named Roger Amiotte in a wash on his land, some distance from the road.[30] Atypically, FBI representation was provided to the BIA police contingent (and area sheriff's deputies) who assembled at the scene shortly after Amiotte phoned the authorities. According to BIA investigators Doug Parisian and Nate Merrick, one of the four agents immediately dispatched by the Bureau to view what it would normally have chalked off as a "stray body report" was David Price.[31]

SA Price knew Aquash well, having arrested her during the September 5, 1975 FBI air assault on Crow Dog's Paradise on the Rosebud Reservation (see Chapter 9). At the time, less than six months before, Price had run up to Aquash shouting, "You! You! I'm so glad I found you! I've been looking for you everywhere!"[32] He subsequently interrogated her at some length in Pierre, S.D. as to the whereabouts of AIM leader Dennis Banks (sought on an interstate flight warrant) as well as Leonard Peltier and others sought in connection with the deaths of SA Jack Coler and Price's close friend SA Ron Williams on June 26, 1975 (again, see Chapter 9). Unable to convince Price otherwise, Aquash—according to the FBI's summary of the interview—finally laid her head upon a table and wearily announced that they could, "Either lock me up or shoot me. That's what you're going to do anyway, and

The only known photo of SA David Price who threatened Anna Mae Aquash, "developed" perjurer Louis Moves Camp, orchestrated Myrtle Poor Bear's "eyewitness" accounts, and engaged in a range of other COINTELPRO-style activities. Currently assigned to the Rochester, Minn. FBI office, his partner William Wood is once again stationed on Pine Ridge. (Photo: Shelley McIntire)

that's the two choices I'm taking."[33] According to statements made by Aquash to friends afterward, Price responded that she was correct, she wouldn't "live out the year" unless she cooperated with the Bureau.[34]

Upon her release from Price's custody, Aquash wrote in a letter to her sister, "My efforts to raise the consciousness of Whites who are so against Indians in the States are bound to be stopped by the FBI sooner or later."[35] Not long after, she was arrested near Vale, Oregon in a motor home believed by the Bureau to have been vacated by both Banks and Peltier only moments earlier (see Chapter 12). SA Price is believed to have been one of the agents who appeared in Vale to hustle Aquash back to South Dakota on a federal fugitive warrant. As she left, she commented to a reporter that, "If they take me back to South Dakota, I'll be murdered."[36] At about the same time, she confided to friends, "They'll execute me. That's what they do to Indians who fight for their people."[37]

Despite the fact that Price was obviously acquainted with Aquash's physical appearance, he professed to be unable to identify the body lying in the wash on February 24. The remains were taken to the Pine Ridge hospital morgue, some 100 miles distant. The following day,

[i]n accordance with normal procedures followed when an unidentified body is found on the reservation, an autopsy was requested by the BIA. No agents of the FBI were present when the autopsy was performed, but SA [Donald] Dealing, SA William B. Wood [Price's partner], and SA David F. Price viewed the body at the PHS [Public Health Service] Hospital, Pine Ridge, South Dakota, prior to the autopsy, and SA John Robert Munis viewed the body after the autopsy...the autopsy was performed by W.O.

Brown, Scottsbluff, Nebraska, who stated in his initial report that the probable cause of death was due to exposure.[38]

Dr. Brown was the same pathologist to whom Delmar Eastman had rushed the body of Pedro Bissonette in the middle of the night some two and one-half years previously and to whom the FBI had turned when an autopsy was needed on the body of Joe Stuntz Killsright on June 25, 1975 (see Chapter 9); on both occasions, Brown had reached findings "confirming" police reports subject to serious debate.

The body was then tabbed as "Jane Doe" for interment in a common grave. According to the FBI,

> ...no identification could be made locally through normal procedures. As is standard in such cases, a decision was made by SA Thomas H. Green to have Dr. Brown sever the hands of the unidentified body in order to send them to the FBI Identification Division for positive identification purposes.[39]

As WKLDOC attorney Bruce Ellison points out, such practice is hardly "standard" because "in order to make this kind of identification, you've got to have a pretty good idea of who you're looking for."[40] In any event, as is noted in a Congressional report, "the BIA [buried] the body on March 2, 1976, prior to the identification. On March 3, 1976, the FBI Identification Division, Washington, D.C., identified the body to be that of Anna Mae Aquash."[41]

On March 5, the Bureau notified Aquash's family in Canada that she had died "by natural causes." The family immediately contacted WKLDOC attorneys in Rapid City and inquired as to whether it would be possible to obtain a second autopsy; Ellison went to work to gain authorization to exhume the body.[42] According to the Bureau's version of events:

> Prior to receiving any information that Ms. Aquash's relatives desired a second autopsy, on March 4, SA Wood contacted Assistant U.S. Attorney Bruce W. Boyd, Rapid City, South Dakota, in order to institute proceedings to obtain a Federal Court order for exhumation and re-examination of the body...An affidavit requesting exhumation was completed on March 8, 1976, and U.S. District Court Judge Andrew Bogue, Rapid City, issued the exhumation order. However, exhumation was delayed after an attorney for Ms. Aquash's family [Ellison] contacted the Rapid City FBI Office that day and requested a pathologist of the family's choosing be present during the second autopsy.[43]

The U.S. Commission on Civil Rights, after investigating the affair, concurs with some of the Bureau's statement, but notes that the affidavit submitted by Wood indicated that the FBI sought exhumation for "purposes of obtaining complete X-rays and further medical examination. X-rays had not been considered necessary during the first examination."[44] This is noted as a "remarkable oversight," given that the initial FBI 302 report filed by one of the four agents on the scene states that, "Because of the distance of the body from the road, [name deleted] also noted that the cause of death may...be manslaughter." Under the circumstances, murder would have been a more logical suspicion and, in either event, *any* suspicion of foul play should have triggered an exceedingly thorough autopsy which would have included complete X-rays.

Ellison arranged for a Minnesota pathologist, Dr. Garry Peterson to represent the family and, in an about-face, the Bureau decided that he should run the second examination absent an "official," governmentally-retained coroner. Hence, upon Peterson's arrival:

> ...on March 11, 1976, the remains of Ms. Aquash were exhumed. Through X-ray examination, conducted by PHS personnel [at Pine Ridge hospital] and Dr. Peterson, it was determined a bullet had entered the skull. FBI SAs Wood and J. Gary Adams were present during the X-ray and subsequent pathological examination of the body. The bullet was recovered from the skull at the time of the second examination by Dr. Peterson.[45]

Even before the X-rays, Peterson "noticed a bulge in the dead woman's left temple and dry blood in her hair," clearly visible to the naked eye even after interment and exhumation; further, "he could see the back of the head had been washed and powdered...a .32 calibre bullet accounting for the bulge in the temple. There were powder burns around the wound in the neck. Anna Mae Aquash...had died from a bullet shot at close range into the back of her head."[46]

The U.S. Commission on Civil Rights officials who investigated the FBI handling of Aquash's death termed it "incredible" that the wound:

> ...was not reported in the first autopsy and [this] gave rise to allegations that the FBI and/or BIA police had covered up the cause of her death. The fact that officers of both agencies examined the body *in situs*, wrapped in a blanket beside the road and far away from any populated area...lends credence to these allegations in the minds of many people. Hospital personnel who received the body at the hospital [on February 24] reportedly expected violence because of the blood on her head.[47]

The Commission report goes on to observe that, "[Many people] are of the opinion that Anna Mae Aquash had been singled out for special attention by the FBI because of her association with AIM leader Dennis Banks and the knowledge she may have had about the shooting of two FBI agents [in the Oglala firefight; see Chapter 9) on the Pine Ridge Reservation last summer."[48] The report concludes that "what was at the very least [an] extremely indifferent and careless investigation of the Aquash murder, [has helped to create a situation] many residents feel reveals an attitude of racism and antagonism on the part of the FBI toward Indian people."[49]

The question was also taken up in Congress, where a truly amazing interchange occurred between James Frier of the FBI's Criminal Investigation Division and two Congressional committee members, clearly demonstrating that Indian interpretations of FBI sentiments were hardly ill-founded:

Mr. Tuchevich: Well, has the FBI made any effort to investigate why a person performing an autopsy could not distinguish between a gunshot wound and exposure as a cause of death?

Mr. Frier: Well, it's very difficult to say why a doctor misidentifies a cause of death...No, we did not do an investigation as to why he misread the cause of death.

Mr. Tuchevich: Do you have any plans to do so, to initiate such an investigation?

Mr. Frier: No sir. It is extremely removed from the time [this testimony occurred in 1981], and I don't think anything would come of it.

Mr. Edwards: How do you know, if you just asked him, he wouldn't say somebody— and I'm not saying who—talked him into it or bribed him or something?

Mr. Frier: Sir, I can't say. I really don't know what his excuses or reasons for missing the identification were. And I really don't know what follow-up was done as to why he did it so poorly...However, we [the FBI] had no involvement at all, and our investigation has been as aggressive as possible in this case.

Mr. Edwards: Well, I'm sure it has been a pain in the neck to you; and it has been to this committee, because we get a lot of mail on it. So we wish somebody would question the doctor. Was he drunk, or what happened? It would be very interesting to know.[50]

In the same hearing, the Bureau itself neatly contradicted Frier's testimony that the FBI had "no plans" to pursue the Aquash investigation further, by fending off queries as follows: "Because the investigation into Ms. Aquash's death is still active and pending, information which would interfere with that investigation has not been disclosed."[51]

While researching a book on the life and death of Anna Mae Aquash, Johanna Brand *did* pose a few of the relevant questions to Dr. W.O. Brown. The pathologist, who acknowledged performing "30-35 autopsies per year on the reservation" (as contracted by the FBI and BIA police), "netting him earnings of about $20,000" annually during the critical period, wanted to know: "Why all the interest in this case? So they found an Indian body—so a body was found."[52] As to the magnitude of "errors" in the matter, the good doctor merely replied rhetorically, "Everybody makes mistakes. Haven't you made mistakes?"[53] And finally, despite the clearly and immediately fatal nature of the gunshot wound at issue, he continued to insist that, "The bullet may have initiated the mechanism of death, the proximate cause of which was frostbite."[54]

All of this lends considerable substance to the observation of Linda Huber of the Washington, D.C. law firm Tigar, Buffone, and Doyle, offered in a letter to the Congressional committee before which Frier testified: "The Aquash matter raises an abundance of troublesome questions...It seems that what is going on is, at the very least, a studied attempt on the part of officials at FBI headquarters to avoid knowing what happened in the field."[55] The answer to Huber's implicit "Why?" may well have been touched upon by the committee itself when it came full circle back to the issue of SA David Price's knowledge of Aquash:

> SA Price had had personal contact with Ms. Aquash in the past and assisted in photographing the body at the PHS morgue on February 25, 1976...SA Price's previous contacts with Ms. Aquash occurred when he interviewed her in connection with an FBI investigation in the early spring of 1975 and again in September 1975...[on the latter occasion] she was arrested...by agents of the FBI, one of whom was SA Price.[56]

The committee report offers SA Price a feeble retort to the obvious by accepting at face value his assertion that "he was unable to recognize the body as that of Anna Mae Aquash due to its decomposition."[57] Such a conclusion is virtually untenable: the morgue photos—pictures that Price himself helped take—reveal a face easily recognizable. David Price, it seems, "missed" recognizing Aquash in precisely the same fashion that W.O. Brown "missed" a .32 calibre hole in the back of her head and the blood that was leaking out upon his morgue table. As WKLDOC attorney Lew Gurwitz put it at the time, "There is a strong possibility of complicity by the FBI in the death of Anna Mae Aquash."[58]

Bad-jacketing

Although charges and countercharges of "being a cop" are inherent among members of any organization targeted for police infiltration and disruption, the terms "bad-jacketing" or "snitch-jacketing" apply only to instances in which a bona fide organizational member is deliberately cast in such a light by those who have infiltrated. Such false portrayals are often consciously facilitated at the "above ground" level by the police agencies from which the real infiltrators emanate. The general purposes of such activity are clear enough:

> This "bad-jacketing" technique, well known in prisons where guards are adept at turning members of a group against each other, also creates a pressure point. When a man is abandoned by his comrades because of a rumor slipped into the prison grapevine, when suspicion and rancor suddenly replace old loyalties, it is easier to turn him into a stoolie, the cooperative, compliant informer the guards tend to see as the ideal prisoner. The man feels cheated and threatened. His loyalties come to reflect the new status thrust upon him by the word put out about him. He abandons those who have abandoned him, becomes the enemy of those who have assumed him [or her] to be one. And, armed with the promise of early parole, given, perhaps, a short stretch in the hole to reinstate him in his [or her] comrades' eyes as no friend of the guards, he is returned to the prison population as the informer he never was before scuttlebutt made him one.[59]

The actual participation in police operations of those targeted is, of course, an "optimal result" from the counterintelligence point of view. More typically, the simple abandonment of "key activists" by their associates—the political "neutralizations" by which COINTELPRO operatives measured their "success"[60]—is deemed quite sufficient. At the juncture in which the bad-jacketing process takes hold within an organization, the police can be reasonably certain that it will begin to unravel, to eat itself alive. Its membership will become increasingly factionalized and isolated from one another; in cases where extreme physical jeopardy has also been imposed by the police (e.g., the BPP), members may also begin literally to liquidate one another as a desperate expedient to perceived self-defense. Each of these outcomes—*including* the "internal" assassination of police-targeted individuals—are consciously calculated COINTELPRO objectives.

In order to employ such a technique "on the street," as opposed to the insular and artificial environment of a prison, it is an absolute requirement that the police place infiltrators within targeted organizations (the higher within the organizational hierarchy, the better). In the case of AIM, as the next chapter will demonstrate, this was accomplished by the FBI with an astonishing degree of effectiveness. It should come as no surprise, then, that the process of bad-jacketing was implemented in various ways and, given the nature and extent of physical repression being visited upon AIM by the Bureau, with particularly grisly results.

The first tangible examples of bad-jacketing being used against AIM occurred in the wake of Wounded Knee, at the organization's national convention held near White Oak, Oklahoma from July 25 through August 5, 1973. The initial focus of suspicion was upon John "Two Birds" Arbuckle, an Anishinabe and former Green Beret who had won the Silver Star in Vietnam and who had recently established an AIM chapter in Lincoln, Nebraska. As a former chapter member remembers:

> We were a new chapter, formed during Wounded Knee, and we were really excited about going to our first national meeting. Arbuckle was our director, had us rolling in high gear, and so about a dozen of us showed up at White Oak...just about the first thing that happened was that a bunch of heavy security guys came around and just interrogated the hell out of John. It seems that some of the national leadership had been put on notice that he [Arbuckle] was working for the police, and they wanted to deal with that...Well, John was pretty cool about it, he dealt with the questions and everything, but it was really humiliating, you could tell...and from that moment on, there was a lot of mistrust and bad feeling between Lincoln AIM and some of the national leadership circles. They were never really able to rely on us, cut us out of what was going on time after time, and we never really forgave *them* for the accusations that were made.[61]

Aaron Two Elk, an Oglala who was at the time a member of the Des Moines, Iowa AIM chapter, recalls that:

> During and right after Wounded Knee, we had what you might call a rush on membership...a whole lot of new people coming in to sign up. One of them was a guy named Doug Durham, who'd been inside the Knee as a reporter or something, and supposedly came out all gung ho...Durham had used to work for the Des Moines police, but he admitted that right up front, so we didn't think much about it at the

Carter Camp (in fringed jacket) with (from left) Kenny Kane, Dennis Banks, and Oscar Bear Runner inside Wounded Knee, 1973. (Photo: *Akwesasne Notes*)

time. In fact, we started off sort of justifying this, that Durham's background sort of gave us a special insight about the way the police worked...and he [Durham] was a pretty good writer, was able to raise money and all sorts of stuff, so we looked at him as a real asset in those early days...Right off, he started telling Ron Petite [AIM's Midwest field coordinator, at the time working out of Des Moines, and a close confidant of Dennis Banks] that John Arbuckle, who was starting up a chapter over in Lincoln, was a pig...an undercover cop. Now, a couple of us knew Arbuckle, and had our doubts about this...but, still, the story got around pretty fast, and I guess a lot of people believed it.[62]

Although no evidence has ever emerged to substantiate the idea that John Arbuckle was in any way associated with police activities, Douglass Durham was very definitely functioning as an FBI infiltrator and provocateur by this point (see next chapter). Nor was Arbuckle the only target of Durham's whispering campaign. For instance, Carter Camp, elected AIM national co-director (along with John Trudell), was rumored to be arranging a "deal with the feds" which would result in the reduction or dismissal of Wounded Knee related charges against him. When Camp sided with Arbuckle, insisting the Lincoln AIM leader was being unfairly impugned, such rumors proliferated.

By the time of the "Sioux Sovereignty Hearings" in early 1974, in Lincoln,[63] matters were coming to a head; "rumors of FBI informers among the leadership...caused a showdown."[64] As Russell Means put it, "Federal officials were paying off some of the AIM leadership to turn on other leaders. Clyde [Bellecourt] thought Camp was being paid off."[65] In any event, Camp borrowed a revolver from Lincoln

Lincoln (later Colorado) AIM member Frank Black Elk. Carter Camp borrowed his gun to shoot Clyde Bellecourt as part of a bad-jacketing scenario orchestrated by FBI infiltrator Doug Durham. (Photo: Arloa Wheeler)

AIM member Frank Black Elk and set off to "straighten things out"; during a violent argument, Camp shot Bellecourt in the stomach at close range.[66] Although Bellecourt survived (refusing to press charges) and quickly joined Leonard Crow Dog in trying to rehabilitate Camp's shattered reputation ("For the sake of unity," he later explained), Means angrily threatened to resign from AIM altogether unless Camp was excommunicated. The issue was never really resolved, despite the fact that Carter Camp was rapidly eclipsed (taking much of AIM's incipient Oklahoma support with him). The fractures within the organization's leadership structure, deepened by the shooting, became increasingly apparent over the next several years. In Two Elk's account:

> By this time, we were becoming very suspicious of Doug Durham in Des Moines. But he'd already gotten real tight with Ron Petite, and this led him into becoming Dennis' [Banks] bodyguard and personal assistant, or something. He'd already moved up from our chapter level to work directly with the national leadership, so there wasn't a lot we could do. When he bad-rapped people, other people listened...I'm not saying that Durham was responsible all by himself for what happened between Carter [Camp] and Clyde [Bellecourt], but he sure helped things along. And, after that, the unity of the Movement really began to come apart.[67]

Over the next year-and-a-half, Durham appears to have been involved in successful efforts to discredit several other AIM members, notably at the outset of the "Skyhorse/Mohawk Case" in California (see Chapter 10). The most serious instance of this FBI-directed disruption is, however, the case of Anna Mae Aquash. Matthiessen refers to "the spreading of rumors that [Aquash] was…an informer" as being part of "the damage done by Douglass Durham" during 1975, and mentions how Leonard Peltier—as an AIM security officer—was assigned by the organization's leaders to confront Aquash with these allegations.[68] He goes on to note that:

> Anna Mae herself took the charges…seriously. Upset and disheartened, she considered going home to Nova Scotia. Instead, she stuck it out on Pine Ridge, returning to her work with the Oglala women.[69]

By this time, Durham had been exposed as an infiltrator, and was thus in no position to further pursue the matter of Aquash's bad-jacketing. It appears that the effort was therefore turned over to a second FBI provocateur named John Stewart. As is noted elsewhere, after her death, "Anna Mae's friends tracked the source of the rumor [that she was a Bureau informant] back to an Oglala village resident, John Stewart, also known as Daryl Blue Lake [*sic;* Blue Legs], and in the summer of 1976, Stewart appeared as a government witness in the trial of two Indians [Butler and Robideau]."[70] As Peter Matthiessen observed:

> Stewart, whose extensive jail record included a conviction for first-degree manslaughter, was one of those who spread the story that Anna Mae Aquash was an informer; he was also rumored to know more than he should about her death. In the spring of 1976, his estranged wife, Dorothy Brings Him Back, showed WKLDOC attorneys a note sent to Stewart at her address which read in part, "I have to talk to you—Dave." Because the handwriting looked familiar, Bruce Ellison compared it to initialed FBI 302 forms, and in his opinion, the "D" is identical to those made by David Price. In a letter to Dorothy in this period, Stewart said he was in jail in Rapid City, doing time for one of his AIM brothers; he gave her a telephone number for leaving messages which turned out to be the local number of the FBI. A month later, he turned up on the list of prosecution witnesses for the trial of Butler and Robideau.[71]

In sum:

> In all likelihood, most people feel, the original suspicions about Anna Mae Aquash were spread by Douglass Durham, who tried to discredit anyone he did not control, and these rumors intensified [after] David Price questioned her in March, 1975; apparently, Price was working with John Stewart, who [then] started the rumors in Oglala.[72]

Given the circumstances of jeopardy under which AIM was existing by late 1975, the peril in which such rumors placed Aquash was quite clear, a situation reflected in a desperately enigmatic statement made by the victim to her sister shortly before her death: "They're out to kill me. They'll get me if the FBI doesn't get me first."[73] This could have referred to the GOONs or any of several area non-Indian vigilante groups, the BIA police or area state and local authorities, or even to other AIM members whom she may well have feared had become convinced she really *was* preparing to finger them for death or long prison sentences. As Russell Means

Anna Mae Pictou Aquash, victim of a whisper campaign initiated by FBI infiltrator Doug Durham, was murdered on Pine Ridge during February of 1976. She was warned by SA David Price that she wouldn't live out the year if she refused to cooperate with the Bureau. (Photo: Kevin Barry McKiernan)

observed: "[Dennis] Banks was so paranoid after Douglass Durham. He thought *everyone* was an informer, even Anna Mae."[74]

The notion that Aquash's bad-jacketing was pursued, or at least sanctioned at a fairly high level within the FBI, receives circumstantial corroboration from an entirely atypical Bureau denial, published in the March 11, 1976 edition of the *Rapid City Journal.* The article, entitled "FBI denies AIM implication that Aquash was informant" appeared on the *day* of the second autopsy on her body and—insofar as no one in AIM had as yet publicly raised such "implications"—seemed designed specifically to make them a topic for discussion and an attempt to divert suspicion concerning the murder to AIM.

Actually, preparation for this move had begun at least as early as March 8, at which time it had become obvious that the victim's family and WKLDOC were going to demand a second autopsy. On that date, David Price's partner, William Wood, hurriedly entered the Bureau's own request for exhumation of Aquash's body. Wood specified as a rationale, "information received from one Anna Mae Tanagale [*sic,* Tanequodle], Tulsa, Oklahoma" that "Anna Mae Aquash was suspected by AIM members as being an FBI informant." Tanequodle, known to AIM by her alias, "Ella Mae Tanegale," had long been considered to be a Bureau informant and had consequently *not* been privy to such inside knowledge for a considerable period.[75] This brings forth the bizarre prospect of agent Wood (and probably Price as well) conjuring up a scenario in which he has an Indian informant inform him that Aquash is thought to be an informant of the FBI.[76] Again, these maneuvers to cast suspicion upon AIM were occurring in the context of a murder the Bureau had ostensibly determined *not* to have happened and, in any event, still maintains it did not yet know about.

In spite of its transparency, the effectiveness of this gambit in sowing confusion about the Aquash murder was quickly revealed in Dennis Banks' cancellation of an AIM investigation into the circumstances of her death; "If AIM was involved, it would crush our movement."[77] As a consequence:

> The suspicion remains that Anna Mae Aquash was killed by an AIM member, who was convinced she was an informer and murdered her in a desperate attempt to stem the flow of information to the FBI and protect hunted leaders. There was no precedent for such treatment of informers within the organization, but according to one observer, "If ever there was to be a first, the time was ripe for it."[78]

The situation was even further compounded (and federal motivations in the Aquash case further revealed) when, a short time later, with specific reference to the death of Anna Mae Aquash, South Dakota Attorney General William Janklow went on the public record openly advocating further "internal" AIM murders: "Some of the best AIM members and leaders are our informants. They would be surprised to learn who our informants are and how many we have."[79]

In the end, as one AIM member (who wishes to remain anonymous) put it,

> I really don't know *who* pulled the trigger of the gun which killed Anna Mae. I doubt very much that it was actually David Price or any other agent of the FBI...they're too smart to do it themselves, at least not directly. It was probably an Indian who killed her, and I won't deny it might have been somebody in AIM. But, I'll tell you this, however it happened, Price and Wood and the rest of the feds were up to their necks in setting it up. They spent a *lot* of time and energy making her out to be an informer, and because of that, she'd become very isolated within AIM. If the GOONs got her— which is very possible—it was because she was isolated and not receiving the protection and security from our guys that she should've been entitled to as an AIM member. And, if one of the AIM people did it, it was because they'd been led to believe she was a serious threat to the well being of others. [According to Bob Robideau, Anna Mae was never isolated from nor suspected of being an FBI informant by the Northwest AIM group to which she, Robideau, the Butlers, and Leonard Peltier belonged.]

> I'm not putting this up as an excuse...There *is* no excuse for what happened to Anna Mae. But, it's a *reason*. And AIM has been paying dues on this ever since, *regardless* of whether or not an organizational member was the guilty party. And maybe that's correct. We don't come off looking very good, no matter *how* it went down. But what I want to know, what's bothered me all these years, is how it is that these feds—guys like Price, and it was a *personal* thing between him and Anna Mae—could've just got off scot free. I mean, how much more blatant could they have been than they were in this case? And *still* nothing happened to them.

Chapter 8

Informers, Infiltrators, Agents Provocateurs

There are reasons why snitches and infiltrators are considered to be the worst scum on the face of the earth. And it has nothing to do with the people holding such opinions being guilty of any crime. All you have to do is look at the reality of the profession involved. I mean, what kind of person is it who makes his living trading on the friendships he develops in order to invent reasons to railroad his friends into prison? Even when he knows them to be blameless...What kind of man uses the trust he gains in political work to get those who trust him killed? What is the character of an individual who has so little conscience or principle that he will tell any lie to destroy a movement that even *he* believes is socially needed and in the right? And what kind of agency is it that habitually employs people of this type for such purposes?
—Aaron Two Elk (Oglala Lakota), AIM Member

The FBI utilized a large number of informers, infiltrators and agents provocateurs against AIM between the years 1972 and 1976. While the full extent of this practice is unknown, it began at least as early as The Trail of Broken Treaties (see Chapter 4) with the introduction of Chicano "Indian militant" John Arellano and other undercover police operatives into the ranks of the group occupying the BIA building. Throughout this book we discuss instances in which the Bureau cynically "turned" people—Myrtle Poor Bear, Marvin Bragg, Louis Moves Camp, Marvin Redshirt, Wish Draper, Mike Anderson and Norman Brown among them—to its own advantage, bearing false witness against AIM members.

Outright infiltrators include: Virginia "Blue Dove" DeLuse, an aging non-Indian Hollywood bit player who helped orchestrate the ugly Skyhorse/Mohawk case in California (Chapter 10); John "Daryl Blue Legs" Stewart, an Oglala who participated in bad-jacketing Anna Mae Aquash (Chapter 9); and Harry ("Gi") and Jill Shafer, non-Indians "who had been inside Wounded Knee and volunteered help with the ensuing legal work...The Shafers had infiltrated Students for a Democratic Society (SDS) in 1969 and later worked in the Red Star Collective, a bogus Communist group which served as an FBI front."[1] The most striking example, however, is that of "secret agent" Douglass Durham.[2]

Durham was a non-Indian[3] with a shady past even for an FBI infiltrator:

> After high school, 1956-59, Durham served in a "special" Special Forces team under
> CIA direction. He was trained in demolitions, sabotage, burglary, and other skills use-
> ful in clandestine warfare. From 1959-61, he was "sheepdipped"—apparently stationed
> at a CIA base in Guatemala...He worked with the CIA's secret army of *gusanos* (Cuban
> counter-revolutionaries) at gun-running, sabotage, and helping with air support for the
> Bay of Pigs invasion of 1961...After the Bay of Pigs fiasco, Durham became a Des
> Moines, Iowa, patrolman and immediately became involved in burglary, prostitution
> and taking bribes—for which he was investigated several times. Apparently, he was
> using various "ethical short circuits" he had been trained in...[4]

Things progressed from there:

> Durham's involvement in prostitution—"running" a string of girls from a cafe called
> *Why Not?*—led to bitter quarrels with his wife. In July, 1964, he beat her brutally; she
> died July 5. Durham was investigated for second-degree manslaughter and, in the
> course of the investigation, was examined by a police psychiatrist...The psychiatrist
> pronounced Durham a violent schizoid, "unfit for office involving public trust," and
> recommended commitment and treatment at a mental institution...He was fired [from
> the police]...in October of 1964. From then on, before he became involved in "politi-
> cal work," he moved rapidly up the ladder of organized crime...He operated several
> restaurants fronting for Mafia interests...He was investigated for large-scale heroin
> smuggling, pandering, receiving stolen goods, and convicted in an odd Mafia/politi-
> cal case in 1971.[5]

This was the background and character of the individual retained by the FBI
in mid-1973 to penetrate AIM and perform a range of tasks within the organization.
He was paid "$1,000 per month, cash," by the Bureau for his services,[6] a matter he
later elaborated upon in Senate subcommittee testimony. The following is an exchange between Durham and Richard Schultz, Chief Counsel to the Senate Subcom-
mitee on the Judiciary, in 1976:

> *Schultz:* ...Mr. Durham, you mentioned that you were a paid operative of the Federal
> Bureau of Investigation. Would you tell us what were the period of time, the dates,
> and approximately what you were paid?

> *Durham:* The period of time was from approximately March, 1973 to March, 1975; on
> an escalating scale for a two year period, it involved approximately $20,000.[7]

In his capacity as a highly paid infiltrator, Durham—who had been inside
Wounded Knee, ostensibly as a reporter/photographer for the radical Midwest
tabloid, *Pax Today*[8]—joined the Des Moines, Iowa AIM chapter headed by Harvey
Major.[9] He quickly became close to AIM Midwest Regional Coordinator Ron Petite,
who was working out of the Des Moines office, and because of Petite's closeness
to AIM leader Dennis Banks was able to rapidly work his way into Banks' inner
circle. In short order, he had assumed a role as Banks' personal "body guard and

pilot" and was designated as AIM National Security Director, a position he himself had created.[10] Later,

[An] AIM national office [was] opened [in January 1974] in St. Paul [Minnesota] by Dennis Banks and Douglass Durham, who was serving [Banks] as an organizer and administrator as well as pilot; Durham was also a cameraman, self-trained, he said, in psychology, and he was now very close to Banks...[and was allowed to become] AIM's first director of security...at Banks' suggestion...[11]

Undermining the Judicial Process

Given his status, Durham was designated coordinator of the defense committee working in behalf of Banks and Russell Means, co-defendants in the "Wounded Knee Leadership Trial" (see Chapter 11):

Banks and Means went to trial on the Wounded Knee charges on January 8, 1974 [and, by then] Durham had become AIM security director and coordinator of the WKLDOC support group. He became AIM's chief bureaucrat, taking charge of the trial records and setting up the AIM national office in St. Paul. He had access to AIM and WKLDOC bank accounts...AIM estimates he may have stolen as much as $100,000 [in organizational and defense funding, during this period].[12]

By Durham's own account:

During this time, I was security director of the American Indian Movement, working with the Wounded Knee Legal Defense Committee in the capacity of security and working to establish the [AIM] national offices at St. Paul.[13]

To this, he immediately added the disclaimer, "I had been advised by the Federal Bureau of Investigation to not involve myself in transmitting defense tactics to them."[14] However, intelligence information gleaned by Durham *was* used improperly to influence the course of the judicial proceedings. Durham, for example, acknowledged that he "immediately reported...to the Federal Bureau of Investigation" both the fact and content of a meeting between Dennis Banks, trial judge Fred Nichol and Nichol's wife at the judge's home subsequent to a pretrial hearing held during October 1973.[15] He also notes that this report to the FBI produced results:

On Monday, March 3, 1974, during the trial in Federal Court in St. Paul, Minn. of Dennis Banks and Russell Means, the U.S. Attorney's Office in Sioux Falls filed a very strongly worded motion of prejudice against Judge Nichol, asking him to disqualify himself for the remainder of the Wounded Knee leadership trial.[16]

Although Judge Nichol was absolved of any misconduct with regard to his handling of the trial, the government's motion resulted in "a hearing conducted [at the insistence of federal attorneys] in the last of May or the first of June, 1974. It was a 7 1/2 hour hearing with about 6 defense attorneys and 2 U.S. Attorneys present."[17]

Outside the Federal Building in St. Paul, 1974, (from right) Douglass Durham, in his capacity as AIM Security Director, Dennis Banks and Harry Belafonte. (Photo: *North Country Anvil*)

The implications of prosecution pressure brought to bear upon a trial judge, in an effort to intimidate him into arriving at the "right" conclusions, are rather obvious here.

Such federal misconduct was compounded when, on April 3, 1974, chief government prosecutor R.D. Hurd submitted an affidavit to the court in response to a defense motion demanding disclosure of "FBI infiltration of the defense team." Hurd's reply stipulated that an exhaustive search of Bureau files "contained no material which could arguably be considered as evidence of the [FBI's] invasion of the defense camp." The prosecution was reinforced on this point by SAC, Minneapolis, Joseph Trimbach, who swore that there were *no* government informers in the defense camp.

The government contention at trial flatly contradicts the reality of the situation, as well as Durham's later testimony that well before the trial began he "advised the FBI that I had been asked to accompany Banks to the trial."[18] After his exposure as a Bureau operative, Durham identified SAs Ray Williams and Robert Taubert to WKLDOC attorneys as his Minneapolis FBI liaisons, to whom he'd reported "regularly" and on "numerous occasions" during the trial itself.[19] Prosecutor Hurd is quoted as having stated that during the trial (his affidavit to the contrary notwithstanding) he'd been informed "by the FBI" that it had an informant "very close to one of the defendents."[20] SAC Trimbach later professed to have "had no knowledge" of Durham's infiltration of AIM or the defense team, despite admitting that just *one* of his agents had "nearly 50" contacts with the infiltrator during the trial.[21]

Durham's significance to the FBI and the prosecution is undeniable:

Durham's job during the eight-month trial was to insure that no government informers were among the attorneys and legal workers who worked on the defense team. He was the only person other than the AIM [WKLDOC] attorneys, legal workers and defendants who had access to the defense strategy room, and he controlled security clearance for both the attorneys and the defense volunteers. As he later described his role, "I exercised so much control you couldn't contact any other chapter without going through me and if you wanted money, you had to see me."[22]

As WKLDOC coordinator Ken Tilsen summed up the situation: "There was no person other than defense counsel and the defendants themselves who knew more about the total plans, concerns and strategems of the defense than Douglass Durham."[23] Such obviously sensitive (and legally protected) information would appear to have been fed directly to the FBI, thence to the prosecuting attorneys, a matter reflected in the Bureau's upgrading of Durham's pay—"for the value of services rendered"—from $900 to $1,000 per month during the trial. Durham himself later tacitly admitted such an information flow (though it is *still* officially denied) when he testified that: "If Dennis [Banks] and I were sitting in a room and an attorney would walk in and start talking, I couldn't jump up and say, 'I can't be here. The FBI won't allow it.'"[24]

Under such circumstances, it is plain that there was no possibility whatsoever of Banks and Means receiving a fair trial. Equally clear is the fact that the FBI and U.S. Attorney's prosecution team had collaborated to bring about this reality, thus deliberately aborting the due process of justice they were mutually charged with upholding. Little could have gone further in validating Judge Nichol's view, offered during his dismissal of all charges against the defendants, that: "I am forced to conclude that the prosecution [and the FBI, personified by SAC Joseph Trimbach] acted in bad faith...and was seeking convictions at the expense of justice." What is far less evident, given that these facts became known shortly after the conclusion of the trial, is why *none* of the principle culprits—Hurd, Trimbach, Williams, Taubert and Durham—was *ever* charged (or in any way penalized) for obstructing justice, perjury, malicious prosecution or other crimes.

"The Violence-Prone American Indian Movement"

While consolidating his wide range of organizational duties in St. Paul, Durham began to indulge his "propensity for visible displays of armed resistance,"[25] openly and persistently advocating "guerrilla warfare" despite the efforts of numerous AIM members to dissuade him.[26] This included the release of several unauthorized memos, disseminated on organizational letterhead, indicating that AIM was preparing to launch a campaign of "systematic violence."[27] Also, as Matthiessen observes: "While subverting the AIM national office, Durham remained active in Iowa; by encouraging rash, inflammatory acts, he all but destroyed Iowa AIM."[28]

In his Senate subcommittee testimony, Durham refers to a number of physical confrontations undertaken by the Des Moines AIM chapter when he was an ac-

Aaron Two Elk, surviving member of the Iowa AIM leadership. (Photo: *Atlanta Constitution*)

tive member, among them the occupation of the Grimes State Office Building during August 1973. He attributes the instigation and leadership of these activities to individuals such as Ron Petite (now deceased), chapter leader Harvey Major (now deceased), and Aaron Two Elk. Two Elk, however, is very clear that it was Durham who was "always right out front, urging everybody to get it on. His thing was that if you didn't have continuous confrontations going on, you weren't really serious, that if we weren't engaged in confrontations, we couldn't generate any sort of progress for Indian people."[29]

Two Elk states it was Durham rather than Ron Petite who issued a somewhat notorious memo over Petite's signature on August 28, 1973, "ordering" all AIM members nationally to "carry arms at all times."[30] Two Elk also recalls:

> It was about this same time that Durham started to bad-rap John Arbuckle [see Chapter 7], and Harvey [Major] was getting to be seriously convinced that there was something really wrong about Durham. But then he [Durham] aired, just picked up and left with Ron [Petite] to go and work for Dennis [Banks]...And we never said much, 'cause we were never sure, and we didn't want to get into being cop-baiters. Besides, Durham was real tight with Banks by then...But it wasn't so long before Harvey turned up dead in a car wreck. The cops claimed it was an accident, and closed the case without really looking into it, but even they admitted that Harvey's brakelines looked to have been messed with.[31]

Meanwhile, Durham was proving his mettle as a slick operator to Banks. During the fall of 1973, the AIM leader was becoming "increasingly paranoid," according to a Minneapolis AIM member (who worked in the national office and wishes to remain anonymous);

...he had this heavy trial coming up because of Wounded Knee, and another on the boards because of the Custer Courthouse confrontation, and so on, and so on. And he was getting phone calls and stuff—we always figured they were from the FBI—saying, "We're gonna get you, Dennis." There was no place that Banks didn't hear footsteps coming up on him from behind. He figured, and you can't blame him for it, that he was gonna get offed before he ever got to trial...To make matters worse, the feds were runnin' this number on him through Doug Durham. Dennis would have a flash about something the feds might try and do to him, and right away Durham would say, "Yeah, you're right. And this is probably how they'll go about it." A day or two later, sure enough, the feds would do something weird, and it always fit Durham's script, although it was always set up that it would happen some place where Dennis wasn't. But it would prove Durham correct, you see? And Dennis would say, "Oh, wow! They're *really* out to get me! What should I do now, Doug?" The whole thing was drivin' all of us nuts because, even though we hadn't tumbled to the fact that he was a cop yet, Durham was such an arrogant asshole...

It was decided that Banks, with Ron Petite as a close advisor, should go into hiding at Rae Lakes, near the town of Yellow Knife in Canada's Northwest Territory, until the Wounded Knee leadership trial began. This action quickly brought about the issue of a federal fugitive warrant for the AIM leader. Further, the location (reputedly suggested by Durham), proved itself far too isolated for AIM's logistical capabilities; in short order, Banks found himself not only wanted on yet another charge, but destitute and cut off from organizational support and communication. At this point:

> Durham salvaged a difficult situation by flying north to Edmonton [Alberta], renting a plane and spiriting Banks illegally across the border. Banks was impressed by Durham's skillful maneuvers, which seemed to have taken him out of the FBI's clutches. His admiration for Durham and the general climate of pursuit meant that the mechanics of Durham's achievements were not closely scrutinized.[32]

This establishes an intriguing scenario wherein the FBI maintained a high level undercover operative specifically to insure that an organizational leader designated as one of the Bureau's "most wanted" fugitives *remained* a fugitive so long as its operative(s) were able to exert decisive influence upon the leader's thinking and upon the evolution of organizational policy. Meanwhile, the Bureau utilized both Banks' status as a fugitive and AIM's policy pronouncements as a propaganda basis for publicly discrediting the organization and "justifying" the increasingly virulent FBI/local police repression of the organization's membership.

In his subsequent Senate subcommittee testimony, Durham indicated that a good deal of the "mechanics" involved in his aerobatic services to Banks came through the funding of a mysterious Los Angeles-based character named George Roberts, who was also involved in the funding of the notorious "AIM Camp 13" and whose idea it was that Banks move from Canada to Cuba in order to "become the new Che Guevara" (Chapter 10).[33] While at least some AIM members concluded that

Roberts was probably a CIA operative, Banks was asking no questions of his "benefactors."

To the contrary, Durham and Roberts were rewarded for their performance by being designated as Banks' *sole* "stateside" conduits of communication.[34] It was at this juncture that Durham's handprints began to appear most clearly on major AIM policy documents. Most notable is a lengthy and "confidential" (immediately passed along to the FBI) memo entitled "Operational Goals of National AIM," released in September 1973 from George Roberts' Los Angeles office over Banks' signature.[35] Point 7 of this document articulates a plan for an AIM "Railroad Operation" by which groups of "traveling warriors" could "move freely in the execution of their appointed tasks" and involving "safe places," vehicle exchanges, and so forth.[36] The document continues, on the following page, that "central [*i.e.,* Banks, Petite, Durham and Roberts] will validate all identities and personnel...know at all times where all personnel are located...[and continually contact] all local chapters."[37] Significantly, in a hand-written note attached to the neatly typed "policy memo," Banks assigned *all* operational authority over the plan to Durham and Roberts.[38]

Also of considerable significance is the fact that the entire, highly centralized paramilitary structure envisioned in the memo (but never actualized) derives from Carlos Marighella's *Mini-Manual of the Urban Guerrilla*, a booklet which Durham refers to in his subcommittee testimony, and which many AIM members recall Durham having "introduced and promoted as the 'bible' of our 'political education' although very few people read it" (see Chapter 10).[39] In any event, no COINTELPRO theorist could have envisioned a neater scenario than one in which an infiltrator was placed in a position to order a targeted organization's membership to engage in clandestine activities, *all* of which were to be reported—directly and immediately—to the infiltrator. Douglass Durham had crossed every conceivable line separating his role from that of an agent provocateur, and it is a clear testament to the real principles of the AIM membership that the Bureau was unable to capitalize on this gambit through criminal prosecutions.

Still, the FBI made the most of the situation, citing its infiltrator's statements (and those engineered by him) as "proof" that AIM was indeed "violence-prone." Durham, in his subsequent testimony, inadvertently acknowledged that "the change from nonviolent to violent," as concerns AIM's public image and policy formation (as opposed to concrete actions), coincided precisely with the time during which he held greatest organizational sway.[40]

In order to separate Durham's impact from the realities of the movement he was assigned to disrupt, the image of AIM as a violence-prone, guerrilla-oriented entity must be contrasted to the AIM positions articulated immediately prior to his ascendency:

> AIM is first a spiritual movement, a religious rebirth, and then a rebirth of Indian dignity. AIM succeeds because it has beliefs to act on. AIM is attempting to connect the realities of the past with the promises of tomorrow...AIM wishes to represent itself as

a peaceful movement...[and as such] AIM represents the *only* true revolutionary group [emphasis added].[41]

It is also noteworthy that AIM abandoned its supposed "armed struggle" posture (as opposed to armed self-defense) a short while after Durham's exit from its "leadership." This again suggests that the whole notion of AIM as an organization actively pursuing violent confrontation was a fabrication of the FBI in general and Douglass Durham in particular. Although this mythology was developed to a much greater extent by the Bureau disinformation specialists after Durham's exposure (see Chapter 10), it is fair to say that he laid a solid groundwork for their endeavors.

William Janklow as Rapist

In his subcommittee testimony, Durham describes an August 1973 plot which he attributes to AIM Midwest Coordinator Ron Petite, in which Petite "advocated kidnapping the Governor [of the State of Iowa, Robert D. Day] to create sympathy for his demands."[42] According to Durham, Petite wanted the kidnapping to be carried out by the Des Moines AIM chapter. This was offered as "proof" of the "violent, or potentially violent" nature of AIM, its members and its supporters. Surviving chapter member Aaron Two Elk, however, remembers that it was Durham who advanced the idea and that the infiltrator/provocateur "really pushed it for a while." In Two Elk's account, Petite joined with Des Moines chapter leader Harvey Major in nixing the plan, dismissing it as "stupid and adventuristic."[43]

Exactly one year later, in August 1974, Durham came forth with a second such proposal, this time focusing upon South Dakota Deputy Attorney General William Janklow (who was campaigning for the Attorney Generalship on an explicitly anti-AIM platform); "Durham tried in vain to persuade AIM to kidnap Janklow as a protest, just before a pre-Election Day rally in Pierre."[44] Russell Means recalls that, when he got wind of the idea, he first "thought it was a bad joke," and then reacted in a fury, seeing to it that:

> Durham was told that AIM was an Indian rights organization. As such, we had absolutely *no* interest in kidnapping and murder and sabotage. He was told that if these were the sorts of actions that appealed to him, he should go join the John Birch Society or the Minutemen, but that AIM did not want to hear any more of that sort of thing...For the record, [Dennis] Banks agreed.[45]

At that point, Durham dropped temporarily out of sight. When he re-emerged he brought with him a young Brulé Lakota woman named Jancita Eagle Deer, who had been living in Iowa. As it turned out, on January 14, 1967, Eagle Deer—then fifteen—had reported to the BIA police on her native Rosebud Reservation that she had been raped the night before. She named her assailant as William Janklow who, at the time, was employed as Tribal Attorney for the Rosebud Sioux, and whose children she had been babysitting during the evening in question (the alleged rape

occurred while Janklow was driving her home). On January 15, then SAC, Minneapolis, Richard G. Held dispatched SA John Penrod to investigate the charge and,
a day later the agent reported back by memo that "it is impossible to determine anything." Six weeks later, Held reported to FBI headquarters that there was "insufficient evidence, the allegations were unfounded; we are closing the matter."[46] In the
interim, Janklow seems to have used his position to close the files on the matter at
the tribal level, then resigned his job and left Rosebud (and tribal jurisdiction) altogether. Eagle Deer, feeling stigmatized by her victimization, also left about a year
later.

For some reason which has never been made clear, SAC Held appears to have
thought it important to keep track of Jancita Eagle Deer's whereabouts. Although
he had no reason to even be aware of the 1967 controversy, other than being informed of it by his FBI liaisons, Douglass Durham was able to immediately find her
in Iowa in 1974. According to Eagle Deer's mother-in-law, Durham easily convinced
the young woman that, if she were to accompany him back to South Dakota, "justice might yet be done in her case."[47] Durham then appears to have gone to work
on Dennis Banks, pointing out that the original FBI investigation of the rape charge
against Janklow had been cursory at best, with the Bureau even missing the fact
that the suspect might have been considered a prior sex offender.[48] Undoubtedly,
he also pointed out that Janklow, as a colleague in "justice and law enforcement,"
was the type of individual whom the FBI would wish to protect on principle and
that the Bureau typically plans ahead; SAC Held might well have calculated that, in
"covering" Janklow at this early stage of his career and then quietly holding the matter over his head, the FBI would garner a useful "ally" to do its bidding.[49] In the context of Janklow's inexplicably virulent anti-AIM campaign in 1974, such logic must
have been persuasive.

Whatever the exact nature of Durham's arguments, Banks became convinced
that the infiltrator/provocateur had discovered a route to undo Janklow (who was
exhibiting a spectacular animus against Banks *personally* at the time) which was
legally, ethically and morally correct. Consequently, against the advice of WKLDOC
coordinator Ken Tilsen, Russell Means and others: "[O]n October 16 [1974], AIM
leader Dennis Banks publicly accused Janklow of [the Eagle Deer] rape charge."[50]
The next day, Banks filed a formal petition before Tribal Judge Mario Gonzales, in
Rosebud Sioux Tribal Court, calling for Janklow's disbarment; Jancita Eagle Deer
testified in support of the petition, and Gonzales duly initiated disbarment proceedings.[51]

On October 18, Judge Gonzales issued subpoenas for William Janklow to appear at the disbarment hearing, scheduled for October 31, and for relevant FBI and
BIA files to be produced. The same day, Janklow publicly announced that the entire matter was nothing more than an "AIM smear campaign."[52] On October 20, BIA
Acting Area Director Harley Zephier (based in Aberdeen, S.D.) followed up by sending a telegram to Acting Special (BIA Police) Officer in Charge Norman Beare, at
Rosebud, ordering him *not* to deliver the requested documents to the court:

Be advised that 68 I.A.M. 5.6 reads as follows: "All reports listed above will be marked U.S. Government Use Only." Thus limiting access to appropriate officials. Furnishing the case reports to other than appropriate federal officials must be cleared prior to release with *the U.S. Attorney*. You are directed by Judge Mario Gonzales and respectively to decline [sic] to produce records on the grounds that the production is prohibited and are considered confidential in nature [emphasis added].

On the day after, the BIA, at the insistence of the Justice Department, "refused to deliver the subpoenaed file," the FBI also "refused to cooperate in any way."[53] Instead, the Bureau announced it had conducted another investigation, apparently in secret and without so much as interviewing anyone on Rosebud or the alleged victim, and reported the charges against Janklow to be "completely unfounded."[54] Thus freed of the spectre of *any* investigative documents being introduced against them, Janklow and his attorney thereupon declined to appear at the disbarment hearing.

Furious at this blatant federal obstructionism and flouting of even the little authority left a tribal judge under American law, Gonzales penned an opinion that "the court is satisfied that the rape allegations against Janklow are proven for the purposes of the hearing today [*i.e.*, to determine whether there was a basis for formal charges],"[55] and promptly filed warrants for the Deputy Attorney General's immediate arrest—should he venture onto the Rosebud Reservation—for "assault with intent to commit rape, and carnal knowledge of a female under 16."[56] Douglass Durham arranged for Jancita Eagle Deer to appear on Sioux Falls television the same evening (October 31, 1974).

Absent documentation, and in the face of the FBI's denial of the validity of her (and AIM's/Gonzales's) charges, Eagle Deer's TV statements left Janklow in a perfect position to build upon his branding of the whole matter as a "crude smear."[57] In South Dakota's intensely racist climate, this translated into overwhelming white voter support for Janklow who won the November 2 election by more than a 2-to-1 margin. Given the complicity of Durham in virtually every phase of this fiasco, and the obvious compatibility of William Janklow's views on AIM with those of the FBI, it is difficult to avoid the conclusion that the entire pre-election rape controversy might have been an extremely thoughtful and sophisticated COINTELPRO maneuver to engineer the landslide victory of the Bureau's preferred candidate, providing him with a Nixonesque "mandate" to "go after" AIM in South Dakota. If so, the undercutting of AIM's credibility nationally that also ensued can only be viewed as an added benefit of one of the FBI's most successful counterintelligence operations.

Young woman (center) thought to be Jancita Eagle Deer during the mid-1960s, about the time she was reputedly raped by future South Dakota Attorney General and Governor William Janklow. She was later a pawn in an elaborate anti-AIM COINTELPRO and subsequently killed while presumably in the company of FBI infiltrator Douglass Durham.

The Strange Death of Jancita Eagle Deer

By the time the Janklow rape controversy reached its culmination, Durham had already made his opening moves in the sensational Skyhorse/Mohawk case in Los Angeles (see Chapter 10). Also by this time, Jancita Eagle Deer had become Durham's "companion":

> Following her appearance on Sioux Falls television, Durham installed Jancita Eagle Deer in his St. Paul apartment. She astounded workers in the [national] AIM office by announcing that she and Durham would marry after his recovery from a [non-existent] deadly illness, as she spoke of Durham's large salary as an AIM director [AIM directors were/are not salaried; this is thought to be in reference to Durham's FBI salary and possibly to his embezzlement of AIM defense funds].[58]

Although Durham occasionally beat Eagle Deer,[59] the young woman became so infatuated and psychologically dependent upon him that she stayed on.

Durham's exposure finally began

> ...in March [1975], AIM [*sic*, WKLDOC] lawyers obtained FBI papers released through court order in one of the Wounded Knee trials. Among the papers was a report signed by Doug Durham. On March 7 Durham was confronted in St. Paul by AIM leaders and lawyers with copies of the incriminating documents.[60]

He quickly admitted the nature of his sordid criminal past and that,

> ...in 1971 [he] began to work as an agent for the Law Enforcement Intelligence Unit of the National Law Enforcement Assistance Administration [LEAA] of the Department of Justice. [When he began working directly for the FBI in] 1973 his assignment to

Wounded Knee required he pose as part Indian, so he obtained brown contact lenses to cover his grey eyes, dyed his hair black, and began passing himself off as "one-quarter Chippewa."[61]

Soon after his exposure and subsequent interviews by WKLDOC attorneys, which ended with a press conference in St. Paul on March 12, "Durham left [the city], pilfering AIM files before he went, and took Eagle Deer with him to Phoenix. When she tried to call her mother en route, he dragged her from a telephone booth and beat her severely. When she appeared at an AIM house in Phoenix, announcing that he was an informer, he beat her again. Two young AIM supporters who witnessed the incident were also beaten by Durham."[62] The pair then apparently went to Los Angeles,[63] before heading to South Dakota.

Eagle Deer was deposited at the home of her brother, Alfred, near Valentine, Nebraska, while Durham began an anti-AIM speaking tour of the high plains, sponsored by the John Birch Society (apparently he had finally taken Russell Means' advice on the matter). However, "[a]round 1:00 p.m. on April 4, 1975, Jancita was picked up at the home of her brother…[Alfred] Eagle Deer said the car was a late '60s blue Chevrolet driven by a dark-haired man he didn't know and didn't get a good look at."[64] In the early evening, her crumpled body was discovered alongside a lonely Nebraska back road:

> At about 9:15 p.m. that day, Jancita's body was examined by a coroner's physician [in Aurora, Nebraska], Dr. Donald J. Larson. No autopsy was performed. "Massive injuries," as a result of being hit by a car was [listed as the cause of] death. In a later interview, Dr. Larson told [WKLDOC researcher Paula Giese] *he thought it possible that she had been beaten, hit over the head or injured when she fell or jumped out of a moving car…*he examined Jancita's body "grossly," as he explained it [to Giese], at the Higbee Mortuary, where Hamilton [Nebraska] County Sheriff W.G. Schultz had had her body taken [emphasis added].[65]

The case was quickly closed by local authorities, despite their failure to conduct anything resembling a proper investigation into the matter—a common enough occurrence when "stray bodies" of Indians turn up south of the Pine Ridge and Rosebud Reservations—on the basis of a "hit and run" finding. Some three months later, however, Giese received an anonymous phone call:

> In mid-July, I received a call at the AIM office [in St. Paul]. The voice sounded like a lawman, but the person wouldn't identify himself. "I understand you're interested in Doug Durham and the death of a young Indian girl, Jancita Eagle Deer. You might like to know that the license of the car that picked her up the afternoon of April 4 was checked. The car belongs to Durham's father." The caller would give no more information, and hung up…

> In October of 1975 I accidently learned a few more facts. Missing from Jancita's things, and not found in AIM's very careful roadside search [conducted by Yankton AIM coordinator Greg Zephier], was Jancita's small black address book. She always carried it

and was very careful about it...Since she had it with her when she left her brother's house, it may be assumed that the dark-haired driver of the blue Chevy had it...

[T]here was a break-in at Jancita's in-law's house [in rural Iowa] a week after her death. Nothing of value was taken, but Jancita's papers appeared to have been gone through. Missing from these papers is a letter of introduction Durham originally brought with him in 1974, ostensibly from Jancita's foster father, saying "trust this man, do what he tells you." In retrospect, the in-laws believe Douglass Durham, an accomplished burglar, performed the break-in. But, as one of them put it, "What can we do? These people have so much power."[66]

WKLDOC researcher Candy Hamilton sums up the situation as being

...one of the most horrible episodes of the whole FBI repression of AIM. I don't know what happened to Jancita Eagle Deer in 1967, but whatever it was really scarred her. She was just lost, a waif, you know? Durham and his handlers in the FBI used her really brutally; never mind the fact that Durham abused her physically—which was *awful*—but the fact that they dragged out all that personal pain of hers, totally misled her for their own purposes. They just used her up...destroyed her. When she was no longer of any use, they tossed her aside like a used kleenex or something. Do you see how cold this was? She wasn't even AIM, she'd offended nobody, had done nothing to anybody—and the FBI *knew* it—and *still* they just used her as a pawn, ruined her. And then, when she was killed—whether Doug Durham actually had a hand in it or not—they just turned their backs. No investigation, no comment, no nothing...it was really sick, from the start to finish.[67]

One AIM member concludes that:

I can't think of any one person who did more damage to AIM than Doug Durham. The kind of pressure the feds were putting on the leadership after Wounded Knee was already causing problems. Some people were beginning to unwrap, Russ and Dennis were continuously tied up in trials, so there wasn't a lot they could do about it. Durham just absolutely destroyed trust inside the organization when he turned out to be a pig...*especially* when it turned out that there were others as well. Nobody could be sure how far it went...This wasn't a joke. The feds were trying to put people in prison on totally bogus charges, remember. And this was for *heavy* time, like 90 years, or 150 years or more than 200 years in a couple of cases. And people were getting killed right and left. So, nobody could afford to be real trusting, if you catch my drift. They were *really* trying to do us in...The game had become as serious as it gets. The thing with Harvey Major proved that, and the thing with Anna Mae [Aquash], no doubt. And then there was Skyhorse and Mohawk, and the thing with Jancita Eagle Deer, and it just kept comin' down. All of that was Doug Durham. And that's not even to mention all the lies and misrepresentations he put out as an "official AIM spokesman," or the speeches he made for the Birchers, or that bullshit he said to Congress, which got AIM labeled as a "terrorist organization."

You could say that a lot of the spirit went out of the movement around what Durham did. Oh, it wasn't just him. The FBI was doin' a lot of other stuff which contributed too. And AIM made its own mistakes. But Dennis [Banks] was never the same after he got taken in. And a whole lot of that early feeling, the *openness* of AIM disappeared.

It got to be small groups who already knew each other real well, who couldn't give up the resistance, but who were thinking more in terms of survival than anything else. That's what AIM was by 1975. And that's what happened at Oglala in the summer of '75 [see Chapter 9]; some feds finally ran into one of these groups which they'd forced into being, and they finally got back what they'd been puttin' out. They took it on the chin for what Doug Durham and the whole damned FBI had been doing to people.[68]

Finally, an elder of the Colorado AIM chapter, Vivian Locust (an Oglala), frames the matter at another, perhaps more important level: "That Durham, he showed us what we were really dealing with. We was trying to act like human beings, reaching out to other human beings, the way Indians always do. But that Durham, he didn't act like no human being. And I'm not sure what to say he *did* act like. No conscience. No guilt. No remorse. No human emotion *at all.* I'd say he acted like a snake, but that's not fair to snakes. Snakes aren't that cold. He was more like some kind of machine, a robot...and then we figured out there was a lot more just like him: that [SA David] Price was one, and that [SA William] Wood was another. And there was that [SA Norman] Zigrossi, and [SAC Joseph] Trimbach, and on and on. *None* of 'em acted human at all. We Indians don't have any way to cope with people like this."[69]

Chapter 9

The Oglala Firefight

That firefight at Oglala, it ruined things for all of us. The feds set it up, then used it as an excuse for all kinds of violence against us that they couldn't have gotten away with otherwise. They broke a lot of people's spirit after that, and the results are still coming down.
—Rick Williams, (AIM Member), Oglala/Cheyenne

By the early summer of 1975, Wilsonite violence had proven so sustained and pervasive that the ION traditionals were requesting that AIM provide armed security for their homes, persons and communities. The FBI, in a memo prepared during the first week of June, noted this trend and pointed out that, as a result, "there are pockets of Indian population which consist almost exclusively of American Indian Movement...members and their supporters on the Reservation."[1] The accuracy of this observation is corroborated by AIM member Nilak Butler, at the time a resident of the Tent City, near the village of Oglala, one of AIM's more important defensive centers. She recalls that the concentration had occurred because, "Oglala was so violent at that time, [that] we were asked to be like a peacekeeping force."[2] Roselyn Jumping Bull, the middle-aged proprietor of the "Jumping Bull Compound"—the property on which the Tent City was located—concurs with both Butler and the Bureau:

We asked...AIM boys to come help us. The boys said "OK. We'll come to help you all we can"...Our [own, non-AIM] boys can't even do nothing. They can't even speak up for themselves 'cause they're so scared of Dick Wilson and his goons.[3]

The Bureau, having put its finger squarely on this bit of reality, nonetheless abandoned truthfulness in its summary, stating: "It is significant that in some of these AIM centers the residents have built bunkers which would literally require military assault forces if it were necessary to overcome resistance emanating from the bunkers."[4] With regard to the Jumping Bull property in particular, the memo goes on:

According to the Agents it had been determined that the Indians were prepared to use these "bunkers" as a defensive position and it was believed they were constructed in such a fashion as to defend against a frontal assault. To successfully overcome automatic or semi-automatic fire from such "bunkers" it appeared as though heavy equipment such as an armored personnel carrier would be required...The "bunkers" in question were observed from a moving automobile for approximately two minutes. The Agents recommended no attempt be made to obtain a closer view as the people residing in the area were AIM members and were known to be unfriendly to the FBI.[5]

This wholly fictional notion of AIM's having constructed fixed fortifications on the Jumping Bull land would, by the end of the month, figure prominently in an FBI disinformation effort (see Chapter 10). In the meantime, however, the camp served as a symbol of the challenge to federal control still being mounted by the AIM/ION amalgam after two solid years of escalating Bureau-fostered repression. Further, the removal of armed defensive enclaves was beyond the capabilities of the GOON squads. The point had been reached where a large-scale intervention by the FBI itself was needed to bring about the final destruction of AIM and allied traditionals. Agents in the area were being "psyched up" for the coming battle.

The only substantial questions which confronted Bureau strategists were simply how, where and when to provoke a confrontation of sufficient magnitude to warrant another massive application of federal force to Pine Ridge. The answers were shortly forthcoming.

The Cowboy Boot Caper

On June 25, 1975, "some time after 4 p.m.," SAs Ronald Williams and Jack Coler accompanied by BIA police officers Robert Ecoffey (an Oglala GOON) and Glenn Little Bird (Nez Perce and a suspected GOON) drove into the Jumping Bull Compound.[6] They claimed to have a warrant for the arrest of a young Oglala AIM supporter named Jimmy Eagle (age nineteen, a grandson of ION leader Gladys Bissonette) who, along with three other reservation youths, was being sought on charges of "kidnapping, aggravated assault and aggravated robbery."[7] In actuality,

What [is difficult] to explain [is] the triviality of the offense for which a federal warrant had been issued...On June 23, Jimmy Eagle and the other three youths sought—Teddy Pourier, Hobart Horse, and Herman Thunder Hawk—had been drinking at Pourier's house with two young white ranch hands whom they had known for most of their lives. A friendly party turned into a free-for-all, in the course of which Horse got into a wrestling match with one of the whites while Eagle removed a pair of cowboy boots from the feet of the other...if the victim had been Indian, it is very unlikely that charges would have been filed at all. The white youths registered a complaint, which was probably justified; what perplexed the Indians was why warrants were issued without investigation, and why a BIA patrolman was not sent out on this errand, which was a matter for tribal court, and why a petty misdemeanor had been transformed overnight into two felonies. For want of a better explanation, one must suppose that a felony was needed to give [FBI] agents jurisdiction on the reservation. The press...were led to believe that a kidnapping (a capital crime) had occurred, when in fact this allega-

A view of the Jumping Bull compound, June 1975, showing the terrain in the background into which the Peltier group escaped after the firefight. (Photo: Kevin Barry McKiernan)

tion had no substance whatsoever, and was dropped quickly without explanation. In fact, the whole episode was so inconsequential that all but Eagle were eventually released on unsecured bonds, or in the custody of others, and Eagle himself was tried only on the robbery charge and then acquitted.[8]

Thus, with scores of unsolved murders clogging the investigative docket of the FBI on Pine Ridge—and the head of the Bureau's Rapid City office, George O'Clock, pleading "lack of manpower" in pursuing these investigations—*two* agents had been dispatched to chase down a teenager who, at most, was guilty of stealing a pair of used cowboy boots. The absurdity of this is compounded by the fact that neither of the agents was even in possession of the warrant they were supposedly trying to serve.[9]

In any event, SAs Coler and Williams and their BIA police counterparts, having first performed a warrantless search on the home of Wanda Siers, the residence closest to Highway 18 within the Jumping Bull property (see map), were informed by AIM member Dusty Nelson (an Oglala, *aka* John Star Yellow Wood) that Jimmy Eagle was not present and had not been seen in the vicinity for several days. From the Siers cabin, "the agents could see a number of Indians watching in silence from the compound, perhaps two hundred yards away…and apparently decided against going any closer."[10] Their preliminary reconnaissance completed, all four law enforcement personnel departed.

Shortly thereafter, Coler and Williams confronted three young AIM members—Norman Charles (Navajo), Mike "Baby AIM" Anderson (Navajo), and Wilford "Wish" Draper (Navajo)—who were walking back to the Tent City along Highway 18 after having gone to Oglala to shower. Arbitrarily, as none of the three was accused of criminal activity or remotely resembled "fugitive" Jimmy Eagle, all three boys were ordered into the FBI car and taken to BIA police headquarters in Pine Ridge village.[11] Although quickly released, they were first interrogated, not so much about Jimmy Eagle's possible presence in the Tent City or elsewhere on the Jumping Bull property, as about who *else* was in residence there. As Peter Matthiessen succinctly points out, it is not difficult to discern why it is widely believed on Pine Ridge that the whole "cowboy boot caper" was contrived by the Bureau as an expedient to gathering tactical intelligence and establishing a prior justification for an already decided-upon confrontation.[12]

The "Shoot-Out"

Between 11 and 11:45 a.m. on June 26, 1975, SAs Coler and Williams returned to the Jumping Bull Compound.[13] They drove past the Siers cabin and proceeded along a lane down a slope leading toward Tent City, positioned at the bottom across a meadow at the edge of the timber surrounding White Clay Creek. According to a 302 Report filed by SA Gerard Waring, who monitored Coler's and Williams' radio communications, the pair of agents were following a "red and white vehicle" in which there seemed "to be some Indians" who "appear[ed] to have rifles."[14]

For reasons which remain quite unclear, the agents stopped their cars at the bottom of the incline and began to fire at an undetermined number of Indians ahead of them. According to Peter Matthiessen, Angie Long Visitor, a young Oglala who lived in the "green house" at the Jumping Bull Compound, later recollected:

> Two strange cars were parked in the pasture west of the compound and below, down toward the horse corral, at the edge of the creek woods. One of the two white men— she assumed they were lawmen because of the radio aerials and good condition of the cars—was removing a gun case from the trunk of [his] car; the other was kneeling and shooting in her direction with a handgun.[15]

Persons in the AIM encampment, believing themselves to be under attack by GOONs or members of a white vigilante group,[16] returned fire. As AIM member Darelle "Dino" Butler (Tuni) remembers it, "I was in the tipi with my wife [Nilak]. We were just getting up, and I heard firing up there. Norman Brown came down and said, 'There is shooting up there, we got to get up there.' So I grabbed my gun and told my wife to take Jean [Bordeaux, a 14-year-old Oglala who was staying with the Butlers] and the other girl out of there."[17] Years later, Butler also recounted how, "them agents could still have got away without any trouble...the agents could have gone back out that way, but they didn't."[18] AIM member Bob Robideau (Chippewa) concurs:

> What we couldn't understand was why them two men stayed right where they were, down in that field; they couldn't have picked a worse place in the first place. The least they could have done was backed them cars down into the woods—that would've

Nilak Butler (Photo: Jenny Vander Wall)

been easy. Or at least run for the corrals, where there was a little cover. They didn't even *try* to take cover; the most they did was kneel down alongside their car. The rest of the time they just stood there, right out in the open.[19]

A clue to understanding such peculiar behavior may be found in a radio transmission made by SA Williams almost as soon as the shooting had begun, requesting someone to "get to the high ground" and provide "covering fire" for him and Coler.[20] Exactly who Williams thought would be in a position to accomplish such a feat in the remote locale of the firefight was quickly clarified.

Almost immediately, someone yelled that two more cars were coming in off Highway 18, one of them a green-and-white BIA patrol car [manned by Fred Two Bulls, an Oglala and a known GOON], and [Norman] Brown ran across to the log cabin to divert the attention of these cars with his .22. Apparently, [Mike] Anderson and [AIM member] Norman Charles were also firing at those cars. At a distance of nearly two hundred yards, the young Indians succeeded in shooting out one tire on each of them, and the cars backed up in a wild zigzagging retreat along [the lane] toward Highway 18, before one of them got stuck in a muddy ditch. After a long-range exchange with a big white man [SA J. Gary Adams] who jumped out of his car and started shooting, Brown returned [to the hill overlooking Williams and Coler].[21]

As Nilak Butler recalls, when the firing gained in intensity she asked others:

[W]ell, what's going on? They said, oh, they're having a firefight over there. And they said it might be police officials [as opposed to GOONs], and they said they were taking off. All this happened really fast; it probably takes longer to tell about it than it actually happened. So we [she, Jean Bordeaux and several children] took off; we were run-

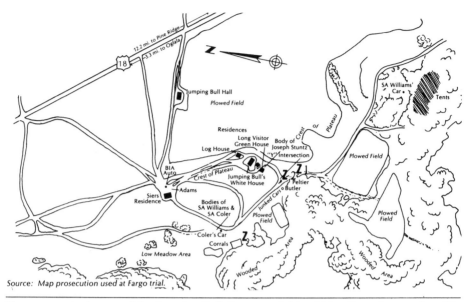

The prosecution's map of the Jumping Bull Compound, Pine Ridge Sioux Reservation, SD, scene of the Oglala firefight. (Prepared by Mary Lea for *The Trial of Leonard Peltier*)

ning into this one area where we knew there was a bridge to get to the main road and try to get the kids out of there, and by the time we hit the main road, there was already a roadblock on it, and a lot of people there. And I was so surprised because it seemed like the shooting had just barely started and already they had roadblocks up...and at this time we saw helicopters, and I remember thinking, what the hell *is* this?[22]

Meanwhile, AIM member Edgar Bear Runner (Oglala), who lived near Oglala, observed that "paramilitary forces had been surrounding the Oglala region all that morning," and had set out on foot to warn the residents of the Tent City that "something ominous was taking place" prior to the beginning of the firefight.[23] At about the same time that the shooting began around the Jumping Bull Compound, Bear Runner was about three-quarters of a mile away. Here, he encountered "Dick Wilson and about 20 GOONs and BIA police" setting up a roadblock. Detouring through a field to get around this obstacle, he came upon a "force of 150 white men—state troopers, U.S. marshals, SWAT teams" at a distance of approximately one-quarter mile from the scene of what the police were already calling "the shoot-out."[24] This corresponds very well with the recollection of Dino Butler that, very early in the fighting:

[T]he Long Visitors were already on their way out, and I told them which way to go; they were hurrying toward the road...Later they said that a car came along right away and picked them up, and that just down the road toward Pine Ridge [Highway 18], there was a big van parked, and someone was handing out weapons to white lawmen. So that was happening within fifteen minutes [after the firing began].[25]

It being physically impossible that the various police agencies involved could simply have responded to Coler's and Williams' distress calls, transmitted from a very isolated location, with such strength and speed, it becomes obvious that large numbers of police and GOONs had been *prepositioned* in the immediate vicinity before the two agents approached the Tent City. This would explain the odd belligerence with which the two "lone" lawmen treated a far larger number of supposedly armed and dangerous opponents, and the cavalier behavior they exhibited once the Indians began to return fire. It appears that their mission, using the spurious warrant for Jimmy Eagle as a cover, was to provoke a shooting altercation which overwhelming numbers of their police and GOON colleagues would then finish. AIM was to be the loser, not only of the immediate "shoot-out," but in the longer term as the Bureau escalated the tactics employed against the organization and increased the number of agents assigned to Pine Ridge. As both Dino Butler and Bob Robideau put it, Coler and Williams acted as they did because "they thought that people were coming in there quick to back them up."[26]

Planning for the operation, however, seems to have been based largely on Coler's and Williams' reconnaissance of the compound the day before and the subsequent interrogation of Mike Anderson, Norman Charles and Wish Draper. On the morning of the 26th, the agents probably expected to encounter only the three boys, Norman Brown, Leonard Peltier, Bob Robideau, Dino Butler, and Dusty Nelson, as well as several unarmed women and children in the AIM camp. However, the actions of the agents on the 25th had alerted AIM members and supporters in the Oglala area that something was seriously amiss. As a consequence, a large number of them—SA David Price has estimated that there were at least thirty[27]—had gravitated to the Jumping Bull property by mid-morning of the fatal day. In addition to the eight fighters who were anticipated to be present when Coler and Williams arrived, the Bureau shortly identified David Sky (Oglala), Sam Loud Hawk (Oglala), Kenny Loud Hawk (Oglala), June Little (Oglala), Bruce "Beau" Little (Oglala), Jerry Mousseau (Oglala), Hobart Horse (Oglala), Cris Westerman (Sisseton-Wahpeton Dakota), Richard Little (Oglala), Frank Black Horse (*aka:* Richard Tall Bull and Frank DeLuca, an Italian from Cleveland who was adopted by a Pine Ridge family), Jimmy Eagle, Leon Eagle (Oglala), Herman Thunder Hawk (Oglala), Melvin Lee Houston (Oglala-Chippewa), Dave Hill (Russell Means' cohort during the Custer Courthouse confrontation and resulting trial; see Chapter 5), and Joe Stuntz Killsright (Coeur D'Alene) as being among those it believed had participated in the firefight.[28]

The reality, of course, was that Coler and Williams were vastly outgunned from the moment they commenced firing, although it is doubtful they realized it at the outset. Further, AIM and its supporters had sufficient firepower available to turn back the initial attempts at reinforcement, sealing the two agents—Custer-like—in their self-made trap. At about the same time that SA Adams and BIA police officer Two Bulls were driven back from their attempt to enter the Jumping Bull Compound, Coler was hit by a rifle bullet fired at long range; the round, a .44 magnum,

FBI agents Jack Coler (left) and Ron Williams were apparently to serve as the "point" elements of an elaborate plan to trap the Tent City AIM group into a gun battle near Oglala on June 26, 1975. They were sent in, cut off and abandoned by their colleagues. (Photos: FBI)

first struck the open door of his car and splayed before nearly severing the agent's right arm near the shoulder.[29] The wound, which was probably fatal, put Coler out of action, leaving Williams truly alone. At this point, the initial cockiness he had displayed deserted him, and the FBI radio log records his desperate transmission, "If someone could get on top of the ridge and give us cover, we might still be able to get out of here." Moments later, his radio communications degenerated to the point of repeating over and over again: "Come on guys. Come on guys." His transmissions are reported to have ended abruptly with the mumbled statement, "I'm hit," a moan and then silence.[30] According to the Rapid City FBI office, there were no further transmissions by either agent "after approximately 12:10 p.m."[31]

Coler and Williams were simply abandoned once Adams and Two Bulls retreated. The tactical commander of the BIA SWAT forces prepositioned near Oglala that day, Marvin Stoldt (an Oglala and a known GOON), later stated in an interview with a WKLDOC investigator that:

> [T]hey [the SWAT team] were to serve as a backup unit to the two FBI agents, that the FBI agents were aware of the explosive atmosphere which existed at the time and in fact were pre-warned [sic] about the same. Mr. Stoldt expressed his belief that the FBI was testing the situation at Pine Ridge...That they had heard the distress call (radio) come over the air from the two FBI agents, that they (SWAT team) were unable to assist the two FBI agents because of the heavy gunfire.[32]

What is most striking about this is not that Stoldt, a relative bit player, might have decided not to risk his neck on behalf of two FBI agents, but that both SA

Adams and BIA police/GOON leader Delmar Eastman *must* have approved the decision to abort the backup effort at the first sign of serious resistance. Rather than attempting to use the perhaps 200 heavily armed men at their disposal to force their way to their embattled comrades barely 200 yards away, they opted to hang back along the main road and engage for "about forty minutes" in "a long-range and sporadic exchange between the cabins [in the Jumping Bull Compound] and the cluster of official cars out on Highway 18."[33]

Meanwhile, reinforcements to the police poured into the area (by dusk, there were more than 250 on the scene) and, as Bob Robideau later wrote, "By noon our defensive positions were completely surrounded by FBI agents, some of whom were SWAT-trained, BIA police, BIA SWAT teams, state law enforcement, and non-law enforcement who were comprised of local white farmers and goons."[34] Nonetheless, using the cover of brush along White Clay Creek, AIM and ION people were beginning to slip away at a rapid rate. SA David Price, who'd blown the engine of his car while en route, received a ride from WKLDOC reseacher Joanna LeDeaux when she happened by. Upon their arrival near the Jumping Bull property at about 12:30 p.m., LeDeaux volunteered to go into the Tent City and attempt to arrange a ceasefire. According to the 302 Report of SA Adams for June 26, she was gone "about an hour" and then returned, stating to BIA Superintendent Kendall Cummings that "no negotiation was possible." Before Adams or other agents could question her, LeDeaux drove away. At about the same time that LeDeaux returned to Highway 18 (1:30 p.m.) another contingent of South Dakota highway patrolmen showed up, followed immediately by a Fall River County "sheriff's posse" headed by South Dakota Attorney General William "Wild Bill" Janklow and his assistant William Delaney.[35]

What LeDeaux had discovered was that both Coler and Williams had been dead for some time and that the remaining people within the AIM positions had thinned to a sort of rear guard covering the retreat of others. By 2 p.m., even this much reduced group had divided itself, leaving two or three people to "pin down" the huge police force with random pot shots while the others evacuated along the creek.[36] Although, as Robideau noted, various groups of agents, police and GOONs had worked themselves around the Jumping Bull property—"flankering," as SA Dean Hughes (head of the FBI SWAT team) was to put it[37]—it was not until 4:20 p.m. that another effort was made to move to Coler's and Williams' assistance. Even then, the FBI's "probe" of the AIM positions came in the form of sending Edgar Bear Runner—with hands raised all the way, lest he be gunned down by a brave Bureau sniper—in to find out what was going on.[38] When Bear Runner returned to Highway 18 approximately a half-hour later, he informed BIA Superintendent Cummings that both agents appeared to be dead, and the Jumping Bull property seemed deserted.[39] Bear Runner and Cummings were then "allowed" to walk back in—*both* with their hands raised—in order to verify that the agents were indeed dead.[40]

At 5:50 p.m., according to SA Hughes' 302 Report, he finally "gave the order to assault the houses." In his testimony at the Cedar Rapids trial of Bob Robideau and Dino Butler, Hughes states that while he was "running zigzag fashion," he "heard

AIM member Joe Stuntz Killsright (left), 18, was recalled by all as staunchly committed to his people's struggle. Killsright lies dead in the mud (below) where his body was dumped on June 26, 1975. Note the absence of blood or a head wound as reported in the FBI autopsy report. (Photo: Kevin Barry McKiernan)

a lot of fire from the group that [SA David] Price had that was assaulting the green house." He goes on that, moments later he "walked over and observed this dead Indian male...I believe he had a bullet hole in the upper part of his head, although I'm not positive about that. The foremost thing I observed, he was wearing an FBI SWAT jacket which I recognized, and it had the letters 'FBI' on the left breast pocket."[41] The assault group proceeded to shoot up and teargas all the structures within the Jumping Bull Compound, but failed to turn up any more Indians.[42]

The dead Indian was Joe Stuntz Killsright, apparently among the last remnant of AIM's rear guard. According to the FBI's autopsy report (echoed by Hughes from the witness stand in Cedar Rapids, although he professed to be "not positive" if it were true), Killsright had been killed by a single, long-range rifle shot to the forehead.[43] However, South Dakota Assistant Attorney General Delaney who—as a prominent member of a vigilante group—was among the first to view the body, stated on June 28, 1975, that: "[T]he dead Indian was lying on his back, and when he was turned over, it appeared he had...received a burst in the back and there was blood coming from the back of his jacket."[44] NPR reporter (and *Minneapolis Tribune* stringer) Kevin McKiernan—who in a momentary, confused lapse in the FBI's usual "security" against on-the-scene press coverage of its anti-AIM operations, was admitted to the Jumping Bull Compound—also contends the Bureau's "bullet-in-the-forehead story is false." McKiernan, who photographed the body from several angles (none of the photos reveals a facial wound) insists that, "The only blood I saw was coming down the jacket sleeve," and suggests that the SWAT jacket may have been put on Killsright's corpse to hide how he had died, "before outside observers were allowed into the area."[45] Finally, AIM member Mike Anderson later recounted how Norman Charles, Killsright's team-mate in the rear guard action, told him shortly afterward that, as the pair was escaping from the FBI's "final assault," Killsright "had been hit and was bleeding too bad to take along."[46]

None of this squares with the official Bureau version of Killsright's death at the hands of a long-range sniper. No FBI investigation into how Killsright died was ever undertaken, and no independent autopsy was ever performed. There is thus a more than passing possibility that SA David Price's assault unit may have capped a day of FBI provocation, bungling and cowardice—ingredients which led to the deaths of two of its agents—with the summary execution of an AIM member. This combination of circumstances goes far toward explaining why, in the face of all facts, Bureau spokesmen began their vehement public insistence that the Indians had held off numerically superior forces for hours by "fighting from bunkers" and that its agents had been unwittingly ambushed while in the normal performance of their duties (see Chapter 10).

In any event, by 5:30 p.m. on June 26, "SAC Joseph Trimbach and a special sniper team from Minneapolis, as well as other [FBI] units from around the **country**" were flying into Rapid City, and "already, armored personnel carriers and high explosives were on the way to Pine Ridge for the second time in not much more than

COINTELPRO specialist Richard G. Held took control of all FBI anti-AIM operations on June 27, 1975. Formerly SAC Chicago where he ran the cover-up of the Hampton and Clark assassinations, he was responsible for the reign of terror on Pine Ridge in July and August 1975, the fraudulent extradition of Leonard Peltier from Canada, *etc.* He was later rewarded with a promotion to second-in-command of the FBI under Clarence Kelly. (Photo: FBI)

two years."[47] The Bureau, as Dino Butler puts it, was now prepared "to clear out the last pocket[s] of real resistance on the reservation."[48]

The Invasion of Pine Ridge

The morning after the Oglala firefight, the FBI moved onto Pine Ridge and the adjoining Rosebud Reservation in force. Approximately 200 agents, augmented by sizable complements of U.S. Marshals Service SOG personnel, BIA police, GOONs and non-Indian vigilantes, utilizing at least nine armored personnel carriers and several Bell (UH-1B) "Huey" helicopters, conducted massive operations in both locales.[49] Numerous incidents of warrantless search (and seizure), breaking and entering, destruction of private property, physical intimidation, false arrest and other systematic deprivations of civil rights accompanied these Vietnam-style operations. As Jim Messerschmidt has pointed out, "assault teams, equipped with M-16s, helicopters, and tracking dogs carried out a series of raids on the reservation in the largest display of strength ever mustered by the Bureau."[50] Bruce Johansen and Roberto Maestes amplify this by observing that:

> The day after the shootout, Richard [G.] Held...arrived in South Dakota with a force of 170 armed agents [more than 40 had already been posted to the Pine Ridge area], who began a military style sweep across the reservation seeking suspects. The agents used M-16s, helicopters, tracking dogs, and armored personnel carriers to conduct a series of raids, during which many Lakota said the FBI broke into homes without warrants, physically abused innocent bystanders...[51]

FBI SWAT personnel on Pine Ridge, June 1975. Massive numbers of Bureau paramilitary specialists were en route to the reservation prior to the firefight on the 26th, suggesting that the whole "shoot-out" was preplanned by the authorities. (Photo Kevin Barry McKiernan)

William Muldrow, of the U.S. Commission on Civil Rights Rocky Mountain Regional Office, who was dispatched to Pine Ridge at the time (specifically to investigate FBI methods employed on the reservation) officially concurred with Johansen and Maestes:

> The FBI immediately launched a large-scale search for the suspected slayers which involved 100 to 200 combat-clad FBI agents, BIA policemen, SWAT teams, helicopters, fixed-wing aircraft and tracking dogs. An increasing volume of requests for information regarding the incident and numerous reports and complaints of threats, harassment, and search procedures conducted without due process of law by the FBI prompted my visit to the reservation to gather firsthand information.[52]

A later Civil Rights Commission report followed up by noting that:

> [T]he BIA and State Police [both of which operated on Pine Ridge during this period under direct control of the FBI] seemed to make a habit of search and seizure without due cause and/or warrant.[53]

The Bureau's official designation for this conduct was the RESMURS (*Reserva-tion Murders*) Investigation. However, "[t]he Reservation Murders Investigation was concerned only with the killings of the agents [Coler and Williams]; it did not con-cern itself with the dozens of murders committed in the past three years on the reservation, almost none of which had been investigated, much less solved."[54] Not unnaturally, the "FBI's tactics caused a great deal of resentment among many tradi-tional Indians, who had watched their friends and relatives killed without a hint of investigation by the FBI."[55]

Indicative of what was going on was the plight of the elderly Jumping Bulls, Harry and Cecelia (parents of Roselyn), who had returned from a trip to sell year-ling calves in Gordon, Nebraska, at about 7 p.m. on the evening of June 26, to find their property literally crawling with FBI, police and GOONs. A feisty woman in her mid-seventies, Cecelia immediately confronted a "white officer lawman," presumab-ly from the FBI, wanting to know what they were doing on her property:

Law Officer: Don't you know two men [were] killed?

Cecelia: Is this one of them? (Pointing to somebody laying there, in front of the Green [Long Visitor] House).

Law Officer: No, down there. (Pointing towards the west, towards the corrals…).

Cecelia: What is that lying there?

Law Officer: That's just an Indian.

Cecelia: Can I see it?

Law Officer: Yes. (Calls to another officer to uncover his [Killsright's] face).

(Cecelia walks over to the body and mourns.)[56]

The elder Jumping Bulls, whose home had been teargassed and shot full of holes (family photos had also been shot at pointblank range), even after it became obvious that the building was harboring no AIM snipers, were summarily evicted. Seventy-nine-year-old Harry spent the next several days unsuccessfully attempting to obtain permission even to visit his home, while Cecelia began to show signs of a nervous breakdown. Finally, "[o]utraged that their respected elders should be for-bidden access to their property, the traditional people of the White Clay District, more than two hundred strong, marched on the BIA roadblocks, which rapidly dis-solved."[57] With that, the Bureau grudgingly "authorized" the Jumping Bulls to return.

On July 2, seventy-five-year-old Wallace Little, Sr.'s residence—near the Jump-ing Bull property—was surrounded by a dozen federal cars and SWAT vans con-taining approximately fifty battle-clad agents. Although Little protested that they had

Oglala elder Cecelia
Jumping Bull stands next to
her bullet-riddled house,
July 1975. Note the picture
on the left was "executed"
by a Bureau gunman, an
indicative example of FBI
performance on Pine Ridge
during this period. (Photo:
Kevin Barry McKiernan)

no right to be on his property and demanded to see a warrant, he was detained at gunpoint while "two agents ransacked his house."[58] On July 12, SA J. Gary Adams led a similar raid on AIM member Oscar Bear Runner's home in Porcupine, by which time the FBI's "[b]ursting into houses and threatening and scaring people had caused the death [by heart attack] of an old man named James Brings Yellow, in Oglala, and as these searches spread across Pine Ridge, the Indians signed a general petition demanding that the FBI leave the reservation."[59]

The breaking-and-entering, threats, harassment, and many other illegal procedures entirely alienated the Lakota, even Wilson supporters who might otherwise have helped; "the Sioux Tribal Council chairmen, after a special meeting on July 12, demanded an immediate withdrawal of most of the FBI agents and U.S. marshals from Pine Ridge and other reservations; they suggested that Oglala tribal officials, Dick Wilson included, be removed from office if they failed to reinstate constitutional procedures, and they also asked [South Dakota] Governor Kneip to reprimand Attorney General Janklow for his inflammatory statements. For once, the BIA's Indian governments were supporting all the Indian people they were supposed to represent."[60]

The U.S. Commission on Civil Rights quickly determined that the operations had assumed the characteristics of "an over-reaction which takes on aspects of a vendetta," and its chairman, Arthur J. Flemming, in a letter of protest to U.S. Attorney General Levi, dated July 22, 1975, described RESMURS as a "full-scale military type invasion" of Pine Ridge. He continued:

> [The FBI's presence in such force] has created a deep resentment on the part of many reservation residents who feel that such a procedure would not be tolerated in any non-Indian community in the United States. They point out that little has been done to solve numerous murders on the reservation, but when two white men are killed, "troops" are brought in from all over the country at a cost of hundreds of millions of dollars.

Flemming's letter might be seen as a followup of sorts to another, written by South Dakota Senator James Abourezk to President Gerald Ford on June 27, requesting that the chief executive intervene directly to forestall the invasion of Pine Ridge. Abourezk noted that he had entered a number of appeals to both the Justice Department and the FBI over the preceding two years, to the effect that they do *something* to curtail the mounting violence on the reservation, only to be met with a "bureaucratic" response and "no action." The Senator concluded that, "[a]t the very least, they [the FBI] have an interest in keeping things stirred up." Ford, of course, did nothing at all.

The Bureau was able to quash such objections through the ample utilization of propaganda, first through a series of press conferences in Rapid City to provide grossly inaccurate information as to what had actually happened to Coler and Williams (see Chapter 10), and then by release of equally fictional documents purporting to show that the Oglala firefight was merely the opening round of an incipient wave of "AIM violence." An example of the latter reads as follows:

> [Area residents have been warned to] get all of their valuables and possessions and themselves out of the [Mt.] Rushmore area as soon as possible because there is going to be a lot of trouble...(deleted) said that AIM has a suicide squad which is extremely well trained in military and guerrilla tactics. The members of this squad are mostly Vietnam veterans, who are heavily armed and have displayed their weapons at AIM meetings in the past. (deleted) believes that there are about thirty members of this AIM suicide squad...AIM people have been telling the general Indian population that on the Fourth of July "the mountain will come down"...(deleted) is thoroughly familiar with the incident at Pine Ridge which resulted in the killings of the two FBI agents. He said that as (deleted) talked he could not help but feel that the two agents who were killed had accidently walked into the holding area for the suicide squad...(deleted) feels that "sniffer dogs" trained to detect explosives should be brought to Mount Rushmore immediately.[61]

Nothing happened at Mt. Rushmore on July 4 and there were no signs at all of the supposed AIM guerrilla campaign, although a group of Indians, tired of being buzzed by an FBI Huey dubbed "Hotel One," shot the helicopter down in the hills north of Pine Ridge village;[62] however the disinformation campaign was largely successful. The Church Committee, for instance, which was then concluding its inves-

Combat-clad FBI personnel boarding a Bell UH-1B "Huey" helicopter, identical to those used in Vietnam, dubbed "Hotel 1." The helicopter was shot down by angry local residents north of Pine Ridge village on July 4, 1975. (Photo: Kevin Barry McKiernan)

tigation of the illegalities surrounding the Bureau's formally designated COIN-TELPRO operations, had announced an intention to investigate the FBI's anti-AIM campaign but suspended that effort on July 3:

> Attached is a letter from the Senate Select Committee (SSC), dated 6-23-75, addressed to [Attorney General] Edward S. Levi. This letter announces the SSC's intent to conduct interviews relating to Douglass Durham, a former Bureau informant. The request obviously relates to our investigation at "Wounded Knee" and our investigation of the American Indian Movement. This request was received 6-27-75, by Legal Division...On 6-27-75, Patrick Shea, staff member of the SSC, requested we hold in abeyance any action on the request in view of the killing of the Agents at Pine Ridge Reservation, South Dakota.[63]

Once "postponed," the investigation of the relationship between the FBI's COINTELPRO methods and what was happening to AIM on Pine Ridge was never reopened.

Thus freed of any restraints, the Bureau increased the intensity of its military operations against "AIM strongpoints." For example, on July 8, SA David Price led a fifty agent "air assault" on the home of AIM member Sylvester "Selo" Black Crow (Oglala), near the remote reservation village of Wanblee. Although no illegal weapons, explosives or fugitives were found—much less bunkers or other fortifications—the heliborne assault force held Black Crow and his wife Irenee, at gunpoint while virtually ripping the house and outbuildings apart, destroying much personal property.[64] The agents left in a cloud of dust and a clatter of rotor blades, presumably off to another warrantless search. All told, more than 500 such "interviews" were conducted across Pine Ridge during the months of July and August 1975.[65]

All of this appears to have been a warm-up for the main event, when a huge force of agents descended in yet another air assault, this time against the adjoining Crow Dog and Running properties on the Rosebud Reservation. As the matter is officially chronicled by Congress:

> As part of the search for suspects in the killings of two agents, on February [sic; September] 5, 1975, in the early morning, nearly 100 FBI agents descended by helicopter and military vehicles upon the property of Al Running and Leonard Crow Dog on the Rosebud Reservation in South Dakota. The ostensible occasion for this raid, accompanied by this massive show of force, were search and arrest warrants arising from a fistfight between two young people. The FBI, however, was also looking for evidence in connection with the June 26, 1975 incident at Oglala regarding the deaths of the agents.[66]

Left out of this dry summary is the fact that the Bureau had been planning the action for weeks, evidenced in a heavily deleted memo prepared by the Rapid City FBI office sometime during the first week of August (when Crow Dog held his annual Sun Dance). Determining that since "approximately 300 to 350 people" were then camping at Crow Dog's Paradise, and since "there is a good chance a gun fight will break out" with this large group if the Sun Dance is interrupted, the Bureau postponed its visit.[67] Another greatly excised memo from the same source and week provides a rationale for the raid: "the desire to 'execute' or 'exterminate' Dick Wilson" was feared to be the prevailing sentiment among the people gathered at Crow Dog's.[68] In view of these plans, the notion that the September 5 air assault had *any* relationship whatsoever to the alleged "fistfight between young people"—actually the eviction of three GOONs who'd come to the Crow Dog residence to pick fights, after being seen in the company of FBI agents (see Chapter 12)—is ludicrous.

Also missed in the Congressional account is the fact that Crow Dog himself, at that time considered AIM's spiritual leader, and acknowledged Brulé Lakota holy man, "was marched out [of his house, where he had been sleeping] naked and even the small frightened children were lined up against the walls as the agents ransacked and all but wrecked every house, tent, cabin, and car on both properties."[69] As AIM member Norman Brown remembers, "These FBI agents came in like they were in Vietnam or something...":

> The one grabbed my hair, he said, All right, motherfucker, lay down. So I laid down and they searched me and then put an M-16 to my head. They said, Who killed those

AIM spiritual leader Leonard Crow Dog in 1975, shortly before the FBI launched a massive air assault upon his home. Upon his arrest, agents humiliated him, ridiculed his religious beliefs, and threatened him with murder. (Photo: Michael Vignes)

FBI agents? Told him I didn't know who, so they picked me up, they pushed me with the M-16 in my back, they pushed me. They said, All right, walk to where the crowd were…And as we were standing there—these women who weren't even dressed yet, people crying and everything—they brought Leonard Crow Dog out and he had nothing on. They wouldn't let him put on his clothes; and we tried to give him his pipe [but they would not let us].[70]

Shep Gurwitz, brother of WKLDOC attorney Lew Gurwitz, who was staying there at the time, shares Brown's assessment: "I had been to Vietnam—airborne—I'd seen all this before."[71]

Having devastated his property for reasons other than specified on their warrants, the agents finally tired of humiliating Crow Dog by forcing him to squat naked in the dust amidst a throng of women and children, gave him his clothing and arrested him. As the car in which he was being transported traveled along the blacktop to Pierre, the agents inside began to ridicule his religion. Finally, the agents pulled to the side of the road, and the following interchange occurred:

Agent (believed to be J. Gary Adams): So you're a spiritual man? So you think you've got special powers?

Crow Dog: I believe in the Sacred Pipe.

Agent: And this Pipe gives you special powers?

Crow Dog: The Pipe has power.

Agent: And you carry the Pipe, so you have special powers.

Crow Dog: (silent)

Agent: So you could use these powers to outrun the bullet from my M-16, couldn't you, Crow Dog?

Crow Dog: (silent)

Agent: (more harshly now) Can you outrun my M-16, Crow Dog?

Crow Dog: No.

Agent: What was that?

Crow Dog: No, I can't outrun the M-16.

Agent: Come on, go for it. I'll give you a head start. All you have to do is run. Give it a try, if you really believe in that Pipe. Just run...[72]

Fun over, the agents drove Crow Dog on to the lockup in Pierre, where, according to Dino Butler, also arrested in the operation: "They said Leonard Crow Dog was a scum bag. They said all Indians were scum bags...I was just a little bitty nobody, a scum bag that didn't deserve to live...The last thing they told me as they walked out was, Dino Butler, you're nothing but a worthless scum bag, and I promise you that some day I am going to shoot you. I am going to blow your fucking head off."[73] Such "methods" seem, by all accounts, to have been entirely characteristic of FBI conduct throughout the RESMURS invasion.

Rick Williams, an AIM member whose family includes the Yellow Woods and Nelsons around Oglala, described what was going on:

> The FBIs weren't really going after the so-called "hard core AIM people" after that firefight. Oh, they were out to get some of 'em, and they did. But the way they did was to go after all these grassroots people. They wanted to terrify a lot of grandmothers and little kids, and they did a good job of it, too. They figured if they put enough pressure on these kinds of people, somebody would crack, somebody would give somebody else up, and then the whole sense of community would just unravel on Pine Ridge. Well, I don't think *that* worked, I don't think any of those grassroots folks cooperated, but the cost was just incredible...And that was the *real* objective of the whole thing. The FBI came in with the idea of beating people down so far that they'd never be able to resist again. And I mean *everybody*. What the FBI did was intentional, and every bit as ugly as anything the army did during the 1800s. It was really criminal, what they did here on Pine Ridge.[74]

Dennis Banks agrees with this assessment, noting that it was 1975 when AIM began to lose a great deal of its basic support on the reservation, "because the killings continued [after Dick Wilson was deposed at the polls] and the people had just been through too much; they didn't want any more trouble."[75] Elsewhere, he has observed that,

...you really can't blame the traditionals on Pine Ridge. Once the FBI came in full force during the summer of '75, they were just overwhelmed by the violence, all the military stuff. They couldn't make the FBI leave and AIM could do no better—hell, we were being shot to pieces by then. So, without ever putting it into words, they sort of asked us to pull back, to do what we had to do to make their pain stop. They had the children to think of, and the old people, and the situation had become just untenable. The feds made sure of it.[76]

The Ordeal of Angie Long Visitor

Aside from the remarkable display of thuggishness with which the Bureau pursued its invasion of Pine Ridge in the field, other methods of raw coercion were employed against the traditionals. A cardinal element in this regard was the use of grand juries, the first of which was convened in Rapid City on July 14 at the request of SAC Richard G. Held and U.S. Attorney William Clayton.[77] The net it attempted to cast was so broad, and so obviously intended to serve purposes other than mere information gathering, that "[WKLDOC attorney] William Kunstler turned up to contest its right to subpoena more than fifteen Indians—none of whom (so far as was known) were from the AIM camp—without an evidentiary hearing."[78]

Referring to the "reign of terror" on the Pine Ridge Reservation, Kunstler declared that unless the situation changed, "there's going to be bloodshed...which is in part initiated by the federal government as a retaliation for Wounded Knee, as a retaliation for the emergence of the American Indian Movement as a force in American affairs, and in order to set up some innocent people as the so-called murderers of FBI agents.[79]

Edgar Bear Runner, one of the few AIM people called to testify, firmly refused, publicly shredding his subpoena (which, in any event, had been improperly served) and announcing his only allegiance was to his own, Oglala Lakota, nation: "I'm not a citizen of this colonial system. I'm not a citizen of this federal government."[80] Although it clearly knew Bear Runner could have had no part in the Oglala firefight— he had, after all, been detained in the federal positions along Highway 18 throughout the shooting on June 26—the Bureau responded by placing his name on the list of "RESMURS Suspects" on July 17.[81] Still, the AIM member's example, in combination with the mounting anger among traditionals at the Bureau's draconian behavior on the reservation itself, created a near-blanket resistance to the Rapid City proceedings:

Because of a stolid refusal by local witnesses to give testimony, the first grand jury had to be disbanded; by the time it reconvened in August, at least fifty Indians had refused to cooperate, among them June Little and Wanda Siers, a small, delicate woman who pointedly shut her mouth and refused to open it every time she was approached by the FBI...no one on Pine Ridge was willing to help out [the Bureau] except law-enforcement officers and goons.[82]

Held, Zigrossi and Clayton seem to have rethought their approach between the point the grand jury was cancelled (July 19) and a second convened in late August. Their decision was apparently to reissue subpoenas to all concerned, and then concentrate on those they perceived to be weakest among the roster of intended "witnesses," requesting that these select few be jailed until such time as they agreed to testify (thus, in theory at least, reversing the "Bear Runner Principle" of absolute noncooperation).[83] Hence, of the fifty or more people refusing to go on the stand, all of whom were equally subject to incarceration for "contempt of a grand jury," only three—Ivis and Angie Long Visitor, and Joanna LeDeaux—were targeted for such treatment.

LeDeaux, the young WKLDOC researcher who had attempted to intervene with AIM to halt the firefight upon her arrival at the Jumping Bull property on June 26, was probably chosen because the Bureau construed her desperate action as signifying some sort of latent sympathy for the FBI. More importantly, she was known by federal officials to be pregnant and it was undoubtedly assumed that she would ultimately cooperate rather than undergo delivery of her child in prison. It was probably such reasoning which led federal Judge Andrew Bogue (who also presided over the Crow Dog trials, see Chapter 12) to inform her, as she was being led away, that, "The keys to your cell are in your mouth."[84] In any event, the federal players completely misjudged the depth of LeDeaux's principles, as she not only had her baby behind bars, but served fully eight months (mostly at the federal women's facility in San Pedro, Calif.) rather than cooperate with her kidnappers in any way at all.[85]

The situation of the Long Visitors, elsewhere described as being "nonpolitical, scared and bewildered,"[86] was even worse. Very poor people, they already had three young children to care for.[87] Unlike LeDeaux, they had also been interrogated by the Bureau in the immediate wake of the firefight and, thoroughly shaken by the pitched battle which had suddenly engulfed their home, had attempted to comply with the demands of their visibly enraged questioners that they "talk." Although it was obvious that the couple had gathered up their children and begun their trek to flee the area with the firing of the first shots on June 26—and that neither was therefore in any position to identify the individual(s) who actually killed agents Coler and Williams—it was from Angie Long Visitor's early interviews that Held's COINTELPRO specialists began to assemble the list of those against whom they wished to pursue prosecution (or target as "key witnesses") in the RESMURS case:

1. BOB LNU [Last Name Unknown], male, Indian, 5'6" tall, 120-130 pounds, 25 years old, medium brown hair, (This is the individual previously referred to as firing on law enforcement officials).

2. NORMAN LNU, age 17-18, male, Navajo Indian, from Arizona, 5'2" tall, 120 pounds, brown hair, (This is the individual previously referred to as firing on law enforcement officials).

3. LEONARD LNU, age 25, male, Indian, tribe unknown, 5'8" tall, 200 pounds, brown hair.

4. DEANO LNU, male, Indian, tribe unknown, age 23-24, 5'6" tall, 140 pounds, dark brown hair.

5. MIKE LNU, also known as BABY AIM, male Navajo Indian, 17 years old, 5'2" tall, 125 pounds, dark brown hair.

6. WISH (Unknown if this is first name, last name or nickname), male Navajo Indian, 18 years old, 5'2" tall, 125 pounds, brown hair.

7. NORMAN LNU, male, Indian, tribe unknown, reportedly from Rapid City, South Dakota, age 18, 5'4", 125 pounds, brown hair.[88]

In addition to the specifically AIM-identified men sifted from the FBI's overall RESMURs suspect list in this compilation (*i.e.*: Bob Robideau, Norman Charles, Leonard Peltier, Dino Butler, Mike Anderson, Wish Draper and Norman Brown), the AIM women (Jean Bordeaux, Lena "Lynn" Gunston, Nilak Butler and Jean Day) are also pinpointed via careful Bureau questioning:

1. JEAN LNU, female, tribe unknown, resides in Rapid City, age 17, 5'1", 110 pounds, dark brown, shoulder length hair. Immediately after the gun fight, her mother came from Rapid City looking for her daughter.

2. LYNN (LNU), female, Indian from Arizona, age 18, 5'5" tall, 110 pounds, dark brown, waist length hair.

3. NILAK (Phonetic), female, Eskimo, reportedly from Alaska, age 19, 5'1", 140 pounds, chunky build. She [Angie Long Visitor] added that NILAK was DEANO's girl friend [sic, wife].

4. JEAN LNU, female, Indian, tribe unknown, from Wisconsin, age 24, 5'7" tall, 160 pounds, wore glasses, light brown hair, light complexion. LONGVISITOR [sic] indicated this JEAN went home approximately one week prior to this shooting and that she was the girlfriend of LEONARD LNU.[89]

The overt COINTELPRO strategy devised by Held, *et al.*, appears to have been to maximize the forms of pressure brought upon local Pine Ridge residents while omitting them altogether from prosecution in the deaths of its agents. In this scenario, the guiding theory is that it would be easier—given the right degree of "persuasion"—for the ION traditionals to "give up outsiders," such as AIM members at Tent City, than other Oglalas (whether AIM members or not). Once this was accomplished, the wedge the FBI had been seeking to drive between AIM as a whole and the Pine Ridge traditional community would be hammered home; the attendant elimination of given AIM leaders and/or members (*i.e.* their conviction for murder) would be only a tasty fringe benefit to the larger RESMURS objective of destroying the political unity achieved among the reservation dissidents. As Peter Matthiessen has put it, the way the Bureau proceeded was calculated to obtain precisely this result, as opposed to discovery of even the true identities of those who killed Coler and Williams:

> [A considerable range of local people] could have come forward and provided testimony against the outside Indians in return, perhaps, for immunity for local families, and almost certainly one or more did, to judge from the details which were provided to Myrtle Poor Bear [in constructing her utterly fabricated "contributions," see Chapter 11] and other potential witnesses.[90]

In getting the ball rolling on this, as well as beginning to consolidate the circumstantial case it was constructing against the Tent City AIM people, "cracking" the Long Visitors was of utmost importance to the Bureau. Consequently, Joanna LeDeaux, Ivis and Angie Long Visitor were all jailed on September 16, 1975.[91] Although the couple had honored their subpoenas, and had merely declined to go beyond their original statements in their testimony (*i.e.*, refused to advance "desirable" testimony, as opposed to the truth as they knew it), they served three months each in lockup before being released at the end of 1975, to "think it over."[92]

Given that Angie's, rather than Ivis', initial statements were more useful to the federal case being erected, he was not called again. Angie, on the other hand, received five more RESMURS-related subpoenas during 1976; on *each* occasion, she honored the papers, but refused to expand upon the information she had provided at the outset.[93] Finally, in obvious frustration that she had not yet been broken, Rapid City FBI head Norman Zigrossi kicked off the new year of 1977 by conjuring up a factual basis (in the form of an affidavit prepared by himself) for her to be re-jailed. The document reads in part:

> ...it will be impractical to obtain the appearance of Angie Long Visitor for the trial of Leonard Peltier solely by means of a subpoena because she has demonstrated reluctance to appear, and because she has avoided contact with Government Agents...Long Visitor eluded intensive effort to locate her by various means, including avoiding contact with known associates and departing the State of South Dakota.[94]

As it turned out, Zigrossi's reference to Long Visitor's "elusive" behavior (a contention which failed to mention the *six* subpoenas she'd honored) concerned her possible testimony at the Butler-Robideau trial in Cedar Rapids in 1976.[95] No evidence was ever submitted to substantiate the notion that Angie Long Visitor had at any time actually "avoided contact with known associates" (to avoid agents, or for any other reason), much less that she'd fled the state in order to avoid subpoena service. For that matter, no evidence was posited to substantiate the contention that an "intensive effort" was undertaken through "various means" by Zigrossi's agents to locate and serve her. To the contrary, the recollection of local Pine Ridge residents is that no such effort was made by the Bureau, a matter which suggests the whole issue was invented by Zigrossi simply to bring additional pressure to bear upon this "unfriendly" witness.[96]

Nonetheless, on January 17, U.S. Attorney Clayton presented Zigrossi's affidavit to federal Judge Paul Benson, obtaining a Warrant for Arrest of a Material Witness.[97] As a result, at about 7:30 a.m. on January 18, three carloads of agents headed by a "red headed" individual believed to have been SA J. Gary Adams drove up to the Deana He Crow residence, near Oglala, the location at which Angie Long Visitor was staying. The agents surrounded the house, kicked in the door and, brandishing shotguns and automatic weapons, thoroughly terrified the occupants (who were accused of no crime, and who included a number of small children). Their intended victim was arrested, handcuffed and whisked away; the He Crow home was simply left with its shattered door, its residents exposed to the freezing winds of a South Dakota winter.[98]

Upon arrival at the Federal Building in Rapid City, Long Visitor's bail was set at $10,000 despite the fact that she had no prior arrests, was accused of no crime and had attempted neither to run nor resist arrest.[99] She was denied permission either to phone or to see WKLDOC attorney Bruce Ellison, who was waiting to meet with her in an ante-room; at noon, Ellison was informed by Federal Magistrate James Wilson that no bail hearing would be held, and that he would be allowed neither to see nor communicate with his client in any way insofar as WKLDOC was "disallowed" from representing her.[100] WKLDOC director Ken Tilsen then telephoned Wilson directly from Minneapolis and arranged for a "neutral" attorney, Alfredo Peña of Denver, to serve as counsel to Long Visitor during mandatory bail review hearings. However, when Peña arrived in Rapid City, he too was informed that no such hearing would be held, and that he was barred from any communication with his client (this provision was dropped temporarily during the late afternoon of January 19).[101]

On January 20, despite the frenzied efforts of her lawyers to obtain due process, Angie Long Visitor was secretly transferred to the jail in Sioux Falls, where she was held pending her transport to Fargo, N.D. to testify "against" Leonard Peltier. There, the final act in the cruel federal charade was carried out: "Although her statements [did] little harm to Peltier, they did serious injury to her self-respect. On the stand, she wept almost continually with shame and fear, her voice all but inaudible."[102] Ivis, afraid that he too would be used as an example of federal power to trample upon human dignity, actually *had* gone into hiding, a circumstance quickly seized upon by the Bureau to foster even more terror and divisiveness within the community. As his mother, Roselyn Jumping Bull, put it:

> They [the FBI] say he has to testify. One of them told my daughter-in-law [Angie] that even after the Leonard Peltier trial is over, he's going to jail if they ever catch him, he's not going to get away with it...Right now they said Pine Ridge people are telling each other that whoever tells where my son is, they're going to get seven hundred dollars [which the agents were offering "out-of-pocket" as an impromptu reward to anyone who would break faith].[103]

Although Fargo was the end of Angie Long Visitor's ordeal, and nothing ever came of the FBI's threats concerning Ivis, much psychic maiming had been gratuitously imposed upon them both. Similarly, the near two-year experience of brutal Bureau harassment could not have failed to scar their young children. The example into which these innocent people were converted for purposes of federal "law enforcement" had exactly the tangible and ugly chilling effect upon the traditional Oglalas which the COINTELPRO planners desired. Theda Nelson (aunt to Dusty), a long-time Oglala resident and AIM member, sums up the effect:

> The way the FBIs worked this, offering money to poor people to tell lies about each other, offering to drop charges against people in exchange for testimony—false testimony—about other people, it was sick. They didn't get many people to take 'em up on it, but all they needed was one or two. Then instead of trust, you had suspicion. Then, instead of a movement, you had individuals, or individual families, trying to look out for themselves, to protect each other no matter who else got hurt. It's a normal human reaction to what the FBIs were doing to people. And, you know what? It never did the FBI no good in court, even though it sure messed up a lot of lives on this reservation. A lot of folks never *have* got back their self-respect after what the FBIs put 'em through. But, maybe that was their point, eh?[104]

Like the invasion of Pine Ridge and the Oglala firefight itself, the FBI's utilization of grand juries, subpoena power and related incarcerations during its RESMURS Investigation had little to do with law enforcement, pursuit of justice or the desire to punish the guilty. Rather, from beginning to end, the entire operation was simply a drive to break the spirit of a people, to break their will and ability to resist the imposition of unjust authority.

Chapter 10

The Disinformation Campaign

Anyone who becomes involved with the media quickly learns that the advantage of the first news reports being favorable to one's own side is overwhelming. The first reports are usually the ones generally believed, and it is hard to reverse an unfavorable first report...Are soldiers obliged to tell the truth to the media, even if it would be damaging to the Government's cause?...[A] soldier appearing before the press and television must obey an order to conceal an unpalatable truth and an order to tell a palatable lie. It is most important that this should be understood by both the press and public.

—Robin Evelegh,
Peace Keeping in a Democratic Society: The Lessons of Northern Ireland

As discussed in our Introduction and Chapter 1, the process described above as a technique of counterinsurgency warfare has been cultivated by the FBI since the earliest days of J. Edgar Hoover's tenure. Indeed, the same dual emphasis upon the spreading of false information intended to discredit its "enemies" while projecting equally inaccurate positive images of itself and its "friends" has been a standard of Bureau counterintelligence activities throughout its history, a matter which reached a zenith of perfection during the COINTELPRO years of the 1960s and early-1970s (see Chapters 2 and 3).

The more virulent Bureau efforts in this regard are often found in the broader context of propaganda exercises undertaken by the supporters/designers of the socio-political *status quo*. In the case of the FBI's anti-AIM media campaign from 1972 onwards, this meant the promotion of certain token Indian "leaders" and federally subsidized organizations, each of which dutifully parroted government-approved views and values, as being the "real" and "legitimate" representatives of Indian Country. In contrast, all Indian dissidents and their organizations were *by definition* illegitimate and non-representative. Among the most obvious examples of this was the injection, by the Departments of Justice and Interior, of the arch-reactionary National Tribal Chairmen's Association (NTCA) into a central position in the public commentary following The Trail of Broken Treaties in 1972.[1]

The ploy involved not only the Washington, D.C. press conference mentioned in Chapter 5, in which NTCA leader Webster Two Hawk denounced AIM as being

"The White Man's Indian,"
National Tribal Chairmen's
Association head Webster Two
Hawk denounces AIM "radicals"
in Washington, D.C., all
expenses paid by the federal
government. (Photo: United
Press International)

"a bunch of irresponsible self-styled revolutionaries" who had no real support from Indians,[2] but a series of more localized denunciations of Trail participants by their (NTCA member) tribal chairmen on reservations across the country.[3] The NTCA statements were then used by such "friend of the Bureau" columnists as Roland Evans and Robert Novak to "substantiate" their own ideological attacks on AIM.[4] Representative of the thrust of this carefully orchestrated editorializing is this excerpt:

> The tragedy is that the stupid and barbaric behavior of a few hundred militants, who probably do not represent the aspirations and needs of the great mass of the Indians, could serve to obscure the real problems and legitimate hopes of their people.[5]

As Malcolm X once aptly noted, "If you are not careful, the newspapers will have you hating the people who are being oppressed and loving the people who are doing the oppressing."[6] The charade continued as, only sixty days after the conclusion of The Trail of Broken Treaties, the government "flew [Two Hawk] into Washington, D.C., at the taxpayers' expense...to ride in Nixon's second inaugural parade, straddling a pathetic horse that must have come from a Washington hackney cab and wearing an Indian suit that could only have come from a costume shop. A war bonnet fluttered over the Rev. Two Hawk's close-cropped crew cut. The effect was one of monstrous parody, a middle-class clergyman posing for 'The End of the Trail.'"[7] On television this was projected, through straightfaced commentary, as being proof that American Indians were indeed pursuing, and included within, the American Dream.

Ultimately, the government's pretentions concerning the nature and attitudes expressive of "typical" Indian sentiment were demolished as each of the NTCA's "Uncle Tomahawks" were deposed by their own people. This was amply demonstrated in 1974 (the year Dick Wilson used massive fraud and force to forestall a similar fate at the hands of Russell Means; see Chapter 6), when the Brulé Lakota of the Rosebud Reservation turned out Webster Two Hawk himself for the outspoken critic of the government, Robert Burnette. Two Hawk's administration had proven as venal, if not as vicious, as that of Wilson on adjoining Pine Ridge and, as Burnette recounts:

> I filed against him for the office of tribal chairman of the Rosebud reservation. When some of the people heard I was running, they told Two Hawk to his face that they didn't even want to sign his nominating petition. The August primary, which winnowed seven preliminary candidates down to two finalists, showed Two Hawk lagging behind me as we both qualified for the final election. On 23 October I beat Two Hawk by close to three hundred votes [a landslide]. The incumbent might have delighted conservative commentators by his attacks on...AIM, and on any Indian who dared question the status quo, but he couldn't win an election on his own reservation, despite his access to almost unlimited federal funds. There wasn't enough money in the mint to bribe the people of Rosebud into accepting another term of Two Hawk, or to second his endorsements of the status quo with their votes.[8]

Such rejection of the federal government's chosen Indian figureheads was not well received by the Bureau. The FBI responded by conscientiously supporting the Pine Ridge's "duly elected tribal government" of Dick Wilson, defending it against both the "outside agitators" of AIM and the "unrepresentative reservation rabble" of OSCRO and the ION. FBI behavior became all the more noble on March 26, 1973 when the Bureau used the pretext of being "unable to insure the safety of reporters" as a rationale to seal off Wounded Knee from the press. Media coverage of the conflict on Pine Ridge was constrained largely to information provided by the FBI itself in the daily press briefings, a situation which immediately led to wide reportage of such "facts" as the non-Indian identity of Frank Clearwater and Russell Means' award of an eagle feather to Frank Black Horse as a result of the latter's wounding of a federal agent.[9]

Although such inaccurate stories were occasionally corrected well after the fact—usually in a small box on the back pages—the results of such "evenhandedness" were, as Evelegh correctly points out, quite irrelevant in terms of shaping public opinion. With this in mind, the FBI maintained a veritable drumbeat of publicity through the end of 1976 which, despite the facts, persistently qualified the use of the acronym "AIM" with the words "violence prone"; AIM tactics were inevitably "violent." Meanwhile, the actions of Wilson and the GOONs were systematically downplayed, omitted from mention in FBI accounts, or, when they cropped up on their own, qualified with such words as "alleged" and "unproven." In short order, the consistent distortions had their desired effect, even among the smallish journals which had originally been sympathetic to AIM and which had attempted to report its struggle in equitable fashion. By mid-1973, even the *Race Relations Reporter* was paying heed to the suggestion by a UPI stringer that "AIM wasn't worth covering any more."[10]

Increasingly isolated from public support or even anything resembling accurate depiction of their circumstances on Pine Ridge, AIM members and supporters were cast adrift to be picked off one by one by GOON hit squads and FBI "technicians." Their casualties were popularly construed as being "what they deserved." Their only alternatives were to give up the fight altogether or to protect themselves through armed self-defense. The latter recourse, while it allowed for the survival of many who might otherwise have been killed, was used to maximum effectiveness by Bureau spokesmen, who contended that it "validated" their earlier assertions as to AIM's "violent character." Clearly, the organization had been placed in a no-win situation by the FBI's cynical propagandists.

While the Bureau's misrepresentation of both AIM and the situation on Pine Ridge was effectively seamless by virtue of being both steady and relatively low-key, more sensational strokes were sometimes needed, usually to divert attention from some particularly gruesome GOON atrocity or to establish a plausible rationale for the next escalation of FBI force. With regard to GOON crimes, the usual gambit seems to have been for agents to deliberately confuse the issue by suggesting for the record that AIM itself might be responsible; notable instances of this occurred in the case of Anna Mae Aquash (see Chapter 7); in the murders of Jeanette Bissonette and Clarence Cross (see Chapter 6); and Dick Wilson's ludicrous contention that it was not he, but Russell Means, who headed the gang of thugs who assaulted Roger Finzel and WKLDOC personnel at the Pine Ridge airport in February 1975. This lie was solemnly repeated to the press by FBI spokesmen.[11]

There are also a number of instances in which the Bureau appears to have fabricated "incidents" out of whole cloth in order to prepare the public to accept intensifications of anti-AIM violence. Among the more striking examples are the following:

The Skyhorse/Mohawk Case

On the night of October 10, 1974, Los Angeles cab driver George Aird was bludgeoned into unconsciousness, abducted in his taxi, dragged by a rope behind the car, stabbed at least seventeen times, and disposed of in a large drainpipe.[12] Two days later, an unknown informant called the Ventura County (California) Sheriff's Department, reporting the location of the body as being in a place called "AIM Camp 13," located in Box Canyon near the infamous Spahn Movie Ranch, once headquarters to mass-murderer Charles Manson's lethal "family."[13] By nightfall, police had arrested a thirty-year-old Oglala named Marvin Redshirt and his non-Indian companion, Holly Broussard, in possession of a knife believed to be the murder weapon, and their personal property smeared with what proved to be Aird's blood. A short time later, an associate of the duo named Marcella "Makes Noise Eaglestaff" McNoise (another non-Indian) was also arrested.[14]

As it turned out, the three non-AIM members—who had been "hanging out" at the former AIM rest facility for some weeks—had visited the home of actor David

Paul "Skyhorse" Durant (left) and Richard "Mohawk" Billings shortly after their arrest by the FBI on October 17, 1974. (Photo: Paulette D'Auteuil Robideau)

Carradine (a substantial AIM contributor) on the evening of October 10, and had become highly intoxicated. At about 10 p.m., they phoned a cab to transport them back to Camp 13. Aird, unfortunately for him, responded to their call: "Somewhere along the way, the meter was pulled out, stopping at $6.00, and Redshirt took over driving."[15] Despite the strong evidence against the suspects, representatives of the Los Angeles office of the FBI intervened shortly after the arrests of Redshirt, Broussard and McNoise. Wasn't it "interesting," the agents suggested, that the location of the murder was something called an *AIM* camp. They then revealed they had information from a "confidential source" that the actual murderers of George Aird were not the three persons in custody in Ventura, but two other individuals named Paul "Skyhorse" Durant (a Chippewa from Minnesota) and Richard "Mohawk" Billings (a Tuscarora/Mohawk from upstate New York) whom the Bureau was ready and willing to assist Ventura County authorities in apprehending.[16]

The two men thus targeted were members of the southern California AIM chapter, a matter which dovetailed neatly with the murder scene being a reputed AIM facility. An odd note and apparent "scalp" had already been recovered by the police, conveniently tacked together on a signpost near Aird's body. The note took credit for the murder in the name of "the American Indian Movement"; the sign on the post, freshly painted, spelled out the organizational acronym in bold lettering.[17] As Skyhorse and Mohawk were attending the National Indian Education Association conference at Arizona State University on October 17, they were arrested and held for extradition to California on the basis of a pair of first degree murder warrants issued in the killing of George Aird.[18] Once safely locked in Ventura County Jail, they were held without bail. Press coverage of the matter, previously lurid, now became truly sensational.[19]

Dennis Banks, also in attendance at the conference, remembers that "AIM security director" Douglass Durham "showed up" and met with Skyhorse and Mohawk shortly before their arrest, a "coincidence" which leaves the impression that he had facilitated their apprehension.[20] AIM had formally disassociated itself

Virginia "Blue Dove" DeLuse, a Hollywood bit player, impersonated an "AIM militant" for the FBI. DeLuse worked with FBI infiltrator Douglass Durham and suspected CIA infiltrator George Roberts to orchestrate the "AIM Camp 13" slaying of cab driver George Aird in 1974 and the subsequent murder charges levied against Skyhorse and Mohawk. (Photo: *Los Angeles Times*)

from Camp 13—due to its habitual use by non-AIM people who engaged in chronic alcohol and drug abuse—several months before the Aird murder.[21] This fact never managed to find its way into press and television accounts of the matter, largely because rent on the site had continued to be paid by a Los Angeles area "AIM coordinator" named "Blue Dove," and because it had continued to bear the organizational acronym in its title (the name had been bestowed by Durham in late 1974).[22] Further, it was Durham who had troubled himself to paint and erect the large, boldly lettered sign captioned "AIM Camp 13," which figured so prominently in media coverage, only a week before the murder.[23]

As detailed in Chapter 8, Douglass Durham was functioning at this time as an FBI "super-provocateur" within AIM. There is a high degree of probability that he was the anonymous caller who tipped Ventura County deputies to the location of Aird's body at the very foot of the "AIM" sign, the mysterious party who penned the note "linking" AIM to the murder and tacked it and the bogus "scalp" to the signpost, and the "reliable source" posited by the FBI as falsely identifying Skyhorse and Mohawk as Aird's killers. In addition, the funds with which Durham's FBI provocateur colleague, Virginia "Blue Dove" DeLuse, rented Camp 13 after AIM abandoned it apparently came from the Bureau for this express purpose.[24]

Not content to rest on his laurels in the midst of such a promising COIN-TELPRO, Durham informed AIM leadership that Skyhorse and Mohawk were "probably guilty" of the sordid crime and recommended that the organization distance itself from them as rapidly as possible.[25] Dennis Banks, in particular, heeded the advice of his trusted lieutenant and consequently the defendants were thoroughly isolated from such outside support as bail money, the raising of legal defense funds, and even legal expertise. (This is reminiscent of the tactics employed by the

FBI against Los Angeles BPP leader Geronimo Pratt only a short time before; see Chapter 3.)[26] Redshirt, Broussard and McNoise—the three individuals originally charged with killing Aird and against whom considerable evidence had been amassed—were then offered immunity from prosecution in exchange for their "eyewitness" testimony against the two AIM members, against whom there was otherwise no case.[27] As Banks recalls:

> For a year and a half, I would not give those guys support...Then one of the prosecution people told me, Dennis, if you repeat this I'll call you a liar, but we gave immunity to the wrong people. I changed my mind about AIM support when I realized that they were going to nail Skyhorse and Mohawk not because they were guilty but because they were AIM.[28]

A defense team consisting of attorneys Wendy Eaton, Leonard Weinglass, Skip Glenn, Dianne Orr and Jack Schwarz was finally put together. A $2 million civil rights suit was filed against the prosecution for having conspired to solicit perjured testimony from those originally charged in order to obtain convictions against Skyhorse and Mohawk.[29] Although the suit did not ultimately result in an award of damages, it did lead to the dismissal of charges against the AIM members when Marvin Redshirt collapsed under cross examination, "...admitting that he himself had struck the first blow against Aird and had participated in an orgy of stabbing which finally killed him...he [also] acknowledged 'lying about a thousand times'" on the witness stand.[30] In the end, Skyhorse and Mohawk had each been imprisoned some thirty-one months for a crime they'd never committed, and were left uncompensated for their ordeal. As to those who actually had participated in killing Aird: Redshirt was sentenced to five years probation while charges were dismissed against Holly Broussard and Marcella McNoise;[31] two other accomplices, known as Black Cloud and Rising Sun, were treated with similar leniency. WKLDOC attorney Jack Schwarz later summed up the case:

> The FBI urged the local Sheriff's Department to charge Skyhorse and Mohawk, and to let the three people found at the scene of the crime covered in blood go free. Two weapons—knives—were recovered, but one was supposedly lost on the way to the police station and the other one supposedly melted in the police lab. One of the knives was traceable to Holly Broussard, the white little rich girl. The case was actually a media campaign—"radical Indians," "ritual murder," and all that—and it worked. But the defense strategy was that the case was a frameup, to financially damage AIM. We proved it; it came across as a vendetta. Although the law doesn't actually recognize frame-ups; that is, the court [Judge Floyd Dodson] would never officially accept the decision that the FBI framed somebody, the jury bought it; they understood.[32]

Schwarz was undoubtedly correct in his analysis of the case. The initial publicity attending the Skyhorse/Mohawk travesty served to dry up an estimated 95 percent of the contributions to AIM in California, a major share of the funds which were then being used to underwrite the organization's national legal defense effort.[33] Nor is it coincidental that the portrayal of AIM as a gaggle of Mansonesque butchers was timed perfectly to place a tremendous damper on public scrutiny and criticism of the Bureau's introduction of a huge paramilitary force onto the Pine Ridge Reservation (see Chapter 9). The diversion and/or suppression of public dialogue in this connection was obtained via the disinformation stratagem sketched in the preceding section.

Recognizing the success of their media COINTELPRO, the Bureau had every incentive to continue it for as long as possible, picking up "residual" press coverage which inevitably presented AIM in the worst possible light. The neutralization of AIM activists Skyhorse and Mohawk throughout the three-year process (and thereafter, as both men seem to have been shattered by their experience) was no doubt seen by the FBI as a "fringe benefit."[34] In an effort to further drag things out, Douglass Durham, in his last known act as an outright provocateur, went into a California courtroom in February 1976 (*after* he'd been unmasked), appearing at a pre-trial hearing in the guise of an "Iowa psychotherapist," and testified that Skyhorse's "mental instability" made him a public menace, unworthy of bail.[35]

In the end, as Los Angeles AIM supporter Laura Kadenahe has observed:

After the arrest of Skyhorse and Mohawk, things just fell apart for the Movement in LA. We started to call the local chapter "lame" instead of LA-AIM, and said the area was a "black hole" into which organizers were sent, never to be seen again. And I think the trial had a lot to do with the demise of the Movement everywhere. After that bust, you know, the feds could do anything they wanted to AIM, and people would just say "So what? You guys asked for it." We've never recovered, in a lot of ways.[36]

Defense lawyer Leonard Weinglass has also pointed out:

Something very important tends to get lost in the controversy over the Skyhorse/Mohawk case. This is that a human being, George Aird, was the victim of an incredibly brutal crime. George Aird, at the very least, had the right to expect that an honest effort be made to bring his killers to justice. But when the FBI decided to become involved, to accomplish political objectives having nothing whatever to do with the case itself, all that got lost in the shuffle. The death of George Aird, the *horrible* thing that happened to him, was converted into little more than a stage prop. Now, I never knew George Aird, but I *am* confident of one thing: who*ever* this man was, he deserved better than to have his fate used in such callous fashion by those who are sworn to serve and protect.[37]

Of Bunkers and Executions

Immediately after the June 26, 1975 firefight near Oglala (see Chapter 8), the FBI issued a series of "field reports" indicating that the Jumping Bull compound—scene of the shooting—was in fact a sophisticated AIM military complex featuring fixed defensive positions such as bunkers. The Bureau, by way of Tom Coll, a media specialist dispatched to Rapid City from Quantico especially for this purpose, also

FBI media specialist Tom Coll lies straight-facedly to the press during a Pine Ridge briefing on June 27, 1975. The agent in sunglasses is thought to be J. Gary Adams who, after the deaths of his colleagues Williams and Coler, launched a personal vendetta against AIM members in several states.
(Photo: Associated Press)

claimed that slain agents Jack Coler and Ron Williams had been ambushed and executed by the occupants of this AIM facility.

> Since the press was banned from the scene of the shooting for two days, the public had to [accept] the propaganda of the authorities...According to the FBI's public relations man [Coll], flown in with a planeload of forty or fifty SWATs from Quantico on that first night to present the story in the right perspective to the American people, Agents Coler and Williams had been murdered in a "cold-blooded ambush" by a large force of well-trained guerrillas in "sophisticated bunkers" and "fortifications," but not before Williams had first pleaded for their lives for the sake of his companion's wife and children. How the Bureau developed this information about Williams' last words in the absence of anyone who could have heard them was not clear. Another FBI spokesman...declared that the bodies had been "riddled with bullets;" their cars were also "riddled by machine-gun bullets." [38]

As a result, press coverage was spectacular. United Press International (UPI) reported the incident on its wire service, shortly after midnight on June 27:

> Oglala, S.D.—(UPI) Two FBI agents were ambushed and killed with repeated blasts of gunfire Thursday in an outbreak of bloodshed appearing to stem from the 1973 occupation of Wounded Knee. The office of South Dakota Gov. Richard Kneip said that the agents, on the Oglala Sioux Reservation to serve a warrant, were sucked into an ambush, dragged from their cars, and shot up to 15 to 20 times with automatic weapons. The FBI confirmed the report. An agent said: "This is a regular coup de gras [*sic*] by

the Indians." The agents were taken from their cars, stripped to their waists, then shot repeatedly in their heads.

The Associated Press (AP) report, issued shortly after that of UPI, was similar:

Oglala, S.D.—(AP) Two FBI agents were dragged out of their cars when they tried to serve warrants on people who were holed up in a house on the Pine Ridge Reservation...

On that first day, the *Rapid City Journal* quoted local authorities and the FBI as stating that, "the two men were lured into an ambush...as many as 30 persons were waiting in the house when the agents arrived." Banner headlines in the *New York Post* on June 27 record that SOUTH DAKOTA INDIANS KILL TWO FBI AGENTS; in the *San Diego Union*, the story was TWO FBI AGENTS SLAIN AT WOUNDED KNEE. The same principle held true in papers as diverse as the *New York Times*, the *Washington Post*, and the *Peoria* (Illinois) *Journal Star*, as well as on all three major television networks. Only the *Minneapolis Tribune*, intimately well-versed in AIM-FBI relations through eight years of conscientious reporting on the subject, was wary enough to conduct a preliminary check of the story's accuracy; its headline, in measured type, read, "Indians, FBI, exchange fire in S.D.; three dead." Minneapolis was thus the only city afforded the opportunity even of realizing that an Indian (Joe Stuntz Killsright), as well as two federal agents, had been killed.

By June 29, the *Rapid City Journal's* headline read "FBI deaths spark agent anger," and agents themselves were quoted as saying, "We'll stay here as long as it takes to round up the people who did this," and "We lost two guys out there, and we're going to pull out all the plugs." They were joined by South Dakota Attorney General William Janklow—who as was noted in Chapter 9, headed a group of prepositioned white vigilantes on June 26—who informed AP and UPI reporters that "it looked like an execution," dubbed the killings (of the agents, *not* Killsright) as "assassinations," and announced that it was time to stop being "soft on Indians just because they're a minority group." He also had considerable commentary to offer on "sob sisters" who were inclined to protect AIM "murderers and others who have no respect for society."[39]

With the "first public impression" now firmly established, FBI Director Clarence Kelly was free to come forward to "set the record straight." This he did in a press conference conducted at the Century Plaza Hotel in Los Angeles five days after the event, on July 1. Accompanied by SAC, Minneapolis, Joseph Trimbach and SA J. Gary Adams, one of the field agents at Pine Ridge, the Director "clarified" that the supposed "bunkers" on the Jumping Bull property were actually root cellars and broken-down cattle shelters of the sort common to any rural area, that neither agent had been shot more than three times (as opposed to the "fifteen to twenty times" each, reported by Coll), that neither agent had been "stripped to the waist" or "dragged from his car" (as reported by Coll) although Williams had apparently ripped off his own shirt in a futile attempt to make a tourniquet for Coler's arm. He also abandoned the contention that the agents had been ambushed, and lowered the official estimate of the number of Indians involved from "thirty" to sixteen. Needless to say, these "corrections" received far less media coverage than the original—superbly distorted—version.[40] Even less attention was paid to (far more accurate) AIM statements, such as John Trudell's that:

> FBI agents armed with M-16s came onto the Pine Ridge Reservation to serve a warrant they didn't have, on someone who wasn't there; they were accompanied by over fifty highly trained military marksmen, also with high-powered automatic weapons. These agents opened fire on a small house in which men, women and children were asleep...On that same day, in Washington, D.C., Dickie Wilson gave away one eighth of the Pine Ridge Reservation to the U.S. government. Now, common sense tells us that something very unusual is going on.[41]

Few members of the press responded seriously to what had happened. Perhaps the most notable exception was *Washington Post* reporter Joel Weisman, who had been barred from the firefight scene—at gunpoint—by an FBI agent on June 27.[42] Incensed by this, and troubled by the way the story was being "played" by the Bureau in absence of any *direct* media coverage, Weisman undertook an in-depth examination of FBI procedures. His conclusions, published in the *Columbia Journalism Review* that fall,[43] were that the Bureau *had* to have been aware, even before the first press conference on the evening of June 26, that neither Coler nor Williams had been "riddled with bullets," as claimed by FBI spokesmen. Further, with scores of agents having already examined the terrain of the firefight, it had to have been clear that there were no "bunkers" or other AIM defensive works in the Jumping Bull compound. The Bureau thus knew that the entire "ambush" thesis, and all the frills about "last words" and the like, were bogus *before* they were ever fed to the media. Weisman therefore noted that the FBI's denial of press access was intended not to preserve crucial evidence but to *conceal* evidence from "premature" journalistic disclosure. In other words, Coll and the Bureau had lied, straight-faced, deliberately and systematically, to the press and the public as a means of creating a completely false image of what had occurred.

Weisman's findings correlate with the observations of PBS reporter Kevin McKiernan, the sole journalist to gain access to the scene during the first 48 hours. Further, both accounts were validated in their impressions of the FBI's intentionally engaging in gross disinformation by the U.S. Commission on Civil Rights, which after its own investigation discovered that:

> Media representatives felt that the FBI had been unnecessarily restrictive in the kind and amount of information it provided. It is patently clear that many of the statements that have been released [by the Bureau] regarding the incident are either false, unsubstantiated, or directly misleading.[44]

The question, of course, is why. In this connection, there is likely a certain truth to the AIM contention, expressed above by John Trudell, that the June 25 firefight had been deliberately provoked to divert attention from the simultaneous transfer of title to the Sheep Mountain Gunnery Range. To the extent that this is true, however, it is equally likely that the correlation is sheerly a matter of timing and convenience. More probably, the Bureau's real objective was the manufacture of an event which would serve to justify its introduction (again) of radically increased force levels on Pine Ridge, obtaining public approval for use of the "horsepower" needed to break the back of AIM, once and for all. In this sense, the cover provided to Dick Wilson's signing of the land transfer agreement was no doubt an afterthought, a "service" to other federal agencies.

This is not to say that the FBI intended agents Coler and Williams to die. To the contrary, all evidence points to the likelihood that they were simply to provoke an altercation which would quickly be wrapped up by the police and civilian paramilitary personnel prepositioned in the area. The AIM encampment near Oglala was to be destroyed, and the very nature of its destruction packaged in such a way as to fuel public sanction for similar destruction of other AIM centers across the reservation. From a Bureau perspective, June 26 must have been an incredibly botched operation.

But, with two agents and one Indian dead, the FBI pulled itself together and followed through, putting the best face on things, barring the press and offering the sort of "information" which would absolutely mask the Bureau's culpability. Coll and other FBI propagandists proved equal to their task, successfully shifting the onus of blame onto the victims before allowing contrary facts to emerge. Ironically, the unintended deaths of Coler and Williams served to greatly strengthen the emotional appeal of the Bureau's disinformation campaign. The false image of AIM as a gang of "executioners," which even the FBI had never been quite bold enough to project, had suddenly concretized. After Oglala, the Bureau could deal with AIM in any manner it chose, a situation which has continued through the present day.

The Douglass Durham Show

In April of 1975, FBI infiltrator/provocateur Douglass Durham appeared before Senator James Eastland's Senate Subcommittee on Internal Security,[45] then "investigating" what it called "revolutionary activities within the United States." Although it was common knowledge, at that point, that Durham had played a highly suspicious role with regard to many of the events, activities, thinking and personalities about which he was to testify, he was the sole witness called by the Subcommittee in relation to AIM; Senator Eastland himself was the only Subcommittee member present to hear this testimony and/or examine the witness.[46]

A result of this rather odd arrangement was that Durham's many assertions concerning AIM, its organizational character and activities were accepted at face value, unchallenged and utterly unsubstantiated. The bias of this "hearing" was so pronounced that Senator Birch Bayh (D-Indiana), a member of the Subcommittee, was led to denounce the whole affair as being "totally unacceptable," based ex-

In his guise as "one-quarter Chippewa" (left), FBI infiltrator/provocateur Douglass Durham became Dennis Banks' personal bodyguard, AIM's security director, manager of the national office, and prosecution mole in the Wounded Knee trials. Unmasked (right), Durham was paid by the FBI to testify before Congress, and pose as a psychotherapist at a hearing relating to the Skyhorse/Mohawk murder trial. (Photos: *North Country Anvil*)

clusively upon "the unchallenged testimony of one solitary witness," and seeming "to have no other purpose than to discredit...the American Indian Movement."[47] Nonetheless, Senator Eastland caused the resulting transcript to be published and widely distributed as an official and extremely inflammatory government report under the title, *Revolutionary Activities Within the United States: The American Indian Movement*.[48] Because of the federal authority with which it is imbued, this maliciously biased document was quickly accepted as a primary source of background information for reportage and scholarship on AIM, and has remained so ever since.

Among the many unfounded allegations made by Durham during his testimony were the following:

- He "established" that AIM was doctrinally committed to violence as a means of accomplishing its objectives:

Schultz: ...let's talk about the violent actions that were participated or involved in AIM activities. Is the American Indian Movement a violent action oriented organization in your view?

Durham: Most obviously the leadership condones this type of action. During Wounded Knee, as an example of their violence, they hung a man from a cross on Easter Sunday...There was a murder in Los Angeles, Calif., in the fall of 1974 where a man was dragged from a cab in an AIM guerrilla camp in Box Canyon, scalped, dismembered, and stuffed down a drain pipe; and the reaction of AIM was, "They should have shoved grass down the throat of the body." There were very grisly and mean events that transpired since then; the assassination, or execution, of the two FBI agents...[49]

Schultz: ...Do they [AIM] have the ability to carry out [these] threats; and, if so, how?

Durham: They have the ability to create great havoc and terror in the United States by guerrilla activities. Some of them are fairly well learned on a "Mini-Manual of the Urban Guerrilla," by one Carlos Marighella, a Brazilian terrorist. This manual espouses different plans and models for terrorism, such as bombing, murder, kidnapping, you know, these types of activity. AIM has been involved in just about every one of these activities, including the kidnapping...Urban Indians tend to identify more with violence...terrorism has been used as a means of [AIM] recruitment...Terrorism and its attendant publicity by the media create a means of release for many of those who would espouse a drastic method of changing the United States...[50]

None of these, and many similar accusations made during Durham's sworn testimony, was ever substantiated. To the contrary, his assertion of an "Easter Sunday Crucifixion" at Wounded Knee is known to have been absolutely false; his account of George Aird's having been scalped and dismembered at an "AIM guerrilla camp" was a fabrication; and the contention that FBI agents Coler and Williams were "executed" on June 26, 1975 was untrue. Further it is known that it was Durham himself who introduced and promoted Marighella's *Mini-Manual of the Urban Guerrilla* to AIM members.

- Durham gave further shape to his charges of AIM "terrorism," as is indicated by the following exchanges:

Schultz: ...do you have information concerning [AIM's] planned activities for the Bicentennial year, 1976?

Durham: ...I will give you a direct quote from some of the leaders of the American Indian Movement, relating to the Bicentennial, and relate to you some of their particular plans...William Kunstler, an attorney for the American Indian Movement, in a speech to Corky Gonzalez's Mexican-American Crusade for Justice in Denver, Col., said, "I promise you revolution in 1976. It is better to die in the streets than to live on your knees. We are stronger together, and the system is getting weaker every day"...At that very same press conference Russell Means told the same members of the press, "The white man has the goddamned gall to celebrate his birthday in 1976, they will have to do it over my blood. Everyone, everywhere should participate in blowing out the white man's birthday candle"...Carter Camp, June 5, 1975, said, "I promise you revolution in '76. It will be America's unhappiest birthday, and AIM guarantees it."

Schultz: Do you know, or are you aware of any targets which have been selected for attack in 1976?

Durham: I was told while I was in the American Indian Movement that any patriotic symbol of the United States would be an immediate target for attack. I was told that

Washington, D.C., and Valley Forge were targets; the Bureau of Indian Affairs Building and branch offices across the United States would be targets, as would be government offices...*Some of the targets are current, confidential [FBI] information that I have received at this time.* [emphasis added].[51]

This statement suggests the witness was still employed by the FBI at the time of his testimony. Later Durham explains that:

Durham: ...Approximately September 15, 1975, Russell Means in Sioux Falls, S. Dak., announced a "counteroffensive" by AIM, saying that the counteroffensive would be directed at the Federal Government and the South Dakota State government. He cited incidents in six states including Minnesota and South Dakota. Although Means refused to divulge specific plans for the counteroffensive, he indicated that they would deal with "the white man's 200th birthday celebration here in South Dakota." On March 18, 1974, Russell Means predicted insurrection in 2 years, while addressing the Mexican-American Crusade for Justice...Veiled threats have been made regarding the invading of the city of Philadelphia by Indian-Americans, Mexican-Americans, Puerto Ricans, Blacks and other racial minorities during the Bicentennial celebration July 4...[52]

These "plans"—which never materialized—were utilized as the basis for an extraordinary FBI disinformation gambit during the summer of 1976 (see below).

- Durham went to great lengths to demonstrate that AIM was part of an international communist/terrorist conspiracy:

Durham: ...I was advised there would be a meeting with the People's Republic of China in Ottawa, Canada, in the last week of September [1974], and received this written set of instructions advising myself, George Roberts, Russell Means, and John Trudell to go to this meeting...[53]

Schultz: Do you have reason to believe, or know that Mr. [George] Roberts [a suspected CIA infiltrator] actually had contacts [in "behalf" of AIM] with embassies around the world?

Durham: I sat in his house while he called Dr. Faustino Perez [a Cuban diplomat] in Mexico City, and the other embassies, and spoke in various tongues to these other embassies. He seemed on a first-name basis with embassy personnel, people from the Irish Republican Army, Mexico, Cuba, Germany, East Germany, and various other parts of the world...[54]

Durham: ...George Roberts advocated spiriting Dennis Banks to Cuba, and in my presence, called Dr. Faustino Perez, in New [*sic*] Mexico, to establish contact with Fidel Castro. Perez was an old friend of Ahmed Ben Bella from Algeria, and was quite involved in the landing in Cuba.

Schultz: The Bay of Pigs?

Durham: No; when Castro first obtained power in Cuba.

Schultz: Alright, when he came out of the mountains.

Durham: Right, out of the mountains. Dr. Fausto—as he is referred to—advised Roberts that he would have the information sent in a diplomatic pouch to Cuba and at that point Roberts advised his wife to travel to Mexico City to meet Faustino Perez, who was supposedly, or allegedly, a friend of hers. Anyway, she returned with the information that Castro had rejected the plan because he felt there would be increasing relations with the United States, and reported one U.S. Senator's actions as being the main reason for there being no further chance for political exile in Cuba for Banks.

Schultz: He was expecting this to disturb the increasingly better relations with the United States?

Durham: That's correct, sir. A suggestion was issued, allegedly from Dr. Faustino Perez, that Banks should approach the People's Republic of China for a move in the direction they would indicate, which would later allow him to go to Latin America and become the new Che Guevara because he was a native American person...[55]

Schultz: ...Could you give us some estimates as to the amount of funds available to AIM from foreign sources?

Durham: There wasn't as much direct funding, such as Moscow sending a check for $400, or something of that nature, to AIM; but through front groups who became involved and ideologically aligned with AIM, and they provided money...As far as actual direct foreign funding committees in other countries that call themselves AIM chapters and send monies to the American Indian Movement, those figures were made available to the FBI, however, I don't have them with me at this time.[56]

• And on the "domestic front":

Schultz: Mr. Durham, you were just about to discuss the activities which occurred at the Omni Center in Atlanta, Ga.; you traveled there with Mr. Banks. Would you continue please?

Durham: Well, we arrived at the 900 block of Juniper Street, in Atlanta, which was the home of the American Indian Movement. The staff of the American Indian Movement consisted of one Indian and five or six non-Indians, sharing the same office facilities with the "Great Speckled Bird," the Georgia power project, and the Georgia Communist League, as I understand it. I'm not positive about the GCL. I understand there were members of the GCL present at this time when we held [a] meeting to discuss an upcoming concert to be held to raise funds for the [Banks/Means] trial.

Schultz: Would you identify for us what the "Speckled Bird" and the Georgia power project is?

Durham: The "Great Speckled Bird" was a newspaper, socialist in nature. A large amount of the staff were from members of the Georgia power project, and again, members of the Georgia Communist League, which later became the October League, Marxist-Leninist...They were working hand in hand, in fact interfacing with members of the AIM staff in this particular office, toward setting up this "People's Concert for Justice," with the assistance of one Troy Donahue, a former Hollywood cowboy...[57]

Schultz: ...Do you have some documents which serve to identify other revolutionary groups which have assisted and participated in the programs of AIM?

Durham: ...the Organization of Arab Students, the Iranian Students Association, the American Servicemen's Union, the Black Panther Party, the New York Consulate of the Republic of New Africa [sic], the Carlos Feliciano Defense Committee, the American Committee on Africa [sic], the Youth Against War and Fascism, the National Alliance against Racist and Political Oppression [sic]—which by the way Clyde Bellecourt is a national officer of; the Lincoln De-Tox [sic] Program, the New York American Indian Movement, the Indo-China [sic] Solidarity Committee, the Prisoner's Day Solidarity Committee...[58]

Schultz: ...What other groups that have advocated terrorism or violence for the Bicentennial have shown support for the American Indian Movement?

Durham: The Weather underground published a full-page ad in the back of their *Osawatomie,* fall 1975 [actually summer 1975] issue, stating "support for the Indian resistance." The Irish Republican Army, as mentioned earlier, met with the leaders of AIM [at Durham's behest] during the trial in St. Paul. Banks claimed to have met with the Palestine Liberation Organization. The Iranian Students Association has demonstrated on AIM's behalf and they do have a history of violence. The Revolutionary Student Brigade has demonstrated on AIM's behalf as have the Puerto Rican Solidarity Committee and Puerto Rican groups hosted by Fidel Castro in Cuba in 1975. *The Militant* has written many articles supportive of AIM and revolution, and they are a strong defender of AIM's "rights." The New World Liberation Front has bombed buildings in support of AIM's actions, two houses in Piedmont, Calif., were firebombed in this reaction. The Symbionese Liberation Army did name AIM as one of the five groups to distribute their "People in Need" program money in 1974. The large amount of support contributed by the National Lawyers Guild, a group which seems to condone violence, is also indicative of the type of groups supporting AIM.[59]

In his preliminary statement, Durham also quoted an earlier subcommittee report:

The Communist Party [U.S.A.] for more than a year now has been supporting the so-called "American Indian Liberation Movement [as Senator Eastland called AIM at the time]." The decision to make the Indian Liberation Movement a major point of emphasis was made at a special "National Conference on Indian Liberation" convened somewhere in the Western United States in November 1969. According to the West Coast *People's World,* which gave the conference extensive coverage in its issues of November 8 and 15, 1969, Communist Party Chairman Henry Winston keynoted the conference by describing the Indian Liberation Movement as "one of the four major struggles in our country...The Conference defined the vanguard role of Communists in the fight, and are leading the fight..."[60]

The whole performance was intended to create the impression, through implication and innuendo of a massive, foreign-directed inter-organizational conspiracy. More, many of the supposed "incidents" recounted by Durham as "evidence" of AIM's ties with communist nations—the meeting in the Toronto consulate of the People's Republic of China, the alleged plan to spirit Dennis Banks away to Latin America, *etc.*—simply never materialized. Castro's alleged refusal to grant Banks sanctuary in Cuba and Durham's "explanation" of why this supposed scheme was not acted upon hardly reconciles with the sanctuary provided to BPP founder Huey P. Newton a short while later, or the Cuban leader's providing refuge to BLA member Assata Shakur later still.[61] There is no corroboration from any quarter that Banks even desired to go to Cuba, never mind that he fancied himself an incipient Che Guevara. Finally, Durham conveniently neglected to bring his supposed "records" of foreign financial support to AIM.

As concerns AIM's alignment with various domestic organizations, Durham tendered no more substantiation than a series of clippings extracted from the publications of various organizations, each bearing some sort of "statement of solidarity" from the respective groups to AIM. These were "reinforced" by clippings from the mainstream media indicating that some of the organizations named had staged rallies or fund-raising events in support of AIM from time to time. No deeper linkages were demonstrated in any connection, not to mention the sort of "communist" or "terrorist" inter-organizational conspiracy which was being alluded to.

Tellingly, Durham failed to make any sort of comparison between AIM's association with these organizations and its closer ties to others, such as the Ecumenical Council, United Methodist Church and Lutheran Church. Finally, virtually every concrete interaction between "AIM" and any of the "suspect" foreign entities posited came, not through *bona fide* AIM members, but through either Durham (a known FBI infiltrator), George Roberts (a suspected CIA infiltrator), or both. The entire spurious issue thus is indelibly marked with the stamp of COINTELPRO-style orchestration.

- Durham repeatedly asserted that federal grant monies awarded to AIM's community service projects had been misappropriated to finance weapons acquisitions and other AIM "terrorist" activities:

Durham: ...the Office of Economic Opportunity contacted [AIM Midwest Coordinator Ron] Petite, as Petite related to me, and urged that we apply for a grant. At this point, Petite suggested we apply for an employment for Indians grant in the Des Moines, Iowa, area. Hired on this grant were, of course, Raymond Slick, one of the [AIM] warriors, [and] Petite's wife; and it was used merely as a means to escape the country a few days later...

Schultz: Do you know what [a portion of this money] was used for?

Durham: Ray Slick had indicated he was supposed to buy some weapons and travel up north with them, for purposes undescribed at this time...[62]

Durham: ...I would like to submit for the record, if I might, the food stamp card of Dennis Banks, since I was signed on as an alternate. I'm aware of the fact that not only did he draw food stamps, but I went down and picked them up for him. The food stamp office in St. Paul [Minnesota] moved for 1 week into the national offices of the American Indian Movement, and signed up everybody they could find for food stamps.

Schultz: What did he do with the food stamps he got?

Durham: Well, a couple of times they were stolen from him. This was the only *violent act* [sic; emphasis added] he ever described to me within AIM, when his food stamps were stolen. Sometimes they were sold for 80 cents on the dollar, and of course arms, weapons, and things like that were purchased for members of AIM.

Schultz: Do you know that, having observed the sale of these food stamps?

Durham: I did *not* [emphasis added] directly observe the sale of Dennis' food stamps. I observed the sale of food stamps of like nature by people in a bar in Minneapolis; it was quite common practice at the time...The arms purchased I definitely observed in Dennis Banks' apartment in St. Paul, in East St. Paul, in Magnolia Court; and a $6,250 social understanding grant brought a carload of arms down by one Nogeesich Aquash. These weapons were of Czechoslovakian nature, and some of them just ordinary high-powered hunting rifles, were brought in from Canada.

Schultz: And these were purchased by Banks, or were they donated by these groups?

Durham: They were purchased by Nogeesich with this social understanding grant money.

Schultz: And where does that money come from?

Durham: I'm not familiar with the exact origin of the grant, but it was to create better understanding between Indians and non-Indians in the north.

Schultz: Are you talking about Federal money?

Durham: It was some sort of Federal money, but I'm not familiar with exactly what program it was...[63]

Predictably enough, nothing was ever unearthed to corroborate Durham's contentions of embezzlement of OEO funds in Des Moines, of a conspiracy between AIM and the St. Paul welfare office to engage in food stamp fraud, or to sell food stamps. Even the $6,250 "social understanding grant" turned out *not* to have been of federal origin, and no questions of financial malfeasance were ever put forward by the sponsor. However, once these assertions were broadly disseminated through the active efforts of the FBI and Senate subcommittee, AIM's sources of funding eroded very rapidly.

John Birch Society advertisement of the type displayed in South Dakota during the 1975 speaking tour of Douglass Durham. It is suspected that Durham continued to work for the Bureau after his exposure and that the tour, billboards, *etc.*, were part of the anti-AIM program which culminated in the fabricated "Dog Soldier Teletypes" of 1976.

Durham's stint as the star witness of the Eastland subcommittee's came as a prelude to a lecture tour he undertook throughout the Midwest, with the sponsorship of the John Birch Society. During this tour, he consistently maintained that AIM was "communist controlled" and "a threat to freedom."[64] At the Hotel Alex Johnson in Rapid City on the evening of October 14, 1975, for example, he informed his rabidly anti-AIM audience that "AIM is a leader in the scheme to disrupt our nation's Bicentennial in 1976. In preparation for the deceleration, AIM has established training camps around the country in which political indoctrination, marksmanship, and guerrilla warfare are taught."[65] A week later, in Mitchell (S.D.), he claimed that AIM's "guerrilla war" was designed to include "indiscriminate killings of whites."[66] The former infiltrator was often accompanied to these talks by FBI personnel, presumably for "security" purposes.[67]

Many of Durham's "revelations," from both the stump and the witness stand, seem to have been designed to whip up the already pronounced anti-AIM sentiments of the rural-midwest racist population. This potentially lethal proposition was manifested during the spring of 1975 in the John Birch Society's wide use of advertisements and billboards. Another indicator may be found in the Society's retention, in the fall of the same year, of its first "in house" Indian speaker and "expert on Indian affairs," Eugene Rooks, a known GOON and one of Dick Wilson's "political proteges."[68] More ominous was the proliferation of white "vigilance committees" which became involved in the events of Pine Ridge during the summer (see Chapter 9). Durham's "information" also provided the basis for FBI reports such as the following, shared with police agencies in the Dakotas in May 1976:

> Analysis of the facts surrounding A.I.M. leads one to the conclusion that this is one of the most violent and extremist-oriented organizations yet encountered by the United States...danger exists in that other radical terrorist and extremist groups, both foreign and domestic, see in A.I.M. a powerful ally for their release of destructive violence against the United States. The assistance of such groups, whether through funds, manpower, weapons, political philosophy or instigation of violence, can be a pertinent threat to the welfare of the United States government and its citizenry of the first magnitude...Due to A.I.M.'s violence potential, which is frequently directed toward local and state governments and police officers, timely dissemination of specific intelligence information affecting their agencies, is of utmost importance.[69]

In other words, the anti-AIM disinformation COINTELPRO in which Douglass Durham played so prominent a part, was to go on and on, both within and without the Bureau.

The Dog Soldier Teletypes

On June 21, 1976, the FBI released to the media the contents of a teletype contending that Crusade for Justice leader Rudolfo "Corky" Gonzales was in possession of "a rocket launcher, rockets, M-16 automatic rifles, and hand grenades," and that in combination with "the American Indian Movement and SDS [a long-defunct white radical organization]," the Crusade was "setting up terrorist groups." The purpose of this was, according to Bureau spokesmen, the launching of a campaign to "kill a cop a day" by using "various ruses" to "lure law enforcement officers into ambush." Coincidental to this anti-police effort, the rather odd "united front" was to assassinate the governor of the state of South Dakota, "burn" farmers, snipe at tourists, and engage in some unspecified "action" at Mt. Rushmore.[70] As Gonzales observed, "This went out across the country,"[71] making the six o'clock news and banner headlines. A week later, the item was still considered juicy enough to be treated as prime subject-matter by news reporters, as it was re-aired on KWTV in Denver on July 1, and by all three national television networks (again) the following day.[72] The entire scenario sounded very much like a verbatim regurgitation of Douglass Durham's testimony before the Eastland "committee" a few months earlier.

The June 21 teletype mentioned that AIM was contributing "2,000 warriors," all "trained in the Northwest Territory [sic]," to the multiracial venture in terrorism.[73]

AIM leader Ted Means tried hard to overcome the impression created by the FBI's fabricated "Dog Soldier Teletypes" that AIM was preparing a "terrorist campaign" in 1976. (Photo: *Akwesasne Notes*)

On June 22, the Bureau followed up by releasing another teletype which, together with the one of the day before, have come to be known as the "Dog Soldier Teletypes." The lengthy text is worth reproducing in its entirety:

28 1765Z May 76
From Director FBI
To Deputy Attorney General
Attn: Analysis and Evaluation Unit Assistant Attorney General, Criminal Division
Attn: Internal Security Section U.S. Marshal's Services U.S. Secret Service (PID)
Department of Interior
Re: American Indian Movement
Unclassified

A source, with whom insufficient contact has been made to determine reliability but who is in a position to furnish reliable information, advised as follows on May 21, 1976, "Dog Soldiers" who are pro-American Indian Movement (AIM) members who will kill for the advancement of AIM objectives have been training since the Wounded Knee, South Dakota, incident in 1973. These Dog Soldiers, approximately 2000 in number have been training in "The Northwest Territory" (not further described) and also an unknown number have been training in the desert of Arizona. These Dog Soldiers allegedly are undergoing guerrilla warfare training experiences (not further described).

The Dog Soldiers are to arrive at the Yankton Sioux Reservation, South Dakota (Wagner, South Dakota) in order to attend the traditional Sioux Sun Dance and International Treaty Conference. The Sun Dance and the conference are to occur on the Yankton Reservation in early June of 1976 and this Sun Dance and conference are to serve as a cover for the influx of Dog Soldiers. (The second biennial International Indian Treaty Conference is scheduled for May 28-June 6, 1976, Yankton Reservation).

At the conclusion of the activities on the Sioux Reservation, the Dog Soldiers are to meet on June 25, 1976, or immediately thereafter, at 20 North Street, Rapid City, South Dakota, the residence of Renee Howell. At this meeting final assignments will be given to the Dog Soldiers for targets throughout the state on the Fourth of July weekend. Currently some Dog Soldiers from the "Northwest Territory" are in the state of South Dakota watching the movements of public employees at public buildings.

The Dog Soldiers' assignments are to be carried out between July 1 and July 5, 1976. Alleged targets are as follows:

1. The Charles Mix County court house, Lake Andes, South Dakota where valves on the heating systems boiler are to be set (including the safety valve) in such a way that the boiler will blow up.
2. State Capitol, Pierre, South Dakota (no further detail).
3. Ft. Randall Dam, Pickstown, South Dakota, would have turbines blown up, short circuiting power.
4. The Dog Soldiers were "on the line" to assassinate the Governor of South Dakota.
5. Sniping of tourists on interstate highways in South Dakota.
6. Taking action to Mt. Rushmore.
7. To "burn farmers" and shooting equipment in the Wagner, South Dakota area.
8. To assault the State Penitentiary at Sioux Falls, South Dakota to assassinate an inmate.
9. To blow up the Bureau of Indian Affairs (BIA Buildings in the Wagner, South Dakota area.)

The Dog Soldiers are allegedly to be armed with M-15s and carbines which are hidden in Porcupine, South Dakota, area, on Rosebud Indian Reservation [sic].

Sam Moves Camp, an acting AIM member, Pine Ridge, South Dakota, allegedly transports the above weapons from Red Man Street, number unknown, Omaha, Nebraska, to the residence of Charlie Abourezk, Porcupine, South Dakota. Abourezk, who is involved with the Dog Soldiers, is the son of a United States Senator James Abourezk, South Dakota. Additionally, Sam Moves Camp allegedly drives an Oldsmobile, four-door black over brown, and resides in Isla Vista, Nebraska, (believed to be a suburb of Omaha, Nebraska).

Source learned that dynamite was stored at the home of Tony Zephier, Green Wood, South Dakota, in September, 1975, and dynamite was also stored at the home of Gregory Francis Zephier, Sr., also known as Greg, Wagner, South Dakota, in February, 1975.

Source has heard that Wilburt Provost, also known as Willie, is one of Russell Means' "hit men" and that Wallace Little, Jr., also known as June Little, who is expert with explosives, was once teacher of the Dog Soldiers in the Northwest Territory.

Greg Zephier, Wagner, South Dakota, is listed as the Director of the AIM, South Dakota, according to Janice Stark, Clerk, Incorporation Records, South Dakota Secretary of State, as of July 18, 1975.

A second source advised that Russell Means holds no national office in AIM; however he is member of the AIM central committee [sic; no such entity ever existed], the decision-making body of AIM.

The American Indian Movement (AIM) was founded in Minnesota in 1968, dedicated to improving conditions for the American Indian. AIM led and participated in confrontations with local authorities in Scottsbluff, Nebraska, and the Rapid City-Custer areas

Senator James Abourezk (left) had by 1975 become an outspoken critic of the FBI operations on Pine Ridge. (Photo: *Washington Star/News*) His son, Charlie (right), was without substantiation branded a terrorist by the Bureau. (Photo: *Rapid City Journal*)

of South Dakota. AIM led the takeover and occupation of Wounded Knee, South Dakota, in February-May, 1973.

Both documents were released at a particularly critical juncture in the Cedar Rapids murder trial of AIM members Dino Butler and Bob Robideau (see Chapter 11). When the jury was becoming disenchanted with the government's case in general and the performance of the FBI in particular, the teletypes reinforced the government's contention that AIM was part of a conspiracy to lure police (and, by implication, federal agents) into ambushes, as Butler and Robideau were accused of doing; that AIM had an elite corps of "hit men," an entity to which Butler and Robideau were accused of belonging; and that AIM was involved in erecting more-or-less formal military facilities, as Butler and Robideau were said to have done.

The general tenor of both documents was that AIM as a whole was a mad-dog organization—an image the Bureau had been striving to create for years—and that members such as the Cedar Rapids defendants were thus a public menace of the sort which might best be locked away, regardless of their guilt or innocence in any specific matter (such as the killing of two FBI agents, for which they were being tried). The media blitz regarding these documents came within two weeks of the verdict at Cedar Rapids.[74]

Tellingly, June Little, the individual pinpointed in the Dog Soldier Teletype as being an "explosives expert" who was training AIM's "dog soldiers" in the "Northwest

Territory," was himself suspected of having been involved in the deaths of SA Coler and Williams on June 26, 1975. The seemingly gratuitous inclusion of the name of Charles Abourezk, a non-Indian, as being "involved with the dog soldiers," was likely intended to discredit Senator James Abourezk of South Dakota who had become one of the Bureau's more outspoken critics (see Chapters 8 and 9). The Senator noted this when, on July 3, 1975, he described the documents as being part of a "smear campaign" which "smacks of a total setup that these unfounded, unverified reports are given such widespread distribution."[75]

The Senator's analysis should be assessed in view of the FBI's own determination that when engaging in a COINTELPRO disinformation campaign, "It is immaterial whether facts exist to substantiate the charge. If facts are present, it aids in the success of the proposal...disruption [of targeted organizations and individuals] can be accomplished [by leveling accusations in the media] without facts to back it up."[76] When FBI Director Clarence Kelly was sworn in as a witness at the Cedar Rapids trial a few days after the teletypes were released, the question was put to him by defense attorney William Kunstler:

Kunstler: Mr. Kelly, is there one shred of evidence to support the allegations made in these teletypes?

Kelly: I know of none...

To further solidify the impression that the entire matter had been manufactured by his agents from whole cloth, Kelly then proceeded to testify that, "It is my very definite knowledge that the American Indian Movement is a movement which has fine goals, has many fine people, and has as its general consideration of what needs to be done, something that is worthwhile; and it is not tabbed by us as an un-American, subversive, or otherwise objectionable organization."[77]

Since no one was ever arrested as a "dog soldier" conspirator and none of the alleged incipient terrorist acts ever materialized, it is impossible to avoid the conclusions reached by Rex Weyler: "The memo[s...were] a completely fabricated creation of the FBI"[78]; or by Peter Matthiessen: "Not a single sliver of hard evidence supported the lies and propaganda being aimed at the Cedar Rapids jury by...the U.S. Attorney's office, and the Federal Bureau of Investigation or that sadly eroded institution, the U.S. Department of Justice."[79] Further, aside from the specific jury-tainting objectives which may be associated with them, the Dog Soldier teletypes fit within the framework of the overall false image of AIM which the FBI's disinformation campaign had been designed to achieve.

Chapter 11

Perjury and Fabrication of Evidence

FBI officials said a principal way to neutralize individuals was to show they were violating Federal, State or local statutes.
—House Report to the Committee on the Judiciary, *FBI Domestic Intelligence Operations—Their Purpose and Scope: Issues That Need to be Resolved*

The FBI will fabricate and suppress evidence in order to tie [radical political] leaders up in the courts and in prison. The FBI also encourages agents to lie; one FBI memo stated that "it is immaterial whether facts exist to substantiate the charge. If facts are present, it aids in the success of the proposal [to "neutralize individuals" through the courts]...but disruption [of legitimate political organizations] can be accomplished without facts to back it up.
—Jim Messerschmidt, *The Trial of Leonard Peltier*

As Messerschmidt has noted, "The state response to collective behavior organizing to resist [state power] contains two essential, but inherently contradictory aspects. First, and most important, it must disrupt and disorganize the [threatening] behavior...In short, the state will repress the activity as soon as possible."[1] As we have seen, the FBI spared little "initiative and imagination"[2] in its 1972-76 campaign to directly repress AIM. However:

...the state cannot merely overtly repress behavior which is considered a menace to [its power]. It must also legitimize that repression. This brings us to the second major aspect of the state response to collective resistance. If the state engages merely in outright repression, it runs the risk of destroying its hegemony, which relies on people believing it is a neutral arbiter. Such a strategy would lead to an *increase* in the political composition of the organized [resistance] movement. The state is therefore confronted with a highly conflicting and contradictory situation...The state is compelled to maintain a legalistic image if it is to limit political, collective resistance in the future.[3]

It follows that "[t]he state solves this inherent problem by appealing to the legal system. This enables the state to dispose of the threatening political behavior while simultaneously legitimizing its repressive acts...[the state] claims to be applying universal codes impartially and not singling out specific groups for special and arbitrary treatment. But as Anatole France ironically notes, 'It is the majestic equality of the...law which forbids both rich and poor from sleeping under the bridges of the Seine.'"[4] In principle then, "[t]he legal system (especially substantive and procedural forms to be applied both to the government and the governed) 'sets definite constraints on the ability of political elites to dispose efficiently' of collective resistance, 'constraints which they can ignore only at the risk of endangering their long-run legitimacy and interest in minimizing' a growing political movement. Nevertheless, the 'immediate pressures' to end collective resistance 'unavoidably dictate serious abrogations of the law.'"[5] Such a dynamic includes legal breaches not only outside, but within the judicial process *per se*.

The following examples are indicative of the vast scope and depth of the FBI practice of systematically engaging in the manufacture of a variety of forms of evidence in order to obtain "legal" convictions of AIM members.

The Louis Moves Camp Affair

From August 5 through 10, 1974, SAs David Price and Ronald Williams met with former AIM member Louis Moves Camp at Ellsworth Air Force Base, near Rapid City.[6] Moves Camp had resigned from AIM on July 4 "after returning to the [Rapid City] AIM house to find his belongings on the sidewalk; the expulsion, ordered by Dennis Banks, would have happened sooner had he not been the son of a respected elder, Ellen Moves Camp, since he had repeatedly broken the AIM house rules in regard to drugs, alcohol, and creating disturbances."[7] A Congressional Report later recorded the FBI's version of what was happening at the air base:

> Mr. Moves Camp first came to the attention of the Government as a possible witness when he voluntarily contacted the FBI's Rapid City Resident Agency on about August 5, 1974, and offered to testify as a Government witness against the defendants [Dennis Banks and Russell Means, at the upcoming Wounded Knee Leadership Trial]. SAs David Price and Ronald Williams then contacted Assistant Special Agent in Charge [ASAC] Philip Enlow [in Minneapolis] with this information on August 7th, who in turn contacted Assistant U.S. Attorney [AUSA] R.D. Hurd [also in Minneapolis, and slated to be the chief prosecutor during the Banks/Means trial].[8]

In cross-examination at the trial, Moves Camp acknowledged that Price and Williams met daily with him from the 5th through the 10th and that on August 9 he had signed "three affidavits [prepared by the agents] that were subsequently turned over to prosecutor Hurd."[9] Missing from both the Bureau account and Moves Camp's statements on the matter were the facts of his personal grudge against Banks for having evicted him, his pique at AIM in general, and that he was "awaiting trial for robbery, assault with a deadly weapon [two counts], and assault causing bodily injury [two counts]...[he was] faced with a possible jail sentence of twenty years."[10] Whether Moves Camp approached the FBI or the other way around, it is not credible that SAs Price and Williams were unaware of Moves Camp's legal situation or that it might be parlayed into the creation of the most "cooperative" possible type of witness.

From Rapid City, Price and Williams transported Moves Camp to Minneapolis, where they checked into the Dyckman Hotel.[11] On August 13, the trio relocated to the J&R Dude Ranch, just across the Wisconsin state line and the next day prosecutor Hurd had his first meeting with the man he expected to be his star witness.[12] Although things seemed to be going smoothly for the government at this juncture,

[On the morning of August 15] Price was distressed because Louis had gotten himself into some sort of trouble...He was, in fact, now in the custody of the River Falls [Wisconsin] police...[where] to quote Ron Williams..."some type of law-enforcement-related person...had been advised that a female had made an oral allegation...that Mr. Moves Camp had raped her"...[Price later] telephoned [Williams] to notify his partner that no rape complaint was going to be filed after all, and that he was on his way home with [Moves Camp]...Curiously...Price and Williams failed to prepare a field report or F.D. "302", on all these exciting events, a standard procedure for agents when on duty.[13]

The subsequent FBI version of what had happened is contained in a Congressional Report:

In a September 19, 1974, signed memorandum to the SAC [Joseph Trimbach], [ASAC Philip] Enlow recounted that on the afternoon of August 16, 1974, SA Price advised him that an allegation had been made by a young woman in River Falls, Wisconsin that Moves Camp had raped her. Mr. Enlow instructed SA Price to take no action whatsoever to interfere with or influence the investigation by the local police department or to persuade local authorities not to prosecute Mr. Moves Camp on the rape charge...As it turned out, no rape charges were, in fact, filed since the prosecutor, after interviewing the complainant, her parents, and the officer involved, determined that there was no evidence that a crime had been committed and the matter was, therefore, not prosecuted...Mr. Enlow [then] spoke with SA [Ray] Gammon and...AUSA Hurd in a conference call and *informed Mr. Hurd of the allegation*, that Mr. Moves Camp was not under arrest, and that no charges had been filed [emphasis added].[14]

Although the FBI introduced sworn statements by local authorities that "neither SA Price nor any Federal Government employee tried to or did exert influence" on them in this matter,[15] the defense established in cross examination at trial that—before the rape charge against Moves Camp was dropped—Price "conferred for several hours with a state prosecutor as well as with the River Falls police, and had made it clear to his fellow lawmen that Moves Camp was a crucial witness in the Banks/Means trial."[16] SA Williams further testified that immediately after Price and Moves Camp had returned from River Falls, the trio had checked out of the J&R Dude Ranch and gone back to Minnesota (out of Wisconsin jurisdiction), because "hostile persons might find out where we were."[17] The victim herself told WKLDOC attorneys that there was "a very active campaign on the part of officials to keep her

AIM leaders Russell Means (left) and Dennis Banks (right) with defense attorney William Kunstler during the "Wounded Knee Leadership Trial" in St. Paul, MN, 1974. (Photo: Dick Bancroft)

from talking to anyone."[18] As WKLDOC attorney Larry Leventhal summed up the situation:

> At the time of the alleged rape incident Louis Moves Camp was spending a few days in the presence of FBI agents Williams and Price...[who] by their own testimony, consumed great amounts of alcohol one evening in the presence of Moves Camp. Moves Camp thereafter left their company. The following morning a young woman attempted to press a rape complaint against Louis Moves Camp, with the county attorney's office. Her complaint was initially processed, and then following contact between the FBI agents and the county attorney the complaint was sidetracked.[19]

All of this calls into question the non-interference or non-influence with which the Bureau has steadfastly characterized its posture. Either way, the Wisconsin rape charge hanging over Moves Camp's head could now be added to the pre-existing tally of pending sentences which the FBI could utilize in bargaining for the witness's "full cooperation." Nonetheless, for his testimony to be viable, the prosecution *had* to keep word of such matters from the jury. It was undoubtedly for this reason that the following exchange occurred between AUSA R.D. Hurd and WKLDOC attorney Mark Lane during the trial:

> *Lane:* I should like to know if Louis Moves Camp was arrested while in Wisconsin; if he was jailed for a serious charge, which may be rape; and if the agents of the FBI or other representatives of the United States government arranged his release; if any of that fact situation [*sic*] is true.

Judge Nichol then asked Hurd if he could provide the requested information.

Hurd: It's my understanding that he was arrested on a public intoxication charge. Now, I'm not sure on the details of that, but it was my understanding that he was arrested on a public intoxication charge. I don't believe there was ever a conviction on it; he was released. I'm not even sure he was arrested...He has not been arrested on anything more than public intoxication.

Lane: Well, I think we're entitled to this information...I think we're entitled to know the date of the arrest, and what role the federal government played in having him released.

Hurd: I don't think any of that is relevant and material; you can't impeach a witness by showing he was arrested for public intoxication.[20]

It was only later in the trial that Hurd, when confronted by Lane with incontrovertible evidence that he had been informed by ASAC Enlow of the rape charge against Moves Camp at least a week prior to the prosecutor's statements in court, dropped his pretense that he had "not known" of the situation.[21] Being caught in an outright lie led to Hurd's being censured by Judge Nichol:

Mr. Hurd deceived the Court up here at the bench in connection with the Moves Camp incident in Wisconsin. It hurts me deeply. It's going to take me a long time to forget it...to that extent, I think the prosecutor in this case was guilty of misconduct; it was certainly not in accord with the highest standards we ought to expect from those officers that represent what I used to think was the majesty of the United States Government. I guess it's been a bad year for justice, a bad year for justice.[22]

Perhaps more important than *how* the FBI obtained Moves Camp's testimony (and what the Bureau was prepared to do in order to retain him as a witness) was the nature of *what* he was expected to testify about. As the trial transcript reveals, Moves Camp was used to fill virtually every hole in the government's "case" against Banks and Means:

Louis Moves Camp...testified that he had witnessed virtually every crime with which the defendants were charged. He told the court that he had been at the Calico meeting [which led to AIM going to Wounded Knee] on February 27, 1973, providing evidence of conspiracy. He told the court he had witnessed both Banks and Means pilfering merchandise from the trading post [at Wounded Knee]. He said he had seen Banks and Means handing out guns and giving orders to others, casting them as instigators in violence against federal officers. If Moves Camp's testimony were true, the defendants would be found guilty of every charge in the eleven-point indictment...[23]

The first crack in this flawless eyewitnessing of crucial events, however, occurred when Moves Camp's mother, Ellen, a major ION leader at Wounded Knee, stood up from among the spectators in the courtroom and shouted, "Louis never stayed at Wounded Knee. Even while he was there, he was in and out. He's lying about everything! Every statement he signed is a lie! Everything he said is a lie!"[24] Shortly thereafter, "the defense established that Price's witness had left Wounded

Knee for the last time about March 11 [1973] and that he was actually in California at the time of most of the events he described:"[25]

Further investigation by WKLDOC revealed that a BIA employee had seen Moves Camp in California from March 17 through the month of June. Records from the Monterey Peninsula Cable Television Company revealed that Moves Camp had appeared on a television show there on April 23 and 26, days that he supposedly witnessed events at Wounded Knee. Other witnesses testified that he had been on the San Jose State College campus in April.[26]

Still further investigation revealed that prosecutor Hurd, as his case began to deteriorate, had requested Moves Camp be administered a polygraph examination before going on the stand, and that SAC Trimbach had refused to allow the Bureau's prize witness to be so tested.[27] When Judge Nichol discovered that the FBI had paid Moves Camp some "$2,074.50 in expenses and *fees* [emphasis added]" for his services as a false witness,[28] he stated that, even in the "most favorable possible finding," Hurd had been "grossly negligent in failing to verify Moves Camp's testimony, and further, in failing to offer an explanation or correction of his testimony in the face of overwhelming contradictory evidence. His conduct here at least borders on violation of the American Bar Association Standards…"[29] As to the Bureau, the Judge observed that:

> I blurted out, maybe unfortunately, in the early part of this trial, that the FBI had certainly deteriorated. I think that statement…has become justified by the manner in which the FBI has operated in this trial [at the time of this statement, Nichol was still unaware of the Bureau's implantation of Douglass Durham within the defense team; see Chapter 8].[30]

The Bureau's illegal behavior with regard to the Moves Camp matter was compounded on August 30, 1974 when,

> …the prosecution and FBI misconduct, which had reached tragic proportions turned, for a moment, comic. While questioning FBI agent Ronald Williams concerning the alleged FBI coverup [of Moves Camp's River Falls rape charge, WKLDOC] attorney William Kunstler noticed a door behind the bench slightly ajar—a door that was usually closed. Continuing his questioning, Kunstler wandered about the courtroom, moving ever closer to the open door. As he got close enough to reach the handle, he quickly swung open the door, at which point two eavesdropping FBI agents almost fell on their faces as they stumbled embarrassingly into the room. An incredulous Judge Nichol stopped the proceedings and took the two agents, Dennis O'Callahan and Patrick Flynn, to his chambers for questioning. FBI agent David Price had been sequestered, awaiting his turn to testify, and Nichol wanted assurance that the two sleuths had not intended to subvert the process of objective testimony by revealing Williams' testimony to Price.[31]

The Moves Camp affair was the death-knell of the government's otherwise almost non-existent case against Banks and Means. Already, "in July, when the government [originally] rested its case, Judge Nichol had dismissed…burglary, arson, illegal

Federal Judge Fred Nichol dismissed all charges against Means and Banks, citing rampant misconduct by the government, and stated that the FBI and prosecution had "stooped so low" in this case as to "pollute the waters of justice." At the time, Nichol still didn't know of the Bureau's infiltration of Douglass Durham into the defense team.
(Photo: *Akwesasne Notes*)

weapons [Molotov cocktails], and theft charges—there being simply no proof to sustain them."[32] A short time later, he also "dismissed two counts of 'interfering or obstructing federal law enforcement officials during a civil disorder' because the government could not show that the presence of the officials was lawful in the first place."[33] As the dimension of the Bureau misconduct in relation to Moves Camp's blatant perjury became obvious, Nichol seized the opportunity to dismiss all remaining charges as well:

> More serious than Louis Moves Camp's lies was the all but inescapable conclusion that Agent Price, and perhaps Agent Williams, had knowingly prepared this man to give false testimony; at the very least, they found his story so convenient that they had not bothered to find out if it was true. More serious still was the likelihood that U.S. Attorney Hurd had also been aware that Moves Camp's testimony was false even before he put him on the stand.[34]

As the judge eloquently summarized the case in the remarks accompanying his final dismissal action:

> Although it hurts me deeply, I am forced to the conclusion that the prosecution in this trial had something other than attaining justice foremost in its mind...The fact that incidents of misconduct formed a pattern throughout the course of the trial leads me to the belief that this case was not prosecuted in good faith or in the spirit of justice. The waters of justice have been polluted, and dismissal, I believe, is the appropriate cure for the pollution in this case.[35]

AIM member Jimmy Eagle is escorted to court by U.S. marshals during August, 1975, as the FBI was arranging the false depositions of Greg Clifford and others to implicate Eagle in the killings of SAs Williams and Coler. (Photo: *Rapid City Journal*)

As concerned the Bureau in particular, Nichol spoke with equal severity: "It's hard for me to believe that the FBI, which I have revered for so long, has stooped so low."[36] Still, as Vine Deloria, Jr. concluded about a year after the trial:

> [T]he trials growing out of the Wounded Knee occupation involved such serious misconduct both by the FBI and the Federal prosecutor that the judge in the case of American Indian Movement leaders Russell Means and Dennis Banks was forced to dismiss all charges...But when lawyers representing Means and Banks asked for disciplining action by the Justice Department against the federal employees who had overstepped their authority, they were told the government planned no such action.[37]

To the contrary, R.D. Hurd was immediately commended and assigned to take the lead role in the remaining "Wounded Knee Leadership" cases, those against Leonard Crow Dog (see next chapter), Stan Holder and Carter Camp (tried in Cedar Rapids, Iowa, during June of 1975 resulting in convictions).[38] Joseph Trimbach continued overseeing the entire FBI anti-AIM operation in South Dakota, while agents Price and Williams were returned to the fray on Pine Ridge itself (Williams was killed there on June 26, 1975; see Chapter 9). As for Louis Moves Camp, his performance on the stand was not punished in any way whatsoever; the River Falls rape charge was allowed to simply drift into oblivion and the sentences on all his twenty-odd years worth of prior convictions were suspended. In April 1975, he was critically wounded by a rifle bullet in the tiny reservation village of Wanblee, in apparent retribution for his recent rape of a Pine Ridge woman.[39]

The Butler/Robideau Trial

During the RESMURS investigation of 1975, the FBI rapidly—and inexplicably—narrowed its list of those wanted in connection with the deaths of SAs Williams and Coler from the original "more than 30 suspects" (see Chapter 9) to just four: Darelle "Dino" Butler, Robert "Bob" Robideau, Leonard Peltier and James Theodore "Jimmy" Eagle. "Coincidentally," this much abbreviated roster of those targeted by the Bureau to face first degree murder charges in the matter were, with the excep-

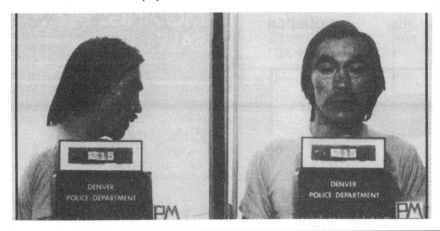

Gregory Dewey Clifford, member of a noted Pine Ridge GOON family, bargained his way out of the Pennington County (SD) Jail and rape charges in July 1975 by fabricating evidence against Jimmy Eagle and Leonard Peltier. Although his bogus confession was not used at trial, the FBI rewarded Clifford with a new life by placing him in the Federal Witness Protection Program and blocking his prosecution in a series of brutal crimes. In March 1987, the buffers of the Bureau wore out: Clifford was arrested for the grisly murder and dismemberment of a woman named Gerri Patton and is currently serving 45 years in Colorado. (Photo: Denver Police Dept.).

tion of Eagle, those identified as being the "key AIM members" present at the Jumping Bull property during the firefight of June 26 that year.[40]

According to the Bureau, the charges against Jimmy Eagle were derived from his having "confessed" his part in the killing of the agents to a cellmate, Gregory Dewey Clifford (an Oglala), after having turned himself in on the "cowboy boot charges" (see Chapter 9) on July 9:

> According to Clifford, Eagle claimed that one agent had come early on June 26 to the Jumping Bull property and had been told to leave; that there were many Indians present, some of them armed with M-14 or M-16 automatic weapons; that when the two agents returned, a warning shot was fired, at which point the agents started shooting; that when they were disabled, a number of Indians including Eagle, moved up close and killed them. Eagle, who said he was standing four feet away, described how one of the agents begged for his life (just as reported in FBI news releases after the deaths); that this man was shot with a Thompson .45 submachine gun, the impact of which knocked him into the air so that he came down hard, denting the car; that Eagle and his companions had taken turns shooting the agents on the ground.[41]

SA William Wood, who took Clifford's statement in the Pennington County Jail (in Rapid City), found "corroboration" in the statements of two other Oglalas, Marion High Bull and Melvin White Wing, who claimed they'd overheard Eagle's "boastful" story, told to Clifford. According to Wood's summary of the High Bull interview, Eagle had not only said what Clifford claimed, but had specifically threatened the life of Wood's partner, SA David Price, as well.[42] On October 15, 1975, Wood recorded White Wing as contending that:

> EAGLE was heard to say that the Agent [Coler] was pulled from his car and then shot..."We all took turns shooting at them." JIMMY EAGLE was emotionally involved when he was telling his story and he, WHITE WING, believed that JIMMY EAGLE was not telling a story as heard from someone else but...as though he, JIMMY EAGLE, was actually there. WHITE WING stated that JIMMY EAGLE...was very proud of the fact that "they" killed the agents.[43]

Meanwhile, Dino Butler had been captured during the FBI air assault on the Crow Dog and Running properties (on the Rosebud Reservation, September 5; see Chapter 9), and, on September 10, Bob Robideau had been arrested when the car in which he had been riding exploded alongside the Kansas Turnpike, near Wichita.[44] Three of the four specified "culprits" in the deaths of agents Williams and Coler were thus in custody within sixty days of the event; only Leonard Peltier remained at large.

Butler and Robideau were moved from their separate locations to the Pennington County Jail in January 1976 to await the beginning of their trial. On April 19, Pennington County Sheriff's Deputies supposedly discovered several hacksaw blades hidden in their cellblock and, for undisclosed reasons, five FBI agents—J. Gary Adams, William Wood, Dean Hughes, Fred Coward and David Price—were "invited" to join Sheriff Mel Larson and three of his deputies in a "more thorough" search of the facility. Despite the fact that the two cells searched by the lawmen housed a total of sixteen prisoners at the time, Robideau was immediately targeted as the "ringleader" of an escape plot with Dino Butler and two other incarcerated AIM members (Kenny Kane and Alonzo Bush, both Oglalas) designated as his "accomplices." These "facts" were supposedly confirmed on April 20, when SAs Coward and Hughes interviewed a young black inmate, Marvin Bragg (aka: Ricky Lee Waters). As Robideau recalls:

> [Bragg was] just a little guy, maybe five foot two, and he was a real terror there in Rapid [City]; had more than ten rapes, and most of them pretty weird, involving old women. A real sad figure—everywhere he went, he was getting beat up, especially after he [fingered] us, because rapists and snitches, well cons don't go for that shit, and Bragg was both...He was going with an Indian woman at the time, and I guess it was her who threw them hacksaw blades in through the window...Bragg was serious about escaping, but he was facing up to eighty years, and when the shit came down, he just switched sides and pinned it all on us, to save himself.[45]

In a second interview between Bragg and SA Coward, on the afternoon of April 21, the rapist identified Butler's WKLDOC attorney, Bruce Ellison, as being the party who, on April 15, 1976, had delivered the hacksaw blades. A Bureau memo, recently released under the FOIA, shows clearly that the FBI was quite aware of the

Bob Robideau and Dino Butler being led to trial in chains, Cedar Rapids, 1976. The heavy security presence of U.S. marshals was a result of the "terrorist threat" frenzy whipped up by FBI propagandists. (Photo: *Cedar Rapids Gazette*)

falsity of Bragg's statements, but it *nonetheless* used this "evidence" to cause Ellison's dismissal as defense counsel:

> [AUSA Boyd] advised that an affidavit had been filed with the Court concerning the involvement of Attorney BRUCE ELLISON in this matter. ELLISON was subsequently dismissed as Defense Counsel. BOYD said he failed to notify the court that ELLISON was actually in St. Louis, Missouri, with USA EVAN HULTMAN on 4/15/76...[46]

On May 7, cast as desperate potential jailbreakers, Butler and Robideau were transferred to the maximum security South Dakota State Penitentiary in Sioux Falls,[47] where they were held under especially stark conditions. WKLDOC attorneys, meanwhile, had secured a change of venue, allowing the case to be heard in Cedar Rapids, Iowa, rather than Rapid City, because of the anti-AIM prejudice so demonstrably running rampant in South Dakota. With that, the Bureau's publicists moved into high gear:

> The FBI warned local law-enforcement personnel that carloads of AIM terrorists were descending upon [Cedar Rapids], and on May 11, U.S. marshals visited every office in the Federal Building, telling folks to prepare for shooting incidents and the seizure of hostages and advising them of the precautions to be taken; the frightened citizens were assured that U.S. marshals on the roof would be on the lookout for marauding Indians. On May 24, Rapid City police, reporting [on the basis of an FBI "informant tip"] a huge

cache of Indian armaments left over from Wounded Knee, tore up a vacant lot with backhoes, exposing three spent shotgun shells in their day's work.[48]

At first, the elaborate, but rather transparent, federal effort to harden public sentiment against AIM—both generally, and with a very specific eye toward obtaining convictions in the RESMURS case—bore fruit. As Nilak Butler recalls the situation, by the time the Butler/Robideau trial opened in Cedar Rapids before Judge Edward McManus,[49] on June 7:

> [T]he police were so paranoid they locked up the whole jail. The headlines at the time were that the Governor was asking for National Guard support during the trial, the feds psyched them up so bad, and *that's* where we were going to get our jury. The citizens were more concerned that no damage happen to their person, place or thing, because they were psyched out—just totally psyched out.[50]

Shortly, however, as "the great scare campaign turned out to be lies as well as nonsense, the citizens of Cedar Rapids began to observe the Justice Department stage directions with more skepticism, and perhaps some resentment, as well."[51] In court, this may have first manifested itself in Judge McManus' decision to allow the defendants' case to be presented on the basis of their having acted in self-defense in the deaths of agents Coler and Williams. This involved elaboration of the context of violence prevailing on Pine Ridge by 1975, and assessment of the FBI's role in fostering or at least allowing the situation, before the jury.

Prosecutor Evan Hultman (a brigadier general in the army reserve), apparently fearing a repeat of the Louis Moves Camp fiasco, quickly began cutting his potential losses. In a remarkable commentary on his belief in the veracity of Bragg's possible testimony against the defendants, Hultman cut the rapist from the prosecution's roster. Bragg later admitted "having benefitted [from his escape plan story] by receiving a concurrent sentence on…three rape convictions…[and, at the time, had] high hopes of an early parole from…two recent sentences on charges of murder."[52] Still, both Butler and Robideau remained charged with planning a jailbreak, entirely on the basis of Bragg's "eyewitness" account. Only at the conclusion of the RESMURS trial—when the propaganda value for the government in court had ended—was the lack of substance attending the whole issue fully revealed and the escape charges were quietly dropped.[53]

Next to go from the lineup of prosecution witnesses was an infiltrator named John "Daryl Blue Legs" Stewart (see Chapter 7), whose testimony Hultman seems to have felt might tend to "taint" the government case. The reason for the prosecutor's decision in this matter appears to have been predicated on the fact that this man, too, was an accused rapist—of a Pine Ridge woman, the winter before—and that he, too, was receiving federal assistance in "mitigating" these charges.[54] Finally, Hultman announced he was eliminating a woman named Myrtle Poor Bear, whom the defense knew well as a sort of "roving eye-witness" used by the FBI in major AIM cases (see next section and Chapter 12). This last provoked a sharp exchange between WKLDOC attorney William Kunstler, Hultman and assistant prosecutor Robert Sikma:

> *Kunstler:* They don't want to call her because they know she is a fake, but they put us in the position of having worked all weekend on this witness and I think they should be required to call this witness to the stand. This is part of the [FBI's and prosecution's] offensive fabrication.
>
> *Sikma:* She is not a fake...
>
> *Kunstler:* Put her on the stand and we will show you. She is an FBI fake. Just as they did in the Banks-Means trial. That is why they are reneging about calling her.
>
> *Hultman:* You have seen the record and what the record shows.
>
> *Kunstler:* They know *it* is a fake, too. Part of our defense is fabrication by the FBI. That is why this witness becomes so crucial. That is why they don't want to call her.
>
> *Hultman:* I object to this. There is no showing of any kind. it is a bald statement of counsel and we have been getting...
>
> *Kunstler:* Put her on![55]

Hultman and Sikma wisely declined to do so. They nonetheless made ample use of witnesses whose false testimony appears quite clearly to have been suborned by the Bureau. For example, there was Wish Draper, one of the Tent City AIM group, to which Butler and Robideau also belonged (see Chapter 9). On January 9, 1976, Draper (then sixteen years old) was arrested on the Navajo Reservation in Arizona on alcohol and robbery charges. That evening, he was "interviewed" in his cell by SAs Charles Stapleton and James Doyle; the two agents strapped Draper to a chair for "about three hours," and eventually extracted his signature on an "eyewitness statement" they'd prepared for him, implicating Butler, Robideau and Leonard Peltier in the deaths of agents Coler and Williams.[56] On January 17, the FBI put the young AIM member on the stand before a federal grand jury in Sioux Falls in order to obtain murder indictments against his three colleagues. Under cross-examination by WKLDOC attorney John Lowe [during the subsequent trial of Leonard Peltier], however, Draper "acknowledged without hesitation that he had lied to the grand jury in January, and also as a prosecution witness [in the Butler/Robideau] trial:

> *Lowe:* On January 13, 1976, at Sioux Falls, South Dakota, did you appear before the Grand Jury?
>
> *Draper:* Yes.
>
> *Lowe:* Did you testify under oath?

Draper: Yes.

Lowe: Would I be correct in saying some of the testimony you gave was false?

Draper: Yes.[57]

The witness also established that his perjury was motivated by the "coaching" of both the prosecutors and the FBI:

Lowe: Who told you [the weapon used to kill Coler and Williams] was not a Thompson [submachinegun]?

Draper: [Prosecutor] Sikma.

Lowe: He told you that it was an AR-15? Didn't he?

Draper: Yes.

Lowe: And that is where you got the information from, isn't that correct?

Draper: Yes.

Lowe: Did he tell you the names of all the other guns as well?

Draper: No. Some of the [FBI] agents did at Sioux Falls when I was testifying.[58]

He also admitted that the Bureau had promised him exoneration on possible RESMURS charges, as well as "assistance" with his local charges, an education, and a "new start in life" in exchange for his bearing false witness against his friends:

Lowe: It is your expectation after you have finished testifying here that any legal problems you have in the criminal area will be taken care of, is it not?

Draper: Yes.[59]

Then there was the case of another member of the Tent City AIM group, Norman Brown (then 17 years old) who was interviewed by SAs J. Gary Adams and O. Victor Harvey on September 22, 1975. He was told by Adams that, "If you don't talk to us, you might never walk the earth again," and "you won't see your family again."[60] According to his own testimony, Brown became "exceptionally frightened" by the agents and, on January 13, 1976, gave false testimony to the federal grand jury hearing RESMURS evidence in Sioux Falls. Although the matter was not brought out clearly during the Butler/Robideau trial, at the subsequent Peltier trial the following exchange occurred between Brown and defense attorney Elliot Taikeff, with interjections by trial judge Paul Benson and U.S. Attorney Evan Hultman:

Taikeff: Were you afraid of the FBI when you were before the Grand Jury?

Brown: Yeah.

Taikeff: When you finished testifying in the Grand Jury and you came out, did you see any of the lawyers sitting at the government table?

Brown: Yeah. It was that guy (indicating).

Taikeff: [Prosecutor] Sikma?

Brown: Yeah.

Taikeff: Did he say anything to you?

Brown: Yeah.

Objection by U.S. Attorney Evan Hultman for the government. Judge Benson asked Counsel to approach the bench, where the following colloquy occurred.

Benson: What do you expect the answer to be?

Taikeff: I expect the answer to be Mr. Sikma said, quote, "You did good. We could have put you away for a long time."

Hultman: I object to that.[61]

At the Peltier trial, Brown repudiated his own testimony as lies, and stipulated that he had been coerced by the prosecution and the FBI, both of which had promised him immunity and other rewards for his "cooperation" in putting Peltier—and, by implication, Butler and Robideau—in prison for life. When prosecutor Hultman attempted to force him to return to the story he'd presented to the grand jury, he countered, "Are you trying to tell me what *I* saw [during the Oglala firefight]? It seems you are calling me a liar. I have just sworn on the sacred pipe." When asked whether he'd sworn on the pipe prior to giving his grand jury testimony, he replied that he had not.[62]

Nor was the federal carrot and stick routine restricted to AIM members. The final prosecution witness against Butler and Robideau was a man named James Harper, produced by the FBI, who claimed that Dino Butler had not only confessed to him a particularly lethal role in the deaths of Coler and Williams, but had implicated virtually everyone on the Bureau's "hit list" of AIM personalities. Harper's contention was that all this was said while he and Butler were incarcerated in the same cell at the Cedar Rapids jail, and "[l]ike Louis Moves Camp in St. Paul, James Harper...filled in the missing pieces in the government case, including the ambush [of

Coler and Williams] that would serve as motivation, and he also dragged in a number of people the FBI wished to see incriminated, or made credible."[63]

Under cross-examination by William Kunstler, Harper stated that he was "presently held on a fugitive warrant from the State of Texas and prosecution in Wisconsin on theft by fraud."[64] The exchange continued:

> *Kunstler:* Would it be fair to say that being in the clutches of the law enforcement agencies and the courts at this point, that you would not mind at all getting some help from anybody that might be in a position to give you help with regard to these charges?
>
> *Harper:* Yes. That is correct...
>
> *Kunstler:* How many times would you say you have lied to police officers...?
>
> *Harper:* Probably every time I have been arrested.[65]

At another point, in response to Kunstler's question of whether there were other occasions in which Harper had "lied in order to get something [he] wanted," the witness replied: "Numerous times in my life."[66] Corroboration of the impression that Harper had been offered a deal by the FBI in tendering just such lies, under oath, against Butler and Robideau may be found in his subsequent suit "against the U.S. Attorney's office and the Justice Department for breach of contract, saying that the assistance with his many career problems had been implicit in his negotiations with the FBI agents and [assistant prosecutor] Robert Sikma."[67] In any event, as jury foreman Robert Bolin put it, Harper's testimony was so obviously fabricated that, "Not one single person [on the jury] believed one single word he said."[68]

In their defense, both Butler and Robideau openly acknowledged that they had participated in the shooting which had killed Coler and Williams (although they denied having "executed" the agents at point blank range, as the government contended). Further, they relied upon the testimony of witnesses such as U.S. Civil Rights Commission investigator William Muldrow to establish that their actions had been justified:

> "A great deal of tension and fear exist on the Reservation," Muldrow testified. "Residents feel that life is cheap, that no one really cares what happens to them...Acts of violence...are commonplace. Numerous complaints were lodged in my office about FBI activities." Muldrow concluded that by the summer of 1975 conditions on Pine Ridge had become so fearful that traditional Indians as well as AIM members had felt obliged to carry weapons at all times.[69]

In his instructions to the all-white jury, Judge McManus specified that:

> In order for a defendant to have been justified in the use of deadly force in self-defense, he must not have provoked the assault on him or have been the aggressor. If the defendant was the aggressor, or if he provoked the assault upon himself, he cannot rely

upon the right of self-defense to justify his use of force. One who deliberately puts himself in a position where he had reason to believe that his presence would provoke trouble cannot claim self-defense.[70]

Further:

The circumstances under which he acted must have been such as to produce in the mind of a reasonably prudent person, similarly situated, the reasonable belief that the other person, was then about to kill him or the Indian women and children or to do them serious bodily harm. In addition, the defendant must have actually believed that he or the Indian women and children were in imminent danger of death or serious bodily harm, and that deadly force must be used to repel it.[71]

And finally:

Even if the other person was the aggressor and the defendant was justified in using force in self-defense, he could not be entitled to use any greater force than he had reasonable grounds to believe and actually did believe to be necessary under the circumstances to save his life or avert serious bodily harm.[72]

Thus cogently informed of the legal nature of self-defense, the jury retired to five full days of deliberation on the matter. On July 16, 1976, they returned to deliver verdicts of "not guilty" against Dino Butler and Bob Robideau on each of the four counts levied against them. As jury foreman Bolin put it in a press statement made immediately afterwards:

The jury agreed with the defense contention that an atmosphere of fear and violence exists on the reservation, and that the defendants arguably could have been shooting in self-defense. While it was shown [indeed, admitted] that the defendants were firing guns in the direction of the agents, it was held that this was not excessive in the heat of passion.[73]

In other words, the jury saw the killing of the agents as a natural and *justifiable* response in the context of the FBI-created violence on Pine Ridge. Bolin also pointed out that the charge of "aiding and abetting in the murder of the agents" had been specifically disallowed, insofar as *no murder had been committed.* By any rational assessment, such a formal determination by a jury should have been the end of the RESMURS affair, a conclusion substantiated by the fact that the verdict "devastated FBI morale," and that: "One of the South Dakota FBI agents close to the case had tears in his eyes as he walked down the federal building hall" after the acquittals.[74] In Rapid City, Norman Zigrossi, Richard G. Held's protege brought in especially to handle RESMURS, commented, "The amount of time we spent on that case—oh God! But the system beat us."[75]

Indeed, at one point, the government seemed to acknowledge the inappropriateness of prosecuting anyone else for murders which a jury had already determined had never occurred. On August 9, 1976, FBI director Clarence Kelly,

Frank Black Horse (Frank DeLuca), an Italian from Cleveland, was naturalized as an Indian via his adoption into a Pine Ridge Oglala family. He was identified by the Bureau as one of the "shooters" at the Oglala firefight and was arrested with Peltier at the Smallboy Camp, but—inexplicably—no effort was made to extradite him. His present whereabouts are unknown.

COINTELPRO specialist Richard G. Held (now Kelly's assistant and "number two man in the FBI") and U.S. Attorney Hultman met in the Bureau's Washington, D.C. headquarters. Their decision was to drop all RESMURS charges against Jimmy Eagle, despite the two earlier descriptions of Eagle's "confession" in the slayings collected by Held's agents from Gregory Clifford and Melvin White Wing in 1975 (see above), and an account of the same conversation obtained from Marvin Bragg by SA Fred Coward on April 23, 1976.[76] However, the decision was not based upon any real recognition of the fundamental absurdity of another RESMURS trial, but "so that the full prosecutive weight of the Federal Government could be directed against Leonard Peltier."[77]

The Trial of Leonard Peltier

On February 6, 1976, Royal Canadian Mounted Police (RCMP) Inspector Edward W.J. Mitchell arrested three men at the camp of traditional Cree chief Robert Smallboy, near the town of Hinton, about 160 miles west of Edmonton, Alberta. One of the three was Leonard Peltier, whom Mitchell had received instructions earlier in the day to pick up "on the request of American authorities." The other two arrested were Frank Black Horse and Ronald Blackman (a.k.a.: Ron Janvier), a Canadian national who was quickly released.[78] Peltier was transported more-or-less directly to the maximum security prison at Oakalla, near Vancouver, to await extradition proceedings concerning his possible return to the U.S. for prosecution in the deaths of SAs Ron Williams and Jack Coler.

On May 11, representatives of the U.S. Department of Justice provided Canadian prosecutor Paul Halprin with a "true copy" of an affidavit signed by Myrtle

Leonard Peltier in the custody of the Royal Canadian Mounted Police, Vancouver, 1976. Peltier was fraudulently extradited to the U.S. on the basis of false "eyewitness" affidavits drawn up by FBI agents David Price and William Wood. (Photo: *Vancouver Sun*)

Poor Bear on February 19, 1976. Poor Bear claimed to have been an eyewitness to the events on the Jumping Bull property on June 26, 1975, and identified Peltier as the unassisted killer of the two agents. As a result, on June 18, 1976, Canadian Justice W.A. Schultz ordered the defendant to be extradited to stand trial; Peltier was moved from Oakalla to the Pennington County Jail in Rapid City on December 16.[79]

By the time Peltier was removed from Canada, it had become apparent that the Poor Bear affidavit was one of three mutually contradictory affidavits signed by her. They had been obtained by FBI agents David Price, William Wood and Fred Coward during a forty-five-day period in which she had been held incommunicado and thoroughly terrorized. Poor Bear had also provided similar, decisive, "eyewitness" testimony against AIM/OSCRO leader Richard Marshall during his South Dakota murder trial (see Chapter 12) and was withdrawn by the government as a credible witness during the Butler-Robideau murder trial. Unaccountably, Justice Schultz continued to view the affidavit submitted to his court as legitimate and allowed the extradition to proceed. Although Canadian Minister of External Affairs Allen MacEachen called for an "urgent investigation" of FBI conduct in the matter during November (before Peltier's extradition),[80] it was not until April 1978 that Canadian Supreme Court Justice R.P. Anderson determined that, "It seems clear to me that the conduct of the U.S. government involved misconduct from inception." By then, unfortunately, the damage had been done.[81]

Meanwhile, the government conducted an analysis of why it had lost the Butler-Robideau case. In a report dated July 20, 1976, the Bureau determined the "reasons why [the] jury found the defendants Robideau and Butler not guilty on July 16, 1976": the defense had been "allowed to question witnesses[!!!]"; Judge McManus had "continually overruled government objections" and had "forced the government to furnish the defense with all 302s prepared by Special Agents who testified for the government"; the court had allowed contextual testimony vital to the defendants' self-defense argument (*i.e.*, "the Court allowed testimony concerning past activities of the FBI relating to COINTELPRO and subsequently allowed the Church Report into evidence"); the "jury was not sequestered"; and the defense was "uncontrolled in its dealings with the news media."[82] Unsatisfied with the prospect of again having to conform to even the most rudimentary forms of due process the prosecution went shopping for a judge who might be more "cooperative":

> Originally the [Peltier] case was assigned to the federal district court in Sioux Falls, where Judge [Fred] Nichol [who had dismissed charges against Russell Means and Dennis Banks] would have presided, but when Nichol excused himself [under pressure], he was replaced by Judge Paul Benson, a former Attorney General of North Dakota and Nixon appointee, whose bias was clear two months before the trial.[83]

After a series of meetings with FBI officials and federal prosecutors in Rapid City,[84] Benson conducted a pretrial hearing in Sioux Falls on January 14, 1977, at which he ordered the trial to be held in his hometown of Fargo, North Dakota.[85]

Once the trial had begun, on March 21, 1977, one of Judge Benson's first acts was to inform Peltier's WKLDOC defense team—composed of Elliott Taikeff of New York, John Lowe of Charlottesville (Va.), Bruce Ellison, Stanley Englestein of New York and Terry Gilbert of Cleveland, Ohio—that evidence would be heavily circumscribed:

> Benson ruled right from the start that evidence would be almost entirely restricted to the events of June 26, 1975—that the suspect affidavits used in Canada, the historical background of Pine Ridge violence, the persecution of AIM by the FBI, the verdict at Cedar Rapids, together with all testimony from that trial, were inadmissable as evidence in his court. The effect of these rulings became clear with the very first prosecution witness: the defense was forbidden to impeach SA [J.] Gary Adams for the glaring contradictions in his testimony at the two trials...Reduced to discussing Adams' zeal in pursuing the Oglala suspects—he traveled to Arizona, Kansas and the state of Washington to serve his subpoenas, although local agents could have done this for him—attorney Taikeff found himself hobbled by the U.S. Attorney's objections, which Benson sustained throughout the trial.[86]

Establishing the background within which the Oglala firefight had occurred, which had allowed the construction of a viable self-defense strategy for Robideau and Butler only a few months before, was disallowed by the court, *a priori*. Lead defense counsel Taikeff seems to have become so rattled by the ruling that he acknowledged—contrary to both reason and the facts—in his opening remarks, that agents Coler and Williams *had* been the victims of "first degree murder."[87] Things went downhill from there.

Upon completion of jury selection, on March 23, Benson also ordered the entire all-white panel of ten women and four men (two of whom were alternates) to be sequestered for the duration of the trial, a practice which is well known to bias juries—ironically—against defendants.[88] He then issued strict sanctions against the defense interacting with the press in any way concerning the course and conduct of the trial. With the government's main criteria for "success" already met, the prosecution's case began.

The first major witness was Mike Anderson, a member of the Tent City AIM group (see Chapter 9), of which Peltier was also a member. Anderson had been arrested along with Bob Robideau, Kamook Banks and others on September 10, 1975, when their car had exploded alongside the Kansas Turnpike. That evening, the 15-year-old was interrogated in his cell by SAs J. Gary Adams and O. Victor Harvey.[89] He asked for an attorney, but none was provided.[90] According to the youngster's later testimony, Adams explained that, "If you don't talk, I will beat you up right here in the cell."[91] Subsequently, he was arrested on probation violation charges in Albuquerque, and "interviewed" again by SA Adams, this time accompanied by SA James Doyle.[92]

Ultimately, Anderson was "convinced" to come into court, although he testified "throughout in a dull, unhappy way," saying "I don't know" and contradicting himself—as well as other government witnesses—continually. He said agents Coler and Williams had followed a red and white van, known to be driven by Leonard Peltier, into the Jumping Bull Compound on the fatal day, rather than a "red pickup" Williams himself had reported he was following just prior to the firefight[93] (see Chapter 9). This exchange occurred during direct examination:

Sikma: The three [Peltier, Joe Stuntz Killsright, and Norman Charles] came back [to the Jumping Bull property] in the red and white van you say?

Anderson: Yes.

Sikma: And what, if anything, happened following their coming back in the red and white van? Just tell us in your own words.

Anderson: They stopped over at the Littles' place and started talking; and I was sitting on top of the roof and then those two FBI agents' cars were coming. So they all hopped in the van and went down the hill...

Sikma: All right. And it was at that time you say you saw the FBI cars come; is that right?

Anderson: Yes.

Sikma: And what if anything took place at that time?

Anderson: He [SA Williams] just asked if Jimmy Eagle was around.

Sikma: And what if anything happened then?

Anderson: Well, I guess they seen the *orange pickup* going down that way [toward the Tent City] and they followed it [emphasis added].

Sikma: Now, when you say "orange pickup" is that the red and white van to which...

John Lowe: Objection, your honor. That's objectionable, it's an outrageously leading question, and I object and ask the jury to be instructed, and counsel to be admonished. He [Sikma] knows very well what he's doing.

The Court: The objection is sustained...

Hultman: Mr. Anderson, tell us what the car was...

Anderson: The orange and white and red and white van was going down the hill.[94]

All of this was contrary, not only to FBI testimony offered during the Butler-Robideau trial,[95] but to the Bureau's own investigative documents, released later under the FOIA. For instance, a memo dated the day after the shootout:

At approximately 6:25 a.m., Minneapolis office telephonically advised that an explosion had occurred at the Visitor's Center, Mt. Rushmore, S.D....There were earlier reports that a *red pickup truck* had been spotted in the vicinity of the Visitor's Center shortly before the explosion and this may have a significant connection to the captioned matter since a *red pickup truck* was also reported in the shooting [of Williams and Coler; emphasis added].[96]

On the other hand, according to FBI Director Clarence Kelly (in his press conference of July 1, 1975; see Chapter 10), and based upon a 302 report filed by SA David Price on June 26, 1975, Williams had been heard to transmit:

He's [Eagle] supposed to be in *a red Scout*...That looks like a *red Scout* over there...There's a lot of people around...They're getting in a *red Scout* with rifles. They're shooting at us [emphasis added].

The combination of all these prior reports and testimony should logically have led to the conclusion that Coler and Williams had been following a red-orange International Scout pickup, possibly containing Jimmy Eagle, when they drove onto the Jumping Bull property, *not* a red and white van containing Leonard Peltier.[97] From there, Sikma led Anderson into making the next links:

Sikma: Did you see any individuals down at the agents' cars at any time?

Anderson: Yes.

Sikma: And tell us who it was you saw at the agents' cars.

Anderson: Butler, Robideau and Peltier.

Sikma: And did they have weapons with them?

Anderson: Yes.

Sikma: Would you tell us starting with Mr. Peltier what kind of weapon he had?

Anderson: AR. [An AR-15, the semi-automatic civilian version of the fully automatic military M-16 assault rifle carried by the FBI, BIA police and GOONs.]

Sikma: And how do you know it's an AR?

Anderson: Because of the handle.[98]

This last was crucially important to the government's case insofar as it had no real ballistics evidence to introduce. No slugs had been recovered from either agent's body, and only fragments of some sort of .22 calibre *series* ammunition—which could have been fired from a .22, a .222, a .223 (such as an AR-15 or M-16) and so on—had been recovered from the ground beneath their bodies. It could not even be determined whether these fragments had been fired on the day in question. The government retained two pathologists—Dr. Robert Bloemendaal of Rapid City, and the celebrated Los Angeles coroner, Thomas Noguchi—to perform the autopsies on the agents' bodies. Neither pathologist could, despite an exhaustive series of tests, firing everything from .22s to .45 calibre automatics into animal parts, determine anything more than that at least one agent had been killed by a "small calibre, high velocity rifle [or rifles] fired at close range."[99] This left the prosecution with the prospect that the weapon or weapons used to kill the agents could have been anything from a .22 long rifle to everything falling within the .30 caliber series, a broad array of weaponry not linkable to anyone at all.

Initially, even the Bureau admitted that it had not so much as a spent brass cartridge which it could establish conclusively as having come from the weapon which killed the two agents. Nothing of the sort had been found by dozens of investigators at the death scene; large numbers of spent cartridges from weapons which fit the general description of the alleged murder weapon were found, but in locations some distance from the bodies. The FBI's theory was that the killer or killers, after dispatching Coler and Williams point blank, had actually stopped in the midst of a firefight, hunted around in the tall grass and picked up *all* of their spent cartridges so the Bureau would find no evidence later.[100]

However, a memo prepared in early July 1975 by unidentified agents in the Rapid City FBI office and submitted for signature to SA Courtland Cunningham, Chief of the FBI Firearms and Toolmarks Division in Washington, D.C., states that on July 1, 1975:

Also in said 1972 Chevrolet Biscayne automobile I found one .223 cartridge case in the trunk which I took in my possession and placed in an envelope marked "Items recovered from trunk, Jack R. Coler automobile."[101]

The Bureau theorized that this cartridge casing had been extracted from the weapon fired by Coler's and Williams' "executioner" and landed in Coler's trunk, open at the time of the shooting. When the defense noted that, in his 302 report for July 1, 1975 (obtained during the Butler-Robideau trial), SA Cunningham made no mention at all of such a major find, the toolmarks expert admitted that he had *not* found the piece of evidence in question.[102] Rather, he said, a fingerprint specialist named Winthrop Lodge had found the cartridge casing on June 29, 1975.[103] Lodge, Cunningham asserted, had taken the casing from the trunk of the car, tagged it, and handed it over to Cunningham.[104]

Further testimony by Lodge revealed once again the unreliability of FBI evidence. At first he testified that items found in Coler's automobile for evidence had not been removed from the vehicle. Shortly after, he stated, "Yes sir. Most of the items were actually taken out of the automobile." A few minutes later he admitted, "all evidence was inventoried and removed from the vehicle."[105]

And it went on. Lodge had been given no receipt (standard FBI procedure) by Cunningham or anyone else for the crucial evidence he'd supposedly unearthed.[106] Later, he completely contradicted his earlier testimony by stating that, "not everything was turned over to Cunningham...since some of the items were [inexplicably] carried back to Pine Ridge and turned over to the agent personally in charge of evidence"; he "couldn't recall" exactly *which* agent this might have been.[107] Nonetheless, it was "established" that this particular cartridge casing—regardless of where and when it was found, or by whom, or in whose custody it had been kept—had come from the "murder weapon." The next trick was to match it to a particular rifle.

This was accomplished by SA Evan Hodge, a specialist in the FBI Firearms and Toolmarks Identification Unit, who compared the casing to another extracted from an AR-15 recovered from the AIM car which exploded near Wichita. At the Peltier trial, Hodge admitted that he had written a report dated October 31, 1975 which stated that the rifle in question could "*not* be connected to the RESMURS investigation."[108] However, said Hodge, he had not compared cartridges extracted from the weapon with the casing supposedly found in the trunk of Coler's car at the time he wrote this report; unaccountably, he claimed to have reversed normal FBI procedure in his investigation, examining those cartridges found furthest from the alleged murder scene prior to those found closest.[109] Consequently, he did not get around to the most crucial evidence attributed to the death scene until "the end of the year or early 1976."[110]

Hodge first attempted a firing pin test which he described under oath as having been "inconclusive" because of "a lack of marks on the bolt face and the condition in which I received it [the AR-15]."[111] What he meant by the last remark was that the Wichita AR had been almost destroyed by the explosion and fire which had engulfed Robideau's car. He therefore set out to perform a test comparison of the marks made by the extractor of the Wichita AR on shell casings ejected from it, and extractor marks on the casing from Coler's trunk. He acknowledged that such tests

were unreliable[112] before making matters even worse: the Wichita AR being disfunc-
tional, he had removed the bolt from the weapon and mounted it in an altogether
different AR chassis in order to perform the extraction.[113] Nonetheless, he
pronounced the comparison conclusive and declared the Wichita AR to be the much
sought after "murder weapon."[114] At this point, the task had become one of linking
this particular rifle to a given individual on June 26, 1975, a matter which—on its
face—presented no little difficulty.

Hodge, however, moved once again into the breach. By testifying that only
one AR-15 had been used by the Indians on the Jumping Bull property (and ignoring "a whole lot of ammunition components" which had been recovered, but neither
identified nor matched to weapons), the firearms identification specialist presented
a scenario wherein whichever Indian could be demonstrated to have carried an AR
during the firefight was the "guilty party." Hence, an eyewitness account placing
Peltier close to the agents, and carrying an AR-15 rifle on June 26 was the linchpin
of the prosecution's case. Obviously, the coerced testimony of Mike Anderson accomplished both objectives. Despite the severe constraints imposed by Judge Benson on defense probes into exactly how the FBI had rendered certain of its witnesses
"willing" to say what was being sworn to in court, John Lowe was able to evoke
testimony from Anderson that both the stick and the carrot had been applied in his
case:

Lowe: [Concerning the threats made to Anderson in his cell by SA J. Gary Adams on
the night of September 10, 1975] And did that make you afraid?

Anderson: Yes.

Lowe: And did you understand that you would get beat up if you didn't give him the
answers he wanted?

Anderson: Yes.

Lowe: And did you give him the answers he wanted?

Anderson: Yes...

Lowe: Did you believe that Special Agent Gary Adams was capable of hurting you if
you didn't do what he wanted?

Anderson: Yes...

Lowe: Did the FBI tell you that they would try to help you on your charges in Wichita
arising out of the exploded car?

Anderson: I don't remember.

Lowe: Have you ever been prosecuted on those charges?

Anderson: No.

Lowe: In fact, those charges have been dropped, haven't they?

Anderson: Yes.[115]

Toward the end of the trial, his federal testimony completed and apparently free of his FBI "protection," Anderson asked whether he might testify on Peltier's behalf. Lead defense counsel Taikeff declined this offer. As Peltier, who disagreed with this decision, recalls:

> Mike Anderson was called and came back to testify for me with the encouragement of his mother and his brother Larry…All our defense witnesses were first interviewed by our investigators, and one of them [Judy Bennett of the Jury Project] told me Mike was going to be a good witness for me. Sure, he was a little scared because of the threats, etc., but she felt he was going to be good. After she was finished, she called Elliott [Taikeff] in, and it could not have been five minutes later he came out and said, No good, he's scared and will destroy us. Our investigator could never understand why Elliott did this…As for the comment of Mike destroying us—to this day I don't know what he meant there because there was nothing truthful Mike could have said that would have destroyed me or anyone at Oglala that day.[116]

The prosecution moved to tighten its circumstantial net around Peltier, calling Wish Draper and Norman Brown as witnesses. Draper testified that he had seen Peltier carrying an AR-15 immediately after Coler and Williams were killed, although he was nowhere near their bodies at the time.[117] Brown testified that, early in the firefight, he had seen Peltier firing at the agents with a weapon that looked "like an M-16" from some distance away.[118] Angie Long Visitor was then forced to go through her degrading session in the witness chair (see Chapter 9), while both Marvin Bragg and Marion High Bull were dropped from the prosecution witness list.[119]

Perhaps fearing that the calibre of the accounts implicating Peltier lacked the authority to compel the jury, Hultman finished with an FBI "eyewitness" who had been conspicuously missing from the prosecution roster during the Butler-Robideau trial:

> Special Agent Fred Coward testified he saw Leonard Peltier on 26 June 1975. This alleged sighting, which he said took place around 3:45 p.m., was made through a 2x7 power rifle scope at a distance of one half mile as he was looking east. He supposedly identified Peltier [whom he had never seen before] running south [at a point close to Coler's and Williams' bodies, moving away from them, and carrying an AR-15]. Therefore, Peltier would have been seen in profile. It was a hot, sunny June day, and the day before had been rainy, so the mirage factor was high.[120]

Myrtle Poor Bear, an unbalanced Lakota woman, was held *incommunicado* and intimidated systematically by agents Price and Wood for over a month, thus induced to provide false affidavits and testimony against Peltier and Richard Marshall. Poor Bear later recanted everything and described the process by which her perjury had been obtained. (Photo: Lan Brookes Ritz)

The defense suggested that Judge Benson attempt to recognize a close ac-quaintance at a half mile's distance through such a low-powered scope, but his honor both declined the invitation and refused to allow the jury to make a similar attempt.[121] James R. Hall, an experienced outdoorsman and manager of a shop specializing in firearms, rifle scopes, and the like, was brought in by the defense to conduct a test in the presence of both a WKLDOC attorney and an FBI agent.[122] Hall subsequently testified that using a scope virtually identical to the one claimed by SA Coward, he had failed to recognize an acquaintance who was standing still and facing him at one half-mile on a crisp, overcast, 38° day with minimal mirage fac-tor; Hall "could not determine *any* facial features [emphasis added]" of his friend through such a scope at the required distance, even under ideal conditions.[123] Still, the "eyewitness i.d." of Peltier by an agent had gone to the jury, while much of the defense counter-argument had not. With that, the prosecution's case closed.

The defense attempted to move to impeach the entire manner in which the FBI and prosecution had obtained the circumstantial evidence presented against Peltier (no concrete evidence of his guilt ever having been offered in the government's case), thus destroying the credibility of the evidence itself. The key to this strategy lay in calling Myrtle Poor Bear whom Hultman had once again declined to put on the stand and whose supposed "eyewitness" accounts of Peltier's involvement in the deaths of Coler and Williams had resulted in his extradition from Canada. Judge Benson refused to allow her to be called by the defense, arguing (as did Hultman and Sikma) that any testimony she might offer concerning her earlier affidavits—and the manner in which they had been obtained by the Bureau—would be "irrelevant, irresponsible and immaterial,"[124] given that it would not pertain "*direct-ly* to the events of June 26, 1975."[125] Benson, however, agreed to hold an "offer of proof" hearing, out of the presence of the jury, in which the defense could attempt to demonstrate why Poor Bear should be allowed to testify, and how this would "shed light" on the nature of the government's case. Elliott Taikeff examined the witness during the hearing:

Taikeff: Do you know a person named Leonard Peltier?

Poor Bear: No...

Taikeff: Did you ever see him in your life?

Poor Bear: No.

Taikeff: Were you ever at the Jumping Bull area on the Pine Ridge Reservation?

Poor Bear: No.

Taikeff: Did you ever live with Leonard Peltier?

Poor Bear: No.

Taikeff: Last night did you tell me you were frightened?

Poor Bear: Yes, I did.

Taikeff: What were you frightened of?

Poor Bear: I don't know. I am scared of the Government.

Judge Benson: What was the answer?

Taikeff: I don't know. I am scared of the Government.

Taikeff: Did anyone from the Government ever say anything to make you afraid?

Poor Bear: The [FBI] agents are always talking about Anna Mae [Aquash].

Taikeff: What did they say about Anna Mae?

Poor Bear: Oh, they just would talk about that time she died.

Taikeff: What did they say about it? You can tell the judge, it's all right (Defense Counsel confer).

Taikeff: May counsel approach, your honor?

Judge Benson: You may.

Taikeff: (At the bench) Your honor, I would ask that your honor briefly advise her that she is under oath and you want to hear what she has to say providing it is the truth and that she has nothing to fear by telling the truth...She is very frightened, Your Honor. She told me last night she is afraid she is going to be killed, and that is why she is so upset at this particular moment.[126]

Shortly thereafter, Taikeff resumed his questioning:

Taikeff: What did [SAs David Price and William Wood] tell you about the American Indian Movement?

Poor Bear: They told me they were going to kill me.

Taikeff: Did Mr. Wood ever say anything about the subject of getting away with killing people?

Poor Bear: I think he did.

Taikeff: Do you recall what he said?

Poor Bear: He said that they could get away with killing because they were agents...[127]

When Assistant Prosecutor Lynn Crooks cross-examined Poor Bear, the following exchange occurred:

Crooks: Has anybody [meaning AIM] threatened to do anything to you if you did not change your story?

Poor Bear: No.

Crooks: Nobody even suggested it?

Poor Bear: No...

Crooks: Why were you signing these affidavits [incriminating Peltier]?

Poor Bear: I don't know.

Crooks: Well did [SA] Bill Wood threaten to harm you or hurt you if you didn't sign?

Poor Bear: (No response.)

Crooks: Can you answer that question?

After a 45 minute recess, the hearing resumed.

Taikeff: Your honor, I would like the record to reflect a 45 minute pause measured by the courtroom clock between the last question and the following question.

Crooks: Can you answer the question, Myrtle?

Poor Bear: I was forced to sign both [*sic:* there were three] of those papers.

Crooks: By whom?

Poor Bear: They said my family members were going to be hurt if I didn't do it. By [SAs] David Price and Bill Wood...[128]

In redirect examination, Taikeff followed up:

Taikeff: Do you remember Mr. Crooks, that's the man with the dark glasses, asked you a couple of times this afternoon about whether you were threatened by Agent Price or Agent Wood...

Poor Bear: Yes, I remember.

Taikeff: Do you remember when he asked you that question you remained silent for a very long time every time he asked you that question?

Poor Bear: Yes.

Taikeff: Why did you remain silent and not answer his question?

Poor Bear: Because they [the FBI] *did* threaten me.

Taikeff: Miss Poor Bear, will you please tell us whether Agent Price ever threatened you?

Poor Bear: Yes, he did.

Taikeff: What did he say to you?

Poor Bear: He told me they were going to plan everything out and if I didn't do it I was going to get hurt.

Taikeff: Did anybody else ever say that to you from the FBI?

Poor Bear: Bill Wood.[129]

This testimony corresponded well with a sworn statement Poor Bear had made in Canada on May 11, 1977, that:

I remember Dave Price and Bill Wood, the two FBI agents, telling me about Anna Mae Aquash. Dave described her body to me. He said from what he had heard she had been burnt and her clothes put back on her and that after her clothes were put back on she was shot...he showed me pictures of the body and said that if I don't cooperate this is what may happen to me...The two FBI agents constantly reminded me of what happened to Anna Mae Aquash. And every so often the FBI agents showed me pictures of Anna Mae Aquash's body and I was really scared...Bill Wood said that all the way along he knew that the body found on Pine Ridge was Anna Mae's body but that he had had her hands severed from her body and sent to Washington for identification and to verify his own observations.[130]

Price and Wood had been holding Poor Bear—on no particular charge—incommunicado in motels in Gordon, Nebraska, and Sturgis, South Dakota. Motel bills, signed receipts and other documents demonstrated conclusively that she had been in these agents' custody on February 19 and 23, 1976, the days on which she had signed false affidavits claiming variously to have witnessed the Oglala firefight first hand, and that she was Leonard Peltier's "girlfriend," to whom he'd confessed his guilt (this was the same story she gave with regard to Dick Marshall during *his* murder trial; see Chapter 12). Supposedly, Price and Wood "relinquished all custody" of Poor Bear on March 24, turning her over to SA Edward Skelly, who kept her—again incommunicado—at a motel in Belle Fourche, South Dakota.[131] She was still being held when she signed a third, again contradictory, affidavit "establishing" Peltier's guilt, on March 31, 1976.

Added to the virtual kidnapping of Poor Bear by Price and Wood, and the intimidation they had used in extracting her statements, was the fact that the FBI and prosecution had opted *not* to follow up on anything she said which did not pertain directly to Peltier. For instance, in the initial affidavit, Price and Wood had Poor Bear declare that she'd overheard Peltier discussing a plan to lure agents into an ambush on the Jumping Bull land. Such a conversation would not only provide proof of premeditation (the essential ingredient in first degree murder), but would lay the groundwork for a whole new charge: *conspiracy* to commit murder. The Bureau, however, proved utterly disinterested—never even posing the question to its "eyewitness"—in the identities of the other "conspirators."

Similarly, Poor Bear claimed to have witnessed not only Leonard Peltier, but an Oglala youth named Ricky Little Boy, "executing" SAs Williams and Coler on the fatal day. No effort was ever made to investigate seriously or to bring charges against Little Boy (there is no indication that this man was anywhere near the Jumping Bull property on June 26, 1975). The FBI extracted other allegations from Poor Bear: that she had been raped by Dino Butler and eight others prior to the firefight, that an Oglala woman named Madonna Slow Bear had forced her to watch the agents being killed, and so on. Cumulatively, such lack of enthusiasm by the Bureau in pursuing Poor Bear's various "leads" added up to the distinct probability that the FBI knew *from the beginning* that *none* of this woman's "evidence" was real. Yet it had nonetheless submitted *precisely* this evidence against Peltier in Canadian courts, a matter which led Canadian prosecutor Paul Halprin to profess "shock" at the Bureau's conduct.[132]

The final piece of the Poor Bear puzzle fell into place with clarification of the criteria by which the FBI seemed to have selected Myrtle Poor Bear as the initial linchpin of its "case": she was a "witness whose mental imbalance is so gross as to render her testimony [for the government, on the stand] unbelievable."[133] As Peltier himself put it:

Leonard Peltier in his cell at the "super-maximum" security federal penitentiary at Marion, IL, 1983. In 1985, he was moved to the standard maximum security facility at Leavenworth, KS. (Photo: Michael DuBois)

She is a poor, sick woman. I have no bad thoughts for her. She was a pawn to them [the FBI], and they used her like they have used so many Indian people.[134]

Unaccountably, lead defense attorney Taikeff made no effort to force Judge Benson to present Poor Bear to the jury. To the contrary, he suddenly agreed—over the vehement objections of co-counsels John Lowe and Bruce Ellison—with the prosecution that such matters were "irrelevant."[135] For his part, Benson then denied the offer of proof and declined to allow the jury to hear Poor Bear's testimony (on grounds that it might "prejudice" the government's case). This was followed by his refusal, in his charge to the jurors, to read them Jury Instruction #19:

Testimony has been given in this case which if believed by you shows that the Government induced witnesses to testify falsely. If you believe that the Government, or any of its agents, induced any witness to testify falsely in this case...this is affirmative evidence of the weakness of the Government's case.[136]

With Peltier's defense in shambles, assistant prosecutor Lynn Crooks felt emboldened to ignore marginal charges such as "aiding and abetting" of which the defendant might be found guilty and go for broke by arguing in his closing statement that the government had established proof of murder in the first degree:

There's no question about it...[the evidence] indicates that Leonard Peltier was not only the leader of [the Tent City AIM] group, he started the fight, he started the shooting, he executed these two human beings at point blank range.[137]

Although John Lowe repeatedly attempted to object that much of what Crooks was telling the jury was simply not a matter of trial record, Judge Benson overruled on each occasion.[138] Thus, on April 18, 1977—after only six hours of deliberation—the jury returned verdicts of guilty on two counts of first degree murder and, on

June 1, Benson imposed two *consecutive* life sentences as punishment. This sentencing, the harshest possible under the circumstances, had been predicted by Peltier in a pre-sentencing statement. Atypically, other than in political cases, the newly made convict—who had no prior felony convictions—was sent directly to the federal "super-maximum security" prison at Marion, Illinois, supposedly the repository for "incorrigible" criminals.

The Ordeal of Leonard Peltier

Elliot Taikeff "resigned" from WKLDOC immediately after the Peltier trial.[139] An appeal team composed of William Kunstler, Washington, D.C. attorney Michael Tigar, and Bruce Ellison (John Lowe continued to consult) was quickly assembled to see what could be salvaged from the disaster.[140] The record of government procedures utilized against Leonard Peltier both in and out of court was so rich in misconduct that by early December 1977, a massive appeal document had been filed in St. Louis with the U.S. Eighth Circuit Court.[141]

During the spring of 1978, a three judge panel composed of William Webster, Donald Ross, and Gerald W. Heaney heard the appeal. On April 12, Myrtle Poor Bear's role in the extradition of Peltier from Canada was taken up. This led to an exchange between Judge Ross and prosecutor Evan Hultman:

> *Judge Ross:* But anybody who read those affidavits would know that they contradict each other. And why the FBI and Prosecutor's office continued to extract more to put into these affidavits in hope to get Mr. Peltier back into the United States is beyond my understanding.
>
> *Hultman:* Yes...
>
> *Judge Ross:* Because you should have known, and the FBI should have known that you were pressuring this woman to add to her statement.
>
> *Hultman:* Your Honor, I personally was not present...[142]

Moments later, Hultman admitted that both he and the Bureau had been aware that "she was [mentally] incompetent in the utter, utter, utter ultimate sense of incompetency."[143] Ross then drew his own conclusion:

> *Judge Ross:* But can't you see, Mr. Hultman, that what happened happened in such a way that it gives some credence to the claim of the...
>
> *Hultman:* I understand, Your Honor...
>
> *Judge Ross:* ...the Indian people that the United States is willing to resort to *any* tactic in order to bring somebody back to the United States from Canada.
>
> *Hultman:* Judge...

Judge Ross: And if they are willing to do that, they must be willing to fabricate other evidence. And it's no wonder they are unhappy and disbelieve the things that happen in our courts when things like this happen.

Hultman: Judge Ross, I in no way do anything but agree with you totally.[144]

The judge then summed up that, "We have an obligation to [AIM people and their supporters], not only to treat them fairly, but not to give the appearance of manufacturing evidence by interrogating incompetent witnesses."[145] In its opinion on the appeal, the Eighth Circuit panel held that, "The use of affidavits of Poor Bear in the extradition proceedings was to say the least, a clear abuse of investigative process by the FBI." A number of other investigative and judicial procedure problems with the handling of Peltier's case were also noted, before it was acknowledged that:

As we stated earlier, Peltier's theory of the case was that the F.B.I. framed him by manufacturing evidence and inducing witnesses to testify in accordance with its theory of the [deaths of Coler and Williams]. The Poor Bear...testimony was certainly consistent with [Peltier's] theory.[146]

As Peter Matthiessen has observed,

Why the defense request for a new trial was denied, under these circumstances, seems somewhat mysterious, since as Judge Ross had pointed out, "If they were willing to [fabricate the Poor Bear affidavits], they must be willing to fabricate other evidence"— in other words, if the government is willing to present coerced or fabricated testimony why would it hesitate to present fabricated circumstantial evidence as well? With this query in mind, the rickety ballistics evidence purporting to link Peltier to the killings [not to mention the "eyewitness" account of SA Coward] becomes even more suspect than before.[147]

The panel's odd decision, in the face of all this, to allow Peltier's conviction to stand is perhaps explained by the fact that the presiding judge, William Webster, had already departed to assume a new title as *Director of the Federal Bureau of Investigation.*[148]

Apparently Webster "saw no impropriety in a future FBI head sitting in judgement on an appeal based on FBI abuses, for he did not remove himself from the case until the nomination had been made public...by this time...the damage to Peltier was done."[149]

Michael Tigar immediately filed an appeal of the Eighth Circuit ruling with the U.S. Supreme Court and,

On January 10, 1979, a round-the-clock vigil sponsored by the Leonard Peltier Defense Committee was begun outside the Supreme Court in Washington, D.C.; this vigil, led by John Trudell, Crow Dog, and others, continued day and night for fifty-five days, through the bitter weather that included some of the worst storms in the city's history...On February 11, in zero-degree temperatures, a protest march demanding a Supreme Court review of Peltier's case was harassed by dozens of police, many of them in riot gear, and the next day the Supreme Court refused to hear the appeal of the Fargo conviction, offering no explanation of its decision.[150]

As an infuriated appeals team member, Lew Gurwitz, put it that evening:

After all, it's their court system, it's all one government. There's so much FBI illegality here that they can't afford to have a new trial. They know he'd be found innocent. [But] this is a case which won't go away.[151]

Gurwitz's assessment was borne out as, in 1981, Amnesty International (AI) published an analysis, not only of Peltier's situation, but also those of BPP leader Geronimo Pratt (see Chapter 3) and AIM/OSCRO leader Richard Marshall (see Chapter 12)—also serving life sentences.[152] AI found strong indications in each of these cases that the activists had been victimized by the FBI's COINTELPRO campaigns, denied due process, and thus unfairly convicted and imprisoned.[153] The respected international human rights organization recommended that Peltier, Marshall and Pratt each be retried, and that a Commission of Inquiry once again be established to look into the nature of COINTELPRO-type operations by intelligence agencies in the U.S.

Also in 1981, after an FOIA suit, the Peltier appeal team received some 12,000 pages of the approximately 18,000 pages of RESMURS documents generated by the FBI during its investigation of the deaths of Coler and Williams. Although the 6,000 odd pages of RESMURS material withheld by the FBI—ostensibly on the basis of national security—undoubtedly contain the most damaging information (to the Bureau), defense attorneys were able to identify a number of exculpatory documents which had been denied to Peltier at trial. The massive stack of paper was found to contain evidence which contradicted testimony given during the trial by prosecution witnesses concerning the type of vehicle being followed by Coler and Williams and SA Coward's incredible scope sighting.[154] The newly released documents also indicated that the FBI had been aware that it could *not* be determined that SA Coler had been killed by a "small calibre, high velocity missile" such as a .223 calibre attributable to the AR-15 "linked" to Peltier.[155] Further, contrary to what the prosecution had insisted at trial, the Bureau had known that it was likely *neither* agent had been killed "at point blank range." Coler was known to have been first mortally wounded by a .44 magnum bullet fired from long range, while pathologist reports indicated that Williams' fatal head wound was probably the *first* injury he suffered, meaning that this bullet, too, was fired from a distance.[156]

Hence, the FBI and the prosecution had suppressed evidence that Coler might not have died from a .223 slug at all, and insisted—contrary to available evidence— that William's head wound had been the *last* injury inflicted upon him, administered after he was already disabled, and at close range. As Crooks had framed it at the trial:

Apparently Special Agent Williams was killed first. He was struck in the face and hand by the bullet...probably begging for his life, and he was shot. The back of his head was blown off by a high powered rifle...Leonard Peltier then turned, as the evidence indicates, to Jack Coler lying on the ground helpless. He shoots him in the top of the head. Apparently feeling he hadn't done a good enough job, he shoots him again through the jaw, and his face explodes. No shell even comes out, just explodes. The whole bottom of his chin is blown out by the force of the concussion. He dies. Blood splattered against the side of the car.[157]

Williams dying with the first bullet to strike him also served to destroy the neat chronology of events assembled by the Bureau, which had a number of FBI employees—including David Price's wife, Linda—testifying at both Cedar Rapids and Fargo that Williams had radioed "I'm hit!" at a certain point in the firefight, and raised the specter of a well-orchestrated and pervasive "game plan" of perjury utilizing not just vulnerable individuals, such as Myrtle Poor Bear and Mike Anderson, but even Bureau employees themselves. Additionally, it cast the FBI's steadfast refusal to release its audio tapes of agent radio transmissions made at Rapid City on June 26, 1975 in an entirely sinister light.[158]

Even more damaging to the government's case was a document which flatly contradicted FBI Firearms and Toolmarks expert Evan Hodge's trial testimony. As was mentioned earlier, Hodge testified that the results of the firing pin test on the Wichita AR-15 were *inconclusive* and he had therefore been forced to rely upon the less definitive extractor mark test to "match" the .223 casing, a test he had not performed until late December 1975 or early 1976. However, a Bureau Teletype dated October 2, 1975 indicated that Hodge performed the firing pin test almost immediately after receiving the Wichita AR with *negative* results:

Recovered .223 cal. Colt Rifle received from S.A. [Michael Gammage; name deleted in original document], BATF, contains *a different firing pin* than that in rifle used at RESMURS scene [emphasis added].[159]

In sum, once the Bureau had been forced to divulge even a portion of the documents it was legally obligated to provide to the defense at trial, the prosecution's "case" began to unravel rapidly. The new evidence destroyed the entire "casing in the trunk" thesis "establishing" that the "murder weapon" was an AR-15 and opened up the possibility that Williams was hit by any of a number of small calibre rifles, spent cartridges from which had been recovered by the Bureau after the firefight at ranges up to 300 meters from the bodies of Williams and Coler.[160] It also demolishes the "execution" scenario and the "lone gunman" idea assistant prosecutor Crooks utilized to such effect with the jury in his closing argument (and which tie so tidily to the "eyewitness" sightings sworn to by Norman Brown, Mike Anderson and SA Fred Coward).

Besides exculpatory documents illegally withheld by the prosecution, the FOIA material was found to contain other documents which indicated that Judge Benson had met with the FBI and U.S. Attorneys prior to the trial to discuss security arrangements. The FBI made an effort to impress upon the judge that there was a high probability of the trial proceeding being disrupted and its security jeopardized by unspecified AIM activities. They offered no proof for this allegation and ignored the fact that no such activities had occurred at the earlier Cedar Rapids RESMURS trial. Nonetheless, it is likely that the allegation had a prejudicial influence on the judge's attitude toward the defendant. The extreme security measures which resulted could not have failed to convey to the jury the idea that the defendant was a member of a dangerous terrorist organization.[161]

Armed with this newly discovered evidence, the appeal team was able to avoid the judicial dead end imposed by the Supreme Court's refusal to even hear Peltier's argument(s) in 1979. In April 1982, motions were filed in the District Court in Fargo, N.D. requesting that Peltier's conviction be dismissed, an evidentiary hearing be held, and the case be retried.[162] The motion was based on legal precedents in which the deliberate withholding of exculpatory evidence by the prosecution constituted grounds for "vacation of judgement" and retrial. A separate motion was filed in December 1982 requesting that Judge Benson remove himself from the case on the grounds that his *ex parte* communication with the prosecution and the FBI had prejudiced him against the defendant. Benson refused and on December 30, 1982 denied the motion for a new trial asserting that the newly discovered evidence had little significance and in any case was merely additive to evidence already presented by the defense.

On appeal of the denial, the Eighth Circuit Court took exception to Benson's opinion. The three judge panel composed of Judges Donald Ross, Gerald Heaney and John Gibson held that the FBI's ballistics evidence was pivotal to the government's successful prosecution of Peltier:

> The importance of [the ballistics evidence] to the government's case against Peltier cannot be ignored. During the argument to the jury at the close of the trial, counsel for the government stated, "One shell casing is ejected into the trunk of the agent's car which was open, one shell casing, perhaps *the single most important piece of evidence in this case.* This little, small cartridge is ejected by the killers into the trunk of the car..." Tr. at 4996 (April 15, 1977). We [the Eighth Circuit Court] recognized the importance of the casing in our opinion on direct appeal. We noted, "The .223 caliber casing *allegedly* found in the trunk of Coler's car was critical evidence against Peltier [emphasis added]."[163]

In April 1984, citing the October 2, 1975 teletype, the panel ordered Judge Benson to reopen the Peltier case to the extent of conducting an evidentiary hearing, albeit on the extremely narrow question of the FBI documents relating to the ballistics evidence. At this hearing, which Benson grudgingly scheduled in Bismarck, North Dakota—with all the "security" fanfare by the Bureau which had accompanied both RESMURS trials—at the end of October 1984, Evan Hodge was called to the stand to explain the glaring discrepancies between his trial testimony and documentary evidence which had subsequently emerged. During direct examination by appeal attorney William Kunstler, Hodge suggested that the whole matter was a misunderstanding, based in "confusion" attending the "interpretation" of various documents, such as the firing pin teletype.

Hodge went on to explain that the October 2 teletype referred not to the cartridge found in the trunk of SA Coler's car but to seven other cartridges from an AR-15 which had been found near the "green house," in the Jumping Bull Compound.[164] The FBI has never determined which AR-15 fired these cartridges. Hence the FBI knew at the time of the Fargo trial that at least one other AR-15 might have been fired at Coler and Williams during the firefight and that the "single AR-15" argument, used in the trial to tie Peltier to the Wichita AR-15, was entirely suspect.[165]

When pressed by the defense to explain why he had waited another three months to perform the extractor test with which he linked the Wichita AR-15 to the cartridge from Coler's trunk, "Agent Hodge...claimed delay in examining the crucial casing [because] he was not aware of any particular urgency connected to the casing, and had not received any priority request concerning it..."[166] He further contended that he was delayed in performing the test due to the large volume of work associated with the RESMURS investigation which had to be completed by him and his sole assistant, Joseph Twardowski. He also claimed that he had personally performed all the critical tests on the RESMURS ballistics evidence.[167] Both of these assertions were patently false.

Concerning his lack of awareness of the significance of the .223 casing, the Eighth Circuit Court was to conclude that it was, "facially inconsistent with the newly-discovered evidence, which included several teletypes from FBI officials, agents requesting [Hodge] to compare submitted AR-15 rifle with .223 casings found at the scene, and [Hodge's] response to these teletypes..."[168] As to his having performed all of the tests himself, Hodge was confronted during the evidentiary hearing with the fact that the critical lab notes which linked the Wichita AR-15 to the .223 casing bore handwriting which was clearly not his. Hodge replied that the handwriting was that of his assistant, Joseph Twardowski.[169] When the defense team asked that the notes be examined by a handwriting expert, Judge Benson granted the request over vigorous objections from the prosecution. Shortly after the hearing adjourned, defense attorneys were summoned to the judge's chambers where an embarrassed Evan Hodge explained that he had "misspoken" (i.e., perjured himself) during the hearing, and that he did not know whose handwriting appeared on the critical notes. The handwriting was eventually identified as that of a laboratory trainee, William Albrecht, thereby casting further doubt on the chain of custody of the evidence and increasing the probability that the cartridge had been deliberately or inadvertently switched in the lab.[170]

By the time of the oral arguments before the Eighth Circuit on October 15, 1985, it was clear that the prosecution's circumstantial ballistics case was disintegrating. Prosecutor Lynn Crooks then attempted a remarkable about-face. Counter to his own grandiloquent presentation to the jury at trial, he now contended that it had never been the government's intention to establish that Leonard Peltier had actually killed Coler and Williams himself: "We can't prove who shot those agents," he admitted.[171] However, he asserted that this was of no consequence since Peltier had been tried for "aiding and abetting" in their deaths. This turnabout seemed to induce a certain bewilderment on the part of Judge Heaney, and Crooks, as well:

Judge Heaney: Aiding and abetting Robideau and Butler?

Crooks: Aiding and abetting whoever did the final shooting. Perhaps aiding and abetting himself. And hopefully the jury would believe that in effect he did it all. But aiding and abetting, nevertheless.[172]

A bit earlier, Judge Heaney had spelled out the seriousness of this reversal for the government's case:

Judge Heaney: Just let me make myself a little more clear. It seems to me that this would have been an entirely different case, both in terms of the manner in which it was presented to the jury and the sentence that the judge imposed, if the only evidence that you have was that Leonard Peltier was participating on the periphery of the fire fight and the agents got killed. Now that would have been an entirely different case. But the evidence here is that the agents were killed at close range and that Peltier was at the vehicles so he could have done the killing and that even though somebody else may have pulled the trigger, he had the AR-15 and was there with those other two men and that therefore they were directly implicated. Because I doubt that if all he had been was, like Brown who was also shooting, and a number of others who were also shooting from the periphery, I don't think this would have been the same case at all.[173]

Confronted with contradictions of this magnitude, Judges Heaney, Ross and Gibson "deliberated" on this matter for nearly a year before tendering their decision on September 11, 1986. All three members of the panel agreed that Lynn Crooks' argument that Peltier had been convicted of aiding and abetting was without merit, the prosecution having clearly argued at the trial that Peltier was "the principal" in a case of first-degree murder. They also agreed that the government's original contention that only Peltier had carried an AR-15 during the firefight was incorrect, evidence of "several" such weapons now having plainly emerged (in other words, the original case against Peltier no longer existed at all). Then they admitted experiencing "discomfort" with their own reasoning before determining that the presentation of the new ballistics information before the Fargo jury might "possibly" have changed the verdict. In conclusion, they observed that recent Supreme Court standards require that such new evidence must add up to the assessment that the jury's verdict would "probably" have been changed, had the jurors been exposed to the information at trial. Therefore, there would be no new trial, and Peltier's conviction would be allowed to stand.

A deeper insight into the panel's motivations in arriving at this conclusion may be readily discerned in a single peripheral paragraph:

There are only two alternatives...to the government's contention that the .223 casing was ejected into the trunk of Coler's car when the Wichita AR-15 was fired at the agents. One alternative is that the .223 casing was planted in the trunk of Coler's car either before its discovery by the investigating agents or by the agents who reported its discovery. The other alternative is that a non-matching casing was originally found in the trunk and sent to the FBI laboratory, only to be replaced by a matching casing when the importance of a match to the Wichita AR-15 became evident... *We recognize that there is evidence in this record of improper conduct on the part of some FBI agents, but we are reluctant to impute even further improprieties to them* [emphasis added].[174]

Thus, it was deemed more appropriate that Leonard Peltier remain locked away in a maximum security cell rather than expose the FBI to further scrutiny concerning the way in which it had obtained his conviction, even *after* a clear pattern of Bureau misconduct had been demonstrated. In desperation, the appeal team filed a motion for an *en banc* hearing, wherein the full Eighth Circuit Court would convene to review the decision of its three judge panel.[175] After several months, this too was denied, essentially on the grounds that such a review would demean the dignity of Judges Heaney, Ross, and Gibson.[176] The only remaining option was the filing of another appeal to the Supreme Court, which was done on the basis that the high court needed to resolve the issue of whether illegally withheld exculpatory evidence need be sufficient to "probably" reverse the original jury verdict, or whether evidence which would "possibly" lead to this outcome is sufficient to warrant ordering of a retrial (as other Appeals Courts had interpreted it).[177] On October 5, 1987, the Supreme Court for the second time refused to consider an appeal in the case of Leonard Peltier. As in the first instance, no reason for this decision was offered.[178]

As of this writing, Leonard Peltier has spent some ten and one-half years in prison (excluding ten months in Oakalla awaiting extradition, and six months jail time before and during his trial)—almost all of this time in maximum security institutions, and much of this in solitary confinement or under conditions of general "lockdown"—without ever experiencing anything approximating a fair hearing.[179] Meanwhile, he has been selected to receive the International Human Rights Prize for 1986 by the Human Rights Commission of Spain.[180] As of late 1986, fifty-one members of the Canadian Parliament had officially issued a call to the United States to undertake a new trial; six of the endorsers held cabinet level positions in the Canadian government (including the post of Solicitor General) at the time of Peltier's extradition. M.P. Jim Fulton, a sponsor of Canada's parliamentary petition supporting Peltier, has gone on record observing:

[The nature of Peltier's extradition] constitutes treaty fraud between our nations and should we sleep on this case we can surely expect a repetition in the future...As a nation we should call for the return of Leonard Peltier. He was fraudulently extradited...[181]

Peltier's case has also been submitted to the United Nations Commission on Human Rights through its Working Group on Indigenous Populations.[182] Some 14,000,000 people world-wide have signed petitions demanding a retrial and in 1987

Peltier requested that the Soviet Union grant him status as a political prisoner and offer him sanctuary on its soil, should the U.S. government agree to his release from confinement under conditions of exile:[183] The request stated:

> No man nor woman who truly loves their homeland wants to leave; however, because there is no justice for myself and because there is no justice for my People, I am making this request for political asylum in your Great Nation.

> My People are living in some of the worst conditions in America, perhaps some of the worst conditions in the world. I can do nothing for my People where I am. For my People, "the American Dream" is a 20th Century Nightmare. I want the world to know this...[184]

International attention to the Peltier case continues to mount, rather than abate, a circumstance which validates Lew Gurwitz's 1979 prediction that it simply "won't go away."

Still, despite such growing exposure and the embarrassment this undoubtedly entails for the government as a whole, all conventional doors of the legal process remain slammed in Peltier's face. At this juncture, only two possibilities present themselves. One is that the matter could be resolved by the granting of a Presidential pardon. Barring this extremely unlikely action, the Congress of the United States could convene a formal investigation into the FBI activities surrounding—indeed, *engulfing*—the Peltier case, forcing for the first time a *full* disclosure by the Bureau of relevant information. While the Congress is not empowered to order Peltier's release or retrial, it is a virtual certainty that any investigation it undertook along these lines would generate another raft of "newly discovered evidence" with which the Peltier appeal team could once again go before the District Court, calling for a new trial. And, in such a changed political environment as would be indicated by a Congressional investigation of FBI abuses, it seems likely a retrial would be finally granted.

Meanwhile, the simple fact that Leonard Peltier remains in prison, even after a truly vicious pattern of federal misconduct in his case has been repeatedly demonstrated (and acknowledged by the courts), offers ample testimony to the ongoing power of the FBI to abort the judicial process. In this sense, not much has really changed since the COINTELPRO era of the late 1960s. By the same token, the lengths to which the Bureau has demonstrably been prepared to go in order to keep Peltier in prison, a symbol of the FBI's ultimate "victory" over AIM, speaks for itself. They have made of this man an example neither he nor they ever intended; the freedom of Leonard Peltier has in many ways become the test of whether the people or the police are ascendant in American life.

Chapter 12

Other Political Abuses of
the Judicial System

AIM's most militant leaders and followers are under indictment, in jail or warrants are out for their arrest. But the government can win, even if no one goes
to jail.

—Colonel Volney Warner, 1974

The Banks-Means "Wounded Knee Leadership Trial" and the RESMURS trials
hardly exhaust the list of instances of federal foul play in subverting, or attempting
to subvert, the judicial process during the height of the FBI's war on AIM. There
were literally thousands of cases filed against AIM members and supporters between
1972 and 1976, the vast bulk of which were demonstrably unfounded; in this sense,
the so-called "Consolidated Wounded Knee Cases" of more than forty grassroots
AIM members and the various trials of individuals around the country who were accused of having tendered material support to AIM/ION, are but the tip of the prover-
bial iceberg. Viewed as a whole, the situation can hardly be described as other than
the cynical use by federal officials of the judicial process itself as an instrument of
political repression. Win, lose or draw in court, AIM was simply overwhelmed by
the unending waves of costly, time consuming and psychologically destructive
"legalisms" advanced by government representatives operating on the basis of in-
exhaustible resources and apparently immune from punishment, regardless of the
misconduct engaged in.

While the general level of legalistic repression visited upon AIM was both
remarkable and deadening, there were times when the magnitude of federal vicious-
ness in particular cases calls them forth for special attention. The Wounded Knee
Leadership Trial and RESMURS trials are proof of this. The following three examples
will establish that these were not isolated instances.

The Case of Leonard Crow Dog

As was noted in Chapter 5, traditional Brulé Lakota (Rosebud Sioux) holy man
Leonard Crow Dog had been a mainstay of the bridge between AIM and reserva-

The famous "postal inspectors" detained at Wounded Knee on March 11, 1973. Although AIM leader Stan Holder took responsibility for the detention and stated that Leonard Crow Dog had no role in it, the AIM spiritual leader was nonetheless convicted of "aiding and abetting." (Photo: *Akwesasne Notes*)

tion grassroots people at Wounded Knee. Insofar as one of the FBI's primary objectives in its anti-AIM campaign was to sever precisely such linkages, isolating AIM and denying it a viable base of support, Crow Dog quickly became a prime target for neutralization. This became apparent in the immediate aftermath of the Wounded Knee siege when, contrary to his actual role as a spiritual practitioner within the hamlet, he was designated by the government—along with such political figures as Russell Means, Dennis Banks, Stan Holder, Carter Camp and Pedro Bissonette—as being among the group constituting "the Wounded Knee leadership." (One can only wonder at what rationale the FBI used in excluding women such as Gladys Bissonette and Ellen Moves Camp from this masculine roster.)[1]

After the Means-Banks charges were dismissed because of federal misconduct in September 1974 (Chapter 11):

> ...the charges against Leonard Crow Dog, Carter Camp and Stan Holder [Pedro Bissonette having by this time been assassinated; see Chapter 7] were reduced from the original eleven counts to three. They were tried eventually, in June, 1975, in Cedar Rapids, Iowa, and once again the prosecutor was R.D. Hurd [who had been cited for misconduct at the end of the Banks-Means trial]; this time, Hurd won his convictions.[2]

Rex Weyler explains the gravity of the case which Hurd had won, and the outcome:

Crow Dog was first brought to trial in U.S. courts for his involvement in an incident on March 11, 1973, during the siege of Wounded Knee. On that day six men entered the Wounded Knee village, four of them claiming to be postal inspectors who were there to "examine the post office in the trading post." The men were detained and searched, and found to be carrying pistols and handcuffs. Two were suspected goons, and photographs later showed them toting guns on a Dickie Wilson roadblock. Crow Dog was among the group that disarmed the men and sent them away...Crow Dog was convicted of "aiding and abetting" an assault, interfering with a federal official and robbery, for which he received a three-year and an eight-year sentence.[3]

Crow Dog was released on probation (Camp and Holder having gone underground and failing to show up for sentencing) by Judge Edward McManus, who would shortly preside over the Butler-Robideau RESMURS trial (see Chapter 11), and at the time dubbed "Speedie Eddie" by AIM people because of his having slammed through the remaining leadership cases in less than a month. Obviously, the FBI was less than satisfied with an outcome which, although it resulted (finally) in some sort of convictions against AIM, left a "guilty party" such as Crow Dog at large to continue organizing. A result of this Bureau perspective was that he "was to become the only one of the leaders brought to trial who ever spent a day in prison on charges directly related to Wounded Knee."[4] But, this too involved a separate case.

Crow Dog's *real* legal "difficulties" may be said to have begun on September 2, 1975, when two known GOONs, William McCloskey and Robert Beck (a non-Indian who had been present at the July 25 shooting death of Crow Dog's nephew, AIM member Andrew Paul Stewart, on Pine Ridge, but who had never been so much as questioned in the matter by the FBI or BIA police) drove out to Crow Dog's home for reasons which have never been explained. Upon arrival at the remote "Crow Dog's Paradise," the two GOONs were met at the gate by another nephew, fifteen-year-old Frank Running, who told them they were unwelcome and asked that they leave. The boy was physically assaulted by both Beck and McCloskey before they drove off.[5] This might have been the end of things but:

> After midnight on the evening of the skirmish, Beck and McCloskey—who acknowledged later that he and Beck had been the aggressors—drove out to Grass Mountain [the location of Crow Dog's Paradise] to pick another fight; this time the Runnings and their friends beat hell out of the goons, after which Beck lodged a complaint with the police.[6]

The next day, September 4, Robert Beck was seen "riding in an FBI car" in the vicinity of the Crow Dog property,[7] and then—at 6 a.m. on September 5—came the massive air assault on Crow Dog's Paradise and the adjoining property of Al Running (see Chapter 9). The whole extravaganza was staged on the ostensible basis of the Bureau's need to serve assault and battery warrants on five people— Crow Dog, Al Running, Frank Running, Gerald Millard and Owen Young, Jr.—pursuant to the second altercation with Beck and McCloskey; "[t]he Indians believe that, whether or not Beck set it up, the episode was used by the FBI in the same way it had used the cowboy-boot episode involving Jimmy Eagle—as an excuse for another paramilitary raid."[8]

The September 5 raid was a direct violation of an official agreement, arrived at between the BIA, traditional spiritual leaders and the Rosebud tribal government in the wake of the Oglala firefight, that the FBI would not conduct such operations on the relatively peaceful reservation without prior notification to both the BIA Superintendent and Tribal president. The Bureau attempted to retroactively justify this breach by conducting a press conference in Rapid City on the evening of September 5. At this time External Affairs Officer Tom Coll grimly announced that "various weapons were seized" in the raid; among the items listed under evidence illustrating this fact were fingernail clippers, string and a tampon.[9]

Despite statements by Rosebud Tribal President Robert Burnette that both Beck and McCloskey were "notorious trouble makers" and protesting the FBI's invasion of his reservation,[10] as well as assertions by witnesses that Crow Dog had not—indeed *could not* have—taken part in the fight with the GOONs, the spiritual leader was held for immediate trial.[11] On its face, this was not so much because of the Beck-McCloskey matter, *per se,* but because of Crow Dog's apparent violation of a constitutionally dubious probation stipulation imposed by Judge McManus after the Wounded Knee trial, forbidding him to "consort with Indian militant types" for five years.[12]

Rather than making an effort to get to the bottom of what had actually occurred at Crow Dog's Paradise in the early morning hours of September 2, the FBI proceeded to disrupt any possibility of Crow Dog mounting a coherent defense. On October 4, 1975, SAC Norman Zigrossi himself led a raid on the Rapid City office of WKLDOC, in which files were dumped and legal papers scattered about; other defense materials were seized.[13] SAs David Price and J. Gary Adams figured prominently in Zigrossi's raid and, two weeks later, Price was a leading actor in a similar Bureau raid conducted on the WKLDOC office in Sioux Falls.[14]

Crow Dog was taken to trial in Rapid City before Federal District Judge Robert Merhige, on loan from Virginia to "clear up South Dakota's docket of AIM cases before Thanksgiving."[15] On November 28, 1975, Crow Dog was found guilty by an all-white jury:

> As at Cedar Rapids, Crow Dog's prosecutor was R.D. Hurd, attired as always in bright sport clothes, who recoiled from the defense suggestion that Crow Dog had been set up for the assault charge. "The Government is here to protect you!" Hurd told the jury. "I am here to protect you!" At this he placed his hand on his heart. "Would you believe, ladies and gentlemen, that the Government, *your* Government, would lie to you?"[16]

Although several witnesses testified that Crow Dog had taken no part in physically ejecting Beck and McCloskey from his property, Judge Merhige honored Hurd's request that "the maximum penalty" be imposed. "As a spiritual leader," said the judge, "[Crow Dog] should have prevented the fight."[17] Gerald Millard, who acknow-

Crow Dog leading a prayer inside Wounded Knee during the siege of 1973. Federal Judge Robert Merhige "reasoned" that the spiritual leader should have utilized his position to prevent his people from demanding their rights, and imposed the harshest possible sentence upon him. (Photo: Kevin Barry McKiernan)

ledged direct participation in the altercation, was sentenced to three years imprisonment, while Crow Dog received a five year sentence for "aiding and abetting" it. Prosecutor Hurd then entered a motion for revocation of Crow Dog's probation—he requested *consecutive* sentencing, which would have totaled ten years—which Judge Edward McManus refused to honor.[18]

During the trial, GOONs had attacked the home of Crow Dog's parents, Henry and Gertrude (both AIM supporters) at Grass Mountain, setting it ablaze; although the two elderly people survived, their home, sacred objects and other personal possessions were completely destroyed.[19] Crow Dog himself was immediately whisked off to the state's maximum security prison at Sioux Falls where he was incarcerated for several weeks before "accommodations" were secured for him in a federal cell. He was transferred, first to the U.S. medium security facility in Wichita, Kan., and then to the maximum security institution in Lewisburg, Pennsylvania.[20]

Unsatisfied that the "dangerous" holy man had been sufficiently neutralized—or that his example was sufficiently "chilling" to AIM members and supporters—the government brought yet a *third* case against him in January 1976. This time, "the charges stemmed from an incident on March 25, 1975 when three white men, previously unknown to Crow Dog, visited his home. Crow Dog, his wife Mary, and other witnesses claim that the three men were drunk and aggressive."[21] As the matter is put by a witness:

One of [the white men], Royer Pfersick, made a crude pass at Mary...in full sight of everybody. Crow Dog tells him: "This is my home, a medicine man's home. You can't do this here." Pfersick answers, "Who the hell are you, telling me what to do?" He hits Crow Dog and splits his lip. A relative and visitor take Crow Dog's part, and Pfersick is finally thrown out in a free-for-all.[22]

Crow Dog was transported from Lewisburg, back to Rapid City for the trial; his judge was once again Robert Merhige (who had failed to meet his Thanksgiving deadline), his prosecutor R.D. Hurd, his jury all-white. In a virtual replay of his successful speech at the previous trial, Hurd argued in his closing: "Ladies and gentlemen [of the jury], we have a good system going here in this country. The government is here to protect you. I am here to protect you."[23] Tellingly, he also announced that it was the government's contention that Pfersick was not "beaten because he made a pass at Crow Dog's wife. He was beaten because the Indians thought he was an [FBI] informer!"[24] With that, Crow Dog was found guilty on all counts and sentenced to yet another five-year prison term, to run consecutively with the one he was already serving.[25]

Crow Dog was immediately removed, *not* back to Lewisberg but to the federal maximum security facility at Terre Haute, Indiana, where he was held for two weeks. From there, he began an odyssey which carried him to at least nine different facilities in barely six months, before he landed in "the grandfather of all prisons" at Leavenworth, Kansas.[26] WKLDOC attorney Lew Gurwitz notes that Crow Dog was always transported incommunicado and without prior notice to either his family or lawyers: "No adequate explanation was ever offered for this amazing series of moves. We could only conclude that the handling of Crow Dog's incarceration amounted to a combination of deliberate psychological torture—both of him *and* his family and friends—and an effort to prevent his receipt of adequate legal counsel on appeal."[27]

Meanwhile, William McCloskey, one of the two GOONs whose alleged assault had led to Crow Dog's being jailed in the first place, had written a letter to Judge Merhige, "expressing regret that he had accused Crow Dog, whom he called a holy man, peacemaker, and healer who should be released."[28] Crow Dog's federal keepers responded to this turn of events by adding a new dimension to the psychological harassment of their prisoner:

Richard Erdoes recalls that his friend Crow Dog lost forty-five pounds in the two weeks at Terre Haute, and in Richmond a medical examiner told Crow Dog that they had found a brain tumor, and that he would need an operation. Crow Dog phoned Erdoes and asked: "Richard, can they do this to me? Cut into my brain without my consent?"[29]

The situation was so grotesque that the "National Council of Churches, the U.S. Civil Rights Commission and Amnesty International took up Crow Dog's case. He avoided brain surgery, but remained in prison [at Leavenworth] until paroled on March 21, 1977."[30] Cumulatively, at the time of his release, he had spent some 27 months under lock-and-key, and under what were particularly ugly conditions, for what amounted—at most—to having observed the commission of three rather petty offenses. As Wallace Black Elk, the Oglala spiritual leader who served as Crow Dog's assistant at Wounded Knee, was to put it several years later: "What them FBI did to Leonard, it took a lot out of him. He just wasn't the same after he came out of prison."[31]

The Dick Marshall Case

At about midnight on the evening of March 1, 1975, a twenty-eight-year-old Oglala named Martin Montileaux was drinking in the Longhorn Bar, in the tiny town of Scenic, S.D., just across the reservation line on the road to Rapid City. Montileaux and several others, including a woman named Marion Poor Bear, had been at the bar since mid-afternoon. Somewhere around 11:40 p.m., another group, including AIM/OSCRO leader Richard "Dick" Marshall,[32] his wife Cleo, Russell Means and AIM member Evelyn Bordeaux arrived. A few minutes later, as the AIM group was leaving, a shot was heard in the men's room of the bar. As Halley Merrill, owner of the Longhorn, later put it: "We found [Martin] Montileaux sitting on the floor of the john, shot in the neck."[33]

Evelyn Bordeaux recalls:

> We were drinking that evening, and we stopped in Scenic to pick up some beer; we were going on, so I never got out of the car. When them guys [Marshall, Means, *et al.*] came out, I never had any feeling they was in a rush or anything was wrong.[34]

Bar owner Merrill, who had been cited by AIM as a probable fence for stolen goods from the reservation and as being a bootlegger, had instructed his grandson to phone Pennington County (S.D.) Sheriff Mel Larson as soon as Means entered the Longhorn; that is, well *before* the shooting of Montileaux. Hence, it appears that sheriff's deputies were moving to intercept the AIM group prior to any "incident" having occurred.[35] Bordeaux continues:

> I was in the convertible—that was the first car—and there were three other cars, and we all headed for Rapid, but none of them other cars was stopped, only the one with Russ in it. When they caught up with us, they were chasing us around this tourist court, and finally the sheriff rammed us from the back so hard that Russ got hurt when his face hit the windshield or the mirror. Then we heard this bullhorn: Come out with your hands up! [Then they] took us to jail...[36]

During the chase, Marshall had exchanged his coat for Means' distinctive brown and white cowhide jacket, in an apparent effort to confuse the pursuers as to who was who. While Sheriff Larson's deputies would attempt to project this as an indication of guilt in the Montileaux shooting, WKLDOC coordinator Ken Tilsen offers the alternative explanation that the group initially imagined they were being chased by GOONs and that Marshall was desperately attempting to protect Means, a prime GOON target who "had already been the victim of two shootings [he would

AIM/OSCRO leader Dick Marshall was expressedly and repeatedly *not* identified as his assailant by victim Martin Montileaux and other eyewitnesses. Subsequent to Montileaux's death, Marshall was given a life sentence on the basis of Myrtle Poor Bear's testimony, fabricated by FBI agents Price and Wood. (Photo: *Oyate Wichaho*)

suffer a third within two months] and several serious beatings. It was the sort of thing Dick [Marshall] would do."[37]

In any event, as the AIM members were taken to the Pennington County Jail in Rapid City on the morning of March 2, Martin Montileaux was rushed to the hospital in the same town. On March 3, the FBI made clear its intentions to become involved in this "purely local law enforcement matter":

> This investigation is based upon information which indicates the subject is engaged in activities which could involve a violation of Title 18, U.S. Code, Section 2383 (Rebellion or Insurrection) or 2384 (Seditious Conspiracy), as indicated hereafter. The subject has been identified as being actively involved in militant activities of AIM...AIM has been actively involved in demonstrations and violent confrontations with local authorities...The above individual was arrested 3/1/75 [sic] with RUSSELL MEANS, AIM leader, after a high speed chase by members of the SD Highway Patrol and Pennington County Sheriff's Office. MEANS and RICHARD MARSHALL are subjects in a shooting at the Scenic, S.D. Bar in which the victim remains paralyzed [*sic*].[38]

"Coincidental" to the issuance of this memorandum, WKLDOC reported that at least twenty AIM leaders and members were arrested within twenty-four hours around the country, a situation which was described as being part of an FBI "national offensive against AIM people in the wake of a civil war on the Pine Ridge reservation."[39] Meanwhile, Pennington County Sheriff's deputy Donald Phillips was interviewing Martin Montileaux in the hospital, attempting to follow up on statements made by Halley Merrill and his daughter, Twila, that they had witnessed both Russell Means and Dick Marshall follow the victim into the restroom on the night of March 1:

Phillips: Martin, can you talk?

Montileaux: Yeah.

Phillips: Do you know who shot you?

Montileaux: No.

Phillips: You told me last night.

Montileaux: No I didn't. I don't know. I don't know him.

Phillips: Could you, how many people were in the bathroom with you?

Montileaux: Just me and that guy [the assailant].[40]

Both Phillips and Twila Merrill were contending that, as the deputy had knelt over Montileaux on the restroom floor at the Longhorn, he had asked the wounded man who had shot him, and that Montileaux had responded, "Means' friend." Thus, despite the victim's flat denial that he'd made any such statement, Phillips kept at it. And, despite Montileaux's clear statements that *only* he and his attacker were in the men's room at the time of the shooting, the deputy made a blatant effort to play upon the victim's fears, attempting to obtain direct incrimination of Means as well:

Phillips: How about the other guy that was in there with him, do you know him? Do you know you're pretty serious Martin? Can you hear me, Martin? Can you hear me?[41]

Phillips proceeded with relentless consistency. As the process is summarized elsewhere:

The following day, when Phillips returned to the hospital a second time, he asked the patient if he could recognize the man who shot him from a photograph, and Montileaux said, "Probably." Despite this answer (or perhaps because of it), he was never shown a photograph, or a suspect either; Phillips said this was because he thought the patient would recover. By now the dying man had come around to Phillips' opinion that there had been not one but two men in the men's room, that they had come in not before [as Montileaux had originally stated], but *after* his arrival, and that one of the two was Russell Means, who he had greeted.[42]

There were still problems with making the victim's account square with the police "theory" of the shooting however: "[Montileaux] insisted that Means had *not* shot him, and he did not know the identity of the other man, who was wearing an 'army coat' and had 'shaggy hair.' In the course of the interview, having led Montileaux to say that he was afraid of AIM and that AIM might kill him if he testified, Phillips said, 'Oh, I think we can prevent that. You are not in good shape now; and I'd hate to see these guys go free, especially if they're some big AIM leaders, wouldn't you?' In the third and final interview, on March 5, Phillips asked Montileaux if he knew Richard Marshall, and he said he did not. Phillips also made two more attempts to get Montileaux to implicate Means, which he would not do."[43]

Even Montileaux's description of his assailant—which the police were trying to make fit Dick Marshall—was very wide of the mark. No one had reported Marshall to be wearing anything which could be considered an "army coat" on the night of March 1, and his hair—worn in his customary neat braid down his back at the time of his arrest—could, by no reasonable interpretation, have been considered "shaggy." Phillips determinedly attempted to correct this problem during the last interview:

Montileaux: [The attacker] was a shaggy-headed guy.

Phillips: Uh-huh. Was his hair in a pony tail?

Montileaux: Yeah. No, it wasn't in a pony tail.

Phillips: No pony tail?

Montileaux: Unh-unh [negative reply].

Phillips: Was...do you know a guy by the name of Richard Marshall?

Montileaux: Unh-unh [negative reply].[44]

On March 15, 1975, Martin Montileaux died of complications stemming from his gunshot wound, and the South Dakota Attorney General's office, "receiving more encouragement from the FBI than from the victim,"[45] filed first degree murder charges against Russell Means and Dick Marshall. The state contended that it had two "eyewitnesses"—both of whom had known Marshall "for years"—who had seen him and Means follow Montileaux into the restroom on the fatal evening; a shot and a thump were heard moments later, and the two AIM leaders were then seen to walk directly from the restroom, through the bar, get into their car and drive away.[46] "They were smiling when they left," said one of the witnesses.[47]

A major difficulty with this tidy prospectus developed for the police, however, when both of these star witnesses—Halley Merrill and Montileaux's girlfriend, Marion Poor Bear—each of whom professed long-term familiarity with Dick Marshall, proved completely unable to pick him out of a standard police lineup.[48] This situation caused the Means-Marshall defense team to move that the cases of their clients be severed and tried separately.[49] This motion was quickly granted.

As the time of Marshall's trial approached, in mid-March 1976, the state's case was virtually non-existent. Despite Deputy Phillips' best efforts, the victim's own description of his killer clearly militated against Marshall being the guilty party; both "eyewitness" accounts were severely undercut by the witnesses' failure to identify him; and a ballistics test had failed to match a .22 caliber revolver found in the Means-Marshall car—which the police had contended was the murder weapon—with the slug which actually struck Martin Montileaux.[50] The state also could come up with no plausible motive as to why Marshall might have wished to kill Montileaux. Marshall was therefore offered a plea bargain arrangement which would have allowed him to eliminate the first degree murder charges against him in exchange for pleading guilty to a lesser, manslaughter charge; he refused this, contending complete innocence.[51]

Suddenly, however, the prosecution was miraculously presented with a witness who could plug the holes in its badly leaking case: the ubiquitous Myrtle Poor Bear (Marion's cousin), who had grown up in the same village as Marshall and was thus well acquainted with his physical appearance. Poor Bear, who had been brought to the Pennington County Sheriff's Office on March 22 by FBI agents David Price and William Wood,[52] had a most interesting tale to tell:

[She] identified herself as a friend of the defendant and his wife, Cleo, and hinted that she had been Dick Marshall's girl friend [the same relationship she simultaneously claimed with Leonard Peltier]. Like Louis Moves Camp [also provided as a witness by SA David Price; see Chapter 11], Myrtle Poor Bear filled in all the missing pieces in the prosecution's case. She testified that Marshall had the motive necessary to sustain the first-degree murder charge, namely, a beating by Montileaux suffered in a Gordon, Nebraska, bar; that Marshall had carried a gun into the Longhorn; that he shot Montileaux; and that he had admitted his crime to her on three separate occasions [again, the same story she put forth regarding Peltier].[53]

Consequently, as the case went to trial on March 29, 1976 in Rapid City, before South Dakota Judge Marshall Young, the defense was confronted with a surprise witness, about whom virtually nothing was known, and for whom there had been absolutely no opportunity to prepare.[54] The following testimony presents one of her versions of Marshall's alleged confessions:

He [Marshall] was dancing and then he stopped and came over to the table where I was sitting and he said, "You know that guy who got killed in Scenic?" I said, "Yeah." He said, 'I asked the guy if that was the right one and he said, 'Yeah,' it was," so he said, 'We waited for him and followed him into the bathroom," and then he said, "I pulled the trigger." He said, 'I'll never forget the look on that son-of-a-bitch's face as he went down."[55]

At another point, she related that, on another occasion, "[Marshall] was dancing and he came over and he said, 'I don't know why I shot [Montileaux].'"[56] Confronted with testimony such as this, the defense collapsed and, on April 6, the jury returned a verdict finding Dick Marshall guilty of murder in the first degree. On the same evening, despite the FBI's official disinterest in the trial, SA David Price sent a rather self-congratulatory teletype to the Director and a number of other Bureau offices:

On April 6, 1976, Richard Marshall was convicted of first degree murder, Pennington County Court, Rapid City, South Dakota. Marshall was immediately given the mandatory sentence of life in prison at hard labor. The Rapid City office of the FBI was helpful to local authorities as the FBI supplied one witness who heard Marshall boast of the murder. Marshall is currently incarcerated.[57]

The Bureau's actions regarding the Marshall trial were designed not so much to neutralize the defendant himself—although this was undoubtedly viewed as a nice "fringe benefit"—as to set the stage for Russell Means' conviction as an accomplice in the Montileaux murder. Despite the obvious intention of Poor Bear's attribution of the pronoun "we" (rather than "I") to Marshall's supposed confessions—language well-reported to prospective Means trial jurors in Rapid City[58]—this portion of the federal game-plan simply flopped. With no plausible testimony which Poor Bear could enter against Means (she was by then being withheld as a key witness in the RESMURS trials of Bob Robideau, Dino Butler and Leonard Peltier; see Chapter 11), the case against the AIM leader proved baseless and he was acquitted on June 17, 1976.[59]

Dick Marshall was sent to the South Dakota maximum security prison at Sioux Falls. WKLDOC attorney Ken Tilsen filed an appeal resulting in a post-conviction hearing at which Myrtle Poor Bear recanted the entirety of her testimony at trial. Tilsen was also able to introduce medical records indicating 105 recent clinical and hospital admissions for "bizarre behavior," "psychosis and depression," as well as "other physical and mental anomalies."[60] Her father, Theodore Poor Bear, took the stand to testify that his daughter was "very disturbed," trapped in "fantasies," and that she habitually "makes up stories and other things."[61] Such evidence notwithstanding, Judge Young found no basis upon which to order a retrial, although Tilsen's points on the nature of FBI involvement were acknowledged:

> While the circumstances and this testimony creates some concern in the mind, yet there is *no articulable basis* upon which this court can find [the FBI] participated in any subornation of perjury or coaching of the witness, Myrtle Poor Bear, in preparation for the Marshall trial. While *[FBI] conduct in some instances seems inappropriate and inconsistent, such is not a sufficient basis to find intentional governmental misconduct* [emphasis added].[62]

In February 1977, Myrtle Poor Bear testified before the Minnesota Citizens Review Commission in Minneapolis concerning the techniques employed by SAs Price and Wood in forcing her to bear false witness against both Dick Marshall and Leonard Peltier.[63] The following month, Tilsen was able to subpoena both Price and Wood to testify before the Review Commission. Wood flatly refused to answer questions regarding his intimidation of Poor Bear, stating, "I don't believe that was within the guidelines I was given to answer, sir."[64] David Price was also extremely evasive, but did acknowledge that he had brought up the matter of Anna Mae Aquash's fate while he and Wood were holding Poor Bear incommunicado; asked whether he'd also shown Poor Bear the FBI's grisly photos of Aquash's corpse, he responded, "I don't recall."[65]

Poor Bear also testified, both in Canada and at the Peltier trial, to the psychological terrorization she had experienced at the hands of Price and Wood as a result of their threats that she would "end up like Anna Mae" Aquash—while showing her photos of the body—unless she "cooperated" by lying about Marshall and Peltier. Federal prosecutor Evan Hultman admitted before the Eighth Circuit Court that there was "not one scintilla" of truth to anything Poor Bear had said about Peltier. It was also rumored that Poor Bear was coming forward with the story of her treatment once again, this time in the pages of *People* magazine.[66]

Thus armed, Tilsen and his co-counsel, Rapid City attorney James Leach, launched an appeal to the South Dakota Supreme Court, asking that Dick Marshall be retried. He argued from the combined record that the "articulable basis" demanded by Judge Young in 1976 to prove that the FBI's pattern of "inappropriate and inconsistent" conduct regarding Myrtle Poor Bear now added up to clearly "intentional government misconduct." This, by conventional interpretation of the law, would compel South Dakota's high court to put the case back before a jury. On May 20, 1981, in a remarkable echo of California Supreme Court decisions concerning the Geronimo Pratt case (see Chapter 3), the court found,

> We are not reasonably well satisfied that [Myrtle] Poor Bear's testimony was false or that, without it, the jury might have reached a different conclusion. We conclude that the petitioner was able to effectively cross-examine Poor Bear at trial...We cannot say that the case findings are contrary to the clear preponderance of the evidence, nor are we left with a definite and firm conviction that a mistake has been committed.[67]

Chief Justice Wollman sharply dissented from the majority decision however. Among other things, the Justice noted:

• Petitioner [Marshall] did not know of the contemporaneous and apparently false affidavits given by Poor Bear with regard to the [Leonard Peltier RESMURS case] and did not even know Poor Bear's true relationship to the FBI.

• Petitioner was unable to review Poor Bear's medical history, which in itself would probably have had a substantial effect on her credibility [and upon that of the government's case more generally]

• Poor Bear was a material witness at [Marshall's] trial and...the jury might have reached a different conclusion without her testimony.

• In addition to [certain stated] inconsistencies, the testimony of Myrtle Poor Bear may have been the key evidence on several critical areas raised during the trial.[68]

Justice Wollman concluded that, "[t]he cumulative effect of this evidence persuades me that Poor Bear testified falsely at [Dick Marshall's] murder trial," and that

Minneapolis attorney Ken
Tilsen founded WKLDOC in
1973 and coordinated AIM's
legal defense through the
mid-1970s, serving as lead
counsel in Richard Marshall's
appeals process.
(Photo: Lan Brookes Ritz)

a new trial was therefore in order.[69] In late 1981, Amnesty International released a
widely distributed report spotlighting the Marshall case, along with those of
Geronimo Pratt and Leonard Peltier, as being primary among the situations which
led AI to conclude that selective criminal prosecution of key political activists was
occurring in the U.S., and calling for a full-scale investigation of the FBI's *ongoing*
COINTELPRO-type activities.[70]

Tilsen and Leach's only avenue of redress for their client was the federal courts,
ultimately the same U.S. Supreme Court which was refusing to hear the appeals of
Leonard Peltier (see Chapter 11) and which, to this day, has yet to consider *any* of
the hundreds of AIM cases which have proliferated during the past fifteen years.
For all the supposed arenas of "due process" technically open to him, Dick Marshall—languishing in his maximum security cell—had reached a complete legal dead
end.

By 1984 considerable international attention was beginning to be focused upon
the political prisoners/prisoners of war being held in the U.S.; the "big three" in this
regard (probably because of the AI report) were Geronimo Pratt, Leonard Peltier
and Dick Marshall, each of whom continued to assert not only their right/respon-
sibility to struggle against the U.S., but their innocence of the specific acts for which
they had ostensibly been placed in prison.[71] There was a growing propaganda need
on the part of U.S. geo-politicians to counter the external awareness of federal
policies of repression.

Consequently, it was somehow arranged that Dick Marshall, as the least recognized of the big-three prisoners, would have his sentence commuted by Governor
Janklow in exchange for a highly publicized admission of guilt.[72] The deal was cut,
the "confession" made and on December 20, 1984 Richard Marshall left the prison
at Sioux Falls a "free," if broken, man.[73] He had served more than eight years in
prison for a crime he, in all probability, never committed.

South Dakota Governor William "Wild Bill" Janklow engaged in a personal vendetta against Dick Marshall, Dennis Banks, and AIM members in general, thereby making himself a willing tool of COINTELPRO. Repeatedly accused of sex offenses during his "public service," Janklow is presently employed by corporate interests in Minnesota. (Photo: *South Dakota Legislative Manual*)

The Case of Dennis Banks, et al.

The central prominence accorded by the FBI to Dennis Banks as a founder and perhaps the pivotal leader of AIM in the mid-1970s leaves little question as to why the Bureau might have targeted him for especially tenacious pursuit. According to Ken Baka, "The [Banks] case has already been one of the longest-running in U.S. history."[74] It has garnered the dubious distinction of becoming the most sustained attempt at a federal prosecution in the history of American jurisprudence. This longevity does much to support the observation, offered by Banks' Brooklyn, N.Y. attorney, Ken Stern, that the matter is "a continuation of a campaign of gross harassment against American Indian Movement activists" begun more than a decade ago.[75] To summarize:

> On July 26 [1975], Banks had been convicted in Custer [S.D.] on charges based on the courthouse riots of 1973 [see Chapter 5]; Banks skipped bail and went underground, advising those who had forfeited his bond that he feared for his life while in state custody...[H]e gave as a reason [then South Dakota Attorney General, later Governor] William Janklow's statement about "putting a bullet through the heads of AIM leaders."[76]

From South Dakota, Banks went to Colorado where he was hidden by local AIM members and Chicano leader Corky Gonzalez's Crusade for Justice organization for a considerable period of time.[77] Then on February 14, 1976:

> ...a state police officer stopped a station wagon and a motor home [belonging to actor Marlon Brando, a highly vocal AIM supporter] near...Ontario, Oregon, a town of 8,000 people located on the Idaho-Oregon border...two men fled the vehicles, police said. One ran into a field and fired at the officer, said police...The two men were thought

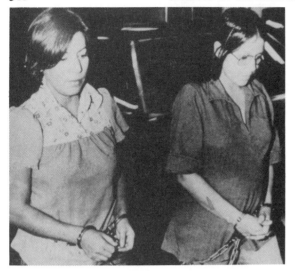

Anna Mae Aquash (left) and Kamook Banks in custody in Vale, Oregon on February 15, 1976. Aquash was quickly returned to South Dakota where she was executed by "person or persons unknown." Banks, eight months pregnant, was shipped to a federal lockup in Kansas City to await trial on spurious weapons and explosives charges. (Photo: FBI)

to be Dennis Banks and Leonard Peltier. Both men were wanted: Banks in South Dakota for sentencing for the Feb. 6, 1973 melee at the Custer County Courthouse, and Peltier in Milwaukee, Wis., in connection with a murder [sic; Peltier was wanted in Milwaukee on a charge of attempted murder. The charge proved to have been fabricated. Peltier was later acquitted after the former girlfriend of the alleged victim, an off-duty Milwaukee policeman named Hlavinka, testified that around the time of the incident he had shown her a photograph of Peltier and boasted his intention of "catching a big one for the FBI"]...Police arrested Banks' wife KaMook [sic, Kamook], then known as Darlene Nichols; Kenneth Loud Hawk, then of Pine Ridge, now of Bozeman, Mont.; Russell Redner [Shoshone], then of Eureka, Calif. and now of Oglala; and the late Anna Mae Aquash, of Nova Scotia, whose body was found in 1976...Federal authorities said they found ammunition and seven cases of dynamite in the vehicles.[78]

Those arrested were charged with interstate transportation of explosives and illegal possession of firearms.[79] "Kamook Banks had [originally] been charged in the Custer Courthouse Battle in 1973, but charges were dropped [in April 1976]...Her bail in Oregon had first been $100,000, then $50,000, then $20,000 and on February 23 [1976], she was released in third-party custody."[80] Redner and Loud Hawk had also been,

...charged by the State of Oregon with "possession of a dangerous weapon with intent to use." The evidence against Russ [Redner] was a Buck knife of the folding variety found in a leather sheath on his belt. Kenny [Loud Hawk] also carried a Buck knife of the folding variety in his pocket, but was not charged for it. Instead, he was charged for a handgun found under the rear seat of the station wagon they were traveling in...Nita Bellows, the Ontario, Oregon, Justice of the Peace, set bail at $50,000 each [the usual Oregon bail in a Class C felony matter being $1,500]...Bill Williams, PR man for the FBI's Portland [Ore.] office [had] "no comment" on how Bellows arrived at such a figure...Redner and Loud Hawk were held in isolation in Vale [Oregon, the jail from which Anna Mae Aquash was removed back to South Dakota by the FBI, and subsequently murdered; see Chapter 11]...the prisoners were taken to Portland via Boise to face federal charges…Riding in the car with Ken Loud Hawk was an FBI agent from Rapid City, South Dakota [thought to have been either SA David Price or SA J. Gary Adams]. He thought Ken might know something about the two FBI agents [Coler and Williams] killed on the Pine Ridge Reservation…" If you tell me who did it," he said, "we could make a deal. Transportation of firearms is a very serious charge."[81]

As all this was going on, the FBI "identified" Dennis Banks as having been one of the two men who had reportedly fled the scene, firing on police as they went. The evidence was exceedingly flimsy:

> …the government claims Banks was there because KaMook [sic] was there, because Banks' briefcase was in the motorhome and because Banks' fingerprints were found on a pickle jar [in the vehicle]…Banks [in hiding, was subsequently] arrested in San Francisco. In April, 1976, Banks [and Kamook, Redner and Loudhawk] appeared in a Portland court and pleaded innocent of five counts of illegal possession and transportation of destructive devices and firearms.[82]

At the trial, the Bureau contended that the dynamite allegedly seized in the Brando motor home had been destroyed; the prosecution attempted to submit polaroid photos of small puffs of smoke in an open field which, it claimed, were evidence of the dynamite being detonated by police demolition experts.[83] The arms undergirding the government's various weapons charges had also been "mislaid." Under such circumstances:

> It took the U.S. District Judge [Belloni] exactly eighteen minutes and 55 seconds on May 12 [1976] to dismiss firearms and explosives charges against [the] four American Indian Movement activists…At the trial, Judge Belloni asked the U.S. to proceed with the prosecution. The prosecutor said he wasn't ready. The defense moved for dismissal, and the motion was granted.[84]

However, "U.S. Attorney Sid Lezak, obviously feeling the pressure of this decisive defeat, vowed he would appeal Belloni's decision to the Ninth Circuit Court of Appeals. Loud Hawk and Redner still face[d] state charges [which were later dropped]."[85] Dennis Banks was returned to California, where a series of hearings were being held concerning a move by the State of South Dakota to extradite him (a federal "fugitive from justice" warrant had been issued) in connection with his conviction in the Custer Courthouse case.

Governor Jerry Brown of California intervened in the judicial proceedings to announce that he would sign no order forcing Banks to return for sentencing and imprisonment, due to William Janklow's several public death threats against the AIM leader. Brown was undoubtedly aided in arriving at this position by receipt of a petition signed by some 150,000 of his constituents urging him to block extradition on this basis, and a second petition with "another half-million signatures from around the U.S."[86] South Dakota Attorney General Janklow, trapped by his own inflammatory rhetoric, was reduced to fuming that Brown's decision was "absolutely absurd" and evidence of "preferential treatment" of Banks.[87] Janklow, elected Governor of South

Kamook Banks (Darlene Nichols) and her baby Iron Door Woman, named in commemoration of her prison birth, after Kamook's release from federal custody. The government's case was dismissed on the basis of vindictive prosecution. (Photo: Bernardine Nichols)

Dakota in 1978, "countered" Brown's all-but-unprecedented granting of political asylum to Banks by an even *more* novel expedient. In 1981, he ordered that parole of South Dakota's more prominent felons be conditioned upon their "deportation" to California.[88] "If Jerry Brown likes our felons," the South Dakota Governor said, "he can have them all."[89]

Banks settled in California to engage in such dangerous pursuits as serving as chancellor of D-Q University, an Indian-run institution established on a former military site near San Francisco in the wake of the Alcatraz occupation in the early '70s (see Chapter 4), and which had drawn heavily on AIM principles in its structure and curriculum. He also remained a solid activist, speaking and fundraising on tours of the state with celebrities such as Cree singer, Buffy Sainte-Marie, working on AIM's "Longest Walk" in 1978,[90] and organizing a tribunal to consider evidence of U.S. human rights violations against indigenous populations—Alaskan and Hawaiian natives as well as American Indians—during September of 1982. The publicity attendant to all of this made him a less than welcome guest to California conservatives. When Republican gubernatorial candidate George Deukmejian campaigned during 1982, one of his positions—loudly voiced—was a promise to "return Dennis Banks to justice in South Dakota."[91]

With Deukmejian's election in November of 1982,[92] Banks immediately went underground, surfacing just after the first of the year at the tiny Onondaga Reservation in upstate New York, invited by and under the sovereign protection of the traditional Onondaga chiefs. The latter promised to offer active resistance to any effort on the part of New York state or federal police to forcibly remove Banks from their sanctuary, and a period of negotiation ensued. After approximately a year and one

Dennis Banks in his cell in the South Dakota maximum security facility in Sioux Falls, 1985. While his parole ended in January 1987, he and codefendants Russ Redner, Kamook Banks and Kenny Loud Hawk were once again faced with federal trial on the three-times-dismissed 1976 weapons and explosives charges. (Photo: Kevin Barry McKiernan)

half, acceptable assurances concerning his safety were obtained from Janklow's office and:

> In September 1984, Dennis Banks left New York to surrender in South Dakota, trying to put behind him the Custer riot and assault conviction although many regarded the trial as having involved fraud by the prosecution. He was sentenced by the South Dakota court to two concurrent sentences of three years. He...served 14 months in prison [mostly at the South Dakota State Penitentiary in Sioux Falls].[93]

Prior to his surrender, Banks' conviction had been appealed to the South Dakota Supreme Court, which upheld it on May 2, 1986, and Banks declined to pursue the matter to the U.S. Supreme Court (largely on the basis of that estimable body's sterling performance on the Peltier matter; see Chapter 11).[94] His parole ended in January of 1987, by which time he had announced his "retirement" as an AIM leader, and had settled into his wife's home community of Oglala, where he busied himself trying to establish an employment program and putting on a weekly country music program for the local (AIM-initiated) FM radio station, KILI, near Porcupine.[95]

For much of the period during which all this was going on, little happened with the federal weapons and explosives case in Oregon. Then, in March 1980, the Ninth Circuit Court of Appeals reversed Judge Belloni's 1976 dismissal of the charges on delayed appeal by U.S. Attorney Charles Turner, who had replaced Sidney

Lezak as chief prosecutor. Judge Shirley Hufstedler, in a dissenting opinion, accused the majority of "contorting legal logic" in reinstating the government's case, but the matter was sent back to the District Court in Portland for trial in January of 1983.[96] In May 1983, Dennis and Kamook Banks, Ken Loud Hawk, and Russell Redner appeared before U.S. District Judge James Redden; their attorneys entered a motion for dismissal based on the argument that the defendants' sixth amendment right to a speedy trial had been violated by the government's long hiatus, the judge agreed, and the charges were once again dismissed.[97]

U.S. Attorney Turner again appealed the dismissal to the Ninth Circuit. This time, the appeals court agreed with Judge Hufstedler, and the government's appeal was denied. *Still* not willing to let the matter rest and having infinite financial resources, Turner appealed to the U.S. Supreme Court and, on January 21, 1986, was rewarded with a decision to reverse the dismissal once again, *despite* the fact that some ninety months had elapsed since the original dismissal on the basis of the *prosecution's* unreadiness to proceed with the trial.[98]

Justice Lewis F. Powell, writing for the majority, determined that the "problem" which resulted in the government's inability to go to trial in the first place had to do with successful defense challenges to the admissibility of supposed federal evidence. Hence, the exercise of the fundamental rights of the accused to mount a defence was somehow construed as "doing everything in their power to delay going to trial" and a *de facto* waiver of sixth amendment rights.[99] Such "reasoning" was strongly dissented from by Justices Thurgood Marshall, William J. Brennan, Harry A. Blackmun and John Paul Stevens. The matter was once again sent back to the District Court in Portland, as a result of a decision which former WKLDOC attorney Lynn Parkinson described as "intellectually dishonest and vindictive."[100]

For once, the lower courts appear to have come to share fully such a "radical" opinion. On July 14, 1986, Judge Redden wrote that—in his court, at least—although the high court had reversed orders that the charges should be dismissed on sixth amendment grounds, those dismissals would stand "because the government has also violated the defendants' due process rights in other regards."[101] The government immediately launched yet another appeal of this, the third consecutive dismissal of its fabricated charges. As of this writing (mid-January 1988), it appears that the case will come before the district court for yet a fourth time in 12 years, although U.S. Attorney Turner has openly admitted that he "may be losing [his] objectivity" in the matter.[102]

In November 1987, Judge Fred Nichol, now retired, was asked his opinion of discovery motions filed in this case by attorney Ken Stern. He responded,

...I ended [the Wounded Knee Leadership] case with the firm conviction that the Government would go to any end...in order to convict Mr. Banks...[T]he total disregard of truth and fairness in the Government's attempt to "get" Dennis Banks "by hook or crook" did not stop at the doorstep of the FBI. The U.S. Attorney's office was an active participant. The Court was intentionally deceived...The fact that both the FBI and the U.S. Attorney's office were active participants in this pollution of justice convinced me there was a systemic, in addition to an individual, desire to convict Mr. Banks by means well beyond those which were ethical and fair. After all, in other cases in my district I had both FBI agents and these attorneys before me regularly. But the willingness to lie and fabricate and withhold evidence was only exhibited against Mr. Banks and his AIM co-defendant. And it was exhibited with a vengeance...If my experience has taught me anything, it is that the past is a good indication of the future. The broad and pervasive nature of the FBI and prosecutors' misconduct in 1973 and 1974 reflected patterns and beliefs that were deeply held. I doubt they would be easily abandoned.[103]

Indeed, the seeds of the FBI's anti-AIM campaign of the mid-1970s have continued to sprout, well into the second half of the 1980s.

Part IV

We Will Remember

In Nazi Germany...first they put the Communists and Jehovah's Witnesses in concentration camps, but I was not a Communist or a Jehovah's Witness so I did nothing. Then they came for the Social Democrats, but I was not a Social Democrat, so I did nothing...Then they arrested the trade unionists, but I did nothing because I was not one. Then they arrested the Jews, and again I did nothing because I was not Jewish. Then they came for the Catholics, but I was not a Catholic so I did nothing again...At last they came and arrested me, but by then it was too late...no one was left to speak up.

—Pastor Martin Neimoller, 1965

It is just my personal feeling, but many [U.S. citizens] are going to have to accept some blame too, because it's *their* federal government...the white Americans are guilty of apathy and self-indulgence to the extent that they have allowed inhumanity to thrive in this country.

—John Trudell, AIM National Chairman, 1977

Chapter 13

A Legacy of Repression

The evidence...does not point to mistakes or excesses within the FBI so much as it points to a police organization with its own political bias, judgements and goals, which is designed to function and does function to achieve those goals consistent with its own vision of what is correct and proper for our country...[I]t is essential...that we recognize that the FBI plays a crucial role in decisions as to who gets arrested, prosecuted, convicted and imprisoned. In making or influencing these decisions, the political outlook of the FBI dominates its actions. The result is that justice in the United States is neither fair nor equal.
—Kenneth Tilsen, WKLDOC Director, 1976

As for us—how are we to make our way through that rosy mist? Whom are we to ask about it? Those who were shot aren't talking, and neither are those who have been scattered to the four winds.
—Aleksandr Solzhenitsyn

As Professor Roxanne Dunbar Ortiz has observed, "During the Nixon era, and during its adjunct Ford administration, hundreds of black organizers were murdered, destabilized or imprisoned. Nearly every case is now traceable to government intelligence sources and outright assassinations and frameups. 'COINTELPRO—New Left,' the government program designed to destabilize and destroy the student movement, was established in 1968 and was used with vigor by the Nixon administration. The attack on Indian demonstrators and particularly on American Indian Movement activists was brutal and grisly, with a far greater ratio of deaths and imprisonments than any other movement."[1]

The brunt of this physical repression by the FBI and other police agencies upon political dissidents within the United States appears to have passed, at least for the moment. However, there are clear indicators that the moderation of many of the Bureau's worst activities after 1976 is linked more to a diminishment of the overt forms of political dissent in America during the ensuing period than it is to any fundamental shift in FBI policies or tactics. In cases where the Bureau perceives the need—where it discovers people organizing for their rights—it has continued to demonstrate itself quite capable of resorting to tried and true methods of repression. As concerns AIM, two prominent examples will illustrate this point.

The Plot to Assassinate Leonard Peltier

Shortly after Leonard Peltier was incarcerated in the federal "super-max" prison at Marion, Illinois, it became obvious that his case would be subject to a major appeals effort. Simultaneously, it became apparent that the FBI would ultimately be forced under provision of the FOIA to disclose a significant portion of the RESMURS investigative documents illegally withheld from the defense during his trial. On both counts, the Bureau was (and is) exposed to the risk of substantial embarrassment and the distinct possibility of criminal culpability applying to agents and high-ranking officials.

Although federal courts have done far more than even the Bureau might have expected in glossing over "FBI improprieties" during Peltier's appeals (see Chapter 11), there was no way Bureau strategists could be sure of this outcome. The one thing which *was* certain was that if Peltier were suddenly to die, the urgent impetus guiding his attorneys and supporters through the appeals and FOIA processes would correspondingly disappear. There is strong evidence suggesting that the FBI developed and implemented a plan to bring about Peltier's assassination in prison, thus closing the books on his case once and for all.

The mechanism by which this was to have been accomplished seems to have been a middle-aged Oneida/Choctaw from Oklahoma named Robert Hugh Wilson, a.k.a. Standing Deer. "By reputation, Wilson, a heavy-set bank robber of 235 pounds, was a very dangerous man; according to his copious prison records, he had 'assaulted every officer who ever attempted to apprehend him, and is considered [by the FBI] to be the most dangerous individual ever apprehended in this [Chicago and northern Illinois] district.'"[2] He was doing time in Marion because of a successful breakout from the Oklahoma State Prison on April 30, 1975, followed by a June 3 armed robbery in Oklahoma City during which a policeman had been shot:

> In addition to the twenty-five-year term he was already serving, he was charged with seven felonies, including bank robberies, auto thefts and the near-fatal wounding of the police officer in Oklahoma City. Because of his previous record, he was technically subject to seven life sentences in prison.[3]

In sum, Standing Deer had reason to believe he was fated to spend every remaining moment of his life squarely "in the belly of the beast."[4] Perhaps worse, from his point of view, he suffered chronically from an excruciating and degenerative spinal disease which rendered him increasingly dependent upon his keepers for medical treatment.[5] He was, in fact, in the prison hospital on March 17, 1978, when he was first approached by Dr. J.R. Plank with the government's proposal that, in exchange for continuing medical attention, he should "help out" Marion Correctional Supervisor (chief guard) R.M. "Max" Carey by informing on the activities of fellow inmate/fellow Indian Leonard Peltier. Guided by instincts developed through a lifetime spent in open confrontation with "the man," Standing Deer flatly refused.[6]

Robert Hugh Wilson, a.k.a. Standing Deer, was retained by the FBI and prison officials to assassinate Leonard Peltier. (Photo: U.S. Bureau of Prisons)

The pay-back for such "obstinance" was quickly forthcoming. On March 27, Dr. Plank informed Standing Deer that, despite the severity of his condition and the fact that no particular disciplinary rationale was given, he was being transferred directly from the prison hospital to the "Hole." For the next six weeks, in spite of repeated written requests for emergency medical assistance, he was denied not only this "privilege," but also a wheelchair and any sleeping arrangement other than a "cot" consisting of a solid steel slab.[7] By May 5, his condition had deteriorated to the point that, when he slipped and fell on his way to the shower, he was unable to regain his feet.[8] At that point, according to Standing Deer's diary, "[Chief guard] Carey asked me if I was ready to cooperate with him in exchange for medical treatment. I told him we could talk about it if he would get me some medical treatment right away."[9]

On May 15, he was finally returned to the hospital, although he still received no treatment. However, as Standing Deer later put it in a deposition:

[O]n the afternoon of May 17, 1978, Chief Correctional Supervisor R.M. Carey unlocked the door to my room and entered. Mr. Carey was accompanied by a well-dressed stranger in a light brown suit and diagonal striped tie. The man accompanying Mr. Carey appeared to be in his late thirties, about six-feet tall and 170 pounds, very erect posture, nearly blond hair with blue eyes. The stranger said that if I would cooperate in "neutralizing Leonard Peltier" he would see that I received immediate medical treatment, and, after I cooperated with him he would get me paroled from the federal system to my Oklahoma detainer; I asked the stranger who he represented and what he meant by "neutralizing" Leonard Peltier. He replied that he was a person who had the power to do what he promised. As to what he meant by "neutralizing Leonard Peltier," he said I would have to weigh that for myself, but that according to my record I was not averse to "going all the way" when faced with a desperate situation.[10]

To the carrot was added the stick:

The stranger asked me how it felt to know I would never make it through the Oklahoma trial alive. He said that shooting a police officer in Oklahoma was a charge that would bring the wrath of all Oklahoma City law enforcement officers on my head. He said that if I did not cooperate, he would personally see to it that I would not survive the trip to Oklahoma. On the other hand, if I would cooperate, he said he would guarantee my safety in Oklahoma by having me held in the federal prison in El Reno, Oklahoma during the trial and never having me in the custody of state authorities without the presence of two United States marshals.[11]

Eventually, the "stranger" (thought to have been SA James Wilkins)[12] agreed that in exchange for Peltier's neutralization he would order immediate resumption of medical treatment, and arrange for the dismissal of all seven pending indictments against Standing Deer in Oklahoma. The newly retained assassin was to work his way into Peltier's confidence, taking his time in the process, and await word—to be transmitted through Carey—that a second assassin was in place and available to help with the job.[13] Upon his departure the stranger warned Standing Deer:

> Don't even think of playing us for fools because, at this point, it's Peltier's life or yours. We don't accept backing out or betrayals. You are now committed to this with your life. If you betray us you will die. If you perform honorably you will be rewarded even more than our arrangement. If you tell about this conversation it will be our word against yours and you won't be believed.[14]

Treatment of Standing Deer's back ailment with drugs, hot packs and liniment was resumed on the same afternoon[15] and, on May 24, the Records Control Supervisor at Marion was notified by Oklahoma authorities that state detainers on the inmate had been removed; on June 1, it was announced that his pending Oklahoma trial had been cancelled altogether.[16] His physical condition much improved by the therapy he had received, Standing Deer was discharged from the hospital at the end of the latter month and assigned a cell giving him easy access to Leonard Peltier. Caught in this dilemma, and *still* unable to let go of the system of "con ethics" he'd absorbed over the years, he noted in his diary at the end of his hospital stay that:

> This is too fucking heavy to even think about. I don't know what to do. If I tell Leonard and he wants me to expose it, they'll probably kill me. If I refuse to act, they can get somebody else and we won't even know who. I'll just have to get back into population and dump the whole thing in Leonard's lap.[17]

This he did at a Fourth of July picnic conducted in the prison yard: "According to Wilson, Peltier was visibly upset by the news that Wilson was supposed to kill him, and asked Wilson to pretend to cooperate so that he would not be replaced by an unknown enemy."[18] Standing Deer, in line with the FBI's instructions, joined an Indian culture group (of which he was shortly elected chair and spokesperson) founded by Peltier and undertook other activities which would seem designed to "gain the target's trust." On September 14, he received word that the State of Oklahoma had dismissed all charges against him.[19] On the afternoon of November 9, Standing Deer's FBI handler reappeared and informed the inmate that "they were just about out of time and so was I."[20] The agent explained that it had been decided Peltier should die during an ostensible escape attempt[21] and that:

> Marion has so much security that planning a successful escape is just about impossible, therefore, unless I had firm plans to neutralize Peltier they intended to move both me and Leonard Peltier to a less secure prison in California where an escape attempt would be hard to resist. He said I would be going to Leavenworth in December. Leonard would go to USP [U.S. Prison] Lompoc about 60 days after I got to Leavenworth. I would not go to Lompoc until they had another Indian situated in Lompoc who would help me neutralize Peltier. He said the Indian I would meet in Lompoc enjoyed their complete trust, and he would be watching me to be sure I performed.[22]

On December 21, 1978, Standing Deer was transferred from Marion to the U.S. prison at Leavenworth, Kansas.[23] The trip aggravated his back condition once more and, upon arrival, he vented his foul humor by threatening a guard.[24] In a hearing on December 27—which he was unable to attend for lack of a wheelchair—Standing Deer was sentenced by prison authorities to be returned to Marion for "special handling" in that prison's infamous Control Unit.[25] Unaccountably, the sentence was never carried out; instead, this most dangerous inmate was suddenly *promoted* to serve as trustee for the first time in his lengthy prison career.[26]

For his part, Peltier was transshipped through Leavenworth in February, arriving in Lompoc on April 10, 1979.[27] On May 24, Charles "Chuck" Richards, a son-in-law of Dick Wilson[28] and notorious Pine Ridge GOON who had a hand in the Byron DeSersa assassination in 1976 (see Chapter 7) and several other reservation murders, also arrived in Lompoc.[29] Adopting the alias "Chuck Richardson," apparently with the cooperation of prison authorities, Richards quickly moved to befriend Peltier (who would have recognized the GOON's name by reputation, but who—having never seen him—had no reason to recognize him by sight). Standing Deer, aware of the GOON's departure and destination, immediately sent word to the intended target—through a circuitous route involving a support group member, Ramona Benke, in Seattle[30]—concerning Richards' real identity and the probability that this was the second assassin called for in the federal plan.

Although Peltier immediately began to shun Richards, limiting the GOON's ability to get to him, he realized that the assassination plot was proceeding apace. In desperation, he enlisted the aid of two other inmates, a twenty-three-year-old Hunkpapa Lakota from the Standing Rock Reservation named Dallas Thundershield (whom Peltier had met at the First International Treaty Council in 1974) and Bobby Garcia, a Chicano from New Mexico who had been convicted of murder and incarcerated in the federal system after an unsuccessful jailbreak during which a guard was killed.[31] The three determined it was necessary to preempt the federal schedule by Peltier's escaping from Lompoc before matters progressed any further.[32] Peltier then recruited the assistance of Roque Duenas, one of his AIM confederates from Washington state.[33] It seems probable that prison authorities intercepted some of these last communications and were thus aware of both the nature and timing of the escape plan.

On the night of July 20, 1979, Peltier, Garcia and Thundershield escaped from Lompoc by climbing the prison's chain-link and barbed wire fence near Guard Tower 4. For reasons never explained, the tower guard, R. Hodgkinson, who observed the prisoners scaling the fence, merely shouted at them to stop rather than firing a warning shot or incapacitating them with his shotgun. Instead, he fired only when the fleeing men—who were running toward an area obscured from view from the prison compound itself—were too far away to be hit. Reportedly, Hodgkinson's fire was returned by a "person or persons unknown" who had been pre-positioned to cover the escapees' flight.[34]

Bobby Garcia became separated from Peltier and Thundershield as the three made their getaway. To divert attention from the other escapees, Garcia gave himself up not far from the prison wall.[35] Meanwhile, Peltier and Thundershield had been pinned in the headlights of an oncoming truck driven by William Guild, an engineer at the prison power plant:

> William Guild, an ex-guard working at the prison's power facility, responded to the escape and shot in the back the first long-haired Indian he saw as the man raised his hands to surrender. This individual was Dallas Thundershield, who from the rear looked similar to Peltier. Did Guild think he was killing Peltier? Only Guild fired a weapon at close range at a prisoner, even though others had the chance. Moreover, according to [subsequent] testimony of William Guild...he *knew* the route the escaping men would take.[36]

Thus, while tower guard Hodgkinson had declined to shoot (from an observable position) with his relatively harmless scatter gun while the targets were in range, Guild—who would ordinarily not even have been carrying a weapon—opted to shoot an unarmed man from behind at close range with an entirely deadly .38 calibre revolver when out of sight of possible witnesses.[37] There is also considerable evidence that Thundershield, once shot, was simply allowed to bleed to death while confusion concerning his identity was cleared up by a small horde of guards and the representatives of "outside agencies" who arrived promptly on the scene.[38] Peltier, in the meantime, had slipped away.

Five days later, Peltier, hungry and exhausted, was spotted by a farmer, Jerry Parker, while attempting to take a pumpkin from his field. Peltier had made it some fifteen miles from Lompoc through very rough country and, unbeknownst to Parker, was now armed with a Ruger Mini-14 rifle. Parker, in a fit of property protection, drove his pickup toward the field, firing a rifle of his own at the man engaged in the theft of a vegetable. When the man ran, Parker pursued, only to be taken prisoner moments later. Recognizing the "cop killer" from television reports of the Lompoc escape, Parker mused audibly that, "I suppose you're going to kill me now." Peltier, who later admitted having been furious that someone had attempted to kill him over a pumpkin, responded, "I ain't no killer." Instead, he relieved Parker of $30 cash, his boots and his pickup and continued his escape attempt.[39]

As subsequent testimony revealed, this proved to be Peltier's undoing; despite his lack of boots, "Jerry Parker hotfooted it to a telephone and reported the theft of his truck to the sheriff's office in Santa Monica."[40] Not much later, the truck was found alongside a gravel road, its clutch ruined. With this discovery, a team from the Santa Monica Police Department commanded by Detective Bruce Correll—but actually led by Detective Bill Turner, a Vietnam combat veteran and experienced tracker—and accompanied by FBI agent James Wilkins moved out in pursuit. A few hours later, Peltier allowed himself to be taken without a fight, despite the fact that all police personnel agreed that from the defensive position he'd selected he could easily have killed several of them, had he desired.[41] As he later put it:

> I seen 'em comin' from a long ways off. I had binoculars and the Mini-14, and I was in a good position to fight from. But I could tell they was cops, not FBI. If it had been FBI, I would have had no choice but to sell myself as dear as possible. But, since it was local cops, I figured I'd live through surrendering, even if a couple of agents was with them. I never killed nobody, and figured I might as well not start.[42]

Peltier was taken to trial on November 14, 1979 on charges of armed robbery, assault, auto theft, escape from a federal prison and conspiracy to escape, among other things. After a month-long trial in which Assistant U.S. Attorneys Lourdes Baird and Robert Biniaz were allowed more than twenty days to present their case, while defense attorney Bruce Ellison was restricted to less than three by evidentiary rulings of Judge Lawrence Lydick, he was convicted of escape and the illegal possession of a weapon by a felon; the conspiracy and assault-related charges, as well as auto theft, resulted in acquittals. On February 4, 1980 he was sentenced and a total of seven years was tacked onto the end of his double-life sentence. He was immediately transported back to Marion with the recommendation, signed by Lompoc Correctional Supervisor Greg Hutson, that he be subjected to an "indefinite period" in the Control Unit.[43]

Bobby Garcia was also convicted of escape at about the same time as Peltier. He was shipped straight into the Marion Control Unit, where he was held for about thirty days, before being transferred to the maximum security facility at Terre Haute, Indiana on March 12, 1980. Perhaps ironically, his cellmate at Terre Haute was none other than Standing Deer, who had been transferred there after being "fired" from his preferred position at Leavenworth on the day of the Lompoc breakout (without explanation, and despite a recent letter of commendation for his on-the-job performance).[44] On August 1, Standing Deer was transferred back to Leavenworth and, on December 1, Bobby Garcia was placed in the "Hole" in Terre Haute for reasons other than disciplinary action. On December 13, 1980 he was found dead in his cell; the official cause of death was listed as suicide by hanging, although his body was found in a position where his feet could reach the floor. Postmortem blood tests showed the presence of eight drugs, including barbiturate levels sufficient to render

Bobby Garcia, who assisted Leonard Peltier escape from Lompoc Prison, was consequently transferred to the control unit at the federal prison in Terre Haute, Indiana. On December 13, 1980, he "committed suicide by hanging himself" in his cell, under virtually impossible circumstances. (Drawing: Bob Robideau)

him unconscious well *before* the time of death. Bobby Garcia was known not to be a drug user and had shown no indication of being suicidal in communications to friends and fellow prisoners immediately before his death.[45]

Roque Duenas, arrested about the same time Peltier was captured, spent the next eight months in jail. He was awaiting his day in court on an array of charges including assault (he was accused of having laid down the diversionary fire on Guard Tower 4 during the escape), smuggling arms into a federal prison, conspiracy and so forth. The trial ended in a hung jury. Rather than try the case again, the government accepted a plea bargain in which Duenas would acknowledge his complicity as an "aider and abettor" of the escape. All other charges would be dropped, with the understanding that he would receive a total sentence of two years. However, the prosecution was in for a mild surprise:

> [U.S. District] Judge Robert Takasugi, who immediately released [Duenas] on proba-tion…also expressed "very deep concern" about possible government misconduct in the Peltier case, citing especially Standing Deer's affidavits; he was eager to know, among other things, if the seven charges against Wilson in Oklahoma had actually been dismissed; if it was unusual for Wilson with his maximum security classification to have been transferred to Leavenworth and then Lompoc (the same might have been asked about Peltier himself); if Wilson had actually been given a clerk's job at Leaven-worth, and if he had been fired on the day of the escape.[46]

Assistant U.S. Attorney Biniaz quickly assured Takasugi that the alleged assas-sination plot had been thoroughly investigated by the Justice Department's Office of Professional Responsibility, and that there was "absolutely no merit" to the story. Moreover, a cynical and rather conservative *Los Angeles Times* reporter named Bill

Hazlett—who was routinely covering the Duenas sentencing for his paper—decided that he would dispel such rumors once and for all. Contrary to his expectations, once he began his investigation:

> Hazlett was disturbed by what he learned of the alleged plot to assassinate Peltier, and also by the uneasiness of the government attorneys...The *Los Angeles Times* sent Hazlett east to Oklahoma, where he discovered that Robert Hugh Wilson's account of the dismissal of seven serious charges on his record was entirely true...Increasingly disturbed, Hazlett extended his researches to four other states, then continued east to Washington, D.C., to discuss his findings with old acquaintances at FBI headquarters and to hear the Bureau's explanation of the strange story.[47]

As Hazlett later put it,

> I've always been a welcome guest back there in Washington, you know; used to get letters from J. Edgar Hoover and Clarence Kelly commending me for stories I'd written concerning the FBI. But when those guys found out I was looking into the Peltier case, I couldn't even get up to the second floor. I mean, there's got to be *something* fishy here, because they stonewalled me entirely; they don't want to discuss this case at all.[48]

In early 1981, Hazlett submitted a five-part, 30,000 word feature series, based upon his investigation, to his employers at the *Times*. The paper, which had underwritten the whole effort—originally intended to exonerate the FBI and Bureau of Prisons—unceremoniously declined to publish the result.[49]

Roque Duenas returned to his home in Seattle. On October 1, 1981, he and his nephew, Kevin Henry, went fishing off Narrows Point in Tacoma Sound. The following morning, at 2:15 a.m., their boat was found capsized approximately 200 yards from shore. Kevin Henry's body was found, a large bruise caused by a blow with a blunt object disfiguring the forehead.[50] Duenas' body is still missing and he is legally presumed dead.

The Murder of John Trudell's Family

The Peltier assassination effort appears to be only one of several abortive but deadly FBI counterintelligence operations directed at the remnants of AIM during the late 1970s and early 1980s. Another, even grimmer example concerns the death of the family of AIM's last national chairman, John Trudell:

> In February 1979, Trudell led a march in Washington, D.C. to draw attention to the difficulties the Indians were having. Although he had received a warning against speaking out, he delivered an address from the steps of the FBI building on the subject of the agency's harassment of Indians...Less than 12 hours later, Trudell's wife, Tina, his three childern, and his wife's mother were burned alive in the family home in Duck Valley, Nevada—the apparent work of an arsonist.[51]

Tina Trudell with her children (from left) Ricarda Star, Eli Changing Sun and Sunshine Karma, shortly before they were murdered at Duck Valley, Utah. (Photo: Collection of Paulette D'Auteuil Robideau)

Further detail is added elsewhere:

On the Shoshone-Paiute Reservation of Duck Valley, straddling the Nevada-Idaho border, at 1:30 a.m., February 12, 1979, a fire ripped through the house of Arthur Manning and his family. Manning was a member of the Duck Valley Tribal Council who was actively working for Shoshone-Paiute treaty rights. Opposition to Manning included local tribal police chief, Benny Richards, a former member of the Wilson goon squad on Pine Ridge [and brother of intended Peltier assassin Chuck Richards; both are of the Pine Ridge "Manson Family"], and the local BIA Director John Artichoker, also from Pine Ridge. Manning's wife, Leah, was a coordinator for social services on the reservation. Their daughter, Tina, had been working actively in a local campaign to preserve the tribe's water rights at Wildhorse Reservoir; she was opposed by the BIA, Elko County [and] Nevada officials, the water recreation industry, and local white ranchers. Tina's husband was John Trudell, national chairman of AIM [from approximately 1974-80]. The Trudells had three children: Ricarda Star [age five], Sunshine Karma [three], and Eli Changing Sun [one]...The fire [caught] the entire family asleep. Dead were Leah Hicks-Manning, her daughter Tina, and the three young children. Arthur Manning survived the blaze. The BIA issued a statement saying the fire was an accident. Trudell believes his family was murdered.[52]

The basis for Trudell's belief rested in his AIM activities in general, and with regard to the Peltier case in particular.

John Trudell, AIM's last national chairman, designated by the FBI as "an extremely effective agitator," engaging in the activity which made him and his family a prime Bureau target.
(Photo: *Akwesasne Notes*)

During the Peltier trial in Fargo, North Dakota, Trudell had returned to the courtroom one day when a marshal informed him that he would not be allowed inside. An argument ensued, and Trudell was evicted. He was later arrested for the incident, charged with contempt of court, convicted before [U.S. District] Judge Ronald Davies, and sentenced to sixty days in jail. He served his time in five institutions in three states [a matter clearly reminiscent of the handling of Leonard Crow Dog; see Chapter 12]. While in Springfield Prison in Missouri, he was told by a fellow inmate that if he did not stop his Indian rights work his family would be killed.[53]

Of course, as is indicated above, the Mannings had no shortage of enemies at Duck Valley, any one or group of which might have perpetrated the fatal arson (assuming it *was* arson—despite the obvious basis for suspicion, and Trudell's repeated allegations in this regard, no formal investigation of the fire was ever conducted by the FBI). However, given the overall context of apparent illegalities involved in the FBI's anti-AIM operations, and the concomitantly high stakes which would be involved in their disclosure, more than usual heed should be paid to Trudell's contentions:

When I got sent up for sixty days, that time in Fargo, I was approached by another inmate, a guy I didn't know, and he started talking about my public statements. You can't go around talking that shit, he says, you'd better get out of the country. You don't know these crazy bastards [the FBI]—they could kill your wife and children. Well, I was suspicious of the guy's so-called warning at the time; *that* was a message John Trudell was *supposed* to receive! I know who did it. What I still don't understand is why; it was so unnecessary. But it *was* arson, and it *was* deliberate—an assassination. Those people did a terrible thing; they should think a long, long time about what they did.[54]

Trudell has explained that, in essence, he believes the death of his family was "set up" by the FBI as a part of its strategy to silence his and other AIM members' attempts to draw broad public attention to the Bureau's pattern of abuses concerning AIM in general and Pine Ridge in particular. He attributes the emphasis placed upon himself and his family in this regard not only to his high position within AIM, but to the FBI's assessment of his special talents as a speaker/organizer, repeated over and over in the investigatory documents amassed on him between 1969 and 1979 (some 17,000 pages of which were released in a FOIA suit in 1986):

> TRUDELL is an intelligent individual and eloquent speaker who has the ability to stimulate people into action. TRUDELL is a known hardliner who openly advocates and encourages the use of violence [*i.e.*: armed self-defense] although he himself never becomes involved in the fighting...TRUDELL has the ability to meet with a group of pacifists and in a short time have them yelling and screaming "right-on!" In short, he is an extremely effective agitator.[55]

As we have seen, a number of people died on Pine Ridge during the period 1972-76, as a result of having tendered far less provocation to the Federal Bureau of Investigation than is entailed in this Bureau "profile" of John Trudell.

Other COINTELPRO-Style Activities in the 1980s

Of course, not all COINTELPRO-type activities during the 1980s have involved murder, nor have they been directed exclusively against AIM. To the contrary, such examples as are brought out above seem to represent extreme cases, the exception rather than the rule. More typical have been the operations of New York's Joint Terrorist Task Force (JTTF), an FBI-police amalgam patterned after those pioneered in Los Angeles and Chicago (see Chapter 3). The JTTF was "formed in 1980 to investigate bombings by an anti-Castro group called Omega 7, a Yugoslavian terrorist group known as the Croatian Liberation Forces, and a Puerto Rican terrorist [*sic*] group called *Fuerzas Armadas de Liberación Nacional Puertorriqueña*, or FALN."[56] Rhetoric concerning "terrorism" notwithstanding, the founding principles of the JTTF—like those of its predecessors in the West and Midwest—concern nothing so much as the suppression of political dissidence within the United States.

In terms of real clandestine organizational activity, the JTTF proved resoundingly inept from the first day. For instance, a Black Liberation Army spin-off calling itself the Revolutionary Armed Task Force (RATF) was able to conduct a series of armed expropriations of armored cars in New York during 1980-81 without the "counter-terrorists" coming up with a clue as to their identities.[57] The supposed "terrorists" were utilizing the proceeds to fund a clinic (the Black Acupuncture Advisory Association of North America, BAAANA) in Harlem and to underwrite health care for the slum community of the South Bronx.[58] It was only after an unsuccessful attempt to rob a Brinks truck in West Nyack, New York on October 20, 1981—an action in which two police officers were killed, and several RATF members captured by the local constabulary—that the FBI and its cohorts were able to "crack the case."[59] The two policemen, Waverly L. Brown and Edward O'Grady, are the only known casualties inflicted by the "Terrorist Family" in its decade of "armed propaganda," a record much less lethal than the FBI and police "counter-terrorists."

The JTTF proved far more effective against non-clandestine groups which supported, but did not engage in, armed struggle. One example concerns a study group formed by Coltrane Chimerenga (slave name: Randolph Simms), an RNA member and associate of BAAANA. Attempting to define this group as "The Son of Brinks," successor organization to the RATF:

> From December 21, 1983...until October 18, 1984...the JTTF wiretapped their telephones, bugged their apartments and dispatched surveillance teams consisting of one hundred or more agents.[60]

They also managed to infiltrate a provocateur named Howard Bonds into the group.[61] In the end, frustrated at having no more than sinister-sounding theorizing to go on—"no armored cars were robbed or [RATF] members broken out of jail"[62]— but still determined to stamp out such dangerous thinking, the JTTF arrested five group members, including Chimerenga. They were charged with various sorts of "criminal conspiracy," much of which involved ideas or "plans" introduced by Bonds.[63] Despite the infiltrator's testimony, and "450 pages of affidavits that included lengthy excerpts from court-ordered wiretaps—all purporting to "prove" the charges—Chimerenga and his co-defendants were acquitted on most counts on August 5, 1985; they were found guilty only of having possession of weapons deemed illegal in the city of New York, and of having false IDs:

> In conversations with defense lawyers following the verdict, the jurors condemned the JTTF surveillance as an infringement of the defendants' civil liberties and said they were worried their own phones were tapped. They dismissed the investigation as guilt by association...[64]

The group was thoroughly crushed by the arrests and trial, and the FBI and police conveyed the message that certain types of political thought, even at the most abstract levels, are simply forbidden. At about the same time, the JTTF was engaged in harassment directed at members of the May 19th Movement and other support organizations,[65] while grand juries were utilized as a mechanism by which to jail activists such as former Weather Underground fugitive Bernardine Dohrn and Fulani Sunni-Ali, wife of RATF member Bilal Sunni-Ali.[66] Little if any of this had to do with suspected violence (*i.e.*: "terrorism") on the part of those targeted. Similar tactics were used in Chicago, where individuals such as *Movimiento de Liberación Nacional* (MLN) activists Ricardo Romero, María Cueto, Steven Guerra, Julio Rosado, and Andrés Rosado were sent to prison for periods of up to three years for the "criminal contempt" of refusing to cooperate with grand juries.[67]

As all this was going on, a concerted effort was being made to destroy those "political hardliners" who were incarcerated in federal prisons. For examples, RATF members Sekou Odinga, Sundiata Acoli, Richard Thompson-El and Timothy Blunk were all placed in the Marion super-max, where the Control Unit, according to U.S. District Judge James Foreman, "has been used to silence prison critics. It has been used to silence religious leaders. It has been used to silence economic and philosophic dissidents."[68] A former Marion warden, Ralph Aron, has joined in Judge Foreman's assessment, observing rather proudly that, "The purpose of the Marion Control Unit is to control revolutionary attitudes in the prison system *and the society at large* [emphasis added]."[69]

Across gender lines, RATF members Susan Rosenberg and Silvia Baraldini, along with FALN leader Alejandrina Torres, were entombed for an indefinite period in the Control Unit of the maximum security women's facility at Lexington, Kentucky. The purpose of the unit, according to noted prison psychologist and criminologist Richard Korn, is equally straightforward:

> [The Control Unit functions] to reduce the prisoners to the state of submission essential for their ideological conversion. That failing, the next step is to reduce them to a state of psychological incompetence sufficient to neutralize them as efficient, self-directed antagonists. That failing, the only alternative is to destroy them, preferably by making them desperate enough to destroy themselves.[70]

The Attack on the Puerto Rican Independence Movement

Beginning with some of the earliest acknowledged COINTELPROs—*circa* 1960 (see Chapter 2)—organizations advocating independence for Puerto Rico have been the targets of FBI counterintelligence programs. Over the years, the Bureau has pioneered some of its ugliest counterintelligence methods against the *independentistas*, including an ample measure of physical violence. With reference to the content of some seventy-five *volumes* of "investigative file material" compiled on him alone, the veteran *independentista* leader Juan Mari Bras testified before the United Nations that:

> They [the files] reflect the general activity of the FBI toward the Movement. But some of the memos are dated 1976 and 1977; long after Cointelpro was [supposedly] ended as an FBI activity...[For example, at] one point, there is a detailed description of the death of my son, in 1976, at the hands of a gun-toting assassin. The bottom of the memo is fully deleted leaving one wondering who the assassin was. The main point, however, is that the memo is almost joyful about the impact his death will undoubtedly have on me...[71]

The Mari Bras files also contain several memos recounting the circumstances of the Puerto Rican leader's several heart attacks and offering suggestions as to how the Bureau might put more pressure on him, a tactic calculated to produce more of the same. One document even contends, "It is hardly idle boasting to say that at

Puerto Rican *independentista* leader Juan Mari Bras was a target of vicious FBI COINTELPRO-type activities throughout the 1970s and 1980s. Among the successful operations reported by Bureau agents was causing the elderly activist to suffer a heart attack. (Photo: *Claridad*)

least some of the Bureau's activities have provoked the situation of Mari Bras."[72] Of course, there have been other targets. Among these was Juan Cabellero, a militant Teamster shop steward who mysteriously disappeared after being questioned by police in mid-October 1977. On the 25th of that month, a body which was supposedly his was discovered, bound hand and foot with electrical wire, in El Yunque rain forest. Police "explained" the matter by suggesting that Cabellero had been executed by fellow Teamsters; the union, police hinted, might have been under the impression that the steward had turned informer. In a second striking parallel to the Anna Mae Aquash case (see Chapter 7) the FBI severed the corpse's hands for purposes of making a "positive identification" at the FBIHQ fingerprint lab in Washington. This time, however, the Bureau "lost" these vital body parts, just as it claimed to have lost exculpatory ELSURS evidence in the case of Geronimo Pratt (Chapter 3). The situation became even more bizarre when it was revealed that x-rays of the rain forest body failed to match up with Cabellero's dental charts. To date, questions concerning the body's real identity and the nature of Cabellero's actual fate have never been resolved.[73]

Such "problems" notwithstanding, prosecutors (assisted by the FBI) felt quite free to enter the alleged "Cabellero execution" into the 1978 case brought against Teamster organizer Miguel Cabrera, accused in the September 1977 murder of a U.S. attorney named Allen Randall (legal counsel to the arch-reactionary National Labor Relations Board in Puerto Rico). The government's star witness at trial was an admitted "professional assassin," Angel Hernandez Tanco, who was "cooperating" with authorities in exchange for much-reduced sentencing on four murder convictions of his own. Although Tanco apparently tried hard, when neither the prosecution's testimony nor the physical evidence jibed with the case brought against Cabrera, the jury acquitted him. But, by this point, he had already spent more than a year in jail and, as Alfredo Lopez sums it up: "There is no doubt about the impact [of Cabellero's disappearance and Cabrera's trial]: it halted the Teamsters' drive at a crucial period and forced the union into a defensive posture. This type of case can be recounted dozens of times: key people tried at key moments and removed from leadership positions by evidence that suddenly falls apart at trial."[74]

In yet another example:

> It is known that FBI personnel met with police prior to the assassination of two *independentistas*, in an ambush in the Cerro Maravilla area in 1978. According to police, the two were on their way to bomb a police station and were accompanied by a police informant who admits having planned and urged the bombing. A *carro publico* driver who witnessed the ambush testified that some three police who were waiting in the bushes shot without giving orders of any kind and without either of the youngsters raising their revolvers. "It was a planned murder," he told a commission set up to investigate, "and it was carried out like that."[75]

As in the Pine Ridge anti-AIM campaign, while the Bureau had abundant resources with which to participate prominently in these sorts of repressive activities, it proved spectacularly unable to come to grips with *any* sort of violence directed at independence advocates:

> [O]ver the last fifteen years, 170 attacks—beatings, shootings, and bombings of independence organizations and activists—have been documented. The offices of the pro-independence newspaper *Claridad* have been bombed three times; its printing press has been bombed twice and burned once. The PIP [*Partido Independentista Puertorriqueña*] offices have been bombed three times. The PSP's [*Partido Socialista Puertorriqueña*] bombed once; Mari Bras' home was burned down once. There have been countless attacks and beatings of people at rallies and pickets, to say nothing of "unsolved" incidents of beatings of *independentistas* walking the streets. These are routine. The 1975 bombing of a rally in Mayaguez that killed two restaurant workers was more dramatic, but like the other 170 attacks, remains unsolved. Although right-wing organizations claimed credit for nearly 70 of these attacks, not one person has ever been arrested or brought to trial.[76]

During the 1980s, the FALN and other organizations devoted to the cause of independence have been the target of some of Bureau's most intense covert operations. FBI activities on the island culminated on August 30, 1985 with a massive paramilitary operation bearing a striking resemblance to the operations on the Pine Ridge and Rosebud Reservations a decade earlier. More than 300 heavily armed FBI agents and U.S. marshals participated in raids throughout Puerto Rico, kicking in doors, conducting warrantless searches, wrecking the contents of homes, impounding personal property and arresting scores of activists on "John Doe" warrants. The operation was staged at the Roosevelt Roads Naval Base and carried out with the active participation of the military. The Puerto Rican government was not notified until after the operation was well under way, which Governor Rafael Hernández Colon termed "an unpardonable omission." In a clarification of Puerto Rico's colonial status, the FBI responded that they were not required to keep the Puerto Rican government informed of their activities and called the governor's objections "lamentable."[77]

Anti-FBI demonstration in San Juan, Puerto Rico, shortly after the Bureau's Palmer Raid-style sweep of the *independentista* movement on the island in 1985. (Photo: *Claridad*)

The pretext for the massive raids was a $7.2 million 1983 Wells-Fargo robbery in Hartford, Connecticut, credited to a clandestine Puerto Rican independence movement, *Los Macheteros*. Eventually sixteen *independentistas* were indicted in connection with this action.[78] As pretrial hearings in the cases enter their third year, a pattern of FBI abuses has emerged with all the hallmarks of a classic COINTELPRO. For example:

- FBI agent José Rodríguez was forced to admit he "mis-spoke" when he testified during the hearings that Cuban arms were discovered in the home of one of the defendants, Hilton Fernández.[79]

- In an attempt to coerce him into collaborating, the FBI bad-jacketed *independentista* Alejandro Martínez Vargas. In a *San Juan Star* article, SA Fernando Rivero referred to Martínez Vargas as a "former *Machetero*, now informant." Martínez Vargas was kept in isolation and subjected to what he termed "fascist means to break [him] down psychologically and physically," which included death threats against his family. Martínez Vargas remained steadfast in his refusal to cooperate.[80]

- One of the bulwarks of the FBI's case is the testimony of informant Carlos Rodríguez Rodríguez. A former activist, Rodríguez Rodríguez traded his testimony for sentence reductions for his wife and himself on charges of bank fraud and possession of heroin with intent to distribute, as well as charge reductions on two counts of homicide and ten weapons charges.[81]

- Two FBI agents have admitted using illegal electronic surveillance (ELSUR) procedures. Federal law requires agents to record all surveillance. Not only did the agents fail to record monitored conversations, they signed affidavits to the effect that they had recorded them. Furthermore, the Puerto Rican constitution specifically prohibits such electronic surveillance.[82]

• An examination by an expert hired by the defense team of ELSUR tapes presented during the hearings revealed that the tapes were not originals and showed signs of tampering.[83]

The case has already cost the government some $15 million and has yet to come to trial. The trial, scheduled for spring 1988, promises to be as lengthy as the pretrial hearings. Two defendants, Juan Segarra Palmer and Filberto Ojeda Ríos, have already been held without bail for twenty-eight months on non-capital charges, longer than anyone in U.S. judicial history.[84] And as the full scope of the FBI's operations is revealed, public disaffection with the program is growing:

...National outrage increased when the Puerto Rican Police Intelligence Division [interlocked with the Bureau in a manner which should, by now, be quite familiar] admitted in court that its massive surveillance efforts against the Independence Movement includes files on 74,000 individuals.[85]

The FBI's SAC in San Juan, Puerto Rico, who oversaw the planning and execution of this incredible preemption of legality was former Los Angeles office COIN-TELPRO specialist Richard Wallace Held,[86] promoted, no doubt, because of the success of his earlier operations against Geronimo Pratt, Bunchy Carter, Jon Huggins, and Jean Seberg, to name but a few (see Chapter 3). Less than two months after the Puerto Rican raid, Held was rewarded again, transferred to serve as SAC, San Francisco.

Harassment of Central America Activists

Nor have the FBI's COINTELPRO-type attentions been devoted exclusively to individuals and organizations which might arguably be considered supporters of armed struggle. For instance, Christic Institute attorney Daniel Sheehan recounts how, in 1986, FBI agents paid personal visits to financial supporters of the Sanctuary Movement—an entirely nonviolent, church-based entity devoted to achieving the safety of refugees from the U.S.-sponsored wars and repression rampaging throughout Central America—to spread the deliberate disinformation that the organization was "terrorist controlled" and devoted to "infiltrating Latin American terrorists into the United States."[87] In the same vein, the Center for Constitutional Rights (CCR) and National Lawyers Guild have jointly released a list of nearly 200 documented instances of suspected counterintelligence activities being directed at Sanctuary activists and members of affiliated organizations, as well as members of other nonviolently dissident political groups within the U.S. between 1984 and the end of 1986. The following examples are indicative of the whole:[88]

- On April 2, 1986, two secretaries at the United Church of Santa Fe in New Mexico discovered that the door to the church's educational area had been broken into and the wood around the deadbolt locks gouged out. Inner offices were entered and an attempt made to break open the exit door. Nothing of monetary value was taken, although petty cash was available, but cabinets and closets were gone through and the church membership lists were left on a desk top. Although it was not officially a sanctuary church, many members are vocal advocates of sanctuary and lobbied to make Santa Fe a sanctuary city and New Mexico a sanctuary state. The incident was reported to city police who "shrugged it off."

- On April 6, 1986, the *Dallas Morning News* released a story about Frank Varelli, a Salvadoran who became a U.S. citizen and was hired by the FBI in 1981 to analyze information received from other FBI offices and the CIA about El Salvador. In 1982 he went to El Salvador to make contact with the intelligence unit of the National Guard. Then, assuming the identity of a refugee named Gilberto Mendoza, he infiltrated Dallas CISPES as part of an FBI covert operation designed to uncover the "terrorist activities" of a number of Dallas organizations. Varelli, who had resigned in 1984, decided to tell his story because he was angry that the FBI had refused to give him back pay.

- On April 7, 1986, the apartment of two Brookline, Massachusetts art instructors involved in cultural exchange programs with Cuban and Nicaraguan artists was broken into. The intruders, who entered by breaking a window, took computer disks, a telephone answering machine and a beeper, but left all other valuables untouched. The police report on the incident termed it "a teenager's prank."

- On April 14, 1986, 150 persons participated in a rally and act of civil disobedience in opposition to Contra aid at 26 Federal Plaza in New York City. One of the persons arrested recognized a member of the Joint Terrorist Task Force (JTTF) who had been pointed out to him about a year ago at a John Brown Anti-Klan demonstration, also in New York City. The agent was watching the participants. The arrestee said to the agent, "I know you're part of the JTTF. Do you think we are all terrorists?" The agent replied, "You may not all be terrorists yet, but I'm sure there is some Soviet infiltration here."

- On the night of May 21-22, 1986, in New York, the offices of the North American Congress on Latin America (NACLA) were burglarized. There were no signs of forced entry. Desk drawers were opened and even the contents of envelopes were examined. One wall was graffitied, but only $20 and a heavy tool box were taken.

- On June 11, 1986, the apartment of a Brooklyn woman whose sister is active in Central America work was burglarized and ransacked. The intruders went through her files, and, ignoring items of value, took only a few of her earrings.

- On June 12, 1986, intruders burglarized and ransacked the apartment of a Michigan woman active in the Central America Solidarity Committee. They rifled her files and threw papers and books all over the floor. Items of value—TV, stereo, and rent money—were ignored.

- On July 29, 1986, a Center for Constitutional Rights staff person reported that when her travel agent telephoned, although she was home and her answering machine on, no message came over. Instead, a man answered who said: "I'm her boyfriend and a policeman, I'll take the message."

- On September 26, 1986, the car of a man active in Witness for Peace was broken into. Items taken were a briefcase containing Nicaraguan newspapers, books and files, a slide projector and slides of Nicaragua, camera, typewriter and suitcase of clothing. One hundred pamphlets on the back seat entitled *What We Have Seen and Heard in Nicaragua* were also taken. A passport, checkbook and overcoat were left behind.

- On November 17, 1986, Centro Presente, a Cambridge organization that helps refugees from El Salvador, was broken into. A computer, disks, files and keys to the file cabinet were taken.

- On November 30, 1986, offices of the International Center for Development Policy (Commission on U.S.-Central American Relations) were broken into. Files were ransacked and documents stolen. One of the documents stolen concerned a covert Southern Air Transport flight which carried arms to the Contras. Southern Air Transport is a CIA "proprietary."

- In early December 1986, the pastor of the Reformed Christian Church in Washington, D.C. received a call from his brother who had recently returned from Nicaragua. On December 14, 1986, the pastor discovered that his office in the church had been burglarized. Files were rifled, old tax returns and checkbooks taken out and examined. The only items removed were an old Walkman and a blood pressure monitor. Computer equipment and an expensive radio were left behind. A second break-in occurred on January 6, 1987. The burglar took a new blood pressure monitor and a Walkman.

- On the night of January 3-4, 1987, a break-in occurred at the Arlington Street Church in Boston. Five locked offices were entered. Files and desk drawers were rifled. The burglars were expert lock pickers and apparently knew which offices to enter. The only missing items were a padlock and $5 in petty cash. The church's vote to become a sanctuary was announced in its newsletter on January 1, 1986 and reported in the *Boston Globe* on January 2. Sanctuary was also the subject of the January 4, 1987 sermon.

The list was extended by a raft of more than 300 comparable incidents of harassment occurring between 1984 and 1988, itemized in a second report issued by CCR and the National Lawyers Guild on January 27, 1988.[89] This time, the compilation was offered in the context of a finding—gleaned from the heavily deleted pages of more than 3,600 investigative documents the Bureau was forced to divulge because of a successful FOIA suit brought by CCR attorneys—that the incidents had been part of a massive and prolonged "probe" of more than 200 U.S. social, religious and political organizations, as well as a large but undetermined number of individual activists.[90]

According to Margaret Ratner, CCR Education Director, the FBI activity had constituted "a sweeping and intrusive investigation" spawning files containing "reports of political beliefs of hundreds of individuals." The latter "show that the FBI widely disseminated thousands of photographs of people who attended peaceful demonstrations, regularly recorded license plate numbers of cars parked near meetings and rallies, monitored radio stations, invaded campuses, and caused FBI files and indices to be searched on countless individuals and organizations." They also "show that the FBI utilized wiretaps, undercover agents, and informants, in addition to the type of intensive physical surveillance that is normally associated with investigations of serious crimes."[91] Ann Mari Buitrago, Director of an intelligence analysis enterprise in New York called FOIA, Inc., followed up by noting that the files had been collected with the active participation of at least "52 FBI field offices," thus establishing clearly that what had happened was truly national in scope.[92]

At the center of the Bureau undertaking was the Committee in Solidarity with the People of El Salvador (CISPES), an organization quite outspoken in its opposition to the Reagan Administration's Central America policies. According to Buitrago, "For two years, 1981 through 1982, the FBI tried *unsuccessfully* to substantiate a charge that CISPES was an agent of a foreign government and thus in violation of the Foreign Agents Registration Act."[93]

When this attempt failed, the FBI, with the approval of Attorney General William French Smith, mounted a Foreign Counterintelligence-International Terrorism investigation on the premise that CISPES might be a terrorist organization. Needless to say, the FBI never had nor ever found any information to support that premise, unless you give credence (which even the FBI did not) to a preposterous story, generated by a Dallas informer, Frank Varelli, that CISPES was running a rehabilitation and reindoctrination camp for Salvadoran refugees, some of whom remained in the U.S. to commit acts of terrorism.[94]

By mid-1984, "finding no evidence to support its obviously fradulent premise, the FBI, in order to keep the investigation going, reached into the bag of tricks it had developed in the Hoover era. Despite the fact that reports from the FBI field offices investigating CISPES made it clear that individuals and groups working with CISPES were 'legitimate' and 'respectable' and CISPES' activities—demonstrating, lobbying, protesting, speaking, publishing newsletters, and occasionally conducting non-violent civil disobedience—were all protected by the First Amendment, the FBI developed two rationales that allowed the investigation to continue.[95] These were:

The "covert programs" rationale. To explain away its negative results, the FBI reasoned that all peaceful legal activities on which CISPES' broad support was based represented an *overt* program designed to cover a sinister *covert* program of which most CISPES members were unaware.

The "Front Group" rationale. The old concept of "front groups" was dredged up to enable the investigation to expand beyond CISPES chapters and affiliates to any of the

"Mr. Clean." Despite his reputation as having cleaned up the FBI's Hoover-era practices, Director William Webster's qualifications include being the judge of the Eighth Circuit Court who scuttled Leonard Peltier's first appeal prior to his promotion to head the Bureau. During the 1980s, Webster oversaw the most systematic operations against political organizations since COINTELPRO prior to his promotion to direct the CIA. (Photo: Teresa Zabala)

hundreds of organizations whose work brought them in touch with CISPES or its members...Since any group *might* be a cover there were no effective limits to the choice of targets or the duration of the investigation. In fact, the logic of these rationales drove the investigation further and deeper; failure to turn up evidence of illegality increased the pressure to expand the hunt for "fronts" and intensify the search for covert activities.[96]

The two rationales combined to spread the Bureau's investigative focus to at least 215 organizations other than CISPES. Included among these were not only such standard "militant" targets as AIM, the BLA, and the Marxist-Leninist Party, USA, but many other *completely* incongruous groups and institutions such as the Maryknoll Sisters, the Moslem Students Association, Amnesty International, the Chicago Interreligious Taskforce, the National Education Association, Wichita State University, Clergy and Laity Concerned, Vanderbilt University, the U.S. Catholic Conference, the Virginia Education Association, and the National Association of Women Religious.[97]

As concerns individuals, not only were mainstay CISPES organizers such as former Rocky Mountain Regional Coordinator Gonzalo Santos targeted for special attention,[98] but also individuals with no tangible connection to CISPES or any other politically dissident group. A classic example of this concerns Paul F. Knitter, a theology professor at Xavier University. Apparently on the basis of the fact that Knitter belonged to a rather staid and mainstream Catholic relief organization taking Central America as one of its areas of concern, he became the subject of Bureau scrutiny. Although Cincinnati SAC Terrence D. Dinan denies that his office opened a formal investigation of Knitter, agents repeatedly questioned the professor's colleagues and administrators at Xavier concerning the possibility of his having engaged in "subversive" activities during the spring of 1985. Xavier being a thoroughly conservative

FBI Director William Sessions during a January 1988 press conference in which he admitted the Bureau's operations against CISPES and more than 200 other dissident organizations during the 1980s had been "poorly directed." Nonetheless, the Director defended his agents' actions. (Photo: Wide World)

school, Knitter was consequently subjected to considerable anxiety as to the status of his job, and admits that his expression of political belief was substantially chilled as a result.[99]

In the wake of these revelations, FBI Director William S. Sessions (a recent replacement for William Webster, who oversaw the entire CISPES affair before being promoted to head up the CIA) acknowledged that the investigation had "not been properly directed" in its entirety. Still, Sessions maintained that it had been "warranted" because the Bureau had a "legitimate concern" that CISPES and "affiliated groups" *might* have been guilty of "violating the Foreign Agents Registration Act," "complicit in terrorism," or "engaged in seditious conspiracy."[100] Ronald Reagan, of course, immediately weighed in with his "full support" for the FBI's conduct, terming it "entirely justified."[101] Neither the Director nor the President cared to bring up the fact that the Bureau had felt similarly "compelled" to "safeguard the national interest" by undertaking dozens of huge seditious conspiracy investigations against "leftist" U.S. organizations since 1950 without *ever* finding a basis for charges or any other demonstration of substance. Nor did they so much as hint that even in instances where violations of the Foreign Agents Registration Act by *right*-wing individuals and organizations were quite clear (*e.g., Soldier of Fortune* magazine publisher Robert K. Brown's running of Rhodesian National Army recruitment posters on the back cover of his publication from 1976-78) no comparable FBI investigation had resulted. Finally, they neglected to mention that where *right*-wing complicity in terrorism was amply demonstrated (*e.g.,* former Major General John Singlaub's unabashed recruitment and fundraising in behalf of the "Contra" troops slaughtering Nicaraguan civilians) the FBI had failed to act in any way whatsoever.

So transparent was official posturing in the matter that "responsible" journals of liberal public opinion such as the *New York Times* and *Boston Globe,* normally abject apologists for the *status quo*, were forced to bemoan the recurrence of FBI "excesses."[102] The *Globe*, ignoring much obvious recent history, even took to momentarily pondering such improbable questions as "how did the FBI go astray?"[103]

Such editorialists needn't have searched far for answers. The philosophical basis for such behavior on the part of the FBI was lucidly articulated in a concept paper prepared by a Bureau task force in 1976, purporting to explain the motivations underlying the ongoing assault on AIM:

> Many Americans tend to overlook the fact that the United States has constitutionally guaranteed rights which are just as inviolate as those of the individual. To accept at face value, an AIM argument, that it is set upon by the CIA, FBI and Bureau of Indian Affairs (BIA), as part of a government conspiracy to destroy the movement, and as a result, back off, would result in eventual abdication of this governmental responsibility...The government's right to continue full investigation of AIM and certain affiliated organizations may create relevant danger to a few citizens' privacy and free expression, but this danger must be weighed against society's [*i.e.,* the government's] *right to protect itself against domestic threats.*[104]

No more blatant expression of the state's "prerogative" to arbitrarily preempt or suspend constitutional rights of its citizenry—or of the FBI's function in enforcing the political, social and economic *status quo*—can be imagined. No society professing to be, or even aspiring to be, free, open and committed to democratic ideals can afford to allow its police agencies anything approaching this degree of cynicism and duplicity, or such latitude in operational discretion. This is all the more true in a period when, once again, we hear the themes of "national security," "internal security," "counter-terrorism," and "domestic intelligence" infesting our national political discourse. Despite all arguments (or wishes) to the contrary, systematic harassment and neutralization remain the prices demanded by America's political police of those who achieve, or even seek, oppositional political effectiveness. We may therefore anticipate that, if the present trend towards rekindling of social conscience and awareness, activism and pressure for a positive change in the United States continues to build into the 1990s, there will be a corresponding upsurge in COINTELPRO-type activities.

Impediments to Change

In April 1984, the U.S. House Subcommittee on Civil and Constitutional Rights released a report,[105] nearly four years in the making, on FBI undercover operations. Chaired by California Congressman Don Edwards, himself an ex-agent with a deserved reputation as one of the Bureau's sharper critics, the Subcommittee produced what in some ways is a very insightful document. Overall, the report held that "undercover operations carry with them the potential for serious damage, both to individuals and to the democratic institutions upon which our society is based."[106]

In the course of these hearings,

the Subcommittee learned a great deal about the pervasiveness of such operations, and the very disturbing impact that they had had on the lives of innocent individuals. As the hearing process continued, the Subcommittee's concerns were compounded by the realization that the technique posed a very real threat to our liberties. Many of the values reflected in our Constitution are directly threatened by these operations. The proper limit of governmental intrusion into individual's [sic] lives and privacy, reflected in the Fourth and Ninth Amendments; the protection of privileged relationships reflected in the First Amendment; and the requirements that criminal investigations and prosecutions be conducted in a fundamentally fair manner, commanded by the Fifth Amendment, are all being endangered by the undercover technique as it is being used today.[107]

The report continues:

The infiltration of government agents, or criminals who are financed by the government, into the private lives of citizens; the spectacle of the United States Government spending large sums of money to tempt people into committing crimes; and the atmosphere of fear, suspicion and paranoia which develops as the use of the technique expands, are all anathema to the values protected and cherished in our Constitution.[108]

Going into more detail, the Subcommittee found that "[undercover] operations are necessarily costly and often of long duration. The increased use of the technique is seen in the Bureau's own statistics. The FBI budget for undercover work has jumped from $1 million in 1977 to $12.5 million for 1984. Undercover operations have climbed from 53 in 1977 to over 300 in 1984."[109] What was involved in this accelerating trend was the FBI's "use of elaborate, lengthy, and deceptive practices [carrying] the need to avoid discovery [which] have resulted in severe harm befalling totally innocent citizens, either through a failure to monitor informants or as a result of careless (even callous) neglect or conscious design on the part of undercover agents."[110] Worse,

...the Subcommittee, in its review of undercover cases, has found that the undercover technique carries with it the potential for subjecting the innocent to opprobrium, prosecution and even conviction. *Because agents create crime, rather than merely detect it, they hold the power to create the appearance of guilt* [emphasis added].[111]

The Subcommittee also found that, "once an undercover operation is unleashed, virtually any individual can be subjected to a full testing of his [or her] morality by investigators armed with the full panoply of power exercised by the FBI in its traditional [sic] law enforcement activities."[112] Although "guidelines and safeguards [theoretically] exist and are directed at several aspects of undercover operations"[113] to prevent abuses, the Bureau simply ignored them whenever it chose. Using "Operation Corkscrew"[114] as an example, "field agents did not even apprise [the oversight body supposedly enforcing the vaunted guidelines and safeguards], much less seek approval, of changes" in their pre-approved plan of action.[115] More, operations such as Corkscrew "are *not* aberrations, but in fact reflect a pattern of recurrent problems which are inherent in the [undercover] process."[116]

The failure to abide not only

> by the letter but also the spirit of the safeguards and guidelines in this instance led to a complete fiasco. Even where, as in other operations [where allegedly legitimate], convictions or recoveries are obtained, and thus produce some measure of accomplishment, it is clear that the FBI and Department of Justice are incapable of adequately implementing their own safeguards and guidelines.[117]

All of this appears to add up to a significant insight on the part of the Subcommittee concerning the real nature of FBI covert operations. One might expect that, under such circumstances, some very far-reaching recommendations for corrective legislation might have been forthcoming. The Subcommittee drew back sharply from doing anything meaningful, however, observing that:

> Notwithstanding the foregoing, the Subcommittee believes that the undercover technique, where used judiciously, can be a valuable weapon in the law enforcement arsenal in appropriate cases...Therefore, the issue for the Subcommittee has been whether, and if so how, the citizens of this nation can reap the benefits of this law enforcement tool without subjecting themselves and the nation to the grave risks inherent in the process.[118]

Having thus set the stage for reduction of its own argument to a *non sequitur*, the Subcommittee proceeded to recommend only cosmetic alterations of the composition of the Undercover Operation Review Committee—which it had already determined was incapable of regulating Bureau operatives once they were set loose—as an antidote.[119] Beyond this, it recommended that warrants be required before undercover operations are begun and that Congress should "clarify" against what sort of targets such "sensitive techniques" might be employed.[120] That such gestures were virtually certain *not* to solve the problems identified as stemming from the Bureau's methods is clearly, albeit tacitly, admitted:

> The sufficiency of legal remedies available to third [or innocent?] parties injured by undercover operations must be monitored to determine whether injured third parties are obtaining compensation for their injuries, and if not, whether appropriate amendments to the Federal Torts Claims Act are necessary.[121]

This last is suggested as the sole "remedy" for FBI misconduct despite the Subcommittee's open acknowledgement that Bureau personnel had been *intentionally*, even "callously," inflicting great damage upon all manner of groups and individuals. In other words, the patently criminal activities of FBI personnel can only "appropriately" be addressed through *civil*, rather than criminal procedures.[122] Put another way, the Bureau was left perfectly free to continue, and possibly even escalate, the very sorts of operations over which the Subcommittee had ostensibly expressed considerable dismay.

Sadly, we have all become thoroughly conditioned to expect and even accept such shoddy performance on the part of Congress, at least where police and intelligence operations are concerned. The Subcommittee has considerable precedent for having waxed eloquently indignant about "excesses" and "abuses" before turning the guilty agencies loose to continue business as usual. The outcome of the earlier mentioned Church Committee offers ample evidence of this.

Worse in some respects has been the Congressional aptitude for sitting on its hands while the FBI systematically squelches those, including both "civilians" and active or former agents, who have attempted to shine even a little light into some of the darker recesses of Bureau violence and illegality. In part, this still assumes the form, covered in Chapter 1, of agents taking as part of their "official responsibility" the discrediting of anyone challenging Bureau mythology. A very recent example occurred when "Southern California's top FBI official [Richard T. Bretzing]...denounced Willie Nelson, Robin Williams and other entertainers for agreeing to appear at a benefit concert" intended to raise funds for the ongoing legal defense of Leonard Peltier.[123] After the attendance (and proceeds) from the October 27, 1987 event had been crippled by Bretzing's gratuitous, inaccurate and highly publicized commentary, the Los Angeles SAC seems to have busied himself inflicting further punishment upon Nelson—for having exercised his constitutional right to free speech in behalf of Peltier's constitutional right to due process—by sending his agents to local radio stations, requesting they cease playing Willie Nelson's music.[124] There has yet to be so much as a murmur of public protest concerning Bretzing's behavior from our duly elected representatives.

What is perhaps a worse case has been going on for several years. In May of 1983, then South Dakota Governor William Janklow filed a libel suit contending that he was entitled to some $4 million in actual and $20 million in punitive damages from the author Peter Matthiessen and his publisher, Viking Press, as well as three South Dakota bookstores which handle Matthiessen titles.[125] Janklow claimed that his character had been "defamed" by the best-selling writer in his exhaustive and extremely accurate study of the FBI's war on AIM, *In the Spirit of Crazy Horse*.[126] Although the suit was repeatedly dismissed as being groundless, Janklow managed to have it reinstated, dragging things out until a final dismissal in January of 1987. In the meantime, FBI agent David Price (now based out of Rochester, Minnesota) had entered a similar suit—reportedly for $40 million in aggregate damages—arguing that he had been "falsely portrayed as a racist" by Matthiessen.[127]

Underwritten in part by the ultra-reactionary Heritage Foundation, and obviously receiving the tacit support of the Bureau, Price's suit sufficiently intimidated Viking Press to cause it to meekly withdraw the title from circulation, "pending litigation."[128] Thus, the public has once again been denied an essential glimpse of the FBI's real workings without any legal or scholarly determination of the merits of a book's content whatsoever. (The suppression of Matthiessen's book was one of the motivations for this book, which relies heavily and intentionally on his material: these issues will *not* go away.) The libel suit tactic, when undertaken by government agencies such as the FBI (or its fronts, such as Price), cuts to the heart of the issue:

> Ultimately the essential rationale for giving the press [and book publishers] the power it has is to create a countervailing force to the use of political power as well as the other pockets of power in our society—economic and social…Unless the press is able to speak freely about the country's enormous power centers, [they] will develop an arrogance of their own that would be intolerable.[129]

On January 16, 1988 Price's lawsuit was thrown out by the U.S. District Court in Minneapolis. In dismissing the suit, Judge Diana Murphy wrote:

> As criticism of the government, the statements [in the book] are entitled to the maximum protection of the First Amendment. They cannot provide the basis for a defamation action.[130]

In the Spirit of Crazy Horse, meanwhile, has been thoroughly suppressed for nearly five years and Price's attorneys intend to appeal the dismissal to the U.S. Eighth Circuit Court of Appeals.

Plainly, in the case of the FBI, the arrogance at issue has *already* become intolerable, as the Bureau's campaign to suppress critical information over the past several decades indicates rather well. This appears to be all the more true when the sources of the Bureau's informational discomfort happen to be "members of the club." This was a lesson learned very well by former COINTELPRO operative Wesley Swearingen (see Chapters 2 and 3) when he left Bureau service and attempted to speak candidly about what was being done in the name of law and order. Even after the Church Committee's "COINTELPRO revelations," Swearingen remains bound by a set of "security guidelines" which prevent him from divulging his knowledge other than to respond to *specific* questions posed by an examiner for the purposes of legal deposition or testimony under oath.[131]

A more topical example concerns John C. Ryan, an agent with twenty-one years service and two commendations, who until very recently headed the counterintelligence section of the Bureau's Peoria, Illinois Resident Agency:

> Ryan's career came completely unraveled when he refused last December [1986] to conduct a local investigation of attacks on 11 military recruiting offices in the Chicago area. The target of the FBI probe was Silo Plowshares, a group in the Chicago area opposed to United States policy in Central America…[He] was headed for a quiet retirement…but 10 months before the big day, he was fired.[132]

Essentially, Ryan's offense was that he rejected the Bureau's classification of the pacifist Plowshares organization as "a terrorist group" and "felt strongly that the FBI should not be involved in surveillance of peace groups."[133] This "transformation from a case-hardened G-man to an unyielding pacifist,"[134] as well as a growing tendency to attempt to communicate with those he was assigned to repress, rendered him "unreliable" in the eyes of Bureau policy makers. He was therefore simply expelled from the FBI and placed under the same restrictive guidelines as those afflicting Swearingen.[135]

Meanwhile, as punishment is visited upon those few agents prompted by their consciences to break with Bureau practice, the shield of Presidential protection is extended over those—equally few—who have actually been called to account for their misdeeds. In this connection, a classic case is that of Ronald Reagan's immediate pardon of SAs W. Mark Felt and Edward S. Miller, agents of the FBI's New York office, convicted in 1983 of burglaries committed in their "investigation" of Weather Underground fugitives.[136] This was on a par with Reagan's 1981 commutation of the prison sentence of the former Democratic governor of Maryland (stripped of office in 1979 after having been convicted of mail fraud and accepting $380,000 in bribes),[137] while refusing to so much as review a single case among the many COINTELPRO victims still languishing in prisons.

In many ways, then, the prospects for securing justice with regard to what the FBI has done over the years—or even bringing the Bureau under some semblance of democratic control—are bleak. We are confronted with a resurgent FBI domestic counterintelligence capability which is no less vicious than it was ten years ago, and which can now rely upon the assistance of a much more evolved and perfected local police apparatus. We are saddled with a judicial system which is heavily weighted in favor of "law enforcement," and a judiciary which in far too many instances shares the reactionary sensibilities of agents and prosecutors, hopelessly biasing even this imperfect system's "due process" safeguards against political defendants. We are cursed with an executive branch which makes it a point of honor to enforce orthodoxy by often overriding whatever pittance of justice leaks through. And we are plagued with a legislature which, while typically professing to be appalled at these circumstances, has failed to *ever* do anything tangible about them. The entire seamy complex is bound up in the context of a public largely propagandized into believing that almost everything is other than it is.

Such an assessment is, no doubt, both accurate and the stuff of agony and despair. Certainly, it would be understandable in the face of such adversity to simply throw up one's hands, admit defeat and retreat into the supposed refuge of acquiescence. Yet the dynamics of institutional growth and consolidation—to which the police establishment is as subject as any other organizational entity—preclude this course. Unchecked, the FBI and its affiliates will inevitably continue to expand their power, spilling into all refuges at the expense of even the most basic human freedoms. The only true alternatives are to abandon ourselves to the totality of a police state, or to move forward in conscious, active opposition to it.

Chapter 14

Moving Forward

Beaten one, who shall avenge you? You on whom the blows are falling, Hear your wounded comrades calling, Weakness gives us strength to lend you. Comrade, come, we shall avenge you. Everything or nothing. All of us or none.
—Bertolt Brecht

Never forget. Never forget what they have done...
—Chris DeBurgh, 1983

The idea of coming to grips with the FBI and its surrogates no doubt seems quite daunting. Despite the fact that a limited range of options presently exists—including conscious non-cooperation with *any* Bureau investigation, the entry of civil suits via such socially responsible legal entities as the Christic Institute and Center for Constitutional Rights, and the maximization of FOIA requests—by which private citizens may engage in some level of confrontation with the domestic counterintelligence apparatus, going toe-to-toe with it "in the street" promises little but horrible consequences for those who attempt to do so. Still, we obviously *must* proceed to bring the agency to heel, and there *are* strategies for beginning to achieve this goal.

The first phase of any such effort is, however, predicated upon a certain alteration of the perspectives prevailing in most quarters of the American opposition today. This goes to the notion that the devoting of individual/organizational time, energy and other resources to attaining curtailment of the FBI's operational latitude is somehow too "reformist" or too "wide of the central issues" to be systematically undertaken. What must be understood, and understood quite clearly by all concerned, is that only through such reform can the "space" be bought within which progressive groupings can hope to pursue successfully broader and more radical agendas of societal transformation. Until such reform can be achieved, and the FBI's license to attack political targets revoked, the Bureau may be counted upon to follow its seventy-year tradition by neutralizing dissident political formations long before they manage to consolidate their potentials.

In terms of issue-orientation, it matters not at all what the focus of a given group may be. Whether one believes that the re-allocation of the means of production to the working class is paramount, thinks that ending women's oppression is most important, wishes to see centralized government dissolved altogether, considers oneself to be a staunch anti-imperialist or follows the visions of cultural nationalism, each central issue represents a flat challenge to the political orthodoxy of the U.S. *status quo*. You and your organization are thus a matter of concern to the FBI and, therefore, subject to one or another level of intelligence and counterintelligence attention. In many instances, the same may be said even if the nature of your activism is less philosophically sweeping. It matters little whether your concern is with tax or draft resistance, seeing treaties with American Indians finally honored, combatting the abuses of the Immigration and Naturalization "Service," forcing open information in the governmental and corporate sectors, combatting defense spending, fighting discrimination in jobs and housing, advocating consumer rights, securing gay/lesbian rights, ending environmental destruction, or humanizing penal and mental health institutions. You are a "deviant" who has thereby become a real or potential threat to one or another tenet of the *status quo*. And, as the histories of both the Bureau and American progressivism amply demonstrate, to the extent that you become effective at advocating and organizing around your agenda, you will be targeted by the FBI for systematic undermining and discrediting, harassment, and—ultimately—outright elimination by counterintelligence operatives. The first task is to understand this unpleasant reality. Avoidance of the facts, and consignment of those who speak of them to the realm of "paranoia"—a common phenomenon during the late 1960s, the very height of the COINTELPRO era— is not helpful. The reality of a nation-wide, highly perfected mechanism of political repression (with the FBI as its hub) must be accepted for what it is, and assigned the high priority it deserves. Regardless of whether the various elements of American progressivism can otherwise so much as agree on the menu for lunch, they must in this case overcome their many deep divisions and face the fact that in this regard they confront a common enemy, occupy common ground and simply *must* act in concert to curb the ability of the FBI to serve as a political regulator.

The most expeditious route to achieving the sort of "united front against FBI repression" which is plainly needed would seem to lie in the formation of some type of national council intended to serve only this purpose. All progressive (or nominally progressive) organizations should be called upon to participate by sending representatives. All such organizations should also be expected to participate at a more grassroots level by assigning a firm portion of their resources—human, financial and otherwise—to combatting police repression of political activism. The proposed council could serve as an overarching coordinative body, allowing for the emergence of a coherent, national anti-FBI strategy. This could also be the entity which oversees implementation of this strategy, develops an effective lobbying effort, disseminates information, raises funds and directs overall energy toward individual local flashpoints.

It appears probable that the initial objectives of such an amalgamation should be to undertake a massive public education campaign concerning the FBI and its affiliates. This book and others like it have been efforts in that direction; sadly, they barely scratch the surface. Vast amounts of information concerning COINTELPRO-type activities undertaken by federal and local police over the past 25 years is presently scattered across the country, and is generally inaccessible. A tremendous and ongoing effort is needed to bring this information into a clearinghouse operation which would make it available to all who have use for it.

Such an effort should not restrict itself to the generation of document copies and "movement" films and literature (although these are sorely needed, and will inevitably carry the brunt of early dissemination), but should push its way into the mainstream media. Ten thousand or 100,000 people from across the nation demanding that *60 Minutes* air a particular program segment, or that the *New York Times* devote coverage to a given topic, has been known to have a certain productive effect. This is all the more true if *20/20* can be convinced to "scoop" its rival news program, or if *Mother Jones* and *Zeta* magazines are fulfilling their potentials. The message to those in power in the United States must be that the body politic is increasingly less afflicted with social amnesia: "We know what the FBI and its cohorts have done, and *we will remember.* An accounting is both overdue and inevitable."

Particular examples drawn from the available information about how political repression has been carried out in the U.S. should be used as the bases upon which to mount the first concrete national campaigns to reverse the "successfulness" of FBI counterintelligence programs. In this regard, the cases of Geronimo Pratt and Leonard Peltier—both used by the Bureau as symbols of the high cost of unswerving resistance to the present social order—should be considered paramount. Continued, detailed exposure of the ways they were targeted for neutralization and railroaded into prison offers an exceedingly important lesson to learn, and their release from the cells in which they are currently incarcerated would be a severe blow to the FBI, not only symbolically, but tactically and in terms of agent morale.

Undertakings of this sort will naturally point up specific and glaring gaps in our information base. These, in combination with the damning information already known, constitute a logical basis for an urgent demand for the re-convening of a formal congressional investigation into the methods employed by the FBI counterintelligence operations past, present and projected. Converting this entirely legitimate demand into actual hearings will undoubtedly require a sustained and highly visible national campaign (*i.e.*: demonstrations, letter writing, petition drives, etc.) directed at Congress. It may well prove necessary to focus national attention on certain members of Congress who, as "friends of the Bureau," would go out of their way to cripple or block such an investigation. The objective in such instances must be to unseat them, bringing national resources to bear in their local campaigns and getting the message across that there are direct consequences attached to championing the agents of repression.

Integral to the call for any investigation of the FBI must be the unequivocal instruction to our elected representatives that a mere repeat of the Church Committee's halfway measures will *not* be acceptable. One way of approaching this is by insisting that any investigation begin where the Church panel left off; with the question of FBI complicity in the assassinations of Mark Clark, Fred Hampton and many other key BPP leaders during the period 1969-71. An even more salient area of exploration, it should be stressed, concerns the FBI's anti-AIM operations related to Pine Ridge, 1972-76, with special emphasis placed upon the assassinations of key leaders such as Pedro Bissonette, Byron DeSersa and Anna Mae Aquash. A consistent theme underlying all demands for an investigation must be that we are entitled not *just* to know precisely what happened, and to receive Bureau assurances that "it will never happen again," but—where given agents can be shown to have been involved in murder, or in the coverup of murder—they be tried, and if convicted, sent to prison. The vacancies created in various penal facilities by the release of Pratt, Peltier and other political prisoners/POWs will surely create room for the accommodation of such FBI personnel.

Similarly, emphasis must be placed upon examination of instances of deliberate fabrication or withholding of evidence related to the criminal prosecutions of political targets. Orchestrating the false imprisonment of an individual is a crime very nearly as bad as murder (some might argue it is even worse), and should be treated as such. Close attention should be paid at the outset to known instances—such as the introduction of Louis Moves Camp as a prosecution witness in the Wounded Knee Leadership Trial of Dennis Banks and Russell Means, the use of Myrtle Poor Bear against Dick Marshall and Leonard Peltier, and the Bureau-contrived perjury of Julius C. Butler in the trial of Geronimo Pratt—where the FBI has obviously engaged in such activities. It hardly seems unlikely that many other, lesser known instances will emerge during any serious investigation. Again, where possible, individual agents (and prosecutors) who can be conclusively shown to have been involved should be routed straight to the nearest penitentiary. In instances where absence of existing legislation and/or the Statute of Limitations preclude outright prosecution, the culpable parties should be summarily dismissed from government service on the grounds of having "engaged in conduct violating public trust."

Another integral aspect of any demand for Congressional investigation must be that it result in *meaningful* legislation to prevent any continuation or recurrence of the FBI's counterintelligence business as usual. It must be impressed upon Congress that the "tuning" of existing rules and guidelines, the formation of "appropriate oversight bodies" (or cosmetic reconfiguration of existing ones), and the like, have already been tried and have failed. They are thus, in themselves, not a successful agenda for resolving the problems at issue. It must be clearly explained that what is expected—at a *minimum*—is that the Bureau be bound hand and foot in terms of its ability to intervene ever again in the domestic political process. Legislation is therefore required making it a criminal offense for a government official to engage in *any* COINTELPRO-style activity such as spreading disinformation about individuals and groups, infiltrating provocateurs into organizations, bad-jacketing any individual, and so forth. Equally, the appropriate statutes must be revised so that criminal prosecution is *required* in any instance where an agent can be shown to have perjured him/herself, suborned perjury from another, tampered with evidence or withheld evidence of any sort. Such principles should also apply to prosecutors and local police.

In order to get any sort of viable oversight of all this, it is essential that the FBI's present ability to classify and withhold information be sharply curtailed. Insofar as the Bureau's "intelligence gathering methods" are precisely what is at issue here, the FOIA exemption allowing secrecy in this area must be dramatically diminished, or abolished altogether. Similarly, given that it can be readily demonstrated that the Bureau habitually uses "informants" (the FBI euphemism covering both agents provocateurs and wholly fabricated sources) for utterly inappropriate, and often illegal purposes, the FOIA exemption in this area must also be dismantled, a matter which pertains as well to much of the Intelligence Identities Protection Act. In instances where the Bureau wishes to contend that information must be withheld for reasons of "national security," it must be forced to demonstrate the involvement of some hostile foreign power before a review board *elected* (not appointed) for this purpose. While the disclosure of actual national security information may well be considered a punishable offense, so too must be the deliberate miscasting of other information in this light.

Another mechanism by which oversight of the FBI might be reinforced, and through which an ever greater degree of popular control over the Bureau might be extended, lies in the possibility of the permanent legislative establishment of localized entities such as the Commission of Inquiry into the Black Panthers and the Police in Chicago (1969-70) and the Minnesota Citizens' Review Commission on the FBI (1977). Such bodies, equipped with subpoena power, etc., have always been in an ideal position to monitor the conduct of the Bureau on a more-or-less grassroots level. The creation of a regularized system of these commissions, reporting directly to the national, elected oversight or review board, would represent another giant step towards defanging the American political police.

It may be anticipated that Congress will, in general, be less than thrilled at the prospect of following through on any such "radical" and sweeping agenda. The legislature will no doubt require considerable encouragement in this regard. Much support will need to be extended to those Congresspeople who prove honest and courageous enough to "stay the course." And, again, massive pressure will need to be brought to bear upon those recalcitrants who actively seek to block the process. Nothing less than a fully national and concerted effort may be expected to wield the clout requisite to force such an issue.

It may also be expected that the FBI itself will fight back strongly against any such diminishment of its power and prerogatives. Organizers will be targeted as subversives and traitors. False information concerning their personal and professional lives will be leaked. Jobs will be lost, careers shattered, families destroyed. Homes and offices will be broken into, files rifled and stolen, rooms bugged and phones tapped. Midnight raids will be conducted on spurious warrants. Passports will be revoked. IRS audits will be ordered against "key extremists." Offices and domiciles will be firebombed. People will be accused, arrested, tried, convicted and sent to prison for crimes they never committed (and which may never have occurred at all). Others will be attacked and beaten, stabbed and otherwise maimed by "patriotic" thugs on city streets, in alleyways and along lonely back country roads. Still others will be murdered "by person or persons unknown."

Still, horrible as these prospects may be, in the final analysis they represent no particular change other than the possible identities of some victims. What has been described is no more than *normal* operating procedures of the FBI where "politically objectionable" targets are concerned. The only real question is whether such atrocities will occur as part of a process which ultimately forces the Bureau to stop, or whether they are allowed to occur unhindered, while we collectively busy ourselves with other, "more important" matters (unless or until, of course, we ourselves happen to become targets).

Objectively, the only way we will *ever* succeed in attaining *any* of our other noble social objectives will be through elimination of the force which systematically destroys us for trying. There is no real alternative but that the FBI and the repressive apparatus it has fostered must be, in its own terms, "neutralized." It is clear that neither the Congress nor the courts can be relied upon as guarantors of political freedom and protectors or our rights. Both the responsibility and the power for ending the abuses of America's secret police lie with the people. At the 1980 Black Hills Survival Gathering, John Trudell spoke of this power:

> When I go around in America and I see the bulk of the white people, they do not feel oppressed; they feel powerless. When I go amongst my people, we do not feel powerless; we feel oppressed. We do not want to make the trade...We must be willing in our lifetime to deal with reality. It's not revolution; it's liberation. We want to be free of a value system that's being imposed upon us. We do not want to participate in that value system. We don't want to change that value system. We want to remove it from our lives forever...We have to assume our responsibilities as power, as individuals, as spirit, as people...

To this we have little to add other than to echo Trudell's own conclusion to his thoughts: "We are the People. We have the potential for power. We must not fool ourselves. We must not mislead ourselves. It takes more than good intentions. It takes commitment. It takes recognizing that at some point in our lives we are going to have to decide that we have a way of life that we follow, and we are going to have to live that way of life...That is the only solution there is for us."

Notes

Introduction

1. Ungar, Sanford, *FBI*, Little, Brown, and Company, Boston, 1976, pp. 387-388.

2. Most scholars on the subject of organized crime in America date the beginning of the ascendency of gangland's "young Turks" such as Lansky and Luciano, and the emergence of modern criminal syndicates, from a conference held among members of their ranks at Atlantic City's President Hotel, May 13-16, 1929; see Kobler, John, *Capone: The Life and World of Al Capone*, G.P. Putnam's Sons, New York, 1971, pp. 246-247. This meeting resulted in the elimination of the old-line urban mob bosses during the subsequent "Castellamarese War" of 1931-32, a matter covered from an insider's point of view in Maas, Peter, *The Valachi Papers*, G.P. Putnam's Sons, New York, 1968, pp. 85-112. By the time of Hoover's "war on crime," the syndicate was rapidly consolidating its gains, and continued to do so, essentially unhampered by the FBI; see Jennings, Dean, *We Only Kill Each Other*, Prentice-Hall, New York, 1967, for an account of one principle member organization—the "Bugs-Meyer Mob" of Benjamin "Bugsy" Siegel and Meyer Lansky—during this growth period.

3. Perhaps the best single chronicle of the campaign against these archaic outlaws during the 1930s may be found in Toland, John, *The Dillinger Days*, Random House, New York, 1963. Attribution of the term "G-men" to Kelly comes at p. 102. Toland's version of events should be contrasted to that contained in the tacitly "official" version contained in Whitehead, Don, *The FBI Story: A Report to the People*, Random House, New York, 1963; the book was adapted, in even more glamorized form, for production as a movie starring James Stewart in 1964.

4. Ungar, *op. cit.*, p. 261. The Hoover biography mentioned in this passage is de Toledano, Ralph, *J. Edgar Hoover: The Man in His Time*, Arlington House Publishers, New York, 1973. In his autobiography, (Karpis, Alvin, with Bill Trent, *The Alvin Karpis Story*, Coward, McCann, & Geoghegan, New York, 1971), Hoover's "first arrest" vehemently denies that the Director had anything at all to do with his actual apprehension, although "the coward took credit for it from his own agents..." As for Buchalter—who, atypically for an FBI target, *was* a big-timer (head of New York's infamous "Murder, Inc.")—even *Playboy's Illustrated History of Organized Crime* demonstrates that the gangster was essentially sacrificed by his peers (forced to give himself up on pain of death) as a means of taking off "heat" brought on the syndicate, not by the Bureau, but by New York's prosecutors Thomas Dewey, William O'Dwyer, and Barton Turkus. The author of *Playboy's* 1975 tract, Richard Hammer, notes at p. 191 that a deal was worked out for Buchalter's peaceful surrender to J. Edgar Hoover by Walter Winchell (acting for Hoover, in exchange for exclusive Bureau information) and New York gang leader Albert Anastasia because it would embellish "the G-man's reputation, which was suffering from competition." The arrest, which occurred at 10 p.m. on August 24, 1939, was thus a carefully orchestrated and entirely safe affair.

5. Ungar, *op. cit.*, p. 373.

6. *Ibid.*, p. 370.

7. *Ibid.*, p. 384.

8. The books mentioned in this passage are: Collins, Frederick L., *The FBI in Peace and War*, (Introduction by J. Edgar Hoover), Books, Inc., New York, 1943; *The Story of the FBI: The Official Picture History of the Federal Bureau of Investigation*, (compiled by the editors of *Look* magazine; Introduction by J. Edgar Hoover), Dutton Publishers, New York, 1947; Tully, Andrew, *The FBI's Most Famous Cases*, (Introduction and Comments by J. Edgar Hoover), William Morrow and Company, New York, 1965; Whitehead, Don, *The FBI Story*, (Introduction by J. Edgar Hoover), *op. cit.*, and Whitehead, Don, *Attack on Terror: The FBI Against the Ku Klux Klan in Mississippi*, Funk and Wagnall's, New York, 1970. The earlier cited de Toledano biography of Hoover should undoubtedly be added to this list.

9. Ungar, *op. cit.*, p. 379. For the best overview of the FBI's self-glamorization process, see Powers, Richard Gid, *G-Men: The FBI in American Popular Culture*, Southern Illinois University Press, Carbondale, 1983.

10. Possibly the best book on this matter is Navasky, Victor S., *Naming Names,* Viking Press, New York, 1980. For an examination of the Bureau's role in portions of the McCarthyite procedures, see Bontecou, Eleanor, *The Federal Loyalty and Security Program,* Cornell University Press, Ithaca, New York, 1953, and Brown, Ralph S., *Loyalty and Security,* Yale University Press, New Haven, Connecticut, 1958. The fullest view of the specifics of what was done in public to members of the movie industry can, of course, be found in U.S. Congress, House Committee on Un-American Activities, *Hearings Regarding the Communist Infiltration of the Motion Picture Industry,* Eightieth Congress, U.S. Government Printing Office, Washington, D.C., 1947.

11. Ungar, *op. cit.,* p. 380. In this reference, Don Whitehead's aforementioned book, *Attack on Terror,* and a subsequent CBS Television *Thursday Night at the Movies* "docudrama" concerning the Bureau's Mississippi performance, both produced with energetic collaboration by the FBI, should be viewed as direct responses to articles such as Nelson's…and as outright attempts to negate the truth.

12. *Ibid.,* pp. 379-380.

13. *Ibid.,* pp. 375-376.

14. *Ibid.,* p. 376. The books mentioned in this passage are Lowenthal, Max, *The Federal Bureau of Investigation,* William Sloan Associates, Inc., New York, 1950; and Cook, Fred J., *The FBI Nobody Knows,* Macmillan, New York, 1964.

15. Ungar, *op. cit.,* pp. 376-377. The book referenced is Demaris, Ovid, *The Director: An Oral History of J. Edgar Hoover,* Harper's Magazine Press, New York, 1975.

16. The books referenced in this passage are Turner, William, *Hoover's FBI: The Men and the Myth,* Dell Publishers, New York, 1971; Ollestad, Norman, *Inside the FBI,* Lyle Stuart Publishers, New York, 1967; and Connors, Benard F., *Don't Embarrass the Bureau,* Bobbs-Merrill Co., Indianapolis, 1972.

17. Among a number of other instances, those which come most immediately to mind with regard to "legal" CIA attempts to silence former employees are the examples of Phillip Agee (*Inside the Company: A CIA Diary,* Stonehill Publishing Co., New York, 1975), Patrick J. McGarvey (*CIA: The Myth and the Madness,* Saturday Review Press, New York, 1972), John Stockwell (*In Search of Enemies: A CIA Story,* W.W. Norton & Co., New York, 1978), Frank Snepp (*Decent Interval,* Random House, New York, 1977), William R. Corson (*Armies of Ignorance,* Dial Press, New York, 1977), Ralph W. McGehee (*Deadly Deceits: My 25 Years in the CIA,* Sheridan Square Publishers, New York, 1983), and Victor Marchetti (with John D. Marks, *The CIA and the Cult of Intelligence,* Alfred A. Knopf, New York, 1974).

18. Quoted in Ungar, *op. cit.,* p. 383.

19. *Ibid.,* pp. 380-381.

20. The lengthy and expensive precursor to the great conspiracy trials of the late 1960s and early 1970s resulted in the following toll among its defendant-victims: nine were acquitted of all charges, mistrial was declared with regard to five others, all charges were dismissed against two, and the thirteenth committed suicide. Needless to say, this example hardly entered the FBI's roster of its "greatest cases." To the contrary, there is evidence that both the Bureau and its Director wished the entire affair quickly forgotten…once they had gleaned the desired utility from it. Further examples of this technique will be drawn on later in this book.

21. Quoted in Ungar, *op. cit.,* p. 392.

22. *Ibid.*

23. *Ibid.,* p. 391.

24. Quoted, *ibid.*

25. Quoted, *ibid.,* p. 393.

26. *Ibid.,* p. 398.

27. The quote is excerpted from a taped interview by Ward Churchill of a lieutenant in the NYPD in 1984. As he is nearing retirement (within the next few years), he has obvious reasons for wishing to remain anonymous. For the record, many of his assertions were rather stronger than those selected for quotation herein, and his view of the FBI seems widely held by members of local police anti-organized-crime units across the nation.

28. Preston, William Jr., "Political Surveillance and the FBI," Introduction to Buitrago, Ann Mari, and Leon Andrew Immerman, *Are You Now or Have You Ever Been in the FBI Files?,* Grove Press, New York, 1981, p. xiii.

29. There is more than passing indication that Hoover/the Bureau has employed the same sorts of blackmailing methods against prominent members of the media, and others, over the years, all in order to maintain a "correct atmosphere" within which to operate as they see fit. Certain examples will be drawn on later in this book.

30. The naming of the new FBI headquarters in Washington, D.C. after Hoover, despite the revelations of his systematic misconduct, is a perfect example of this phenomenon. Another, and more nauseating, instance was the publication by the U.S. Congress of *J. Edgar Hoover: Memorial Tributes in the Congress of the United States and Various Articles and Editorials Relating to His Life and Work*, U.S. Government Printing Office, Washington, D.C., 1974. Be it noted that many of those who allowed their names to be attached to this tome had ample reason to absolutely detest Hoover; they were thus *far* less than honest with their constituents in providing a eulogy of this sort for public consumption. The whole thing can only be construed as reinforcing, rather than undermining the Hooverian legacy. Much of the impetus toward this may be found in Sorretino, Dr. Frank M., *Ideological Warfare: The FBI's Path Toward Power*, National University Press Publications, New York, 1985.

31. Prominent examples of this trend include Executive Order 12356, signed on April 2, 1983, increasing the scope of material which can be withheld under the FOIA, and authorizing (for the first time) the CIA to engage in domestic intelligence operations. About a year earlier, on March 31, 1982, National Security Decision Directive Number 84 (NSDD 84) established new procedures and penalties concerning "unauthorized leaks" of government information to the press, thus clamping the mantle of secrecy even more tightly around counterintelligence activities. The measure was signed into law by Ronald Reagan on March 11, 1983. On June 23, 1982 Reagan also signed the Intelligence Identities Protection Act, making it a crime punishable by three years imprisonment and a $15,000 fine (five years and $25,000 for those holding a security clearance at the time of their act) to disclose the identity of any U.S. intelligence operative; this law means that anyone "blowing the cover" of an infiltrator/provocateur—even an agent within one's own organization who is engaged in the advocacy or commission of felonies—could then be convicted of the "crime" of having done so. The Act dovetails neatly with Executive Order 12333, signed by Reagan on December 4, 1981, affording much broader latitude to U.S. intelligence agencies in their domestic counterintelligence operations. All of this should be viewed in light of the superficially innocuous Paperwork Reduction Act of 1980, which curtails U.S. Government Printing Office publication/dissemination of even that executive branch information still deemed "legal." These factors combined to create a context in which, on May 7, 1983, Attorney General William French Smith could release revised FBI guidelines officially entitling the Bureau to launch full-scale investigations of individuals and groups which it feels "advocate criminal activity or indicate an apparent intent to engage in crime." This last led *Chicago Tribune* columnist Stephen Chapman to observe in June 1983 that, "There is reason to suspect that the administration may be more interested in discouraging radical dissent than in attacking terrorism. The old guidelines worked well to protect constitutional rights of Americans, and no one has offered credible evidence that they impair legitimate FBI work. The new ones are liable to sacrifice those rights while doing little for law enforcement." For further information, see Pell, Eve, *The Big Chill: How the Reagan administration, corporate America, and religious conservatives are subverting free speech and the public's right to know*, Beacon Press, Boston, 1984.

Chapter 1

1. United States Congress, *Appropriations to the Budget of the United States of America, 1872*, Section VII, *United States Department of Justice*, Washington, D.C., 1871, p. 31.

2. Lowenthal, Max, *The Federal Bureau of Investigation,* William Sloan Associates, Inc., New York, 1950, pp. 9-10.

3. Quoted in Ungar, Sanford, *FBI*, Little, Brown, and Company, 1976, p. 39.

4. United States Congress, *Hearings Before the Congress of United States of America Concerning the National Budget for the Year 1907,* Washington, D.C., 1906, (Vol. 9, p. 57, p. 81).

5. Enforcement of the Mann Act, under a novel Supreme Court interpretation stipulating that "pecuniary gain need not be proved" in order for the crimes of prostitution and pandering to pertain, led the Bureau of Investigation directly into the sordid Jack Johnson case. In this matter, the then-reigning (black) world heavyweight boxing champion, Johnson, was arrested, convicted and sent to prison for having committed the offense of transporting his (adult, white) fiancé across state lines. The episode was a clear precursor of the similar, but extralegal, racist and puritanical moralism on the part of the FBI in future years.

6. The best succinct account of this period is in Zinn, Howard, *A People's History of the United States,* Harper and Row, New York, 1980, pp. 350-358.

7. Ungar, *op. cit.,* p. 41.

8. *Ibid.,* p. 42. This situation, too, is an obvious precursor to later "*ad hoc* arrangements" effected by the FBI.

9. Zinn, *op. cit.,* p. 364. For a full account of the IWW, see Dubofsky, Melvyn, *We Shall Be All: A History of the Industrial Workers of the World,* Quadrangle Books, New York, 1974. Of additional interest is Haywood, Bill, *The Autobiography of Big Bill Haywood,* International Publishers, New York, 1929 (recently reprinted). In any event, both the mass raid technique and political conspiracy trial were to become FBI trademarks over the next fifty years.

10. Kornbluh, Joyce L. (ed.), *Rebel Voices: An I.W.W. Anthology,* University of Michigan Press, Ann Arbor, (2nd Printing) 1972, p. 306. For an excellent overview of the context in Butte at the time, see Duffy, J.H., *Butte Was Like That,* Tom Greenfield Press, Butte, Montana, 1941.

11. Archer, Jules, *Strikes, Bombs, and Bullets: Big Bill Haywood and the IWW,* Julian Messner, New York, 1972, p. 169. The best available overview of the situation prevailing in Centralia at the time of Everest's lynching is probably Tyler, Robert L., "Violence at Centralia, 1919," *Pacific Northwest Quarterly,* 65, October 1954, pp. 116-124. An interesting topical perspective on the national context in which the repression of the IWW occurred is to be found in Bing, Alexander M., *War Time Strikes and Their Adjustments,* E.P. Dutton, New York, 1921.

12. Undoubtedly the best account of the Goldman/Berkman affair may still be found in Goldman's autobiography, *Living My Life,* Vol. 2, Dover Publications, New York, 1970, pp. 608-692.

13. Quoted in Zinn, *op. cit.,* p. 363.

14. *Ibid.,* p. 392.

15. Ungar, *op. cit.,* p. 42.

16. *Ibid.,* p. 43.

17. Quoted in Zinn, *op. cit.,* p. 366.

18. Ungar, *op. cit.,* p. 43.

19. Zinn, *op. cit.,* p. 366.

20. Ungar, *op. cit.,* pp. 43-44.

21. Weeks, Robert P., (ed.), *The Commonwealth versus Sacco and Vanzetti*, Prentice-Hall, Inc., 1958, p. 1 (citing Post, Louis F., *The Deportation Delirium of Nineteen-Twenty*, Chicago, 1923, p. 167.)

22. Messerschmidt, Jim, *The Trial of Leonard Peltier*, South End Press, Boston, 1984, p. 13.

23. Zinn, *op. cit.*, p. 367.

24. Ungar, *op. cit.*, pp. 44-45.

25. *Ibid.*, pp. 45-46.

26. *Ibid.* Again, all of this plainly foreshadows aspects of Hoover's later conception of the FBI's "discrete" methods of maintaining itself and growing within the labyrinth of Washington bureaucracy.

27. *Ibid.*, p. 46. The systematic leveling of charges for which there was no real hope of obtaining conviction, but as a means of "tying up" radicals in court procedures, draining their finances through the posting of bails, and the like—as well as possibly generating secondary charges, such as contempt of court, which *would* stick—became an integral aspect of FBI procedure forever after.

28. *Ibid.*, p. 47. The deployment of FBI agents to repress "subversion" where no federal statute pertained, and the enlistment of local police and other agencies as "cooperating entities" in this regard, has also become a hallowed Bureau tradition. Meanwhile, as has been noted, many large-scale violations of *real* federal law have gone unattended by the FBI.

29. See Belknap, Michael R., "The Mechanics of Repression: J. Edgar Hoover, The Bureau of Investigation and the Radicals, 1917-1925," *Crime and Social Justice*, Spring/Summer, 1972, pp. 51-52. According to Ungar (p. 59), Hoover was such an acknowledged "anti-Bolshevik" specialist by 1923, that he was called upon to draft the brief used by Secretary of State Charles Evans Hughes before the Senate Foreign Relations Committee to block U.S. recognition of the Soviet Union.

30. Ungar, *op. cit.*, pp. 47-48.

31. *Ibid.*, p. 48. The whole matter smacks of the later Watergate era intelligence scandals, during which Congress became incensed and reacted mightily to the turning of "investigatory" tactics upon themselves and other members of the mainstream establishment which had *always* been standard practice of the FBI in its anti-radical work.

32. *Ibid.*

33. Quoted in *ibid.*, p. 48.

34. Quoted in *ibid.*

35. Messerschmidt, *op. cit.*, p. 13.

36. Ungar, *op. cit.*, p. 54.

37. *Ibid.*, p. 49.

38. *Ibid.*

39. *Ibid.*, p. 57.

40. *Ibid.*, pp. 151-152.

41. *Ibid.*, pp. 55-56.

42. *Ibid.*, p. 59.

43. *Ibid.*, p. 55.

44. Taylor, Flynt, and Margaret Van Houten, *Counterintelligence: A Documentary Look at America's Secret Police*, National Lawyers Guild Task Force on Counterintelligence and the Secret Police, Chicago, 1978, p. 3.

45. For a succinct overview of the Garvey movement, see Pinkney, Alphonso, *Red, Black, and Green: Black Nationalism in the United States*, Cambridge University Press, New York, 1976, pp. 37-56.

46. Quoted in Whitehead (1956), *op. cit.*, pp. 159-160.

47. *U.S. Senate Select Committee to Study Governmental Operations, Intelligence Activities and the Rights of Americans, Book II*, U.S. Government Printing Office, Washington, D.C., 1976, p. 32.

48. *Ibid.*, pp. 36-38.

49. Ungar, *op. cit.*, p. 103.

50. Zinn, *op. cit.*, p. 411.

51. Ungar, *op. cit.*, p. 103.

52. *Ibid.*, pp. 103-104. Such massive predawn raids, the deprivation of the basic rights of the accused in the immediate wake of arrest, and the display of the arrested in chains, etc., had by then become—and have remained—a signature of the FBI's political operations (and those of local police units trained at the Bureau's "National Police Academy").

53. *Ibid.*, p. 104.

54. Zinn, *op. cit.*, p. 411.

55. Quoted in Ungar, *op. cit.*, p. 106.

56. *Ibid.*, p. 105.

57. Higham, Charles, *Trading with the Enemy: An Exposé of the Nazi-American Money Plot 1933-1949*, Dell Publishing Co., Inc., New York, 1983, pp. 53-82.

58. *Ibid.*, pp. 113-135. Also see Sampson, Anthony, *The Sovereign State of ITT*, Fawcett Publications, Greenwich, Connecticut, 1973, pp. 20-46.

59. Higham, Charles, *op. cit.*, pp. 175-199.

60. ITT and GM eventually met with justice, of a sort, for their wartime support of the Nazis. In 1967, the U.S. Foreign Claims Settlement Commission awarded GM $33 million in tax exemptions for "trouble and destruction occasioned to its airplane and motorized factories in Germany and Austria in World War II", *i.e.* for its factories producing Nazi war materiel which were destroyed by Allied air raids. Similarly, ITT received $27 million in reparations including $5 million for damages to its Focke-Wulf aircraft plants. See Higham, *op. cit.*, p. 199 and Sampson, *op. cit.*, p. 45.

61. Higham, *op. cit.*, p. 132.

62. *Ibid.*, p. 104.

63. *Ibid.*, pp. 104-106.

64. Ungar, *op. cit.*, p. 57.

65. Zinn, *op. cit.*, pp. 418-419. An insight into exactly what is meant by this is provided by Edward Bernays, a leading and seminal figure in the public relations field, when he coined the phrase "engineering of consent" in the 1947 issue of *Annals of the American Academy of Political and Social Science:*

...quite simply [this] means the application of scientific principles and tried practices to the task of getting people to support ideas and programs...The engineering of consent is the very essence of the democratic process...A leader frequently cannot wait for the people to arrive at an understanding...democratic leaders must play their part in...engineering...consent to socially constructive goals and values.

Hence "the people" must be told what—and *only* what—is necessary to get them to believe what their "leaders" wish them to believe, and to do what these leaders want them to do, even if what they are told must be made up from whole cloth. This novel sense of "democratic process" clearly guided many or most of the government's informational activities during the McCarthy era, and may be seen to be very much alive today.

66. Ungar, *op. cit.*, p. 108.

67. *Ibid.*, pp. 108-109.

68. For the best quick rendering of this subject, see Chomsky, Noam, *Toward a New Cold War*, Pantheon Books, New York, 1983, pp. 21-23.

69. Zinn, *op. cit.*, pp. 423-424. It should be noted that the Humphrey-Lehman proposal was adopted, and was not rescinded until 1968.

70. *Ibid.*, p. 422. It is worth noting that while McCarthy was rooting around the State Department looking for Communists, the Central Intelligence Agency (CIA) was infested with Nazis. In 1946 the CIA's predecessor, the Office of Secret Services (OSS), recruited the former head of Nazi intelligence operations for the Eastern Front, Reinhard Gehlen. With OSS funding, Gehlen rebuilt the Nazi intelligence apparatus in Eastern bloc countries, staffing it with former SD, Abwehr and Gestapo officers. In 1949, Gehlen's organization became part of the newly formed CIA. Gehlen was rabidly anti-Soviet and created the myth that the Soviets intended to overrun Western Europe and that war between the U.S. and the Soviet Union was inevitable. This was based on Gehlen's ideological bent rather than intelligence data. From 1946 to 1954, virtually all U.S. intelligence on the Eastern bloc countries was filtered through Gehlen's organization and slanted accordingly. This was, in all probability, the major contributing factor to the genesis of the Cold War. Given McCarthy's association with U.S. pro-fascist forces, it is likely that he knew and approved of this infiltration of the CIA. For a more detailed account of the CIA's recruitment of Nazis, see Higham, Charles, *American Swastika*, Doubleday & Co., Inc., Garden City, N.Y., 1985, pp. 241-301.

71. Cook, Fred J., *The FBI Nobody Knows*, Macmillan, New York, 1964, p. 191.

72. Ungar, *op. cit.*, p. 128.

73. *Ibid.*, *op. cit.*, p. 109.

74. None of the substantive issues raised by Cook *(op. cit.)*, for example, was resolved by the documents released by the Bureau during the mid-70s.

75. The best account of the Rosenberg case can be found in Schneir, Walter and Miriam, *Invitation to an Inquest*, Pantheon Books, New York, 1983.

76. Zinn, *op. cit.*, p. 426. Also see Schneir, *op. cit.*, pp. 261-479.

77. Zinn, *op. cit.*, pp. 427-428. There is ample evidence that the FBI was up to its neck in the disinformation blitz. For example, the Senate Select (Church) Committee, in its earlier cited *Intelligence Activities and the Rights of Americans*, states on p. 49 that the Bureau consistently provided "a distorted picture of communist 'infiltration'..." Ungar, *op. cit.*, p. 372, notes that: "The FBI took no hand in *I Led Three Lives*, the early television series based on the adventures of FBI counterspy Herbert Philbrick, but it had earlier helped Philbrick with his book [*i.e.* the Bureau had written it for him with his approval] and was very favorably portrayed on the program;" see Philbrick, Herbert A., *I Led Three Lives: Citizen—Communist—Counterspy*, Grosset & Dunlap Publishers, New York, 1952. The "liaison" function of Bureau personnel with various elements of the media was covered more substantially in the Introduction to this book.

78. *Ibid.*, p. 422.

79. *Ibid.*, pp. 422-423.

80. Miller, Douglas, and Marion Nowak, *The Fifties: The Way We Really Were*, Doubleday, New York, 1977, p. 231.

81. *Intelligence Activities and the Rights of Americans*, *op. cit.*, p. 49.

82. Mills, C. Wright, *The Socialist Imagination*, Oxford University Press, New York, 1959, p. 178.

Chapter 2

1. 1974 statement issued by the U.S. Department of Justice; quoted in Ungar, *op. cit.*, p. 178.

2. *Intelligence Activities and the Rights of Americans*, *op. cit.*, p. 67.

3. Quoted in *ibid.*, p. 66.

4. Buitrago and Immerman, *op. cit.*, pp. 18-19, make the following observations concerning related but technically non-COINTELPRO matters: "'JUNE' (or 'JUNE mail') documents contain the fruits of the FBI burglaries and electronic surveillances, and also record the preparation and authorization for such activities...The 'JUNE' system was begun in June, 1949, to keep information on electronic surveillance separate [and secret]. It was a response to the FBI's embarrassment over the Judith Coplan case, in which documents released by court order revealed that the FBI was obtaining political information through wiretaps...ELSUR (electronic surveillance) logs...include both TESUR (technical surveillance, i.e. wiretaps) and MISUR (microphone surveillance)..." As the Church Committee (*Intelligence Activities and the Rights of Americans*, *op. cit.*, p. 137) put it, these non-COINTELPRO procedures involved many "unlawful and improper acts," and the Bureau knew it, as is evidenced by an internal memo (quoted by Norrock, Nicholas, "238 Break-Ins Committed by FBI Over 26 Years", *New York Times*, November 11, 1974, p. 15): "Such techniques involve trespassing and are clearly illegal...Break-ins...have [nonetheless] been used because they represent an invaluable technique in combatting subversive activities of a clandestine nature..."

5. Kunstler, William, "FBI Letters: New Writers of the Purple Rage," *Nation*, December 30, 1978, p. 721. Also see Robins, Natalie, "The Defiling of Writers: The F.B.I. and American Lit," *Nation*, October 10, 1987.

6. For analysis and reproduction of key documents, see Perkus, Cathy, (ed.), *COINTELPRO: The FBI's Secret War on Political Freedom*, Monad Press, New York, 1976. Also see Taylor and Vanhouten, *op. cit.*

7. U.S. Senate Select Committee to Study Government Operations, *The FBI's Covert Program to Destroy the Black Panther Party*, U.S. Government Printing Office, Washington, D.C., 1976, pp. 200-207.

8. Zimroth, Peter L., *Perversions of Justice: The Prosecution and Acquittal of the Panther 21*, Viking Press, New York, 1974, p. 398.

9. *The FBI's Covert Action Program to Destroy the Black Panther Party*, *op. cit.*, pp. 189-194.

10. See Volkman, Ernest, "Othello," *Penthouse*, April 1979.

11. Luce, Phillip Abbott, *The New Left*, David McKay, Inc., New York, 1966.

12. Divalo, William Tulio, with James, Joseph, *I Lived Inside the Campus Revolution*, Cowles Book Company, Los Angeles, 1973.

13. Grathwohl, Larry (as told to Frank Reagan), *Bringing Down America: An FBI Informer with the Weathermen*, Arlington House Publishers, New Rochelle, New York, 1976.

14. Lubash, Arnold H., "316 Used by FBI in Informer Role," *New York Times*, September 5, 1976, p. 24.

15. At least one of the infiltrators has placed the number at a level double this amount. See Tackwood,

Lewis E., "My Assignment Was to Kill George Jackson, "*Black Panther,* April 21, 1980.

16. Ungar, *op. cit.,* p. 469.

17. See Cooper, Lynn, *et al., The Iron Fist and the Velvet Glove: An Analysis of U.S. Police,* Center for Research on Criminal Justice, Berkeley, 1975, p. 134.

18. Kitson, Frank, *Low Intensity Operations: Subversion, Insurgency, Peace-keeping,* Stackpole Books, Harrisburg, PA, 1971, p. 100.

19. Lawrence, Ken, *The New State Repression,* International Network Against the New State Repression, Chicago, 1985, pp. 4-5.

20. Reprinted in Newton, Huey P., *To Die for the People,* Vintage Books, New York, 1972, p. 191.

21. Durden-Smith, Jo, *Who Killed George Jackson? Fantasies, Paranoia, and the Revolution,* Alfred A. Knopf, New York, 1976; Bennett, pp. 104-107, Carr, pp. 113-126.

22. See Epstein, Jason, *The Great Conspiracy Trial,* Random House, New York, 1970.

23. For the best detailed account and analysis of the case itself, see Mitford, Jessica, *The Trial of Dr. Spock, Reverend William Sloan Coffin, Jr., Michael Ferber, Mitchell Goodman and Marcus Raskin,* Alfred A. Knopf, New York, 1969; for placement of it within the broader context of government repression attending Vietnam War-related dissent, see Smith, Robert, "Disaffection, Delegitimation and Consequences: Aggregate Trends for World War II, Korea and Vietnam," in Charles Moskos, (ed.), *Public Opinion and the Military Establishment,* Sage Publications, Beverly Hills, CA, 1971, p. 235.

24. See Kempton, Murray, *The Briar Patch: The People of the State of New York v. Lumumba Shakur, et al.,* E.P. Dutton Co., Inc., New York, 1973; and Zimroth, *op. cit.*

25. See Freed, Donald, *Agony in New Haven: The Trial of Bobby Seale, Ericka Huggins, and the Black Panther Party,* Simon and Schuster, New York, 1973.

26. See Newton, *op. cit.,* p. 224.

27. FBI Director to SAC, San Juan (marked *PERSONAL ATTENTION*), dated August 4, 1960, and captioned GROUPS SEEKING INDEPENDENCE FOR PUERTO RICO (SUBVERSIVE CONTROL). The document was also routed to the Chicago, New York and Washington field offices; hand inscribed "Counterintelligence Programs."

28. Memorandum, SAC, New York, to Director, FBI, dated 11/15/60, type-captioned as a COUNTERINTELLIGENCE PROGRAM document pertaining to GROUPS SEEKING INDEPENDENCE FOR PUERTO RICO (SUBVERSIVE CONTROL).

29. SAC, San Juan, to Director, FBI, June 12, 1961; same caption as 27 above. For more on FBI repression of the Puerto Rican independence movement, see Lopez, Alfredo, *Dona Licha's Island,* South End Press, Boston, 1987.

30. Memorandum, Director to SAC, Atlanta, May 11, 1962, captioned MARTIN LUTHER KING, JR., SM-C. For more information concerning the FBI's thinking on the detention of political dissidents during the period, see Goldstein, Robert J., "An American Gulag? Summary Arrest and Detention of Political Dissidents in the United States," *Columbia Human Rights Law Review 10,* 1978, pp. 541-573.

31. In a memorandum to Attorney General Robert F. Kennedy on April 20, 1962, Hoover wrote that "The Bureau has recently received...information showing the influence of Stanley David Levinson, a secret member of the Communist Party, upon Martin Luther King, Jr." The Director cited "a confidential source who has proven reliable in the past"—which turned out to be an illegal wiretap of Levinson's office—as the basis of this information. Hoover was apparently under the impression that O'Dell had been elected to the National Committee of the CPUSA under the pseudonym "Cornelius Jones" in 1959; Memorandum to Kennedy captioned MARTIN LUTHER KING, JR., SM-C, June 25, 1962. Meanwhile, the report to the Director, bearing the same caption, had been sent by the SAC, Atlanta, to Hoover on April 25, 1962.

32. See Garrow, David J., *The FBI and Martin Luther King, Jr.,* Penguin Books, New York, 1981, pp. 59-60: "Not reported to Kennedy or the White House was information from [FBI informer] Jack Childs that...in mid-March [1962] he had to report that Levinson was 'disenchanted' with the CP. The FBI kept this news strictly to itself." O'Dell's membership in the CP's National Committee—under any name—was never established, and his relationship to King was, at most, remote in terms of influence. The major offenses of both seem to have centered more than anything upon their refusals to cooperate with various witch-hunting committees: Levinson having taken the Fifth Amendment—upon advice of his attorney William Kunstler—to all questions posed by the Eastland Senate Committee in 1962, and O'Dell before HUAC after his expulsion from the National Maritime Union in the late 1940s.

33. Fred J. Baumgardner to William C. Sullivan, captioned COMINFIL SCLC, IS-C, October 22, 1962. Memorandum, SAC, New York, to Director, captioned CPUSA, COINTELPRO, IS-C, September 28, 1962.

The articles which appeared as a result of the latter were "Red Aids King's Efforts," *Atlanta Chronicle*, October 25, 1962, p. 4A; "Communist Revealed as King's Aid," *St. Louis Globe Democrat*, October 26, 1962, p. 1; "A Communist has Infiltrated Martin Luther King's Top Ranks," *Long Island Star Journal*, October 26, 1962, pp. 1-2. Tellingly, all the papers attributed their information to "a highly authoritative source."

34. Garrow, *op. cit.*, p. 54.

35. Zinn, Howard, *Albany: A Study in National Responsibility*, Southern Regional Council, Atlanta, November 14, 1962 (this was an expansion of an earlier report Zinn had completed for the Council on January 8, 1962). For additional information of FBI performance *vis a vis* the civil rights movement at this time, see Wechsler, James, "The FBI's Failure in the South," *The Progressive* 27, December, 1963, pp. 20-23.

36. See "Dr. Martin Luther King Says F.B.I. in Albany, Ga., Favors Segregationists," *New York Times*, November 19, 1962, p. 21; reprinted in the *Atlanta Constitution*, November 19, 1962, p. 18.

37. Memorandum, C.D. DeLoach to John Mohr, captioned "Racial Situation, Albany, Georgia, RM," January 15, 1963.

38. Memorandum, Hoover to Attorney General Kennedy, caption unknown, January 18, 1963.

39. See FBI reporting documents from Birmingham reproduced as pp. 6-7 of Taylor and Vanhouten, *op. cit.* Also see "Documents detail FBI-Klan links in early rights strife," *Chicago Tribune*, 8/14/78, reproduced on p. 6. Additional information may be obtained from "Informer Scores FBI on Violence," *New York Times*, December 3, 1976, p. 23. It should be noted, as Taylor and van Houten observe on p. 3, that among the Klan's 1963 activities in Birmingham were the bombing of a church in which four black children were killed and the killing of another black man during a "racial disturbance."

40. Garrow, *op. cit.*, p. 115. It is noteworthy that the Bureau was fully aware that the IRS had already attempted—and failed—to find "problems" with the tax returns of both King and SCLC (p. 114). Also, a "trash cover" amounts to sifting the garbage discarded by a "suspect" in hopes of turning up something incriminating.

41. Memorandum from Director to SAC, Atlanta, dated October 4, 1965 and captioned COMINFIL SCLC, IS-C. Also see Memoranda from SAC, Atlanta to Director, dated November 9, 18, and 19, 1965, each captioned COMINFIL SCLC, IS-C. At p. 287, Garrow (*op. cit.*) notes that "Harrison publicly admits his role as an FBI informant" and that "The FBI's Atlanta office also had another informant, a young, itinerant black minister, who on occasion could obtain information from the SCLC headquarters that the Bureau needed." For further information, see Good, Paul, "An Uneasy Life for Man Who Spied on King," and Lee, Dallas, "SCLC Had Been Aware of Informants," both in the *Atlanta Constitution*, November 16, 1980, at p. 1A and 16A respectively.

42. Memorandum from W.C. Sullivan to Alan H. Belmont, dated January 6, 1964 and captioned CPUSA, NEGRO QUESTION; CRM, IS-C; Sullivan observed that "trespass is involved" in the installation of the bug, which was nonetheless planted in King's room by Belmont or one of his subordinates.

43. William C. Sullivan's account quoted in Garrow, *op. cit.*, p. 106.

44. Hoover is quoted in a Memorandum, Fred J. Baumgardner to W.C. Sullivan, dated January 23, 1964 and captioned COMMUNIST PARTY, USA, NEGRO QUESTION; COMMUNIST INFLUENCE IN RACIAL MATTERS, IS-C (JUNE).

45. Garrow, *op. cit.*, pp. 107-124.

46. A more complete text of the letter is to be found in *ibid.*, pp. 125-126.

47. Memoranda from Baumgardner to Sullivan, dated November 19 and 20, 1964, each captioned MARTIN LUTHER KING, JR., SM-C. Memorandum from Clarence B. Jones to DeLoach, dated December 1, 1964 and captioned MARTIN LUTHER KING, JR. For further information on this matter, see Schlesinger, Arthur M., *Robert Kennedy and His Times*, Houghton-Mifflin Co., Boston, 1978, pp. 364-365. Also see Horrock, Nicholas M., "Ex-Officials Say FBI Harassed Dr. King to Stop His Criticism" (*New York Times*, March 9, 1975, p. 40) and "Senate Intelligence Panel Told of FBI Attempt to Discredit Dr. King in 1964" (*New York Times*, March 19, 1975. p. 16).

48. King, Coretta Scott, *My Life With Martin Luther King, Jr.*, Holt Rinehart, & Winston, New York, 1969, p. 247.

49. Wise, David, *The American Police State*, Random House, New York, 1976, pp. 303-306. Also see Bray, Howard, *Pillars of the Post*, W.W. Norton & Co., New York, 1980, pp. 109-111. DeLoach having approached Bradlee before the Senate Select Committee (see his testimony in *Hearings—Federal Bureau of Investigation*, 94th Congress, 1st Session, Vol. 6, U.S. Government Printing Office, Washington, D.C., 1976, at p. 210), but it is known that the FBI is withholding a Memorandum, DeLoach to John Mohr,

dated December 1, 1964, in which it is said he announced his intention to do so. As to the other person approached, see Garrow, *op. cit.*, pp. 130-31, and Clancy, Paul, "The Bureau and the bureaus," *Quill*, February, 1976, pp. 12-18.

50. See, for example, Riesel, Victor, "Hoover Bided Time to Answer King," *Memphis Commercial Appeal*, November 26, 1964, p. 7.

51. Quoted in Garrow, *op. cit.*, p. 134.

52. U.S. Congress, Senate Select Committee to Study Government Operations with Respect to Intelligence Activities, *Final Report—Book III: Supplementary Detailed Staff Reports on Intelligence Activities and the Rights of Americans*, 94th Congress, 2nd Session, U.S. Government Printing Office, Washington, D.C., 1976, p. 95. Also see U.S. Congress, House Select Committee on Assassinations, *The Final Report*, Bantam Books, New York, 1979, p. 570. The question of "other motivations" attending the FBI's persecution of King was addressed in a Memorandum from Sullivan to Belmont, dated January 8, 1964 and captioned MARTIN LUTHER KING, JR. in which he stated among other things, that "The right kind of national Negro leader could...be gradually developed so as to overshadow Dr. King..." "Sullivan had in mind a specific man who would be this 'right kind' of leader...New York attorney Samuel R. Pierce..." an extreme conservative.

53. Government documents "clearing" the FBI of direct involvement in the King assassination include U.S. Congress, House Select Committee on Assassinations, *Hearings on Investigation of the Assassination of Dr. Martin Luther King, Jr.*, 95th Congress, 2nd Session, Vols. 1, 6, 7, U.S. Government Printing Office, Washington, D.C., 1979, and the subsequent *Final Report*, *op. cit.* Also see the U.S. Department of Justice, *Report of the Task Force to Review the FBI, Martin Luther King, Jr., Security and Assassination Investigations*, Washington, D.C., January 11, 1977. For a sample of items raising questions concerning the FBI not answered by the official summaries, see Lane, Mark, and Dick Gregory, *Code Name "Zorro": The Murder of Martin Luther King, Jr.*, Prentice-Hall, Inc., Englewood Cliffs, N.J., 1977; Lewis, David L., *King: A Biography*, University of Illinois Press, Urbana, 1978; Lawton, James, "And the Character Assassination That Followed," *Civil Liberties Review* 5, July-August, 1978, pp. 30-32; and Hatcher, Ed, and Amy Shaw, "Kunstler Blames FBI in King Killing," *Durham (North Carolina) Morning Herald*, November 17, 1978, p. 5B.

54. In the case of Halstead, a Bureau AIRTEL dated 7/23/68 outlines a plan to engage in redbaiting designed to incite violence against the candidate during his planned trip to visit GIs in Vietnam that year; the anonymous author of this document observed that this "should be an interesting experience for Mr. HALSTED [sic]..." Franklin's case was much earlier: a Memorandum from the SAC, New York to the Director, dated 10/20/61 and captioned SOCIALIST WORKERS PARTY (SWP), IS-SWP, DISRUPTION PROGRAM, details a strategy to utilize information on the candidate's criminal record in "causing embarrassment to the SWP." The plan was actualized in the "On the Town" column of Charles McHarry in the *New York Daily News* on November 7, 1961. Other SWP candidates known to have been subverted in this fashion include Judy White (Memorandum, SAC, New York to Director, 10/24/66), Barbara Taplin and Howard Wallace (Memorandum, SAC, Denver to Director, 5/4/65), and Paul Boutelle (fragmentary FBI documentation originating in New York sometime in 1969); reproduced in Perkus, *op. cit.*, pp. 52-53.

55. In his testimony before the Supplemental and Deficiencies Subcommittee of the Senate Appropriations Committee on November 27, 1970, Hoover announced that a group "composed of Catholic priests and nuns, teachers, students, and former students who have manifested opposition to the war in Vietnam by acts of [undisclosed] violence against Government agencies and private corporations," led by "Philip and Daniel Berrigan...plans to blow up underground electrical conduits and steam pipes serving the Washington, D.C. area in order to disrupt Federal Government operations. The plotters are also concocting a scheme to kidnap a highly placed government official. The name of a White House staff member [later identified as being Henry Kissinger] has been mentioned as a possible victim." Despite massive FBI efforts to obtain conviction in this matter—including use of an infiltrator named Boyd Douglas—the "East Coast Conspiracy to Save Lives," as the Berrigan group was called, was acquitted of all charges *en masse* on April 2, 1971. For comprehensive information on this aspect of COINTELPRO, see Nelson, Jack, and Roland J. Ostrow, *The FBI and the Berrigans: The Making of a Conspiracy*, Coward, McCann & Geoghegan, Inc., New York, 1972.

56. An analysis of FBI documents removed during the earlier-mentioned raid on the Media, PA resident agency in 1971 revealed the following: 40% devoted to political action and surveillance (95% of the targets being leftist groups and individuals); 14% devoted to draft resistance and military desertion; 25% devoted to bank robberies (including those attributed to "politicals"); 1% devoted to investigation of or-

ganized crime (mostly gambling). For further information, see "From the Citizens Commission to Investigate the FBI," *Win*, Vol. VIII, Nos. 4 & 5, March 1 & 15, 1972, p. 9.

57. Memorandum from the Director, FBI to SAC, Albany (New York; routed simultaneously to 22 other field offices) dated August 25, 1967 and captioned COUNTERINTELLIGENCE PROGRAM, BLACK NATIONALIST—HATE GROUPS, INTERNAL SECURITY. At another point in this document, Hoover cautions his agents that, "the nature of this new endeavor is such that under no circumstances should the existence of the program be made known outside the Bureau and appropriate within-office security should be afforded to the sensitive operations and techniques considered under this program."

58. Memorandum from the Director, FBI to SAC, Albany (routed simultaneously to 40 other field offices) dated 3/44/68 and captioned COUNTERINTELLIGENCE PROGRAM, BLACK NATIONALIST—HATE GROUPS, RACIAL INTELLIGENCE (marked to the personal attention of the SACs). The document concludes with the observation that, "Because of the nature of this program each operation must be designed to protect the Bureau's interest so there is no possibility of embarrassment to the Bureau."

59. See Breitman, George, Herman Porter and Baxter Smith, *The Assassination of Malcolm X*, Pathfinder Press, New York, 1976. Among other things, Malcolm's personal bodyguard, Eugene Roberts, was later discovered to have been serving as an infiltrator on the New York Police Department's "subversives" unit, an entity revealed to have worked in very close liaison with the Bureau's anti-"black extremist" COINTELPRO personnel. Roberts later emerged as an infiltrating "charter member" of the New York chapter of the Black Panther Party and testified against the defendants in the earlier-mentioned Panther 21 case.

60. Garrow, *op. cit.*, p. 154. Also see a Memorandum, Hoover to Herbert Brownell, dated December 31, 1956 and captioned ELIJA MOHAMMED [sic], INTERNAL SECURITY—MUSLIM CULT OF ISLAM; Fred J. Baumgardner to William C. Sullivan, dated September 8, 1961 and captioned NATION OF ISLAM—IS-NOI; SAC, Phoenix to Director, FBI, dated June 30, 1965 and captioned NATION OF ISLAM—NOI; Hoover to Katzenbach, dated July 1, 1966 and captioned NATION OF ISLAM—IS-NOI.

61. The best account of what happened to Brown is contained in his autobiography *Die Nigger Die!*, Dial Press, New York, 1969. It should be noted that the 1968 Senate appropriations rider attached to civil rights legislation which established the so-called "interstate conspiracy law" under which the Chicago 8 trial occurred was actually aimed at Brown personally, and for a time referred to as the "Rap Brown Act." SNCC itself is better known by its earlier designation as the Student *Nonviolent* Coordinating Committee (this being changed to National at the behest of Brown and SNCC leader Stokely Carmichael in 1965); for the best account of FBI performance *vis a vis* SNCC in this earlier period, see Zinn, Howard, *SNCC: The New Abolitionists*, Beacon Press, Boston, 1964.

62. Shirk, Martha, "Cairo Pastor Says FBI Lied to Bishop," *St. Louis Post Dispatch*, November 30, 1975, describes "anonymous letters" containing false information about Koen, fabricated by the Bureau's St. Louis field office and disseminated to the press and his employer in 1971. "Bare Hoover's smear tactic," *Chicago Daily News*, December 3, 1975, reveals another such letter, prepared by the SAC, St. Louis, in 1971, and designed to "alienate [Koen] from his wife"; this last is the actual intent of the FBI, as expressed in its covering memo.

63. Memorandum from SAC, Chicago, to Director, FBI, dated May 15, 1968 and captioned COUNTERINTELLIGENCE PROGRAM, BLACK NATIONALIST—HATE GROUPS, RACIAL INTELLIGENCE (RICHARD CLAXTON GREGORY), marked to the personal attention of Hoover. The document reads in part, "Consider the use of [Gregory's statements condemning the mob] in developing a counterintelligence operation to alert La Cosa Nostra (LCN) to Gregory's attack on the LCN." The memo concludes with the observation that, "The Director noted, on the informative note of [a 3/30/68 New Orleans field office] teletype which said we should recommend counterintelligence action against Gregory when warranted, 'right.'"

64. See Raymond, John, "Files Recently Released: FBI Spying on Black Student Union Revealed," *Common Ground*, Vol. III, No. 7, University of California, Santa Barbara, April 18-25, 1978, p. 1.

65. Memorandum, Director, FBI, to SACs, New York, Chicago, Washington Field, dated July 15, 1964 and caption deleted. Also routed to Belmont, Sullivan, D.E. Moore, Baumgardner, Branigan, Smith and Ryan at FBI headquarters.

66. Deposition of former FBI agent M. Wesley Swearingen, taken in October 1980, in Honolulu, Hawaii, p. 2.

Chapter 3

1. Memorandum from Director, FBI, to SAC, Baltimore, dated 11/25/68 and captioned COUNTERIN-TELLIGENCE PROGRAM, BLACK NATIONALIST HATE GROUPS, RACIAL INTELLIGENCE (BLACK PANTHER PARTY); routed also to Chicago and, later, 40 other field offices.

2. Newton was ordered to prison for three years on March 12, 1987 despite the fact that the felony conviction at issue had long since been overturned as having been unconstitutionally obtained. His attorney apparently failed to file a necessary paper at the time of the constitutional decision (1976) which would have resulted in the conviction being officially "set aside" in California. Hence, when he was subsequently arrested in possession of a .22 calibre pistol, he was still "technically" recorded as a felon in that state despite the felony itself having been negated. He was convicted on this basis in 1978. In his appeal to the Ninth Circuit Court, he argued, reasonably enough, that "in good faith, I believed I was *not* a convicted felon at the time of my arrest." In essence, the federal court ruled this irrelevant and he served time as a result. A similar ploy was used by the state in Newton's celebrated 1968 murder trial in the death of Oakland policeman John Frey; see Keating, Edward M., *Free Huey! The True Story of the Trial of Huey Newton*, Ramparts Press, San Francisco, 1971.

3. Introduction to Perkus, *op. cit.*, p. 16.

4. Interview with Bob Brown, All-African Peoples Revolutionary Party office, Washington, D.C., September, 1984.

5. Certain documents at issue here were introduced as evidence in the case of *Iberia Hampton, et. al., Plaintiffs-Appellants v. Edward V. Hanrahan, et al., Defendants-Appellees* (Nos. 77-1968, 77-1210 and 77-1370; hereinafter referred to as *Appeal*), and will be recorded by their evidentiary numbering on appeal, for purposes of this study. As pertains to informer placement within the Maywood NAACP office, see *Appeal*, PL # 39, 71; SD # 111-118. (The term *Transcript* will also refer to this case.)

6. *Appeal*, PL # 313, 111.

7. On placement on Agitator Index, see *Appeal*, PL # 69; also see *Transcript* at 8985. On designation as "key militant leader," see *Appeal*, PL # 69.

8. See *Transcript* at 21741-62 and 21807-18. *Appeal*, PL WON # 3 also shows that Mitchell had personally posted a $300 cash bond on the latter charge. O'Neal was never prosecuted in either matter.

9. See *Transcript* at 28321, 6210-23 and 21820. *Appeal*, PL # 16-17 and WON # 3, as well as *Transcript* at 6558-9 and 6566 all show that Mitchell began indoctrination of O'Neal in counterintelligence principles and tactics prior to the infiltrator's enlistment in the BPP.

10. *Appeal*, PL WON # 3.

11. Letterhead Memorandum, SAC, Chicago, to Director, FBI dated 12/20/68 and captioned COUNTERINTELLIGENCE PROGRAM, BLACK NATIONALIST—HATE GROUPS, RACIAL INTELLIGENCE MATTER (BLACK PANTHER PARTY). The document reads in part: "Source advised nothing was decided about the two groups joining forces, however, a decision was made to meet again on Christmas day. Source stated Fort did relate that the Rangers were behind the Panthers but that they were not to be considered members. Fort wanted the Panthers to join the Rangers and Hampton wanted the opposite, stating that if the Rangers joined the Panthers, then together they would be able to absorb all the other Chicago gangs...Source advised that based on conversations during this meeting, Fort did not appear over anxious to join forces with the Panthers, however, neither did it appear that he wanted to terminate meeting for this purpose." The "source"—who was William O'Neal—also reported in some detail about the Rangers' weaponry, including eight ".45 calibre machine guns," several "sawed off carbines," *etc.* It is clear that the FBI knew the Blackstone Rangers to be a heavily armed and violence-prone organization.

12. The COINTELPRO was apparently intended to exacerbate tensions which O'Neal had (correctly) reported as attending the question of whether the Rangers joined the Panthers, or *vice versa*. In a memorandum from SAC, Chicago to the Director, FBI, dated 1/10/69 requesting authorization for the letter to Fort, Johnson "justified" the idea by observing that: "It is believed the above [draft letter] may intensify the degree of animosity between the two groups and occasion Forte [*sic*] to take retaliatory action which could disrupt the BPP or lead to *reprisals against its leadership*... Consideration has been given to a similar letter to the BPP alleging a Ranger plot against the BPP leadership; however, it is not felt this would be *productive* principally because the BPP...is not believed to be as violence prone as the Rangers to whom violent type activity—shooting and the like—is second nature [!!!]" (emphasis added). Marlin Johnson later attempted the pretense—under oath in federal court—that nothing violent was intended

as an outcome of the FBI's behavior in this matter, even going so far as to assert that he believed "a hit," such as was threatened to Fort, to be "something nonviolent in nature"; see Greene, Bob, "Laundered box score? No hits, no guns, no terror," *Chicago Sun-Times*, Thursday, February 12, 1976.

13. Internal field office memorandum from SA Mitchell to SAC, Chicago (Johnson), dated 1/28/69 and reporting on Informant (O'Neal) Report.

14. *Appeal*, PL WON # 3.

15. *Appeal*, PL # 16-17 and *Transcript* at 4113-4.

16. The request for approval of the Mau Mau letter was made in a memorandum from SAC, Chicago, to Director, FBI, under a COINTELPRO-BPP heading on 12/30/68; approval by the Director was relayed back by a memo referencing the 12/30 document on 1/30/69.

17. Approval for the letter to Hampton was sought under the heading COINTELPRO-BPP in a memorandum from SAC, Chicago, to Director, FBI, dated 3/24/69; approval was conveyed by a memorandum from the Director referencing the 3/24 document on 4/8/69.

18. Senate Select Committee staff interview with BPP Deputy Minister of Defense Bobby Rush on 11/26/75; reported at p. 198 of *The FBI's Covert Action Program to Destroy the Black Panther Party, op. cit.*

19. *Appeal*, PL # 306 shows that the pay increase was sought by Mitchell, with Johnson's endorsement, in late February, and approved by FBI headquarters on March 11; *Appeal*, PL WON # 3 shows that the raise was to $450 per month, plus $125 monthly expenses.

20. It should be borne in mind that the BPP in Chicago was committed, as were all Party chapters, to following the basic Panther philosophy of building upon the so-called "lumpen proletariat" (or simply "lumpen," as it was termed in Party vernacular) of permanently unemployed, "criminalized," inner-city blacks as a first priority. See Newton, Huey P., "The Brothers on the Block," in *Revolutionary Suicide*, Harcourt, Brace and Jovanovich, New York, 1973, pp. 73-77, for a succinct rendering of the original impetus. Eldridge Cleaver took this notion, via his interpretation of Frantz Fanon, to extreme lengths, beginning in mid-1968; see Lockwood, Lee, *Conversation With Eldridge Cleaver*, Delta Books, New York, 1970.

21. *Appeal*, PL # 26-28 and WON 5. Also see *Transcript* at 6579 and 8907.

22. *Appeal*, PL # 29-30.

23. *Appeal*, PL # 26. The Young Lords were a former Puerto Rican street gang converted to a political organization championing independence for Puerto Rico by Enrique "Cha Cha" Jimenez; Jimenez was subsequently targeted with a spurious kidnapping charge, of which he was first convicted in late 1969, and then acquitted after an appeal finding government misconduct. The Young Patriots were a group founded by former SDS national office organizer Mike James, and composed of white street gang members on Chicago's near-west side in early 1969; the group fashioned itself in the mold of Detroit's White Panther Party and for a time published a radical newspaper, *Rising Up Angry*.

24. There is considerable indication that Mitchell, with both Johnson's and Piper's knowledge and approval, was seeking to establish a federal/local counterintelligence consortium similar to that which was being established simultaneously in California, albeit at a somewhat lower level. On the special relationship between Mitchell, Hanrahan and Jalovec, see *Appeal*, PL # 413 and *Transcript* at 26909.

25. *Transcript* at 27001.

26. On unit formation, see *Appeal*, PL # 413 and FGJ, pp. 88-89. For Hanrahan's statement, see article in the *Chicago Sun-Times*, 6/10/69; also see *Transcript* at 29687-9 and 29672.

27. Perhaps "detached from the police" is not the right phrase. University of Chicago professor Dan Stern, who has researched the matter rather thoroughly, contends that Groth *never* had a normal police assignment, but was deployed all along in a counterintelligence capacity, having earlier focused his attentions upon such entities as the Fair Play for Cuba Committee. Groth's record also reveals several lengthy "training leaves" to Washington, D.C. where it is believed he underwent specialized counterintelligence training under the auspices of both the FBI and CIA.

28. Davis was notorious in Chicago for his wanton brutality, mostly directed against blacks. His nickname, "Gloves," derived from his propensity to don a pair of kidskin gloves before dispensing summary punishment for alleged offenses on the sidewalk prior to, or rather than, making arrests. His personal record, before being assigned to the State's Attorney's "elite" anti-Panther unit contained upwards of 60 disciplinary actions against him, including a civil settlement of damages to Ferris Young, a black man he had beaten comatose at curbside in 1968; most of the disciplinary actions involved similar sorts of physical assault. See CPD disciplinary files entered in *Appeal* as PL # 579-80 *op.cit.* It should be noted that Davis was himself a black man, as were Jones and Howard.

29. The temporary transfers of each of these men to the new "special duty" formation was personally approved by Chicago Police Superintendant William Conlisk; see *Appeal Brief* (prepared by Flint Taylor and Jeff Haas, People's Law Office, Chicago), p. 16.

30. *Appeal*, PL # 422 (Dep. pp. 286-87); also see *Transcript* at 24832-44. Jalovec has acknowledged receiving non-criminal information on the BPP from Mitchell, including nocturnal calls to his residence, "on many occasions" during 1969; see *Transcript* at 6871 and 24534. Mitchell has stated that it was Jalovec's primary "function" to receive such "intelligence"; see *Appeal*, PL # 442 (SSGJ, pp. 4-5).

31. Mitchell retained a copy of this plan in his files, as "evidence" of the BPP's being "violence-prone." *Appeal*, PL # 44; also see *Transcript* at 6487. For further information on Hampton's and Rush's rejection of O'Neal's many efforts to instigate Panther violence, see *Transcript* at 14341-59.

32. Concerning O'Neal's electric chair, see *Transcript* at 29186-90 and 28323. On the bullwhipping, see *Transcript* at 28828-32. He is known to have also bad-jacketed another Party member, Louis Truelock, in December, 1969; see *Transcript*, 9/22/76 *op. cit.*

33. *Transcript* at 29186-90 and 28324-6.

34. *Transcript* at 28339-43. Bruce later testified that such activities were clearly in violation of BPP policy, as articulated by Hampton; see *Transcript* at 28339 and 28343. It should also be noted that Bruce had returned to Chicago with intent to turn himself in, but O'Neal dissuaded him from doing so for several months; see *Transcript* at 28394-6.

35. See *Transcript* at 28369-71 and *Appeal*, WON # 1, 9/25/69 entry.

36. See *Appeal*, PL 78-82. *Appeal*, WON # 2 shows that Mitchell posted bond for O'Neal in this matter, paying $1,000 out-of-pocket.

37. *Appeal*, PL # 19, p. 2, demonstrates Johnson's personal approval of Mitchell's plan for O'Neal to "impel" illegal actions on the part of BPP members. In federal court, years later, Johnson testified under oath that he believed the word "impel" in this document meant "to restrain"; see *Transcript* at 4277-83.

38. Concerning the .45 see *Transcript* at 28340. On the "personal inventory," see *Transcript* at 29954-7.

39. Concerning acquisition of weapons, see *Transcript* at 21979-80 and 23592. On falsification of documents, see *Transcript* at 21979-80. About the training on a farm in Michigan, see *Transcript* at 28491.

40. *Transcript* at 13306. Although it was always a basic tenet of Panther philosophy—indeed, its predication as the Black Panther Party *for Self-Defense* in 1966—that armed self-defense was a necessary and inherent right, the direction taken by O'Neal and other infiltrators had little to do with the practice espoused by Huey P. Newton, Bobby Seale and other early Panther leaders.

41. By SAC Johnson's own later admission, the raid was a part of COINTELPRO-BPP rather than any sort of attempt to enforce the law; see *Appeal*, PL # 20. It was conducted using a floorplan provided by O'Neal (see *Appeal*, PL # 43 and *Transcript* at 4954-67 and 6921-32) and on which the (completely legal) cache of weapons was indicated. Impounded was a quantity of other non-criminal BPP property aside from weapons: posters, literature, cash, financial records, membership lists and lists of contributors, for example; see *Appeal Brief* at p. 11. Although not a shot was fired (see *Transcript* at 6921-32), several Panthers were arrested for "menacing" the raiders (charges were dropped; see *Appeal*, PL # 20 and 115, *Transcript* at 22106-12). Sams, the ostensible basis for the raid, was *not* arrested; see *Appeal Brief* at p. 11. His case is extremely interesting insofar as the Bureau used his "fugitive status" as a pretext to raid Panther offices in a number of cities, including Denver, Baltimore, Jersey City and Detroit during the summer of 1969, with results similar to those obtained in Chicago.

42. AIRTEL, dated 5/15/69, from Director, FBI to 27 SACs (names deleted; locations deleted other than Chicago) captioned BLACK PANTHER PARTY (BPP), RACIAL MATTERS (BREAKFAST FOR CHILDREN PROGRAM), the censor neglected to delete routing to SAC, Albany, from p. 2 of this document. It is worth mentioning that the censor, in "conforming" to the intent of the Freedom of Information Act, also deleted J. Edgar Hoover's name as Director of the FBI (sensitive information, no doubt).

43. *Appeal*, PL # 90.

44. *Appeal*, PL # 90, 106, 107, and 326; a handwritten notation (by Johnson) at the bottom of PL # 106 indicates the SAC called Piper in on at least one occasion to strategize how best to prevent young ghetto children from receiving free breakfasts. This COINTELPRO seems to have consisted primarily of a sustained smear campaign in the Chicago press.

45. *Appeal*, PL # 102 and 103.

46. *Appeal*, PL # 106. The COINTELPRO to destroy distribution of *The Black Panther* became fully national and quite sophisticated over the following year. For example, a memorandum from Director, FBI, to the SACs in 39 cities, dated 11/10/70 and captioned COUNTERINTELLIGENCE PROGRAM, RA-

CIAL MATTERS, BLACK PANTHER PARTY (BPP), BLACK PANTHER NEWSPAPER, reads in part: "Enclosed for each office are 50 copies of a column by Victor Riesel regarding the Black Panther Party (BPP)... Portions of the column deal with a proposal that union members refuse to handle shipments of BPP newspapers. Obviously, if such a boycott gains national support it will result in effectively cutting off BPP propaganda and finances, therefore, it is most desirable that this proposal be brought to the attention of members and officials of unions such as the Teamsters and others involved in the handling and shipment of the BPP newspapers... Each office [should] anonymously mail copies of enclosed to officials of appropriate unions, police organizations and other individuals within its territory who could encourage such a boycott."

47. *Appeal,* PL # 97. As with most of the COINTELPROs, this was hardly restricted to Chicago; the basis of Johnson's order was a memorandum from Director, FBI, to SAC, San Francisco, routed to Chicago and 27 other field offices, dated 6/25/69 and captioned RACIAL INFORMANTS, BLACK PANTHER PARTY, RACIAL MATTERS; it called upon all recipient offices to assign their BPP infiltrators to accomplish such thefts. In Chicago, O'Neal had furnished Mitchell with a duplicate key to the BPP office at least as early as January of 1969 (facilitating surreptitious entry); see *Appeal,* PL # 106, handwritten notation by Mitchell. Although he testified under oath in federal court that the Bureau had only one infiltrator besides O'Neal inside the Chicago BPP in 1969, and that this individual was "handled" by SA Herman Scott of the Racial Matters Squad, evidence was presented that Mitchell alone was responsible for "eight to ten" informants inside the Party; see *Transcript* at 6330-2 and 6377. All told, the FBI was known to have a total of 67 infiltrators within the BPP nationally in that year; see *Appeal* PL # 106, offer of proof.

48. *Appeal,* D # 108 and SD # 15-18; also see *Transcript* at 13931-5. Most of the charges were later dropped.

49. *Transcript* at 28990 and 8392-401; also see *Appeal,* SD # 15-38. O'Neal provided information to SA Mitchell on each of these confrontations, which was then used to manufacture "news stories."

50. *Transcript,* at 6783-7.

51. The former Maywood mayor testified at Hampton's trial that it was common knowledge in that community that the key police witness had a personal "vendetta" against the BPP leader and had pointed him out in a lineup to the complaining witness. He later publicly expressed "considerable doubts" as to whether justice had been done in the case; see *Transcript* at 32429-30 and 32450-1. Another individual confessed to the offense immediately prior to Hampton's death, but the matter was quietly dropped by the Maywood police thereafter; see *Transcript* at 13912-3.

52. See *Appeal Brief* at p. 19.

53. *Appeal,* PL # 47-48. Hanrahan went to court opposing the appeal bond on this petty offense on grounds that Hampton was "a professed revolutionary."

54. Hampton was coming into his own as a brilliantly effective orator. Bobby Rush compared him favorably to Malcolm X, Martin Luther King, Jr., Stokely Carmichael and the other "messiahs" of the Black Liberation Movement whom J. Edgar Hoover had expressly targeted for silencing; see *Transcript* at 29202-3. Even O'Neal testified that Hampton was an eloquent speaker and charismatic and intelligent leader, whom he'd respected; see *Transcript* at 24017-018.

55. See *Appeal Brief* at p. 20.

56. *Transcript* at 29002-4 and 29680-87, o.p., John and Michael Soto were two brothers from the West Side of Chicago who were killed by police in the fall of 1969. John was killed while on leave from Vietnam to attend the funeral of Michael. The Sotos were two of eleven black youths the BPP contended had been murdered by the CPD up to that point in 1969.

57. *Transcript* at 22433-40.

58. On weapons transfer, see *Transcript* at 22433-40. Concerning the use of the apartment by other Panthers, see *Appeal,* PL # 49, 22, and 308; also see *Transcript* at 9244-51 and 28985. Handwritten notes on the documents indicate Mitchell discussed O'Neal's reports on these matters with Piper.

59. *Transcript* at 28911-15. Hampton called for an alliance between black and white activists, a matter which was anathema to the Bureau (see note 12, above).

60. *Transcript* at 29037-8 and 29183-4.

61. *Transcript* at 29030-38.

62. *Appeal,* PL # 50-51, 53 and 55.

63. *Transcript* at 6212-15 and 6682-705. The possibility of Hampton's assuming the number one position in the BPP must have seemed especially menacing to the FBI, given the energy which had already been devoted to shattering the Party's leadership. At the time, Panther founder Huey P. Newton, released on appeal, was facing retrial in the death of Oakland police officer John Frey; Party Chairman

Bobby Seale was facing trial in New Haven on charges of conspiring to murder Alex Rackley and being held without bond; Minister of Information Eldridge Cleaver, on parole, had been ordered returned to San Quentin and had gone into exile in Algeria; Chief of Staff Hilliard had been indicted for "threatening the life of the President" in a public speech; Los Angeles Panther leaders Jon Huggins and Bunchy Carter had been killed by US assassins; the entire New York leadership was being held without bond in a bizarre case involving conspiracy to blow up department stores; and nationally, more than a score of BPP members had been gunned down. The spectre of Fred Hampton rapidly putting the staggering organization back on its feet across the country—as he seemed to have done in Chicago—could not have been comforting to the Bureau.

64. *Transcript* 68910-50. O'Neal *Transcript* at 22841-2, has acknowledged that the *sole* purpose of assembling the floorplan was "for use in a raid." Mitchell, in his deposition on the matter (*Appeal*, PL # 422, pp. 234-5), has admitted that this is the only reason he had O'Neal draw it up.

65. Both O'Neal and Mitchell were aware that Winters had been expelled from the BPP at least as early as September 1969; see *Appeal*, D # 89. Mitchell (and the press) apparently made much over Winter's former BPP membership, and Hampton's eulogy to him as "a fallen comrade"—much as he spoke of other non-Panthers killed by the police—as a "link" between the Party and the November 13 shootout; see *Appeal*, WON # 10-11.

66. *Appeal*, PL # 21. Also see *Transcript* at 6988-9.

67. This was in large part Mitchell's influence; see *Transcript* at 6988-9.

68. *Transcript* at 6927-9 and 9291-2.

69. *Transcript* at 5026 and 5032. Johnson, *Transcript* at 5028-31, later admitted having made an "unusual" call to Lyons at the last moment, trying to ascertain that the planned raid was going forward.

70. As concerns Mitchell's interaction with Jalovec at this point, see *Transcript* at 6875, 24398-9, 24592-3, and 9430; also see *Appeal*, PL # 57-58 and 422 (Dep., p. 274). On the meeting between Mitchell, Jalovec and Groth, see *Transcript* at 7002, 7017, 9302, 9502, 9708-11; also see *Appeal*, PL # 412 (Dep., pp. 307-308 and 310) and 413 (Dep., pp. 234 and 305-07). For additional reference, see *Appeal*, PL # 21.

71. *Transcript* at 25068-78, 25084-5, 25126-30, 25141, 25157-63 and 25308-10.

72. Concerning the meeting itself, see *Transcript* at 25182-7 and 25241-6. As concerns the plan, see *Appeal*, PL # 413 (Dep., pp. 244-7, o.p.) for consideration of the submachinegun; PL # 413 (Dep., p. 244) about Groth's command and additional manpower; PL # 413 (FGJ, pp. 37-38) as to the predawn timing. *Transcript* at 25383-4 and 25389 reveals that Groth had never used a submachinegun in any other action in Chicago; at 25384 it is revealed that Groth had never taken more than 8 men on any similar assignment; at 23612-6 it is demonstrated that Jalovec had to intervene personally with an Officer Cagney to secure the additional 6 men; at 25437 and 25448-9 it is revealed that the planners selected their time so as to catch apartment occupants in their sleep; at 25618 it is admitted that no discussion occurred concerning the use of sound equipment, tear gas or other means short of a violent, forced entry to the apartment. The roster of raid personnel, and their dispositions during the event, are provided at the front of *Appeal Brief*.

73. *Transcript* at 24410-11 shows that Groth swore to the warrant based upon information provided by the FBI, and that the warrant was issued to Hanrahan by Circuit Court Judge Robert Collins, a former employee of Hanrahan. At 24570 and 25278, it is shown that although SA Mitchell was involved in the preparation of the warrant, only Jalovec's and Groth's names were mentioned, so as "not to get Mitchell involved." *Appeal*, PL # 25, offers the memorandum submitted to Hoover by SAC Johnson and SA Piper on December 3, and indicates that Johnson, Piper and Mitchell were all aware of the nature of the planned SPU raid at this time. Both Hanrahan and Groth later acknowledged (*Transcript* at 25460-76, o.p., and 27172-4, o.p.) they were aware that the FBI often got "local police to do its dirty work" and (*Appeal*, PL # 409) the arms raid was conducted specifically at the solicitation of the Bureau.

74. *Brief* at p. 35.

75. *Transcript* at 17783, 29203-05.

76. *Appeal*, PL # 58, p. 2. *Transcript* at 15643 indicates that O'Neal may also have tampered with the Panther armaments in the apartment at some point on December 3.

77. *Transcript* at 15664.

78. *Transcript* at 15664 concerning O'Neal's departure; *Brief* at p. 36 concerning the odd nature of Hampton's falling asleep.

79. *Transcript* at 25398, 25406-7.

80. *Transcript* at 25449-50 reveals that the raiders maintained strict secrecy by traveling in three unmarked cars and an unmarked telephone truck and by failing to inform the CPD of the raid until they

were two blocks from the apartment. As to weaponry, *Transcript* at 25431-2 posits that, in addition to the submachinegun and three 12 gauge riot guns obtained from the CPD armory, the raiders were allowed to carry personal items such as Gloves Davis' M-1 carbine and a sawed-off shotgun utilized by George Jones. *Transcript* at 19515 and 25435 confirms that super-lethal, non-regulation ammunition, including dumdum and hollow-point bullets, were also carried and used by Gloves Davis to kill Mark Clark. *Transcript* at 25433, 25436-7, indicates that, in contrast to their extreme preoccupation with lethal force, the raiders paid virtually no attention at all to non-lethal alternatives, such as tear gas.

81. *Transcript* at 34401 defines the front door subteam as being composed of Daniel Groth, Gloves Davis, Joseph Gorman, George Jones, Robert Hughes, Lynwood Harris, Fred Howard and John Marusich. Edward Carmody, John Ciszewski, Raymond Broderick, William Corbett, William Kelly and Phillip Joseph comprised the rear door subteam.

82. *Transcript* at 33842-33855, 33970.

83. *Transcript* at 17810.

84. Davis acknowledged shooting Harris while she was in bed (*ibid*). His shot seems to have struck her in the leg.

85. *Transcript* at 17803-07; Groth's shot seems to have hit Harris in the hand as she attempted to shield her face.

86. *Transcript* at 18802.

87. *Ibid.*

88. *Transcript* at 19483-94; *Brief* at p. 44. That Hampton was asleep when hit is virtually beyond doubt. Both Truelock and Bell later testified that they shook and otherwise attempted to wake him, without success, in the first moments of the raid (*Transcript* at 14118-19). Eleanor Berman, Chief Toxicologist of the Cook County Hospital, testified that Hampton was heavily sedated at the time of his death; her ultraviolet spectrometer test of his blood revealed a 4.5 mg. dosage of secobarbitol; a thin-layer chromatography performed somewhat later indicated a 3.0 mg. dosage. Dr. Berman further testifies that the discrepancy between test results was caused by the fact that secobarbitol deteriorates rapidly, even when refrigerated. She concluded that the results would have indicated much higher concentrations of the sedative had not the relevant blood samples been denied her for several days by Dr. Victor Levine, a Cook County Coroner who had performed an autopsy on Hampton's body (without showing the barbiturate concentration in his results). Levine apparently colluded in this matter with an FBI chemist named Gormley. See *Transcript* at 21212-21398, 32940-33021, 35411-20, 35445-524; also see *Brief* at pp. 41-42. Both BPP member Bell (*Transcript* at 23150) and FBI infiltrator O'Neal (*Transcript* at 14070-1) testified that Hampton *never* used drugs of any sort. This leaves open the widespread suspicion that O'Neal drugged Hampton before the raid via the medium of a glass of kool-aid, prepared by O'Neal, which the chairman had consumed at dinner.

89. *Transcript* at 201-262, 26190.

90. Harold Bell testified to this exchange (*Transcript* at 14128-40), as did Deborah Johnson (*Transcript* at 16876-78, 16694).

91. Johnson testimony, *Transcript* at 16457. Both bullets, believed to have been fired by Carmody, passed completely through Hampton's head and—according to police—were never recovered for ballistics examination. One entered the right forehead and exited below the left ear. The other entered the right temple and exited from the left side of the throat (see *Brief* at p. 43).

92. See photographs of Hampton's body in *Brief*, Figure 6A. On Carmody dragging Hampton's body, see *Transcript* at 26401, 26560.

93. *Transcript* at 33716. Jones also fired a shotgun into the bedroom (*Transcript* at 34413) and Broderick a revolver (*Transcript* at 34385).

94. See photograph of Satchell's wounds, extending in a line from the right hip to the lower right rib-cage (the lower wound created the need for surgical removal of one-third of his colon), *Brief*, Figure 7A. Anderson was shot in the hip and penis, Brewer in the thigh and kneecap (the latter wound permanently disabling her); see *Brief* at p. 45. As to the Panthers being unarmed when this occurred, see *Brief* at p. 46, and *Transcript* at 3462-3.

95. *Brief* at pp. 46-47. Bell and Truelock were not shot during the raid, but both were severely beaten after surrendering. Deborah Johnson was also not shot and, apparently because she was nine months pregnant, less severely beaten; see photographs of her immediately after her arrest in *Brief*, Figure 7B.

96. *Appeal*, PL #87.

97. *Transcript* at 8412, 8446, 9537-8.

98. *Transcript* at 8408-20 on meeting and its length. Concerning timing and content of the press conference, see *Transcript* at 27097-101.

99. Appeal, PL # 530-45, *op. cit.* Also see *Brief* at p. 54., concerning bail and denial of preliminary hearing on December 5. In late January 1970, proceeding largely on false ballistics information presented by Hanrahan, the Cook County Grand Jury returned indictments against all seven Panther survivors; see *Transcript* at 27651. It was not until May 8, 1970, with his "evidence" unraveling in all directions, that Hanrahan dismissed the indictments and dropped all remaining attempts to prosecute; see *Transcript* at 28182, 28302-8.

100. *Transcript* at 27103-9.

101. *Transcript* at 27471.

102. See reproduction of the *Tribune* front page in question in *Brief,* Figure 9B. Concerning the procedure by which the story was assembled, see *Transcript* at 28182, 28302-8.

103. *Transcript* at 27541-42, 24690, 25628-36, and 27750-51.

104. *Transcript* at 24701-2.

105. *Brief* at pp. 58-59. Citizens Research and Investigation Committee and Louis E. Tackwood, *The Glass House Tapes: The Story of an Agent Provocateur and the New Police-Intelligence Complex,* Avon Books, New York, 1973, p. 100 reveals that the SPU fired "82-100" shots, while the Panthers fired only *one,* by Mark Clark as a convulsive death reflex.

106. On Hanrahan's anger and evasiveness, see *Transcript* at 27109-17. On ordering the IID, see *Transcript* at 27864.

107. For Ervanian's use of the word "whitewash," see *Appeal,* PL #406 (Federal Grand Jury transcript, p. 174, o.p.); the other statements will be found in the same exhibit at p. 177. Examples of the sorts of problems at issue in the IID findings include the facts that ballistic examiner Sadunas received direct pressure from the State's Attorney's Office, including contact from raiders Carmody and Ciszewski, to conclude his part of the investigation prior to examining *any* of the SPU team's personal firearms (he complied with this; *Appeal,* PL # 425 [Federal Grand Jury transcript, pp. 126-27]), the fact that each of the raiders was provided with questions and answers prior to their interrogation (*Appeal,* PL # 425 [Federal Grand Jury transcript, p. 426] and PL #423 [FGJ transcript, p. 42]).

108. The term "exoneration" was actually first publicly used by Superintendent Conlisk in connection with the IID findings on December 19, 1969; Hanrahan repeated it from that point onward (see *Appeal,* PL #425 [FGJ transcript, p. 259].

109. AIRTEL from Piper to DIRECTOR, FBI (caption deleted), dated 12/11/69; reproduced fully in Taylor and Vanhouten, *op. cit.,* p. 44.

110. *Ibid.;* Piper used the term "success" to describe the murders of Hampton and Clark in open court (*Transcript* at 9529). Also see Fisher, Dennis D., "Panther raid 'success'—agent," *Chicago Sun Times,* April 30, 1976.

111. See "Panther Trial," *New Times,* February 18, 1977: "FBI documents in evidence show that O'Neal was rewarded for his efforts with a $300 bonus." The article notes that, "In 1969-70, O'Neal earned $30,000 as a paid FBI informant..." *Appeal,* PL # 94, is a Bureau memo, dated 12/17/69 authorizing bonus payment to O'Neal; he received the money on 12/23/69.

112. *Appeal,* PL # 23. Contrary to his coverup memo of 12/12/69, PL #61 is a memo, also written by SA Mitchell stating that all weapons revealed by O'Neal to be in the Monroe Street apartment were "legally purchased." PL #83 is a memo written by SA Piper the day *before* the coverup memo (that is, on 12/11/69) which also states flatly that the weapons in question were legally purchased. There is no reason to believe that either the FBI or the SPU ever really thought the apartment contained an illegal arsenal they were duty-bound to capture by force.

113. *Transcript* at 5325. Johnson may have been prompted to proceed in this direction by receipt of a Civil Rights Commission request for FBI investigation into the matter, also on December 13 (*Transcript* at 27704-5).

114. The secret intelligence unit in which Leonard was a member, to Mitchell's knowledge, was dubbed the Special Disturbances Group and was aimed quite specifically at "black militants"; it contained representation from the CIA, FBI, Justice Department and other agencies. See *The Rockefeller Report,* pp. 116-125.

115. *Transcript* at 5325. It was arranged that Johnson and his agents would proceed only in accordance with Leonard's "instructions" with regard to evidence (*Transcript* at 5197).

116. *Brief* at p. 68.

117. Virtually all the crucial assertions made before the coroner's panel were proven false in open court. With regard to Groth's testimony in particular, see *Transcript* at 25497-502, 25511-14, 25525-30. Also see *Brief* at p. 68.

118. *Appeal,* PL # 414 (FGJ transcript, pp. 117-27).

119. *Appeal,* PL #91, p. 6.

120. Enclosed with this memo was a copy of the confidential index of the Federal Grand Jury Report (FGJ), complete with a draft first chapter; presented in *Appeal* as PL #24, pp. 1, 3-16. When the FGJ finally finished its work on May 15, 1970, Jerris Leonard disingenuously blamed the lack of indictments on the Panther survivors' refusal to participate in the proceedings; see *Brief* at p. 81; also see *Appeal,* PL #126, o.p.

121. The most blatant of these problems at the time concerned the supposed ballistics evidence prepared by CPD expert John Sadunas, which had been used both as a cover for the raiders and as a principal plank in the indictment of the Panther survivors. When, in compliance with the standard FGJ requirements, the Sadunas "evidence" was reviewed by FBI ballistics specialist Robert Zimmers, it was found to be so erroneous as to be untenable (*e.g.*, police rounds had been attributed to Panther weapons, *etc.*). It then came out that Sadunas had never even examined the raiders' personal weapons prior to submitting his "exonerating" IID report. This left Hanrahan no real alternative but to drop the indictments against the Panther survivors, a matter he managed to parlay into the deal with Jerris Leonard whereby he and his men would not be indicted on matters such as obstruction of justice, perjury, violation of civil rights, aggravated assault and murder. The outcome of the FGJ was thus, as Attorney General Mitchell, Leonard, and SAC Johnson intended, to abort rather than to serve the process of justice. See *Transcript* at 19705, 19708-10, 19804, and 20384; also see *Appeal,* PL #RZ93, p. 6, PL #98, o.p., and PL #427, inclusive. An excellent summary of what was actually known at this point in the case may be found in Wilkins, Roy, and Ramsey Clark, *Search and Destroy: A Report by the Commission of Inquiry into the Black Panthers and the Police,* Metropolitan Applied Research Center, Inc., New York, 1973.

122. The plaintiffs in the *Hampton v. Hanrahan* case were Brenda Harris, Fannie Clark (Mark Clark's mother), Harold Bell, Louis Truelock, Deborah Johnson, Iberia Hampton (Fred Hampton's mother), Blair Anderson, Verlina Brewer, Doc Satchell and Fred Johnson (Hampton's posthumous child). The defendants were ultimately Marlin Johnson, Robert Piper, Roy Martin Mitchell, and William McKinley O'Neal of the FBI; Edward V. Hanrahan, Richard Jalovec, James Metreger and Heldon Sorosky of the Cook County State's Attorney's Office; Daniel Groth, James Davis, Joseph Gorman, George Jones, Robert Hughes, Lynwood Harris, Fred Howard, John Marusich, Edward Carmody, John Ciszewski, Raymond Broderick, William Corbett, William Kelly and Phillip Joseph of the SPU; John Koludrovic, John Sadunas and David Purtell of the CPD Crime Lab; and John Mulchrone, John Meade, Harry Ervanian and Robert Kukowinski of IID. Another 49 individuals—including J. Edgar Hoover, William C. Sullivan, Charles Brennan, George Moore, Larry Deaton, Maria Fisher, Joseph Gormley, Richard G. Held, Joseph McCabe, Thomas Payton, Joseph Stanley, Alan Stephens, Robert Stoetzel and Robert Zimmers of the FBI—were also listed as "Unsued Conspirators" or "Non-Party Participants" in the case.

123. For example, see Eaton, William J., "Charge FBI informer was 'hit man'," *Chicago Daily News,* December 3, 1975.

124. *Brief* at p. 43.

125. Interview with Flint Taylor conducted at the People's Law Office, 343 South Dearborn St., Chicago, IL; July 1986.

126. *Iberia Hampton, et al.,* (600 F2d 600 [1979]), p. 1.

127. *Ibid.,* Findings.

128. Levin, S.K., "Black Panthers Get Bittersweet Revenge," *Colorado Daily,* November 10, 1982. Concerning the Supreme Court appeal and sanctions on the FBI, see *Plantiff's Motion for Sanctions Against Certain Defendants and Lawyers for Violation of the Rules, Abuse of Privilege, Bad Faith and Obstruction of Justice,* Nos. 70-C-3026, 70-C-2371, and 70-C-1384, Northern District of Illinois, United States District Court, 1982 (inclusive).

129. This personal background information on Pratt derives from an amalgam of sources, including FBI documents and conversations with several of his attorneys, such as Stuart Hanlon and Mary O'Melveny and conversations with Pratt himself.

130. The information concerning Pratt's discharge, re-entry into civil life and recruitment into the BPP derives from a comprehensive summary of his case assembled anonymously by various members of his defense (at p. 4, under the heading "G's Life and Times—1968-72"). Hereafter, this document—a copy of which is on file, and which can be made available through the law offices of Jonathan Lubell in

New York City—will be referenced simply as *Summary.* A good overview of the Panther/police atmosphere into which Pratt was recruited may be found in Major, Reginald, *A Panther Is a Black Cat: A Study in Depth of the Black Panther Party, Its Origins, Its Goals, Its Struggle for Survival,* William Morrow and Company, New York, 1971.

131. Interview, *New York Times,* September 8, 1968.

132. Cleaver had, as he explains in his book *Soul on Ice* (Delta Books, New York, 1968, pp. 3-17), written in San Quentin Prison, been convicted twice on felonies in California; the first time as a teenager in possession of marijuana and the second for rape. He was paroled in 1967 after having served approximately five years of the second sentence, upon the guarantee that he would be employed as a writer by *Ramparts* magazine in San Francisco. It was in this capacity that he first met Huey P. Newton and Bobby Seale, and was immediately recruited to become the BPP Minister of Information and editor of the Party newspaper, *The Black Panther.* Cleaver's talents as an orator, as well as a writer and theorist, quickly made him a major actor in the Party's public affairs, particularly as COINTELPRO tactics began to decimate the BPP leadership in early 1968. He became even more prominent as his outspoken advocacy of forming coalitions with white radicals became better known, a matter which led to his selection as presidential candidate by the Peace and Freedom Party. Obviously, he was a prime target for neutralization by this point and, on the evening of April 6, 1968 a group of Panthers, including Cleaver, was attacked (there really is no other adequate word for what happened) by Oakland police on a quiet residential street. Although there is no indication that Cleaver was armed or that he in any way threatened the police, he was wounded; a 17-year-old companion, Robert "Li'l Bobby" Hutton, was shot to death (five rounds in the back at point-blank range). Despite the fact that he was charged with no crime, the California State Parole Board moved to revoke Cleaver's parole. Cleaver challenged this, appealing to the California Superior Court of Judge Charles Sherwin. Upon review the judge found that:

> The uncontradicted evidence presented to this court indicated that the petitioner had been a model parolee. The peril to his parole status stemmed from no failure of personal rehabilitation, but from his undue eloquence in pursuing political goals, goals which were offensive to many of his contemporaries. Not only was there absence of cause for the cancellation of parole, it was a type of pressure unbecoming, to say the least, of the law-enforcement paraphernalia of this state.

Sherwin then ordered Cleaver released on $25 bond. The State, of course, appealed the outcome of Cleaver's appeal, and achieved a ruling that the judicial system held no power to impose due process on the Parole Board procedures, and ordered Cleaver remanded to San Quentin. It was at this point that he went into exile, first in Cuba, and later in Algeria where, convinced by his experience that there was absolutely no possibility of a peaceful alternative for social change in the United States, he came to rely increasingly upon theories of armed struggle to achieve black liberation (see Lockwood, Lee, *Conversations with Eldridge Cleaver: Algiers,* op. cit., and Cleaver's own *Post-Prison Writings and Speeches,* Vintage Books, New York, 1969). The overemphasis on militarism by Cleaver's International Section of the BPP led to increasing tension with the original Newton group, a situation which was heavily exploited by COINTELPRO (see above), and which led to his almost total isolation from former colleagues. Apparently, he eventually went mad, abandoned all his revolutionary positions and returned to the United States, where he is now a spokesperson for the evangelical right (for a personal account of his collapse, see *Soul on Fire,* Word Books, Waco, Texas, 1978). The best source on Cleaver's stateside Panther period is probably Marine, *op. cit.*

133. *Summary,* p. 5.

134. As is revealed in *Summary,* p. 6. Pratt's first arrest occurred on January 11, 1968—the very evening of the Carter-Huggins assassination—while he and 17 other Panthers, including Huggins' widow, Ericka, were sharing their grief and attempting to overcome their shock. No charges were filed, as the police seem to have considered this to have been merely a "routine roust." Pratt, though, undoubtedly observed when, as Freed, *op. cit.,* recounts on p. 65: "The night Jon was killed, Los Angeles police arrested her [Ericka Huggins] and put a gun to [her and Jon's] baby's head, laughed and said, 'You're next.'" FBI involvement in this nasty, but ostensibly local, matter is clearly indicated in a 1/28/69 memo from SAC, Los Angeles, to the Director, captioned BLACK PANTHER PARTY, RACIAL MATTERS, providing a detailed inventory of the (all legal) weapons confiscated and stating that "Special Agents of the FBI photographed those items..."

135. The "Key Black Extremist" tag seems to have been adopted for local use by the LA office COINTELPRO group from at least as early as January 20, 1969, based upon internal office memos. A memo from SAC, Los Angeles to the Director, dated 4/21/69 and captioned BLACK PANTHER PARTY—AR-

RESTS, RACIAL MATTERS, recommended placing both Pratt and his second in command, Roger Lee Lewis, in the National Security Index.

136. *The Glass House Tapes, op. cit.,* pp. 34-35.

137. Durden-Smith, *op. cit.,* pp. 145-46.

138. This is readily borne out in a Bureau document, LA 157-3436 which, in Section V (MISCEL-LANEOUS ITEMS RELATING TO ACTIVITIES ASSOCIATED WITH THE BPP), describes how Pratt and several other Panthers, in a private residence, had sawn off the barrels of "15 to 20 weapons" (a legal act, so long as resulting barrel length is not less than 18 inches) during January of 1969; for no apparent reason, it stated that "it was believed the weapons were obtained in a burglary." The document then goes on to itemize other legal activities in which Pratt had engaged, such as target practice in the Mojave Desert, travel to and from Kansas City, providing a guided tour of the local BPP office for Angela Davis, *etc.* This is intermixed with suggestions (no reference to evidence of any sort) that Pratt illegally possessed at least one .45 caliber submachinegun and engaged in other criminal behavior.

139. An AIRTEL from SAC, Los Angeles, to the Director, FBI, dated 4/21/69 and captioned BLACK PANTHER PARTY—ARRESTS, RACIAL MATTERS, also routed to the Secret Service, Norton Air Force Base, NISO (San Diego) and the LA Alcohol and Tax Unit, contains the following inventory of what was supposedly found by the LAPD in Pratt's 1967 GTO convertible: "...one metal pipe eight inches long with caps on both ends; one Elect blasting cap three inches long with yellow and green wires; one Elect blasting cap two inches long with copper wire." The document then goes on to detail (somewhat inaccurately) Pratt's military background. Whatever substance there might have been to this "evidence," which was "released to the LAPD Bombing [sic] Squad" was negated by its being "unavailable" when the case finally went to trial three years later. Rather, the LAPD introduced two other items mentioned later in the FBI document—"a paper notebook containing instructions on bomb making and some miscellaneous bullets and shell casings"—as "proof" that Pratt and Lewis had possessed the makings of a pipebomb (or three), *sans* explosive.

140. According to a Los Angeles Office Field Report, LA 157-3416, dated 6/9/69, the Panthers—other than Butler and Pratt—who were arrested in the matter were Ronald Freeman, Richard Jones, John William ("Long John") Washington, Nathaniel Clark and Roger Lee Lewis. As is brought out in *Summary* at p. 78, there was virtually no evidence presented at trial that Ollie Taylor had been kidnapped, by Pratt or anyone else. What *was* shown was that an FBI infiltrator named Julius Carl ("Julio") Butler had viciously pistolwhipped the youngster on April 23, 1969, a situation ended by Pratt's intervention. It was also shown that Butler had similarly beaten another Panther—referred to as "Little Bobby"—and had earlier exacerbated tensions between US and the BPP by machinegunning the apartment of James Doss, Vice Chairman of the Karenga organization, on August 5, 1969. Ultimately, and apparently on the basis of services rendered, Butler was allowed to plead guilty to four serious felonies and received a five-year probation for the lot; the infiltrator never served a day in jail for his crimes.

141. The notion that Pratt might have killed Frank Diggs supposedly derives from a letter Julio C. Butler submitted to Sergeant Rice of the LAPD. It should be noted, however, that Captain Franco was Butler's immediate superior within the Panther organization, might have stumbled upon indication of the infiltrator's true identity, and could easily have suffered his "execution-style" fate as a result (see *Summary* at p. 98). It is also noteworthy that the Bureau itself seems to have had a considerable interest in associating Pratt with the Diggs murder, as is evidenced by LA 157-3436, which claims, "PRATT also bragged that he had killed more people than anyone else in the BPP organization. He intimated he had killed MELVIN "X", and FRANK DIGGS...FRANK DIGGS is a former BPP Area Captain murdered in 1968, in an execution-style slaying...MELVIN BISHOP WILLIAMS, also known as Melvin X, former co-founder of the Black Student Alliance (BSA)...was murdered in the fall of 1970 in another execution-style slaying." No evidence has ever been introduced to substantiate any of this, and all indications are that Pratt and Diggs were close...with Diggs often serving as Pratt's driver and having free use of Pratt's car (see *Summary* at pp. 97-98).

142. This last caused both Pratt and the LA-BPP more generally a considerable philosophical problem. As Marine, *op. cit.,* puts it on p. 210: "The question that confronts militant blacks in the Los Angeles area now, and may confront others in other areas soon, is simple: Are the Panthers playing by their own revolutionary rules when they cooperate with the very police they detest...? Or to put it more simply: Ought an organization with the stated values of the Panthers ever cooperate with the police at all?"

143. Memo from SCA, Los Angeles to the Director, FBI, dated 5/6/69 and captioned ELMER PRATT, BR—CONSPIRACY states, "As the Bureau is aware, Los Angeles is investigating one bank robbery com-

mitted by persons known to be involved in 'US' [several words deleted] UNSUBS [3]; BANK OF AMERICA, NT & SA, Jefferson Hill Branch, 3320 South Hill Street, Los Angeles, California, 1/10/69, BR')." The document then goes on, for no logical reason, to announce that BPP members "have possibly been involved in bank robbery matters in the Los Angeles area," singles Pratt out by name in a heavily deleted passage, and ends with the observation that, "A bank robbery conspiracy case is being opened in the Los Angeles Office on ELMER PRATT...appropriate investigation *to attempt to develop a conspiracy case* will be conducted [emphasis added]." In a memo to the Director dated 6/5/69 and captioned "ELMER PRATT, BR—CONSPIRACY," the SAC, Los Angeles, eventually acknowledged that the matter was being dropped because "no information has been developed to indicate that any Black Panther Party (BPP) members have been plotting bank robberies in Los Angeles or elsewhere." The document concludes that the "captioned case is...subject to being reopened at any time information is received to indicate that Pratt or other members of the BPP are plotting or are responsible for bank robberies."

144. Los Angeles office Field Report, LA 157-3553, dated 5/14/69. The character of the case reported upon is described as, "RM—SMITH ACT OF 1940; SEDITIOUS CONSPIRACY AND INSURRECTION." The document was circulated to 8 Bureau offices, the Norton Air Force Base Office of Strategic Intelligence, 115th Military Intelligence Group, and the Secret Service in its initial distribution.

145. Los Angeles office Field Report, LA 157-3436, dated 6/2/69, titled "ELMER GERARD PRATT, aka 'Gee,' 'Geronimo,' 'G.'"

146. Memo from Director, FBI, to SAC, Los Angeles, dated 6/4/69.

147. See Counterintelligence Report from the SAC, Los Angeles, to Director, FBI, (LA 157-17511), dated 6/3/69 and captioned "COUNTERINTELLIGENCE PROGRAM, BLACK NATIONALIST-HATE GROUPS, RACIAL INTELLIGENCE (BLACK PANTHER PARTY)." As to the younger Held's position in the LA-COINTELPRO operation, see Swearingen deposition, *op. cit.*, p. 1: "I knew RICHARD WALLACE HELD as head of the COINTELPRO section in Los Angeles [during this period]."

148. Along with Sekou Odinga (Michael Tabor) in New York, who had experienced similar experiences of attempted neutralization as a defendant in the Panther 21 trial, Pratt is credited with having been an operational founding member of the BLA.

149. Durden-Smith, *op. cit.*, pp. 134-35. There is absolutely *no* evidence that Pratt aimed a weapon at police.

150. *Summary* at p. 6.

151. Durden-Smith, *op. cit.*, p. 136, quotes Tackwood describing Cotton Smith before the raid, "cutting up this cardboard and making this building, and he's putting little dolls with names on them, where they were, and associations and such and such." The LA version of the O'Neal floorplan in Chicago was thus apparently in three dimensions.

152. Although not so straightforward as the Chicago memoranda in the aftermath of the Hampton-Clark assassinations, a memo from SAC, Los Angeles to Director, FBI, dated 12/8/69 and captioned BLACK PANTHER PARTY, ARRESTS—RACIAL MATTERS, indicates the Bureau was directly involved in the LA raid and that the local FBI office sought credit for this "success." Among the BPP members listed in this document as having been arrested on (spurious) attempted murder charges and other offenses as a result of Bureau/police efforts on 12/8 are Robert Bryan, Roland Freeman, Craig Williams, Jackie Johnson, Wayne L. Pharr, Isiah Houston, Elmer Pratt, Sandra Lane Pratt (wife), Willie Stafford, Tommy E. Williams, Renee Moore, Paul Redd, Albert Armor, Melvin Smith and George Young. The situation seems to have sparked substantial interest at the very highest levels of the FBI, as is indicated by a memo on the matter between national COINTELPRO head W.C. Sullivan and his primary operational coordinator, G.C. Moore, dated 12/17/69, in which Moore expresses delight that, "Both Pratts were arrested for their participation in the shooting battle with the Los Angeles Police Department on 12-8-69."

153. *The Glass House Tapes, op. cit.*, p. 104.

154. See "63 Verdicts End Panther Trial", *Los Angeles Times*, December 24, 1971.

155. *The Glass House Tapes, op. cit.*, pp. 104-105.

156. See memorandum from (deleted), Los Angeles, to (deleted) Intelligence Division, dated February 9, 1970, and captioned "Elmer Gerard Pratt."

157. Pratt, Elmer Gerard ("Geronimo"), *The New Urban Guerrilla,* introduced by Zayd Malik Shakur, Revolutionary People's Communication Network (RPCN), New York, 1971, and *Humanity, Freedom,*

Peace, RPCN, New York, 1972. Pratt apparently never intended this material for publication, and indicates many of his ideas were changed during the "editing" process.

158. For example, a Teletype, dated May 21, 1970 and captioned BLACK PANTHER PARTY (BPP)—TRAVEL OF LEADERSHIP, distributed by the Atlanta Field Office to Los Angeles, San Francisco, and Chicago, has "Jeronimo" speaking to an SCLC rally in Georgia on that date.

159. See Durden-Smith, *op. cit.*, p. 136-137. Pratt indicates this is untrue.

160. Los Angeles office Field Report, LA-3436, dated 2/26/70 and captioned ELMER GERARD PRATT, aka "Gee," "G," P.C. The lengthy document provides another comprehensive Bureau version of Pratt's biography and informs recipients (once again including Military Intelligence and the Secret Service) that: *"IN VIEW OF PRATT'S VIOLENT HISTORY AND PRESENT AFFILIATION WITH THE BPP, PRATT SHOULD BE CONSIDERED ARMED AND EXTREMELY DANGEROUS."* In police parlance this language is typically intended as a rather transparently coded invitation to shoot first and justify the act later.

161. *Summary* at p. 6.

162. Durden-Smith, *op. cit.*, p. 155.

163. This is brought out rather clearly in an AIRTEL from SAC, Los Angeles, to the Director, FBI, dated 8/10/70 and captioned COUNTERINTELLIGENCE PROGRAMS, BLACK NATIONALIST—HATE GROUPS, RACIAL INTELLIGENCE—BLACK PANTHER PARTY, in which it is proposed to send a letter to Newton critical of Pratt and serving "to acutely impair Los Angeles BPP operations by dividing the loyalties of BPP members between the two aforementioned individuals [i.e., Cleaver and Newton]." The distancing of Cleaver from Pratt was brought out somewhat obliquely by Kathleen Cleaver in a television interview on the "Ralph Storey Program," KABC-TV, Los Angeles, October 21, 1971; the interview was transcribed by the FBI. At p. 9, Ms. Cleaver attributes the distancing to the fact that, "We in Algeria did not have adequate information to move on this..." Oddly, the Bureau itself seemed to be unaware of the true effectiveness with which it had been able to isolate Pratt, as is evidenced by a heavily deleted intelligence summary produced by the Los Angeles Field Office on September 11, 1970, titled *ELMER GERARD PRATT*, which indicates the belief that Pratt might have gone to Algeria to join Cleaver and "to organize a contingent of BPP members which would eventually travel to North Vietnam and actively participate in guerrilla activities to be directed against the Armed Forces of the United States in South Vietnam."

164. On Marin County, see Section 3, this chapter. On the Pratt group's relocation to Texas, see Durden-Smith, *op. cit.*, p. 155. On the missed court appearance, see a Los Angeles Teletype to FBI Headquarters, dated 8-19-70 and captioned "ELMER G. PRATT, RM-BPP": "SUBJ, DEPUTY MINISTER BPP, FAILED TO APPEAR AT TRIAL AUGUST SEVENTEEN LAST AND LOCAL BENCH WARRANT ISSUED. LA COUNTY SO IN POSSESSION OF WARRANT."

165. Circular (43 LA CODE) issued to the FBI Special Investigations Division via Director, FBI, by SAC, Los Angeles, dated 9/15/70 and captioned "ELMER GERARD PRATT, aka Elmer Pratt, Geronimo, Gee, 'G'—FUGITIVE, UFAP—FALSE IMPRISONMENT AND ADW."

166. *Summary* at p. 7 concerning CCS. Also see Richardson, *op. cit.*, p. 31, for infiltrator Smith's recollections: "The FBI agent [George Aiken], Smith said, gave him a list of possible murders which could be pinned on Pratt." According to Smith, Aiken also offered $3,000-$5,000 for testimony that would convict Pratt of murder.

167. *The Glass House Tapes*, *op. cit.*, pp. 213-14. The FBI version of this, as contained in a Bureau report dated 12/16/70 (no other identifying information available) is that "[Pratt] was advised of the identities of the arresting agents as Special Agents of the FBI and taken into custody...On December 9, 1970, PRATT and [deleted] appeared before acting US Commissioner BAILEY RANKIN, Northern District of Texas, at which time they admitted their identities and were released from federal custody to custody of the Dallas County Sheriff's Office for further release to California authorities." Either way, normal extradition proceedings are not mentioned; the Bureau later contended Pratt "waived" his right to an extradition hearing.

168. *Summary* at p. 7.

169. "Let Us Hold High the Banner of Intercommunalism and the Invincible Thoughts of Huey P. Newton, Minister of Defense and Supreme Commander of the Black Panther Party!" *The Black Panther*, Center Section, January 23, 1971; the statement is believed to have been written by BPP Central Committee member Elaine Brown, acting under Newton's direct instructions.

170. These points are noted approvingly in a Teletype sent to the Director, FBI from "San Francisco" on *1/21/71*—two days *before* the newspaper was released—and apparently served as the basis for an LA Field Office attempt to enmesh Pratt even more deeply in the gambit (see memo from SAC, Los Angeles, to Director, FBI, dated 1/29/71 and captioned "COINTELPRO, BLACK NATIONALIST HATE

GROUPS, RACIAL INTELLIGENCE, BLACK PANTHER PARTY [BPP]") by advising him that freedom of speech was a right guaranteed by the Constitution, and in so being, it was his prerogative to write letters critical of the BPP to anyone he desired." The document closes with the note that, "Los Angeles will maintain discrete contact with PRATT and appropriate COINTELPRO recommendations will be forwarded."

171. Los Angeles office Field Report, dated 7/1/71 and captioned "BLACK PANTHER PARTY," recounts the Newton-Cleaver television debate.

172. The authors have on file 11 separate Bureau documents from the spring of 1971 pertaining to FBI attempts to link Pratt to the Camp Pendleton robbery, each of which is too heavily deleted to offer useful citation, but which in combination point to the energy put into this effort.

173. *Summary* at p. 7. A Los Angeles Field Office reporting document dated January 14, 1972, and captioned BLACK PANTHER PARTY, LOS ANGELES DIVISION, EXTREMIST MATTER, and reveals Sandra Lane Pratt had been shot five times at point-blank range.

174. It is worth noting that, by 1980, Johnnie Cochran was the third ranking member of the District Attorney's Office in Los Angeles, and was still adamantly insisting that not only was Pratt innocent of the tennis court murder, but that if he'd had access to COINTELPRO documents withheld at trial, the case would have been "no contest."

175. *Summary* at pp. 1-2.

176. On prosecution presentation, see *ibid.* at pp. 2-3; on Newton faction refusal to testify for Pratt, see pp. 94-96.

177. AIRTEL from SAC, Los Angeles, to Acting Director, FBI, dated 7/18/72 (caption deleted).

178. An "URGENT" Teletype, sent at 1:26 PM, 7-28-72, from the Los Angeles Field Office to the Acting Director, FBI, and reading, "LOS ANGELES SHERIFF'S OFFICE INTELLIGENCE, ADVISED INSTANT DATE ELMER GERARD PRATT FOUND GUILTY FIRST DEGREE MURDER...DETAILS TO FOLLOW," gives some indication of the ownership and priority the Bureau felt in this case.

179. See Amnesty International, *Proposal for a commission of inquiry into the effect of domestic intelligence activities on criminal trials in the United States of America* (hereinafter referred to as *AI*), Amnesty International, New York, 1980, p. 29: "[The defense obtained] over 7,000 pages of FBI surveillance records dated after 2 January 1969. Elmer Pratt claimed earlier records would reveal that he was at a meeting in Oakland at the time of the murder on 18 December 1968 but the FBI's initial response to this was that there had been no surveillance before 1969. This was later shown to be untrue."

180. See *Elmer G. Pratt v. William Webster, et al.*, United States Court of Appeals in the District of Columbia (No. 81-1907) for presentation of the case, and *Pratt v. Webster, et. al.* (508 F. Supp. 751 [1981]) for the ruling. The federal "national security" argument may be found in the reply brief (No. 81-1907).

181. For Judge J. Dunn's dissenting remarks, see his minority opinion *In Re: Pratt, 112 Cal. App. 3d. 795;—Cal. Rptr.—(Crim. No. 37534. Second Dist., Div. One. 3 December 1980)*; hereinafter referred to as *"Minority"* and *"Majority."*

182. *Pratt Trial Transcript*, Vol. II, pp. 390-91.

183. *AI, op. cit.*, pp. 107-110. Informant Reports and related memoranda on file.

184. *Summary* at p. 15.

185. *Ibid.* at p. 79, Butler was able to hold a job as legislative assistant to Los Angeles City Councilman David Cunningham while attending West Los Angeles University Law School during the late 1970s.

186. Richardson, Lee, "Ex-FBI Agent Exposes Use of Informants to Destroy the BPP," *Freedom Magazine.* 18:5, January 1985, p. 31.

187. *AI, op. cit.*, p. 25.

188. *Summary* at p. 3; this was a matter raised in a motion for retrial by Johnnie Cochran, which was denied by trial judge Kathleen Parker.

189. *Ibid.* at p. 2.

190. *Ibid.* at pp. 91-93.

191. *Summary* at p. 4.

192. *AI, op. cit.*, p. 22.

193. *"Majority,"* p. 13.

194. Order Denying Writ of *Habeas Corpus,* (Criminal No. 21826), California Supreme Court *en Banc.* 1 April 1981.

195. *Pratt v. D.J. McCarthy, et al., NO. CR. 81-3407-PAR (K),* United States District Court, Central District of California, 1985; Vol. 3[A], pp.452-53.

196. *Ibid.* at p. 463.

197. *Summary* at p. 4.

198. Conversation with Stuart Hanlon, May, 1987; it seems noteworthy, in view of the major focus of this study, that—in a statement released after the 1987 parole denial—Pratt consciously linked his case to those of American Indian Movement COINTELPRO victims such as Leonard Peltier and Anna Mae Aquash (see Part III). During Pratt's parole hearing (part of which was shown on the November 29, 1987 *60 Minutes* segment on the Pratt case), L.A. Deputy District Attorney Diane Visanni again made explicit the political nature of his imprisonment: "The time Mr. Pratt left Vietnam he was a walking time bomb. He was mentally, physically and emotionally in a combat mode. Are we dealing with a time bomb or are we really dealing with a man that has changed? *I think we still have a revolutionary man. He does have this network out there. If he chooses to set up a revolutionary organization upon release from prison, it would be easy for him to do so* [emphasis added]."

199. San Francisco Field Office Investigative Report, dated August 30, 1974 and captioned "ELMER GERARD PRATT, Also Known As Geronimo." Less than two years later, on May 19, 1976, a Los Angeles Field Office Investigative Report captioned "ELMER GERARD PRATT" reveals that, "inmates within San Quentin Prison consider Elmer Pratt to be the top man in the Black Liberation Army (BLA) within the California prison system and therefore was highly thought of by members of the BGF [Black Guerrilla Family]. (Deleted) described Pratt as a top organizer within the prison system with many outside contacts." Clearly, the days of Newton's ability to isolate him had ended, albeit Pratt himself claims no position within the BGF.

200. The document also posits "*the absolute necessity*" for intensive investigative efforts in [political] matters (emphasis added)."

201. Select Committee, *Final Report,* Book III, *op. cit.,* p. 517.

202. An excellent account of the events surrounding the Jackson case may be found in Armstrong, Gregory, *The Dragon Has Come: The Last Fourteen Months in the Life of George Jackson,* Harper and Row, New York, 1974. Armstrong was Jackson's editor and apparently close friend.

203. The Soledad Brothers case may be capsulized as follows: On January 13, 1970, three black inmates at California's Soledad prison—W.L. Nolen, Cleveland Edwards and Alvin "Jug" Miller—were shot at close range by a tower guard, Opie G. Miller, an expert marksman, using a .30 calibre carbine. The victims were left lying where they fell in the prison's O-Wing courtyard until it was too late for them to be saved by medical treatment. Nolan, in particular, had been instrumental in organizing protests of guard killings of two other black inmates—Clarence Causey and William A. Powell—at Soledad in the recent past, and was consequently both a thorn in the side of the prison officials and a hero to the black inmate population. All told, the killings of Nolen, Edwards and Miller were thus widely perceived as amounting to outright summary execution; the view was shared even by prisoners such as Billie D. "Buzzard" Harris, a self-proclaimed "white racist" with "a long chaw of hate for niggers" and who headed the prison's "Aryan Brotherhood" organization. (Harris, in his deposition as an eye-witness to the shootings, asserted they were "in cold blood" and that Miller "had no right to shoot them coons that way.") When Opie G. Miller was exonerated of any wrongdoing by a Board of Inquiry some two weeks after the fact, a guard named John V. Mills was killed in apparent retaliation. Charged in the Mills slaying were George Jackson, Fleeta Drumgo and John Cluchette, all black; Jackson, as a "lifer," faced the death penalty if convicted. These three, and their case, quickly became known as "The Soledad Brothers." The best account of the overall situation is to be found in Yee, Min S., *The Melancholy History of Soledad Prison: In Which a Utopian Scheme Turns Bedlam,* Harpers Magazine Press, New York, 1973.

204. Jackson, George L., *Soledad Brother: The Prison Letters of George Jackson,* (Introduction by Jean Genet), Coward McCann Publishers, New York, 1970. Jackson had a second book, *Blood in My Eye,* (Random House, New York, 1972), published posthumously, which was not so well received.

205. It is worth noting that Tackwood passed—with flying colors—a polygraph examination regarding the substance of his version of the FBI/CCS/SII/CII operations surrounding the entire Jackson affair. The test was administered by Chris Gugas, a former FBI agent and president of the American Polygraph Association. Further, much of what he's had to say has been at least circumstantially corroborated by subsequently released FBI documents, as well as the statements of other former infiltrators and FBI agents. As concerns the latter group, see Richardson, *op. cit.,* pp. 28-40, for an interview with Melvin "Cotton" Smith (currently serving a life sentence for murder in the Kentucky State Prison). Also see "Othello," *op. cit.;* according to former FBI COINTELPRO specialist Wesley Swearingen, Othello was the Bureau code-name for California Panther infiltrator Darthard Perry (Swearingen deposition, *op. cit.,* p. 2).

206. Durden-Smith, *op. cit.,* pp. 127-172.

207. *Ibid.,* p. 156.

208. *Ibid.,* p. 155.

209. As to what CCS representatives were doing orchestrating a firing squad outside the Marin County Civic Center in San Rafael, more than 300 miles north of their ostensible jurisdiction, Tackwood offers the following observation: "...you've got the FBI, CCS, SII and you got State, Federal and Local. I'll tell you something else, they don't work with the counties, no way. CCS's jurisdiction is California, they're based in Los Angeles, are paid by the city, and their jurisdiction is the state. And there ain't no place they can't go..."; Tackwood, *The Glass House Tapes, op. cit.,* p. 213. Tackwood also noted that, under FBI ausplices, CCS was known to work on an interstate basis. At pp. 237-238, he states, "And the FBI works hand in hand with all of them...Los Angeles has more power as a Police Department goes, because of the proximity of working with the CII and also the FBI." At p. 214, he notes, "There ain't nowhere they can't go. CCS, like they're federally sponsored." As to how the San Quentin guards managed to make their timely appearance, Yee (*op. cit.,* pp. 165-66) recounts the state's version that they "were on their way back [to the prison] from a session at a nearby rifle range when they heard broadcasts of the...escape attempt." They claimed "not to hear" an order by Sheriff Louis Mountanos not to fire.

210. Durden-Smith, *op. cit.,* p. 156. As to direct FBI involvement, Tackwood, in *The Glass House Tapes* (*op. cit.,* p. 221), observes, "This vanguard of FBI agents was stationed at Santa Cruz at the Moon Bay Motel. Had the whole motel covered. And CCS got permission from somebody to use the FBI agents that were connected to them—they didn't want to use no Northern California people, see; they never liked to use Northern California people cause they don't trust 'em."

211. Durden-Smith, *op. cit.,* p. 160. This is very much in line with Tackwood's observation in *The Glass House Tapes* (*op. cit.,* p. 183) that, "What CII was fearful of is that a coalition with the Revolutionary Union would come about, they didn't want a coalition...For the first time up North there was a coalition of the black militants and the white militants, and they didn't want it to spread down here. They wanted to destroy it before it got started..." At p. 208, he also remarks that "CII sent me to Berkeley to work on the coalition. I was to get information on the Revolutionary Union and the Panthers and everyone involved in militant organizations." Another RU leader who was targeted less successfully was Bob Avakian, an Oakland judge's son who had become Huey Newton's errand boy during the early days of the BPP and who was consequently designated as the party's liaison with Berkeley SDS in 1967; Avakian is presently chairman of the Revolutionary Communist Party, USA (RCP) and "politically exiled" in Paris.

212. See Moore, Howard, Jr., "Angela—Symbol of Resistance," in Davis, Angela Y., *et al., If They Come in the Morning,* Signet Books, New York, 1971, pp. 203-212.

213. See Abt, John, "From New York to California: The Extradition of Angela Davis," in Davis, *et al., op. cit.,* pp. 213-219.

214. See Tackwood, Louis E., "My Assignment Was to Kill George Jackson," *The Black Panther,* April 21-May 4, 1980, p. 4.

215. Durden-Smith (*op. cit.,* p. 227) summarizes this nicely.

216. Quoted in *ibid.,* p. 227.

217. Armstrong, *op. cit.,* at pp. 226-27, notes that Jackson's autopsy reveals he had been shot twice, rather than once, as initially stated by prison officials. Further, the first round had shattered his ankle, leaving it somewhat less than probable that he was "running" when killed by a "bullet in the head." Finally, the second, and fatal, bullet had entered the small of Jackson's back, traveled upward through his body and exited through the top of his head. The last shot was apparently administered at close range from behind as the victim was kneeling on all fours. All of this lends considerable credence to the notion that George Jackson was summarily executed.

218. The weapon in question had been impounded by the FBI when Williams was arrested in Denver, Colorado on June 5, 1969 and charged with interstate flight to avoid prosecution in New Haven, Connecticut in connection with the "murder conspiracy" surrounding the death of Alex Rackley (see Chapter 2). The Bureau (and Denver Police) later claimed to have "lost" their records pertaining to the impounded weapon, suggesting it had been returned to Williams after the conspiracy charges against him were dropped in the wake of the acquittal of Bobby Seale and Ericka Huggins in the same case. Williams, for his part, contends that the weapon was not returned. Its turning up as evidence in the Jackson case, under incredibly suspicious circumstances, suggests that the Williams version is correct. This would place the Bureau in a position of direct involvement in the Jackson affair. See *The Glass House Tapes, op. cit.,* p. 121.

219. On August 28, 1971, the *San Francisco Chronicle* carried a story concerning its attempts to duplicate the feat Jackson supposedly accomplished. Using a black model, an automatic identical to the one supposedly secreted on top of Jackson's head and an Afro wig comparable to the one he allegedly utilized in hiding it, they reached the following conclusion: "The model's attempt to hide the gun by lifting the front

of the wig and sliding the weapon onto the top of his head failed...He eventually removed the wig, placed the gun inside and forced the hairpiece back on his head with some struggle. The wig was obviously askew, and with every step he took, the gun wobbled dangerously, bringing his hands instinctively to his head." An accompanying photograph showed the muzzle of the pistol protruding some 3" out from under the wig. The weapon in question, an Astra-600, is 8 1/8" long, 1 1/4" thick and 5 1/2" wide, weighing 2 1/2 pounds when unloaded. It is thus ill-suited for use in the state's scenario.

220. Despite the patent absurdity of its case, the state never dropped charges against Stephen Bingham. As a result, the attorney remained in hiding for nearly 15 years, finally surfacing in the spring of 1986. He was brought to trial before being acquitted on all counts.

221. *The Glass House Tapes, op. cit.*, p. 180. For more on this "overall plan," see Appendix in Katsiaficas, George, *Imagination of the New Left*, South End Press, Boston, 1987.

Chapter 4

1. The full text of the "Treaty of Fort Laramie with the Sioux, Etc., 1851," appears in Kappler, Charles J., *Indian Treaties, 1778-1883*, Interland Publishing Company, New York, (second printing) 1972, pp. 594-96. Also see Nadeau, Remi, *Fort Laramie and the Sioux*, University of Nebraska Press, Lincoln, 1967.

2. The best succinct description may be found in Olson, James C., *Red Cloud and the Sioux Problem*, University of Nebraska Press, Lincoln, 1965, pp. 3-41. For a more comprehensive account (and a stark expression of the white point of view) see Hebard, Grace, and E.A. Brininstool, *The Bozeman Trail* (2 vols.), Arthur H. Clark Co., Cleveland, 1922.

3. The seven divisions or "bands" of the Lakota are the Oglala, Brulé (Sekunjou), Hunkpapa, Minneconjou, Two Kettles, Sans Arc, and Black Feet (this last should not be confused with the Montana/Idaho/Canada confederation of the same name).

4. See Hafen, Le Roy R., and Francis Marion Young, *Fort Laramie and the Pageant of the West, 1834-1890*, University of Nebraska Press, Lincoln, 1938, pp. 331-35; at p. 334, the authors estimate the main force of "Sioux, Cheyennes and Arapahoe" sealing off the Bozeman Trail as being "3,000 warriors."

5. Brown, Dee, *Fort Phil Kearney: An American Saga*, University of Nebraska Press, Lincoln, 1971, pp. 184-90.

6. *The Omaha Weekly Herald*, June 10, 1868 quotes a message sent by Red Cloud to the government peace commission as saying, "We are on the mountains looking down on the soldiers and forts. When we see the soldiers moving away and the forts abandoned, we will come down and talk."

7. Brown, *op. cit.*, p. 225; it is noted that although the 1868 Fort Laramie Treaty is officially dated April 29 (the point of the first Indian signatures), Red Cloud did not dignify or consummate the arrangement until November 6 (after he was well and truly sure the Bozeman Trail had been abandoned).

8. *Treaty of Fort Laramie with the Sioux, Cheyenne and Arapahoe*, April 29, 1868, U.S. *Stat.* 635.

9. Article 17 reads: "It is espressedly understood and agreed by and between the respective parties to this treaty that the execution of this treaty and its ratification by the United States Senate shall have the effect, and shall be construed as abrogating and annulling all treaties and agreements heretofore entered into by the respective parties hereto, so far as such treaties and agreements obligate the United States to furnish and provide money, clothing, or other articles of property to such Indians and bands of Indians as become party to this treaty, *but no further* [emphasis added]."

10. This interpretation of treaty-making to construe formal recognition of one nation by another derives not only from customary international practice, but from the United States Constitition itself. Under Article I, Section 10, the Constitution holds that "No State shall enter into any Treaty, Alliance, or Confederation" and reserves such powers to the federal government (a principle which is reaffirmed in the U.S. Articles of Confederation). It follows that the federal government cannot enter into such agreements with states or other subordinate sovereignties, and treaties are thus rendered inherently nation-to-nation in their stature. Insofar as this is true, the terms and provisions of the various treaties entered into by the U.S. comprises a body of law superior to any domestic body of law (i.e. federal, state, and local laws cannot contravene the contents of any standing treaty; treaty law is thus on a par with the law of the Constitution itself). This is borne out in the Constitution under Article VI, Section 2: "This Constitution, and the laws of the United States which shall be made in pursuance thereof; and *all the Treaties made, or which shall be made*, under the Authority of the United States, *shall be the Supreme Law of the Land*, and the Judges in every State shall be bound thereby and any Thing in the Constitution or Laws of the States to the Contrary notwithstanding [emphasis added]." For a further elaboration on the meaning of all this, see Churchill, Ward, "Implications of Treaty Relationships Between the United States of America

and Various Indian Nations," *Akwesasne Notes*, Vol. 16, No. 2, Mohawk Nation via Rooseveltown, N.Y., February 1984.

11. Jackson, Donald, *Custer's Gold: The United States Cavalry Expedition of 1874*, University of Nebraska Press, Lincoln, 1966, p. 8. On p. 9 Jackson notes that Collins, editor of the *Sioux City Times*, was "an active leader of the move to invade the Hills" and violate the treaty.

12. Editorial, *Yankton (S.D.) Press and Dakotan*, September 3, 1874.

13. *Yankton Press*, March 20, 1872; this is the earlier title of the publication cited in notes 12 and 14.

14. The text of this order, signed on June 8, was reproduced in the *Yankton Press and Dakotan* on July 2, 1874, with the observation that "the Army has finally come to its senses!" Custer was a brevet (reserve) major general at the end of the Civil War—hence, the "General Custer" characterization, although his formal rank was never higher than Lt. Colonel.

15. For details on Custer's preparations for the Black Hills expedition, see *Special Orders and Circulars from Headquarters, Black Hills Expedition, 1874*, Fort Abraham Lincoln, RG 98 NA.

16. Jackson, *op. cit.*, pp. 17-18.

17. The major findings of this group are in Ludlow, William, *Report of a Reconnaissance of the Black Hills of Dakota*, U.S. Government Printing Office, Washington, D.C., 1875; Ludlow's preliminary report was published in Chief of [Military] Engineers, *Annual Report*, Washington, D.C., 1874 and the *Army and Navy Journal*, September 19, 1874. The latter also found its way into a number of civilian newspapers (e.g., the *New York Tribune*, September 19, 1874). Jackson, *op. cit.*, at p. 144, rosters the scientists as being not only Ludlow, but George Bird Grinnell, Newton H. Winchell, A.B. Donaldson, and Luther North; two professional miners—Horatio Nelson Ross and William McKay—also went along.

18. In an interview given in Sioux City on August 13, 1874, and reported in the Bismarck (N.D.) *Tribune* on August 19, Reynolds stated clearly that he himself had seen no gold, and that he knew of no one on the expedition who had. A scientist, Newton H. Winchell, who was also a part of the expedition later said precisely the same thing, a matter reported in the *New York Times*, September 14, 1874, p. 2. Custer himself, despite having expressed certain reservations as to the discovery of gold in his dispatch of August 2, was later adamant on having discovered a "New Eldorado," stating in a letter to the *New York World*, published on December 13, 1874: "The reason Professor Winchell saw no gold was simply due to the fact he neglected to look for it"; this was reprinted in *The Army and Navy Journal* on January 9, 1875.

19. Jackson, *op. cit.*, at p. 114, estimates that there were approximately 800 miners illegally in the Black Hills at this point.

20. The Jenny Expedition had been first proposed on August 3, 1874, while the Custer Expedition was still in progress, by William Eleroy Curtis, a member of Custer's scientific party; see Curtis's letter in the *New York World*, August 16, 1874. The military contingent of the second expedition (six companies of cavalry and two of infantry) was commanded by General George Crook, a matter recorded in the introduction to Jenny, Walter P., *Report on the Mineral Wealth, Climate and Rainfall and Natural Resources of the Black Hills of Dakota*, 44th Congress, 1st Session, Exec. Doc. No. 51, Washington, D.C., 1876.

21. The full extent of Custer's correspondence is unknown. Package 31 of the Elizabeth Bacon Custer Collection, Custer Battlefield National Monument (Crow Indian Agency, Montana) contains a letter to Custer from *New York Herald* editor James Gordon Bennet, dated April 1, 1875: Custer is solicited to contribute stories, "signed or unsigned," on "the Black Hills situation" and assigned him the code name "Alta."

22. See Hyde, George E., *Red Cloud's Folk: A History of the Oglala Sioux Indians*, University of Oklahoma Press, Norman, 1937, pp. 230-48, for the most comprehensive account of the failed treaty commission. Also see *Annual Report of the Commissioner of Indian Affairs, 1875*, U.S. Department of Interior, Washington, D.C., 1875 for verbatim transcripts of the rejections by Lakota leaders Red Cloud, Spotted Tail, Little Bear and Red Dog, among others.

23. Neither Red Cloud or Spotted Tail, principal leaders of the Oglala and Brulé respectively, left the South Dakota agencies for the Powder River; apparently both were convinced that military resistance would be fruitless. In any event, by November 9, 1875, the exodus of people from the agencies was so pronounced that Indian Bureau Special Investigator E.T. Watkins recommended a military campaign to "*whip* them into submission [emphasis in original];" 44th Congress, 1st Session, Exec. Doc. 184, pp. 8-9. Mari Sandoz, in her *Crazy Horse: Strange Man of the Oglalas* (University of Nebraska Press, Lincoln, 1942, pp. 302-316) lays out the Lakota intentions of gathering in the Powder River country quite clearly, mostly on the basis of Indian accounts.

24. U.S. Secretary of War, *Report*, Washington, D.C., 1875, p. 21.

25. Exec. Doc. 184, *op. cit.*, pp. 10, 17-18; on February 1, 1876, after the "hostiles" had failed to meet Smith's deadline, the Secretary of Interior turned the matter over to the War Department; see U.S. Secretary of War, *Report*, Washington, D.C., 1876, p. 441.

26. U.S. Secretary of War, 1876, *ibid.* Sheridan's exact quote from which the aphorism was extracted was uttered to a Comanche leader named Tosawi in 1869: "The only good Indians I ever saw were dead"; the definitive reference on this is in Ellis, Edward S., *The History of Our Country*, Vol. 6, Indianapolis, 1900, p. 1483.

27. U.S. Secretary of War, 1876, *op. cit.*

28. Sandoz, Mari, *The Battle of Little Bighorn*, Curtis Books, New York, 1966, gives a good description of the strategy at pp. 1-32.

29. Brown, Dee, *Bury My Heart at Wounded Knee: An Indian History of the American West*, Holt, Rinehart, and Winston, New York, 1970, says of Crazy Horse at p. 289: "In all the years since the Fetterman fight at Fort Phil Kearny, he had studied the soldiers and their ways of fighting. Each time he went into the Black Hills to seek visions, he had asked Wakantanka to give him secret powers so that he could lead the Oglalas to victory if the white men ever came again to make war upon his people."

30. Trebbel, John, *The Compact History of the Indian Wars*, Tower Books, New York, 1966, p. 277.

31. There is considerable indication that Custer was pursuing the same tactical approach which had allowed him to massacre some 200 peaceful Cheyennes at the Washita River in Oklahoma on November 30, 1868, an atrocity he seems to have felt added considerable luster to his reputation (see Hoig, Stan, *The Battle of the Washita*, University of Oklahoma Press, Norman, 1976). There was also a rumor, remarked upon in much of the literature, that Custer had presidential aspirations and that this motivated him to attack rather blindly, seeking one more great and glorious "victory" to lay before the American people.

32. This explanation, of Custer's attempting to run down what he believed were a fleeing mass of people, is offered by General Philip Sheridan in an official report reproduced in Graham, W.A., *The Custer Myth: A Source Book of Custeriana*, University of Nebraska Press, Lincoln, 1986, pp. 116-17. Although the good general would undoubtedly not have viewed matters in such terms, this thesis lends considerable credence to the idea that Custer had in mind to reproduce the war crimes he committed at the Washita when he entered the Little Bighorn valley. *The Battle of the Little Big Horn*, *op. cit.*, p. 24, notes government reports from the Department of the Platte, dated in April and May of 1876, "Verifying that there were three thousand lodges of hostile Indians in the Yellowstone country...this meant 3,500 to 4,000 warriors at least." Custer, it seems, unwittingly attacked the entire group.

33. Exactly how Custer's immediate command was destroyed remains somewhat shrouded in mystery insofar as the Indian accounts of the battle appear contradictory in some respects. Perhaps the best attempt at overall reconstruction may be found in Connell, Evan S., *Son of Morning Star: Custer and the Little Bighorn*, North Point Press, San Francisco, 1984, pp. 264-422. Also see *The Custer Myth*, *op. cit.*

34. Andrist, Ralph K., *The Long Death: Last Days of the Plains Indians*, Collier Books, New York, 1964, pp. 276-92. Reno is quoted as sending the frantic message: "For God's sake, Benteen, help me. I've lost half my men!"

35. Brown, *Bury My Heart at Wounded Knee*, *op. cit.*, p. 297.

36. The quote is from General Philip Sheridan, *U.S. War Department, Report*, Washington, D.C., 1869, p. 47.

37. Brown, *Bury My Heart at Wounded Knee*, *op. cit.*, p. 297.

38. Washburn, Wilcomb E., "Indian Land Claims in the Mainstream," in Imre Sutton (ed.), *Irredeemable America: The Indians' Estate and Land Claims*, University of New Mexico Press, Albuquerque, 1985, p. 25. Note how both ends were being played against the middle as great care was taken to coerce *some* written consent on the part of the Lakota—a pretention to legitimacy and due process—while the three-quarters expressed consent of all adult male Lakotas to the land cession, required by the 1868 treaty, was patently ignored.

39. Sheridan's tactical approach had been pioneered in 1864 by Colonel John M. Chivington and the 3rd Colorado Volunteers, an SS-type unit raised specifically to "exterminate" (the term used by then Colorado Territorial Governor John Evans, Chivington and many others) Cheyenne and Arapaho Indians. Using the rubric "nits make lice" to explain his instruction to his troops to "kill all, big and little" where Indians were concerned, Chivington led his troops to a spot on the Sand Creek, in southeastern Colorado, where at dawn on November 29, they attacked a camp of Cheyennes and Arapaho assembled there by order of the U.S. Army (the Indians were flying both a white flag and an American flag); at least 130 Indians—virtually all of them women, children and old people—were thereupon butchered; the troops then proceeded to mutilate the bodies (see Hoig, Stan, *The Sand Creek Massacre*, University of Oklahoma

Press, Norman, 1961). Sheridan, in a letter to Kansas Governor Samuel J. Crawford, dated September 10, 1868, posited that such tactics should be (more or less informally) adopted by the military as a whole: not only would winter campaigning provide an ideal medium for doing maximum damage, but the army would "make war on the stock and *families* of these Indians [emphasis added]." Such a policy, of course, led to the massacre on the Washita (see note 31, above).

40. See Greene, Jerome A., *Slim Buttes, 1876: An Episode of the Great Sioux War*, University of Oklahoma Press, Norman, 1982.

41. Andrist, *op. cit.*, p. 297. McKenzie, who was described by President Ulysses S. Grant as "the most promising young officer in the army," has been elsewhere characterized as being "cold, remote, taciturn, utterly professional, a 'monk in boots' who had no other interests except in carrying out combat missions." He would make his reputation on September 28, 1874, by tracking and attacking a village of Kuhtsooehkuh Comanches camped in Palo Duro Canyon, in the Texas Panhandle, while commanding some 450 men of the 4th Cavalry; earlier (in 1873) his relentless winter pursuits had carried him deep into Mexico, where he attacked Kickapoo, Lipan and Mescalero Apache villages. See Fehrenbach, T.R., *Comanches: The Destruction of a People*, Alfred A. Knopf, New York, 1974, pp. 516-21.

42. Andrist, *op. cit.*, pp. 297-98.

43. Brown, *Bury My Heart at Wounded Knee, op. cit.*, pp. 308-310; Red Cloud was used by the army to convey these assurances to Crazy Horse.

44. Sandoz, *Crazy Horse, op. cit.*, p. 361.

45. Brown, *Bury My Heart at Wounded Knee, op. cit.*, p. 312, notes that Crazy Horse was arrested by a squad of special Oglala police headed by Little Big Man (not to be confused with the idiot of the same name played by Dustin Hoffman in a Hollywood epic). When the Oglala leader resisted being locked in a guardhouse, his arms were pinioned by Little Big Man; he was then bayonetted in the midsection by an army private, William Gentles, and died the same evening. Sandoz, in *Crazy Horse, op. cit.*, pp. 408-10, gives essentially the same account, but omits Gentles' name. In all reconstructions of the incident, it is agreed that there was little or no reason for the man's arrest in the first place.

46. Quoted in Erdoes, Richard, *The Sun Dance People: The Plains Indians, Their Past and Present*, Vintage Books, New York, 1972, p. 174.

47. *Ibid.*, p. 175. The Sun Dance, the most central of all Lakota ceremonies, remained technically illegal right into the late 1950s when the laws prohibiting its practice were quietly dropped, largely through the efforts of Oglalas such as Frank Fools Crow who, as elders, became the guiding force behind the American Indian Movement during the 1970s (see Mails, Thomas, *Fools Crow*, Avon Books, New York, 1979); the ceremonies had been covertly conducted all along.

48. See Fuchs, Estelle, and Robert J. Havighurst, *To Live On This Earth: American Indian Education*, Doubleday/Anchor Books, New York, pp. 6-14. It should be noted that although its use has been very much diminished over the past quarter-century, the boarding school system is still in use today.

49. As Deloria, Vine, Jr., and Clifford M. Lytle note in their *American Indians, American Justice*, University of Texas Press, Austin, 1983, p. 11: "Prior to the Major Crimes Act these offenses fell under the exclusive jurisdiction of the Indian Tribes. The act was passed by Congress after the Supreme Court held that an Indian named Crow Dog, who had killed Spotted Tail, a noted Brulé chief, could not be tried by the federal government because the crime had been preserved to the Sioux by treaty (*Ex Parte Crow Dog*, 109 U.S. 556 [1883]). When the court overturned Crow Dog's conviction, releasing to tribal jurisdiction a 'murderer' whom many people felt should be hanged, the incensed legislators responded by stripping the tribes of their right to handle crimes according to traditional customs." It should also be noted that Crow Dog was a reputed Lakota recalcitrant, while Spotted Tail had been considered (perhaps unfairly) by the government to be one of its primary puppets since at least as early as 1876-77. For further information, see Clinton, T.R., "Development of Criminal Jurisdiction Over Indian Lands: The Historical Perspective," *Arizona Law Review*, Number 17, Winter 1975.

50. Deloria and Lytle, *American Indians, American Justice, op. cit.*, p. 9. Also see, Otis, S.D., *The Dawes Act and Allotment of Indian Lands*, University of Oklahoma Press, Norman, 1973, and Kicking Bird, Kirk, and Karen Duchenaux, *One Hundred Million Acres*, Macmillan Publishing, New York, 1973.

51. Deloria and Lytle, *American Indians, American Justice, op. cit.*, p. 10. The Lakotas alone lost some 11,000,000 acres as a result of the Dawes Act. The "leasing rights" assigned to the agents has resulted in the "checkerboard" phenomenon wherein even what little good land is left within the reservations ends up being used for the profit of non-Indians. For more information on the subject, see Jacobs, Wil-

bur R., *Dispossessing the American Indian: Indians and Whites on the Colonial Frontier*, Charles Scribner's Sons, New York, 1972.

52. Brown, *Bury My Heart at Wounded Knee*, *op. cit.*, p. 431.

53. LaBarre, Weston, *The Ghost Dance: The Origins of Religion*, Delta Books, New York, 1970, p. 230.

54. *Bury My Heart at Wounded Knee*, *op. cit.*, pp. 432-34.

55. To the contrary, Brown (*ibid.*, p. 435) notes one of Wovoka's "commandments" as being: "You must not hurt anybody or do harm to anyone. You must not fight. You must do right always."

56. The quotations and other information in this passage accrue from Andrist, *op. cit.*, p. 342.

57. U.S. Commissioner on Indian Affairs, *Report*, Washington, D.C., 1891, p. 333.

58. Utley, Robert M., *The Last Days of the Sioux Nation*, Yale University Press, New Haven, 1963, p. 159.

59. Brown, *Bury My Heart at Wounded Knee*, *op. cit.*, pp. 439-40.

60. Utley, *op. cit.*, p. 195.

61. Andrist, *op. cit.*, p. 348. It should be noted that, not only did the troopers of the 7th Cavalry have a very heavy ax to grind with the Lakota after the Little Bighorn, but that Forsyth had been head of an irregular Indian fighting unit which had been very nearly wiped out by the Cheyenne at Beecher's Island on the Kansas-Colorado line during the summer of 1868; the colonel had been badly wounded and was known to be no friend of the Indians (for what is probably the best overall account of the Beecher Island fight, see Grinnell, George Bird, *The Fighting Cheyennes*, University of Oklahoma Press, Norman, 1956 [first published by an unknown New York publisher in 1915], pp. 277-297).

62. Andrist, *op. cit.*, pp. 351-52.

63. *Ibid.*

64. Some of Eastman's better known works include *Old Indian Days* (McClure Publishers, New York, 1907), *The Soul of the Indian: An Interpretation* (Johnson Reprint Corporation, New York, 1971; originally published in 1911), *From the Deep Woods to Civilization: Chapters in the Autobiography of an Indian* (Little, Brown, Boston, 1916) and *Indian Heroes and Great Chieftains* (Little, Brown, Boston, 1918). The definitive biography of Eastman is Wilson, Raymond, *Ohiyesa: Charles Eastman, Santee Sioux*, University of Illinois Press, Urbana, 1983; Eastman's experiences during the Ghost Dance are recounted therein, pp. 40-46.

65. The 1924 Citizenship Act, in its own right and especially in combination with the 1934 Indian Reorganization Act, is directly contrary to the United Nations *Declaration on the Granting of Independence to Colonial Countries and Peoples* (General Assembly Resolution 1514 [XV], December 14, 1960), as endorsed by the United States. The declaration reads in part, "All peoples have the right to self-determination; by virtue of that right they freely determine their political status and freely pursue their economic, social and cultural development." See Brownlie, Ian (ed.), *Basic Documents on Human Rights*, Clarendon Press, Oxford University, 1981, p. 29.

66. Vine Deloria, Jr. and Clifford Lytle, in their sympathetic study of the Indian Reorganization Act, *The Nations Within: The Past and Future of American Indian Sovereignty* (Pantheon, New York, 1984, p. 144), address the question of corporate board structure within the tribal council governments: "Under the IRA, the secretary of interior, upon receiving a petition from at least one-third of the adult reservation Indians [in practice drawn almost exclusively from Indians employed by or otherwise closely associated with the federal bureaucracy, and often organized by federal officials themselves], could issue a charter of incorporation [euphemistically dubbed a "constitution"] to the tribe. The charter would become operative when ratified [through a process administered by the federal authorities and fraught with voting irregularities such as designation of abstentions as aye votes in the Hopi referendum of 1936] by a majority vote of the adult tribal members...The chartered corporation permitted tribes to engage for the first time in a number of business enterprises [*i.e.*, "normalizing" and "legitimating" the expropriation of Indian assets]. The corporation could obtain loans, acquire and manage property, issue certificates of interest in the corporate property, transfer land, and exercise other powers that were incidental to the conduct of corporate business...Once a charter was issued to a tribe, it could not be revoked except by act of Congress...[At which point, the] tribe could elect its own corporate officials, draft bylaws, pay dividends, and otherwise function independently of the Bureau of Indian Affairs." This last, of course, was illusory. Commissioner of Indian Affairs John Collier noted at the time of its passage that, within provisions of the IRA, the relationship of the federal government, "with all of its plenary power," to Indian nations would "be kept intact," albeit transformed from the BIA to a "board of supervision...distinct from the board of directors of the tribe" (see U.S. Senate, *Hearings on S.4165 Incorporation of the Klamath Indian Corporation*,

U.S. Government Printing Office, Washington, D.C., 1930, p. 17). The process involved here closely resembles that described by Edward S. Herman and Frank Brodhead as being employed by the U.S. in other countries during the 1960s and 1970s; see *Demonstration Elections: U.S. Staged Elections in the Dominican Republic, Vietnam, and El Salvador,* South End Press, Boston, 1984.

67. As the noted Lakota legal scholar Vine Deloria, Jr. put it in a talk during the American Indian Awareness Week at the University of Colorado/Boulder in 1981 (tape on file): "You can understand how the Claims Commission works through a little analogy. Let's say I steal your Porsche. Okay, I drive off in the Porsche, a cop catches me, and I'm hauled in for car theft while the Porsche is impounded. Now, they haul me up before the judge and he asks, 'How do you plead?' I look around, and I know the law, so I answer, 'Guilty as sin, your honor.' So the judge—he knows the law too, y'understand—he says, 'Alright, your sentence is to pay whatever you think the car is worth.' So I write you out a check for, say $5, and that's it for my punishment. But wait, there's still a catch here. *I* now retain possession of your Porsche. The instant you cash my punishment check, title legally passes to me. If you don't cash my check, I *still* retain possession of your Porsche while we negotiate whether maybe I shouldn't be paying you $10, or $15 or even $50. Any way you cut it, there's no possibility that you can get your car back once I've stolen it, no way you'll ever get remotely what it was worth—even assuming you decided you wished to sell it—and no way I'll undergo anything but a pretense of consequences to atone for my theft. Nice system, eh? Well that's the stuff of federal Indian law."

68. Quoted in Armstrong, Virginia I., *I Have Spoken: American History Through the Voices of Indians,* Pocket Books, New York, 1975, p. 175.

69. Of the two large nations terminated during the mid-1950s, the Menominee were, in the mid-1970s, able to be "restored"; the best account of this process is to be found in Peroff, Nicholas C., *Menominee Drums: Tribal Termination and Restoration, 1954-1974,* University of Oklahoma Press, Norman, 1982. The Klamaths, on the other hand, remain dissolved; see Stern, Theodore, *The Klamath Tribe: The People and Their Reservation,* University of Washington Press, Seattle, 1965. Of the smaller terminated groups, only the Siletz have regained something of their original status; for an overview of the context in which the Oregon-Washington terminations occurred, see Deloria, Vine, Jr., *Indians of the Pacific Northwest: From the Coming of the White Man to the Present Day,* Doubleday, New York, 1977.

70. What Public Law 280 clearly represents is a further diminishing of Indian sovereign national status from that of "quasi- sovereignties" subordinate to the federal government (but superior to individual states of the union) to a level below that of the states. Indian nations became approximately equivalent to counties within this "logic" (a constitutional impossibility).

71. The best overall account of the Pick-Sloan Plan may be found in Lawson, Michael L., *The Damned Indians: The Pick-Sloan Plan and the Missouri River Sioux, 1944-1980,* University of Oklahoma Press, Norman, 1982.

72. The filing of this suit required a special Act of Congress (41 *Stat.* 738). It was dismissed by the Court of Claims in 1942 (*Sioux Tribes v. U.S.,* 97 Ct. Cl. 613 [1942], *cert. denied,* 318 U.S. 789 [1943]).

73. The Claims Commission, under such circumstances, delayed hearing the Black Hills Land Claims case for nearly two decades. Ultimately, however, its decision (33 *Ind. Cl. Comm.* 151 [1974]) was that it had no alternative but to review the matter. It then determined (*U.S. v. Sioux Nation of Indians,* 207 *Ct. Cl.* 234, 518 F. 2d 1298, *cert. denied,* 423 U.S. 1016 [1975]) that the Lakota were entitled to a total of $17.5 million in compensation for the taking of the virtual entirety of the huge 1868 treaty territory; further appeal of the case was barred *res judicata.* The Lakotas nonetheless rejected payment, leaving the western South Dakota land titles clouded and possibly inhibiting real estate transactions in the area to some extent (not to mention setting up a potential embarrassment for the U.S. internationally). Consequently, Congress passed an act in 1978 (P.L. 95-243, 25 U.S.C. 70s [Supp. II, 1978]) providing—without regard to *res judicata*—for the *de novo* review of the Claims Commission finding. In 1979, the Court of Claims determined (*Sioux Nation of Indians v. U.S.,* 220 *Ct. Cl.* 442, 601 F. 2d 1157 [1979]) that the Lakotas were entitled to 5% annual simple interest accrued on their $17.5 million since 1877, making the government's compensatory offer $122.5 million. As of this writing, the Lakota—a very impoverished people—have continued to reject such payment and continue to insist upon return of their stolen lands under the slogan "The Black Hills are not for sale!"

74. See, for example, Dixon, Joseph K., *The Vanishing Race: The Last Great Indian Council,* Popular Library, New York, 1972. It is interesting to note that in Europe, at about the same time, the myth had already been reversed; see Fiedler, Leslie A., *The Return of the Vanishing American,* Paladin Publishers, London, 1972. When the realization of this took hold in the U.S., things were carried to their other extreme; see Steiner, Stan, *The Vanishing White Man,* Harper-Colophon Books, New York, 1976.

75. This was hardly the last consideration in the Indians' minds; see O'Brien, Sharon, "Federal Indian Policies and the International Protection of Human Rights," in Vine Deloria, Jr. (ed.), *American Indian Policy in the Twentieth Century*, University of Oklahoma Press, Norman, 1985, pp. 35-62.

76. The best placement of Clyde Warrior in his context of emergent Indian activism can probably be found in Josephy, Alvin, Jr., *Red Power: The American Indians' Fight for Freedom*, McGraw-Hill Book Co., New York, 1971.

77. Quoted in Steiner, Stan, *The New Indians*, Delta Books, New York, 1968, p. 68.

78. Deloria's thinking during this period is perhaps best encapsulated in a small book, *The Indian Affair*, he published rather after the fact through Friendship Press, New York, in 1974. On the other hand, his NCAI experiences gave birth to the more robust articulations found in his seminal and much celebrated *Custer Died for Your Sins: An Indian Manifesto* (Macmillan, New York, 1969) and *We Talk, You Listen: New Tribes, New Turf* (Macmillan, New York, 1970); taken together, these last two books served as something of a "bible" for Indian activism throughout the 1970s.

79. An excellent examination of the Northwest fishing rights struggle may be found in American Friends Service Committee, *Uncommon Controversy: The Fishing Rights of the Muckleshoot, Puyallup, and Nisqually Indians*, University of Washington Press, Seattle, 1970.

80. A succinct overview of these diverse struggles is contained in Meyer, William, *Native Americans: The New Indian Resistance*, International Publishers, New York, 1971.

81. Concerning the founding of AIM, see Burnette, Robert, with John Koster, *The Road to Wounded Knee*, Bantam Books, New York, 1974, pp. 196-97; on the BPP community self-defense program, see Marine, *op. cit.*, pp. 10-65. It should also be noted that it is often contended that it was Clyde Bellecourt rather than George Mitchell who was cofounder of AIM, along with Dennis Banks. It has also been erroneously posited that Russell Means was a cofounder; Means was the founder of the first AIM chapter (Cleveland) outside of Minneapolis.

82. Although born on Pine Ridge, Means grew up in the slums of Oakland where, by his own account, he'd been an alcoholic and heroin addict, ballroom dance instructor and certified public accountant. He was well aware of the BPP Oakland community self-defense effort. He relocated to Cleveland in late 1967 to direct the Cleveland Indian Center and used this position as a basis from which to form an AIM chapter; see Means, Russell, "Penthouse Interview," *Penthouse*, November 1982, pp. 136-38.

83. The shift in emphasis from urban to reservation, and from civil rights to treaty rights, was entirely intended, according to interviews conducted by the authors with Dennis Banks, Russell Means and Joe Locust.

84. Quoted in Blue Cloud, Peter (ed.), *Alcatraz is Not an Island*, Wingbow Press, Berkeley, Calif., 1972, p. 40.

85. An example of the widespread and articulate non-Indian support which was beginning to be brought to bear almost from the outset of the occupation is a widely distributed article, "Alcatraz: What It Means," authored by University of California/Davis professor Jack D. Forbes (reproduced in Blue Cloud, *op. cit.*, pp. 44-45).

86. *Ibid.*, p. 51.

87. *Ibid.*, p. 56.

88. *Ibid.*, p. 65.

89. Quoted in *ibid.*, p. 68.

90. *Ibid.*, p. 69.

91. Quoted in *ibid.* There is evidence that, as early as August of 1970, the Coast Guard planned to transport 100-200 U.S. marshals to Alcatraz in an operation code-named "Operation Parks" and designed to clear the island of militants. The plan was apparently called off at the last moment due to its premature disclosure by columnist Herb Caen of the *San Francisco Chronicle*.

92. See "End of a Squalid Sit-In," *San Francisco Chronicle* (editorial), June 15, 1971, for an especially ugly account of the removal.

93. On the California actions, see Blue Cloud, *op. cit.*, pp. 86-96. As concerns the Chicago NIKE base, see Jerry Aronson's 1979 academy award nominated short documentary film, "The Divided Trail: A Native American Odyssey." For more on Pit River see Jaimes, M. Annette, "The Pit River Indian Land Claim Dispute in Northern California," *Journal of Ethnic Studies*, Vol. 14, No. 4, Winter 1987, pp. 47-64.

94. On the Adams shooting, see Weyler, Rex, *Blood of the Land: The Government and Corporate War Against the American Indian Movement*, Vintage Books, New York, 1984, p. 44 (first printed by Everest House Publishers, New York, 1982).

95. Burnette and Koster, *op. cit.*, pp. 196-97.

96. Weyler, *op. cit.*, p. 48.

97. Quoted in *ibid.*, p. 49.

98. Josephy, Alvin M., Jr., *Now That the Buffalo's Gone: A Study of Today's American Indians*, Alfred A. Knopf, New York, 1982, p. 237.

99. This account of the inception of the Trail of Broken Treaties comes from Robert Burnette (Burnette and Koster, *op. cit.*, pp. 197-99); Burnette claims credit for actually articulating the idea at the Crow Dog's Paradise meeting.

100. *Ibid.*, pp. 199-203.

101. Oaks was apparently ambushed while walking, unarmed, through the woods near Santa Rosa, CA; Morgan, who was known to have fired a weapon at the IAT leader before, shot him to death with a 9 mm. automatic at pointblank range. Morgan, who was charged only with manslaughter in the slaying, was acquitted even of this after he testified that Oaks had "jumped" him; see Weyler, *op. cit.*, pp. 48-49.

102. The Hare brothers ultimately served only a year apiece for their leading role in the ritual murder of Raymond Yellow Thunder; *ibid.*, p. 49. Phillip Celay was shot in the back at close range by Deputy David Bosman, who subsequently claimed he'd fired because Celay had taken the gun of fellow deputy Mike Wilson during an altercation attending their arrest of the youth on a routine traffic offense. Ajo, Arizona Justice of the Peace M.F. Anderson then ruled the killing "justifiable homicide" despite the fact that several Indian witnesses testified that Celay never disarmed Wilson, and that he'd merely pushed back when Bosman began "pushing him around" after the deputies stopped his truck for a broken taillight. The Indians uniformly contended that Celay became frightened when Bosman thereupon drew his revolver, attempted to run, and was shot down in cold blood; *ibid.*, p. 48. Leroy Shenandoah was "brutally beaten and shot to death by police, who justified the act as 'excusable homicide'" in Philadelphia during February 1972; Josephy, *op. cit.*, p. 235. The nature and frequency of these murders lent considerable credence to AIM's contention articulated by Russell Means, that: "Indian-killing is still the national pastime, and it's our job to stop it."

103. Deloria, Vine, Jr., *Behind the Trail of Broken Treaties: An Indian Declaration of Independence*, Delta Books, New York, 1974, pp. 47-48.

104. Akwesasne Notes, *BIA, I'm not Your Indian Any More: Trail of Broken Treaties*, Akwesasne Notes, Mohawk Nation via Rooseveltown, New York, 1973, p. 8.

105. *Ibid.*, p. 9.

106. *Ibid.*, pp. 10-11.

107. Quoted in *ibid.*, p. 9.

108. Both parties are quoted in *ibid.*, p. 12.

109. *Ibid.*; the eviction order was signed at the request of the White House by Federal Judge John H. Pratt.

110. *Ibid.*, p. 13.

111. Deloria, *Behind the Trail of Broken Treaties, op. cit.*, pp. 54-55.

112. Akwesasne Notes, *BIA, I'm Not Your Indian Any More, op. cit.*, p. 16; Weyler, *op. cit.*, p. 53.

113. Deloria, *Behind the Trail of Broken Treaties, op. cit.*, p. 56.

114. *Ibid.*, p. 58.

115. *Ibid.*, p. 59.

116. *Ibid.*, pp. 59-60.

117. *Ibid.*, p. 58.

118. *Ibid.*, p. 57.

119. Akwesasne Notes, *BIA, I'm Not Your Indian Any More, op. cit.*, p. 40; some of those arrested and tried as a result of this duplicity were Alida and Andrea Quiroz of Rialto, Ca.; Myron Thomas, of Chicago; David Molino, of Redlands, Ca.; Whitney Grey, of the Salt River Reservation in southern Arizona; Steve Mesa, from the Los Angeles area; and Cynthia J. deVaughn, a companion of Mesa.

120. Burnette and Koster, *op. cit.*, p. 217.

121. *Ibid.*, p. 220; Burnette recounts calling the White House directly on the matter of Means' arrest.

122. Quoted in *ibid.*, p. 221. Also arrested in Scottsbluff at the same time as Means, were Nebraska AIM leader John "Two Birds" Arbuckle (later the victim of a badjacketing plot; see Chapter 7), National AIM leaders Stan Holder and Carter Camp, and Leroy Casades, a member of the Denver-based Crusade for Justice suspected of being an FBI informant; see "Another AIM leader arrested in Scottsbluff," *Rapid City Journal*, January 16, 1973, p. 1.

123. Stevens, Don and Jane, *South Dakota: The Mississippi of the North, or Stories Jack Anderson Never Told You,* Self-published booklet (P.O. Box 241, Custer, S.D.), 1977.

124. Quoted in LaCourse, Rick, *Race Relations* (reprinted in *Akwesasne Notes,* Mohawk Nation via Rooseveltown, New York, Winter, 1975, p. 31).

125. Interview with Dennis Banks, Boulder, Colorado, April 16, 1987 (tape on file).

126. Weyler, *op. cit.,* pp. 262-63.

127. Lawson, Michael L., *op. cit.,* pp. 179-80. The author refers to "the multi-billion dollar engineering wonder known as the Pick-Sloan Plan;" at p. 185, he indicates the cost of the smallish Garrison Irrigation Project (along the North and South Dakota Boundary) *alone* as being $248 million, with an initial authorization of some $695 million.

128. South Dakota Department of Tourism, *Summary Report,* Pierre, S.D., 1975, p. 3.

129. See Irvin, Amelia, "Energy Development and the Effect of Mining on the Lakota Nation," *Journal of Ethnic Studies,* Vol. 10, No. 1, Winter, 1982, pp. 89-102.

130. For further details on Edgemont/Igloo, and a broader view of the entire question at issue, see Churchill, Ward, and Winona LaDuke, "Native America: The Political Economy of Radioactive Colonialism," *Journal of Ethnic Studies,* Vol. 13, No. 3, Fall, 1985, pp. 107-32.

131. Irvin, *op. cit.*

132. Weyler, *op. cit.,* pp. 261-63.

133. See *Status of Mineral Resource Information on the Pine Ridge Indian Reservation,* BIA Report No. 12, U.S. Department of Interior, Washington, D.C., 1976.

134. *Ibid.*

135. Quoted in Matthiessen, Peter, *In the Spirit of Crazy Horse,* Viking Press, New York, 1975, p. 426.

136. Quoted by Rex Weyler in *New Age Magazine,* January 1981. In line with this assertion, a 1980 Indian Health Service report concerning water contamination on Pine Ridge revealed that well tests in the village of Slim Buttes, on the Red Shirt Table (adjoining the Gunnery Range area) showed gross levels of alpha radiation three times the national safety standard, while newer wells have tested at *fourteen* times the standard; Gilbert (Thunderhawk), Madonna, "Radioactive Water Contamination on the Red Shirt Table," Women of All Red Nations (WARN), Porcupine, S.D., March 1980. WARN attributes these alpha levels to both the presence of substantial uranium deposits in the Gunnery Range area and the 1962 Edgemont tailings wash.

137. See Huber, Jacqueline, *et al., The Gunnery Range Report,* Oglala Sioux Tribe, Office of the Tribal President, Pine Ridge, S.D., 1981, for details on the entire, sordid Gunnery Range transaction, from 1942 onward. As concerns the language found in P.L. 90-468, one is hard pressed to conceive of how even the U.S. Congress could see itself as *reacquiring* land which it had never possessed, but which had all along been reserved by the Lakotas—this *is,* after all, the meaning of the term "reservation"—for themselves. In any event, the final version of the Wilson agreement, dated 2 January 1976, can be had from the Department of the Interior under the title *Memorandum of Agreement Between the Oglala Sioux Tribe of South Dakota and the National Park Service of the Department of the Interior to Facilitate Establishment, Development, Administration and Public Use of the Oglala Sioux Tribal Lands, Badlands National Monument.* The use—or lack of it—to which the Park Service put its new acquisition is covered in National Park Service, *Master Plan Badlands National Monument* (Rocky Mountain Region: National Park Service, Denver, 1978).

138. Matthiessen, *op. cit.,* p. 104.

139. National Academy of Sciences (NAS) and National Academy of Engineering (joint report), *Rehabilitation of Western Coal Lands: A Report to the Energy Policy Project of the Ford Foundation,* Ballinger Publishing Co., Cambridge, MA, 1974. A fuller NAS articulation of this theme may be found in its publication, *Energy and Climate,* Washington, D.C., 1977.

140. Matthiessen, *op. cit.,* p. 104; also see *North Central Power Study, Vol. I: Study of Mine-Mouth Thermal Power Plants with Extra-High Voltage for Delivery to Load Centers,* U.S. Bureau of Reclamation, Billings, Montana, October 1971.

141. Wasserman, Henry, "The Sioux's Last Fight for the Black Hills," *Rocky Mountain News,* August 24, 1980.

142. Meinhart, Nick, *Water and Energy,* pamphlet produced by the Black Hills Alliance (P.O. Box 2508, Rapid City, S.D.), 1982, p. 4; an acre foot is the amount of water required to submerge one acre of land one foot deep.

143. U.S. Bureau of Reclamation, *Water for Energy* (final environmental impact statement on the Black Hills Region), U.S. Department of Interior, Washington, D.C., December 1, 1977, p. 1.

144. Means, Russell, "The Same Old Song," in Ward Churchill (ed.), *Marxism and Native Americans*, South End Press, Boston, 1984, p. 25.

145. See Churchill and LaDuke, *op. cit.*

146. Los Alamos National Laboratory, *Mini-Report*, Los Alamos, N.M., February 1978.

147. As concerns the Edgemont proposal, see "Nuclear Waste Facility Proposed Near Edgemont," *Rapid City Journal*, November 19, 1982, p. 3, and "Edgemont Waste Facility No Hazard Says Chemical Nuclear Corp.," *Rapid City Journal*, December 10, 1982, p. 5. Concerning the Gunnery Range site, see Women of All Red Nations, "Radiation: Dangerous to Pine Ridge Women," *Akwesasne Notes*, Mohawk Nation via Rooseveltown, New York, Spring, 1980, p. 22.

148. U.S. Commission on Civil Rights, *Hearing Before the United States Commission on Civil Rights: National Indian Civil Rights Issues*, (Hearing Held in Washington, D.C., March 19-20, 1979), *Vol. I: Testimony*, U.S. Government Printing Office, Washington, D.C., 1979, p. 31.

149. Cited in Matthiessen, *op. cit.*, pp. 106-107.

150. The environmental issues raised in this chapter have by no means gone away. Although they are largely wide of the scope of this book and will therefore not be dealt with in further depth, they represent an obvious and grotesque danger, not only to the regional populations involved, but to living things everywhere. About the best that can be said is that the temporary depression in the domestic uranium market and momentary "surplus" in U.S. oil stocks, among other factors, have recently slowed the pace of development in both national sacrifice areas.

Chapter 5

1. Deloria, *Behind the Trail of Broken Treaties*, *op. cit.*, p. 71.

2. The clearest and most developed articulation of Means' platform came with the publication of *TREATY: Russell Means, Candidate for President of the Oglala Sioux Tribe (Overview Platform)*, 444 Crazy Horse Dr., Porcupine, S.D., 1982. It is interesting to note that response to this call for sovereignty remained sufficient nine years after Wounded Knee that the BIA "disqualified" Means as a candidate at the last moment, on the basis that he was a "convicted felon" (in South Dakota, *not* under Lakota or even federal law). His brother Ted—also a convicted felon in South Dakota—who ran for tribal council the same year and on the same platform (but who was apparently not considered so much of a threat by the BIA) was not disqualified and won a seat by a wide margin.

3. Weyler, *op. cit.*, p. 70.

4. *Ibid.*, p. 71. Wilson was able to accomplish this under language on BIA Lease Form 5-5525—which does not provide for an Indian "ward" to refuse to lease his/her land—but which does provide that lease money is "deposited in accordance with the regulations of the Department of Interior," *i.e.* with the reservation superintendent or with "the treasurer of [the] tribe, where the tribe is organized under the [IRA]."

5. Burnette and Koster, *op. cit.*, p. 221.

6. The statement is taken from Wilson's testimony before a Congressional Hearing on the matter of Pine Ridge violence, included in the film *Voices from Wounded Knee*, by Saul Landau, Institute for Policy Studies, Washington, D.C., 1974.

7. Quoted in Weyler, *op. cit.*, p. 61.

8. Burnette and Koster, *op. cit.*, p. 225.

9. *Ibid.*, p. 221.

10. Weyler, *op. cit.*, p. 68. Also see "Unity conference of minorities held in Scottsbluff," *Rapid City Journal*, January 15, 1973, p. 3.

11. Burnette and Koster, *op. cit.*, pp. 221-22.

12. Quoted in *ibid.*, p. 222.

13. *Ibid.*, pp. 222-23.

14. Weyler, *op. cit.*, pp. 68-69. Concerning the FBI presence at Custer, see Matthiessen, *op. cit.*, p. 64. A smaller fire at an oil storage facility near the Chamber of Commerce building was possibly set by enraged AIM members or supporters.

15. Deloria, *Behind the Trail of Broken Treaties*, *op. cit.*, p. 71.

16. *Ibid.*

17. Weyler, *op. cit.*, pp. 71-72. Also see "Pine Ridge conspiracy charge made," *Rapid City Journal*, February 17, 1973, p. 1.

18. *Ibid.*, pp. 72-73.

19. *Ibid.* p. 73.

20. Probably the best overall account of the Wilson impeachment process may be found in *Voices From Wounded Knee, 1973*, Akwesasne Notes, Mohawk Nation via Rooseveltown, NY, 1974, pp. 17-26.

21. *Ibid.*, p. 28. Also see "Impeachment charges against Wilson dropped," *Rapid City Journal*, February 17, 1973, p. 1.

22. Weyler, *op. cit.*, p. 74.

23. Interview with Dennis Banks, *op. cit.* See a selection of three articles—"Police, AIM team to keep things cool," "Coalition to work on race issues," and Harold Higgins' "Hot Springs discussion 'productive'"—all on p. 1 of the *Rapid City Journal*, February 16, 1973, for context.

24. Burnette and Koster, *op. cit.*, p. 74.

25. Quoted in *ibid.*, p. 226; Burnette points out quite accurately that Means, as an enrolled member of the Oglala Sioux Tribe, and a Pine Ridge landowner to boot, had *every* right to be on the reservation. He also observes that the assembled federal forces stood ready to enforce Wilson's blatantly illegal barring of Means from his home.

26. Quoted in Matthiessen, *op. cit.*, p. 66.

27. Quoted in *ibid.*, p. 67.

28. Testimony of Dennis J. Banks before Judge Fred Nichol, *U.S. v. Dennis Banks and Russell Means*, February 12, 1974. AIM's going to Wounded Knee was endorsed by the traditional Oglala Chiefs: Frank Fools Crow, Pete Catches, Ellis Chips, Edgar Red Cloud, Jake Kills Enemy, Morris Wounded, Severt Young Bear, and Everette Catches (*Voices From Wounded Knee, op. cit.*, p. 36).

29. The best overall account of this is Weyler, *op. cit.*, pp. 76-78. For a local view, see "Indians control, hold nine hostages at Wounded Knee," *Rapid City Journal*, February 29, 1973, p. 1.

30. Quoted in Matthiessen, *op. cit.*, p. 68.

31. Testimony of Agnes Lamont *United States (Plantiff) v. Consolidated Wounded Knee Cases (Defendants)*(CR. 73-5019, "The Sioux Sovereignty Hearings"), before Judge Warren K. Urbom, December 20, 1974; excerpt published in Dunbar-Ortiz, Roxanne (ed.), *The Great Sioux Nation: Sitting in Judgement on America*, International Indian Treaty Council/Mood Books, New York/San Francisco, 1977, pp. 47-49.

32. Akwesasne Notes, *Voices From Wounded Knee, op. cit.*, p. 23. The demands, and a separate statement by Russell Means, made their way—courtesy of Terronez—into the *Rapid City Journal* on March 1.

33. Weyler, *op. cit.*, pp. 80-81. For further information, see *The Nation*, November 9, 1974, and *University Review*, the same month. Also see *Akwesasne Notes*, Early Summer, 1974. The California Civil Disorder Management School is a program associated with the California Specialized Training Institute (CSTI), then headed by Louis Giuffrida. Giuffrida developed a program at CSTI which attempted to apply the counterinsurgency strategies of Frank Kitson and Robin Evelegh to the suppression of domestic dissent in the U.S. See Lawrence, Ken, *The New State Repression*, International Network Against the New State Repression, Chicago, 1985, pp. 5-8 for more information on the CTSI. Giuffrida is currently head of the Federal Emergency Management Agency (FEMA).

34. Weyler, *op. cit.*, p. 81.

35. The term "siege of Wounded Knee" is attributed to Russell Means, as a response to the governmental/media insistence on inaccurately describing what was happening as "the Wounded Knee occupation." The latter phrase was coined by Seattle activist/author Roberto Maestas, and used as the title of a book he later coauthored with Bruce Johansen; see *Wasi'chu: The Continuing Indian Wars*, Monthly Review Press, New York, 1978. For use of the term in a more establishment source, see the special eight part reprint by the *Denver Post* of Jim Richardson and John Aloysius Farrell, "The New Indian Wars," originally run November 20-27, 1983.

36. The "hostages" were mostly elderly residents of Wounded Knee and consisted of Wilbert A. Riegert (age 86), Girlie Clark (75), Clive Guildersleeve (73), Agnes Guildersleeve (68), Bill Cole (82), Mary Pike (72), Adrienne Fritze (12), Guy Fritze (49), Jeane Fritze (47), Father Paul Manhart (46) and Annie Hunts Horse (78).

37. Burnette and Koster, *op. cit.*, pp. 227-28. Also see "Senators fly to reservation," *Rapid City Journal*, March 1, 1973, p. 1.

38. Quoted in *Voices From Wounded Knee, op. cit.*, p. 39.

39. *Ibid.* Also see Gladstone, Lyn, "Senators sample feeling of Pine Ridge people," *Rapid City Journal,* March 1, 1973, p. 1.

40. *Ibid.,* p. 45.

41. *Ibid.* Also see Ciccone, F. Richard, "Lawyers meet with Indians," *Rapid City Journal,* March 4, 1973, p. 1.

42. *Ibid.,* p. 41.

43. The most graphic depiction of the buildup of AIM's position inside Wounded Knee, and the various supply and reinforcement expedients used to effect this, may be found in Lan Brookes Ritz's documentary film, *Annie Mae: A Brave-Hearted Woman,* Brown Bird Productions, Los Angeles, 1979.

44. Quoted in *Voices From Wounded Knee, op. cit.,* pp. 46-7.

45. Quoted in Burnette and Koster, *op. cit.,* p. 226; Burnette also notes that Wilson stated that "when Means was captured [Wilson] would shave his head, stuff him into a woman's dress, and dump him beyond the reservation boundaries, never more to return."

46. Quoted in Akwesasne Notes, *Voices From Wounded Knee, op. cit.,* p. 51.

47. *Ibid.*

48. *Ibid.,* pp. 51-52.

49. *Ibid.,* p. 51. Also see "Militant Indians demanding ouster of Wilson," *Rapid City Journal,* March 7, 1973, p. 3.

50. Burnette and Koster, *op. cit.,* p. 234, identify one of those wounded as being Webster Poor Bear.

51. On AIM firepower, see Weyler, *op. cit.,* p. 82; on the M-60 report, see Akwesasne Notes, *Voices From Wounded Knee, op. cit.,* p. 41.

52. *Ibid.,* p. 52; Adams credits Russell Means with agreeing to "pull back his men from one sector," thus bringing the shooting to a halt.

53. *Ibid.,* p. 54. Also see Ciccone, F. Richard, "New peace talks set with Indians," *Rapid City Journal,* March 7, 1973, p. 3.

54. Quoted in *ibid.* Also see "Tentative agreement reached," *Rapid City Journal,* p. 1.

55. Weyler, *op. cit.,* p. 83. Also see "Abernathy visits Wounded Knee; Kunstler, Berrigan plan to come," *Rapid City Journal,* March 8, 1973, p. 1.

56. *Voices From Wounded Knee, op. cit.,* p. 54.

57. Burnette and Koster, *op. cit.,* p. 58; Burnette suggests (p. 238) that a female U.S. Marshal infiltrated the meeting going on in Wounded Knee on March 11, disguised as a reporter.

58. On general scenario, see *ibid.,* p. 237; on Held's presence and function, see Matthiessen, *op. cit.,* p. 109. Also see Gladstone, Lyn, "Tension grows on reservation," *Rapid City Journal,* March 9, 1973, p. 1.

59. Burnette and Koster, *op. cit.,* p. 237.

60. *Ibid.,* pp. 237-38. Also see Ciccone, F. Richard, "FBI agent shot, 'sovereign state' proclaimed: Wounded Knee circumstances jury topic," *Rapid City Journal,* March 12, 1973, p. 1.

61. *Ibid.,* p. 238. Also see Ciccone, F. Richard, "Indians seek removal of lawmen at Wounded Knee," *Rapid City Journal,* March 10, 1973, p. 1.

62. The Held report is covered in Matthiessen, *op. cit.,* p. 134. Also see Ciccone, F. Richard, "Federal authorities re-establish barriers around Wounded Knee," *Rapid City Journal,* March 13, 1973, p. 1.

63. The BIA police are always and by statute subordinate to the FBI; insofar as the GOONs on Pine Ridge were subordinate to the BIA police (by virtue of overlapping membership/commanders) their relationship to the Bureau would be even more pronounced, albeit less formally so. A Memorandum from SAC, Rapid City to Director, June 26, 1975, caption deleted, elaborates on the FBI's preeminent responsibility for reservation "law enforcement": "[BIA] Superintendent [Kendall] CUMMINGS advised Special Agent [J. Gary] ADAMS and members of the South Dakota Highway Patrol that he was in charge of the Pine Ridge Indian Reservation and would run the operation [concerning the investigation of the June 26 firefight near Oglala, see Chapter 9]. Special Agent ADAMS instructed Superintendent CUMMINGS that *the FBI was in charge of criminal activity [sic!] and criminal investigation on the Pine Ridge Indian Reservation* and the FBI would coordinate [all police] activity…[emphasis added]." Although the slip concerning the FBI being "in charge of al criminal activity" is positively Freudian, the jurisdictional intent of the memo is quite clear.

64. Quoted in Burnette and Koster, *op. cit.,* p. 238. Rather constrasting public sentiments were simultaneously being expressed; for example, see "Getting beyond Wounded Knee," *Christian Science Monitor,* March 10, 1973.

65. Quoted in Akwesasne Notes, *Voices From Wounded Knee, op. cit.,* p. 77.

66. Quoted in Weyler, *op. cit.*, p. 83.

67. Akwesasne Notes, *Voices From Wounded Knee*, *op. cit.*, pp. 112-13.

68. Quoted in *ibid.*, p. 112.

69. Quoted in *ibid.*

70. The Young Bear arrest is covered in *ibid.*, pp. 101-102; "FBIs, I think, pressed the charges. They had eight charges against me, saying that I was at Wounded Knee, and that I destroyed a post office box at Wounded Knee, and that I was an AIM organizer and that they used my house as a supply center and they seen boxes of weapons and ammo and food being transferred into my house on March 7. But on March 7 I was in Rapid City." It turned out that Young Bear had not only not been present when his home was used as a "supply center," but that he'd never been one of the Wounded Knee "occupiers" and that the Bureau *knew* this when it filed charges, having had the council member under continuous surveillance since at least as early as February 28. Charges were unceremoniously dropped, but not before they had been used to "neutralize" this opponent on Dick Wilson's behalf.

71. Burnette and Koster, *op. cit.*, pp. 239-40.

72. Akwesasne Notes, *Voices From Wounded Knee*, *op. cit.*, p. 115. Also see Lundquist, John, "Guarded optimism latest report from Wounded Knee," *Rapid City Journal*, March 16, 1973, p. 1.

73. Akwesasne Notes, *Voices From Wounded Knee*, *op. cit.*, pp. 114-15.

74. Quoted in *ibid.*, p. 115.

75. Quoted in Weyler, *op. cit.*, p. 83.

76. The best account of this period of escalation is found in *Voices From Wounded Knee*, *op. cit.*, pp. 118-23. Betsy Dudley was arrested by the FBI on May 7, 1973, while attempting to leave Wounded Knee; her notes were impounded. Tom Cook had much the same experience.

77. Quoted in *ibid.*, pp. 124-25. Author Ward Churchill was arrested and jailed in Chadron, Nebraska, en route to Wounded Knee, on March 21, 1973. He was held for approximately 50 hours on a "routine warrant check," requested from local police relative to all out-of-state traffic "apparently headed to Pine Ridge" by the FBI on or about March 20. Upon release from jail, he was ordered to drive southward, away from Pine Ridge, and was followed by a Nebraska state police car all the way to the Wyoming line. Of related interest is "Wounded Knee support rally forms," *Rapid City Journal*, March 17, 1973, p. 3.

78. Brand, Johanna, *The Life and Death of Anna Mae Aquash*, James Lorimer & Company, Publishers, Toronto (Ontario), 1978, p. 41.

79. Akwesasne Notes, *Voices From Wounded Knee*, *op. cit.*, pp. 124-25.

80. Quoted in *ibid.*, p. 128.

81. Interview with Dennis Banks, *op. cit.*

82. Burnette and Koster, *op. cit.*, p. 243; Akwesasne Notes, *Voices From Wounded Knee*, *op. cit.*, p. 128. Many Wounded Knee veterans contend that Grimm was actually hit by a GOON round fired from behind his position.

83. Quoted in Weyler, *op. cit.*, p. 81.

84. Akwesasne Notes, *Voices From Wounded Knee*, *op. cit.*, pp. 124-25.

85. Burnette had been meeting with Nixon administration representative Bradley Patterson throughout the siege (Burnette and Koster, *op. cit.*, pp. 236-37; Means is quoted at pp. 241-42).

86. *Ibid.*, p. 130.

87. Akwesasne Notes, *Voices From Wounded Knee*, *op. cit.*, p. 130.

88. For example, *ibid.*, p. 123, offers the account of LeRoy Little Ghost, a Hunkpapa from the Fort Totten Reservation in North Dakota, who was recruited on March 3, 1973 to infiltrate AIM inside Wounded Knee and to relay information to federal forces at a compensation of $2,000 to $20,000, depending on how well he did. It is doubtful that Little Ghost was ever paid for his services, insofar as he shortly "defected" to AIM.

89. *Ibid.*, p. 130.

90. The playing of the tape is covered in *ibid.*, p. 131. An excellent example of the government view being regurgitated verbatim as "analysis" by the press may be found in Ciccone, F. Richard, "The anatomy of a takeover at Wounded Knee," *Rapid City Journal*, March 18, 1973, p. 1.

91. Transcript quoted in *ibid.*, p. 145.

92. Quoted in *ibid.*, p. 145.

93. The summarization is taken from Burnette and Koster, *op. cit.*, pp. 244-45.

94. Quoted in *ibid.*, p. 245.

95. *Voices From Wounded Knee*, *op. cit.*, p. 148.

96. *Ibid.*

97. Burnette and Koster, *op. cit.*, p. 245.

98. Quoted in *ibid.*

99. *Voices From Wounded Knee, op. cit.*, p. 176.

100. *Ibid.* It should also be noted that Bill Zimmerman, a pilot of one of the three planes involved, records in his book, *Airlift to Wounded Knee* (The Swallow Press, Inc., Chicago, 1976, p. 275) that: "The [FBI] radio log was subpoenaed by defense lawyers several months after the end of the occupation [sic]. The entry for 7:02 a.m., exactly one hour and fifty-six minutes *after* the airdrop, reads as follows, '0702— Red Arrow reports shots fired at FBI helicopter Snoopy. Snoopy advised to leave area' [emphasis added]." For context underlying the air drop, see Devine, Terry, "Negotiations halted by storm; Indians low on supplies," *Rapid City Journal*, March 15, 1973, p. 1.

101. *Ibid.*, p. 277. The entire cargo manifest for the three-plane Wounded Knee airlift, reproduced at p. 274 of Zimmerman, reveals that *nothing* but food, soap, and cigarette tobacco was dropped. Further, as Zimmerman rhetorically queries on p. 275: "How does it happen that federal law enforcement officers riding in a helicopter come to shoot at two adults and 'a whole flock of small kids' walking down a road" for any reason whatsoever?

102. *Ibid.*, p. 277.

103. *Ibid.*

104. *Ibid.*, p. 278.

105. *Ibid.*

106. Quoted in *Voices From Wounded Knee, op. cit.*, p. 178.

107. Quoted in *ibid.*, p. 179.

108. Zimmerman, *op. cit.*, p. 305.

109. Quoted in Burnette and Koster, *op. cit.*, p. 245.

110. *Ibid.*, p. 247.

111. Brand, *op. cit.*, p. 41. Matthiessen, *op. cit.*, p. 78, quotes the FBI's character assassination of Clearwater: "A check of military records revealed that Frank Clearwater was not an Indian but a white man, dishonorably discharged from the army, who later fraudulently re-enlisted."

112. Burnette and Koster, *op. cit.*, p. 247-48.

113. Quoted in *Voices From Wounded Knee, op. cit.*, p. 189.

114. *Akwesasne Notes*, Early Summer, 1973, pp. 18-20. Also see *Voices From Wounded Knee, op. cit.*, p. 189. Another account is found in the Minnesota Citizens Review Commission on the FBI's Hearing Board Report (*op. cit.*, p. 7): "There is a marked contrast between the FBI's response to incidents which can be used as an excuse for the arrest of American Indian Movement Supporters and the response to incidents which involve violence by friends of the FBI...One notable example of the latter occurred in April, 1973, when a group of anti-AIM armed vigilantes set up a roadblock on the Bigfoot Trail leading into Wounded Knee. The Chief United States Marshal and the Solicitor General of the Department of Interior were stopped and prevented from proceeding. A rifle was pointed at the Solicitor General's head. The FBI broke up the confrontation, but because these people were opposing AIM, no arrests were made."

115. *Ibid.*, p. 190.

116. Weyler, *op. cit.*, p. 60; Matthiessen, *op. cit.*, p. 62, notes that both Eastman and Brewer were "notorious" on Pine Ridge in this regard.

117. *Voices From Wounded Knee, op. cit.*

118. *Ibid.*

119. *Ibid.*, p. 193. In Burnette and Koster, *op. cit.*, p. 248, the Rosebud Tribal President recounts how, "[Solicitor General] Kent Frizzell...called me to request that I come to Wounded Knee with two FBI agents in an attempt to find eight graves that were rumored to be around the perimeter. The activists who spoke of these graves believed they contained the bodies of Indians murdered by white vigilantes or Wilson's men [or both]."

120. *Voices From Wounded Knee, op. cit.*, p. 213.

121. Weyler, *op. cit.*, pp. 92-93.

122. *Ibid.*, p. 93.

123. Burnette and Koster, *op. cit.*, p. 248; Lamont had specifically requested burial at Wounded Knee in the event he was killed there.

124. *Voices From Wounded Knee, op. cit.*, p. 213.

125. *Ibid.*, pp. 219-20.

126. *Ibid.*, p. 220.

127. *Ibid.*, p. 224.

128. *Ibid.*, pp. 224-27.

129. *Ibid.*, p. 228.

130. *Ibid.*, p. 231.

131. *Ibid.*; in its final form, the government allowed its roadblocks to remain in place, monitoring the attendance of Lamont's funeral, and specified that a letter from the White House guaranteeing the treaty commission meeting in late May would be sufficient. The other provisions remained unchanged.

132. *Ibid.*

133. *Ibid.*, p. 240.

134. *Ibid.*

135. *Ibid.*, p. 243.

136. Quoted in *ibid.*

137. The church has never been rebuilt and serves, along with the grave of Buddy Lamont, as a sort of monument to Wounded Knee, 1973; see Burnette and Koster, *op. cit.*, pp. 253-54.

138. *Ibid.*, p. 249.

139. Quoted in *Voices From Wounded Knee*, *op. cit.*, p. 244.

140. Weyler, *op. cit.*, p. 95. Burnette and Koster, *op. cit.*, p. 253; it took WKLDOC attorney Ramon Roubideaux over a month to arrange bail for all arrested.

141. Northcott, Karen, "The FBI in Indian Communities," unpublished account of the FBI operations conducted on Pine Ridge from 1973-75. Tilsen, Ken, "The FBI, Wounded Knee and Politics," *The Iowa Journal of Social Work*, Fall, 1976, p. 20, notes that 562 people had been arrested between February 28 and May 7, 1973, in the immediate vicinity of Wounded Knee.

142. *Voices From Wounded Knee*, *op. cit.*, p. 252.

143. *Ibid.*

144. *Ibid.*, p. 251.

145. Quoted in *ibid.*, p. 252.

146. Transcript quoted in *ibid.*

147. Quoted in *ibid.*, p. 253.

148. *Ibid.*, pp. 253-54.

149. *Ibid.*, p. 255.

150. Quoted in *ibid.*, p. 256.

151. Quoted in *ibid.*, pp. 256-57.

152. Letter quoted in *ibid.*, pp. 257-58.

153. Quoted in *ibid.*, p. 250.

154. Quoted in *ibid.*, p. 256.

155. Weyler, *op. cit.*, p. 95.

156. These data are the compilation of former WKLDOC researcher Candy Hamilton, who performed site investigations at the time of the actual events; Hamilton suggests that her information is "undoubtedly incomplete." FBI and BIA documents bear out much of the substance of her records.

157. Johansen and Maestes, *op. cit.*, pp. 83-84.

158. *The New York Times*, January 24, 1974.

159. U.S. Commission on Civil Rights, *Report of Investigation: Oglala Sioux Tribe, General Election, 1974*, Civil Rights Commission, Washington, D.C., October, 1974.

160. Johansen and Maestes, *op. cit.*, p. 88. As is noted in U.S. Department of Justice, *Report of the Task Force on Indian Matters* (Washington, D.C., 1975, pp. 42-3), "...when Indians complain about the lack of investigation and prosecution on reservation crime, they are usually told the Federal government does not have the resources to handle the work."

161. Johansen and Maestes, *op. cit.*

162. FBI Special Agent Jack Coler, who was killed on Pine Ridge on June 26, 1975, was assigned to the SWAT contingent; see Matthiessen, *op. cit.*, p. 173.

163. See Johansen and Maestes, *op. cit.*, p. 93, for ratio. See *Report of the Task Force on Indian Affairs*, *op. cit.*, pp. 42-3, concerning the super-saturation of Pine Ridge with agents in 1975.

164. U.S. Senate, Committee on the Judiciary, Subcommittee on Internal Security (Eastland Subcommittee), *Revolutionary Activities Within the United States: The American Indian Movement*, U.S. Government Printing Office, Washington, D.C., 1976, p. 61. Such statistics give the lie to right-wing publications which very selectively use FBI documents to discredit AIM; see, for example, Dewing, Roland, *The FBI Files on the American Indian Movement and Wounded Knee*, University Publications of America, 1987,

in which some 26,000 documents of the hundreds of thousands compiled are presented as "definitive." It should be noted that Dewing had considerable assistance from the Bureau in assembling his hopelessly distorted collection.

165. U.S. House of Representatives, *Hearings Before the Subcommittee on Civil and Constitutional Rights, 97th Congress, 1st Session on FBI Authorization, March 19, 24, 25; April 2 and 8, 1981*, U.S. Government Printing Office, Washington, D.C., 1981; Johansen and Maestes, *op. cit.*, at pp. 88-89, reveal that five of these 15 cases were on charges of "interfering with a federal officer."

166. Statement by WKLDOC attorney Ken Tilsen during the 1974 "Wounded Knee Leadership Trials" in St. Paul, Minnesota.

167. Johansen and Maestes, *op. cit.*, p. 89; Means was ultimately convicted of "assaulting a peace officer" who physically attacked him in court after Means refused to rise in honor of the entry of the trial judge. Means, in a recent conversation with Ward Churchill, still contends that the matter was a clear-cut case of self-defense.

168. For U.S. government usage of the terms "colonized," "colonial," and "colony" with regard to American Indian nations, see the quote from FBI agent Norman Zigrossi corresponding to note 171, below. For a less rabid example, see U.S. Commission on Civil Rights, *The Navajo Nation: An American Colony*, A Report of the U.S. Commission on Civil Rights, Washington, D.C., September 1975.

169. The authors are in no way resorting to doctrinaire name-calling by using the word "imperial" in this context. Rather, we are simply adhering to the dictionary definition (*Webster's College Dictionary*, G.&C. Merriam Publishers, Springfield, MA, 5th Edition, 1942, p. 500) corresponding to the government's own use of colonial terminology: "Of or pertaining to a state as sovereign and supreme over colonies, and the like."

170. U.S. House of Representatives, *Report of the Commissioner on Indian Affairs, 58th Annual Report*, U.S. Government Printing Office, Washington, D.C., October 1, 1889.

171. Quoted in Weir, David, and Lowell Bergman, "The Killing of Anna Mae Aquash," *Rolling Stone*, April 7, 1977, p. 55.

Chapter 6

1. The names of those slain are James Waller, Sandra Neely Smith, William Sampson, Michael Nathan and César Vicente Cauce. The most comprehensive title available on this subject is Bermanzohm, Paul C. (M.D.), and Sally A. Bermanzohm, *The True Story of the Greensboro Massacre*, César Cauce Publishers and Distributors, Inc., New York, 1980.

2. *New York Times*, July 25, 1980.

3. Pinsky, Mark, "Government Infiltration an Issue in Greensboro Trial," *Newsday*, July 31, 1980.

4. *The Charlotte (North Carolina) Observer*, November 16, 1979.

5. Statement of SA Andrew Pelczar, head of the FBI Greensboro task force, quoted in *The Greensboro (North Carolina) Record*, November 8, 1979.

6. Zoccino, Nanda, "Ex-FBI Informer Describes Terrorist Role," *The Los Angeles Times*, January 26, 1976. Also see Michael Parenti, *Democracy for the Few*, St. Martin's Press, New York, 1980, p. 24.

7. *The Glass House Tapes*, *op. cit.*, p. 161.

8. *Ibid.*, pp. 161-62.

9. *Ibid.*, p. 161.

10. *Ibid.*, pp. 161-62.

11. *Ibid.*

12. *Ibid.*, p. 161.

13. *Ibid.*, p. 163.

14. *Ibid.*, p. 164.

15. See Lernoux, Penny, *The Cry of the People: United States Involvement in the Rise of Fascism, Torture, and Murder, and the Persecution of the Catholic Church in Latin America*, Doubleday & Co., New York, 1980.

16. Burnette and Koster, *op. cit.*, p. 228.

17. *Ibid.*, p. 266.

18. Weyler, *op. cit.*, p. 106.

19. Burnette and Koster, *op. cit.*, pp. 265-66.

20. *Ibid.*, p. 282.

21. *Ibid.*

22. *Ibid.*, p. 283.

23. *Ibid.*

24. Weyler, *op. cit.*, pp. 172-73; see Matthiessen, *op. cit.*, p. 130, concerning the administration of polygraph examinations to the victims. In this case, Wilson and his cohorts were actually indicted by a federal grand jury. However, before the matter could be brought to court, Wilson had the group charged with the same offense in tribal court, pleaded guilty, and walked away with a $10 fine. He was then able to successfully argue "double jeopardy" and receive a dismissal of federal charges. This astute legal strategy carries with it an obvious whiff of federal coaching.

25. Weyler, *op. cit.*, p. 174; on the Wilson "assurance" to Fools Crow—who after all, had already suffered vehicular assault at the hands of the GOONs (see Chapter 5)—see p. 106. Concerning the attack on Fools Crow's home, see Matthiessen, *op. cit.*, p. 133.

26. Weyler, *op. cit.*, p. 174.

27. Information on this matter, including the Abourezk quote, can be found in *ibid.*, p. 175.

28. Matthiessen, *op. cit.*, pp. 147-48.

29. *Akwesasne Notes*, Vol. 7, No. 4, Early Autumn, 1975, p. 6.

30. *Ibid.*

31. Matthiessen, *op. cit.*, p. 270.

32. Unlike Pine Ridge, the Yankton Reservation comes under P.L.-280-type state jurisdiction. Consequently, Means' and Thomas' assailants were arrested by South Dakota State Police and arraigned before U.S. Magistrate David Vrooman in Sioux Falls on May 7; they were later given probation. The FBI seems to have been of virtually no assistance in obtaining even this laughable result.

33. Quoted in Matthiessen, *op. cit.*, p. 132; Trimble's son was pistol-whipped by GOONs in 1974, and the vigilantes warned the superintendent himself to "get a bodyguard because we're going to get you."

34. *Ibid.*, p. 129.

35. FBI Headquarters Report, titled "Law Enforcement on Pine Ridge Indian Reservation," dated June 5, 1975.

36. Quoted in Matthiessen, *op. cit.*, p. 129.

37. Burnette and Koster, *op. cit.*, p. 283.

38. Quoted in Weyler, *op. cit.*, p. 110.

39. U.S. Commission on Civil Rights, *Report of Investigation: Oglala Sioux Tribe, General Election, 1974, op. cit.*, inclusive; for Abourezk data, see Burnette and Koster, *op. cit.*, p. 257.

40. See Kobler, *op. cit.*, pp. 206-210; at pp. 107-109, the author sketches how Capone had practiced the same "techniques" on a smaller scale in the Cicero (Illinois) municipal election of 1923.

41. *Ibid.*, pp. 9-13; Kobler recounts how Frank Loesch, head of the Chicago Crime Commission—a group supported directly by the White House—negotiated directly with Capone to forestall a repeat of the gangster's "Pineapple Primary" performance during the 1928 Illinois state elections. The result was that the Thompson machine was deposed, not only in Chicago, but throughout the state. This, in the end, was a prelude to the U.S. Internal Revenue Service's successful prosecution of Capone—now politically uncovered—for income tax evasion in 1930 and 1931. Clearly, no similar actions were taken against the Wilsonites in the Pine Ridge example.

42. For Jim Wilson's salary, see the *New York Times*, April 22, 1975; on Pine Ridge per capita income and standard of living, see McCall, Cheryl, "Life at Pine Ridge Bleak," *Colorado Daily*, May 16, 1975. *Voices From Wounded Knee, op. cit.*, p. 21, notes that, in addition to his salary for 1972, Jim Wilson had received some $15,000 in "consulting fees" from the tribe.

43. Quoted in *BIA, I'm Not Your Indian Anymore, op. cit.*, p. 34.

44. *Voices From Wounded Knee, op. cit.*, p. 20.

45. Matthiessen, *op. cit.*, p. 61.

46. *Voices From Wounded Knee, op. cit.*, p. 21; Matthiessen, *op. cit.*, p. 62. It appears that, while serving as tribal president with a salary which had already been tripled, Wilson was also paying *himself* supplements as a "consultant" to the tribe.

47. Affidavit quoted in *Voices From Wounded Knee, op. cit.*, p. 19.

48. *Ibid.*, p. 15.

49. Matthiessen, *op. cit.*, p. 62.

50. Brand, *op. cit.*, p. 34.

51. *Ibid.*

52. *Ibid.*

53. Matthiessen, *op. cit.*, p. 130.

54. U.S. Congress, Senate Select Committee to Study Government Operations with Respect to Intelligence Activities, *Intelligence Activities and the Rights of Americans*, *op. cit.*

55. This reality corresponds well with the most abstract analysis of "The Pacification Model" provided in *The Iron Fist and the Velvet Glove*, *op. cit.*, pp. 126-31.

56. For a concise overall view, see Stanton, Shelby L., *Vietnam Order of Battle* (Chapter 28, "MACV Special Operations"), U.S. News Books, Washington, D.C., 1981, pp. 251-53.

57. See Simpson, Charles M. (III), *Inside the Green Berets: The First Thirty Years* (Chapter 14, "Special Operations and Unconventional Warfare [UW]"), Presidio Press, Novato, CA, 1983, pp. 135-150. All of this is very much in line with the recent observation of former (1961-63) Department of Defense Director of Internal Intelligence Charles Maechling, Jr., that: "Notably absent [from the initial 1962 *U.S. Overseas Internal Defense Document* outlining counterinsurgency methods] was any reference to human rights, international law, the Geneva Conventions on prisoner treatment, U.S. legislative authority or the conditions of its application other than presidential fiat. Repeated efforts to include even cursory mention of these factors were rejected by the Pentagon and General [Maxwell] Taylor's office as 'superfluous'"; "Counterinsurgency: the First Ordeal by Fire," in Michael T. Klare and Peter Kornbluh, *Low Intensity Warfare: Counterinsurgency, Proinsurgency and Antiterrorism in the Eighties*, Pantheon, New York, 1988, p. 30. For recent U.S. counterinsurgency strategy see Barnett, Frank R., B. Hugh Tovar, and Richard H. Schultz (eds.), *Special Operations in US Strategy*, National Defense University Press, Washington, D.C., 1984. This tome, which expounds the theoretical basis for the Iran/Contra operation, is truly chilling in its expressed contempt for human rights, international law and democratic process and its willingness to sacrifice these to its overweening goal of "anti-communism."

58. *Akwesasne Notes*, Mohawk Nation via Rooseveltown, N.Y., Winter, 1975, p. 31.

59. Butz, Tim, "Garden Plot—'Flowers of Evil,'" *Akwesasne Notes*, Vol. 7, No. 5, Early Winter, 1975, p. 6. Also see, Garbus, Martin, "General Haig of Wounded Knee," *The Nation*, November 9, 1974; Warner also notes that General Creighton Abrams, one-time commander of U.S. forces in Vietnam, reviewed all proposals on the Wounded Knee buildup.

60. This was part of Warner's testimony at the Wounded Knee trials in St. Paul, Minn., in 1974.

61. As Frank Kitson (a consultant to the Pentagon on counterinsurgency, who as a British Brigadier headed operations against both the guerrillas in Malaya and the so-called Mau Mau in Kenya) puts it on p. 77 of his book, *Low Intensity Operations: Subversion, Insurgency and Peace-Keeping* (Stackpole Books, Harrisburg, Pa., 1971): "The army has an important role to play in the business, firstly by insuring that its own requirements are met, and secondly by making a direct contribution in terms of men and material as required..."

62. At p. 77, Kitson, *op. cit.*, observes: "...the armed forces should be brought into the business from the very beginning. There is no danger of political repercussions to this course of action, because the consultation can be carried out in the strictest secrecy." As Michael Klare has recently observed, "Although intended to free U.S. military personnel to operate as they see fit on foreign soil, the domestic political measures advocated by ardent [Low Intensity Conflict] enthusiasts would inevitably erode the integrity of our democratic values. Once we surrender a free press and key democratic values to the exigencies of war, we may find that other barriers to the authoritarianism will disappear as well"; Klare and Kornbluh, *op. cit.*, p. 79. For the record, according to Mitchell M. Zais, writing in *Military Review*, August 1986, p. 93, the currently fashionable term "Low Intensity Conflict" is merely a new name for an old concept: counterinsurgency.

63. Butz, Tim, *op. cit.*, p. 7.

64. *Ibid.*; Matthiessen, *op. cit.*, p. 73, notes Warner later acknowledged that, on March 12, 1973, he and Potter had submitted a draft plan of such an operation to Haig.

65. FBI infiltrator/*provocateur* Douglass Durham, in his testimony before the Senate Committee on the Judiciary at transcript p. 5, put his, and the Bureau's, count at "258."

66. Langguth, A.J., *Hidden Terrors: The Truth About U.S. Police Operations in Latin America*, Pantheon, New York, 1978. Of related interest, see Herman, Edward S., *The Real Terror Network: Terrorism in Fact and Propaganda*, South End Press, Boston, MA, 1982.

67. See *U.S. v. Dennis Banks and Russell Means*, 374 F. Supp. 321,331 (S.D. 1974), before Judge Fred J. Nichol, Chief Judge, United States District Court of South Dakota; February 12 to September 16, 1974; St. Paul, Minnesota, and a separate account of the trial compiled from the court record by WKLDOC attorney Larry Leventhal.

68. See *Counter Spy*, Fall, 1974. The premise here is entirely in line with a recent statement of the U.S. military's Joint Chiefs of Staff that: "Low intensity conflict is a limited politico-military struggle to achieve political, social, economic, or psychological objectives. It is often protracted and ranges from diplomatic, economic, and psycho-social pressures through terrorism and insurgency. Low-intensity conflict is generally confined to a geographic area and is often characterized by constraints on the weaponry, tactics, and the level of violence"; US Army Training and Doctrine Command, *US Army Operational Concept for Low Intensity Conflict*, TRADOC Pamphlet No. 525-44, Fort Monroe, Va., 1986, p. 2.

Chapter 7

1. Information on the "deal" and Bissonette's potential sentence may be found in Matthiessen, *op. cit.*, p. 100.

2. Quoted in *Voices From Wounded Knee, op. cit.*, p. 259.

3. Matthiessen, *op. cit.*, p. 101, terms the federal position as being "gross government misconduct" and notes that this resulted in Bissonette's being "set free."

4. *Ibid*. "Because he [Bissonette] knew every last detail about the Wilson regime and its dealings with the U.S. government, he would have been a crucial witness for the defense." More threateningly, he would have been a crucial witness against the prosecution.

5. Richards' identity has been suggested to one of the authors by former AIM member Frank Black Elk.

6. Oglala Sioux Civil Rights Organization, *The Murder of Pedro Bissonette*, circular released from Manderson, S.D., October 18, 1973.

7. Quoted in *Rapid City Journal*, October 18, 1973; it is noteworthy that the accounts of "official sources" such as Cunningham, Eastman and Dick Wilson were the only versions allowed into print at the time.

8. Incident Report of BIA Police Officer Joe Clifford, filed the night of October 17, 1973 at BIA Police headquarters, Pine Ridge, S.D.

9. The emergency log at Pine Ridge hospital (a facility of the federal Indian Health Service) for October 17, 1973, records the arrival time of Bissonette's body.

10. These witness accounts, made in the form of depositions, were taken by WKLDOC attorneys and researchers at the time. Although copies were provided to then head of the Rapid City FBI office, George O'Clock, no action was ever taken by the Bureau to investigate the matter. They are mentioned in Weyler, *op. cit.*, p. 109.

11. Quoted in *ibid*.

12. *Ibid*. This is confirmed by WKLDOC files.

13. According to Gladys Bissonette, this was already her intention; unpublished interview with WKLDOC researcher Candy Hamilton, conducted in early 1974.

14. Weyler, *op. cit.*; Theda Nelson, a medical practitioner at the Pine Ridge hospital and long-time AIM member, has told author Churchill that the body was removed in a BIA ambulance.

15. *Rapid City Journal*, October 19, 1973; Eastman contended that such instructions from Clayton were "not particularly" unusual. On the same date, Dick Wilson went on record as saying of Bissonette that, "He was not killed because he was in AIM."

16. See Weyler, *op. cit.*

17. The sealed coffin, WKLDOC attorney Mark Lane was informed by the FBI, was ordered because "the nature and thoroughness" of the autopsy had so greatly disfigured Bissonette's remains, that the government wished to spare his family the "unpleasantness" of viewing it. WKLDOC records reveal that it was decided a second autopsy would "probably not be worthwhile," given that the police had ample opportunity to remove the slugs from the body, etc.

18. The BIA police scrutiny of the burial ceremony was explained by Dick Wilson in the *Rapid City Journal* (October 24, 1973) as being based on the need to "keep order," to continue the ban on AIM activities—and presence—on the reservation and to avert possible "AIM inspired violence."

19. Quoted in Matthiessen, *op. cit.*, p. 102.

20. *Ibid.*, p. 258.

21. The description of GOON equipment comes from *ibid.*; it is widely remembered by Wanblee residents to this day.

22. Matthiessen, *op. cit.*, pp. 258-59; the authors would like to express their appreciation to Vivian Locust of Colorado AIM for her description of DeSersa's activities between 1972 and his death.

23. Matthiessen, *op. cit.*, p. 259; Guy Dull Knife was a descendent of the Cheyenne Chief, Dull Knife (see Chapter 4), who fought at the Little Big Horn and later led his people from their exile in Oklahoma to the Red Cloud Agency during the so-called "Cheyenne Breakout of 1878." For further information on this last, see Sandoz, Mari, *Cheyenne Autumn*, Hastings House, New York, 1953.

24. Matthiessen, *op. cit.*, p. 259.

25. Hill Witt, Shirley, and William Muldrow, *Events Surrounding Recent Murders on the Pine Ridge Reservation in South Dakota*, report issued by the Rocky Mountain Regional Office, U.S. Commission on Civil Rights, Denver, March 31, 1976, pp. 1-2.

26. U.S. Commission on Civil Rights, *Hearing Held Before the U.S. Commission on Civil Rights: American Indian Issues in South Dakota*, Hearing Held in Rapid City, South Dakota, July 27-28, 1978, U.S. Government Printing Office, Washington, D.C., 1978, p. 33.

27. Hill Witt and Muldrow, *op. cit.*, p. 2.

28. Matthiessen, *op. cit.*, p. 259.

29. The tally of trial outcomes may be found in *ibid.*; the sentencing should be compared to that visited upon AIM members and supporters after their far less weighty convictions (*e.g.* Leonard Crow Dog, Dennis Banks) or in far more dubious cases (*e.g.* Leonard Peltier, Dick Marshall), matters covered elsewhere in this book.

30. Amiotte is interviewed in the documentary film, *Annie Mae: A Brave Hearted Woman, op. cit.*; he shows the exact location in which he found the body and recalls that he immediately noticed she was wearing "very distinctive" turquoise jewelry which, Aquash's friends point out, was her "trademark."

31. The Parisian/Merrick report is mentioned in Matthiessen, *op. cit.*, p. 260.

32. Price is quoted in Brand, *op. cit.*, p. 131. The official FBI report of the incident, filed late in the day at the Minneapolis FBI office is a bit more sedate: "SA DAVID PRICE and SA CHARLES ENGAR...called out words to the effect 'FBI, come out of the tent!' A female voice answered approximately a minute later. A person identified herself as ANNA MAE PICTOU, Indian, female, came out of the tent by unzipping the bottom flap and crawling out...PICTOU identified herself at the request of SA PRICE and was advised of SA PRICE's official identity...PICTOU was advised that SA PRICE *remembered her* from earlier interview concerning the murder of JEANETTE BISSONETTE and was asked several questions concerning the events surrounding the murder of BISSONETTE. PICTOU advised that she would not answer questions concerning the BISSONETTE murder [emphasis added]."

33. Aquash was interviewed by SA Fred Coward. Coward's summary of the interview dated September 5, 1975, reads in part that, "PICTOU was specifically asked if she knew DENNIS BANKS, LEONARD PELTIER, FRANK BLACK HORSE and ROBERT ROBIDEAU." In her own account, Aquash states that, at a certain point, Price "came in and...started referring to the June twenty-sixth incident that happened in Oglala where two men were killed, and I told him three, and he said, Okay, three. He kept insisting that I used to live there, and I kept insisting back to him that I have never lived there, and he just wouldn't believe me. He just kept asking me questions like whether I knew Harry and Cecelia Jumping Bull. You know, I've never even had the opportunity of meeting these people, let alone knowing them. Finally, I just refused to talk, so he left me alone. But they would come through periodically and ask me something. I was there three hours, and they finally took me over to the county jail in Pierre (quoted in Matthiessen, *op. cit.*, pp. 236-37)." Coward's summary is more specific on the latter phase of the active interview: "At this point in the interview there was a brief pause by PICTOU who put her head down on the desk to [*sic*] which she was sitting and did not reply to the question. The interviewing agents again specifically asked PICTOU if she knew these individuals just mentioned. PICTOU advised at this point that 'you can either shoot me or throw me in jail as those are the two choices I'm taking.' PICTOU was asked specifically what she meant by this to which she replied, 'that's what you're going to do with me anyway.'" The formulation of these last statements found in our text comes from WKLDOC researcher Candy Hamilton, a close friend of Aquash, to whom she reported her version.

34. Attribution of this statement to Price was made by Aquash to Candy Hamilton on at least two occasions. Colorado AIM member Troy Lynn Yellow Wood, another close friend of Aquash, also recalls being told this.

35. Kevin McKiernan quotes this letter in "Indian woman's death raises many troubling questions," *Minneapolis Tribune*, May 30, 1976. It is also quoted in *Annie Mae: A Brave Hearted Woman, op. cit.*

36. Brand, *op. cit.*, p. 135.

37. *Ibid.*, pp. 133-34. Candy Hamilton also offers this quotation, along with that concerning the Price death threat in an article in the *Minneapolis Tribune,* May 30, 1976.

38. U.S. House of Representatives, *First Session on FBI Authorization (1981),* 97th Congress, First Session, March 19, 24, 25; April 2, and 8, 1981, U.S. Government Printing Office, Washington, D.C., 1981, p. 276.

39. *Ibid.* Also see Oppenheimer, Jerry, "Questions raised about the FBI's handling of Aquash Case," *Rapid City Journal,* May 25, 1976.

40. Ellison is quoted in *Annie Mae: A Brave Hearted Woman, op. cit.*; he has also made similar observations to the authors.

41. *First Session on FBI Authorization (1981), op. cit.*

42. This sequence is provided both by Ellison and Aquash's sister in *Annie Mae: A Brave Hearted Woman, op. cit.*

43. *First Session on FBI Authorization (1981), op. cit.*, pp. 267-68.

44. Hill Witt and Muldrow, *op. cit.*, p. 3.

45. *First Session on FBI Authorization (1981), op. cit.*, p. 277. Hill Witt and Muldrow, *op. cit.*, p. 3, generally concur on behalf of the U.S. Commission on Civil Rights: "On March 11, the body was exhumed in the presence of FBI agents and Dr. Garry Peterson, a pathologist from Minneapolis, Minnesota, who had been brought in by Aquash's family to examine the body. X-rays revealed a bullet of approximately .32 calibre in her head. Peterson's examination revealed a bullet wound in the back of the head surrounded by a 5x5 cm. area of subgaleal reddish discoloration."

46. Brand, *op. cit.*, p. 131. Attorney Bruce Ellison has indicated to the authors that the slug recovered from Aquash's head was of the unjacketed lead type and had distorted greatly upon impact with her skull. Thus it was impossible to determine the exact calibre; Ellison says, "it was consistent with being from either a .32 or .38 calibre handgun."

47. Hill Witt and Muldrow, *op. cit.*, p. 3.

48. *Ibid.*

49. *Ibid.*

50. *First Session on FBI Authorization (1981), op. cit.*, p. 666.

51. *Ibid.*, p. 275.

52. Brand, *op. cit.*, p. 21.

53. *Ibid.*, pp. 21-22.

54. *Ibid.*, p. 22.

55. The Haber letter is reproduced in *First Session on FBI Authorization (1981), op. cit.*, pp. 247-49.

56. *Ibid.*, p. 278.

57. *Ibid.*

58. "Lawyer questions FBI's dependability," *Rapid City Journal,* May 23, 1976.

59. Durden-Smith, *op. cit.*, p. 119.

60. The exact quote is, "You don't measure success in this area [counterintelligence] in terms of apprehension, but in terms of neutralization"; Ungar, *op. cit.*, p. 120. Although Ungar makes no attribution of the quote, implying only that it came from a high level Bureau expert on the subject, the authors believe the statement was made by Richard G. Held (serving at the time as chief of the FBI Internal Security Section).

61. Interview with Richard B. Williams, Boulder, Colorado, November 1986.

62. Interview with Aaron Two Elk, Denver, Colorado, April 1987.

63. The Sovereignty Hearings were conducted as a pretrial aspect of the government's "Consolidated Wounded Knee Cases"; AIM and the ION, via their WKLDOC attorneys, had entered a motion, based in the sovereignty of the Oglala implicit to the 1868 Fort Laramie Treaty, challenging the idea that the U.S. held jurisdiction to try the cases at all. See Dunbar Ortiz, *The Great Sioux Nation, op. cit.*

64. Quoted in Matthiessen, *op. cit.*, pp. 86-87; Means today says that he doesn't know whether Camp was ever a federal informer *per se,* but that the shooting of Bellecourt "was and will always be absolutely inexcusable...if Carter wasn't a cop, he definitely did a cop's work in this case." Means also notes that Camp's subsequent, publicly announced ban on AIM organizers entering the state of Oklahoma, while "obviously unenforceable," was "the same thing Dickie Wilson attempted on Pine Ridge," and therefore "speaks for itself." Dennis Banks, quoted in Matthiessen, *op. cit.*, p. 86, is more charitable: "Carter was very eloquent, but he wasn't ready for leadership."

65. There is no evidence that Carter Camp ever cooperated with federal authorities in this matter. To the contrary, "On June 5, [1975] in Cedar Rapids, Iowa, Leonard Crow Dog, Carter Camp, and Stan Holder were convicted on Wounded Knee charges after a brief trial..." (Matthiessen, *op. cit.*, p. 146). Camp and Holder both went underground for a period to avoid sentencing and incarceration; when they surfaced, they were both imprisoned for a year, not on the original conviction, but for having fled.

66. *Ibid.*, p. 86; the information concerning ownership of the weapon comes from Black Elk personally.

67. Interview with Aaron Two Elk, *op. cit.*

68. Matthiessen, *op. cit.*, p. 147; Peltier's "conversation" with Aquash occurred, in a situation reminiscent of the John Arbuckle matter, at AIM's 8th national convention, held in Farmington, New Mexico, June 6-18, 1975.

69. *Ibid.*

70. Johansen and Maestes, *op. cit.*, p. 105; Stewart did *not* actually testify at the trial of Butler and Robideau. He was on the prosecution witness list, but was among the various informers and infiltrators who were not used, given a prosecution assessment that their testimony might "taint" the government's case before the jury.

71. Matthiessen, *op. cit.*, pp. 289-90; Stewart was also on the prosecution witness list for the trial of Leonard Peltier, but again was not called to testify.

72. *Ibid.*, p. 445.

73. Quoted in McKiernan, *op. cit.*

74. Quoted in Matthiessen, *op. cit.*, p. 256. Bob Robideau disagrees with this assessment of Banks' suspicion of Aquash.

75. Aaron Two Elk remembers that "Nobody trusted that woman with *any* sort of sensitive information."

76. According to Johansen and Maestes, *op. cit.*, Tanequodle subsequently denied ever talking to Wood, or anyone else from the FBI, with regard to Anna Mae Aquash.

77. Quoted in Brand, *op. cit.*, p. 143.

78. *Ibid.*, pp. 143-44.

79. Quoted in Weir and Bergman, *op. cit.*, p. 54.

Chapter 8

1. Weyler, *op. cit.*, pp. 169-70. Also see Lawrence, Ken, *op. cit.*, pp. 4-5.

2. The term derives from a pamphlet published by WKLDOC researcher Paula Geise under the title "Secret Agent Douglass Durham and the Death of Jancita Eagle Deer" in 1976. The pamphlet is still available from the *North Country Anvil*, Minneapolis.

3. The characterization of Durham, who portrayed himself variously as "a one-quarter Chippewa" and as "a Minneconjou Lakota" during his time inside AIM, as a non-Indian comes from his own 1976 testimony before Senator James Eastland's Subcommittee on Internal Security. The following exchange between Durham and Richard Schultz, Chief Counsel to the Senate Committee on the Judiciary, is recorded at p. 3 (*Revolutionary Activities Within the United States: The American Indian Movement, op. cit.*):

Schultz: Are you an American Indian?

Durham: No Sir. I am not.

Schultz: What is your nationality [*sic*]?

Durham: Scotch-Irish, English and German.

4. Geise, Paula, "Profile of an Informer," *Covert Action Information Bulletin*, Number 24, Summer 1985, pp. 18-19.

5. *Ibid.* In a taped interview with WKLDOC attorneys conducted in Chicago, March 9-12, 1975 (immediately after Durham's identity was exposed) he acknowledged that he had been "considered [by local police officials] to be the head of the largest criminal organization in the State of Iowa."

6. AIM National Headquarters (Minneapolis) released a pamphlet entitled *Anatomy of an Informer* in 1975, composed of transcriptions from the interviews mentioned in the preceding note. Durham's statement that "I was paid $1,000 per month, cash," is contained therein.

7. *Revolutionary Activities Within the United States: The American Indian Movement, op. cit.,* p. 10. It is worth noting that the "escalating scale" involved in Durham's payment simply means that as his activities grew tangibly worse, he was paid more by the Bureau.

8. *Ibid.,* p. 11.

9. Durham's joining the Des Moines AIM chapter is recalled by Aaron Two Elk, a chapter member described by Durham at *ibid.,* p. 17, as being "the resident militant."

10. On Durham's being Banks' "bodyguard and pilot," see Matthiessen, *op. cit.,* p. 109.

11. *Ibid.,* p. 88.

12. Brand, *op. cit.,* pp. 98-99. As concerns the $100,000, Matthiessen, *op. cit.,* p. 123, quotes Nilak Butler to the effect that, "the money was going into a second acount under the name of Douglass Durham."

13. *Revolutionary Activities Within the United States: The American Indian Movement, op. cit.,* pp. 6-7.

14. *Ibid.,* p. 7.

15. *Ibid.,* p. 55.

16. *Ibid.*

17. *Ibid.*

18. *Ibid.,* p. 61.

19. Chicago interview, *op. cit.;* Durham also identified his Des Moines FBI liaison as having been SA David Hedgecock.

20. Quoted in Brand, *op. cit.,* p. 99.

21. Quoted in *ibid.*

22. *Ibid.* Durham's last statement conforms very well with his testimony, recorded at p. 61 of *Revolutionary Activities Within the United States: The American Indian Movement, op. cit.,* that "I was the person who issued the passes for the defense attorneys to get into their own rooms. I was the one who cleared the defense attorneys...I controlled security all around them."

23. Quoted in Matthiessen, *op. cit.,* p.123; Durham's salary increase is noted on the same page.

24. *Revolutionary Activities Within the United States: The American Indian Movement, op. cit.,* p. 61. On the same page, Durham makes a feeble attempt to gloss over the situation, insisting that, "I tried to ease out [of the defense strategy meetings] as rapidly and subtly as I could" and that although "I was charged with, for a short period, maintaining the [defense trial] records I never once glanced at those records, or related any of the information I overheard relating to defense tactics, to the FBI." One is left to wonder, in this ludicrous scenario, what engendered Durham's pay increase at the same time, and what—exactly—was the subject matter of his "nearly 50" meetings with the FBI during the trial.

25. The description is offered in Weyler, *op. cit.,* p. 114.

26. According to both Candy Hamilton and Nilak Butler, Anna Mae Aquash was one of those who was most insistent that Durham was "out of line" with such statements. Both women are certain that Durham developed a deep animus for Aquash at this time, and that his efforts to discredit (bad-jacket) her began in St. Paul.

27. The term "systematic violence" comes from a memorandum, SAC, Minneapolis, to Director, FBI, caption deleted, dated February 9, 1974, speculating upon AIM "plans for the immediate future," and citing a memo released on AIM letterhead by Durham three days previously.

28. Matthiessen, *op. cit.,* p. 124.

29. Two Elk interview, *op. cit.*

30. This is the date given for the memo in an article on the topic published in the *Des Moines [Iowa] Tribune,* August 28, 1973.

31. Two Elk interview, *op. cit.*

32. Brand, *op. cit.,* p. 98.

33. *Revolutionary Activities Within the United States: The American Indian Movement, op. cit.,* pp. 45-47; Roberts underwrote Durham's airplane rentals "in part." See also, Brand, *op. cit.,* p. 98.

34. *Revolutionary Activities Within the United States: The American Indian Movement, op. cit.,* p. 46.

35. This document is reproduced in *ibid.,* as Exhibit 31, at pp. 152-72. The first known FBI reference to it is in a memorandum from SAC, Minneapolis, to the Director, FBI, captioned THE AMERICAN INDIAN MOVEMENT—VIOLENT ACTIVITIES, and dated September 21, 1973. In other words, the Bureau had the document as soon as it was released (or sooner).

36. Point 7 may be found at p. 161 of *Revolutionary Activities Within the United States: The American Indian Movement, op. cit.*

37. *Ibid.*, p. 162.

38. The handwritten Banks note is included in *ibid.*, as Exhibit 20, at pp. 132-33.

39. This statement comes from the same AIM member, who requests anonymity, quoted earlier in this section.

40. *Revolutionary Activities Within the United States: The American Indian Movement, op. cit.*, p. 69.

41. The quotation is from *Fact Sheet: The American Indian Movement*, an AIM circular included in *ibid.*, as Exhibit 6, pp. 90-92 (the specific quote is at p. 92).

42. *Ibid.*, p. 31.

43. Two Elk interview, *op. cit.*

44. Matthiessen, *op. cit.*, p. 110.

45. Means interview, *op. cit.* Russell Means also contends that he always considered Durham to be "a punk" and "Dennis Banks' errand boy," as did Bill Means and "the rest of the leadership aside from Banks. We *never* trusted the guy." Banks concurs that this assessment is, to some extent, true.

46. The case is covered, and FBI documents cited, in Matthiessen, op. cit., pp. 108-12.

47. "Secret Agent Douglass Durham and the Death of Jancita Eagle Deer," *op. cit.*; Eagle Deer had married, after moving to Iowa, but was separated from her husband and living with her in-laws at the time Durham "found" her in 1974.

48. Weyler, *op. cit.*, p. 125, notes that Janklow's election opponent, incumbent South Dakota Attorney General Kermit Sande, had brought up the fact that in 1955, as a juvenile, Janklow had been accused of sexual assault upon a 17-year-old Moody County, S.D., woman. Sande contended that the charge lodged in the confidential juvenile record was "rape." Janklow countered that it wasn't rape: "It didn't go that far. It was a preliminary sort of thing." Durham would hardly have been inaccurate or unjustified in pointing out to Banks that *any* FBI investigation of the Eagle Deer charges (worthy of the name) *must* have turned up this information.

49. This is not to suggest that Held and the Bureau already "knew" William Janklow would later become Deputy Attorney General, Attorney General and the Governor of the State of South Dakota. Rather, such thinking would no doubt have been couched in terms of "solidifying" the "support" of an articulate and potentially prominent member of South Dakota's "professional community." If, and to the extent that this is true, Janklow's "pay off" to the Bureau—in terms of services rendered—must have surpassed Held's wildest expectations.

50. Weyler, *op. cit.*, p. 125; Tilsen described Eagle Deer as a "confused person" who was "easily intimidated," and warned Banks that the charges would not hold up in court without further documentation.

51. This was a preliminary hearing at which Janklow had not been ordered to appear. Taking the matter into tribal court has been described by Banks as an expedient attempt to acquire the documentation held by the FBI and BIA which Tilsen had said was necessary for the matter to be pursued further.

52. See the *Rapid City Journal*, October 18, 1974; also see the *Sioux Falls Argus Leader*, the same date.

53. Matthiessen, *op. cit.*, p. 112.

54. Weyler, *op. cit.*, p. 126, states: "…in the summer of 1975, Janklow having been appointed to the Board of Directors of the Legal Services Corporation, the FBI conducted a second [sic, *third*] investigation, again reviewing each of the charges, and again counseling that they were unfounded. Further investigations by both the White House and the U.S. Senate Committee on Labor and Public Welfare ruled unequivocally that there was no truth either to the charges of the alleged rape of Jancita Eagle Deer, or to any of the other charges brought against Janklow. In a letter dated June 10, 1975, White House Counsel Philip W. Buchen made particular reference to the White House investigations, concluding, 'The results of this investigation and two previous investigations which have been communicated to the [Senate] committee indicate that these allegations are simply unfounded…'"

55. Gonzales, Mario, Chief Justice, Rosebud Sioux Tribal Court, Rosebud, South Dakota, *Judicial Opinion*, CIV. NO. 74-2840, October 31, 1974.

56. Copies of the warrants, as well as subpoenas issued in the case, are on file in the archives of the Rosebud Sioux Tribal Court.

57. See the *Rapid City Journal*, November 1, 1974.

58. Brand, *op. cit.*, p. 103.

59. Matthiessen, *op. cit.*, p. 111, notes that, "one of the first AIM people to suspect Douglass Durham was some sort of government agent was Anna Mae Aquash..." Weyler, *op. cit.*, pp. 167-68, observes that, "While she was working in the St. Paul AIM office during the Banks/Means trials an antagonism had developed between [Anna Mae] Aquash and AIM security officer Doug Durham. Durham's treatment of women seemed abusive to Aquash, and she was suspicious of his motives." In personal conversation with the authors, Nilak Butler, who also had first-hand knowledge, has said, "I never really thought much about Doug Durham being a cop. But he beat his woman [Jancita Eagle Deer], and that was enough for me." WKLDOC researchers Candy Hamilton and Paula Geise both agree that Durham physically abused Eagle Deer and Dennis Banks has somewhat ruefully admitted he was aware that his aide was "a total sexist pig," but that nothing was done about it by the AIM leadership.

60. Weyler, *op. cit.*, p. 169.

61. *Ibid.*

62. Brand, *op. cit.*, p. 103.

63. This was the point at which Durham misrepresented himself in court as an "Iowa psychologist" during the Skyhorse/Mohawk case (see Chapter 7).

64. "Portrait of an Informer," *op. cit.*, p. 18.

65. *Ibid.*

66. *Ibid.*

67. Candy Hamilton interview, *op. cit.*; Hamilton says that although she has no proof which would stand up in court, she believes Eagle Deer was killed as a means of covering up the nature and extent of FBI involvement in orchestrating the Janklow rape controversy. She also believes Eagle Deer may have become aware of other actions Durham undertook as a *provocateur* and thus was "even more of a threat to the Bureau than we thought at the time." She says she's uncertain whether Durham himself actually killed Eagle Deer, but that "it would certainly not have been out of character. He was a real nasty man, any way you look at it."

68. These comments derive from the anonymous source quoted earlier in this chapter.

69. Interview with Vivian Locust, Denver, Colo., July 1987; notes on file.

Chapter 9

1. Memorandum, SAC, Minneapolis (Joseph Trimbach) to Director, FBI, dated June 3, 1975 and captioned "Law Enforcement on the Pine Ridge Indian Reservation"; the memo was actually prepared by three unidentified Bureau inspectors.

2. Quoted in Matthiessen, *op. cit.*, p. 145.

3. Quoted from unpublished manuscript prepared by WKLDOC researcher Candy Hamilton; copy on file.

4. "Law Enforcement on the Pine Ridge Indian Reservation," *op. cit.*

5. *Ibid.*

6. Matthiessen, *op. cit.*, p. 156.

7. Recap of the precise charges was provided by Bruce Ellison, WKLDOC attorney.

8. Matthiessen, *op. cit.*, 173; the whites were Jerry Schwarting (age 23) and Robert Dinsmore (age 14).

9. *Ibid.*, p. 212; "When early reports that the agents had been carrying a warrant on the [25th and] twenty-sixth turned out to be untrue, the Bureau explained that agents were not required to carry warrants in order to make arrests so long as they knew that a warrant was outstanding." That personnel in the field believed that a warrant for Eagle existed seems beyond doubt; the document is mentioned in the 302 Report of SA Gerard Waring on June 26, 1975, as well as a memo by BIA police officer Glenn Littlebird, Sr., on the same date. However, when the warrant for Eagle was finally produced, it was for robbery *only* and dated July 9, 1975, two weeks *after* Coler and Williams were killed while allegedly trying to serve it.

10. *Ibid.*, p. 156.

11. *Ibid.*

12. Discussion with Richard B. "Rick" Williams, October 11, 1986.

13. The time-frame is established by noting that Coler and Williams were present at the BIA police headquarters in Pine Ridge, where they met with SAs Dean Hughes (head of the FBI SWAT Team on the reservation) and David Price at 11 a.m. This is according to 302 Reports submitted by both Hughes and

Price for June 26, 1975. The FBI radio logs for that date reveal Williams transmitting from inside the Jumping Bull property at 11:45 a.m.

14. A 302 Report is the account an FBI agent is required to write up concerning any significant event in which he participates while on duty. 302s are typically more candid and often more complete than Bureau documents prepared for circulation. They are, however, as subject to modification, revision, rewriting and fabrication (for use as evidence) as any other FBI document.

15. The paraphrase of Angie Long Visitor's statement comes from Matthiessen, *op. cit.*, p. 157.

16. As Matthiessen, *op. cit.*, observes at p. 186, both agents were dressed casually. Jack Coler was wearing a "green shirt and white T-shirt, red-belted tan jeans, white socks, [and] tan moccasins." Ron Williams was wearing a white sport shirt, "blue-checkered slacks, black socks, and red-brown loafers." This attire, in combination with their unmarked cars might well have made them initially appear to be civilian gunmen rather than FBI agents.

17. Quoted in *ibid.*, pp. 157-58.

18. Quoted in *ibid.*, p. 558.

19. Quoted in *ibid.*, pp. 558-59.

20. The reconstruction of Williams' transmission is from the 302 Report filed by SA J. Gary Adams on June 26, 1975.

21. Matthiessen, *op. cit.*, p. 158.

22. Quoted in *ibid.*, p. 159.

23. *Ibid.*, p. 194; Bear Runner's estimates of the numbers of police personnel involved were confirmed in the *New York Times* on June 27, 1975.

24. Bear Runner's account is capsulized in Matthiessen, *op. cit.*, p. 194; author Richard Erdoes, who did much to publicize what was happening on Pine Ridge, recalls receiving a frantic phone call from Gladys Bissonette on the morning of June 26 (that is, *before* the firefight) concerning a federal "invasion" of the reservation.

25. *Ibid.*, pp. 557-58.

26. Butler's and Robideau's statements are quoted in *ibid.*, pp. 558-59; Robideau's view has also been obtained by the authors in personal conversation.

27. Price's estimate is cited in Matthiessen, *op. cit.*, p. 485; it is noted that an FBI suspect list dated July 23, 1975 contained 29 names, *excluding* those of Wish Draper and Norman Brown (who were there, and who participated in the shooting).

28. The names gleaned from *ibid.*, pp. 483-85; it should be noted that several of the names—such as those of Herman and Homer Thunder Hawk—probably do not belong on the lists the FBI compiled. Joe Stuntz Killsright's last two names should be reversed; however, Leonard Peltier states that Joe would wish to be remembered by his Indian name.

29. Coler's arm wound is described in Matthiessen, *op. cit.*, p. 186; the massive tissue loss led to bleeding and shock which would have proven quickly fatal, even with a tourniquet applied by Williams, without prompt and proper medical attention.

30. These derivations of the FBI radio log accrue from an interview conducted with Linda Price, an FBI stenographer charged with recording Williams' transmissions as they came in on June 26, 1975. The interview was conducted at the Rapid City FBI office on June 27, by SA George O'Clock and unidentified agents. The statements she attributes to Williams correspond very well to the frantic appeals for help addressed by Major Marcus Reno to Captain Frederick Benteen during the battle of the Little Big Horn almost exactly a century earlier (see Chapter 4).

31. 302 Report of SA (name deleted), filed June 30, 1975 (MP70-10289).

32. Stoldt's statement, as recorded by the interviewer, is unpublished but is filed at the office of attorney Bruce Ellison in Rapid City, S.D. Stoldt, who quit his BIA SWAT job immediately after the firefight on July 2, 1975, and relocated to Denver, also insists that the order to "pull back" his SWAT Team "came directly from Del Eastman," who reported *directly* to SA J. Gary Adams on the day in question; Matthiessen, *op. cit.*, pp. 554-57.

33. Matthiessen, *op. cit.*, p. 160.

34. Letter from Bob Robideau to WKLDOC attorney Jack Schwartz, June 11, 1976.

35. Janklow was in Hot Springs that day, trying Dennis Banks in the Custer Courthouse case. Upon receiving news of the firefight, he raised a "posse" which was ready to go on such short notice that it lends additional credence to the notion that forces had been pre-positioned for this purpose. The whole group then made the approximate 30 minute (high speed) drive to Oglala. Clearly, not a minute was wasted in bringing these vigilantes to bear. A June 26, 1975 Rapid City FBI office Radio Log entry

(transcribed 7/16/75; transcriber's initials, "m.j.r") mentions the arrival of the Janklow group and that they were "armed with M-16s."

36. At p. 161, Matthiessen, *op. cit.*, names the final rear guard as being composed of Joe Stuntz Killsright and Norman Charles, who were covering the retreat of Leonard Peltier, Bob Robideau and Dino Butler. Together, these five would have been the initial rear guard group encountered by LeDeaux.

37. Quoted in *ibid.*, p. 183.

38. *Ibid.*, p. 185.

39. *Ibid.*, p. 186.

40. *Ibid.* Also see the 302 Report of SA Dean Hughes for June 26, 1975.

41. Transcript quoted in *ibid.*, pp. 189-90.

42. *Ibid.*, p. 190. As he had in the case of Frank Clearwater (see Chapter 5), Dick Wilson attempted to block Killsright's burial on Pine Ridge. In this case, he was simply overridden by AIM and the ION; see "Wake service begins for slain Indian," *Rapid City Journal*, July 2, 1975, p. 1. (Killsright was buried near the Jumping Bull property; Anna Mae Aquash was later buried alongside him.) Agents Coler and Williams were removed for burial elsewhere; see "Slain FBI agents buried in California," *Rapid City Journal*, July 2, 1975, p. 1.

43. The "long-range shot" has been variously attributed to SA Gerard Waring, and to BIA police officer Gerald Hill. In either event, it supposedly was fired at approximately 3 p.m. from a group which had worked its way along the creek for some distance, and which included Waring and Hill, as well as SA Dean Hughes, SA David Price, BIA police/GOON chief Delmar Eastman and six other BIA police officers; Matthiessen, *op. cit.*, p. 183.

44. Quoted in *ibid.*, p. 199.

45. *Ibid.*, p. 200. McKiernan also told this story to author Churchill in San Francisco during September of 1982. McKiernan stated that it looked as if Killsright's body had been "dragged over and dumped in a mud puddle"; this correlates well with Roselyn Jumping Bull's contention—expressed to Bruce Ellison—that Killsright's body had been moved several yards from a "big pool of blood" where she believed he had been killed.

46. Matthiessen, *op. cit.*, p. 199. Bruce Ellison is in possession of a full-face picture of Killsright's body taken by an FBI photographer some time after McKiernan's photos were taken; the FBI photo reveals the forehead shot which appears absent in the McKiernan pictures. In the FBI photo, Killsright's head wound is remarkably clean, indicating it had either been cleaned of gore for the occasion, or that it had been administered after the victim had died and blood had drained from the body. No official medical estimation of the range at which the head shot was fired has ever been forthcoming, insofar as no autopsy was performed; Killsright's body was handled by W.O. Brown, the FBI-retained Nebraska pathologist who performed suspect autopsies on Pedro Bissonette and Anna Mae Aquash (see Chapter 7).

47. *Ibid.*, p. 187. According to the Radio Log of the Rapid City FBI office for June 26, 1975 (pp. 23-24) "MP-1 [SAC Joseph Trimbach]" and his SWAT team were en route from Minneapolis almost as soon as the firing began. A memo, caption deleted, from B.H. Cooke to Mr. Gebhart at FBIHQ on the following day indicates proudly that the Minneapolis SWAT team was on-site at Oglala, under command of SA David Price "by 4:25 p.m." on the 26th. Page 24 of the Log indicates that high explosive rounds for M-79 grenade launchers were also being flown in from the Marine base at Quantico, Va. to Ellsworth Air Force Base by Marine jet during the same afternoon. The speed with which these long-distance maneuvers were executed strongly suggests that the FBI anticipated the firefight, as well as its timing and location.

48. Quoted in *ibid.*, p. 549.

49. Author Churchill experienced one of these sweeps firsthand when, while driving across Pine Ridge on June 27, 1975, he stopped to urinate alongside the road, about five miles south of Porcupine. Over the ridge came an APC, accompanied by some 20 FBI and BIA police personnel, moving "on line," carrying M-16s, and dressed in Vietnam-style jungle fatigues, boots and bush hats. Most of the group were also wearing military-issue flack-jackets. Needless to say, the whole scene afforded a sense of *deja vu* to the viewer, given that he had spent a year in Southeast Asia in combat.

50. Messerschmidt, *op. cit.*, p. 30.

51. Johansen and Maestes, *op. cit.*, p. 95. A June 27, 1975 internal memorandum from R.E. Gebhart to Mr. O'Connell at FBIHQ mentions that Richard G. Held, SAC Chicago, was contacted *in Minneapolis* at "12:30 a.m." on the morning of June 26, 1975. This clearly suggests that Held, who was slated to assume overall command of the FBI's Pine Ridge operations in the wake of the firefight, had been pre-positioned for this purpose. This, again, supports the thesis that provocation of a major incident on the

reservation was part of a clearly thought out Bureau strategy. Also see Worster, Terry, "FBI combing Pine Ridge," *Rapid City Journal*, June 28, 1975, p. 1.

52. Muldrow, William, *Monitoring of Events Related to the Shooting of Two FBI Agents on the Pine Ridge Indian Reservation* (Report to Ms. Shirley Hill Witt, Regional Director), U.S. Commission on Civil Rights, Rocky Mountain Regional Office, Denver, July 9, 1975.

53. U.S. Commission on Civil Rights, *Hearing Before the U.S. Commission on Civil Rights: Indian Issues in South Dakota* (Hearings held in Rapid City, South Dakota, July 27-28, 1978), U.S. Government Printing Office, Washington, D.C., 1978, p. 334.

54. Matthiessen, *op. cit.*, p. 195.

55. Johansen and Maestes, *op. cit.*, p. 96. The flavor of this comes through clearly in an article by Thomas E. Slaughter, titled "FBI establishing identity of suspects," *Rapid City Journal*, July 3, 1975, p. 1.

56. The reconstruction of dialogue is from a deposition taken from Cecelia Jumping Bull by the WKLDOC staff during July of 1975; the transcript is on file at the office of attorney Bruce Ellison in Rapid City.

57. Matthiessen, *op.cit.*, p. 203.

58. *Ibid.* WKLDOC attempted to halt the Bureau's search and destroy operation through legal action; see "Injunction to be filed for FBI removal," *Rapid City Journal*, July 9, 1975, p. 3.

59. *Ibid.*, p. 211; the petition was reported in *The New York Times*, June 30, 1975. For counterpoint from the area's non-Indian community, see the editorial titled "FBI is in middle of factional dispute," *Rapid City Journal*, July 6, 1975, p.3.

60. Matthiessen, *op. cit.* Also see "Lakota council approves resolution asking FBI removal," *Rapid City Journal*, July 14, 1975, p. 3.

61. Memorandum from SAC Minneapolis (Richard G. Held) to Director, FBI, dated July 2, 1975, and captioned THE THREAT TO DESTROY MOUNT RUSHMORE (DESTRUCTION OF GOVERNMENT PROPERTY); the memo was apparently prepared in response to a July 1 statement by AIM spokesperson Ted Means that the organization would conduct a peaceful march to Mount Rushmore on July 4, in honor of "our brother who died near Oglala [Killsright]." Author Churchill was at Mt. Rushmore on the day in question; the most "militant" or "dangerous" act observed on the part of relatively few Indian people who gathered there was a tobacco ceremony. The federal security personnel in the area, on the other hand, proved both belligerent and menacing. For an establishment press account of what actually transpired at Mt. Rushmore, see Slaughter, Thomas E., "Banks says whites on trial," *Rapid City Journal*, July 5, 1975, p. 3.

62. This July 5, 1975 incident, is recorded in Matthiessen, *op. cit.*, p. 205; no FBI personnel were injured, although the helicopter was seriously damaged. Also see "FAA to probe 'copter crash at Pine Ridge," *Rapid City Journal*, July 5, 1975, p. 3. The Bureau later unsuccessfully attempted to deny the cause of the helicopter crash; see "Shots did not hit 'copter says FBI," *Rapid City Journal*, July 8, 1975, p. 11. The 302 Report of SA (name deleted) on July 4, 1975, p. 2, is, however, unequivocal; he quotes the pilot of the $140,000 helicopter as exclaiming, "We're hit! They got us! We're going to crash land! Hold on!" This version is reinforced by a joint 302 Report of two Quantico-trained SWAT team members (names deleted), who were also aboard the helicopter; this document was also filed on July 4, 1975.

63. This response by the Church Committee, which was and remains somewhat illogical (did the deaths of two agents, under *whatever* circumstances, somehow suddenly make COINTELPRO an "okay proposition?"), may well have been exactly what the Bureau had in mind when provoking a firefight on June 26, 1975. One should not discount the bureaucratic savvy of the FBI's top leadership; once stalled, it is usually almost impossible to reinvigorate congressional investigations.

64. The incident is marginally recounted in Matthiessen, *op. cit.*, p. 211. The authors are otherwise familiar with the incident, and are aware that SA Price bore a personal animosity towards Black Crow, based upon the latter's exercising his right to physically evict the agent from his property the preceding winter. Price had come around, "claiming he was investigating a cow theft, without a warrant, and I threw him out," according to Black Crow. Also see "Wanblee man charges FBI with searching without warrant," *Rapid City Journal*, July 5, 1975, p. 1.

65. This is probably a conservative estimate, accruing from WKLDOC researcher Candy Hamilton, who attempted to keep track of such events—on a day by day basis—at the time.

66. U.S. House of Representatives, *Hearings Before the Subcommittee on Civil and Constitutional Rights of the Committee of the Judiciary, 97th Congress, First Session on FBI Authorization*, March 19, 24, 25; April 2 and 8, 1981, U.S. Government Printing Office, Washington, D.C., 1981.

67. FBI teletype, SAC, Rapid City, to Director, FBI, 8/2/75.

68. Quoted in Matthiessen, *op. cit.*, pp. 218-19.

69. *Ibid.*, p. 228.

70. Quoted in *ibid.*

71. Quoted in Weyler, *op. cit.*, p. 183.

72. Reconstruction of dialogue by Leonard Crow Dog on various occasions. A variation may be found in the film *Annie Mae: A Brave Hearted Woman*, directed by Lan Brookes Ritz, Brown Bird Productions, Los Angeles, 1979.

73. Quoted in Matthiessen, *op. cit.*, p. 233; the death threat is believed to be attributable to SA David Price.

74. Interview with Rick Williams, October 17, 1986; Williams, who was a member of the Lincoln (Nebraska) AIM chapter from 1972-75 presently resides in Broomfield, Colorado. Williams' view corresponds with topical assessments; see Gladstone, Lyn, "Feeling on reservation building for inquiry into FBI activities," *Rapid City Journal*, July 1, 1975, p. 1.

75. Quoted in Matthiessen, *op. cit.*, p. 427.

76. Interview with Dennis Banks, *op. cit.*

77. On the date of grand jury commencement, see Matthiessen, op. cit., p. 216; on its being convened at the specific request of Held and Clayton, see p. 210. Also see Kroese, Ron, "Material witness to testify on killings," *Rapid City Journal*, July 2, 1975, p. 1.

78. Matthiessen, *op. cit.*, p. 216.

79. Quoted in *ibid.*

80. Quoted in the *Rapid City Journal*, July 14, 1975; Matthiessen, op. cit., p. 216, observes that Bear Runner's subpoena had actually been served upon his elderly mother, rather than upon the intended witness himself, as required by law. Bear Runner ultimately paid dearly for his expression of Oglala sovereignty. In September 1975 his mother, Grace, was assaulted by a GOON named Charlie Winters and in October his brother, Dennis, was run off the road and beaten by GOONs near Porcupine. In November, Edgar himself was beaten in the Pine Ridge supermarket by Manny Wilson and two other GOONs. In January of 1976, he was seized by FBI agents who kicked in his door and held him for "questioning" after nearly freezing him to death on the ride from Porcupine to Rapid City. Finally, in February of 1977, he was arrested, convicted and sentenced to 1-5 years in the Nebraska State Penitentiary on the charge of "obstructing" a police officer who was pistol-whipping him on the street in Gordon; Matthiessen, *op. cit.*, p. 250.

81. *Ibid.*, the adding of Bear Runner's name to the suspect list was done on the instructions of SAC Richard G. Held, apparently as retaliation for the AIM member's public statements.

82. *Ibid.*

83. By law, witnesses subpoenaed by a grand jury must appear without benefit of counsel. Normal Fifth Amendment protections do not pertain. Failure to "cooperate" with this travesty of justice is arbitrarily punishable by incarceration for the duration of the jury's impanelment (*i.e.*, as long as 18 months). Worse, the reluctant witness, upon release from jail or prison, can then simply be re-subpoenaed, starting the whole procedure over again. In principle, an individual could serve a *de facto* life sentence under such circumstances without ever being "entitled" to his/her due process of a trial. Should the federal prosecutor decide to indict the witness on a charge of "criminal contempt," the defendant could, after a minimal trial (Did she/he refuse to testify? Yes. Guilty as charged!) receive an *actual* life sentence. This is not simply a theoretical danger. In April of 1981, five members of the *Movimiento de Liberación Nacional* (MLN), María Cueto, Steven Guerra, Ricardo Romero, Julio Rosado and Andrés Rosado, were subpoenaed, charged with criminal contempt for refusal to testify, and sentenced to three years imprisonment. The prosecutor in the case moved for life imprisonment.

84. Quoted in Matthiessen, *op. cit.*, p. 217.

85. LeDeaux later stated that, "I had no objection to participating in a process to see justice done. But what was going on had nothing whatsoever to do with justice. It had to do with politics, a witchhunt worse than anything ever done by Joseph McCarthy. I didn't want to go to jail, of course. But I *couldn't cooperate in any way with what the FBI was doing.*" (LeDeaux, Joanna, "Personal Statement," unpublished, written during the summer of 1976; on file.)

86. Matthiessen, *op. cit.*, p. 216.

87. "STATEMENT OF SUPPORT FOR ANGIE LONG VISITOR FROM CANTE OHITIKA WIN," Oglala, S.D., January 21, 1977, p. 1: "It is unthinkable for the U.S. government to hold Angie in jail away from her home, her job and her three children."

88. Attachment to FBI interview transcription, re: ANGIE LONGVISITOR [sic], dated June 27, 1975 (thought to have been compiled by SA David Price; No. MP 70-10239).

89. *Ibid.*

90. Matthiessen, *op. cit.*, p. 485.

91. The date is fixed in *ibid.*, p. 217.

92. "STATEMENT OF SUPPORT FOR ANGIE LONG VISITOR FROM CANTE OHITIKA WIN," *op. cit.*

93. "Motion to Review Conditions of Release and Petition for Extraordinary Remedies in the Matter of Angie Long Visitor, Material Witness," (Number 77-1080, submitted to the United States Eighth Circuit Court of Appeals, January 27, 1977, by Jaqueline Quick, Tilsen and Quick, Attorneys, counsel to the plaintiff, p. 3): "She [Angie Long Visitor] has appeared repeatedly at various judicial proceedings involving her possible testimony in this matter, including the Grand Jury, without arrest or bail." See also "STATEMENT OF SUPPORT FOR ANGIE LONG VISITOR FROM CANTE OHITIKA WIN," *op. cit.*: "...she [Angie Long Visitor] has honored more than six subpoenas for court appearances in connection with the June 26, 1975, incident in Oglala, S.D."

94. AFFIDAVIT FOR DETENTION OF ANGIE LONG VISITOR AS A MATERIAL WITNESS, in the matter of *United States of America v. Leonard Peltier*, CR-75-5106-1, signed by Norman Zigrossi and dated January 17, 1977.

95. *Ibid.*: "Extensive efforts were made on two occasions by the FBI to serve her with subpoenas in case No. CR 76-11 [*United States v. Darelle Dean Butler and Robert Eugene Robideau*, N.D. Ia]...and all such efforts were unsuccessful."

96. All indications are that, although Angie Long Visitor's name indeed appeared on the prosecution's witness list for the Cedar Rapids trial, it was decided that her testimony would not be helpful (about all she could be counted upon to say was that both defendants had been present on the Jumping Bull property at the outset of the June 26 firefight, and that Robideau had fired—long range—at police; these were matters already agreed to by the defense.) Hence, there is a great likelihood that the FBI never attempted subpoena service in this matter; as is noted in the January 27, 1977 motion to the U.S. 8th Circuit, noted above, Jaqueline Quick observes (p. 1) simply that: "There is... no indication that Petitioner [Angie Long Visitor] was aware of the existence of the subpoena in question," and could thus hardly be accused—in any rational sense—of having sought to avoid its service.

97. ORDER OF ARREST AND DETENTION OF ANGIE LONG VISITOR PENDING POSTING BOND in the matter of *United States of America v. Leonard Peltier*, No. CR-5106-1, dated Jan. 17, 1977, and signed by Paul Benson, Judge, United States District Court, District of North Dakota, posits that Long Visitor "is a material witness in the above proceedings." The relevant statute in this matter is 18 U.S.C. § 3149: "If it appears by affidavit that the testimony of a person is material in any criminal proceeding, and if it is shown that it may become impractical to secure his [sic] presence by subpena [sic], a judicial officer shall impose conditions of [arrest and] release [such that appearance is insured]." However, as Jaqueline Quick notes in her January 27, 1977, motion to the 8th Circuit, Zigrossi's own records of Long Visitor's possible testimony in the Peltier trial showed plainly that "she was present near the crime scene, saw there individuals shooting, none of them the defendant" (p. 5). Thus, the Bureau knew that Angie Long Visitor was *not* a material witness when it caused a material witness warrant to be issued for her arrest and detention; similarly, Judge Benson failed to meet *any* test of proof before issuing his order in this regard.

98. The account of the FBI raid on the He Crow residence derives from depositions of witnesses (notably Deana He Crow, Ernest Lame, Vincent Two Lances, Floyd Hernandez and Ben Little) compiled by WKLDOC researcher Candy Hamilton on January 18-19, 1977, and filed with William Muldrow of the Rocky Mountain Regional Office of the U.S. Commission on Civil Rights (Denver) on January 28.

99. The amount of $10,000 was penciled into the blank for bail specification on Paul Benson's earlier signed arrest warrant; the figure was apparently arrived at via a telephone conversation between U.S. Magistrate James Wilson and Benson (who was in Bismarck at the time) without benefit of a hearing.

100. 18 U.S.C. § 3149 clearly states that "No material witness shall be detained because of inability to comply with any condition of release if the testimony of such witness can adequately be secured by deposition, and further detention is not necessary to prevent a failure of justice." Given that Angie Long Visitor's statements concerning the events of June 26, 1975, had been recorded by federal authorities on at least seven occasions, six of them under oath (*i.e.*, meeting the burden of a deposition), a hearing to allow her to achieve a level of bail which she could meet was *clearly* required by law. This would be true, even if her anticipated testimony could reasonably have been considered as that of a *material* witness in the Peltier case, which—as was noted above—it could not. The denial of her rights to a phone call after arrest, and to adequate legal counsel tend to speak for themselves.

101. "Appeal from Order Setting Conditions of Release in the Matter of Angie Long Visitor, Material Witness, Pursuant to 18 U.S.C. § 3147, (b)(2)," submitted to the United States Court of Appeals for the Eighth Circuit by Kenneth E. Tilsen, counsel for the plaintiff, January 19, 1977, p. 3.

102. Matthiessen, *op. cit.*, p. 339.

103. Quoted in *ibid.*, p. 338.

104. Conversation with Theda Nelson, Oglala, S.D., May, 1986.

Chapter 10

1. With regard to NTCA being a federally funded organization, Robert Burnette notes (Burnette and Koster, *op. cit.*, p. 217) that, "The National Congress of American Indians, the nation's oldest and most respected Indian lobby, charged that the Secretary of the Interior, the Bureau of Land Management and the National Council on Indian Opportunity had worked clandestinely to muster elected tribal officials to support the [Nixon] administration. The NCAI charges would surprise no one who knew the national headquarters of the NTCA were in the executive offices of the president and that the puppet chairmen were receiving fifty thousand dollars in federal funding per meeting."

2. Quoted in *ibid.;* Burnette goes on to observe that, "A great many right-wing groups seized on Two Hawk's statements and presented him to an unknowing public as a responsible Indian leader." FBI infiltrator/provocateur Douglass Durham also introduced the NTCA position articulated by Two Hawk to "prove" AIM lacked Indian support during his 1976 subcommittee testimony; see U.S. Senate, Committee on the Judiciary, Subcommittee on Internal Security, *Revolutionary Activities Within the United States: American Indian Movement*, 94th Congress, 2nd Session, U.S. Government Printing Office, Washington, D.C., 1976, p. 4.

3. Sometimes the media methods used went from the vicious to the sublime. For instance, an ad placed in the *Navajo Times* on November 28, 1972 reads: "Why not get off the 'Trail of Broken Treaties' and get on the trail that leads to peace, joy, happiness and heaven. Why walk the 'Trail of Broken Treaties' any longer? When you can have something better now and for eternity." The language is attributed to Reverend Roger Glenn Davis of the Newcomb (N.M.) Assembly of God.

4. See the Evans-Novak column distributed by the Publishers-Hall Syndicate on November 27, 1972 in which the authors demand that the government take a tougher stand with regard to "Indian excesses," helping to temper public sentiment for the repression which was shortly to follow. Also see Kinsolving, Reverend Lester, "Inside Indian Religion: Indian Vandal Aid Denounced," run in 31 papers nationally on the same date and the editorial by Bobbie Greene Kilberg—a former staff member in the Nixon White House under John Erhlichman—run in the *Washington Post* on December 2, 1972, among *many* others.

5. Hempstone, Smith, (associate editor), *Washington (D.C.) Star-News*, November 27, 1972.

6. Quoted in *BIA, I'm Not Your Indian Anymore*, p. 37.

7. Burnette and Koster, *op. cit.*, pp. 269-70.

8. *Ibid.*, p. 270. It is interesting to note that Two Hawk was shortly awarded a professorship in American Indian Studies at the University of South Dakota in Vermillion, where he is presently tenured and still teaching—Indians and non-Indians alike—the "realities" of how Indians view the world. The situation is anything but uncommon within the arena of "objective" academic scholarship today.

9. Once again, the technique was borrowed directly from the military practice in Vietnam, where the daily military press conferences, replacing journalistic access to the sites of events, were so steadily misleading as to be dubbed "The Five O'Clock Follies." See Herr, Michael, *Dispatches*, Discus Books, New York, 1980, pp. 228-38.

10. Burnette and Koster, *op. cit.*, p. 258.

11. The Associated Press story, carried on the wire on February 28, 1975, quoted only Wilson and BIA administrative manager Wayne Adkinson (a Wilson adherent). According to Wilson, "What I can gather, mostly through rumor, is that it was a group of AIM people led by Russell Means. They shot at the airplane and a couple of our vehicles, and then headed east." The *Rapid City Journal*, on the same date, quoted Adkinson as stating that Delmar Eastman's BIA police were stymied in the matter: "[S]ince we have no data, we can't blame anyone." None of this, of course, explains why Wilson pled himself guilty in tribal court in order to avoid federal prosecution over precisely the same incident which he attempted to blame on Means, or who coached him to pursue such an astute legal strategy.

12. Weyler, *op. cit.*, p. 169.

13. Matthiessen, *op. cit.*, p. 113.

14. *Ibid.*

15. Weyler, *op. cit.*, p. 168; Carradine was not at home on the evening in question.

16. This is a reconstruction, based upon known Bureau methods of "becoming involved" in a local police investigation, its agenda *vis a vis* AIM at the time, the major scenario before the fact and the eventual evolution of the case. Skyhorse and Mohawk had co-founded the Illinois chapter of AIM during January of 1973 and were thus long-time "notables" to the FBI.

17. As Matthiessen, *op. cit.*, observes on pp. 115-16, the placement of Aird's body in proximity to the sign virtually guaranteed that, a) the note and "scalp" would be immediately discovered by police after they received the anonymous tip, and b) the AIM acronym would be prominently displayed in all crime-scene photos run in the press and/or introduced at trial.

18. Weyler, *op. cit.*, pp. 168-69, notes that Skyhorse and Mohawk had been taken to a rally in Los Angeles for Sarah Bad Heart Bull by a local AIM member called Blue Dove. Matthiessen, *op. cit.*, p. 115, states that Tempe (Ariz.) police were in possession of identifying photos of the AIM leaders taken at the same rally by Blue Dove.

19. See, for example, the headlines and accounts in the *Los Angeles Times*, on October 12 and 13, 1975 and again on October 18-21, 1975 (*e.g.:* AIM LEADERS ACCUSED IN RITUAL SLAYING OF CAB DRIVER; October 18). For a fuller view of the impact of the "scalp" and the "AIM connection" on press coverage of the case, see Kanter, *op. cit.*, p. 16, as well as the account in *The Nation*, December 24, 1977. The disinformation campaign also had its effect on the left; see "FBI pins brutal slaying on AIM," *The Guardian*, December 1, 1974, p. 4.

20. Banks' recollections of this are contained in Matthiessen, *op. cit.*, p. 114.

21. *Ibid.*, p. 113: "Although AIM (which took it over after Wounded Knee from a Chumash shaman named Paul 'Semu' Huaute) had intended [Camp 13] as a wooded retreat for spiritual ceremonies and renewal, it soon attracted a fallout of non-Indians (some of them from the Hollywood community) addicted to strong drink, drugs, and *kinky violence*. Because of its bad reputation, the Movement withdrew support from Camp 13...[emphasis added]."

22. *Ibid.*

23. *Ibid.*, pp. 115-16.

24. Weyler, *op. cit.*, p. 169, suggests the "scalp" was actually just a lock of hair. See Matthiessen, *op. cit.*, p. 113, concerning funds. This is not to argue that Durham, DeLuse, or anyone else affiliated with the FBI actually staged Aird's murder as a means of discrediting AIM. To the contrary, as is noted by Brand, *op. cit.*, p. 107, there is evidence that "Los Angeles area police had some pre-existing plan to raid the camp." It is likely that the Bureau was in the process of orchestrating some rather less gruesome "event" to discredit AIM when the Aird murder occurred. From there, the Bureau and their operatives seem to have simply availed themselves of a sterling opportunity. Infiltrator Durham, in his Senate subcommittee testimony (p. 7) contends that the original "arrangements for renting this camp were made by George Roberts." Roberts is a suspected CIA infiltrator.

25. See Weyler, *op. cit.*, p. 169.

26. Not only WKLDOC declined to represent Skyhorse and Mohawk. In February of 1981, Los Angeles ACLU attorney Mark Rosenbaum recalled how he, too, would not defend the pair because of AIM's refusal to do so.

27. Matthiessen, *op. cit.*, pp. 113-14, observes that these "blood spattered people" were granted bail and set free in exchange for their testimony while, as Weyler, *op. cit.*, p. 169, notes, Skyhorse and Mohawk "languished in jail."

28. Quoted in Matthiessen, *op. cit.*, p. 115.

29. See Weyler, *op. cit.*, p. 171.

30. Quoted in Matthiessen, *op. cit.*, p. 116; "After Redshirt's collapse on the witness stand, the discouraged prosecution offered a plea bargain based on the two and a half years that the defendants had already spent in prison [without being convicted of *anything*]. Although the deal was acceptable to the defendants [who had—for obvious reasons—little faith in the judicial process, and simply wanted *out* of their cages], it was prohibited by Judge Floyd Dodson, *who appeared eager to prolong this trial as long as possible*, the trial wandered on for another ten months [with Skyhorse and Mohawk locked up the whole time] before the whole travesty came to an end [emphasis added]."

31. Far from being punished for his admitted leading role in butchering George Aird, Marvin Redshirt was provided a federal subsidy to attend college in South Dakota shortly after commencing his California probation (a remarkable similarity to the treatment of FBI infiltrator Julius C. Butler in the Pratt case; see Chapter 3). As Matthiessen, *op. cit.*, notes at p. 116, however, "in 1978, his college career was

interrupted in his hometown of Hot Springs, South Dakota, when he was charged in the near-fatal stabbing of his Box Canyon consort, Holly Broussard." Redshirt was subsequently convicted of attempted murder and was incarcerated in the South Dakota State Penitentiary at Sioux Falls until mid-1987. He now resides in Denver, Colorado.

32. Quoted in Weyler, *op. cit.*, p. 172.

33. Matthiessen, *op. cit.*, p. 115.

34. This assessment of the purpose of the Skyhorse/Mohawk case, goes far towards undercutting the more liberal view, articulated by Hank di Suvero, former president of the National Lawyers Guild, that: "In a fundamental way, the acquittals [of Skyhorse and Mohawk] demonstrated that a basically unfair and repressive judicial system can be overcome when there is popular support and resistance and thorough legal work." (Quoted in Weyler, *op. cit.*, p. 172). This outlook inherently assumes that the FBI's objective was to obtain convictions which it most probably was not.

35. Matthiessen, *op. cit.*, p. 114. Weyler, *op. cit.*, at p. 171, cites the California hearing transcript to the effect that Durham portrayed himself as "an Indian professor of clinical psychology at the University of Iowa."

36. Interview with Laura Kadenahe, Big Mountain, Ariz., March 16, 1984; tape on file. Kadenahe's assessment corresponds to that of the broader movement; see "Skyhorse/Mohawk Acquitted," *Akwesasne Notes,* Mohawk Nation via Rooseveltown, N.Y., Late Spring, 1978, p. 22.

37. Statement of Leonard Weinglass, University of California at Berkeley, August 19, 1977.

38. Matthiessen, *op. cit.*, pp. 195-96.

39. Janklow's last set of statements, made in a radio interview on June 29, 1975, are quoted by Weisman, Joel D., "About that 'ambush' at Wounded Knee," *Columbia Journalism Review,* September/October 1975, pp. 28-31.

40. See, for example, the relevant story and headlines (or lack of the same) in the *Los Angeles Times* on July 1, 1975. Perhaps the reporter was late in filing his full copy. In the *Rapid City Journal,* the story—"Kelly clarifies death situation"—was run on p. 1 on July 2, but says nothing at all about the retraction of the "ambush theory," the absence of bunkers at the firefight scene, *etc.*

41. Quoted in Matthiessen, *op. cit.*, p. 199. The FBI's initial lies, despite being dropped by the Bureau, had taken on a certain life of their own. In late July of 1975, the *Washington Observer Newsletter*—house organ of the ultra-conservative Liberty Lobby—released a story which not only regurgitated all the FBI-generated nonsense about bunkers and ambushes and executioners, but added the fabrication (reportedly provided by a Bureau source) that the two dead agents had been scalped, an idea which may later have played into the Bureau's handling of media with regard to the Skyhorse/Mohawk case. Trudell's viewpoint received a bit of exposure at the time in an article by *Rapid City Journal* reporter Ron Kroese, titled "AIM doesn't apologize for two dead agents" and published on June 30, 1975. Other AIM leaders concurred—see "[Stan] Holder blames government for killings," *Rapid City Journal,* June 27, 1975, p. 3—but were largely frozen out of print. The FBI's original story continues to be parroted by cooperative propogandists to this day. See, for example, Dershowitz, Alan, "Can Leonard Peltier be the Andrei Sakharov of America?" The *Denver Post,* October 21, 1984. The nationally syndicated column ran in many newspapers under various titles on that date.

42. Weyler, *op. cit.*, p. 180.

43. Weisman, *op. cit.*

44. U.S. Commission on Civil Rights, *Monitoring of Events Related to the Shootings of Two FBI Agents on the Pine Ridge Reservation,* U.S. Commission on Civil Rights, Mountain States Regional Office, Denver, Co., July 9, 1975.

45. The Senate Subcommittee on Internal Security was the heir apparent to the House UnAmerican Activities Committee (HUAC) which gained notoriety during the McCarthy era (see Chapter 1). The Senate variant was disbanded in early 1977, shortly after the report at issue herein was released. Such solo testimony before the subcommittee was not without precedent. For example, in 1969, Senator Eastland and two colleagues allowed FBI Director J. Edgar Hoover to testify secretly and alone as to the supposed conspiracy headed by Fathers Daniel and Philip Berrigan, to blow up the storm drain system in Washington, D.C. and kidnap Henry Kissinger. The result of this was an increase in FBI appropriations for 1970 and the arrest/incarceration of "the Berrigan gang," but *no* substantiable crimes; see Nelson and Ostrow, *op. cit.*

46. Matthiessen, *op. cit.*, p. 324.

47. Quoted in Brand, *op. cit.*, pp. 108-109.

48. U.S. Senate, Committee on the Judiciary, Subcommittee on Internal Security, *Revolutionary Activities Within the United States: American Indian Movement, op. cit.* It should be noted that this report was introduced by U.S. government prosecutor R.D. Hurd into the sentence reduction hearing of Leonard Crow Dog, as a showing of "cause" why the AIM spiritual leader should be dealt with harshly (see Chapter 12). It was also introduced by representatives of the Justice Department in the Canadian extradition hearings of Leonard Peltier, this time to show "cause" as to why Peltier, as an AIM member, should be returned to U.S. jurisdiction (see Chapter 11).

49. *Ibid.,* p. 67.

50. *Ibid.,* pp. 68-69.

51. *Ibid.,* pp. 67-68.

52. *Ibid.,* p. 76.

53. *Ibid.,* p. 45; at p. 14, Durham makes much of a letter to Dennis Banks from *New Times* magazine correspondent I. Andronov, in 1973, which begins with the customary greeting, "Dear Friends."

54. *Ibid.,* p. 49. at p. 7, Durham observes that Canadian AIM leader "Ed Bernstick [sic, Burnstick]" met with "the Provisional Revolutionary Government of Vietnam to celebrate their common victory over imperialism and the United States Government" (substantiated by a clipping from the May 25, 1975 edition of the *Berkeley Barb*).

55. *Ibid.,* p. 63.

56. *Ibid.,* p. 71.

57. *Ibid.,* p. 59.

58. *Ibid.,* p. 73; at p. 12, Durham posits Vietnam Veterans Against the War as being an organization "ideologically aligned" with AIM.

59. *Ibid.,* p. 77.

60. U.S. Senate, Committee on the Judiciary, Subcommittee on Internal Security, *The Assault on Freedom: A Compendium of Theoretical and Policy Statements by the Communist Movement, Domestic and International, and by Other Organizations Committed to the Violent Overthrow of Free Institutions,* 92nd Congress, 1st Session, U.S. Government Printing Office, Washington, D.C., 1971, p. 101; quoted in *ibid.,* p. 2.

61. See Newton, Huey P., *To Die For the People, op. cit.* Author Churchill had occasion to meet with Assata Shakur in Havana, where she had been living as a political refugee for some time, during December of 1984. Her whereabouts have now become public knowledge with the publication of *Assata: An Autobiography,* Lawrence Hill, Westport, Conn., 1987.

62. *Revolutionary Activities in the United States: The American Indian Movement, op. cit.,* pp. 38-39; Durham also pointed to paychecks issued to Cheryl Petite under her maiden name (DeCora) and "exorbitant phone bills" as examples of misappropriation; on p. 40, he complains about checks written to Community Concerns—a local Des Moines non-profit agency—for rental of the AIM/OEO office; on p. 41, he suddenly corrects himself, noting that the amount of the OEO grant in question was $4,060, rather than the "$12,000" amount upon which he was basing his contention of misappropriation.

63. *Ibid.,* pp. 64-65.

64. Quoted in Weyler, *op. cit.,* p. 170.

65. Quoted in Matthiessen, *op. cit.,* p. 244.

66. Quoted in *ibid.*

67. This was witnessed by a number of AIM people, among them Bill Means, during the spring, summer and fall of 1975.

68. See Weyler, *op. cit.,* p. 172.

69. FBI report titled "The American Indian Movement," no specific date, 1976.

70. The memo, captioned "Internal Security" and file numbered 281785Z, had actually been prepared in May 1975, but was apparently held for release at an opportune moment. It read, in part: "Rudolfo 'Corky' Gonzales, a leader of the Brown Berets, reportedly has a rocket launcher and rockets either in his possession or available to him along with explosives, hand grenades and ten to fifteen M-16 rifles with banana clips." It should be noted that Gonzales was never a leader of the Brown Berets, a southern California organization which, like Students for a Democratic Society (SDS; mentioned in the teletype as participating with Gonzales in the plan to put these weapons to use), had been defunct for years at the time of the Bureau's writing. Gonzales' actual organization, the Crusade for Justice, was a different radical Chicano group, Denver-based.

71. Quoted in Matthiessen, *op. cit.,* p. 310.

72. *Ibid.*

73. FBI teletype 281785Z, *op. cit.*

74. Matthiessen, *op. cit.*

75. Quoted in *ibid.*, pp. 288-89.

76. See Taylor and Van Houten, *op. cit.*

77. *United States v. Butler and Robideau*, CR76-11 N.D. Ia., July 7, 1976, Appendix A, p. 3. Director Kelley's testimony in this regard hardly squares with a Bureau memorandum, dated March 3, 1975 and captioned "Predication for Investigation of Members and Supporters of AIM," which states in part: "This investigation is based on information that the subject is engaged in activities which could involve a violation of title 19, U.S. Code, Section 2383 (Rebellion and Insurrection) or 2384 (Seditious Conspiracy)...AIM has been actively involved in demonstrations and violent confrontations with local authorities..." This is *precisely* the same language used in an earlier FBI memo justifying the Bureau's involvement in the case of Geronimo Pratt on state murder charges (see Chapter 3); the BPP, of which Pratt was a leader, was expressly "tabbed" by the Bureau as being *all* the things Kelley denied as applying to AIM. A second FBI Memorandum, Director, FBI, to SAC, Minneapolis, dated August 19, 1975 and captioned "RESMURS Investigation", cites "the possibility of additional A.I.M. inspired violence in the future" and stipulates that "all indications of the accumulation of weapons and explosives, 'hit teams' or similar groups, or the existence of safe houses and hideouts must be promptly resolved." The Director also failed to explain why, if the FBI viewed AIM as being such an upstanding organization, the Bureau was—at the very time of his testimony—carrying an "expose" of AIM in its *Domestic Terrorist Digest* (June 18, 1975 edition), distributed to police agencies across the country.

78. Weyler, *op. cit.*, p. 198.

79. Matthiessen, *op. cit.*, p. 109; the author notes that, by the first week of July, the FBI was providing "intelligence information to Pennington County (South Dakota) Sheriff Mel Larson, and that Larson had responded by "beefing up" security in the Rapid City area and cancelling all leaves for his men, despite—by his own admission—having been presented with *no* evidence to substantiate the federal assertions that a murderous "dog soldiers" campaign was about to commence.

Chapter 11

1. Messerschmidt, *op. cit.*, pp. 118-19.

2. The phrase accrues from an FBI COINTELPRO memo quoted in U.S. Senate Select Committee to Study Government Operations, *Intelligence Activities and the Rights of Americans*, Book II, U.S. Government Printing Office, Washington, D.C., 1976, p. 91.

3. Messerschmidt, *op. cit.*, p. 119; the author is drawing his argument from Balbus, Isaac, *The Dialectic of Legal Repression*, Russell Sage Foundation, New York, 1973, Chapter 1.

4. Messerschmidt, *op. cit.*

5. *Ibid.*, the quotations used by the author are drawn from Balbus, *op. cit.*, pp. 3-4. It should be noted that the argument advanced here is very similar to that developed by Jurgen Habermas in *Legitimation Crisis*, Beacon Press, Boston, 1975.

6. It has only been established with clarity that one of the agents' day-long meetings with Moves Camp occurred in facilities at the huge Strategic Air Command base outside Rapid City. The location in which the other five such meetings occurred during the week in question remain somewhat mysterious, but may also have occurred at Ellsworth.

7. Matthiessen, *op. cit.*, pp. 93-94.

8. *First Session on FBI Authorization (1981)*, *op. cit.*, p. 281.

9. Matthiessen, *op. cit.*, p. 94.

10. *Ibid.*

11. This is borne out in the 302 report filed by SA David Price on August 12, 1974; Price and Moves Camp occupied adjoining rooms, while Williams stayed in the Senatorial Suite, across the hall.

12. The location is specified in SA Ronald Williams' 302 report for August 13, 1974; The meeting with Hurd is mentioned in the 302 report of SA David Price for August 14, 1974.

13. Matthiessen, *op. cit.*, pp. 95-96.

14. *First Session on FBI Authorization (1981)*, *op. cit.*, p. 284.

15. *Ibid.*, p. 289.

16. Matthiessen, *op. cit.*, p. 97.

17. Transcript quoted in *ibid.*, p. 96.

18. The woman, whose identity is withheld for obvious reasons, was formally deposed by the defense; the deposition is lodged in WKLDOC files retained by Ken Tilsen in Minneapolis. Tilsen himself, as quoted in Matthiessen, *op. cit.*, p. 97, is unequivocal: "That girl was raped, and all those sexual details [used by the county attorney to justify the dropping of charges against Moves Camp] were probably made up by agents to discredit her. She was so stunned by what had happened that she wanted to sue everyone involved in dropping the charges, not only the FBI but the local police and her own parents."

19. Quoted in Weyler, *op. cit.*, p. 119.

20. Transcript quoted in *ibid.*, p. 120.

21. A discussion at the bench on September 4, 1974, is quoted in *ibid.*: "Attorney Lane had called Hurd to the bench again, and had asked him, 'Did you have a conversation with [ASAC] Enlow on the 16th day of August?' Hurd answered, 'Yes I did...He told me that [Moves Camp]...had been intoxicated in Wisconsin, and that there had been a girl who was alleging that [there had been intercourse, and that she had been raped.'" In a taped interview made with NPR reporter Kevin McKiernan later in 1974, Hurd was still trying to rationalize what he had done, contending that he saw no reason to believe—rape allegation notwithstanding—that Moves Camp had not engaged in a "consensual act between two adults. I have seen no evidence yet that there was any rape...I don't think this effects [Moves Camp's] believability."

22. Transcript quoted in Weyler, *op. cit.*, p. 121; at 120, Weyler comments that, "Up to this point, Judge Nichol had shown leniency toward Hurd's behavior. But now Hurd had been caught in a direct lie to the court, and Nichol was shocked that a...U.S. attorney would so deceive a federal judge. Nichol called Hurd into his chambers and informed him that, according to Nichol, 'The sordid story of what went on over in Wisconsin was going to come out.' During that session in the judge's chambers, Hurd broke down and cried..."

23. *Ibid.*, p. 119.

24. Ellen Moves Camp recounted her remarks in an interview with NPR reporter Kevin McKiernan later in 1974.

25. Matthiessen, *op. cit.*, p. 94; he notes that, "Judge Nichol expressed astonishment that the FBI, which had been 'developing' this witness for six weeks, had not verified a story that the defense shot to pieces almost overnight."

26. Weyler, *op. cit.*, p. 119.

27. This is the Bureau's own account, as recorded in *First Session on FBI Authorization (1981)*, *op. cit.*, pp. 282-84: "[Prosecutor] Hurd himself met with the witness [Moves Camp] three times before putting him on the stand, and apparently he had some doubts about his truthfulness, since he requested a lie detector test that [SAC] Trimbach refused; Hurd could have insisted upon the test but for one reason or another did not do so," and, "an appropriate request [for the polygraph examination of Moves Camp], was sent to FBI Headquarters seeking authority for such an examination at an appropriate time, and this request was subsequently approved on August 9...according to the affidavit fo SA Ray Gammon, he discussed the possibility of a polygraph of Mr. Moves Camp with [SAC] Trimbach. Mr. Trimbach, who was aware that agents were in the process of securing signed statements from Mr. Moves Camp, told SA Gammon that *he thought it inappropriate and unwise to give the witness a polygraph examination at that time since it might harm the rapport between the witness and the government* [emphasis added]...[Still, AUSA] Hurd could have requested or ordered one."

28. Weyler, *op. cit.*, p. 119.

29. Transcript, quoted in *ibid.*

30. Transcript, quoted in *ibid.*, p. 121.

31. *Ibid.*, p. 118.

32. Matthiessen, *op. cit.*, p. 98.

33. *Ibid.* This was with regard to "Garden Plot" and the government's violation of the Constitution and *Posse Comitatus* Act by introducing military force into the "domestic disturbance" at Wounded Knee (see Chapter 5). With reference to this "unlawful military involvement at Wounded Knee," Nichol commented that, "We don't want the military running the civil affairs of this country, or having anything to do with the execution of the laws."

34. *Ibid.* As Weyler, *op. cit.*, points out at pp. 116-17, Nichol was also outraged at the government's withholding of potentially exculpatory evidence from the defense. The judge is quoted from the transcript: "It is my feeling that the prosecutor's offering of testimony that was directly contradicted by a document [FBI affidavits signed by another discredited witness, Alexander Richards] that was in his possession was inexcusable and possibly a violation of American Bar Association Standards on the Prosecution Func-

tion...If [this] was not deliberate deception, it was grossly negligent conduct...131 discoverable or arguably discoverable pieces of [exculpatory] evidence which haven't been turned over [to the defense]...The defendants have expressed a profound mistrust of the FBI...This expression of mistrust is understandable...The FBI was negligent at best...if our system of freedom is to be preserved [at all], the FBI must be servile to our system of justice."

35. There are two versions of this statement. One (quoted herein) comes from the transcript as recorded in the *New York Times*, September 17, 1974. A second, somewhat longer and more refined articulation was recorded by Nichol in a memorandum submitted along with his decision in the case. The relevant passage reads: "I am forced to conclude that the prosecution acted in bad faith at various times throughout the course of the trial and was seeking convictions at the expense of justice...I have taken into consideration the prosecution's conduct throughout the entire trial. The fact that incidents of misconduct formed a pattern throughout the course of the trial leads me to the belief that this case was not prosecuted in good faith or in the spirit of justice. The waters of justice have been polluted, and dismissal, I believe, is the appropriate cure for the pollution in this case."

36. Transcript, quoted in Matthiessen, *op. cit.*, p. 99.

37. Deloria, Vine, Jr., "Who Knows What Violence We Can Expect?" *The Los Angeles Times*, August 17, 1975.

38. Matthiessen, *op. cit.*, p. 100.

39. *Ibid.*, p. 133. The FBI, probably mindful that it had deliberately freed Moves Camp from the consequences of the River Falls rape, and had turned him loose on Pine Ridge to repeat the crime, contended that his shooting was "unrelated" to his latest atrocity. Rather, the Bureau suggested, AIM had waited all those months to punish Moves Camp for his false testimony against Banks and Means.

40. In a memo to the Director, FBI, dated October 16, 1975, and captioned "RESMURS Investigation," COINTELPRO specialist Richard G. Held, who had been assigned to special duty heading up the operation, made this clear, and added: "SAC, CHICAGO [Held] has been on the scene since the early morning hours of Friday, June 27, 1975...The case is in the final stages of being prepared for prosecution." Implicitly congratulating himself on a job well done, Held announced that his job was "finished," and that he planned to return to his post in Chicago within "two days."

41. The summary of Clifford's statement is taken from Matthiessen, *op. cit.*, pp. 214-15. Subsequent to his testimony against Jimmy Eagle, Clifford served three years in a federal penitentiary for sexual assault. Upon his release, he was placed in the federal witness protection program by AUSA Larry Von Wald and given a new identity. On November 9, 1987 Clifford was indicted for first degree murder in Golden, Colorado, in the mutilation slaying of an Edgewater, Colorado, woman. The victim's dismembered body was found in a box in the kitchen of Clifford's home. She had been strangled and stabbed 18 times. See "Man held in mutilation death allegedly testified in killings," *Rocky Mountain News*, November 9, 1987. Also see Hogan, Frank, "Witness for the Prosecution: Accused murderer Gregory Clifford doesn't have many friends—except in the FBI," *Westword*, Vol. 11, Number 20, January 13-19, 1988.

42. In Wood's summary of the interview with High Bull (date deleted), it is put that, "HIGH BULL advised that EAGLE mentioned the name of FBI Agent PRICE and EAGLE said that if he ever got the chance he would blow away FBI Agent PRICE, as he didn't like Agent PRICE's tactics." This interview is believed to have occurred on or about July 15, 1975. Concerning Eagle's turning himself in, see "Last man sought by FBI surrenders," *Rapid City Journal*, July 10, 1975, p. 3; as concerns his codefendants, see "Porcupine men bound over to district court," *Rapid City Journal*, July 9, 1975, p. 3.

43. White Wing had first been interviewed by Wood at approximately the same time as Marion High Bull, some three months earlier.

44. According to Robideau, he had left Crow Dog's Paradise in a 1964 Mercury station wagon he was "trying to fix up," shortly before the September 5th raid. Traveling with him were Kamook Nichols (Banks) and her sister Bernardine, Mike Anderson, Norman Charles and Jean Bordeaux. The group camped in the bluffs near the reservation community of Parmalee for several days, and were joined by a young Oglala named Keith DeMaris. When word came of the air assault at Crow Dog's, they packed the car with their personal gear, and a considerable quantity of ammunition to go along with a number of weapons they had collected, and set out southward to "get as much distance between us and South Dakota as possible." Near Wichita, Anderson noticed the car was trailing a large cloud of smoke, and Robideau pulled to the shoulder to investigate. As Robideau was under the car, attempting to identify the source of the fire (caused by a defective muffler), the ammunition stored in the rear began to detonate from the heat; he was blinded for several weeks by asphalt driven by the force of the explosion into his eyes. The entire group was apprehended shortly thereafter by the Kansas State Patrol. Ultimately, Robideau

was sentenced to 10 years for possession of weapons and explosives and served several months in the federal prison at Leavenworth before his conviction was overturned. Kamook Nichols was also charged in the matter and served several months in jail in Kansas City—where her first child, named "Iron Door Woman" in acknowledgement of the surroundings, was born—before the case was dismissed on the basis of "vindictive prosecution" on the part of U.S. Attorneys and the FBI.

45. Quoted in Matthiessen, *op. cit.*, p. 286.

46. Memorandum from SA (name deleted), Rapid City, to SAC Minneapolis, captioned "Evelyn Bordeaux, Et. Al.; EFP—Conspiracy," dated 9/27/77.

47. See the sensational headlines and stories on this matter in the *Rapid City Journal*, April 20 through May 9, 1976.

48. Matthiessen, *op. cit.*, p. 287.

49. Had the trial occurred in Rapid City, as originally scheduled, rather than Cedar Rapids, the trial judge would have been Andrew Bogue, and the outcome would very likely have been different. See, for example, the examination of Bogue's miserable conduct in the Crow Dog case, covered in Chapter 12.

50. Quoted in Matthiessen, *op. cit.*, p. 290.

51. *Ibid.*

52. *Ibid.*, p. 356.

53. *Ibid.*, p. 320.

54. *Ibid.*, p. 299.

55. Transcript, quoted in *ibid.*, pp. 297-98.

56. Peltier trial transcript, pp. 1085-88, 1115; Draper named a BIA police officer, Frank Gadake, as having assisted SA Stapleton with the interrogation.

57. *Ibid.*, p. 1098. At pp. 1087, 1097, and 1098 Draper states that the day prior to his grand jury testimony, he was "interviewed" by SA James Doyle for approximately 9 hours, SA J. Gary Adams for about 5 hours, and Assistant U.S. Attorney Sikma for approximately 8 hours.

58. Transcript, quoted in Matthiessen, *op. cit.*, p. 295.

59. Transcript, quoted in *ibid.*, p. 296.

60. See Peltier trial transcript, at 4799, 4801, 4803-04; SAs Adams and Harvey, according to Brown's statements, also threatened his mother during the "interview."

61. *Ibid.*, pp. 4842-43.

62. Transcript, quoted in Matthiessen, *op. cit.*, p. 337.

63. *Ibid.*, p. 302. Among those implicated by Harper's testimony aside from Butler and Robideau, were Jimmy Eagle, Norman Brown, Norman Charles, Charlie Abourezk, Wish Draper, Leonard Peltier, and Edgar Bear Runner. Among those supposedly rendered credible were Myrtle Poor Bear and John Stewart.

64. Transcript, quoted in *ibid.*, p. 299.

65. Transcript, quoted in *ibid.*, p. 302.

66. Transcript, quoted in *ibid.*

67. *Ibid.*, p. 319. Harper lost his suit, but was *not* indicted for his blatant perjury.

68. Quoted in *ibid.*

69. Transcript, quoted in *ibid.*, p. 318.

70. Transcript, quoted in *ibid.*, p. 316.

71. Transcript, quoted in *ibid.*

72. Transcript, quoted in *ibid.*, pp. 316-17.

73. Quoted in *ibid.*, p. 318.

74. See the *Cedar Rapids Gazette*, July 19, 1976.

75. Quoted in *ibid.*

76. Concerning Bragg's statement that he, too, had overheard Eagle's jailhouse "confession" nearly a year earlier, and SA Coward's involvement in this charade, see Matthiessen, *op. cit.*, p. 286.

77. The quotation is taken from an FBI memorandum recording the meeting, dated August 9, 1976, and initialed by Kelley, Held and Hultman.

78. This reconstruction of events derives from Inspector Mitchell's RCMP events report, completed and filed on the evening of February 6, 1976.

79. See Matthiessen, *op. cit.*, pp. 281-83, 325.

80. Quoted in *ibid.*, p. 283.

81. Quoted in *ibid.*, p. 325.

82. This document is quoted and analyzed in Messerschmidt, *op. cit.*, pp. 38-41.

83. Matthiessen, *op. cit.*, p. 325.

84. Benson later declared that his meetings with the prosecution side—from which the defense was excluded, and of which it was not even notified—concerned only "security matters" pertaining to the upcoming trial.

85. Matthiessen, *op. cit.*, p. 326.

86. Transcript, quoted in Messerschmidt, *op. cit.*, pp. 40-41.

87. Transcript, quoted in Matthiessen, *op. cit.*, p. 327. Taikeff's precise statement was, "The only question is, did the defendant participate...The government doesn't have to prove first-degree murder, we concede first-degree murder."

88. The principle involved here is truly perverse. Jurors are typically given to understand that they are being sequestered because of some, often intangible, threat to their safety. Given the "fact" that the government would never constitute such a threat, it follows that the jurors believe they are being effectively jailed for an indeterminate period because of the dangerous nature of the defendant(s) or his/her associates. In the instance of the Peltier trial, the intent to bias the jury in this fashion was blatant; after all the many AIM trials during the preceding three years—including the earlier Cedar Rapids RESMURS trial—not *one* juror had ever claimed to have been threatened by AIM. There was thus absolutely *no* basis for the judge, the prosecution, or the FBI to believe things would be different in Fargo.

89. Messerschmidt, *op. cit.*, p. 72; the author notes that each of two charges—one each of transporting weapons and transporting explosives across state lines—levied against Anderson carried a potential ten-year sentence. There was also a pending burglary charge against the youth in Arizona, where he was already on probation for participating in a robbery. After he "cooperated" in the Peltier case, all of this heavy time miraculously disappeared. Also see Peltier trial transcript at 837-38, and 845.

90. Peltier trial transcript at 841.

91. *Ibid.*, pp. 841-42.

92. As Messerschmidt, *op. cit.*, p. 73, puts it: "On February 1, 1977, Special Agents James Doyle and Gary Adams arrested Anderson in Albuquerque, New Mexico, for probation violation. At approximately 10:50 a.m. of that day these agents attempted to interview Anderson and his reply was that he did not wish to be interviewed about his activities of 26 June 1975. The agents brought him to the marshal's office to await his hearing on the probation violation. At 1:40 p.m. Anderson [unaccountably] signed a waiver of his constitutional rights and signed a statement that in effect said...he did in fact see Peltier, Robideau, and Butler down by the agents' cars [*i.e.* exactly where the FBI wished the three to have been seen, in order to place them directly in the 'kill zone' of the Oglala firefight]." Also see Peltier trial transcript at 4203, 4205 and 4298.

93. The "red and white van" story is directly contrary to SA J. Gary Adams' testimony during the Butler-Robideau trial that he personally heard Williams radio that he and Coler were following a vehicle into the Jumping Bull Compound on the morning of June 26, and referring to it as a "pickup." BIA police officer Robert Ecoffey also testified—at a point when the government had not dropped charges against Jimmy Eagle—that Eagle was known to ride around in a red pickup, and that Williams had chased a "red vehicle, van or pickup" onto the Jumping Bull property.

94. Peltier trial transcript at 774-75.

95. During the Butler-Robideau trial, Ann M. Johnson testified that at 12:18 p.m. on June 26, 1975, SA J. Gary Adams had radioed the Rapid City office that he himself had just witnessed a red pickup leave the Jumping Bull property. Johnson, whose job it was to log the radio communications of agents in the field, also testified that at 1:26 p.m. on the 26th, Adams had radioed to SA Fred Coward that a red pickup with only a driver in it had entered the Jumping Bull property, and that it had left with three people inside. On the stand at Cedar Rapids, Adams confirmed the accuracy of Johnson's logs; on the stand in Fargo, he flatly denied making any such transmissions.

96. Memorandum, B.H. Cooke to Gebhardt, captioned UNKNOWN SUBJECTS; SA JACK R. COLER—VICTIM, SA RONALD A. WILLIAMS—VICTIM, and date 6/27/75 (this originated in the Rapid City FBI office).

97. An interesting alternative is that the agents were following an orange-red Scout belonging to an ostensible Crusade for Justice member (and reputed "explosives expert") named Leroy Casades, long suspected of being an FBI infiltrator. With its top detached—which is common enough in summer—the Casades vehicle would have resembled a pickup truck from behind. In any event, the Scout theory is further bolstered by other FBI documents from the time of the shootout. SA Dean Howard Hughes, in his 302 filed that day, essentially corroborated Price's recall in this matter, although he recapitulated the transmission as involving a "red jeep" (it should be noted that the term "jeep" has come to generically

connote *all* 4-wheel drive vehicles such as a Scout, much as "Coke" has come to signify cola); an unidentified agent working at his desk at the Rapid City office did likewise, stating in his (name deleted) 302 that "I paid little attention to the transmission at that moment, but did hear him [Williams] mention the name Jimmy Eagle and something about chasing a "*red jeep.*" Finally, a Bureau teletype from SAC Minneapolis to the Director, *et al.*, captioned RESMURS and dated 7/3/75 observed: "Radio transmissions...from SA Williams determined SA Williams was under fire by unknown individuals from the *the red jeep* [emphasis added]."

98. Peltier trial transcript at p. 777.

99. Bloemendaal had also testified at the Butler-Robideau trial. He agreed with the defense contention that no good purpose would be served by exposing the jury to scores of gory photographs of Williams and Coler after death. Judge McManus also agreed, expressed concern that such exposure might unduly prejudice the jury against the defendants, and limited the number Hultman and Sikma might pass around. In Fargo, Bloemendaal again agreed with the defense on this point. Judge Benson, however, stating that "this type of evidence outweighs its possible prejudice," allowed the prosecution to deploy whatever photos they wished, for whatever shock value they could obtain. Bloemendaal's autopsy had also concluded that only one agent had been killed by a " high-velocity shoulder weapon," and in other important respects tended to undercut the "lone gunman" theory used in court against Peltier (though obviously not against Butler and Robideau). It was for this reason that Noguchi was retained, to reach conclusions more "compatible" with the FBI's new premise.

100. See the *Rapid City Journal*, June 27, 1975.

101. The preparation of such ostensibly personal accounts in resident agencies, for signature by Washington higher-ups, is irregular, even in the FBI.

102. Peltier trial transcript at 2114.

103. *Ibid.*, at 3012-13.

104. *Ibid.*, at 3079-80.

105. Messerschmidt, *op. cit.*, p. 89.

106. Peltier trial transcript at 3137-38 and 3162-63.

107. *Ibid.*, at 3163.

108. Hodge affirmed that the report was indeed his, under oath; *ibid.*, at 3342 and 3388.

109. *Ibid.*, at 3235.

110. The actual date was February 10, 1976, according to the subsequently released FBI documents; Hodge's testimony on the dating is to be found in the Peltier trial transcripts at 3388.

111. *Ibid.*, at 3235 and 3247.

112. *Ibid.*, at 3248.

113. *Ibid.*, at 3234.

114. *Ibid.*, at 3247.

115. *Ibid.*, at 841-42; Anderson was never charged in connection with RESMURS either.

116. Quoted in Matthiessen, *op. cit.*, p. 356; it was possibly this offer which led to Anderson's death, less than two years later, in a car chased by BIA police on the Navajo Reservation. No autopsy was ever performed and no investigation was conducted into the circumstances attending his death (see *ibid.*, p. 439).

117. Peltier trial transcript at 1020-22; Draper also testified that Bob Robideau was carrying a shotgun marked "Denver FBI" at this point.

118. *Ibid.*, at 1446; Brown was the only one of the three former Tent City AIM members who acknowledged having actually engaged in the firefight. At 1492 he recounts how he and Norman Charles fired on the cars of SA J. Gary Adams and BIA police officer Glenn Little Bird early in the firefight, causing them to retreat all the way back to Highway 18.

119. See Matthiessen, *op. cit.*, pp. 355-56.

120. Messerschmidt, *op. cit.*, pp. 50-51. Also see Peltier trial transcript at 1305.

121. *Ibid.*, at 1797.

122. *Ibid.*, at 3786.

123. *Ibid.*, at 3790.

124. This seems to have been one of Hultman's favorite phrases. It is sprinkled liberally throughout both the Butler-Robideau and Peltier trial transcripts.

125. The inability of the defense to adequately test the credibility of the testimony of the government's various witnesses was a built-in aspect—whether intended or not—of Benson's restrictive evidentiary rulings, designed primarily to prevent the building of a self-defense argument for Peltier.

126. Peltier trial transcript at 3790.

127. *Ibid.*

128. *Ibid.*, pp. 4623-26.

129. *Ibid.*, pp. 4649-50.

130. This statement is very similar to the one made by Poor Bear in an interview included in the film, *Annie Mae: A Brave Hearted Woman*, *op. cit.*

131. As Matthiessen, *op. cit.*, p. 454, notes, "For most of February 1976, [Poor Bear's] whereabouts were unknown, and her family became extremely worried...Motel bills, signed receipts and other documents established that Poor Bear was in the custody of Agents Price and Wood between February 19 and February 23, which were also the dates of the first and second affidavits in the Peltier case." Weyler, *op. cit.*, p. 195, also observes that FBI hotel receipts signed by SA David Price on March 21 and 29, 1976, show Poor Bear had been held in the Hacienda Motel in Gordon, Nebraska on those dates; the latter date is five days *after* Price and Wood claim to have turned their captive over to SA Skelly—who supposedly took her to Belle Fourche—and only two days before the final affidavit was signed. In other words, it is likely that this aspect of the FBI's version of what happened is as inaccurate as most of the rest, and that Price and Wood were responsible for the third affidavit, as well as the first two.

132. As the true dimensions of the fraud involved in Peltier's extradition from Canada became clear during the spring of 1977, WKLDOC attorneys accused Canadian prosecutor Halprin, who had presented the U.S. case in court, of complicity. He immediately filed a suit claiming he was libeled, and stated under oath (in May 1977) that he had had no knowledge of the true nature of the Poor Bear situation, and that he was "shocked that the United States government and the F.B.I. had suppressed this evidence [*i.e.*: that the Bureau had two other Poor Bear affidavits which directly contradicted the one Halprin was led to submit in court]." Federal prosecutor Evan Hultman later also testified before the U.S. 8th Circuit Court of Appeals that *he* had had no knowledge of the contradictory affidavits at the time he filed for Peltier's extradition. Hence, the onus in this matter lies *squarely* on the FBI.

133. Statement of WKLDOC attorney John Lowe, from the Peltier trial transcript, quoted in Matthiessen, *op. cit.*, p. 347.

134. Similar statements by Peltier concerning Poor Bear appeared in both *Akwesasne Notes* and *New Age* during 1980 and 1981.

135. Taikeff's strange capitulation also included the submission of evidence concerning the death of Anna Mae Aquash, a matter clearly and closely related to the sorts of coercion employed by SAs Price and Wood to extort false evidence from Myrtle Poor Bear. These decisions, coupled with Taikeff's refusal to use Mike Anderson's rebuttal of his own testimony for the government and the acknowledgement that first degree murder had occurred even after the Cedar Rapids jury found otherwise, went very far toward destroying any possibility of Peltier's mounting a defense. Both John Lowe and Bruce Ellison were enraged by Taikeff's apparent incompetence; Peltier stops little short of suggesting that Taikeff was working for the other side, *a la* Douglass Durham.

136. To the contrary, Benson instructed the defense that it would not be allowed to point up inconsistencies and contradictions in the FBI's ballistics evidence as a part of its closing arguments. This strange ruling has never been explained. Nor has the judge's refusal to deliver full instructions to the jury.

137. Peltier trial transcript, quoted in Matthiessen, *op. cit.*, p. 362.

138. Crooks' closing argument was begun on April 15, 1977. Contrary to the conditions imposed upon the defense, which was prevented from even mentioning crucial aspects of the evidence, Crooks was allowed to theorize before the jury on matters which had absolutely no evidentiary basis (or at least none which had been presented during the trial).

139. Taikeff's version is that he resigned; others say he was fired.

140. Boston attorney Lew Gurwitz was added to the roster shortly thereafter and others, such as Vine Deloria, Jr., and Washington, D.C. attorney John Privatera have been involved since.

141. See Matthiessen, *op. cit.*, p. 371.

142. *United States v. Leonard Peltier*, Criminal No. C77-3003, "Motion to Vacate Judgement and for a New Trial," (submitted by Michael Tigar and Bruce Ellison) at 7326.

143. *Ibid.*, at 7327-28.

144. *Ibid.*, at 7326-27.

145. *Ibid.*

146. Finding of the United States Eighth Circuit Court of Appeals in the Matter of the *United States v. Leonard Peltier*, C77-3003, Motion to Vacate Judgement and for a New Trial, St. Louis, Missouri, September 14, 1978.

147. Matthiessen, *op. cit.*, p. 374. The final panel decision is articulated in *United States v. Peltier*, 858 F.2d 314, 335 (8th Cir. 1978), *cert. denied*, 440 U.S. 945 (1979).

148. William Webster enjoyed a poor reputation concerning civil rights, even in 1977. He was particularly noted for having expressed strongly anti-AIM sentiments in the judicial record of a WKLDOC suit concerning the FBI's performance on Pine Ridge in 1973, concerning the Means-Wilson election travesty on the reservation in 1974, in resisting the reversals of the convictions of Leonard Crow Dog, Carter Camp and Stan Holder in 1975, and so forth. He also belonged to at least two "social clubs" in St. Louis—one of them called The Mysterious Order of the Veiled Prophets—which explicitly excluded women and blacks.

149. Matthiessen, *op. cit.*, p. 371; the author observes that Webster had been informed of his nomination to head up the FBI by Attorney General Griffin Bell *before* he undertook to preside over the Peltier appeal. Such sterling demonstrations of "intelligence and integrity" are no doubt what has lately caused him to be placed in the position of Director of the Central Intelligence Agency, having served as FBI director for nearly a decade.

150. *Ibid.*, p. 375.

151. Gurwitz's statement was made at a Leonard Peltier Defense Committee rally held in front of the Supreme Court Building on the evening of February 12, 1979.

152. *Proposal for a commission of inquiry into the effect of domestic intelligence activities on criminal trials in the United States of America, op. cit.*

153. Amnesty International stopped short of declaring any of the three inmates highlighted in its study to be "prisoners of conscience" because of stipulations in its by-laws that those so designated must be "non-violent." Apparently, all a repressive state need do to avoid being accused of holding such prisoners is to accuse those it wishes to neutralize politically of having engaged in violent acts, *whether or not* this can be proven. Another interpretation of the AI by-laws is that they are designed to preclude even the *advocacy* of armed self-defense on the part of dissidents within politically repressive states. To the extent that this is true, AI's position seems more likely to foster an unending stream of opposition martyrs than to resolve tangible human rights issues.

154. See "Motion to Vacate Judgement and for a New Trial," *United States v. Peltier*, U.S. District Court for the District of North Dakota, April 20, 1982, pp. 18-40.

155. See a heavily deleted teletype from the Rapid City FBI office to the Director, captioned RES-MURS INVESTIGATION and dated February 12, 1976; the document shows clearly the Bureau was aware the pathologist [Dr. Bloemendaal] held that only SA Williams had been killed by a small bullet of "very high velocity," such as the .223 calibre round fired from an AR-15. A copy of this teletype is attached to *ibid.*

156. A teletype from SAC, Minneapolis (Richard G. Held) to Director, FBI, dated July 27, 1975 and captioned RESMURS—PHYSICAL EVIDENCE states in part: "It was the general conclusion of the pathologist [Dr. Bloemendaal] that the bullet which entered SA Williams' head was the *first* in the sequence, and caused death instantaneously [emphasis added]." FBI Director Clarence Kelley also stated, in his Los Angeles press conference, held July 1, 1975, that Williams had been killed by the first bullet to strike him.

157. Peltier trial transcript at 5011.

158. According to the *Washington Post*, July 9, 1975: "The South Dakota law enforcement communications department tape-recorded the conversation between the slain agents prior to the shoot-out and recorded their plea for help after the gunfire began. South Dakota Attorney General William Janklow, whose office oversees the law enforcement communications network, confirmed that the state did record the FBI communication but declined to say what was on the recording. He said the FBI had asked him to keep the information confidential." At the Butler-Robideau trial in Cedar Rapids—in an obvious replay of the Geronimo Pratt case (see Chapter 3)—defense attorneys were informed by federal representatives that no such tapes were in existence.

159. Teletype, Director, FBI, to SAC, Rapid City [Norman Zigrossi], dated October 2, 1975 and captioned RESMURS—PHYSICAL EVIDENCE—[deleted].

160. As was revealed by FBI Firearms and Toolmarks specialist Evan Hodge in his testimony at trial (see Peltier trial transcript at 3314-23), other ammunition components found in the area immediately after the firefight which fit the general configuration of the weapon from which the bullet which killed SA Williams was fired included .30-06 Springfield, .30-06 M-1 (Garand), .303 Lee-Enfield (British), .222 Remington or Savage, .225 Winchester, .223 Ruger Mini-14, .270 Winchester and .22-250 Remington. In several

categories, more than one weapon of the calibre listed were known to have been fired at Williams and Coler from a distance.

161. See "Motion to Vacate Judgement and for a New Trial", *United States v. Peltier*, U.S. District Court for the District of North Dakota, April 20, 1982.

162. The Justice Department fiercely resisted the motion; see "Response to Petition for Rehearing in the Case of the *United States v. Leonard Peltier*," No. 85-5192, (prepared by U.S. Attorney Rodney S. Webb and Assistant U.S. Attorneys Lynn E. Crooks and Richard Vospeka), submitted to the Eighth Circuit Court of Appeals.

163. See United States Court of Appeals for the Eighth Circuit, *United States v. Leonard Peltier*, 731 F.2d 550, 555 (8th Cir. 1984), p. 4.

164. Hearing Transcript, at 200, 344-45.

165. As Crooks "explained" to the jury (Peltier trial transcript at 5007): "There is no other gun that could have extracted that bullet or that shell, and that evidence stands completely unimpeached by any evidence in this case."

166. United States Court of Appeals for the Eighth District, "Appeal from the United States District Court for the District of North Dakota, *United States v. Leonard Peltier*", No. 95-5192, *op. cit.*, September 11, 1986, p. 9.

167. At trial, Hodge had led the jury to believe that he and he *alone* had performed the RESMURS ballistics examinations; see Peltier trial transcript at 3181, 3198-99, 3233-34 and 3238. Joseph Twardowski is still employed by the Bureau, but has since become a full-fledged Special Agent.

168. United States Court of Appeals for the Eighth District, "Appeal from the United States District Court for the District of North Dakota, *United States v. Leonard Peltier*," No. 95-5192 (written by Judge Heaney), September 11, 1986, p. 9.

169. See Bismarck Hearing Transcript at 409-10; at 474, Hodge states that "He [Twardowski] was the only other person making notes on this case." Perhaps tellingly, Twardowski himself was not called to corroborate his former boss's testimony in this matter.

170. Evan Hodge has, since his original "faulty" testimony in the Peltier trial, been promoted to head up the entire FBI Firearms and Toolmarks Identification Division. This, no doubt, was for the excellence of services rendered.

171. Crooks' admission was made on October 22, 1985, and may be found at p. 18 of the Peltier oral arguments transcript.

172. *Ibid.* Crooks' 1985 position should be contrasted to prosecutor Evan Hultman's bald assertion to the press in 1981, that: "There's no doubt in my mind that Peltier shot the agents. He was the enforcer on the reservation—everybody knew that."

173. Judge Heaney's statement was made in the midst of an interchange with assistant prosecutor Lynn Crooks during oral arguments on October 15, 1985.

174. United States Court of Appeals for the Eighth District, "Appeal from the United States District Court for the District of North Dakota, *United States v. Leonard Peltier*," No. 95-5192, *op. cit.*, September 11, 1986, p. 16.

175. "Petition for Rehearing and Suggestion for Rehearing En Banc for Appellant Leonard Peltier, *United States v. Leonard Peltier*," United States Court of Appeals for the Eighth District (1986); at 11-12, the appeals team argues that, "With all due respect, rather than being 'unlikely' that there was tampering with the 'most important piece of evidence in the case,' the newly discovered evidence and the government explanations therefor [sic], raise a substantial likelihood there was such tampering..." See also "Petition for Reconsideration of the Denial of the Petition for Rehearing and Suggestion of Rehearing En Banc, *United States v. Leonard Peltier*," No. 85-5192, submitted to the U.S. Eighth Circuit Court of Appeals.

176. This all begins to sound as if we were dealing with royalty. With a man's life hanging in the balance, the judges are more concerned with preserving one another's dignity and not "imputing improprieties" to federal colleagues than with seeing anything remotely resembling justice actually done.

177. Peltier's second Supreme Court appeal was based on the need for clarification of the high court's decision on the extent of new evidence required to cause reversal of an earlier trial decision; *United States v. Bagley*, U.S. 105 S. Ct. 3375 (1985).

178. See "Court refuses to hear Peltier appeal," *Rapid City Journal*, October 6, 1987.

179. Of Peltier's approximate ten and one-half years in federal penal facilities, some eight years have been spent in the "super-max" prison at Marion, Illinois (the replacement for the notorious Alcatraz Island facility), one year at the maximum security prison at Leavenworth, Kansas, six months at the federal

medical facility at Springfield, Missouri, and the remainder at a minimum security facility at Lompoc, California (see concluding chapter). He is currently incarcerated at Leavenworth. Of this total time, approximately three and one-half years have been spent in solitary confinement, and another 6 months under the conditions of the infamous "Marion Lockdown" of 1983-84; see Cunningham, Dennis, and Jan Susler, *A Public Report About a Violent Mass Assault Against Prisoners and Continuing Illegal Punishment and Torture of the Prison Population at the U.S. Penitentiary at Marion, Illinois*, Marion Prisoners' Rights Project, c/o People's Law Office, Chicago, 1983. Also Committee to End the Marion Lockdown, *Marion Prison: Inside the Lockdown*, People's Law Office, Chicago, 1986, and Amnesty International, *Allegations of Mistreatment in Marion Prison, Illinois, U.S.A.*, New York, 1987.

180. See "Peltier back in Penitentiary, wins prize in Spain," *Rapid City Journal*, December 12, 1986; according to Commission President José Antonio Martin Pallin, Peltier was chosen "because he was defending the historical and cultural rights of his people against the genocide of his race."

181. See "External Affairs: Canada-U.S. Extradition Treaty—Case of Leonard Peltier, Statement of Mr. James Fulton," in *House of Commons Debate, Canada*, Vol. 128, No. 129, 1st Session, 33rd Parliament, Official Report, Thursday, April 17, 1986. Also see DiLauro, Liz, "Press Release," the Cathedral of St. John the Divine, 1047 Amsterdam Ave., New York, April 1986.

182. See "Petition to the United Nations Commission on Human Rights and Sub-Commission on Prevention of Discrimination and Protection of Minorities: HUMAN RIGHTS VIOLATIONS IN THE UNITED STATES," submitted by the National Conference of Black Lawyers, the National Alliance Against Racist and Political Repression, and the United Church of Christ Commission for Racial Justice, during December of 1978. Interventions on the Peltier case have also been submitted to the U.N. Working Group on Indigenous Populations at the Palace of Nations in Geneva, Switzerland, by AIM's International Indian Treaty Council (IITC, a U.N. Class II [consultative] Non-Governmental Organization) in 1979, 1980, 1982, 1984, and 1985.

183. See "Indian seeks Soviet asylum," *Denver Post*, August 20, 1987.

184. See "Request to the Government of the USSR," Leonard Peltier, Leavenworth Federal Penitentiary, Leavenworth, Kansas, July 9, 1987.

Chapter 12

1. It should be noted that Clyde Bellecourt was also considered by the FBI to have been one of the Wounded Knee leaders. However, much to the Bureau's dismay, the evidence against him was deemed so paltry by Judge Fred Nichol that all eleven counts were dismissed without even being brought to trial. This was the same fate encountered by a dozen other charges against Bellecourt—ten of them felonies—the FBI had tried to bring in the wake of the Trail of Broken Treaties in 1972-73.

2. Matthiessen, *op. cit.*, p. 100; at p. 447, the author observes that Hurd had been officially commended by the Justice Department for his "superior performance" during the Banks-Means trial; that is, during the period when he was engaging in misconduct serious enough to cause the government's case to be thrown out. In 1981, Hurd was further rewarded for the quality of his services by being named to serve as a *judge* in South Dakota, replacing Richard Braithwaite—who had sentenced Russell Means to four years for defending himself from a police assault in a Minnehaha County courtroom. Braithwaite had resigned after pleading guilty to a shoplifting charge.

3. Weyler, *op. cit.*, p. 187; this was the FBI's attempt (see Chapter 5) to infiltrate the AIM/ION positions during a truce. The detention of the "postal inspectors" was actually undertaken by Stan Holder—by his *own* account—not Leonard Crow Dog.

4. Matthiessen, *op. cit.*, p. 100.

5. This reconstruction derives from Crow Dog's account in the film, *Annie Mae: Brave-Hearted Woman*, *op. cit.*, as well as information contained in Matthiessen, *op. cit.*, p. 227, and in several oral accounts. It is also noteworthy that Stewart was not the only Crow Dog relative to die violently during this period; in late November of 1974, Leonard's sister, Delphine—stepmother of Jancita Eagle Deer (see Chapter 8)—was badly beaten by BIA police, left lying in a field, and died of exposure.

6. Matthiessen, *op. cit.*, p. 227.

7. Al Running says his sons witnessed Beck in a plain sedan which looked like a Bureau motor pool vehicle. Another rumor places Beck in the company of SAs David Price and William Wood in the off-reservation town of Mitchell (S.D.) on the afternoon of September 4, 1975.

8. Matthiessen, *op. cit.*, p. 227.

9. See "Reign of Terror Continues in South Dakota," *Akwesasne Notes*, Vol. 7, No. 4, Early Autumn, 1975, pp. 4-9.

10. See *Rapid City Journal*, September 5-7, 1975, for Burnette's statements. Matthiessen, *op. cit.*, p. 234, observes that "Beck had terrorized the region" for some time prior to the incidents at Crow Dog's Paradise and, in 1977, "was finally jailed for the senseless killing of an Indian woman named No Moccasins in broad daylight in the reservation community of Parmalee." No action was *ever* taken by the FBI with regard to Beck's involvement in the earlier murder of Crow Dog's nephew, Andrew Paul Stewart.

11. A part of the traditional Lakota punishment imposed upon the original Crow Dog for his killing of Spotted Tail in 1884 (see Chapter 4) was that no member of his family would be allowed to fight or bear arms under *any* circumstances for the next seven generations. The Crow Dog family has—generation after generation—abided by this proscription although it has forced them to rely entirely upon their community for defense and often for sustenance. Leonard Crow Dog is of the seventh generation; even his enemies among the Lakota acknowledge that he has never engaged in acts of physical violence.

12. Ruling quoted in Weyler, *op. cit.*, p. 188. The McManus proscription on Crow Dog's associations would have been legal only if it had disallowed him from interaction with "known criminals," *i.e.* those who had been convicted of felonies. As it was, the probation order was designed to curtail *political* associations. This was quite similar to the probation conditions imposed by South Dakota Judge Braithwaite on Russell Means: "...the defendant will refrain from participating in any American Indian Movement activities except...fundraising...the International Treaty Organization...[and] activities of the American Indian Movement within the courts..." (*State vs. Russell Means* 257 NW 2d. 595, 596). In 1977, the Eighth Circuit Court of Appeals found Braithwaite's conditions of probation—which Means had gone to prison for violating—to be unconstitutional: "[The] condition serves only to stifle [Means'] freedom of expression and association while giving judicial credence to the unfair and unjustified inference that violence is the shibboleth of the American Indian Movement" (440 F. Supp. 553 at 12, 1977).

13. With a rationale strikingly similar to that employed to justify raids on BPP offices during 1969-70, SA David Price later testified that, "We received information that a federal fugitive named Harold Goggle Eyes, who is also known as Poncho, who is listed as armed and dangerous, was staying at that place." Asked whether he felt it likely the agents might locate the fugitive hiding inside a legal file cabinet and why a law office had been considered a likely hiding place at all, Price—who had often harassed WKLDOC legal workers—replied, "I did not know it formally as such"; Matthiessen, *op. cit.*, pp. 243-44. Meanwhile, the Bureau had already disrupted the WKLDOC operation in Council Bluffs, Iowa by convincing the city fathers to evict the group from its office in a municipal building; see "Wounded Knee group faces eviction," *Rapid City Journal*, July 3, 1975, p. 2.

14. The Bureau still maintained it was pursuing Harold Goggle Eyes, apparently from law office to law office. It should be noted that, despite the importance the Bureau claimed to attach to his apprehension, Goggle Eyes was *not* taken to trial.

15. Quoted in the *Rapid City Journal*, October 28, 1975. One is forced to wonder why, if the federal concern really was to "clear its docket of AIM cases," most of which were going nowhere in a judicial sense, the FBI was allowed to continue to proliferate petty charges.

16. Crow Dog trial transcript, quoted in Matthiessen, *op. cit.*, p. 234. After Hurd's personal participation in the Louis Moves Camp affair (see Chapter 11), the brass-plated mendacity of his rhetorical question speaks for itself.

17. Crow Dog trial transcript, quoted in *Akwesasne Notes*, Vol. 8, No. 1, Early Spring, 1976, p. 12.

18. *Ibid.* It seems that "Speedy Eddie" had begun to realize what was going on.

19. This incident is covered in Weyler, *op. cit.*, p. 188.

20. *Ibid.*

21. *Ibid.*

22. See Erdoes, Richard, "Crow Dog's Third Trial," *Akwesasne Notes*, Vol. 8, No. 1, Early Spring, 1976, p. 13. Pfersick testified at this trial that Crow Dog "threatened him with the chain off a chain saw," contrary to the testimony of any other witness. Although this whole affair simply reeks of being an FBI provocation, no relationship between Royer Pfersick and the Bureau has been demonstrated, largely because the Bureau has refused to divulge whether such a relationship in fact existed (the rationale used to cover nondisclosure included "protection of intelligence-gathering methods," a situation which tends to speak for itself).

23. *Ibid.*

24. *Ibid.*

25. The advantage, from the federal perspective, in securing even a concurrent sentence in this case—aside from solidifying support for the government's thesis that Crow Dog was a "dangerous" and "violent" man—lay in the fact that it rendered his parole much more difficult to achieve. Even assuming that an early parole might be granted *vis a vis* the Beck-McCloskey sentence, Crow Dog would *still* remain incarcerated on the Pfersick sentence.

26. Crow Dog's description of Leavenworth accrues from a letter written to his wife, quoted in Weyler, *op. cit.*, p. 189.

27. Gurwitz's assessment was made verbally to author Churchill in September of 1987.

28. McCloskey's letter is covered in Matthiessen, *op. cit.*, p. 234.

29. Weyler, *op. cit.*, p. 189. There has never been *any* evidence that Leonard Crow Dog suffered from a brain tumor, or required brain surgery for other valid medical reasons. The fear of Crow Dog, his family and his supporters at the time—hardly unwarranted under the circumstances—was that the government was preparing to perform a lobotomy or other form of psycho-surgery on its victim. The whole matter was, at the least, an instance of psychological torture.

30. *Ibid.* There is every appearance that the government was cutting its potential losses by granting the parole. It seems clear that the federal assessment was that its desired point had been made, and sufficient damage had been done to Crow Dog that he would be unlikely to resume his full range of activities as an AIM leader. The government could also count on WKLDOC being too busy pursuing pending cases and appeals of those still incarcerated to continue to push the questions of wrongful incarceration and other abuse of a man already released. With the matter effectively dropped, there was little threat of official disclosure of what had been done to Crow Dog.

31. Wallace Black Elk's statement was made to author Churchill in August of 1980.

32. Dick Marshall was, at the time, twenty-four years old. In addition to serving AIM as a "Means lieutenant on the reservation" (according to the FBI), he was an officer in OSCRO's Pine Ridge Committee for Better Tribal Government.

33. Statement of Halley Merrill, taken by the Pennington County (S.D.) Sheriff's Department, March 2, 1975. The reconstruction of events in this paragraph generally conforms to Merrill's version, as well as those of other witnesses.

34. Quoted in Matthiessen, *op. cit.*, pp. 271-72.

35. Merrill statement, *op. cit.* The Pennington County Sheriff's log for March 1, 1975 also reflects that a call was received from Scenic at about 11:45 p.m., nearly twenty minutes before the call reporting the shooting of Martin Montileaux.

36. Quoted in Matthiessen, *op. cit.*, p. 272.

37. Quoted in *ibid.* Means' own explanation of the jacket switch is simply that, "It was cold. We just grabbed the wrong jackets when we jumped out of the car."

38. Memorandum from SAC, Minneapolis (Joseph Trimbach) to Director, FBI (Clarence Kelley), dated March 3, 1975, and captioned "Predication for Investigation of Members and Supporters of AIM—Re: Richard Marshall." It should be noted that the language used is *precisely* the same as that justifying Bureau involvement in the Pratt murder case several years earlier (see Chapter 3).

39. WKLDOC Press Release, Minneapolis, March 4, 1975. Among those arrested—aside from Russell Means and Evelyn Bordeaux—were Bill Means and five others in Denver on March 3, charged with possession of marijuana and tied up in court for months before the case was dismissed. Also on March 3, Milwaukee AIM leader Herb Powless (Oneida) and six others were arrested in a van south of Rapid City, allegedly for transporting an illegal cache of weapons. Although the weapons charges themselves ultimately came to naught, Powless was returned to a federal prison on a parole violation, being technically "a felon in possession of a firearm." Such is the process of political neutralization.

40. Transcript of first Montileaux inteview, quoted in Matthiessen, *op. cit.*, pp. 273-74.

41. Transcript of first Montileaux interview, *ibid.*, p. 274.

42. *Ibid.*

43. *Ibid.*

44. *Ibid.*, p. 275. Marshall had worn a down-filled jacket into the Longhorn Bar on March 1, 1975.

45. *Ibid.*, pp. 274-75. The bullet severed Montileaux's spinal cord at the neck, totally paralyzing him; he died of pneumonia precipitated by this general physical trauma.

46. *Rapid City Journal*, March 7, 1975. These were also the accounts to which both witnesses swore at the Marshall trial and at the subsequent Means trial, both in 1976.

47. The witness was Marion Poor Bear, quoted in Matthiessen, *op. cit.*, p. 275.

48. *Ibid.*

49. According to WKLDOC attorney Bruce Ellison, this strategy was undertaken to free Marshall from the notoriety of Means, a factor all parties were concerned would negatively influence the jury, despite the state's lack of evidence. Insofar as Means was charged, not as being the shooter, but as being the shooter's accomplice, it stood to reason that the Marshall case would have to be tried first. In the event that Marshall was acquitted, the case against Means would virtually collapse before it got started. Hence, the defendants each stood a far better chance on their own than they would have tried together.

50. According to their report, South Dakota's (and presumably, the FBI's) ballistics experts could only determine that the shearing marks scoring the slug which killed Montileaux were "characteristic of those made by most cheap revolvers, due to misalignment of the cylinders and barrel."

51. Matthiessen, *op. cit.*, p. 275.

52. The dating accrues from "Motion to Endorse the Name of Myrtle Poor Bear on the Information," attached to the Marshall trial transcript. As is demonstrated in the preceding chapter, Poor Bear is known to have been in the custody of SAs Price and Wood on this date.

53. Matthiessen, *op. cit.*, p. 276.

54. Poor Bear testified at trial that she had notified the FBI of Marshall's "confession" to her at some point late in 1975. As with the rest of her testimony, this is probably untrue. If accurate, however, at least to the extent that this is when SAs Wood and Price began to coach her with regard to what she would be expected to say against Marshall, this would mean that the Bureau deliberately withheld information from the defense for more than three months concerning the fact that she would be a witness. Marshall's attorneys were finally notified of Poor Bear's existence on March 25, 1976; that is, *three days* before the trial was set to begin. Even had Poor Bear's testimony been truthful, such a withholding of witness identity is absolutely contrary to due process rules of disclosure.

55. Marshall trial transcript, quoted in Matthiessen, *op. cit.*, p. 276.

56. Marshall trial transcript, quoted in *ibid.*

57. This teletype bears a very clear resemblance to the one sent by the Los Angeles FBI office, probably written by Richard W. Held, in the aftermath of Geronimo Pratt's murder conviction; see Chapter 3. It should also be noted that, as is reflected in the motion to bring Poor Bear forward as a witness (note 21, above), Bureau support extended to underwriting Poor Bear's living expenses for the three days she was involved in the trial.

58. See the *Rapid City Journal*, April 2, 3, 6, and 7, 1976.

59. In a conversation with author Churchill in September 1987, Means described the charges levied against him as having been "the most bogus of all the bogus raps they ever tried to lay on me."

60. The record is quoted in *Win Magazine*, December 1, 1980.

61. Theodore Poor Bear's testimony is quoted in *ibid.*

62. Judge Young's finding is quoted in Tilsen's "Appelant's Brief" to the South Dakota Supreme Court on Marshall's behalf, April 1980, at p. 3.

63. The videotape of Poor Bear's testimony before the Review Commission was made by WKLDOC researcher Karen Northcott and is filed at the office of former WKLDOC coordinator Kenneth Tilsen in Minneapolis.

64. Minnesota Review Commission transcript, quoted in Matthiessen, *op. cit.*, p. 455.

65. Minnesota Review Commission transcript, quoted in *ibid.*, pp. 455-56.

66. The story in *People* appeared on April 20, 1981.

67. South Dakota Supreme Court, "Opinion," in *Richard Marshall v. State of South Dakota* (argued September 9, 1980), pp. 9-10.

68. Justice Wollman's dissenting points may be found in *ibid.* at pp. 12-22.

69. *Ibid.*, p. 22.

70. *Proposal for a commission of inquiry into the effect of domestic intelligence activities on criminal trials in the United States of America, op. cit.* It is worth noting that in this document, while AI found itself bound *not* to adopt Pratt, Peltier and Marshall as "prisoners of conscience" because their cases were not nonviolent in nature, it *did* specify (p. 69) that only his release from the South Dakota State Penitentiary at Sioux Falls had prevented AIM leader Russell Means from being designated as the first such (acknowledged) prisoner in the U.S.: "Amnesty International would have considered the adoption of Russell Means as a prisoner of conscience before his release by the federal court. He was, in the words of the federal district court...imprisoned 'solely' because of his infringement of [a] constitutionally invalid bond order [which, like the Marshall conviction, had been reviewed and upheld by the South Dakota Supreme Court, with only Justice Wollman dissenting]." Co-counsel Jim Leach apparently seriously considered a

Federal appeal at this time; see Tucker, Bob, "AIM leader to request new murder trial," *Rapid City Journal*, February 14, 1982, p. 1.

71. Contrary to popular belief, professions that they have not engaged in the acts cited as a basis for their incarcerations are *not* "standard" among prisoners of war in the U.S. A classic example is that of the so-called "Brinks truck robbers," a descendant group of the BLA, most of whom were charged—among other things—with murder pursuant to an armored car robbery attempt in Nyack, New York on October 20, 1981. Of those ultimately tried in this matter, most—Sekou Odinga, Chui Ferguson, Bilal Sunni-Ali, Iliana Robertson, Edward L. Joseph, Silvia Baraldini, Kuwasi Balagoon, David Gilbert, Judy Clark and Mutulu Shakur—adopted the "freedom fighter defense" of denying nothing, rejecting the legitimacy of the court purporting to try them, and refusing (to varying degrees) to participate in the proceedings. A similar posture was adopted by others—including Marilyn Buck, Linda Evans, Kamay Bayete, Tim Blunk, Dr. Alan Berkman and Susan Rosenberg—associated with the case. Only two persons, Kathy Boudin and Sam Brown, argued that the actions ascribed to them by the police were false or inaccurate.

72. "Convicted murderer admits to shooting death," *Rapid City Journal*, January 28, 1984, p. 2; "Marshall's sentence commuted to 99 years," *Rapid City Journal*, August 7, 1984, p. 3.

73. "Janklow commutes Marshall's life sentence," *Rapid City Journal*, December 28, 1984, p. 1. Also see "Janklow impressed with Marshall's courage," *Rapid City Journal*, December 30, 1984, p. 7.

74. Baka, Ken, "Oregon Banks case frustrates prosecutor," in the *Rapid City Journal*, July 24, 1986.

75. Quoted in *ibid*.

76. Matthiessen, *op. cit.*, p. 224.

77. AIM member Nilak Butler is quoted in *ibid.*, pp. 224-25: "In Colorado, we had the support of the Chicano community, which provided safe housing all over the state," in addition to the similar support provided by the area AIM chapter. She and her husband Dino, Bob Robideau, Mike Anderson, Norman Brown, Anna Mae Aquash, Carter Camp, Leonard Peltier and Dennis Banks are among those who benefitted from this alliance before "some of [the] Chicano volunteers got killed in a big fight...among themselves." After that, the AIM fugitives scattered.

78. Baka, *op. cit.*; the information on the Milwaukee attempted murder charge against Peltier, which—in addition to the Myrtle Poor Bear affidavit on the RESMURS matter—was used to obtain his fraudulent extradition from Canada, derives from Matthiessen, *op. cit.*, pp. 56-58.

79. See "Charges Dismissed in Oregon Trial," *Akwesasne Notes*, Vol. 8, No. 2, Early Summer, 1976, p. 10.

80. *Ibid*. Kamook Banks was, at the time, on bail concerning federal charges of interstate transportation of weapons and explosives, derived from the explosion of the car in which she, Bob Robideau and others had been riding, near Wichita, Kansas, on September 10, 1975; see Chapter 11.

81. See "The Arrest of Redner and Loudhawk," *Akwesasne Notes*, Vol. 8, No. 2, Early Summer, 1976, p. 11.

82. Baka, *op. cit.*

83. "Charges Dismissed in Oregon Trial," *op. cit.*

84. *Ibid*.

85. *Ibid*.

86. *Ibid*.

87. Quoted in *ibid*.

88. *Rapid City Journal*, April 7, 1981; Janklow contended the scheme was appropriate because Brown was already "providing a haven for outcasts."

89. Quoted in *ibid*.

90. The Longest Walk was undertaken during the spring of 1978, beginning in San Francisco with a group of about 150 marchers setting out to march all the way across the U.S., ending up in Washington, D.C. All along the way, speaking engagements were scheduled at which the walk's purpose—to dramatize American Indian grievances—would be explained. Additional marchers were recruited at many of these speeches and rallies. Thus, by the time the marchers arrived at the nation's capital in late October (having covered a nearly 3,000 mile route) the ranks had swelled to about 500. The Longest Walk received considerable favorable publicity and might be considered one of AIM's more successful public information efforts of the late 1970s. For further information see the documentary film, *The Longest Walk*, American Indian Information Society, Bismarck, North Dakota, 1979.

91. See Deukmejian's remarks, quoted at p. 8 of the *San Francisco Examiner*, October 24, 1982. These should be construed as the promises of one Republican governor to another.

92. It is worth noting that Deukmejian's successful campaign was not mounted against Brown who had already served two back-to-back terms as California governor.

93. *Freedom Notes,* June-September 1986, p. 3.

94. Brokaw, Chet, "Supreme Court says Banks received fair trial," *Rapid City Journal,* May 2, 1986.

95. Banks headquartered his effort in the Loneman School, in Oglala. Although several companies were involved, he seems to have been primarily concerned with attracting an electronic components assembly contract from the Honeywell Corporation in Minneapolis. Interestingly, Banks contends—and Honeywell has done nothing to challenge it—that he was employed by Honeywell as a "community relations specialist" during the period when he helped found AIM in Minneapolis (1968), and that he was carried on the payroll through mid-1973. This is to say, in effect, that the Honeywell Corporation paid a salary to a major AIM leader during the time he engaged in some of his most "radical" activities (*e.g.* The Trail of Broken Treaties, the Custer Courthouse confrontation, and the Siege of Wounded Knee). Such a circumstance does much to corroborate Banks' contention, consistently voiced, that—contrary to the "new Che Guevara" image manufactured for him by Douglass Durham—his own agenda was always essentially liberal, to see existing laws covering American Indian rights actually enforced. "We in AIM were never perfect," says Banks, "but the whole idea of us pursuing violent tactics, or attempting to bring about some sort of violent revolution is completely false. The violence in which AIM as an organization was involved was *entirely* imposed by the federal government, by the FBI and other agencies, because of the federal government's absolute refusal to abide by its *own* laws." Russell Means, among others, has publicly agreed: "One of the most important things AIM has always tried to do is to help the United States government live up to its own constitution, and its own treaty obligations, which it has always refused to do, and *still* refuses to do. I find it to be the ultimate irony that we Indians have been getting killed for upholding the *U.S. Constitution,* by the very government which is supposedly based on it."

96. See Rubin, James H., "Court rules Banks can be prosecuted on firearms charges," *Rapid City Journal,* January 21, 1986.

97. See "Four Indians face trial on 1975 charges," *Denver Post,* January 25, 1986.

98. Rubin, *op. cit.*

99. This concrete example, far more than any abstract analysis, demonstrates the extreme peril in which we are all placed by the mentality of the "conservative" (*i.e.,* neo-fascist) Reagan appointees to the Supreme Court. The recent and narrowly averted attempt to seat Robert Bork on the high court would have spelled the final dissolution of even token legal protections of human rights within the U.S. With regard to Bork, it is worth noting that after Judge Fred Nichol's dismissal of charges in the "Wounded Knee leadership" trial for gross governmental misconduct, it was then Solicitor General Robert Bork who ordered the U.S. Attorneys in the case to appeal the dismissal.

100. Quoted in Baka, *op. cit.*

101. Quoted in Rubin, *op. cit.*

102. Quoted in Baka, *op. cit.*

103. Letter from The Honorable Fred Nichol to Kenneth S. Stern, November 17, 1987.

Chapter 13

1. Dunbar Ortiz, Roxanne, "Foreword," in Jack D. Forbes, *Native Americans and Nixon: Presidential Politics and Minority Self-Determination,* American Indian Studies Center, UCLA, 1981, p. 12.

2. Matthiessen, *op. cit.,* p. 380. The document he is quoting from is "Medical Record of Federal Prisoner in Transit: Wilson, Robert H., No. 01499-164, from M.C.C., Chicago, IL to U.S.P., Marion, IL, 10-29-76."

3. Matthiessen, *op. cit.* At p. 502, he quotes Standing Deer summing up his own career: "In 1963, I received my first prison sentence. I was sentenced to ten years in Leavenworth for Interstate Transportation of Counterfeit Securities. I served from 3/26/63 to 2/11/70 in Leavenworth. On 11/30/71, I was charged with Armed Robbery and Larceny of an auto in Oklahoma City. I was sentenced to 25 years in the state penitentiary. On July 27, 1973 I was involved in a $27 million riot during which the state prison was burned to the ground. I was on deadlock solitary confinement for a year during which time my 5' x 8' cell door was never opened. On April 29, 1975 I took over a bus when the guards were attempting to transport me and I was on escape until April 6, 1976. I was recaptured in Chicago. It was on June 3, 1975 that a police officer in Okla City was following a robbery and I was accused of shooting. This resulted in seven indictments filed against me, each carrying a possible life sentence. These were the

charges Capt Carey and the stranger had dismissed in the Peltier case. I was tried and convicted of a $40,000 bank robbery in Indianapolis and sentenced to 15 years. I was tried for interstate transportation of stolen jewelry in Chicago and sentenced to 10 years concurrent. I was tried and convicted for a $279,000 jewel robbery in Houston and given three concurrent life sentences. I am indicted on a $51,000 bank robbery in St. Louis which is pending along with several other robberies. The FBI has written on court documents 'considered to be the most dangerous individual ever apprehended in Chicago.'"

4. The phrase is taken from the title of a book written by another Marion inmate during the same period; see Abbott, Jack Henry, *In the Belly of the Beast: Letters from Prison*, Random House, New York, 1981.

5. According to "Clinical Record: Wilson, Robert H., 01499-164, 4-13-77," and "Medical Record of Federal Prisoner in Transit: Wilson, Robert H., 01499-164, from U.S.P., Marion IL to Harris County, Houston TX, 9-28-76," Standing Deer suffered (and suffers) from a "degenerative disk disease of the L5-S1" and "osteophyte formation of the L4-5 vertebral bodies." He was diagnosed as experiencing severe and chronic lower back pain and constant medication was prescribed to offset this.

6. Plank's visit is recounted in a sworn affidavit by Standing Deer dated 9/4/79.

7. See, for example, "Request for Administrative Remedy," submitted by Robert Hugh Wilson, 01499-164, on 3/23/78. Also see U.S. Department of Prisons, "Inmate Request to Staff Member," Wilson, Robert H., (No. 01499-164) to Dr. J.R. Plank, 4/5/78.

8. Matthiessen, *op. cit.*, p. 381. In another "Inmate Request to Staff Member," Standing Deer informed Dr. Plank that, "I am in severe pain in my lower back and left leg. I have a hard time getting to and from the shower. My knee locks and I have lower back spasms and cramping which cause me to fall to the ground. I cannot climb the stairs in the unit and I need a wheelchair."

9. During all his years in various prisons, Standing Deer habitually kept a daily diary. Pertinent sections of his Marion and Leavenworth journals were turned over to Peltier's attorneys in 1979, and are quoted here.

10. Sworn affidavit of Robert Hugh Wilson, *op. cit.*, p. 1.

11. *Ibid.*, p. 5.

12. The actual identity of the FBI agent making this visit has not been established. SA Wilkins is suspected insofar as he is known to have been involved in later aspects of the case.

13. Sworn affidavit of Robert Hugh Wilson, *op. cit.*, pp. 6-7; the notion that Standing Deer might convince Peltier to attempt an escape, during which he might be "legitimately" killed by a guard, was also discussed as "an optional scenario" during this first meeting.

14. *Ibid.*, p. 10.

15. "Chronological Record of Medical Care: Wilson, Robert H., 01499-164," shows at its 5/12/78 entry that a Dr. McMillan recommended that Standing Deer be immediately "transferred to the hospital for local anesthesia and hydrocortisone injections in the tender area plus physiotherapy and medicine." The record reflects a nearly two-month absence of any such treatments, and that they were actually resumed on 5/17/78.

16. As concerns the removal of detainers, see a letter from Larry D. Hayes (Sheriff's Office, Oklahoma County, OK) to Ms. Bonnie L. Streed (Records Control Supervisor, Marion Federal Penitentiary), dated May 24, 1978. Streed notified Oklahoma that Marion had complied—U.S. Department of Justice, Bureau of Prisons, "Comply with Request to Remove Detainer"—June 1, 1978.

17. Standing Deer Diary, *op. cit.*, June 27, 1978.

18. Sworn affidavit of Robert Hugh Wilson, *op. cit.*, p. 2.

19. U.S. Penitentiary, Marion, Illinois, "Memorandum," Bonnie Streed, Manager Records Office to C.B. Faulkner, Regional Legal Counsel, September 15, 1978.

20. Sworn affidavit of Robert Hugh Wilson, *op. cit.*, p. 8.

21. The overall similarity between the Peltier assassination plan and the one by which George Jackson was "taken out" in San Quentin should not be overlooked; see Chapter 3.

22. Sworn affidavit of Robert Hugh Wilson, *op. cit.*, p. 9.

23. "Movement Summary: Wilson, Robert H., 01499-164," December 21, 1978.

24. The sentence is covered in the hearing report for 12/27/78 filed in the records section of the federal facility at Leavenworth. As Peter Matthiessen observes (*op. cit.*, p. 386), "Standing Deer had already served a three-month term in [the Control] unit, a clangorous metal zoo of 6x6x8 foot cell boxes with steel-slab beds where captive humans were (and are) subject to pseudoscientific experiments and 'character invalidation' techniques devised by a certain Dr. Edgar Schein." In a 1962 address to the wardens of all federal maximum security prisons, assembled for the occasion in Washington, D.C., Schein

observed, "In order to produce marked changes in behavior, it is necessary to weaken, undermine, or remove supports for old attitudes. I would like you to think of brainwashing not in terms of politics, ethics and morals, but in terms of the deliberate changing of human behavior by a group of men who have relatively complete control over the environment in which the captives live...[These changes can then be induced by] isolation, sensory deprivation, segregation of leaders, spying, tricking men into written statements which are then shown to others, placing individuals whose willpower has been severely weakened into a living situation with others more advanced in *thought reform*, character invalidation, humiliations, sleeplessness, rewarding subservience, and fear [emphasis added].'" Schein has also been repeatedly documented as having prescribed psychosurgery (*e.g.*: lobotomies), electroshock "treatment" and/or drug "therapy" to "cure" particularly strong-willed inmates of autonomous thought. See National Committee to Support the Marion Brothers, *Breaking Men's Minds*, Chicago, Illinois, 1978. For a study of certain very close parallels in "medical" practice, see Lifton, Robert Jay, *The Nazi Doctors: Medical Killing and the Psychology of Genocide*, Basic Books, New York, 1986.

25. Sworn affidavit of Robert Hugh Wilson, *op. cit.*, p. 3.

26. *Ibid.*

27. Messerschmidt, *op. cit.*, p. 135. Peltier had arrived in Leavenworth on February 23, but was isolated from Standing Deer, Bob Robideau and other prisoners during his six week stay there.

28. Richards was married to Dick Wilson's daughter Saunie.

29. Chuck Richards was a member of one of the very worst GOON clans on Pine Ridge, a group so vicious that it was called "the Manson Family" by local residents. Richards himself was usually referred to as "Charles Manson." Although nothing was ever done about his lethal and well-documented GOON activities, he was finally convicted in 1977 for having detained BIA police officer Pat Mills at shotgun point during an altercation. Even then he was sentenced to only three years.

30. The reason for this convoluted communication process was not so much related to informational security as to the fact that federal inmates are not allowed to correspond directly with one another through the mail.

31. Bobby Garcia had admittedly shot and killed his sister-in-law during a family dispute on November 9, 1966. Later, Garcia was accused of killing a guard during an attempted jailbreak in Tucumcari, New Mexico. His execution was set for March 28, 1968, but commuted to life imprisonment in early 1969 under proviso that he be transferred to the Control Unit at Marion. After five months of behavior modification, he was released into the prison's general population, but remained extremely withdrawn until he warmed to Leonard Peltier nearly a decade later.

32. Peltier's concern that he might actually be killed inside Lompoc is hardly unfounded. According to a communication from L.G. Grossman, California Regional Director for the U.S. Bureau of Prisons, dated November 8, 1979: "By August of 1979 seven individuals had already been murdered at Lompoc."

33. Duenas, a Chicano, had been with Peltier during the mass arrest at the Fort Lawton occupation in 1970 (see Chapter 5) and was subsequently arrested with him again, on September 20, 1974, charged with possession of illegal weapons during a fishing rights confrontation involving the Kootenai people of Idaho. In late 1975, Duenas had assisted Peltier in slipping across the border into Canada to avoid capture after the firefight on Pine Ridge (see Chapter 9).

34. The details of the escape itself are covered very well in Matthiessen, *op. cit.*, pp. 390-91. It seems the prisoners were in possession of three keys to the J Wing Building at the time they made their break. Dallas Thundershield, who had only a few months to go on his sentence, had not been slated to escape; he seems to have decided to go along only about five minutes before the fact. Neither Peltier nor Garcia was able to dissuade him.

35. According to the report of Lompoc Guard John B. Hughes, made on the morning of July 21, 1979: "At approximately 10:30 p.m. [on the night of July 20] I was engaged in making a search of the area in a northerly direction from the Institution toward the F.C.I. [Federal Correctional Institution] Firing Range. As I was proceeding toward the Range at a point about 75-80 yards east of Sewage Pond #1 I was alerted by a voice saying '*This is Garcia. I'm unarmed. Don't shoot.*' Or words to that effect. While a light was held on Garcia, who was lying knee deep in grass, I approached him and put the flexible emergency handcuffs on the suspect, after performing a frisk search of his person [emphasis in the original]."

36. Messerschmidt, *op. cit.*, p. 137.

37. Guild and the rest of the participating guards made much of the fact that the .38 calibre revolver (Serial Number 4454497) had been "issued" to him at the time of the escape. In fact, they are so careful to establish this claim that one is immediately drawn to suspect that the facts are otherwise. Given that Guild's vehicle approached Peltier and Thundershield from the wrong direction—heading not from

the prison, but toward it—it is rather difficult to determine exactly how he might have been issued a revolver at the time of the escape and in response to it. The appearance is that he already had the weapon and was assigned to head off the fleeing men from a point well outside the prison. This scenario corresponds very well with Guild's own admission under oath that he was aware of the escape route before the fact. If this is so, it immediately suggests the possibility that Guild summarily executed Dallas Thundershield, thinking the victim was Leonard Peltier.

38. William Guild's report on the shooting of Dallas Thundershield, submitted on the morning of July 21, 1979, establishes the time of the event as being "about 9:45 p.m. [on July 20]." The report of guard D.A. Blackburn, who had been on routine fence patrol at the time of the breakout indicates that he was first on the scene after Guild, that Thundershield was still alive, and that he (Blackburn) had talked with the wounded man. In the report of Lieutenant Greg Hutson, Correctional Supervisor at Lompoc, it is stated that "outside agencies [*i.e.*: the FBI] began arriving at the scene" and "a picture of the downed person was brought to the area of Dallas THUNDERSHIELD, 03301-073J, with the downed person being identified as Thundershield." Only then, "at approximately 10:45 p.m.," according to Lt. Hutson, was it that a "Dr. Hudson arrived and officially pronounced Thundershield dead." In other words, until it was absolutely established that the wounded man was *not* Leonard Peltier the prison doctor was not allowed to traverse the few yards from the prison gate to administer medical aid. By then, a full *hour* had elapsed and Thundershield had bled to death. This seems to have been the same expedient used to kill Pedro Bissonette; see Chapter 7.

39. An excellent account of this incident may be found in Matthiessen, *op. cit.*, pp 396-97.

40. *Ibid.*, p. 397.

41. *Ibid.*, p. 399. It should be noted that the 302 report of SA James R. Wilkins for this date reflects that Peltier had occupied such a position, and that he appeared to expect to be killed upon allowing himself to be captured. The agent also noted that Peltier had not only a Mini-14 rifle and ammunition, but binoculars, Forest Service topographical maps of the area, a glass water bottle, a red address book and a complete outfit of civilian clothes ("levis, a denim jacket, a black t-shirt and white tennis shoes. He was also wearing leather gloves.")

42. This account comes from a telephone conversation between Peltier and author Churchill in 1985.

43. Matthiessen, *op. cit.*, p. 407. It should be noted that, for whatever reason, Peltier was never placed in the Control Unit. He has, however, been consigned to lengthy periods in the "Hole" during the past seven years.

44. *Ibid.*, pp. 504-505. U.S. Department of Justice, "Extra Good-Time Recommendation for Robert H. Wilson, 01499-164," dated 25 June, 1979: "Inmate Wilson has been assigned as a CCS Clerk since February 1979 and has exceeded all requirements of the job. In addition to very high quality of daily work (seven day a week) he frequently puts in additional time in the evenings to insure smooth operation in this office. Wilson provides helpful suggestions that aid the efficient discharge of the CCS Clerk's duties." This hardly squares with his being summarily fired from this same position on July 20, 1979—the day of the Lompoc breakout—and then transferred to another institution.

45. Garcia had been placed in Terre Haute's N-2 "death unit," where guards habitually ask each inmate, "Are you alive?" in the process of making hourly rounds of the isolation cells, a frequency that fails to jibe with the official pronouncement that he might have been dead "for hours" prior to being discovered by a guard. His cell was situated immediately across the hall from the guards' office, a proximity which virtually guaranteed that they would hear the death throes caused by anyone suffering "fractures of the neck and secondary strangulation," whether self-inflicted or otherwise. Further, Wisconsin AIM leader Herb Powless, who spent time in the N-2 unit shortly before Garcia, insists that all inmates there are continuously monitored by a closed circuit television system. All of this adds up to a not inconsiderable validation of the conclusion reached by inmates Fidel Ramos and Haneef Shabazz (slave name: Beaumont Gereau), who investigated the circumstances of Garcia's death as best they could, that he had not committed suicide. Rather, they say, he was simply murdered by the guards. See Matthiessen, *op. cit.*, p. 512.

46. Matthiessen, *op. cit.*, p. 407.

47. *Ibid.*, p. 408.

48. Hazlett is quoted in *ibid.*, p. 409.

49. Interestingly, because Hazlett was on the *Times* payroll throughout the investigation (as he had been for nearly twenty years, while he became an "ace" police reporter), and because the paper had footed the bills involved, the editors claimed to "own" the story. Hence, while refusing to publish it themselves, they exercised their legal option to also prevent its publication elsewhere, effectively burying it

altogether. Small wonder the *Los Angeles Times* has long been considered by the FBI to be an organization "friendly to the Bureau."

50. See Messerschmidt, *op. cit.*, p. 139.

51. *Freedom*, September 1986, p. 7.

52. Weyler, *op. cit.*, pp. 209-10.

53. *Ibid.*

54. Quoted in Matthiessen, *op. cit.*, pp. 533-34.

55. This is the standard FBI description of Trudell, attached as a matter of course to other documents in which his name is mentioned from approximately late 1973 onward. It is not an atypical Bureau procedure in the case of political subjects.

56. It should be noted that the FALN was the *real* target of the "law" among these organizations, the activities of which were publicly advanced as a justifying rationale for the formation of the JTTF. One will search in vain for the record of any meaningful action ever taken with regard to the Croatian Liberation Forces, a tiny anti-communist grouping whose minor bombings during the late 1970s placed them briefly in the limelight. As for Omega 7, its very reason for existence since its founding in 1961 appears more than anything to have been the provision of trained paramilitary cadres for the CIA, both within the U.S. and throughout Latin America (Omega 7 has functioned for the CIA in much the same way the GOONs functioned for the FBI). Examples of this are legion, and include Omega 7's provision of several of the "technicians"—Guillermo Novo and Alvin Ross among them—who carried out the car-bomb assassinations of Orlando Letelier, a former Chilean government official under Salvador Allende, and researcher Ronni Moffitt in Washington, D.C., on September 21, 1976; see Dinges, John, and Saul Landau, *Assassination on Embassy Row*, Pantheon Books, New York, 1981. The inclusion of right-wing organizations in the JTTF's initial list of targets appears to have had no other function than to provide the public impression of "balance" necessary to make the new unit seem focused on criminal rather than political matters.

57. The 1980-81 expropriations and expropriation attempts include the holdup of a Purolator truck at the European American Bank Branch in Inglewood, New York on April 22, 1980; two foiled attempts to hit Brinks trucks at the Chemical Bank in Nanuet, New York during the fall of 1980; two unsuccessful attempts to hold up a Purolator truck outside Reed's department store in Danbury, Connecticut during the winter of 1980-81; a failed attempt to rob a Purolator truck outside the Danbury, Conneticut Ramada Inn of March 23, 1981; two unsuccessful attempts to rob a Brinks truck at the Chase Manhattan Bank in the Bronx during May of 1981; another two unsuccessful attempts to hit a Brinks truck at the Nanuet Chemical Bank branch in the same month; the robbery of a Brinks truck at the Bronx Chase Manhattan Bank branch on June 2, 1981; and a final two unsuccessful attempts to rob a Brinks truck at the Nanuet Chemical Bank branch in October of 1981. Earlier successful Family operations included the holdup of a Citibank branch in Mount Vernon, New York on October 19, 1977; the October 12, 1978 robbery of a Chase Manhattan Bank branch in Lower Manhattan; the robbery of two Purolator trucks inside Bamberger's department store in the Livingston, New Jersey shopping mall on December 19, 1978; the hold-up of two more Purolator trucks at Bamberger's store in Paramus, New Jersey on September 11, 1979; and breaking Assata Shakur (slave name: Joanne Chesimard) out of a New Jersey women's penal facility on November 2, 1979.

58. The Nyack Police Department captured RATF members Kathy Boudin, David Gilbert, Judy Clark and Sam Brown on the scene of the Brinks truck robbery attempt on October 20, 1981. The JTTF was then able to capture Sekou Odinga (slave name: Nathaniel Burns, a former Panther 21 defendant) and kill Mtyari Sundiata (slave name: Samuel Lee Smith) in New York City on October 23. On January 7, 1982, the FBI led Philadelphia police to Anthony LaBorde and, on January 20, the JTTF captured Kuwasi Balagoon (slave name: Donald Weems) in the Bronx. On March 26, 1982, the JTTF captured Edward Joseph (another Panther 21 defendant) and Chui Ferguson in a Manhattan apartment. On November 9, Silvia Baraldini was arrested the by FBI in Manhattan and, on November 15, Bilal Sunni-Ali was arrested in Belize. It wasn't until November 29, 1984 that the FBI managed to catch up with RATF members Susan Rosenberg and Timothy Blunk, and the capture of Marilyn Jean Buck and Linda Sue Evans did not occur until May 11, 1985. The final pair, Dr. Alan Berkman and Mutulu Shakur, were not tracked down until 1986, five years after the fact.

59. See Castelluci, John, *The Big Dance: The Untold Story of Weatherman Kathy Boudin and the Terrorist Family that Committed the Brink's Truck Robbery Murders*, Dodd, Meade & Co., New York, 1986.

60. *Ibid.*, p. 291.

61. See Bonds' testimony in *U.S. v. Chimerenga, et al.*

62. Castelluci, *op. cit.*

63. Tate, Greg, "Dirty Tricks versus the Right to Dissent," *The Village Voice*, July 2, 1985. Also see Larsen, Jonathan Z., "The Son of Brinks?", *New York Magazine*, May 6, 1985.

64. One very middle-class juror is known to have termed the whole proceeding as "fascist" and "absurd."

65. A prime target within the May 19th Movement was attorney Susan Tipograph, who had devoted her practice to defending radicals accused of engaging in armed struggle. At one point, she was accused of having smuggled weapons to imprisoned FALN leader Willie Morales, in an obvious replay of the successful strategy used against the legal supporters of George Jackson; see Chapter 3. For further information on Tipograph, see Frankfort, Ellen, *Kathy Boudin and the Dance of Death*, Stein and Day, New York, 1983.

66. Both Dohrn and Fulani Sunni-Ali were jailed for several months in 1982-83 for refusing to testify before a grand jury purporting to investigate the radical underground in general, and the RATF contact network in particular. According to Castelluci (p. 242), "the grand jury resisters would steadfastly refuse to talk or provide fingerprints, photographs, handwriting, and hair samples. They would hold press conferences denouncing the grand jury as an instrument of political repression..."; the whole thing was a "sideshow," designed to neutralize certain "key activists" by forcing them to destroy their own credibility through overt cooperation with the state (*e.g.*: the police already had fingerprints, photos, writing samples, etc., concerning Dohrn and Sunni-Ali; what they were seeking was the "voluntary" submission of these items by the two women, in order to establish publicly that they had "sold out" and were cooperating.) For more on the use of grand juries as instruments of political repression, see Chapter 9, Note 83.

67. See Calhoun, Patricia, "Grand Slam," *Westword*, Denver, Co., December 14, 1983, pp. 7-8.

68. Judge Foreman is quoted in *Breaking Men's Minds, op. cit.*

69. Former warden Aron is quoted in *ibid.* Also see Lyden, Jacki, and Paula Schiller, "The Prison that Defies Reform," *Student Lawyer*, May 1987, for further information on procedures at Marion.

70. Dr. Korn is quoted in "Can't Kill the Spirit," insert to *Breakthrough: Political Journal of the Prairie Fire Organizing Committee*, Vol. XI, No. 2, Fall 1987. Also see Reuben, William A., and Carlos Norman, "Brainwashing in America? The Women of Lexington Prison," *The Nation*, June 27, 1987.

71. Mari Bras, Juan, "Speech Before the United Nations Commission on Human Rights," New York, September 24, 1977.

72. Quoted in Lopez, Alfredo, *Doña Licha's Island*, South End Press, Boston, 1987, p. 145.

73. *Ibid.*, pp. 147-51.

74. *Ibid.*, p. 149.

75. *Ibid.* In a case remarkably similar to that emerging from the 1969 Hampton-Clark assassinations in Chicago (see Chapter 3), the families of the victims filed a civil rights suit against the police, federal authorities and FBI. In March 1987, the plaintiffs were awarded a $1.3 million settlement. Once again, no members of the police establishment faced any sort of criminal charges as a result of their participation in and cover-up of what the state acknowledged as being outright murder.

76. *Ibid.*, p. 146.

77. See the September 12, 1985 issue of *Claridad* (San Juan, Puerto Rico), especially Coss, Manuelo, "Cobardes, Viva Puerto Rico Libre"; Delgado, Augusto, "La invasión del viernes 30"; Cotto, Candida, "Madrugada del 30 del agosto"; and "Repudio masivo al FBI."

78. See Walker, Annette, "FBI discredited before Hartford trial even begins," *Guardian*, January 20, 1988, p. 9.

79. See "Continúan las vistas en Hartford," *Claridad*, Sept. 20-26, 1985, p. 3.

80. See Coss, Manolo, "Martínez Vargas niega ser informante," *Claridad*, Sept. 20-26, 1985, p. 5.

81. See Coss, Manolo, "Delicuente al servicio del FBI," *Claridad*, Sept. 20-26, 1975, p. 5.

82. Walker, Annette, *op. cit.*

83. *Ibid.*

84. *Ibid.*

85. "Can't Kill the Spirit," *op. cit.*

86. See Bras, Juan Mari, "El escirro Richard Held," *Claridad*, Sept. 13-19, 1975. It will be remembered that, while the Puerto Rican operation was commanded by Richard W. Held, that on Pine Ridge was commanded by his father, COINTELPRO architect Richard G. Held. The old adage, "like father, like son," surely applies in this case. It will also be remembered that, like Richard W. Held, Richard G. was well rewarded for the atrocities he orchestrated or covered up; he retired from Bureau service in 1981 as Assistant Director of the FBI.

87. See the videotape, *The Secret Team Behind Iran/Contragate*, a lecture given by Daniel Sheehan, Chief Counsel of the Christic Institute, at the Forum West, Los Angeles, February 1, 1987.

88. All incident accounts are excerpted from *Harassment Update: Chronological List of FBI and Other Harassment Incidents*, Movement Support Network, and Anti-Repression Project for the Center for Constitutional Rights and the National Lawyers Guild, New York, January 1987 (Sixth Edition).

89. *Harassment Update*, Center for Constitutional Rights, New York, January 27, 1988.

90. *CCR News*, Center for Constitutional Rights, New York, January 27, 1988, p. 1.

91. Ratner, Margaret, "Statement," Center for Constitutional Rights, New York, January 27, 1988, p. 1.

92. Buitrago, Ann Mari, *Report on CISPES Files Maintained by FBI Headquarters and Released Under the Freedom of Information Act*, FOIA, Inc., New York, January 1988, p. 1.

93. *Ibid.*, p. 2.

94. *Ibid.*; for more on Varelli, see King, Wayne, "F.B.I.'s Papers Portray Inquiry Fed by Informer," *New York Times*, February 13, 1988.

95. Buitrago, *op. cit.*

96. *Ibid.*, p. 4.

97. Press Release, "GROUPS INCLUDED IN THE CISPES FILES OBTAINED FROM FBI HEADQUARTERS," Center for Constitutional Rights, New York, January 27, 1988.

98. FBI Teletype, Denver to Director (routed also to the Dallas, Houston, and San Antonio Field Offices), dated 27 June 1985 and captioned COMMITTEE IN SOLIDARITY WITH THE PEOPLE OF EL SALVADOR (CISPES), p. 2. In 1986, having become the subject of considerable controversy because of his political activities, Santos left his position as a mathematics coordinator with the University Learning Center at the University of Colorado/Boulder. He is presently a doctoral student at SUNY/Binghamton.

99. Hirschorn, Michael W., "Newly Released Documents Provide Rare Look at How FBI Monitors Students and Professors," *The Chronicle of Higher Education*, February 10, 1988, p. A-1.

100. Quoted in part from Shenon, Philip, "F.B.I.'s Chief Says Surveillance Was Justified," *New York Times*, February 3, 1988, and in part from clips of a press conference shown on Cable News Network (CNN) on the same date.

101. Shenon, Philip, "Reagan Backs F.B.I. Surveillance: Accepts Bureau Report That There Was Solid Basis for Effort Aimed at Critics," *New York Times*, February 4, 1988.

102. See, for example, Shenon, Philip, "Dubious Tactics: F.B.I. Once Again Lax on Liberty," *New York Times*, January 31, 1988, and McGrory, Mary, "FBI's Shabby Sleuthing," *Boston Globe*, February 3, 1988.

103. "How Did the F.B.I. Go Astray?" *Boston Globe*, February 6, 1988.

104. FBIHQ, "Predication for the Investigation of the Members and Supporters of A.I.M.," Washington, D.C., 1976, p. 1.

105. United States House of Representatives, Committee on the Judiciary, *FBI Undercover Operations: Report of the Subcommittee on Civil and Constitutional Rights*, (H. Doc. 98-267), 98th Congress, 2d Session, U.S. Government Printing Office, Washington, D.C., April 1984.

106. *Ibid.*, p. 4.

107. *Ibid.*, p. 2.

108. *Ibid.*, pp. 2-3.

109. *Ibid.*, p. 1. At p. 13, however, the subcommittee admits that these figures are probably misleadingly low estimates: "these sums include only those items that the Bureau has chosen to segregate out as special cost of the operations, such as informant payments, bribes, lease expenses, *etc.* The bulk of the expenses—FBI salaries and general overhead—are excluded, and present FBI record-keeping practices do not readily permit retrieval of the actual total costs associated with undercover operations."

110. *Ibid.*, p. 5.

111. *Ibid.*

112. *Ibid.*, p. 6.

113. *Ibid.*

114. *Ibid.*, pp. 7-9; Operation Corkscrew was a "sting" gambit, conducted from 1978-82, to ostensibly "obtain evidence of case-fixing in the Cleveland [Ohio] Municipal Court. In the end, it failed to do so, but ruined the careers of several apparently honest local judges while simultaneously "undermining public confidence in a public institution."

115. *Ibid.*, p. 8.

116. *Ibid.*, pp. 8-9.

117. *Ibid.*, p. 8.

118. *Ibid.*, p. 3.

119. *Ibid.*, p. 10.

120. *Ibid.*, pp. 10-11.

121. *Ibid.*, p. 10.

122. Anyone believing that there is any real utility in addressing criminal acts via civil courts should review the matter of the Hampton/Clark assassinations (Chapter 3): more than a decade of litigation was involved, at a cost of hundreds of thousands of dollars, with the FBI allowed to obstruct the process at every step along the way. Worse, no one was ultimately punished for outright murder, even after it was clearly established as having occurred.

123. Aside from Willie Nelson and Robin Williams, other entertainers involved were Kris Kristofferson, Joni Mitchell, Billy Vera, John Trudell and Jesse Ed Davis. See "Official denounces concert for Peltier," *Rapid City Journal*, October 25, 1987, p. 6. Also see "FBI blasts benefit for Indian activist who killed agents," *Rocky Mountain News*, October 25, 1987, p. 10.

124. Concert organizer Peter Coyote estimated that the benefit grossed "about a third" of the monies anticipated. The Bureau's conduct regarding the concert in general and Nelson in particular was so outrageous that it attracted the attention of *Los Angeles Herald Examiner* editorials editor Timothy Lange. The result was that Lange published one of the most accurate and incisive editorials concerning the Peltier case and the FBI's anti-AIM campaign ever to see print in the mainstream press. See Lange, Timothy, "Cowboys and Indians, FBI style," *Los Angeles Herald Examiner*, November 17, 1987, p. 13.

125. Pell, *op. cit.*, p. 176. The bookstore ploy is particularly ugly. As Pell observes, "[I]f Janklow is permitted to sue the sellers, bookstores may become reluctant to stock controversial works." Although Janklow's suit ultimately ended up exactly where it belonged, the chilling effect on dissemination of information it was intended to achieve—simply by being filed—seems undeniable.

126. It should be noted that the information Janklow claims to have considered objectionable had already appeared in Weyler (*op. cit.*), Messerschmidt (*op. cit.*) and elsewhere. It has also been subsequently published by author Churchill; see "The Strange Case of 'Wild Bill' Janklow," *Covert Action/Information Bulletin*. Janklow showed no interest in filing suits in these instances despite the fact that he had been treated even more harshly by certain of the writers in question than he had by Matthiessen. The rule of thumb at issue seems to be one is free to speak the truth so long as no one, or very few people, will hear you.

127. On June 1, 1983, the Pine Ridge Tribal Council passed, by an eighteen to zero vote, Resolution No. 83-103 demanding that SA Price be permanently removed from the reservation. It read, in part, "Special agent Price's past conduct demonstrates that he is a danger to the well being of the Lakota people, and...has proven to be of unsavory character..." As attorneys Michael E. Tigar, Linda Huber, and John H. Privatera pointed out in a brief to the Subcommittee on Civil and Constitutional Rights, "It is...distressing that the FBI's internal review procedures do not appear to have taken into account the fact that Agents Price and Wood figure again and again in...allegations of misconduct." (Subcommittee on Civil and Constitutional Rights, Committee on the Judiciary, U.S. House of Representatives, *First Session on FBI Authorization, op. cit.*, pp. 244-45.)

128. The suit was dismissed by the U.S. District Court in January 1988. See note 130 below. It had been repeatedly delayed by the inordinate amount of time required for the FBI to produce documents requested by discovery motions.

129. Goodale, James C., "Tavoularis and the *Washington Post*—Getting Even with the Press," unpublished manuscript quoted by Pell, *op. cit.*, p. 172. Goodale's observation should be placed in the context of the massive suits entered by Israeli defense head Ariel Sharon and retired U.S. Army general William Westmoreland to attempt to collect "damages" from television networks which had accurately depicted certain of their past activities.

130. See "Agent's suit over book dismissed," *Rapid City Journal*, January 16, 1988, p. C6.

131. This, of course, places both attorneys and researchers in the position of having to *already* know about the details of COINTELPRO activities in order to pose the questions which will allow Swearingen to reveal his information. Given that COINTELPRO methods are supposedly not part of current counterintelligence techniques, and the discussion of them can thus hardly be construed as a "security breach," one can only conclude that imposition of such Catch-22 guidelines are designed primarily to prevent the disclosure of past FBI illegalities which still carry possible implications of culpability. The only crime on the books carrying a Statute of Limitations long enough to cover the COINTELPRO era proper is murder.

132. "Once a G-Man, Now a Pacifist: A costly conversion," *Newsweek*, November 23, 1987, p. 24.

133. *Ibid.*

134. *Ibid.* Author Churchill can readily attest to the magnitude of the transformation insofar as Ryan appears to have headed up a COINTELPRO directed at him, *circa* 1969-70, when he served as head of the Peoria at-large SDS chapter.

135. Reportedly, California Congressman Don Edwards, chair of the House Judiciary Subcommittee on Civil and Constitutional Rights, intends to look into Ryan's firing, as well as "question [the FBI] about how it classifies dissident groups"; *ibid.*

136. Pell, *op. cit.,* p. 193.

137. "A New Verdict for Mandel," *Time,* November 23, 1987, p. 31.

Selected Bibliography

Abbott, Jack Henry, *In the Belly of the Beast: Letters from Prison*, Random House, New York, 1981.

Agee, Philip, *Inside the Company: CIA Diary*, Stonehill Publishing Co., New York, 1975.

Akwesasne Notes, *Voices From Wounded Knee, 1973*, Mohawk Nation via Rooseveltown, New York, 1974.

American Friends Service Committee, *Uncommon Controversy: The Fishing Rights of the Muckleshoot, Puyallup, and Nisqually Indians*, University of Washington Press, Seattle, 1970.

Amnesty International, *Allegations of Mistreatment in Marion Prison, Illinois, U.S.A.*, New York, 1987.

_____, *Proposal for a commission of inquiry into the effect of domestic intelligence activities on criminal trials in the United States of America*, Amnesty International, New York, 1980.

Andrist, Ralph K., *The Long Death: Last Days of the Plains Indians*, Collier Books, New York.

Archer, Jules, *Strikes, Bombs, and Bullets: Big Bill Haywood and the IWW*, Julian Messner, New York, 1972.

Armstrong, Gregory, *The Dragon Has Come: The Last Fourteen Months in the Life of George Jackson*, Harper and Row, New York, 1974.

Armstrong, Virginia I., *I Have Spoken: American History Through the Voices of Indians*, Pocket Books, New York, 1975.

Balbus, Isaac, *The Dialectic of Legal Repression*, Russell Sage Foundation, New York, 1973.

Barnett, Frank R., B. Hugh Tovar, and Richard H. Schultz (eds.), *Special Operations in US Strategy*, National Defense University Press, Washington, D.C., 1984.

Bermanzohm, Paul C. (M.D.), and Sally A. Bermanzohm, *The True Story of the Greensboro Massacre*, César Cauce Publishers and Distributors, Inc., New York, 1980.

Bing, Alexander M., *War Time Strikes and Their Adjustments*, E.P. Dutton, New York, 1921.

Blue Cloud, Peter, (ed.), *Alcatraz is Not an Island*, Wingbow Press, Berkeley, Calif., 1972.

Bontecou, Eleanor, *The Federal Loyalty and Security Program*, Cornell University Press, Ithaca, New York, 1953.

Brand, Johanna, *The Life and Death of Anna Mae Aquash*, James Lorimer & Company, Publishers, Toronto (Ontario), 1978.

Bray, Howard, *Pillars of the Post*, W.W. Norton & Co., New York, 1980.

Breitman, George, Herman Porter and Baxter Smith, *The Assassination of Malcolm X*, Pathfinder Press, New York, 1976.

Brown, Dee, *Bury My Heart at Wounded Knee: An Indian History of the American West*, Holt, Rinehart, and Winston, New York, 1970.

_____, *Fort Phil Kearny: An American Saga*, University of Nebraska Press, Lincoln, 1971.

Brown, H. "Rap", *Die Nigger Die!*, Dial Press, New York, 1969.

Brown, Ralph S., *Loyalty and Security*, Yale University Press, New Haven, Connecticut, 1958.

Brownlie, Ian, (ed.), *Basic Documents on Human Rights*, Clarendon Press, Oxford University, 1981.

Buitrago, Ann Mari, *Report on CISPES Files Maintained by FBI Headquarters and Released Under the Freedom of Information Act*, FOIA, Inc., New York, 1988.

Buitrago, Ann Mari, and Leon Andrew Immerman, *Are You Now or Have You Ever Been in the FBI Files?*, Grove Press, New York, 1981.

Burnette, Robert, with John Koster, *The Road to Wounded Knee*, Bantam Books, New York, 1974.

Butz, Tim, "Garden Plot—'Flowers of Evil,'" *Akwesasne Notes*, Vol. 7, No. 5, Early Winter, 1975, p. 6.

Castellucci, John, *The Big Dance: The Untold Story of Weatherman Kathy Boudin and the Terrorist Family That Committed the Brink's Robbery Murders*, Dodd, Meade & Company, New York, 1986.

Chomsky, Noam, *Toward a New Cold War*, Pantheon Books, New York, 1983.

Churchill, Ward (ed.), *Marxism and Native Americans*, South End Press, Boston, 1984.

Citizens Research and Investigation Committee and Louis E. Tackwood, *The Glass House Tapes: The Story of an Agent Provocateur and the New Police-Intelligence Complex*, Avon Books, New York, 1973.

Cleaver, Eldridge, *Soul on Fire*, Word Books, Waco, Texas, 1978.

_____, *Soul on Ice*, Delta Books, New York, 1968.

_____, *Post-Prison Writings and Speeches*, Vintage Books, New York, 1969.

Clinton, T.R., "Development of Criminal Jurisdiction Over Indian Lands: The Historical Perspective," *Arizona Law Review*, Number 17, Winter 1975.

Collins, Frederick L., *The FBI in Peace and War*, (Introduction by J. Edgar Hoover), Books, Inc., New York, 1943.

Committee to End the Marion Lockdown, *Marion Prison: Inside the Lockdown*, People's Law Office, Chicago, 1986.

Connell, Evan S., *Son of Morning Star: Custer and the Little Bighorn*, North Point Press, San Francisco, 1984.

Connors, Bernard F., *Don't Embarrass the Bureau*, Bobbs-Merrill Co., Indianapolis, 1972.

Cook, Fred J., *The FBI Nobody Knows*, Macmillan, New York, 1964.

Cooper, Lynn, *et al.*, *The Iron Fist and the Velvet Glove: An Analysis of U.S. Police*, Center for Research on Criminal Justice, Berkeley, 1975.

Corson, William R., *Armies of Ignorance*, Dial Press, New York, 1977.

Cunningham, Dennis, and Jan Susler, *A Public Report About a Violent Mass Assault Against Prisoners and Continuing Illegal Punishment and Torture of the Prison Population at the U.S. Penitentiary at Marion, Illinois*, Marion Prisoners' Rights Project, c/o People's Law Office, Chicago, 1983.

Davis, Angela Y., *et al.*, *If They Come in the Morning*, Signet Books, New York, 1971.

de Toledano, Ralph, *J. Edgar Hoover: The Man in His Time*, Arlington House Publishers, New York, 1973.

Deloria, Vine, Jr., *Behind the Trail of Broken Treaties: An Indian Declaration of Independence*, Delta Books, New York, 1974.

_____, *Custer Died for Your Sins: An Indian Manifesto*, Macmillan, New York, 1969.

_____, *Indians of the Pacific Northwest: From the Coming of the White Man to the Present Day*, Doubleday, New York, 1977.

_____, *The Indian Affair*, Friendship Press, New York, 1974.

_____, *We Talk, You Listen: New Tribes, New Turf*, Macmillan, New York, 1970.

Deloria, Vine, Jr., (ed.), *American Indian Policy in the Twentieth Century*, University of Oklahoma Press, Norman, 1985.

Deloria, Vine Jr., and Clifford M. Lytle, *American Indians, American Justice*, University of Texas Press, Austin, 1983.

_____, *The Nations Within: The Past and Future of American Indian Sovereignty*, Pantheon, New York, 1984.

Demaris, Ovid, *The Director: An Oral History of J. Edgar Hoover*, Harper's Magazine Press, New York, 1975.

Dewing, Roland, *The FBI Files on the American Indian Movement and Wounded Knee*, University Publications of America, 1987.

Dinges, John, and Saul Landau, *Assassination on Embassy Row*, Pantheon Books, New York, 1981.

Divalo, William Tulio, with James, Joseph, *I Lived Inside the Campus Revolution*, Cowles Book Company, Los Angeles, 1973.

Dixon, Joseph K., *The Vanishing Race: The Last Great Indian Council*, Popular Library, New York, 1972.

Dubofsky, Melvyn, *We Shall Be All: A History of the Industrial Workers of the World*, Quadrangle Books, New York, 1974.

Duffy, J.H., *Butte Was Like That*, Tom Greenfield Press, Butte, Montana, 1941.

Durden-Smith, Jo, *Who Killed George Jackson? Fantasies, Paranoia, and the Revolution*, Alfred A. Knopf, New York, 1976.

Eastman, Charles, *From the Deep Woods to Civilization: Chapters in the Autobiography of an Indian*, Little, Brown, Boston, 1916.

_____, *Indian Heroes and Great Chieftains*, Little, Brown, Boston, 1918.

_____, *Old Indian Days*, McClure Publishers, New York, 1907.

_____, *The Soul of the Indian: An Interpretation*, Johnson Reprint Corporation, New York, 1971; originally published in 1911.

Ellis, Edward S., *The History of Our Country*, Vol. 6, Indianapolis, 1900.

Epstein, Jason, *The Great Conspiracy Trial*, Random House, New York, 1970.

Erdoes, Richard, *The Sun Dance People: The Plains Indians, Their Past and Present*, Vintage Books, New York, 1972.

Evelegh, Robin, *Peace-Keeping in a Democratic Society: The Lessons of Northern Ireland*, C. Hurst & Company, London, 1978.

FBI Headquarters Report, titled "Law Enforcement on Pine Ridge Indian Reservation," dated June 5, 1975.

Fehrenbach, T.R., *Comanches: The Destruction of a People*, Alfred A. Knopf, New York, 1974.

Fiedler, Leslie A., *The Return of the Vanishing American*, Paladin Publishers, London, 1972.

Forbes, Jack D., *Native Americans and Nixon: Presidential Politics and Minority Self-Determination*, American Indian Studies Center, UCLA, 1981.

Frankfort, Ellen, *Kathy Boudin and the Dance of Death*, Stein and Day, New York, 1983.

Freed, Donald, *Agony in New Haven: The Trial of Bobby Seale, Ericka Huggins, and the Black Panther Party*, Simon and Schuster, New York, 1973.

Fuchs, Estelle, and Robert J. Havighurst, *To Live On This Earth: American Indian Education*, Doubleday/Anchor Books, New York, 1974.

Garrow, David J., *The FBI and Martin Luther King, Jr.*, Penguin Books, New York, 1981.

Geise, Paula, "Profile of an Informer," *CovertAction/Information Bulletin*, Number 24, Summer 1985, pp. 18-19.

_____, "Secret Agent Douglass Durham and the Death of Jancita Eagle Deer," *North Country Anvil*, Minneapolis, 1976.

Goldman, Emma, *Living My Life*, Dover Publications, New York, 1970.

Graham, W.A., *The Custer Myth: A Source Book of Custeriana*, University of Nebraska Press, Lincoln.

Grathwohl, Larry (as told to Frank Reagan), *Bringing Down America: An FBI Informer with the Weathermen*, Arlington House Publishers, New Rochelle, New York, 1976.

Greene, Jerome A., *Slim Buttes, 1876: An Episode of the Great Sioux War*, University of Oklahoma Press, Norman, 1982.

Grinnell, George Bird, *The Fighting Cheyennes*, University of Oklahoma Press, Norman, 1956 (first published by an unknown New York publisher in 1915).

Habermas, Jurgen, *Legitimation Crisis*, Beacon Press, Boston, 1975.

Hafen, Le Roy R., and Francis Marion Young, *Fort Laramie and the Pageant of the West, 1834-1890*, University of Nebraska Press, Lincoln, 1938.

Hayden, Tom, *Rebellion and Repression*, Hard Times Books, New York, 1969.

Haywood, Bill, *The Autobiography of Big Bill Haywood*, International Publishers, New York, 1929 (recently reprinted).

Hebard, Grace, and E.A. Brininstool, *The Bozeman Trail* (2 vols.), Arthur H. Clark Co., Cleveland, 1922.

Herman, Edward S., *The Real Terror Network: Terrorism in Fact and Propaganda*, South End Press, Boston, MA, 1982.

Herman, Edward S., and Frank Brodhead, *Demonstration Elections: U.S. Staged Elections in the Dominican Republic, Vietnam, and El Salvador*, South End Press, Boston, 1984.

Herr, Michael, *Dispatches*, Discus Books, New York, 1980.

Higham, Charles, *American Swastika*, Doubleday & Co., Inc., Garden City, NY, 1985.

_____, *Trading with the Enemy: An Exposé of the Nazi-American Money Plot 1933-1949*, Dell Publishing Co., Inc., New York, 1983.

Hill Witt, Shirley, and William Muldrow, "Events Surrounding Recent Murders on the Pine Ridge Reservation in South Dakota," report issued by the Rocky Mountain Regional Office, U.S. Commission on Civil Rights, Denver, March 31, 1976.

Hoig, Stan, *The Battle of the Washita*, University of Oklahoma Press, Norman, 1976.

_____, *The Sand Creek Massacre*, University of Oklahoma Press, Norman, 1961.

Hyde, George E., *Red Cloud's Folk: A History of the Oglala Sioux Indians*, University of Oklahoma Press, Norman, 1937.

Jackson, Donald, *Custer's Gold: The United States Cavalry Expedition of 1874*, University of Nebraska Press, Lincoln, 1966.

Jackson, George L., *Blood in My Eye*, Random House, New York, 1972.

_____, *Soledad Brother: The Prison Letters of George Jackson* (Introduction by Jean Genet), Coward McCann Publishers, New York, 1970.

Jacobs, Wilbur R., *Dispossessing the American Indian: Indians and Whites on the Colonial Frontier*, Charles Scribner's Sons, New York, 1972.

Jennings, Dean, *We Only Kill Each Other*, Prentice-Hall, New York, 1967.

Josephy, Alvin M., Jr., *Now That the Buffalo's Gone: A Study of Today's American Indians*, Alfred A. Knopf, New York, 1982.

_____, *Red Power: The American Indians' Fight for Freedom*, McGraw-Hill Book Co., New York, 1971.

Kammer, Jerry, *The Second Long Walk: The Navajo-Hopi Land Dispute*, University of New Mexico Press, Albuquerque, 1978.

Kappler, Charles J., *Indian Treaties, 1778-1883*, Interland Publishing Company, New York, (second printing) 1972.

Karpis, Alvin, with Bill Trent, *The Alvin Karpis Story*, Coward, McCann, & Geoghegan, New York, 1971.

Katsiaficas, George, *Imagination of the New Left*, South End Press, Boston, 1987.

Keating, Edward M., *Free Huey! The True Story of the Trial of Huey Newton*, Ramparts Press, San Francisco, 1971.

Kempton, Murray, *The Briar Patch: The People of the State of New York v. Lumumba Shakur, et al.*, E.P. Dutton Co., Inc., New York, 1973.

Kicking Bird, Kirk, and Karen Duchenaux, *One Hundred Million Acres*, Macmillan Publishing, New York, 1973.

Kitson, Frank, *Low Intensity Operations: Subversion, Insurgency and Peace-Keeping*, Stackpole Books, Harrisburg, PA, 1971.

Klare, Michael T., and Peter Kornbluh, *Low Intensity Warfare: Counterinsurgency, Proinsurgency and Antiterrorism in the Eighties*, Pantheon, New York, 1988.

Kobler, John, *Capone: The Life and World of Al Capone*, G.P. Putnam's Sons, New York, 1971.

Kornbluh, Joyce L. (ed.), *Rebel Voices: An I.W.W. Anthology*, University of Michigan Press, Ann Arbor, (2nd Printing) 1972.

LaBarre, Weston, *The Ghost Dance: The Origins of Religion*, Delta Books, New York, 1970.

Lane, Mark, and Dick Gregory, *Code Name "Zorro": The Murder of Martin Luther King, Jr.*, Prentice-Hall, Inc., Englewood Cliffs, N.J., 1977.

Langguth, A.J., *Hidden Terrors: The Truth About U.S. Police Operations in Latin America*, Pantheon, New York, 1978.

Lawrence, Ken, *The New State Repression*, International Network Against the New State Repression, Chicago, 1985.

Lawson, Michael L., *The Dammed Indians: The Pick-Sloan Plan and the Missouri River Sioux, 1944-1980*, University of Oklahoma Press, Norman, 1982.

Lernoux, Penny, *The Cry of the People: United States Involvement in the Rise of Fascism, Torture, and Murder, and the Persecution of the Catholic Church in Latin America*, Doubleday & Co., New York, 1980.

Lewis, David L., *King: A Biography*, University of Illinois Press, Urbana, 1978.

Lifton, Robert Jay, *The Nazi Doctors: Medical Killing and the Psychology of Genocide*, Basic Books, New York, 1986.

Lockwood, Lee, *Conversation With Eldridge Cleaver*, Delta Books, New York, 1970.

Look magazine, editors of, *The Story of the FBI: The Official Picture History of the Federal Bureau of Investigation*, (Introduction by J. Edgar Hoover), Dutton Publishers, New York, 1947.

Lopez, Alfredo, *Doña Licha's Island: Modern Colonialism in Puerto Rico*, South End Press, Boston, 1987.

Lowenthal, Max, *The Federal Bureau of Investigation*, William Sloan Associates, Inc., New York, 1950.

Luce, Phillip Abbott, *The New Left*, David McKay, Inc., New York, 1966.

Maas, Peter, *The Valachi Papers*, G.P. Putnam's Sons, New York, 1968.

Maestas, Roberto, and Bruce Johansen, *Wasi'chu: The Continuing Indian Wars*, Monthly Review Press, New York, 1978.

Major, Reginald, *A Panther Is a Black Cat: A Study in Depth of the Black Panther Party, Its Origins, Its Goals, Its Struggle for Survival*, William Morrow and Company, New York, 1971.

Marchetti, Victor, with John D. Marks, *The CIA and the Cult of Intelligence*, Alfred A. Knopf, New York, 1974.

Marine, Gene, *The Black Panthers*, Signet Books, New York, 1969.

Matthiessen, Peter, *In the Spirit of Crazy Horse*, Viking Press, New York, 1984.

McGarvey, Patrick J., *CIA: The Myth and the Madness*, Saturday Review Press, New York, 1972.

McGehee, Ralph W., *Deadly Deceits: My 25 Years in the CIA*, Sheridan Square Publishers, New York, 1983.

Means, Russell, "Penthouse Interview," *Penthouse*, November, 1982, pp. 136-38.

Meinhart, Nick, *Water and Energy*, pamphlet produced by the Black Hills Alliance (P.O. Box 2508, Rapid City, S.D.), 1982.

Messerschmidt, Jim, *The Trial of Leonard Peltier*, South End Press, Boston, 1984.

Meyer, William, *Native Americans: The New Indian Resistance*, International Publishers, New York, 1971.

Miller, Douglas, and Marion Nowak, *The Fifties: The Way We Really Were*, Doubleday, New York, 1977.

Mills, C. Wright, *The Socialist Imagination*, Oxford University Press, New York, 1959.

Mitford, Jessica, *The Trial of Dr. Spock, Reverend William Sloane Coffin, Jr., Michael Ferber, Mitchell Goodman and Marcus Raskin*, Alfred A. Knopf, New York, 1969.

Moskos, Charles, (ed.), *Public Opinion and the Military Establishment*, Sage Publications, Beverly Hills, CA, 1971.

Muldrow, William, *Monitoring of Events Related to the Shooting of Two FBI Agents on the Pine Ridge Indian Reservation* (Report to Ms. Shirley Hill Witt, Regional Director), U.S. Commission on Civil Rights, Rocky Mountain Regional Office, Denver, July 9, 1975.

Nadeau, Remi, *Fort Laramie and the Sioux*, University of Nebraska Press, Lincoln, 1967.

National Academy of Sciences (NAS) and National Academy of Engineering (joint report), *Rehabilitation of Western Coal Lands: A Report to the Energy Policy Project of the Ford Foundation*, Ballinger Publishing Co., Cambridge, MA, 1974.

_____, *Energy and Climate*, Washington, D.C., 1977.

National Committee to Support the Marion Brothers, *Breaking Men's Minds*, Chicago, IL, 1978.

Navasky, Victor S., *Naming Names*, Viking Press, New York, 1980.

Newton, Huey P., *Revolutionary Suicide*, Harcourt, Brace and Jovanovich, New York, 1973.

_____, *To Die for the People*, Vintage Books, New York, 1972.

Ollestad, Norman, *Inside the FBI*, Lyle Stuart Publishers, New York, 1967.

Olson, James C., *Red Cloud and the Sioux Problem*, University of Nebraska Press, Lincoln, 1965.

Otis, S.D., *The Dawes Act and Allotment of Indian Lands*, University of Oklahoma Press, Norman, 1973.

Parenti, Michael, *Democracy for the Few*, St. Martins Press, New York, 1980.

Pell, Eve, *The Big Chill: How the Reagan administration, corporate America, and religious conservatives are subverting free speech and the public's right to know*, Beacon Press, Boston, 1984.

Perkus, Cathy, (ed.), *COINTELPRO: The FBI's Secret War on Political Freedom*, (Introduction by Noam Chomsky), Monad Press, New York, 1976.

Philbrick, Herbert A., *I Led Three Lives: Citizen—Communist—Counterspy*, Grosset & Dunlap Publishers, New York, 1952.

Pinkney, Alphonso, *Red, Black, and Green: Black Nationalism in the United States*, Cambridge University Press, New York, 1976.

Post, Louis F., *The Deportation Delirium of Nineteen-Twenty*, Chicago, 1923.

Pratt, Elmer Gerard ("Geronimo"), *The New Urban Guerrilla*, (Introduction by Zayd Malik Shakur), Revolutionary People's Communication Network (RPCN), New York, 1971.

_____, *Humanity, Freedom, Peace*, RPCN, New York, 1972.

Sampson, Anthony, *The Sovereign State of ITT*, Fawcett Publications, Greenwich, CT, 1973.

Sandoz, Mari, *Cheyenne Autumn*, New York, Hastings House, 1953.

_____, *Crazy Horse: Strange Man of the Oglalas*, University of Nebraska Press, Lincoln, 1942.

_____, *The Battle of Little Bighorn*, Curtis Books, New York, 1966.

Schneir, Walter and Miriam, *Invitation to an Inquest*, Pantheon Books, New York, 1983.

Shakur, Assata, *Assata: An Autobiography*, Lawrence Hill, Westport, CT, 1987.

Simpson, Charles M. (III), *Inside the Green Berets: The First Thirty Years*, Presidio Press, Novato, CA, 1983.

Snepp, Frank, *Decent Interval*, Random House, New York, 1977.

Stanton, Shelby L., *Vietnam Order of Battle*, U.S. News Books, Washington, D.C., 1981.

Steiner, Stan, *The New Indians*, Delta Books, New York, 1968.

_____, *The Vanishing White Man*, Harper-Colophon Books, New York, 1976.

Stern, Theodore, *The Klamath Tribe: The People and Their Reservation*, University of Washington Press, Seattle, 1965.

Stevens, Don and Jane, *South Dakota: The Mississippi of the North, or Stories Jack Anderson Never Told You*, Self-published booklet, (P.O. Box 241, Custer, S.D.), 1977.

Stockwell, John, *In Search of Enemies: A CIA Story*, W.W. Norton & Co., New York, 1978.

Sutton, Imre, (ed.), *Irredeemable America: The Indians' Estate and Land Claims*, University of New Mexico Press, Albuquerque, 1985.

Swearingen, M. Wesley, Deposition taken in October, 1980, in Honolulu, Hawaii.

Taylor, Flint, and Margaret Vanhouten, *Counterintelligence: A Documentary Look at America's Secret Police*, National Lawyer's Guild Task Force on Counter Intelligence and the Secret Police, Chicago, 1978.

Toland, John, *The Dillinger Days*, Random House, New York, 1963.

Trebbel, John, *The Compact History of the Indian Wars*, Tower Books, New York, 1966.

Tully, Andrew, *The FBI's Most Famous Cases* (Introduction and Comments by J. Edgar Hoover), William Morrow and Company, New York, 1965.

Turner, William, *Hoover's FBI: The Men and the Myth*, Dell Publishers, New York, 1971.

U.S. Army Training and Doctrine Command, *US Army Operational Concept for Low Intensity Conflict*, TRADOC Pamphlet No. 525-44, Fort Monroe, Va., 1986.

U.S. Bureau of Indian Affairs, *Status of Mineral Resource Information on the Pine Ridge Indian Reservation*, BIA Report No. 12, U.S. Department of Interior, Washington, D.C., 1976.

U.S. Bureau of Reclamation, *North Central Power Study, Vol. I: Study of Mine-Mouth Thermal Power Plants with Extra-High Voltage for Delivery to Load Centers*, Billings, Mont., October, 1971.

U.S. Bureau of Reclamation, *Water for Energy*, (final environmental impact statement on the Black Hills Region), U.S. Department of Interior, Washington, D.C., December 1, 1977.

U.S. Commission on Civil Rights, *Hearing Before the United States Commission on Civil Rights: National Indian Civil Rights Issues*, (Hearing Held in Washington, D.C., March 19-20, 1979), Vol. I: Testimony, U.S. Government Printing Office, Washington, D.C., 1979.

_____, *Report of Investigation: Oglala Sioux Tribe, General Election, 1974*, U.S. Commission on Civil Rights, Washington, D.C., October, 1974.

_____, *The Navajo Nation: An American Colony, A Report of the U.S. Commission on Civil Rights*, Washingtion, D.C., September, 1975.

_____, *Hearing Held Before the U.S. Commission on Civil Rights: American Indian Issues in South Dakota*, Hearing Held in Rapid City, South Dakota, July 27-28, 1978, U.S. Government Printing Office, Washington, D.C., 1978.

_____, *Monitoring of Events Related to the Shootings of Two FBI Agents on the Pine Ridge Reservation*, U.S. Commission on Civil Rights, Mountain States Regional Office, Denver, Co., July, 9, 1975.

U.S. Congress, *Appropriations to the Budget of the United States of America, 1872, Section VII, United States Department of Justice*, Washington, D.C., 1871.

_____, *J. Edgar Hoover: Memorial Tributes in the Congress of the United States and Various Articles and Editorials Relating to His Life and Work*, U.S. Government Printing Office, Washington, D.C., 1974.

_____, *Hearings Before the Congress of United States of America Concerning the National Budget for the Year 1907*, Washington, D.C., 1906.

U.S. Congress, House Committee on UnAmerican Activities, *Hearings Regarding the Communist Infiltration of the Motion Picture Industry*, Eightieth Congress, U.S. Government Printing Office, Washington, D.C., 1947.

U.S. Congress, House Select Committee on Assassinations, *The Final Report*, Bantam Books, New York, 1979.

_____, *Hearings on Investigation of the Assassination of Dr. Martin Luther King, Jr.*, 95th Congress, 2nd Session, Vols. 1, 6, 7, U.S. Government Printing Office, Washington, DC, 1979.

U.S. Congress, Senate Select Committee to Study Government Operations with Respect to Intelligence Activities, *Final Report—Book III: Supplementary Detailed Staff Reports on Intelligence Activities and the Rights of Americans*, 94th Congress, 2nd Session, U.S. Government Printing Office, Washington, D.C., 1976.

U.S. Department of Justice, *Report of the Task Force on Indian Matters*, Washington, D.C., 1975.

_____, *Report of the Task Force to Review the FBI, Martin Luther King, Jr., Security and Assassination Investigations*, Washington, D.C., January 11, 1977.

U.S. House of Representatives, Committee on the Judiciary, *FBI Undercover Operations: Report of the Subcommittee on Civil and Constitutional Rights*, (H. Doc. 98-267), 98th Congress, 2d Session, U.S. Government Printing Office, Washington, D.C., April 1984.

_____, *Hearings Before the Subcommittee on Civil and Constitutional Rights of the Committee of the Judiciary, 97th Congress, First Session on FBI Authorization*, March 19, 24, 25; April 2 and 8, 1981, U.S. Government Printing Office, Washington, D.C., 1981.

U.S. Senate Select Committee to Study Governmental Operations, *Intelligence Activities and the Rights of Americans*, Book II, U.S. Government Printing Office, Washington, D.C., 1976.

U.S. Senate Select Committee to Study Government Operations, *The FBI's Covert Program to Destroy the Black Panther Party*, U.S. Government Printing Office, Washington, D.C., 1976.

U.S. Senate, Committee on the Judiciary, Subcommittee on Internal Security (Eastland Subcommittee), *Revolutionary Activities Within the United States: The American Indian Movement*, U.S. Government Printing Office, Washington, D.C., 1976.

_____, *The Assault on Freedom: A Compendium of Theoretical and Policy Statements by the Communist Movement, Domestic and International, and by Other Organizations Committed to the Violent Overthrow of Free Institutions*, 92nd Congress, 1st Session, U.S. Government Printing Office, Washington, D.C., 1971.

Ungar, Sanford, *FBI*, Little, Brown, and Company, Boston, 1976.

Utley, Robert M., *The Last Days of the Sioux Nation*, Yale University Press, New Haven, 1963.

Volkman, Ernest, "Othello," *Penthouse*, April 1979.

Weeks, Robert P., (ed.), *The Commonwealth versus Sacco and Vanzetti*, Prentice-Hall, Inc., 1958.

Weisman, Joel D., "About that 'ambush' at Wounded Knee," *Columbia Journalism Review*, September/October, 1975, pp. 28-31.

Weyler, Rex, *Blood of the Land: The Government and Corporate War Against the American Indian Movement*, Vintage Books, New York, 1984.

Whitehead, Don, *Attack on Terror: The FBI Against the Ku Klux Klan in Mississippi*, Funk and Wagnall's, New York, 1970.

_____, *The FBI Story: A Report to the People*, Random House, New York, 1963.

Wilkins, Roy, and Ramsey Clark, *Search and Destroy: A Report by the Commission of Inquiry into the Black Panthers and the Police*, Metropolitan Applied Research Center, Inc., New York, 1973.

Wilson, Raymond, *Ohiyesa: Charles Eastman, Santee Sioux*, University of Illinois Press, Urbana, 1983.

Wise, David, *The American Police State*, Random House, New York, 1976.

Yee, Min S., *The Melancholy History of Soledad Prison: In Which a Utopian Scheme Turns Bedlam*, Harpers Magazine Press, New York, 1973.

Zimmerman, Bill, *Airlift to Wounded Knee*, The Swallow Press, Inc., Chicago, 1976.

Zimroth, Peter L., *Perversions of Justice: The Prosecution and Acquittal of the Panther 21*, Viking Press, New York, 1974.

Zinn, Howard, *A People's History of the United States*, Harper and Row, New York, 1980.

_____, *SNCC: The New Abolitionists*, Beacon Press, Boston, 1964.

Zocchino, Nanda, "Ex-FBI Informer Describes Terrorist Role," *The Los Angeles Times*, January 26, 1976.

About South End Press

South End Press is a nonprofit, collectively run book publisher with over 150 titles in print. Since our founding in 1977, we have tried to meet the needs of readers who are exploring, or are already committed to, the politics of radical social change.

Our goal is to publish books that encourage critical thinking and constructive action on the key political, cultural, social, economic, and ecological issues shaping life in the United States and in the world. In this way, we hope to give expression to a wide diversity of democratic social movements and to provide an alternative to the products of corporate publishing.

If you would like a free catalog of South End Press books or information about our membership program—which offers two free books and a 40% discount on all titles—please write us at South End Press, 116 St. Botolph Street, Boston, MA 02115.

Other titles of interest from South End Press:

War at Home:
Covert Action Against U.S. Activists and What We Can Do About It
Brian Glick

Marxism and Native Americans
edited by Ward Churchill

The Trial of Leonard Peltier
Jim Messerschmidt

Cointelpro Papers:
Documents from the FBI's Secret Wars
Against Dissent in the United States
Ward Churchill and Jim Vander Wall

Freedom Under Fire:
U.S. Civil Liberties in Times of War
Michael Linfield

They Should've Served That Cup of Coffee:
Seven Radicals Remember the '60s
edited by Dick Cluster